BARNET & STUBBS
PRACTICAL GUIDE TO

WRITING

BARNET & STUBBS'S PRACTICAL GUIDE TO
WRITING

Sylvan Barnet
Tufts University

Marcia Stubbs
Wellesley College

LITTLE, BROWN AND COMPANY
Boston · Toronto

Library of Congress Catalog Card No. 74–26405

First printing

Published simultaneously in Canada
by Little, Brown & Company (Canada) Limited

Printed in the United States of America

ACKNOWLEDGMENTS

Epigraphs

Page 1: Reprinted with permission of Macmillan Publishing Co., Inc. from *Collected Poems* by William Butler Yeats, p. 358. Copyright 1919 by Macmillan Publishing Co., Inc., renewed 1947 by Bertha Georgie Yeats. Also by permission of M. B. Yeats, Miss Anne Yeats, and the Macmillan Company of Canada.
Page 173: Reprinted with permission of Macmillan Publishing Co., Inc. from *The Variorum Edition of the Poems of W. B. Yeats,* edited by Peter Allt and Russell K. Alspach, p. 778. Copyright 1957 by Macmillan Publishing Co., Inc. Also by permission of M. B. Yeats, Miss Anne Yeats, and Macmillan Co. of Canada.
Page 175: From *Predilections* (New York: Viking Press, 1944), p. 9.
Page 223: From the short story "Guy de Maupassant" in *The Collected Stories,* ed. Walter Morison (New York: Criterion Books, 1955).
Page 283: From *Zen Flesh, Zen Bones,* compiled by Paul Reps (Tokyo: Charles E. Tuttle Co., 1957), p. 114. Reprinted with permission.
Page 286: From the Preface to Edward Arlington Robinson, *King Jasper* (New York: Macmillan, 1935), p. xiii. Copyright 1935 by Macmillan Publishing Co., Inc., renewed 1963 by Macmillan Publishing Co., Inc.

Illustrations

Pages 38, 39: Courtesy of Museum of Fine Arts, Boston. Reprinted with permission.
Page 69: Reprinted from *Mazes 2* by Vladimir Koziakin. Copyright

© 1972 by Vladimir Koziakin. Published by Grosset & Dunlap, Inc. Reprinted with permission.
Page 123: Reproduced from "The New Yorker." Reprinted with the permission of the Atlanta Chamber of Commerce and The New Yorker Magazine, Inc.
Page 136: Material from *The Reader's Guide to Periodical Literature* is reproduced by permission of the H. W. Wilson Company.
Page 176: Copyright, 1974, G. B. Trudeau / distributed by Universal Press Syndicate. Reprinted with permission.

The publisher is also grateful to the following persons:
ASSOCIATED PRESS   For permission to quote in entirety the release "Dodgers Keep Perfect Record in Knocking out Southpaws," *Michigan Daily*, September 29, 1955.
ERNEST BENN LTD.   For permission to quote from *Organization of Thought* by Alfred North Whitehead (Williams & Norgate, 1917). (Reprinted in *The Aims of Education* [New York: Macmillan, 1959].)
ROBERT BLY   For permission to quote in entirety the poem "Love Poem." Reprinted from *Silence in the Snowy Fields*, Wesleyan University Press, Copyright © 1962 by Robert Bly, by his permission.
THE BOBBS-MERRILL COMPANY, INC.   For permission to quote from *The Comic Mind*, copyright © 1973 by Gerald Mast, reprinted by permission of the publisher, The Bobbs-Merrill Company, Inc.
BOSTON GLOBE   For permission to quote in entirety the article "Poetry Class at Norfolk Prison," by Sayre P. Sheldon, May 22, 1974.
COMMENTARY   For permission to quote from Robert Garis, "Persona," December 1967.
CORNELL UNIVERSITY PRESS   For permission to quote from Joseph Wood Krutch, *"Modernism" in Modern Drama*. Copyright 1953 by Cornell University.
THE DIAL PRESS   For permission to quote material excerpted from *Coming of Age in Mississippi* by Anne Moody. Copyright © 1968 by Anne Moody. Used with permission of The Dial Press.
DOUBLEDAY & COMPANY, INC.   For permission to quote from Richard M. Dorson, "Africa and the Folklorist," in Richard M. Dorson, ed., *African Folklore*. Copyright © 1972 by Richard M. Dorson.
ESTATE OF ALBERT EINSTEIN   For permission to quote from Albert Einstein and Leopold Infeld, *The Evolution of Physics* (New York: Simon & Schuster, 1942).
FARRAR, STRAUSS & GIROUX, INC.   For permission to quote material reprinted with the permission of Farrar, Strauss & Giroux, Inc., from *Mystery and Manners* by Flannery O'Connor. Copyright © 1957, 1961, 1963, 1964, 1966, 1967, 1969, by the Estate of Mary Flannery O'Connor, copyright © 1962 by Flannery O'Connor, copyright © 1961 by Farrar, Straus and Cudahy, Inc.
W. H. FREEMAN AND COMPANY   For permission to quote from "Hyperactivity and Drugs," *Scientific American*, July 1974. Copyright © 1974 by Scientific American, Inc. All rights reserved.

GROVE PRESS, INC. For permission to quote from Malcolm X and Alex Haley, *The Autobiography of Malcolm X*. Reprinted by permission of Grove Press, Inc. Copyright © 1964 by Alex Haley and Malcolm X.

INDIANA UNIVERSITY PRESS For permission to quote material reprinted from *The Well-Tempered Critic* by Northrop Frye. Copyright © 1963 by Indiana University Press, Bloomington. Reprinted by permission of the publisher.

INTERNATIONAL FAMOUS AGENCY For permission to quote from the review by William Gass, *New York Review of Books*, 27 June 1974.

LITTLE, BROWN AND COMPANY For permission to quote from X. J. Kennedy, *An Introduction to Poetry*, third edition, p. 170. Copyright © 1966, 1971, 1974 by X. J. Kennedy. Reprinted by permission. Also for permission to quote from *Nobody Ever Died of Old Age* by Sharon R. Curtin, by permission of Little, Brown and Co. in association with The Atlantic Monthly Press. Copyright © 1972 by Sharon R. Curtin.

LOS ANGELES TIMES For permission to quote from "Say One Word and I'll Cut Your Throat" by Charles T. Powers, January 13, 1974. Copyright, 1974, Los Angeles Times. Reprinted by permission.

MACMILLAN PUBLISHING COMPANY, INC. For material reprinted with permission of Macmillan Publishing Co., Inc. from *Sociological Theory and Modern Society* by Talcott Parsons. Copyright © 1967 by The Free Press, a Division of Macmillan Publishing Co., Inc. Also for material reprinted with permission of Macmillan Publishing Co., Inc. from *The Bible and the Common Reader* by Mary Ellen Chase. Copyright 1944 by Mary Ellen Chase, renewed 1972 by Mary Ellen Chase.

JACK S. MARGOLIS For permission to quote in entirety the poem "And All Those Others" from *The Poetry of Richard Milhous Nixon* (Los Angeles: Cliff House Books, 1974).

MC GRAW-HILL BOOK COMPANY For permission to quote from *Soul on Ice* by Eldridge Cleaver. Copyright 1968 by Eldridge Cleaver. Used with permission of McGraw-Hill Book Company.

SCOTT MEREDITH LITERARY AGENCY For permission to quote from Norman Mailer, *Existential Errands*. Reprinted by permission of the author and the author's agents, Scott Meredith Literary Agency, Inc., 580 Fifth Avenue, New York, New York 10036.

THE MUSEUM OF MODERN ART For permission to quote from *Looking at Photographs / 100 Pictures from the Collection of The Museum of Modern Art* by John Szarkowski. Copyright © 1973 The Museum of Modern Art, New York. All rights reserved. Reprinted by permission of The Museum of Modern Art.

THE JOHN G. NEIHARDT TRUST For permission to quote from *Black Elk Speaks* by John G. Neihardt. Copyright John G. Neihardt 1932, 1959, and 1961.

NEW DIRECTIONS For permission to quote in entirety the poem "Hitch Haiku" from Gary Snyder, *The Back Country*. Copyright © 1968 by Gary Snyder. Reprinted by permission of New Directions Publishing Corporation.

THE NEW REPUBLIC For permission to quote in entirety the review

"Family Man," by W. T. Lhamon, Jr., June 1, 1974. Reprinted by permission of *The New Republic,* © 1974 The New Republic, Inc.

NEWSWEEK For permission to quote from "On the Road," July 21, 1969. Copyright Newsweek, Inc. 1969, reprinted by permission.

THE NEW YORK REVIEW OF BOOKS For permission to quote from Peter Farb, "Baby Talk," February 21, 1974. Reprinted with permission from *The New York Review of Books.* Copyright © 1974 Nyrev, Inc.

NEW YORK TIMES For permission to quote in entirety the articles "Topics: Reflections on the Death of a Library" (retitled "The Newark Public Library") by Philip Roth, March 1, 1969; "Columbo Knows the Butler Didn't Do It" by Jeff Greenfield, April 22, 1973; "The New Black Poetry" by Mel Watkins, August 13, 1972; "In Search of the Elusive Pingo," May 5, 1974; "The Right to Choose Death" by O. Ruth Russell, February 14, 1972; "The Rayburn Building" by Ada Louise Huxtable, March 30, 1965; and "Putting the Outside Inside the Fence of Law" by Christopher D. Stone, August 29, 1974. Also for permission to quote from the article "Moby Balloon" by David Royce, May 26, 1974; and from the book review of *Soledad Brother* by Julius Lester, November 22, 1970. © 1974/69/73 1972/65/70 by The New York Times Company. Reprinted by permission.

W. W. NORTON & COMPANY, INC. For permission to quote material reprinted from *Re-Appraisals: Some Commonsense Readings in American Literature,* by Martin Green. By permission of W. W. Norton & Company, Inc. Copyright © 1965, 1963 by Martin Green.

UNIVERSITY OF NOTRE DAME PRESS For permission to quote from Ernesto Galarza, *Barrio Boy.*

PRENTICE-HALL, INC. For permission to quote from Talcott Parsons, *Societies: Evolutionary and Comparative Perspectives.* © 1966. Reprinted by permission of Prentice-Hall, Inc., Englewood Cliffs, New Jersey.

RANDOM HOUSE, INC. For permission to quote from Maya Angelou, *I Know Why the Caged Bird Sings.* Copyright © 1969 by Maya Angelou.

REUTERS For permission to quote in entirety the release "Fish Eat Brazilian Fisherman," *Boston Globe,* January 17, 1971.

PHILIP ROTH For permission to quote in entirety the article "Topics: Reflections on the Death of a Library" (retitled "The Newark Public Library"), *New York Times,* March 1, 1969.

O. RUTH RUSSELL For permission to quote in entirety the article "The Right to Choose Death," *New York Times,* February 14, 1972.

SAYRE P. SHELDON For permission to quote in entirety the article "Poetry Class at Norfolk Prison," *Boston Globe,* May 22, 1974.

SIMON & SCHUSTER, INC. For permission to quote from Leonard Cammer, *Up From Depression.* Reprinted by permission of Simon & Schuster. Copyright, © 1969, by Leonard Cammer, M.D.

CHRISTOPHER D. STONE For permission to quote in entirety the article "Putting the Outside Inside the Fence of Law," *New York Times,* August 29, 1974.

TIME For permission to quote in entirety the article "A View of

Skiers as a Subculture" (retitled "Skiers as a Subculture" by David Boroff. Reprinted by permission from *Sports Illustrated*, November 23, 1964. © 1964 Time Inc. Also for permission to quote from "Lord, They've Done It All," *Time*, May 6, 1974. Reprinted by permission from *Time*, The Weekly Newsmagazine; Copyright Time Inc.

TIMES NEWSPAPERS LIMITED   For permission to quote from a review of Sir Kenneth Clark, *The Nude*, January 11, 1957. Reproduced from the Times Literary Supplement by permission.

VANGUARD PRESS   For permission to quote material reprinted by permission of the publishers, The Vanguard Press, from "The Victim" by Saul Bellow. Copyright, 1947, by Saul Bellow. Copyright renewed 1974 by Saul Bellow.

HELEN VENDLER   For permission to quote in entirety the address "Literature and the Undergraduate," delivered at Boston University.

THE VIKING PRESS, INC.   For permission to quote from *The Liberal Imagination* by Lionel Trilling. Copyright 1950 by Lionel Trilling. All rights reserved. Reprinted by permission of The Viking Press, Inc.

THE WRITER, INC.   For permission to quote from John Holmes, *Writing Poetry*.

PREFACE

> Where there is too much,
> something is missing.

We have tried to keep this proverb in mind; we hope we have written a short, judicious book rather than a long, undiscriminating one.

The book is designed for college courses in which students write essays, instructors read them, and students and instructors together discuss them. We hope we offer a practical guide to all three activities. The student, looking for information about choosing a topic, writing an analysis, constructing a paragraph, using a semicolon, can use the text as a guide to writing the week's essay. The instructor, after reading the essay, can suggest chapters or passages the student should consult in revising the essay or in writing the next one. Students and instructors together can discuss the exercises, the techniques used in the reprinted essays, the assumptions we make and the suggestions we offer.

Although we include discussions and examples of description and narration, we emphasize analysis, exposition, and argument because those are the chief activities, usually rolled into one, that we all engage in, both in school and later. When students write papers for a course, or professors write reports for a committee, or psychiatric social workers write case studies, most of what they write is exposition, a statement of what's what; usually they have come to see what's what by analyzing or dividing the subject into parts, and because they want to be be-lieved they construct as persuasive an argument as possible.

We have included nineteen short essays, as well as numerous paragraphs from books and essays, the work for the most part of first-rate contemporary writers. We include them both to illustrate ways of writing and to provide students with some-thing to write about. Similarly, the suggested exercises often require the students to write about something outside of them-selves. The usual Polonian advice, offered to Laertes—"This above all, to thine own self be true"—seems to us as useless to most people of college ages as it is to Laertes. As Erik Erikson has helped us to see, most young people are engaged in a "search for something and somebody to be true to." They experiment with roles in a search for "the rock-bottom of some truth."[1] Asked to write about how they spent last summer, they may feel a profound uneasiness; however necessary last summer was, they are not sure what it added up to, and though they probably would not spend the next summer in the same way, they are not yet distant enough from their experience to be articulate about it. Some of our exercises do present clear opportunities for in-trospection, and all of them in fact require it, but we think that much of students' writing should be directed outward, not solely a look into the heart but a look around—at people, at places, and especially at ideas.

We have tried therefore to balance the advice "Trust your feelings," "Ask yourself questions," with prescriptions: "Avoid clichés," "Keep your reader in mind." We have tried to in-crease the student's awareness that writing is both an explora-tion of self ("Choose a topic you can write about honestly") and a communication with others ("Revise for clarity").

In Chapter 1, two informal exercises introduce two important points: that one learns to write by writing (Asking Questions and Answering Them); and that generalizations should be sup-ported by specific, concrete details (Clarifying Ideas). Instructors may find these passages useful in the first few class meetings. The book can be read, we hope, from beginning to end, but because each chapter can stand by itself, the instructor can assign chapters in whatever seems a suitable order, and the stu-

[1] *Identity: Youth and Crisis* (New York: W. W. Norton, 1968), pp. 235–36.

dent can consult whatever passages seem most relevant to writing and revising a particular essay. After all, it has never been established that in a college course in English certain topics must be taught before others. Listen to Boswell describing a conversation, more than two hundred years ago, with Dr. Johnson:

We talked of the education of children; and I asked him what he thought was best to teach them first. JOHNSON: "Sir, it is no matter what you teach them first, any more than what leg you shall put into your breeches first. Sir, you may stand disputing which is best to put in first, but in the meantime your breech is bare. Sir, while you are considering which of two things you should teach your child first, another boy has learnt them both."

So much by way of explanation; the reader will be the only judge of how well we have fulfilled our aims. If we have come near, we owe debts to Mary Adams, Jacob Alexander, Morton Berman, William Burto, Joan Carberg, Sally Carson, Charles Christensen, John M. Clum, Leah Creque, Mary Bryan H. Curd, Leopold Damrosch, Aviva Diamond, Denise Ferguson, Jan Fontein, Yolette Garcia, Thomas J. Gasque, Walker Gibson, David Giele, Owen Jenkins, Joseph Keefe, Nancy Kolodny, Joseph Komidar, Andrea La Sane, George Marcopoulos, Lynda Martin, Richard Milburn, Gerald Mimno, Nancy Mimno, Betty Morgan, Rose Moss, Stanley Moss, Robert A. Myers, William Scott, Patrick W. Shaw, Edward Sims, Audrey Smith, Gail Stewart, Eugene Stubbs, Kathy Valdespino, Renita Weems, Elizabeth Wood, Haruo Yanagi; and to all our students, from whose mistakes we hope to profit. It should be noted, too, that several passages in the book appeared earlier in slightly different form in Sylvan Barnet, *A Short Guide to Writing about Literature*.

Sylvan Barnet
Marcia Stubbs

CONTENTS

1. WRITING

CHAPTER FIVE

EXPOSITION AND DEFINITION   84

CHAPTER SIX

ARGUMENT AND PERSUASION   96

CHAPTER SEVEN

DESCRIPTION AND NARRATION

CHAPTER EIGHT

THE RESEARCH PAPER

2. REVISING

CHAPTER ELEVEN

REVISING FOR CLARITY

3. EDITING

CHAPTER FOURTEEN

PUNCTUATION

CHAPTER FIFTEEN

SPELLING

CHAPTER NINETEEN

BARNET & STUBBS'S
PRACTICAL GUIDE TO
WRITING

1. WRITING

THE BALLOON OF THE MIND

Hands, do what you're bid:
Bring the balloon of the mind
That bellies and drags in the wind
Into its narrow shed.

—William Butler Yeats

CHAPTER ONE

FROM SUBJECT TO ESSAY

STARTING

How to Write: Writing as a Physical Act

"One takes a piece of paper," William Carlos Williams wrote, "anything, the flat of a shingle, slate, cardboard and with anything handy to the purpose begins to put down the words after the desired expression in mind." Good advice, from a writer who produced novels, plays, articles, book reviews, an autobiography, a voluminous correspondence, and more than twenty-five books of poetry while raising a family, enjoying a wide circle of friends, and practicing medicine in Rutherford, New Jersey. Not the last word on writing (we have approximately 85,000 of our own to add), but where we would like to begin: "One takes a piece of paper . . . and . . . begins to put down the words. . . ."

Writing is a physical act. It requires materials and energy. And like most physical acts, to be performed skillfully, to bring pleasure to both performer and audience, it requires practice. Talent helps. But few of us are born to be great writers, just as few of us are born to be great athletes. When Mark Spitz won seven gold medals in the 1972 Olympics, *Time* described him as having hands like "a pair of scoop-shovels . . . that can pull him cleanly through the water with scarcely a ripple," and noted his "curious ability to flex his lower legs slightly forward at the knees, which allows him to kick 6 to 12 inches deeper in the water than his opponents." Most of us are not born with the "curious ability" of the great writer or the great swimmer. But we can learn to write, as we can learn to swim, for all practical purposes, including pleasure.

In this book we offer some suggestions, definitions, rules, and examples to help you learn not simply to write, but to write well. We hope they will help you avoid some of the trials and errors—and the fear of drowning—of uninstructed practice. Our first suggestion is this: buy a notebook that you can carry with you (so you won't waste time looking for loose shingles) and write in it regularly.

Why Write? Writing as a Mental Activity

Born writers often describe their need to write as a compulsion, an inner drive to put their feelings and ideas into words. Despite that compulsion, or because of it, they also regularly complain that writing is hard work: "hard labor for life" was Joseph Conrad's summary of his own career. For the rest of us, perhaps, writing is easier because it is not our vocation and we demand less than perfection from ourselves. But it's still hard work, and we accept the occasional sentence to "hard labor" only if we have made some commitment or anticipate some reward. In real life (as opposed to school) people are regularly committed by their jobs and other interests to communicating their ideas in writing. Even television and tape have not diminished the importance of the written word. Scientists and social scientists, to secure contracts, must put their proposals in writing, and then again in writing, report the results of their work to their sponsors and colleagues. Citizens and parents write their petitions and grievances to lawmakers and school boards; through prepared talks and newsletters, volunteers reach the communities they serve. In short, anyone who is engaged with ideas or who wants to influence the course of events finds it necessary to put what Dr. Williams called "the desired expression in mind" into words.

As students, you may or may not make the connection between the assignment you are given today and the need you will have several years hence to put your ideas in writing. The rewards—getting the contract, serving your community—are probably a bit distant to motivate you to write 500 words on a possibly irrelevant topic this week. There is, though, a closer reward: "To be learning something new," said Aristotle, "is ever the chief pleasure of mankind." We believe that. We also believe that writing is not simply a way to express ideas, but a way to acquire them. For, to quote Aristotle again, "What is expressed is impressed."

We emphasize ideas because we are making some assumptions about you: that you are an adult, that you're acquiring an education, either in school or on your own, and that the writing skill you need most help with is the expression of ideas in clear expository essays. Most of our book will concentrate on that skill. We begin, then, with some ideas about ideas.

Some Ideas about Ideas

Would-be writers have one of two complaints: either "I have the ideas but I don't know how to express them," or "I have nothing to say." They are really the same complaint, known to both professional writers and novices as "writer's block." But let's treat them, to begin with, as if they were indeed separate.

Starting to Write by Writing

If you have the ideas but don't know how to express them, sit down and start writing. It doesn't matter where you begin, only that you begin. Resist the temptation to sharpen another pencil, to make yourself a cup of tea, to call your mother. Now is *not* the time to do your laundry or make your bed. Sit down and start putting one word after another. One of the writers of this book finds it useful to start writing notes on three-by-five-inch file cards, then to arrange the cards, and from that arrangement to jot down a sort of outline. Not a formal outline, with capital and lower case letters and roman and arabic numerals, but simply a list of key phrases in some reasonable order. If that way of starting helps you, fine, do it. It doesn't help me, and I'm writing this chapter.

Let's assume you either have an outline or you don't. Again, start writing. As you write, forget any rules you may have learned. In particular forget anything you've heard about opening paragraphs. Forget there is a paper shortage. (The shortage of decent writers is more critical.) If, after writing a sentence, a paragraph, a half page, you find yourself going in the wrong direction (not just a direction you hadn't anticipated—that's probably a good one—but toward a dead end), throw the page away. Take another sheet and start again. After a few false starts, your ideas, if you really have some, will begin to take visible form, and it's much easier to improve ideas once you see them in front of you than it is to do the job in your head. On paper, one word leads to another. In your head, one word often blocks another.

You may realize, as you near the end of a sentence, that you no longer believe it. Never mind. Be glad that your first idea led you to a better one, pick up the better one and keep going with it. By now, you don't need to throw pages away. Take a pencil and cross out the false sentence if it distracts you. Don't erase it; that takes too much time, and you may make something of that sentence later on if you have a record of it. Again, keep going.

At some point you will begin to see where the words already on paper promise to lead you. That's the point at which I would make a rough outline (and my colleague would be revising his). Now you begin to see which ideas must be developed, which discarded, where ideas must be clarified by specific details and examples, and where connections between ideas must be made. When you get these thoughts into notes on paper—and you must write them down or you'll forget them—you are close to having a first draft. We'll have more to say in a while about first drafts and how to pull them into shape. But for the moment, you can go ahead and make your bed and, if you like, climb into it. Now we have something to say to those who "have nothing to say."

Asking Questions and Answering Them

If you have nothing to say about a particular topic, ask yourself questions and answer them. Here is an example of how to go about it. First, read the following editorial from the *New York Times.*

THE NEWARK PUBLIC LIBRARY [1]

Philip Roth

What will the readers of Newark do if the City Council goes ahead with its money-saving plan to shut down the public library system on April 1? Will they loot the stacks as Newarkers looted furniture and appliance stores in the riot of 1967? Will police be called in to Mace down thieves racing off with the *Encyclopedia Britannica*? Will scholars take up sniping positions at reference room windows and school children "seize" the main Washington Street building in order to complete their term papers? If the City Council locks up the books, will library card holders band together to "liberate" them?

I suppose one should hope not. Apparently there must be respect for Law and Order, even where there is none for aspiration and curiosity and quiet pleasure, for language, learning, scholarship, intelligence, reason, wit, beauty, and knowledge.

When I was growing up in Newark in the forties we assumed that the books in the public library belonged to the public. Since my family did not own many books, or have much money for a child to buy them, it was good to know that solely by virtue of my municipal citizenship I had access to any book I wanted from that grandly austere building downtown on Washington Street, or from the branch library I could walk to in my neighborhood. No less satisfying was the idea of communal ownership, property held in common for the common good. Why I had to care for the books I borrowed, return them unscarred and on time, was because they weren't mine alone, they were everybody's. That idea had as much to do with civilizing me as any I was ever to come upon in the books themselves.

If the idea of a *public* library was civilizing so was the place, with its comforting quiet, its tidy shelves, its knowledgeable, dutiful employees who weren't teachers. The library wasn't simply where one had to go to get the books, it was a kind of exacting haven to which a city youngster willingly went for his lesson in restraint and his training in self-control. And then there was the lesson in order, the enormous institution itself serving as instructor. What trust it inspired—in both oneself and in systems—first to decode the catalogue card, then to

[1] In February 1969, after riots had already destroyed much of Newark's black slum neighborhoods, the Newark City Council voted to strike from the city budget the $2.8 million required to finance the Newark Museum and the Newark Public Library. Hundreds of Newark residents vehemently opposed this move, which would have shut down two exceptional civic institutions. In the face of the protest, the Council eventually rescinded their decision. This article appeared on the editorial page of the *New York Times*, March 1, 1969, about two weeks after the Council had announced the budget cutback.

make it through the corridors and stairwells into the open stacks, and there to discover, exactly where it was supposed to be, the desired book. For a ten-year-old to find he actually can steer himself through tens of thousands of volumes to the very one he wants is not without its satisfactions. Nor did it count for nothing to carry a library card in one's pocket; to pay a fine if need be; to sit in a strange place, beyond the reach of parent and school, and read whatever one chose, in anonymity and peace; finally, to carry home across the city and even into bed at night a book with a local lineage of its own, a family-tree of Newark readers to which one's name had now been added.

In the forties, when Newark was mostly white and I was being raised there, it was simply an unassailable fact of life that the books were "ours" and that the public library had much to teach us about the rules of civilized life, as well as civilized pleasures to offer. It is strange, to put it politely, that now when Newark is mostly black, the City Council (for fiscal reasons, we are told) has reached a decision that suggests that the books don't really belong to the public after all, and that the lessons and pleasures a library provides for the young are no longer essential to an education. In a city seething with social grievances there is, in fact, probably little that could be *more* essential to the development and sanity of the thoughtful and ambitious young than access to those libraries and books. For the moment the Newark City Council may, to be sure, have solved a fiscal problem; it is too bad, however, that they are unable to calculate the frustration, cynicism, and rage that such an insult must inevitably generate, or to imagine what shutting down the libraries may cost the community in the end.

Now read the following questions, and imagine how you might answer them, in writing.

1. a. What was the occasion for this editorial? (One sentence)
   b. Summarize Roth's response. (One sentence)
2. a. *How* does he support his position in paragraph 3? Describe his strategy. (One sentence)
   b. What are the two main reasons he gives in paragraph 3 in support of his position? (One or two sentences)
3. Explain what he means by "civilizing" in paragraphs 3 and 4. (Two to four sentences)
4. In paragraph 5, what new reasons does he state or imply in support of his position? (Two to four sentences)
5. Describe and explain his strategy in paragraph 1 and paragraph 2. (Write one short paragraph.)
6. Optional: Evaluate Philip Roth's editorial.

If you were now to take your answers and revise them a bit, you'd have an essay something like the one that follows. We subtitle it "A Composite Essay" because we composed it from the best answers written by twenty students in a freshman class in expository writing.

ON PHILIP ROTH'S "THE NEWARK PUBLIC LIBRARY" (A COMPOSITE ESSAY)

The City Council of Newark introduced a plan to shut down the public library system in order to save money. (1a) Philip Roth, in his editorial (the *New York Times*, March 1, 1969), argues that the closing of the libraries will be a costly mistake, and that the action will be an insult to the citizens of Newark. (1b)

He supports his position by telling how the library helped him when he was young. (2a) He says that the public library gave him a chance to use books that his family couldn't afford, but more important, the very idea of a public library, of the communal ownership of books, played a part in civilizing him. (2b) By civilizing Roth means socializing. The quiet and orderly fashion in which the library was arranged and run taught him restraint, and taught him to value solitude, privacy, and self-control. Looking for books was itself a lesson in order; he learned, for example, that he could find, through the card catalog, one book among the many thousands there. (3)

Roth suggests that since Newark has become predominantly black, the City Council's attitude toward the library's functions and importance has changed. He implies that the Council's plan is irresponsible and discriminatory. He points out that in a city with as many social problems as Newark's, the lessons and pleasures given to the young by the library are more, not less, essential to their education. He says that although the Council's move may solve an immediate fiscal problem, it will in the end create greater social problems because of the frustration and rage it will generate. (4)

He questions what the readers might do if the library is shut down. He hypothesizes that they might riot and loot the library, or they might seize the library and liberate the books. His questions are, of course, ironic. By overdramatizing the possible reactions, he gains the interest of the reader, and he shows the senselessness of the Council's plan. Through sarcasm, he discloses a further irony: the City Council, whose members are the first to insist on respect for law and order, have no respect themselves for communal as opposed to private property, or for the civilized qualities law and order should foster and support: beauty, knowledge, pleasure, aspiration. (5, 6)

Organizing Ideas

In the preceding example we have, of course, prearranged the questions so that the answers, put one after another, would compose a clear and emphatic essay. Clear because in the opening paragraph the essay gives a reader who has not read Roth's editorial enough information to understand what we are writing about. It brings the topic into focus: by summarizing the circumstances that provoked Roth's editorial, by summarizing the gist of Roth's argument, and by indicating (in the word "argues") what kind of essay Roth's essay is. The organization of our essay is emphatic because it moves from what we were less interested in (what happened in Newark) to what we were more interested in (Roth's strategies for persuasion). We were, that is, less interested in a summary of events than we were in an analysis of a good piece of persuasive writing.

When, in preparing to write, you ask yourself questions, some will present themselves to you spontaneously. They'll pop into your head while you read or while you reflect about an experience, and you'll wisely write them down before you forget them. But if you get stuck, think of the four categories into which our specific questions on Roth's editorial fall, and see if these generate specific questions about your topic. Here are the four general questions and methods of answering them.

1. What happened?   Summarize or narrate
2. What does the happening mean? Or,   Interpret or paraphrase
   what do the words mean?
3. What is it? How does it work? How   Analyze
   does it yield meaning?
4. How good is it? What makes it good?   Evaluate
   Or, what makes it bad?

To generate ideas, then, if you have a topic but nothing to say about it, ask yourself questions and answer them. You may write your questions down in whatever order they occur to you, but before you write your essay rearrange your answers with your reader in mind. Your arrangement should be clear: it should make sense to someone who isn't inside your head. And it should be emphatic: that is, it should show by its climactic order what you have found to be the most interesting questions to answer.

Note that arranging answers to questions in clear and climactic order is equivalent to arranging note cards, or to writing an outline after the shape of your ideas has become visible to you. So, whether you see your problem as having ideas but not knowing how to express them or as not having any ideas to express, the solution may be either to start writing or to ask yourself questions and answer them. Either way you'll end up with a least a first draft of an essay.

EXERCISE

Analyze and evaluate a current or recent editorial. Include a copy of the editorial with your essay, but write for a reader who does not have access to the editorial. Suggested length: 350 words.

CLARIFYING IDEAS

On page 6 we wrote "Now you begin to see which ideas must be . . . clarified by specific details and examples." You'll find more discussion of this point on pages 65–67 (about topic ideas) and pages 192–95 (on revising sentences). Here we consider two directions in which the mind of the essayist frequently moves as he expresses and clarifies his ideas. The procedure involves writing fiction, but it does strengthen some techniques for writing expository prose. First, read the following two paragraphs from Saul Bellow's novel *The Victim*.

Leventhal's apartment was spacious. In a better neighborhood, or three stories lower, it would have rented for twice the amount he paid. But the staircase was narrow and stifling and full of turns. Though he went up slowly, he was out of breath when he reached the fourth floor, and his heart beat thickly. He rested before unlocking the door. Entering, he threw down his raincoat and flung himself on the tapestry-covered low bed in the front room. Mary had moved some of the chairs into the corners and covered them with sheets. She could not depend on him to keep the windows shut and the shades and curtains drawn during the day. This afternoon the cleaning woman had been in and there was a pervasive odor of soap powder. He got up and opened a window. The curtains waved once and then were as motionless as before. There was a movie house strung with lights across the street; on its roof a water tank sat heavily uneven on its timbers; the cowls of the chimneys, which rattled in the slightest stir of air, were still.

The motor of the refrigerator began to run. The ice trays were empty and rattled. Wilma, the cleaning woman, had defrosted the machine and forgotten to refill them. He looked for a bottle of beer he had noticed yesterday; it was gone. There was nothing inside except a few lemons and some milk. He drank a glass of milk and it refreshed him. He had already taken off his shirt and was sitting on the bed unlacing his shoes when there was a short ring of the bell. Eagerly he pulled open the door and shouted, "Who is it?" The flat was unbearably empty. He hoped someone had remembered that Mary was away and had come to keep him company. There was no response below. He called out again, impatiently. It was very probable that someone had pushed the wrong button, but he heard no other doors opening. Could it be a prank? This was not the season for it. Nothing moved in the stair well, and it only added to his depression to discover how he longed for a visitor. He stretched out on the bed, pulling a pillow from beneath the spread and doubling it up. He thought he would doze off. But a little later he found himself standing at the window, holding the curtains with both hands. He was under the impression that he had slept. It was only eight-thirty by the whirring electric clock on the night table, however. Only five minutes had passed.[2]

Now try making what is implicit, explicit (practice generalizing from specific details). Write one sentence in which you summarize what Bellow's paragraphs imply about (a) the weather and (b) Leventhal's mood. Your sentence should ascribe two qualities to each. Here is the format:

It was *bright* and *crisp*, and Leventhal was *angry* and *suspicious*.

Obviously the words in the blanks are wrong. You supply the right words.

To write the sentence, you must abstract (deduce) certain qualities of the weather and of Leventhal's mood that are implied by the concrete (specific) details in the paragraphs. Many sentences might do the job, but let's take one:

It was hot and humid and Leventhal was lonely and depressed.

That it was hot and humid is implied by many details in the

first paragraph. Some of them are: the staircase was stifling; Leventhal carried a raincoat; Mary had covered the chairs (to protect them from the sun); the curtains were almost motionless; the cowls (coverings to improve the draft) of the chimneys were still. What details in the second paragraph imply that Leventhal was lonely and depressed?

Next, try making what is explicit, implicit—that is, practice presenting evidence. First, write a sentence in which you again ascribe two abstract qualities to the weather and two to the mood of a character. This time the circumstances, place, and character will be of your own invention. Limitations are helpful: limit yourself, for example, to one scene and to one action that can take place in five or ten minutes, or at most half an hour. Like all writers, you will doubtless base your inventions in part on a scene and a person you actually know. The form of your sentence will be:

It was_____ and _____, and X was _____

and _____.

Now write a paragraph or two in which you imply through specific, concrete details the qualities you have chosen. Name your character and describe him or her performing some action. But don't use the abstract words of your sentence in your paragraphs.

You can measure the success of your description by seeing how close someone else can come to reconstructing your original sentence from the concrete details in your paragraphs.

Abstract and Concrete

We've said that the two operations you have just performed introduce two directions in which the mind of the essayist frequently moves as he expresses and clarifies his ideas. The two directions are from concrete to abstract and from abstract to concrete. An abstraction is said to be "thinner" than the objects or persons—real or imagined—of the concrete world. Words like "weather" and "cheerfulness" do not have the same reality or density that a particular snowy day or a child whistling has. Abstractions can be talked about but they cannot exist apart from concrete objects. "Mankind" or "man" is abstract compared with "this man, Leventhal."

Most good writing offers a judicious mixture of the abstract, by means of generalizations, and the concrete, by means of specific details. A page of highly abstract writing may seem bloodless; a page of concrete details may seem a kleptomaniac's trunkful of bric-a-brac. To keep your reader's attention, try to unify your concrete details with abstractions and generalizations, and to enliven your abstractions and generalizations with specific details and examples. Since students tend to write too abstractly rather than too concretely, it is good to keep in mind Nietzsche's advice: "The more abstract the truth you want to teach, the more thoroughly you must seduce the senses to accept it."

Suppose, for example, a writer offered us the following paragraph:

Certain biological changes which occur as we grow older are apparent whenever you look at an old person. These age changes in the surface of the body are gradual, and vary according to diet, genetic factors, even climate. Like all other aspects of aging, it is not the biological changes themselves (because they are quite natural) but the subsequent changes in self-regard which have the most impact on the individual.

Well, it makes sense, we get the gist of it, and it is even moderately interesting, but could we read many pages of such writing?

Here is what the author really wrote—the previous sentences, but rich with details. Notice how the details clarify and add interest to the generalizations.

Certain biological changes which occur as we grow older are apparent whenever you look at an old person. The hair becomes thin, brittle, dull, and gray. The skin becomes paler and may become blotchy; it takes on a parchmentlike texture and loses its elasticity. The loss of subcutaneous fat and elastic tissue leads to a wrinkled appearance. Sweat gland activity and oil secretion decrease and the skin may look dry and scaly. These age changes in the surface of the body are gradual, and vary according to diet, genetic factors, even climate. Like all other aspects of aging, it is not the biological changes themselves (because they are, after all, quite natural) but the subsequent changes in self-regard which have the most impact on the individual. Gray hair can be softening and becoming to a woman; and look quite distinguished on a man. Yet the individual may resent the change, and regard gray hair as the external sign of all the internal effects—slowness, muscular weakness, waning sexual powers.[3]

   —Sharon R. Curtin

Our eviscerated version made all of the points—but how weakly, without the specific details that enliven them.

EXERCISES

1. The following passages are pretty bloodless. Revise them into something with life:

   a. Women are not officially allowed to engage in contact sports, with a few exceptions. Probably this practice reflects our cultural principle of protecting women. But possibly, too, it reflects physical differences between men and women.

   b. What bothers students about nontraditional methods of grading is a concern about their chances of being accepted at the next level of education.

   c. The city has plenty of sights to offer, but greenery is rarely among them. Yet many people have a need for some contact with nature, and of the various ways of satisfying this need one of the cheapest and easiest is growing houseplants.

2. In reading the following passages note which sentences move toward the abstract, through generalization, and which toward the concrete, through specific details and examples.

   a. The really fascinating thing about baby talk is the universality of its linguistic form and content, as demonstrated by a comparison of the way it is spoken in six quite different languages: American English, Spanish, Syrian Arabic, Marathi of India, Gilyak of Siberia, and Comanche Indian of North America. The actual baby-talk vocabularies in the six languages are of course different; nevertheless, the words reveal surprising similarities in linguistic characteristics. All six languages simplify clusters of consonants (as English speakers do when they substitute *tummy* for *stomach*); they reduplicate syllables (*choo-choo*); they alter words in consistent ways to form diminutives (such as the *y* in *doggy*); they eliminate pronouns (*daddy wants* instead of *I want*); and most of the languages drop unstressed syllables (as when *good-bye* becomes *bye* or *bye-bye*). The existence of such similarities in widely different languages suggests that adults with no knowledge of one another's tongues have arrived at much the same linguistic formulas.[4]

   —Peter Farb

---

[3] *Nobody Ever Died of Old Age* (Little, Brown, 1972), pp. 22–23.
[4] "Baby Talk," *The New York Review*, 21 Feb. 1974, p. 24.

b. I never really liked the doctrine of Indulgences — the notion that you could say five Hail Marys and knock off a year in Purgatory.[5]
—Mary McCarthy

c. What a country calls its vital economic interests are not the things which enable its citizens to live, but the things which enable it to make war. Gasoline is much more likely than wheat to be a cause of international conflict.[6]
—Simone Weil

d. There is no such thing as a free lunch.

FOCUSING

What to Write About: Finding a Topic

If a specific topic is assigned, write on it.

If you're taking a course in composition you will probably receive assignments to write on something you are reading or on something out of your personal experience, which may of course include your experience of books. In other courses it's usually up to you to choose a subject from those covered in the course material, to focus on a topic within the subject, and to explore it in some depth. Any assignment requires you to narrow the topic so that you can treat it thoroughly in the allotted space and time. A good general rule in narrowing a topic is to follow your inclinations: focus on something that interests you.

Suppose you're in a composition course and the class has been assigned to read the Book of Ruth in the Old Testament and to write an essay of 500–1000 words on it. If you start with a topic like "The Book of Ruth, A Charming Idyll" you're in trouble. The topic is much too vague. To write about it you'll find yourself hopping around from one place in the book to another, and in desperation saying insincere things like "The Book of Ruth is probably one of the most charming idylls in all literature" when of course you haven't read all literature, and have precious little idea of what idyll means, and couldn't define charm precisely if your life depended on it.

What to do? Focus on something that interested you about

---

[5] *Memories of a Catholic Girlhood* (New York: Berkley Publishing Corp., 1963), p. 30.

[6] Quoted in W. H. Auden, *A Certain World* (New York: Viking Press, 1970), p. 384.

the book. (If you've read the book with pencil in hand, taking some notes, underlining some passages, putting question marks at others, you'll have some good clues to start with.) The book is named after Ruth, but perhaps you find Naomi the more interesting character. If so, you might say: "Although the Book of Ruth is named after Ruth, I find the character of Naomi more interesting."

Stuck again? Ask yourself questions. Why do you find her more interesting? To answer that question, reread the book, focusing your attention on all the passages in which Naomi acts or speaks or is spoken of by others. Ruth's actions, you may find, are always clearly motivated by her love for and obedience to Naomi. But Naomi's actions are more complex, more puzzling. If you're puzzled, trust your feeling—*there is something puzzling there.* What motivated Naomi? Convert your question to "Naomi's Motivation" and you have a topic. If you explore Naomi's actions one by one you may conclude that "Although Naomi shows in many of her actions her concern for her daughter-in-law, her actions also reveal self-interest." Now you have a thesis. It's a bit awkwardly worded, but you can work on a smoother, more natural expression later. Now you have other things to do: selecting, clarifying, and arranging evidence to support your thesis.

"Naomi's Motivation" is a topic in literary criticism. Unless you've been specifically assigned a literary analysis, if you would prefer not to do one, focus on something that interests you more and that you know something about. If your special interest is, for example, economics, or sociology, or law, your topic might be one of these:

Economic Motivation in the Book of Ruth

Attitudes toward Intermarriage in the Book of Ruth

The Status of Women in the Book of Ruth

Any one of these topics can be managed in 500–1000 words. But remember, you were assigned to write on the Book of Ruth. Formulate a thesis and focus on the passages in the book that illuminate it. Suppress the impulse to put everything you know about economics or intermarriage or the-status-of-women-through-the-ages in between two thin slices, an opening sentence and a concluding sentence, on the Book of Ruth.

Or take another example: You're in a composition course and you're asked to write about something out of your own experience. You try to think of something interesting you've done but you've led a most unremarkable life. Your classmates, all strangers, seem to know more than you do about almost everything. They've all been to Europe—well, most of them. All you did last summer was file cards and run errands in an office full of boring people.

Let's examine two essays, each written by a student during the first weeks of the semester. The first is on a boring job; the second, on an unremarkable incident.

As I look back at it, my first thought is that my job was a waste of time. It consisted of compiling information from the files of the Water and Assessors Department in a form suitable for putting on the city's computer. Supposedly this would bring the water billing and property taxing to an efficient level. If the job sounds interesting, don't be deceived. After the first week of work, I seriously doubted that I would survive through the summer.

But I was able to salvage a lesson in the self-discipline of coping with people. Of course we all know how to succeed with friends, family, acquaintances, and employers. But try it in a situation where you have a distinct disadvantage, where you are the seller and they are the customers. And remember, the customer is always right.

By observing the situation, though I was not a participant, I learned that patience, kindness, and understanding can remove the difficulties you cross at the time.

Not a bad topic, really. One can learn something valuable from a boring, menial, frustrating job. Or if not, one can examine boredom (what exactly is it? how does it come about? how does it feel?) and write about it without boring the reader. (Try to name a half-dozen recent films *not* about boredom.) But this essay doesn't teach us anything about boredom. It doesn't allow us through concrete, specific details to feel with the writer that we too would have doubted we could survive the summer. Expressions such as "compiling information from the files" and "form suitable for putting on the city's computer" give us no sense of the tedium of daily transferring numbers from five hundred manila index cards to five hundred gray index cards. Nor does the essay present any evidence that the experience was redeemed by a lesson in "patience, kindness, and understanding."

As it turns out, there was no such lesson. In class discussion, the student frankly admitted the job *was* a waste of time. She had, out of habit, tried to come up with some "pious thought" to please the instructor. The habit had short-circuited the connection between the student's feelings and the words she was writing. The class discussion led to some genuinely interesting questions. Why, for example, are we reluctant to admit that something we've done was in fact a waste of time? "The job was a waste of time" would have been, for most of us, a more productive thesis than "I was able to salvage a lesson." What experiences lead to the conclusions: I must write what the instructor expects; the instructor expects a pious thought? (We'd like to hear from a student willing to explore that topic in 500–1000 words.)

Here is the second student essay.

LIVE FREE OR DIE

Idaho. Famous potatoes. The two identically yellow Volkswagens were parked on either side of the '57 multicolored pick-up truck like flies on a dead cat. The other one was from Wisconsin, America's dairyland. Kent stood with one foot on the battered running board and I waited, reading license plates and kicking the tire. I wanted to talk, but my mind was resting on each tiny thing in the parking lot, Kent's knees, and my feet.

Do you know what it's like to think about someone every second until you almost feel embarrassed about his control over you, then by chance you happen to mention that you love him even though that phrase has never meant a whole lot to you because you've never felt the same about any two people; after all that, do you know what it feels like to have him shake his head and say, "No, you don't love me, you're just fooling yourself"? It feels somewhat like a kick in the teeth. You're taken aback for a minute, considering. Then the pain comes; a sharp clear pain that makes you want to give up. You begin to wonder how often you kid yourself. Of course you deny his statement over and over trying to convince yourself that you really do love him, what ever the hell that means. But I didn't say it. I looked at my October hands still brown and thin from summer work in the sun. They were my hands, I recognized the rings.

I could see the two of us standing there by the truck, silent and tired. It was as though I'd been suspended slightly, or set aside from my life with the unappealing chance to look back and down on everything so far. We were told shadows are nothing, only eels breed in the Sargasso Sea, and History is real. We wrote everything down and have it still, crammed into notebooks that allow us to forget things. And what seeming innocence amid the plotting and twisting of the formed-in-the-air ideas, the humor, the grudges, the silence! Each time we began to slide away from their logic that turned the walls white and made the world as inaccessible as a glazed winter day, we were drawn back by their trust and our insecurity. And not one thing we learned, or were learning, or would ever learn was going to help me now, standing three feet from the only thing I cared about.

My head hurt. The kind of hurt that goes right through my head so for a split second I could feel the center of my mind. I took a step back. Kent didn't move, just stood with his hands deep in his pockets, filtered through me like a literary creation.

"See ya Kent."

"See ya." My mind grabbed every word as I walked. Massachusetts. Massachusetts. Massachusetts. New Hampshire. "Live free or die."

Clearly—examining these essays should make it clear—there is no such thing as an uninteresting life, or moment in life. There are only uninteresting ways to talk about them. It's also clear that some people are more interested in introspection and in talking and writing about their personal experiences than others. The others may be suffering from the Groucho Marx Complex: as Groucho put it, "I don't want to belong to any club that would have me as a member." Students who freeze at the notion of writing about themselves often feel that everything they have done is so ordinary, no one else could possibly be interested in it; anything they know is so obvious, surely everyone else must know it already. If this is your problem, remember that no one else does know exactly what you know; no one else can know what it feels like to live inside your skin. Remember too that writing from your own experience does not necessarily mean writing about private experience. We all have areas of experience we'd rather keep private, and have a right to remain private about. The important thing in writing about experience is, as Marianne Moore said, "we must be as clear as our natural reticence allows us to be." Think, then, of experiences that you are willing to share and to be clear about. If, for example, you have just learned in a psychology course what "operant conditioning" means, define it for someone unfamiliar with the term. You might find yourself narrating an experience of your own to exemplify it; to be clear, you will have to provide an example. Or if an object in a local museum or craft exhibit or store interests you, ask yourself questions— Why do I like it?—and you'll probably be able to turn an object into experience.

Let's turn now to some examples of writing assignments outside of composition courses.

You're in a course in African history and you're asked to write a critique of Chinua Achebe's novel *Things Fall Apart*. What's a critique? you might ask your instructor. It will help, before you ask, if you look at our comments on analysis (pages 28–55) and on writing a book review (pages 163–64). Then you can ask if the assignment is to do an analysis or a book review of *Things Fall Apart*. If the answer is "an analysis" you now know you must focus on a manageable topic. You can't analyze the whole book in 1000 words. Some manageable topics on *Things Fall Apart*:

Nwoye's Conversion to Christianity

The Function of the Proverbs in *Things Fall Apart*

Okonkwo: Hero or Victim?

The Conflict Between Ibo and Christian Beliefs: Where the Narrator's Sympathies Lie

Or suppose that in a course on Modern Revolutionary Movements you're assigned a term paper on any subject covered by the readings or lectures. A term paper is usually about 3000 words and requires research. You're interested in Mexican history, and after a preliminary search you decide to focus on the Revolution of 1910 or some events leading up to it. Depending upon what is available in your library, you might narrow your topic to one of these:

Mexican Bandits—The First Twentieth-Century Revolutionaries

The Exploits of Joaquin Murieta and Tiburcio Vasquez—Romantic Legend and Fact

(See also pages 132–33, on research.)

In short, it is not enough to have a topic (the Book of Ruth, a boring summer, revolutions); you must concentrate your vision on a significant part of the broad topic, just as a landscape painter or photographer selects a portion of the landscape and then focuses on it. Your interests are your most trustworthy guides to which part of the landscape to focus on.

The Writer's Role: The Writer as Teacher

It will help you to focus on a manageable topic and to develop it thoroughly if you keep in mind that, although you are writing because of an assignment from a teacher, *when you write you are the teacher.* It's your job to clarify and share your responses to what you have read or experienced with another person who is not you and who has something to learn from you. If you imagine that other person to be your teacher, you're likely to feel defeated from the beginning. It's probably easier to assume the role of the essayist, the teacher, if you imagine your reader to be someone in your class, that is, someone intelligent and reasonably well informed who shares some of your interests but who does not happen to be you, and who therefore can't know your thoughts and responses unless you explain them clearly and thoroughly.

Writing an essay, then, requires that you look not only outside of you, in front of you, but within you. You not only explore the text or the topic you're writing about, you also explore your responses to it and make them accessible to someone else.

We'll discuss some specific patterns of organization in later chapters, but if you remember that when you write you are teaching, you'll organize your essay to be clear, and to present your ideas at a pace that sustains your reader's interest. It's not enough to present your ideas as they happened to occur to you; your reader should profit from the trials and errors of your early drafts, not labor through them. On the other hand, if you present a mere summary of your conclusions, your reader will be bored. Specific details and examples that support generalizations incorporate some of the drama of your discoveries, and help persuade your reader of their truth. Examples also help you to reveal your ideas at a rate appropriate to their importance and complexity.

On the whole, build toward a climax. Your reader should feel that in following your lead he is going someplace, not going around in circles, and not marking time.

The Writer's "I"

It is seldom necessary in writing an essay, even on a personal experience, to repeat "I think that" or "in my opinion." Your reader knows that what you write is your opinion. Nor is it necessary, if you've done your job well, to apologize. "After reading the story over several times I'm not really sure what it is about but . . ." Write about something you are reasonably sure of. Occasionally, though, when there is a real problem in the text, it is not only permissible to disclose doubts and to reveal tentative conclusions; it is necessary to do so.

Note also that there is no reason to avoid the pronoun "I" when you are in fact writing about yourself. Attempts to avoid "I" (weak passives, "this writer," "we," and the like) are noticeably awkward and distracting. And sometimes you may want to focus on your subjective response to a topic in order to clarify a point. The following opening paragraph of a movie review provides an example:

I take the chance of writing about Bergman's *Persona* so long after its first showing because this seems to me a movie there's no hurry about. It will be with us a long time, just as it has been on my mind for a long time. Right now, when I am perhaps still under its spell, it seems to me Bergman's masterpiece, but I can't imagine ever thinking it less than one of the great movies. This of course is opinion; what I know for certain is that *Persona* is also one of the most difficult movies I will ever see; and I am afraid that in this case there is a direct connection between difficulty and value. It isn't only that *Persona* is no harder than it has to be; its peculiar haunting power, its spell, and its value come directly from the fact that it's so hard to get a firm grasp on.[7]

—Robert Garis

SOME PRELIMINARY REMARKS ON REVISING

Why Revise?

We spoke earlier of writer's block: the fear or anxiety that seems to stand like a stone wall between the writer's thoughts and the blank page. The way to break the block, or leap over the wall, is, we repeat, to start writing. But once the words are

---

[7] *Commentary*, Dec. 1967, p. 80.

on paper in a workable first draft, the experienced writer begins to knock down other blocks, to clear out other obstructions that stand not like a wall, but more like a semi-opaque screen or a smudged window, between the writer's image of his thoughts and the image his words offer the reader. Or, to change the figure, once the writer has found his way through the maze of his thoughts, he sets up road signs, eliminating ill-paved, bumpy detours, so that the reader can more efficiently and more pleasurably get to the same destination.

In reorganizing paragraphs, in clearing deadwood out of sentences, in replacing a period with a semicolon, the writer clarifies his ideas and emotions for his reader. In a sense, the imagined reader becomes a collaborator in the revision, posing questions, demanding clarification. At the same time, the writer clarifies his ideas for himself. Successful revision is, after all, a re-vision, a new and clearer view.

Revision by Destruction and Addition

Picasso said that in painting a picture he advanced by a series of destructions. A story about a sculptor makes a similar point. When asked how he had made such a lifelike image of an elephant from a block of wood, the sculptor answered, "Well, I just knocked off everything that didn't look like elephant." In Part II, on revising, we show you for the most part what to cut away. Where we can, we also suggest what might be put back in (an advantage the writer has over the sculptor).

But only you can say for sure what you mean. Your readers can point to places in your writing where they are puzzled or irritated or lost; in revising, try to anticipate those places. Only you can transform, step by step, "the desired expression in mind" into words on paper.

AN OVERVIEW: FROM SUBJECT TO ESSAY

Everyone must work out his own procedures and rituals (John C. Calhoun liked to plough his farm before writing), but the following suggestions may be helpful. The rest of this book will give you more detailed help.

1. *Turn a subject into a topic.* The day the assignment is given, if the exact topic is not assigned, try to settle on some-

thing that excites or at least interests you and that can be sensibly discussed in the assigned length. Unfortunately, almost none of us can in a few pages write anything of interest on a large subject. We simply cannot in 500 words say anything readable (that is, true and interesting to others) on subjects as broad as music, sports, ourselves. We have to narrow such subject areas down to more specific topics (country music, commercialization of athletics, a term with a roommate) and we then have to shape these smaller topics by seeing them in a particular focus, by having a thesis, an attitude, a point: Country music is popular because . . . ; College athletes are exploited . . . ; How I came to know that I want a single room. Probably you won't find your exact focus or thesis on the first day, but you will be able to jot down a few things, including some questions to yourself, that come to mind on the topic you have carved out of the broad subject. It doesn't matter whether these jottings are made on cards or as a list on a sheet or in a few roughly sketched paragraphs; the important thing is to write something, perhaps a few generalizations, perhaps a few striking details, perhaps a combination of these.

2. *Turn your reveries into notes.* Put your jottings aside for a day or two (assuming you have a week to do the essay) but be prepared to add to them at any moment; useful thoughts may come to you while you are at lunch, while you read a newspaper or magazine, while your mind wanders in class. Write down these thoughts; do not assume that you will remember them when you come to draft your essay.

3. *Sort things out.* About two days before the essay is due, look over your jottings (you ought to have at least a dozen phrases by now), try to settle on your thesis, and reject what is not relevant. Arrange the surviving half-dozen or so jottings into what looks like a reasonable sequence. Perhaps now is the time to choose a provisional title for your essay. A title will help you to keep your thesis in focus. Now add what comes to mind. If you have asked yourself questions, try to jot down the answers. Draw arrows to indicate the sequence you think the phrases should be in.

4. *Write.* As soon as you think you may have an organization for your thesis—that is, an orderly way of making your point—start putting words on paper. Even if you are not sure that you

have a thesis and an organization, start writing. Don't delay; you have some jottings, and you have a mind that, however casually, has already been thinking. Don't worry about writing an effective opening paragraph (your opening paragraph will almost surely have to be revised later anyway); just try to state and develop your argument, based on the phrases or sentences you have accumulated, with all of the details that flow to mind as you write. Leave lots of space between lines, and leave wide margins; you'll fill these in later with additional details, additional generalizations, and revisions of sentences. Keep going until you have nothing left to say.

5. *Save what you can.* Immediately after writing the draft or a few hours later, look it over to see how much is salvageable. Don't worry about getting the exact word here or there; just see whether or not you have a thesis, whether or not you keep the thesis in view, and whether or not the points flow reasonably. Delete irrelevant paragraphs, however interesting; shift paragraphs that are relevant but that should be somewhere else. You can do this best by scissoring the sheets and gluing the pieces in the right order. Don't assume that you will be able to remember that the paragraph near the bottom of page 3 will go into the middle of page 2. Scissor and glue it now, so that when you next read the essay you will easily be able to tell whether in fact the paragraph does belong in the middle of page 2. Probably you can't do much more with your manuscript at this moment. Put it aside until tomorrow.

6. *Revise.* Reread your draft, first with an eye toward large matters: revise your opening paragraph or write one to provide the reader with a focus; make sure the paragraphs grow out of each other; make sure you keep the thesis in view. Next, after making the necessary large revisions, read the draft with an eye toward smaller matters: make sure that each sentence is clear and shapely, and that the necessary details and generalizations are there. Keep pushing the words, the sentences, the paragraphs into shape until they say what you want them to say from the title onward. Correct anything that disturbs you—for instance, awkward repetitions that grate, inflated utterances that bore.

7. *Edit.* When your draft is as good as you can make it, take care of the mechanical matters: if you are unsure of the spelling

of a word, check it in a dictionary; if you are unsure about a matter of punctuation, check it in this book. You will also find footnote form and manuscript form (where to put the title, what margins to leave, and so forth) in this book in the section on editing.

8. *Prepare the final copy.* Now write or type the final copy; if you are on schedule, you will be doing this a day before the essay is due. After writing or typing it, you will probably want to proofread it; there is no harm in doing so, but you will have to proofread it again because at the moment you are too close to your essay. If you put the essay aside for a few hours and then reread it, you will be more likely to catch omitted words, transposed letters, inconsistent spelling of names, and so forth. Change these neatly (see pages 226–27).

9. *Hand the essay in on time.*

In short, the whole business of moving from a subject to a finished essay on a focused topic adds up to Mrs. Beeton's famous recipe: "First catch your hare, then cook it."

CHAPTER TWO

ANALYSIS

SORTING AND THINKING

Analysis is, literally, a separating into parts. It is a kind of adult version of sorting out cards with pictures of baseball players on them. Now, if you have identical items—for instance, one hundred bricks to unload from a truck—you can't sort them; you can only divide them into groups of, say, ten, for easier handling, or into armloads. But if the items vary in some way you can sort them out. You can, for example, put socks into one drawer, underwear into another, trousers or dresses in a closet—all this is an effort to make life a little more manageable. Similarly, you can sort books by size or by color or by topic or by author; you do this, again, in order to make them manageable, to make easier the job of finding the right one later, and so, ultimately, to learn about what is in the book.

When you think seriously or when you talk about almost anything, you also sort or classify. When you think about choosing courses at school, you sort the courses by subject matter or by degree of difficulty ("Since I'm taking two hard courses, I ought to look for an easy course") or by the hour at which they are offered, or by their merit as determined through the grapevine or by the degree to which they interest you. When you sort, you break down the curriculum into parts, putting into each category things that significantly resemble each other but that are not identical. We need categories or classifications; we simply cannot get through life treating every object as unique. Almost everything has an almost infinite number of characteristics and can therefore be placed in any number of categories, but for certain purposes (and we must know our purposes) certain characteristics are significant. It is on these significant characteristics that we fasten.

In sorting, the categories must be established on a single basis of division: you cannot sort dogs into thoroughbreds and small dogs, for some dogs would belong in both categories. You must sort them into consistent, coordinate categories, let us say either by breeding or by size. Of course you can first sort dogs into thoroughbreds and mutts and then sort each of those two categories into two subordinate categories, dogs under twelve inches at the shoulder and dogs twelve inches or more at the shoulder. The categories, as we shall see in a few minutes, will depend on your purpose. That the categories into which any things are sorted should be coordinate is, alas, unknown to the American Kennel Club, which divides dogs into six groups. The first four seem reasonable enough: (1) sporting dogs (for example, retrievers, pointers, spaniels), (2) hounds (bassets, beagles, whippets), (3) working dogs (sheepdogs, St. Bernards, collies), (4) terriers (airedales, Irish terriers, Scottish terriers). Trouble begins with the fifth classification, toy dogs (Maltese, Chihuahuas, toy poodles), for size has not been a criterion up to now. The sixth category is desperate: nonsporting dogs (chow chow, poodle, dalmatian). Nonsporting! What a category. Why not nonworking or nonhound? And is a poodle really more like a chow chow than like a toy poodle? Still, the classifications are by now established, and every thoroughbred must fit into one and only one, and thus every thoroughbred can be measured against all of the dogs that in significant ways are thought to resemble it. In fact, even people who don't judge in dog shows often have to push a creature into one category or another, or, to put it more politely, must interpret and analyze. In England a train passenger had to buy a "dog ticket" to take a pet aboard. Of course a dog ticket also covered cats. What to do about a child's pet turtle? The trainmaster consulted the rule book, thought awhile, and then announced: "Dogs is dogs, and cats is dogs, and squirrels in cages is parrots. But this here turkle is an inseck."

Most serious thinking is analysis. If, for example, we turn our minds to thinking about punishment for killers, we will distinguish at least between those killers whose actions are premeditated, and those killers whose actions are not. And in the first category we might distinguish between professional killers who carefully contrive a death, killers who are irrational except in their ability to contrive a death, and robbers who contrive a property crime and who kill only when they believe that killing is necessary in order to commit the crime. One can hardly talk usefully about capital punishment or imprisonment without making some such analysis of killers. You have, then, taken killers and sorted or separated or classified them, not for the fun of inventing complications but for the sake of educating yourself and those persons with whom you discuss the topic. Unless your attitude is the mad Red Queen's "Off with their heads," the topic has to be divided into parts before it can be seen for what it really is.

Often, too, in the best analyses we are shown not only what parts are in the whole, but what is *not* there—what is missing in relation to a larger context that we can imagine. For example, if we analyze the women in the best-known fairy tales, we will probably find that most women are either sleeping beauties or wicked stepmothers. (These categories are general: "sleeping beauties" includes all passive women valued only for their appearance, and "wicked stepmothers" includes Cinderella's cruel older sisters. Fairy godmothers form another category, but they are not human beings.) We notice the near total absence of resourceful, productive women, and a thoughtful analysis of women in fairy tales will point out this fact. Another example of an analysis that forces us to call to mind what is not there is a single sentence, the Chicano saying "There are only two kinds of Anglos who are interested in us—the sociologists and the police."

When we begin to analyze a topic, whether it is the appropriate treatment of killers or the function of a character in a parable, of course we don't instantly see what the parts are and how we can separate and discuss them. Only when we get into the topic do we begin to see the need for subtle distinctions. It is useful to practice with familiar materials. Any subject that you are interested in and already know something about can be treated analytically. Let's say, for example, you are interested in blues. You have noticed that singers of blues often sing about traveling. Maybe you recall the lines

When a woman takes the blues
She tucks her head and cries
But when a man catches the blues
He catches a freight and rides

and you wonder, among other things: Why all this talk of traveling? You decide you want to look into this question, so you search your memory of blues, play whatever records are available, perhaps read some anthologies that include blues, and generally try to sort things out, that is, try to set your thoughts in order. You find that blues often talk about traveling, but the travel is not all of the same kind, and you begin to analyze the blues that use this motif. You begin to jot down words or phrases:

> disappointed lover
> travel to a job
> from the South
> fantasy travel
> back to the South
> life is a trip
> jail

You are making a scratch outline, for you are establishing categories, fiddling with them until you have established categories as nearly coordinate as possible; and you are indicating the order in which you will discuss these categories. Then perhaps you find it useful to describe your categories a bit more fully:

1. travel as an escape from unhappy love
2. travel as an economic necessity when jobs are not available at home
3. travel as an escape from the South to the North
4. travel as an escape from the North back to the South

5. travel as sheer wishful thinking, an image of escape from the unhappiness of life
6. travel as an image of the hard job of living until death releases one, as in "It's a long old road, but I'm gonna find the end"
7. enforced travel to prison

You have now taken the theme of travel and separated it into various parts; you are educating yourself and you will educate your reader. Having made these or similar distinctions you can go on to say some interesting things about one or all of these superficially similar but really different motifs of travel. The motif of "travel" has had to be divided into parts before it can be seen for what it is.

Once you have established your categories and tentatively settled on the order in which you will treat them, your job is half done. Possibly a finished essay will make the following points, in the order given below, but with convincing detail to support them.

1. Singers of blues sing of traveling, but the travel is of different sorts.
2. Often it is because of economic, social, or even physical pressure (to get a job; to get to a more congenial environment; to get to jail).
3. Most often, however, and perhaps in the most memorable songs, it is for another reason: it is an attempt to reduce the pain of a betrayal in love, and the hearer senses that it can have no successful outcome.
4. In such songs it is usually the men who travel, because they are more mobile than women (women are left to take care of the children), but whether it is the man who has deserted the woman, or the woman who has deserted the man, both are pathetic figures because even the deserter will be haunted by the memory of the beloved.
5. But all of these variations on the theme of travel overlap, and almost always there is a sense that the trip—whether to the North or South, to a job or to jail, to a man or to a woman or to nowhere in particular—is an image or metaphor for the trip through life, the long, painful road that everyone must walk.

Although we are chiefly concerned with how to write an analytic essay, it should be mentioned that sometimes analysis in its starkest form—little more than an enumeration of categories—may be effective writing. A good example is a report issued by the United States Commission on Civil Rights called "Mexican Americans and the Administration of Justice in the Southwest." It is scarcely more than an outline; the simple, apparently objective presentation of categories, with brief specifications under them, suggests a kind of scientific or dispassionate study. The report, which is too long to quote in full here, establishes thirteen categories, such as "Underrepresentation of Mexican Americans on juries," "Police misconduct," "Language disability," and "Courts and prosecutors." Here is one category with its items:

6. *Underrepresentation of Mexican Americans on juries*
There is a serious and widespread underrepresentation of Mexican Americans on grand and petit State juries in the Southwest:
(a) neither lack of knowledge of the English language nor low-incomes of Mexican Americans can explain the wide disparities between the Mexican American percentage of the population and their representation on juries;
(b) judges or jury commissioners frequently do not make affirmative efforts to obtain a representative cross section of the community for jury service;
(c) the peremptory challenge is used frequently both by prosecutors and defendants' lawyers to remove Mexican Americans from petit jury venires.
The underrepresentation of Mexican Americans on grand and petit juries results in distrust by Mexican Americans of the impartiality of verdicts.[1]

Ordinarily you will not number categories and letter the items, as shown here, but you will be doing something close to it when you say "A further point . . ." or "Another example . . ."

ANALYSIS COMPARED WITH SUMMARY AND INTERPRETATION

Analysis should be clearly distinguished from summary and from interpretation, though of course, as the essay on Roth's editorial illustrates (page 9), an essay may contain all three in

[1] (Washington, D.C.: GPO, 1970), p. 88.

varying proportions. Let us assume we are going to analyze a piece of literature. A summary will tell, without personal comment, what happens; an interpretation will tell what the happenings mean; but an analysis, by examining the parts and relating them to the whole, will tell *how* the meanings are revealed. We analyze—that is, separate into parts—in order better to understand the whole. Analysis poses and answers such questions as "What is the function of this character?" or "Why do we get dialogue here rather than the author's summary of what was said?" Similarly, if you write an essay on the function of school vacations, or the purpose of the gasoline tax, you will be writing an analysis—provided that you don't lapse into a mere summary of the history of these topics.

Probably most of your writing will be about other writing—an analysis (including passages of summary and of interpretation) of What X said happened at Little Bighorn, of Y's account of role-playing, of Z's argument on the dangers of cloning. Let us look at a brief piece of inspired writing, Jesus' Parable of the Prodigal Son (Luke 15), and then compare a summary, an interpretation, and an analysis of it.

PARABLE OF THE PRODIGAL SON

And he said, "A certain man had two sons: and the younger of them said to his father, 'Father, give me the portion of goods that falleth to me.' And he divided unto them his living. And not many days after, the younger son gathered all together, and took his journey into a far country, and there wasted his substance with riotous living. And when he had spent all, there arose a mighty famine in that land, and he began to be in want. And he went and joined himself to a citizen of that country, and he sent him into his fields to feed swine. And he would fain have filled his belly with the husks that the swine did eat: and no man gave unto him. And when he came to himself, he said, 'How many hired servants of my father's have bread enough and to spare, and I perish with hunger? I will arise and go to my father, and will say unto him, "Father, I have sinned against heaven, and before thee. And am no more worthy to be called thy son: make me as one of thy hired servants."' And he arose, and came to his father. But when he was yet a great way off, his father saw him, and had compassion, and ran, and fell on his neck, and kissed him. And the son said unto him, 'Father, I have sinned against heaven, and in thy sight, and am no more worthy to be called thy son.' But the father said to his servants, 'Bring forth the best robe, and put it on him, and put a ring on his hand, and shoes on his feet. And bring hither the fatted calf, and kill it, and let us eat, and be merry. For this my son was dead, and is alive again; he was lost, and is found.' And they began to be merry. Now his elder son was in the field, and as he came and drew nigh to the house, he heard music and dancing. And he called one of the servants, and asked what these things meant. And he said unto him, 'Thy brother is come, and thy father hath killed the fatted calf, because he hath received him safe and sound.' And he was angry, and would not go in: therefore came his father out, and entreated him. And he answering said to his father, 'Lo, these many years do I serve thee, neither transgressed I at any time thy commandment, and yet thou never gavest me a kid, that I might make merry with my friends: but as soon as this thy son was come, which hath devoured thy living with harlots, thou hast killed for him the fatted calf.' And he said unto him, 'Son, thou art ever with me, and all that I have is thine. It was meet that we should make merry, and be glad: for this thy brother was dead, and is alive again: and was lost, and is found.' "

A *summary* (not an interpretation or an analysis) would in a few sentences retell the plot, perhaps like this: "A younger son asks his father for his inheritance, receives it, and journeys far away, where he wastes his money. When he is destitute, a famine arises, and he is forced to take the lowly job of swineherd, eating with the swine. Miserable, he remembers the prosperous life at his father's house, penitently returns, and is joyously welcomed by his father. The older son, who had dutifully served their father, protests at the father's generous forgiveness, but the father explains that the younger son was like a dead man brought back to life."

An *interpretation* would explain that Jesus is teaching his followers the meaning of love and compassion. The father represents God; the older son represents those who obey God's commandments; the younger son represents sinners. The father's house represents heaven. The parable makes the point that the repentant sinner is received as joyously in heaven as the non-sinner. A well-developed interpretation, though, would probably include a summary, quotations, some paraphrasing, and some analysis.

The writer of an *analysis* would ask himself such a question as "What is the function of the older son in this story?" The question is a good one, because the parable is traditionally called the Parable of the Prodigal Son, referring to the younger son. The older son in no way influences the younger son's actions. And we notice that the story of the younger son is complete two-thirds of the way through the parable. Why does Jesus go on to talk about the older son? Possibly we will conclude that the story is badly told, ending with an anticlimax; more likely we will come to sense the function of the ending. An analytical essay on the topic might run along the following lines. (Notice that this essay, although primarily analytical, includes summary and interpretation: summary to remind the reader of the gist of the story, since he may not have it clearly in mind, and interpretation to touch on the larger significance.)

THE OTHER SON

Among the stories that Jesus tells is the parable traditionally called The Prodigal Son, in Luke 15. In this story, a son who leaves his father and squanders his inheritance comes to see that he has been foolish and he returns, penitent. His father, seeing the son approach, joyfully welcomes him even before the son utters a speech of repentance. But an older son, who has dutifully remained with the father, complains that the father welcomes the prodigal with a generosity not shown to the dutiful son. The father explains: "Son, thou art ever with me, and all that I have is thine. It was meet that we should make merry, and be glad: for this thy brother was dead, and is alive again: and was lost, and is found."

It is understandable that this parable of repentance and forgiveness is called the Prodigal Son, for we can easily identify ourselves with the prodigal and we too, knowing that we are sinners, can hope for God's forgiveness. Yet the story does not end with the forgiveness of the prodigal; the last third of the story is largely about the dutiful and resentful older son. If we hold too tightly to the traditional title, we may feel that the ending is anticlimactic, but a closer look at the story reveals the function of the older son.

The older son serves two purposes: (1) he provides, in a special way, a contrast to the younger son, and (2) he is a representative or surrogate for the listener or reader, who wonders, as he learns of the father's forgiveness, if the forgiveness may not be a foolish father's sentimentalism. To take the first point: the young son is clearly impetuous, first in leaving home, second in squandering his fortune. But the older son is not his virtuous opposite; the older son is self-righteous and resentful ("Lo, these many years do I serve thee, neither transgressed I at any time thy commandment; and yet thou never gavest me a kid"). In a sense, then, the older son too was far away from his loving father even though he toiled at home. Perhaps the most wonderful touch is the older son's disdainful reference to "this thy son," evoking the father's tender reply, "This thy brother was dead, and is alive again: and was lost, and is found." The second point is closely related: without the older son *we* might be tempted to find the father's forgiveness too easy. The older brother utters our unspoken half-formulated ungenerous thought; he is answered, and therefore *we* are answered and satisfied.

COMPARING

Analysis frequently involves comparing; things are examined for their resemblances to and differences from other things. Strictly speaking, if one emphasizes the differences rather than the similarities, one is contrasting rather than comparing, but here we need not preserve this distinction; we can call both processes "comparing."

An essay that is not entirely devoted to comparison may include a paragraph or two of comparison to explain, for example, something unfamiliar by comparing it to something familiar ("The heart is like a pump. . . ."). The first part of a paragraph making a comparison may announce the topic, the next part may discuss one of the two items, and the last part may discuss the other. Or the discussion of the two items may run throughout the entire paragraph, the writer perhaps devoting alternate sentences to each. Because almost all writing is designed to help the reader to *see* what the writer has in mind, it may be especially useful here to illustrate this last structure with a discussion of visible distinctions. This comparison of a Japanese statue of the Buddha with a Chinese statue of a bodhisattva (a slightly lower spiritual being, dedicated to saving mankind) may make clear the way in which a comparison can run throughout a paragraph.

The Buddha is recognizable by the cranial bump, representing a super mind. Because the Buddha is free from attachment to things of this world, he wears only a simple monk's robe and his head is unadorned, in contrast to the bodhisattva, whose rich garments and crown symbolize his power as a spiritual creature who still moves on this earth. Moreover, the Buddha is, or was, gilded, symbolizing his heavenly, sun-like nature, whereas the bodhisattva is more or less naturalistically colored. These differences, however, are immediately obvious and, in a sense, superficial. The distinction between the two kinds of spiritual beings, one awesome and one compassionate, is chiefly conveyed by the pose and the carving. The Buddha sits erect and austere, in the lotus position (legs crossed, each foot with the sole upward on the opposite thigh), in full control of his body. The carved folds of his garment, equally severe, form a highly disciplined pattern. The more earthly bodhisattva wears naturalistically carved flowing garments, and sits in a languid, sensuous posture known as "royal ease," the head pensively tilted downward, one knee elevated, one leg hanging down. Both figures are spiritual but the Buddha is remote, constrained, and austere, the bodhisattva is accessible, relaxed, and compassionate.

Buddha (wood, 33½"; Japanese, late tenth century).

Bodhisattva (wood, 56½"; Chinese, twelfth century).

Let us now talk about a comparison or contrast that runs through an entire essay, say a comparison between the characters in two novels, or between the symbolism of two poems. Probably your first thought, after making some jottings, is to discuss one half of the comparison and then to go on to the second half. Instructors and textbooks usually condemn such an organization, arguing that the essay breaks into two parts and that the second part involves a good deal of repetition of categories set up in the first part. Let's say the topic is a comparison of the narrator of *Huckleberry Finn* with the narrator of *Catcher in the Rye*. The organization that is usually recommended is something like this:

1. first similarity (the narrator and his quest)
   a. Huck
   b. Holden
2. second similarity (the corrupt world surrounding the narrator)
   a. society in *Huckleberry Finn*
   b. society in *The Catcher*
3. first difference (degree to which the narrator fulfills his quest and escapes from society)
   a. Huck's plan to "light out" to the frontier
   b. Holden's breakdown

And so on, for as many additional differences as seem relevant. Here is another way of organizing a comparison and contrast:

1. first point: the narrator and his quest
   a. similarities between Huck and Holden
   b. differences between Huck and Holden
2. second point: the corrupt world
   a. similarities between the worlds in *Huck* and *The Catcher*
   b. differences between the worlds in *Huck* and *The Catcher*
3. third point: degree of success
   a. similarities between Huck and Holden
   b. differences between Huck and Holden

But a comparison need not employ either of these structures. There is even the danger that an essay employing either of them may not come into focus until the essayist stands back from his seven-layer cake and announces, in his concluding paragraph, that the odd layers taste better. In one's preparatory thinking one may want to make comparisons in pairs, but one must come to some conclusions about what these add up to before writing the final version. The final version should not duplicate the thought processes; rather, it should be organized so as to make the point clearly and effectively. The point of the essay presumably is not to list pairs of similarities or differences, but to illuminate a topic by making thoughtful comparisons. Although in a long essay one cannot postpone until page 30 a discussion of the second half of the comparison, in an essay of, say less than ten pages nothing is wrong with setting forth one half of the comparison and then, in light of it, the second half. The essay will break into two unrelated parts if the second half makes no use of the first, or if it fails to modify the first half, but not if the second half looks back to the first half and calls attention to differences that the new material reveals. A student ought to learn how to write an essay with interwoven comparisons, but he ought also to know that there is another, simpler and clearer way to write a comparison.

The following summary, paragraph by paragraph, of Stanley Kauffmann's comparison of film versions of Joyce's *Ulysses* and *Finnegans Wake* illustrates this last method; it treats one item chiefly in the first part of the essay, the second chiefly in the second part. Kauffmann's essay, published in the *New American Review 2*, is, of course, filled with concrete details that here are omitted, but the gist of the eleven paragraphs is as follows:

1. Because subjectivity fascinates film-makers, it is natural that Joyce's two great novels of subjectivity would be filmed. One film is good, the other poor.
2. The poor film is *Ulysses,* a book that summarizes a vast amount of life.
3. The film of *Ulysses* has two motifs: tolerance and sexual candor. But these are only minor parts of the novel.
4. The film cannot be said to be faithful to the novel. True, it adds almost nothing; but it omits an enormous amount.
5. Some things of course simply cannot be filmed, so let us look at what is present rather than what is absent in the film. The opening is good, but . . . and . . . and . . . are poor.
6. In general, the acting is poor.
7. On the other hand, the film of *Finnegans Wake* is pretty successful, capturing the effect of a dream.
8. Though a bit long, and with some of the faults of the film of *Ulysses,* the film of *Finnegans Wake* is interesting, imaginative, and inventive.

9. The director uses subtitles, an effective device because Joyce's words (often puns) are "visual objects."
10. The actors effectively convey in their lines the sense of a dream.
11. The film of *Finnegans Wake* captures the mythic quality that the film of *Ulysses* fails to capture.

As this skeleton of the essay shows, Kauffmann introduces both halves of the comparison in his opening paragraph; paragraphs 2–6 concentrate on one half (the film of *Ulysses*); paragraphs 7 and 8 concentrate on the second half of the comparison, but they remind the reader of the first half; paragraphs 9 and 10 discuss more fully the second—more important—film; and paragraph 11, the conclusion, offers a final judgment on both films.

Finally, the point of a comparison is to call attention to the unique features of something by holding it up against something similar but significantly different. If the differences are great and apparent, a comparison is a waste of effort. ("Blueberries are different from elephants. Blueberries do not have trunks. And elephants do not grow on bushes.") Indeed, a comparison between essentially and evidently unlike things can only obscure, for by making the comparison the writer implies there are significant similarities, and the reader can only wonder why he does not see them. The essays that do break into two halves are essays that make uninstructive comparisons: the first half tells the reader about five qualities in Dickens, the second half tells the reader about five different qualities in Dylan Thomas.

EXERCISES

1. Analyze the seating pattern in the cafeteria. Are groups, including groups of empty chairs, perceptible?

2. Look over the birthday cards in a store. What images of girls and women are presented? Are they stereotyped images of passivity and domesticity? If such images predominate, what exceptions are there? Do the exceptions fall into categories? What images of boys and men are presented? Are they stereotyped images of vigor and authority? Again, if there are exceptions, do they form a pattern? (After you have studied the rack for a while, and jotted down some notes, you may find it useful to buy two or three cards so that when you write your essay you will have some evidence at hand.)

3. Write an essay of 500–1000 words on either why people have house plants or why people have pets.

4. Write a brief essay of not more than three paragraphs on the function of one of the following:

credit-noncredit grading
a minor character in a TV series
the gasoline tax
the death penalty
the preface to this book
the Twenty-fifth Amendment to the Constitution
pay toilets
school i.d. cards
monumental fountains near public buildings
Mother's Day

5. An aunt has offered to buy you a subscription to *Time* or *Newsweek*. Compare in 300–500 words the contents of the current issues and explain which magazine you will choose. (If neither magazine is of interest, try comparing *Cosmopolitan* and *Ms.*)

6. Compare the function of the setting in *All in the Family* with that of *The Waltons*.

ANALYSIS AT WORK: FOUR ESSAYS

Here are four essays that are primarily analytic. The first is the most obviously so: it sorts or classifies skiers, from the wretches who go on packaged bus tours up to the glamorous ski instructors.

SKIERS AS A SUBCULTURE
David Boroff

Skiing was once supposed—by sentimentalists—to be the sport of a heroic elite. In a simpler time, when rope tows creaked, the outdoor ideal was untarnished. "It was all fresh air during the day and singing in front of a fire at night," an old-timer recalled. There were even those who, in Norse fashion, made long cross-country trips on skis. (This has become the fashion again.) But the dynamics of popular sport are irresistible. You start with a Spartan idyll, the sport catches on, and there is an inescapable expansion—and melancholy decline—into crowds, technology, motels.

Ski operators are inclined to be impatient with elitist nostalgia. As the sport gains popularity, the facilities become more lavish—so lavish and so expensive that ever larger crowds become economically imperative. Mount Snow has led the way with such peripheral things as outdoor swimming and indoor ice skating, saunas—and girl watching for the predatory. Who has to ski?

Nearly everybody is the answer. For what saves skiing finally is a respect—amounting to reverence—for the sheer skill of the sport. No snobbery is fiercer than that of the *echt* skier. Skiers discuss refinements of technique and equipment with a passion and a minuteness that suggest scholars engaged in esoteric studies.

Technique snobbery is remorseless. The wedelners perform their choreography like movie stars. They come spinning down the mountain with negligent grace and churn into the tow line in a haughty spume of snow. On the mountainside the serfs laboriously make their way down the slope, picking the easy spots, eying the moguls like enemies. But they, in turn, lord it over the beginners. And even the beginners feel a lofty superiority over the snow bunnies, those fellow travelers of sport.

Another system of snobbery has to do with where you ski. The farther you go, the more dash you have. The lower Catskills—Grossinger's, the Concord, Davos—are simply out of the question. Skiers love to boast about prodigies of driving that they perform ("We made Stowe in six and a half hours"), and the whole point of a ski weekend is to cram as much as possible into the weekend with the least amount of sleep. The ultimate refinement in this distance steeplechase is the junket to Switzerland—"just for a few days of skiing" —to Chile or even to that final outpost, New Zealand.

The spirit in which you go also yields points in the status rat race. Skiing is big business today, but skiers like to maintain the illusion of a certain nonchalance—Renaissance Italians called it *sprezzatura,* a highly prized quality among courtiers.

Low man on this totem pole is the square who makes arrangements to go on a packaged bus tour, a kind of grubby welfare state in which meals, lodging and instruction are written into the contract. Bus tours are scorned even by ski operators, a group notable for their magnanimity. The operators' quarrel with bus tours is that they carry their own ski instructors, who, allegedly, are uncertified. There are also recurrent reports of ungentlemanly drinking during the day. The package planners have the last word. They argue that skiers should be relieved of the anxieties of travel and lodging. The ski instructors, they insist, are often certified and have the advantage of knowing their students before they teach them. And in this fresh-air democracy, why shouldn't secretaries and salesmen take a crack at skiing?

One would expect that people who make their living from skiing would be free from the status nonsense. But they tend to be as hierarchical as their customers. The pecking order, in ascending order, is ski bum, ski patrolman and ski instructor. The ski bum is really a beatnik with a suntan and an implausible passion for skiing. He— or she—works part-time in a lodge in exchange for board and a season ski pass. He is often a college kid on the lam, a member of that army of restless students who take a semester or year off. Sometimes he is just out of school, determined to squeeze in a full season of skiing before graduate school or career closes in. Ski bums provide a touch of bohemia in a sport which is becoming big business. (There are even ski bum entertainers whose job it is to sing folk songs in front of the fire.) But, in the end, the Organization will be their undoing. Already, ski operators are nervous about the term ski bums. "Please call them lodge staff," a slope operator suggested primly.

Ski patrolmen, the medical corpsmen of the slopes, are the dray horses of the sport. Brightly costumed, with medical packs bulging around their middle, they maintain safety, take down the injured and make a final sweep of trails and slopes at the end of the day. They are the beefy cops of the ski area—steady, sturdy, utterly reliable.

But ski instructors are the glamour boys of the sport—the gods of the mountain. Handsomely attired (they must be good-looking and wear stretch pants), deeply tanned, highly visible, they are tirelessly pursued by women. And they must be available. They rotate at ski lodge tables, they talk skiing in the evening and they must maintain an aura of manly vigor. Soon or late, they begin to believe the legends about themselves.

The reality underneath is somewhat less than glittering. Many ski instructors are just small-town boys who in the summer are prosaic cabinetmakers, construction workers or telephone linesmen. Recently some professional types have been recruited—engineers, attorneys and nurses (among the women). Of course, there are the European ski instructors, for some of whom the role of gigolo-athlete comes easily. But European instructors are sometimes hired sight unseen—a chancy business. As a result, ski operators often settle for the kid next door. The result is winter head-turning and summer devaluation.

But even the glamorous winter season has its asperities. Instructors are expected to turn up in fair weather and foul, in sickness or in health. And there is a curious reversal of the sexual roles of male and female instructors. It is the men who are courted and petted and spoiled. They are the starlets of the slopes, and narcissism is a serious occupational hazard. The women, on the other hand, are like a cartoon version of wartime WACs—hard-bitten, tough, masculine.

If there is some ambiguity about the life of ski instructors, the ski towns too are not quite certain whether they are blessed or damned. Wilmington, Vermont, near Mount Snow, is not untypical. Years ago it drowsed all winter and waited for a small flurry of summer tourists. Now it swings all winter and people say commiseratingly, "It must be dead here in the summer." And, along with the skiers, there has been a torrent of dollars. Nevertheless, all is not well. This old community, which has its origins in the eighteenth century, finds itself overrun. To many townspeople—flinty Vermonters all —the term skier means foreigner. The town likes the money but hates the people. Wee Moran, who runs a ski shop in Wilmington with a Vermonter's crotchetiness, posted a sign that reads: "Your credit is not good here based on my experience in the past. If this does not apply to you, I am sure you will not be offended." And on the blackboard he is prone to write little homilies, e.g., "If you steal from a crook, you're a clever crook. But if you betray a trust, you're a damned fool."

As a symptom of change, Wilmington now has an authentic Greenwich Village type coffeehouse. The proprietor, Phil Capy, is a singer and dancer with a passion for skiing. During the day, he is the hard-working, paid leader of the ski patrol at Haystack Mountain. Evenings he runs a small dormitory for skiers and sings folk songs in the cellar establishment. To some of the townsmen the coffeehouse is like a hint of Sodom or Babylon in its wicked heyday.

But these are merely the growing pains of a new sport. Skiing has emerged as one of the country's durable activities—esthetically gratifying, technically demanding and bracingly elemental.

The pure mystique of skiing was expressed by a young woman in New York, dark-haired and intricate of psyche: "I was sitting in a lodge feeling outside. And there were all these tall, handsome, blond skiers. And I had a longing for the blue-eyed and blond-haired."[2]

In a way, analytic writing presupposes detective work: the writer looks over the evidence, finds some clues, pursues the trail from one place to the next, and makes the arrest. Here is an analysis of a TV detective series. Jeff Greenfield presents and solves a case: Why is the TV series *Columbo* so popular? As you will see, Greenfield looks at the characterization of the hero and villains, then at the underlying conflict, and finally at the implicit meaning; that is, he breaks the program down

[2] *Sports Illustrated*, 23 Nov. 1964, pp. 9–14.

into parts: character, plot, theme. All three elements contribute to the popularity of the program. Not surprisingly, Greenfield discloses his clues and his interpretations in a climactic order.

COLUMBO KNOWS THE BUTLER DIDN'T DO IT
Jeff Greenfield

The popularity of *Columbo* is as intense as it is puzzling. Dinner parties are adjourned, trips to movies postponed, and telephone calls hastily concluded ("It's starting now, I gotta go." "Migod, it's 8:40, what did I miss?"), all for a detective show that tells us whodunit, howhedunit, and whyhedunit all before the first commercial.

Why? Peter Falk's characterization is part of the answer of course; he plays Lieutenant Columbo with sleepy-eyed, slow-footed, crazy-like-a-fox charm. But shtick—even first-class shtick—goes only so far. Nor is it especially fascinating to watch Columbo piece together clues that are often telegraphed far in advance. No, there is something else which gives *Columbo* a special appeal—something almost never seen on commercial television. That something is a strong, healthy dose of class antagonism. The one constant in *Columbo* is that, with every episode, a working-class hero brings to justice a member of America's social and economic elite.

The homicide files in Columbo's office must contain the highest per-capita income group of any criminals outside of antitrust law. We never see a robber shooting a grocery store owner out of panic or savagery; there are no barroom quarrels settled with a Saturday Night Special; no murderous shootouts between drug dealers or numbers runners. The killers in Columbo's world are art collectors, surgeons, high-priced lawyers, sports executives, a symphony conductor of Bernsteinian charisma—even a world chess champion. They are rich and white (if Columbo ever does track down a black killer, it will surely be a famous writer or singer or athlete or politician, rather than a product of Watts).

Columbo's villains are not simply rich; they are privileged. They live the lives that are for most of us hopeless daydreams: houses on top of mountains, with pools, servants, and sliding doors; parties with women in slinky dresses, and endless food and drink; plush, enclosed box seats at professional sports events; the envy and admiration of the Crowd. While we choose between Johnny Carson and *Invasion of the Body-Snatchers,* they are at screenings of movies the rest of us wait in line for on Third Avenue three months later.

Into the lives of these privileged rich stumbles Lieutenant Columbo —a dweller in another world. His suspects are Los Angeles paradigms: sleek, shiny, impeccably dressed, tanned by the omnipresent sun. Columbo, on the other hand, appears to have been plucked from Queens Boulevard by helicopter, and set down an instant later in Topanga Canyon. His hair is tousled, not styled and sprayed. His chin is pale and stubbled. He has even forgotten to take off his raincoat, a garment thoroughly out of place in Los Angeles eight months of the year. Columbo is also unabashedly stunned by and envious of the life style of his quarry.

"Geez, that is some car," he tells the symphony conductor. "Ya know, I'll bet that car costs more than I make in a year."

"Say, can I ask you something personal?" he says to a suspect wearing $50-dollar shoes. "Ya know where I can buy a pair of shoes like that for $8.95?"

"Boy, I bet this house musta cost—I dunno, hundred, what, hundred fifty thousand?"

His aristocratic adversaries tolerate Columbo at first because they misjudge him. They are amused by him, scornful of his manners, certain that while he possesses the legal authority to demand their cooperation, he has neither the grace nor wit to discover their misdeeds. Only at the end, in a last look of consternation before the final fadeout, do they comprehend that intelligence may indeed find a home in the Robert Hall set. All of them are done in, in some measure, by their contempt for Columbo's background, breeding, and income. Anyone who has worked the wrong side of the counter at Bergdorf's, or who has waited on tables in high-priced restaurants, must feel a wave of satisfaction. ("Yeah, baby, *that's* how dumb we working stiffs are!")

Further, Columbo knows about these people what the rest of us suspect: that they are on top not because they are smarter or work harder than we do, but because they are more amoral and devious. Time after time, the motive for murder in *Columbo* stems from the shakiness of the villain's own status in high society. The chess champion knows his challenger is his better; murder is his only chance to stay king. The surgeon fears that a cooperative research project will endanger his status; he must do in his chief to retain sole credit. The conductor owes his position to the status of his mother-in-law; he must silence his mistress lest she spill the beans and strip him of his wealth and position.

This is, perhaps, the most thorough-going satisfaction *Columbo* offers us: the assurance that those who dwell in marble and satin, those whose clothes, food, cars, and mates are the very best, *do not deserve it*. They are, instead, driven by fear and compulsion to murder. And they are done in by a man of street wit, who is afraid to fly, who can't stand the sight of blood, and who never uses force to take his prey. They are done in by Mosholu Parkway and P. S. 106, by

Fordham U. and a balcony seat at Madison Square Garden, by a man who pulls down $11,800 a year and never ate an anchovy in his life.

It is delicious. I wait only for the ultimate episode: Columbo knocks on the door of 1600 Pennsylvania Avenue one day. "Gee, Mr. President, I really hate to bother you again, but there's *just one thing. . . .*" [3]

In the following essay the categories are less obviously established than in the two preceding essays, but notice that the author builds his essay on a series of contrasts: old-style black poetry / new black poetry; strengths of the new poetry / weaknesses of the new poetry; white criticism / black criticism; poetry as fervor / poetry as technique.

THE NEW BLACK POETRY
Mel Watkins

In the July 30 Book Review David Kalstone said of Jay Wright: "His book ["The Homecoming Singer"] is partly informed by a young black's sense of exclusion. He stands apart from the white society of his childhood . . . but he also, as a child, stood apart from the mysteries of his own blackness." Wright's poetry, then, was cast in a familiar literary mold—the alienated artist struggling for rapprochement with his past and with his *society*. That traditional posture has a further complication for the black artist, for his exclusion from American society is real, not psychological, and, as yet, unresolved. With the increased publication of young black poets, however, one aspect of that dual alienation is being eliminated. Many black poets are accepting their separation from American society a priori, consequently, their work is focused on reappraising their ethnic experience and attempting to shape a "positive" black consciousness.

The approach of these "new black poets" breaks with established, academic poetic tradition in style and content. There is, moreover, a clear distinction in intent between the poetry of most contemporary black poets and that of their predecessors. To move from Phyllis Wheatley's,

> 'Twas not long ago since I left my native shore
> The land of errors, and Egyptian gloom.
> Father of mercy, 'twas thy gracious hand
> Brought me in safety from those dark abodes . . .
> (—From "To the University of Cambridge in England," 1767)

---

[3] *New York Sunday Times*, 22 April 1973, Arts and Leisure sec., p. 19.

to Countee Cullen's,

> Now I was eight and very small,
> And he was no whit bigger,
> And so I smiled, but he poked out
> His tongue, and called me, "Nigger."
>
> I saw the whole of Baltimore
> From May until December;
> Of all the things that happened there
> That's all that I remember . . .
>   (—From "Incident," 1925)

to these lines by Gwendolyn Brooks,

> Be deaf to music and to beauty blind.
> Win war. Rise bloody, maybe not too late
> For having first to civilize a space
> Wherein to play your violin with Grace . . .
>   (—From "First Fight. Then Fiddle," 1963)

is to move from an artistic consciousness riddled by self-abnegation and helpless passivity to one defined by defiance and self-assertion.

For the poets who have made that transformation of sensibility, there is an increased opportunity to explore the black psyche and life style without restrictions. Contemporary poets such as Don L. Lee in "We Walk the Way of the New World" and Nikki Giovanni in "Nikki-Rosa" have demonstrated that this can be done with resonance and amplification. And, working both within and without that tradition, poets such as Imamu Amiri Baraka, Gwendolyn Brooks, Larry Neal, Ishmael Reed, Quincy Troup, Calvin Hernton and David Henderson have continually produced successful work.

But there are pitfalls. Since much of the new black poetry is dedicated to "consciousness raising," "teaching," or "coatpulling," as Carolyn M. Rodgers calls it, and is aimed at the black masses, it often tends toward shrill exhortations and direct propaganda of the "Off the Pig!" variety. Elevating the need for black unification (a realistic and effective goal) above all other considerations, as some poets have, has resulted in a lessening of treating the subjective experiences that initially compelled that urgency. Therefore, dramatization, metaphorical speech and ironic illumination growing out of personal experience and insights are often replaced by abstract, staccato commands: "Get up, get up, get up!/Black man." But despite writer-critic Baraka's rightful assertion that "all art is propaganda," it does not follow that *all propaganda is art*—or poetry.

Moreover, if black poetry is to be judged only by its capacity to communicate and its effectiveness at expanding black consciousness, then it should be measured against today's popular rhythm & blues songs, for their influence on the black audience is much more immediate and intense. Few poems, for instance, have equalled James Brown's "I'm Black and I'm Proud" in reaching black audiences and raising their consciousness. Certainly songwriters such as Brown, Bill Withers and Curtiss Mayfield have produced lyrics that have elicited more response in black communities and, often, those lyrics have reflected a poetic sensibility missing in the more strident works of legitimate "poets."

How is one to judge contemporary black poetry then? Establishment critics have provided no answers. Often they have reacted negatively to what seems like nothing more than an implicit self-assertive attitude and a reversal of traditional values and images— something that was being done as early as the 19th century in W. E. B. DuBois's "The Song of Smoke" when he portrayed blackness as just and divine and whiteness as hell. There are also those who, as Baraka has suggested, insist that a good poem cannot be written about killing white people. Their critical faculties, however, do not function with the same sensitivity when they are assessing the merits of the writing of H. L. Mencken or a film such as D. W. Griffith's "Birth of a Nation."

The new black poetry, then, functions largely in a critical void. Most black critics and spokesmen assess these works *only* in terms of their revolutionary fervor and the poet's commitment to black unification; there is little discussion of how well the poet has handled the rudimentary elements of poetic construction. Most white critics are either so defensive about what is being said or so confounded by black linguistic mannerisms and inner-cultural puns and ironies that they debunk these works as "mere verse" or pretend that they don't exist. Still, there are critical and evaluative distinctions to be made about the raft of contemporary black poetry that is now being published. At its best it incorporates the current positive black awareness and consciousness and, by creating new images and employing the elements of black speech, produces imaginative, relevant poetic works. At worst, it is dull, repetitive and simplistically propagandistic. For the sake of the poets themselves, someone should begin making critical distinctions.[4]

The next essay, originally given as an address to parents of freshmen at Boston University, distinguishes between what literature offers to the undergraduate and what other academic subjects offer, and between what literature offers and what life

[4] *New York Sunday Times*, 13 Aug. 1972, Book Review sec., p. 35.

outside of books offers. The essay as a whole answers the question: What is the function of the study of literature in the undergraduate curriculum?

LITERATURE AND THE UNDERGRADUATE
Helen Vendler

Many students who come to Boston University will probably elect some courses offered by the Department of English, and some will decide to stay with us as concentrators in literature. But most of our students will go on to be doctors or government workers or businessmen or any number of other things, and we have to ask ourselves what good our courses can do them. What is it that literature, and literature alone, can give our students? What can they find in literature that they cannot find in history, or philosophy, or science? And what is it, we must ask even more seriously, that literature can give them that they cannot find in lived life, outside of books? In what ways can poetry, novels, and plays, as they are encountered in our courses, help our students live their lives, wherever those lives may be lived, and in whatever work they may be engaged?

Our purpose, in the undergraduate college, is not to make specialists, but rather to make readers. Facts disappear quickly after college: four hundred years ago an Elizabethan poet said "We learn so little, and forget so much." But the quality of experience does not disappear: the soul, says Wordsworth, remembers *how* she felt even if she forgets *what* she felt. Writers make their feelings permanent by recording them, and all our courses, in the Department of English, are an invitation to acquaintance with those writers—the only people in the history of the world to specialize in the recording of feeling, in the transcription of what it feels like to lead a given life. History can tell us what people did, but only literature and the other arts can tell us how they felt while they were living their lives. Philosophy can ask the meaning of our categories, but only the arts can make us suffer through that meaning; Keats spoke not of "reading through" *King Lear* but instead of "burning through" the story of Lear's tragedy:

> Once again, the fierce dispute
> Betwixt damnation and impassion'd clay
> Must I burn through.

And yet, for all its resemblance to lived life, literature is not life and cannot substitute for it. Why, we might ask, should we go to life in literature when life itself is all around us to be looked at directly? Even Henry James, the novelist's novelist, spoke through one of his characters to a young man, saying, "Live all you can: it's a mistake not to." Should any of the time of life, which is brief enough in itself, be spent reading books about life? That question is the one most often put to us, implicitly or explicitly, by our students, and it brings to bear once more the old debate between the active and the contemplative lives. Each of us has a different answer to that question, and I can only give you one response.

In philosophy and psychology, life is reduced to analytical and skeletal versions of itself, whereas in literature we see life almost full and in the round: in history, life appears random and sequential and all-inclusive, whereas in literature it is given a definitive and consoling shape and intent. In literature, in short, we meet life in a peculiar half-way house; somewhere between the analytic skeleton and the historical totality lies literature, containing more vivid flesh and blood than sociology or anthropology or psychology, and yet being less overwhelmingly and confusingly populated than the chaos of history. In literature we find selection without reduction, shape without abstraction, emotion still alive and not yet embalmed into social science.

Each of the common literary forms has its own claim on us, and each answers some of those ravenous questions that each generation of adolescents must once again begin to put to life. "Those men and women in the streets," asked Walt Whitman when he was a young man, "if they are not flashes and specks what are they?" To give those random flashes and specks a richly conceived life is the aim of the novelist, who wishes to affirm, as though on oath in the witness stand (as George Eliot put it), his own authentic version of life. The novel satisfies us particularly in telling us what it was like to live in nineteenth-century Moscow, or eighteenth-century France, or even what it was like to live on Main Street in America in the early years of this century. We learn from novels what it felt like to be a foreign immigrant in the 1890's in Brooklyn, what it was like to go through the potato famine in Ireland, how it felt to be a girl up for sale in the nineteenth-century marriage market, what kinds of experiences fall to the lot of an expatriate black American, and so on. Through the novel, we can live "as if we lived all lives," especially lives we have no hope of touching in our own life because those lives are already dead, or far away from us in space and culture. To have lived someone's life through with him, if only in a book, makes for a permanent sympathy. The global village existed in novels long before the twentieth century made it a fact of everyday life.

Plays, on the other hand, though they too let us enter other lives, make us enter them purely through events and in a violently compressed form. The descriptive leisure and the large cast of the novel disappear, and in their place we have a strict and unswervable momentum leading to an inevitable end. The shape of life stands out so clearly, the connections of one act to the next are so unmistakable in a play, that instead of naturalizing us in a totally different environment, as the novel does, the play makes us feel how much all men's lives resemble each other in fate, convinces us that time, place, and circumstance separate us, in truth, much less than they sometimes seem to do in life.

And finally, in poems, we come to the most general expressions of feeling about life. To transcend time and space is peculiarly the essence of lyric poetry, since it is the form of literature least bound to national consciousness, age, sex, class, or geography. Poetry has no heroes, no cast of characters, no houses, no rooms, no setting, no plot—it rises above the specificities of life to the common human feelings found in every time and in every country. If poetry should ever be forgotten among us, we would at once become more provincial and more eccentric, less conscious of our humanity held in common both with the human beings of the past and with the human beings of other cultures.

These are the social uses of literature, but it should be added that its personal uses are at least equally great. Besides recognizing the otherness of literature, as we see life in other countries and other times, we also recognize the principle of identity—that what we feel, others have felt; that our predicaments have been experienced before; that we are not alone in our sadness; that we need not be ashamed of our secret hopes or fears. It reinforces us in our own selfhood. It also admits the preeminence of fantasy as practical life cannot: the free and relaxed liberty in which the mind encounters "life" in literature is quite different from the practical way it must encounter such situations in reality. Literature has rehearsal value, and it also permits us to repeat, in another mode, what we have experienced in lived life. When we move within the mind of the author, we are arranging things rather than being the victims of fate's arrangements; illusory though the feeling may be, we seem momentarily in control, and I think we are strengthened by the illusion.

That phrase we are all accustomed to, "The Great Society," came originally from the poet Wordsworth, who said,

> There is
> One great society alone on earth,
> The noble living and the noble dead.

Anyone, in life, can become a member of the first group of that great society, the noble living: but it is chiefly through books that we meet the second group, and can know the noble dead. If each generation is not to be wholly cut off from the lives and feelings of the generations preceding it, it must find, in the living records left by earlier ancestors, a sense of human passions continuing through time—the sense of that human life which is always, as Santayana said, lyrical in its essence, tragic in its fate, and comic in its existence. Our rôle as teachers is to act as mediators between our students and that sense of the human past: "What we have loved," Wordsworth said, "others will love, and we will teach them how."

CHAPTER THREE

OUTLINING

When you write an outline, you do pretty much what an artist does when he draws an outline: you give, without detail and shading, the general shape of your subject.

An outline is a kind of ground plan or blueprint, a diagram showing the arrangement of the parts. It is, then, essentially an analysis of your essay, a classification of its parts. Not all writers use outlines, but those who use them report that an outline helps to make clear to them, before or while they labor through a first draft, what their thesis is, what the main points are, and what the subordinate points are. When the outline is drawn, they not only have a guide that will help them to subordinate what is subordinate, but they can easily see if the development from part to part is clear, consistent, and reasonable.

An outline drafted before you write, however, is necessarily tentative. Don't assume that once you have constructed an outline your plan is fixed. If, as you begin to write, previously neglected points come to mind, or if you see that in any way the outline is unsatisfactory, revise or scrap the outline.

SCRATCH OUTLINE

The simplest outline is a *scratch outline*, half a dozen phrases jotted down, revised, rearranged, listing the topics to be covered. These phrases serve as milestones rather than a roadmap. Most writers do at least this much.

PARAGRAPH OUTLINE

A *paragraph outline* is more developed: it states the thesis (usually in a sentence, but sometimes in a phrase) and then it gives the topic sentence (or a phrase summarizing the topic sentence) of each paragraph. Thus, a paragraph outline of Jeff Greenfield's "Columbo Knows the Butler Didn't Do It" (pages 47–49) might begin like this:

> Thesis: *Columbo* is popular because it shows a privileged, undeserving elite brought down by a fellow like us.
>
> I. *Columbo* is popular.
>
> II. Its popularity is largely due to its hostility toward a social and economic elite.
>
> III. The killers are all rich and white.
>
> IV. Their lives are privileged.

And so on, one roman numeral for each remaining paragraph. A paragraph outline has its uses, especially for papers under, say, a thousand words; it can help you to write unified paragraphs, and it can help you to write a reasonably organized essay. But after you write your essay, check to see if your paragraphs really are developments of what you assert to be the topic sentences, and check to see if you have made the organization clear to the reader, chiefly by means of transitional words and phrases (see pages 68–71). If your essay departs from your outline, the departures should be improvements.

FORMAL OUTLINE

For longer papers such as a research paper (usually at least eight pages of double-spaced typing) a more complicated outline is usually needed. The outline will show relationships, distinguishing between major parts of the essay and subordinate parts. Major parts are indicated by capital roman numerals. These should clearly bear on the thesis. Chief divisions within a major part are indicated by capital letters. Subdivisions within these divisions are indicated by arabic numerals. Still smaller subdivisions—although they are rarely needed because they are apt to provide too much detail for an outline—are indicated by small roman numerals. The first major part of an unusually complicated essay might be outlined as follows; the second major part, not given here, would of course begin with II.

  I.
    A.
      1.
      2.
        a.
        b.
        c.
    B.
      1.
        a.
        b.
          i.
          ii.
        c.
      2.
    C.
      1.
      2.

Such an outline tells you that—at least for the moment—you are planning to begin with a major point (I) which has three large divisions (A, B, C). A, B, and C are roughly coordinate; they are going to be treated as things of equal rank. Let's look at A. It is subdivided into two chief parts, 1 and 2. Subdivision 2 itself is subdivided into three parts, a, b, and c. (If we glance ahead to B, we can see that a further subdivision uses lower case roman numerals.)

Notice that you cannot have a single subdivision. In the example just given, I is divided into A, B, and C. Part I cannot have only a part A; it must be divided into at least A and B. Similarly, part B cannot be "divided" into 1 (without 2). If you have a single subdivision, eliminate it and work the material into the previous heading.

Here is an outline (other versions are of course possible) for Greenfield's "Columbo." In order to illustrate the form of divisions and subdivisions we have written a much fuller outline than is usual for such a short essay.

Thesis: *Columbo* is popular because it shows the undeserving rich brought low by a member of the working class.

I. Popularity of *Columbo*
   A. What it is *not* due to
      1. Acting
      2. Clever detection of surprising criminal plot
   B. What it is due to
      1. Hostility to privileged elite
      2. Columbo is poor and shoddy.
      3. The high are brought low.
         a. No black (minority) villains
         b. The villains live far above us.

II. The hero
   A. Physical appearance
      1. Dress
      2. Hair, beard
   B. Manner
   C. Success as an investigator
      1. Adversaries mistakenly treat him as negligible.
         a. They assume his poverty indicates lack of intelligence.
         b. They learn too late.
      2. Columbo understands the elite.
         a. They are not superior mentally or in diligence.
         b. They are in a shaky position.

III. Our satisfaction with the program
   A. The villains do not deserve their privileges.
   B. Villains are undone by a man in the street.
   C. We look forward to an episode when Columbo visits the most privileged house.

Some authorities require that an outline be consistent in using either phrases or sentences (not a mixture). But when you are writing an outline for yourself, you need not worry about mixing phrases with sentences.

There is, of course, no evidence that Greenfield wrote an outline before he wrote his essay. But he may have roughed out something along these lines, thereby providing himself with a groundplan or a roadmap. And while he looked at it he may have readjusted a few parts to give more emphasis here (changing a subdivision into a major division) or to establish a more reasonable connection there (say, reversing A and B in one of the parts). Even if you don't write from an outline, when an essay is completed you ought to be able to outline it; that is, you ought to be able to sketch its parts. An outline made from a finished essay may help to reveal disproportion or faulty organization that should be remedied before you hand in your essay.

CHAPTER FOUR

PARAGRAPHS

UNIFIED PARAGRAPHS

A paragraph is a group of sentences (rarely a single sentence) presenting one of your major points. The point may have several twists or subdivisions, but you should be able to summarize it in one sentence. If the paragraph contains a sentence that has no relevance to your mental summary, that irrelevant sentence, sure to distract the reader, doesn't belong in the paragraph.

A paragraph may tell an anecdote, define a term, describe a person or a place, explain a process, make a comparison, summarize an opinion, draw a conclusion; it may do almost anything, but it is a major unit of your essay, a room in the house you are building. If your essay is some five hundred words long (about two double-spaced typewritten pages) you probably will not break it down into more than four or five parts or paragraphs. Of course hard-and-fast rules cannot be made about the lengths of paragraphs, but more often than not a good paragraph is between one hundred and two hundred words, consisting of more than one or two but fewer than eight or ten sentences. It is not a matter, however, of counting words or sentences; paragraphs are coherent blocks, substantial units of your essay, and the spaces between them are brief resting places allowing the reader to take in what you have said. One page of typing (approximately 250 words) is about as much as the reader can take before requiring a slight break. On the other hand, one page of typing with half a dozen paragraphs is probably faulty, not because it has too many ideas but because it has too few *developed* ideas; it keeps forcing the reader to stop for unnecessary breaths. Don't be misled by the one-line paragraphs of newspapers.

Read the following horrible example, a newspaper account—chiefly in paragraphs of one sentence each—of an unfortunate happening.

FISH EAT BRAZILIAN FISHERMAN
Reuters

MANAUS, BRAZIL—Man-eating piranha fish devoured fisherman Zeca Vicente when he tumbled into the water during a battle with 300 farmers for possession of an Amazon jungle lake.

Vicente, a leader of a group of 30 fishermen, was eaten alive in minutes by shoals of the ferocious fish lurking in Lake Januaca.

He died when the farmers—packed in an armada of small boats—attacked the fishermen with hunting rifles, knives, and bows and arrows after they refused to leave.

The farmers, who claimed the fishermen were depleting the lake's fish stocks, one of their main sources of food, boarded the fishing vessels and destroyed cold storage installations.

Last to give way was Vicente, who tried to cut down the farmers' leader with a knife. But farmers shot him and he fell wounded into the water, and into the jaws of the piranhas.

Fifteen persons have been charged with the attack which caused Vicente's death and the injury of several other fishermen.

Lake Januaca, about four hours from this Amazon River town by launch, is famous for its pirarucu and tucunare fish which are regarded as table delicacies.[1]

Most marvelously wrong is the final paragraph, with its cool guidebook voice uttering as inappropriate a fact as imaginable, but what concerns us at the moment is the writer's failure to build his sentences into paragraphs. Probably all six paragraphs (the seventh, final paragraph is irrelevant) can be effectively combined into one paragraph. Better, perhaps, the material can be divided into two paragraphs, one describing the event and another describing the cause or background. At the most, there

---

[1] *Boston Globe*, 17 Jan. 1971, p. 79.

is the stuff of three paragraphs, one on the background, one on the event itself, and one on the consequences (fifteen people are charged with the attack). Imagine how it could be presented in one paragraph, in two paragraphs, and in three; which do you think would be most effective? Even the present final paragraph can be worked in; how?

THE USE AND ABUSE OF SHORT PARAGRAPHS

A short paragraph can be effective when it summarizes a highly detailed previous paragraph or group of paragraphs, or when it serves as a transition between two complicated paragraphs, but unless you are sure that the reader needs a break, avoid thin paragraphs. A paragraph that is nothing but a transition can usually be altered into a transitional phrase or clause or sentence at the start of the next paragraph. But of course there are times when a short paragraph is exactly right. Notice the effect of the two-sentence paragraph between two longer paragraphs:

After I returned to prison, I took a long look at myself and, for the first time in my life, admitted that I was wrong, that I had gone astray —astray not so much from the white man's law as from being human, civilized—for I could not approve the act of rape. Even though I had some insight into my own motivations, I did not feel justified. I lost my self-respect. My pride as a man dissolved and my whole fragile moral structure seemed to collapse, completely shattered.

That is why I started to write. To save myself.

I realized that no one could save me but myself. The prison authorities were both uninterested and unable to help me. I had to seek out the truth and unravel the snarled web of my motivations. I had to find out who I am and what I want to be, what type of man I should be, and what I could do to become the best of which I was capable. I understood that what had happened to me had also happened to countless other blacks and it would happen to many, many more.[2]

—Eldridge Cleaver

If the content of the second paragraph were less momentous, it would hardly merit a paragraph. Here the brevity helps to contribute to the enormous impact; those two simple little sen-

[2] *Soul on Ice* (New York: Dell Publishing Company, 1968), p. 15.

tences, set off by themselves, are meant to be equal in weight, so to speak, to the longer paragraphs that precede and follow. They are the hinge on which the door turns.

BUILDING UNIFIED PARAGRAPHS

Although we emphasize unity in paragraphs, don't assume that every development or refinement or alteration of your thought requires a new paragraph. Such an assumption would lead to an essay consisting entirely of one-sentence paragraphs. A good paragraph may, for instance, both ask a question and answer it, or describe an effect and then explain the cause, or set forth details and then offer a generalization. Indeed, if the question or the effect or the details can be set forth in a sentence or two, and the answer or the cause or the generalization can be set forth in a sentence or two, the two halves of the topic should be pulled together into a single paragraph. It is only if the question (for example) is long and complex (say eight or ten sentences) and the answer equally long or longer that you need two or more paragraphs—or, to put it more precisely, that your reader needs two or more paragraphs.

Let's consider three paragraphs from an essay on ballooning. Now, one can write a single sentence on ballooning ("Ballooning is the sport of floating in the air, supported by a bag filled with heated air or gas lighter than air") or one can write a thick book on ballooning—or one can write something in between: say, an essay of twenty pages with perhaps fifty paragraphs. In the essay from which the following three paragraphs were taken, the writer has already explained that ballooning was born in late eighteenth-century France and that almost from its start there were two types of balloons, gas and hot air. Notice that in the paragraphs printed below the first is on gas, the second is chiefly on air (but it wisely makes comparisons with gas), and the third is on the length of flights—of both gas and air balloons. In other words, each paragraph is about one thing— gas balloons, air balloons, length of flight—but each paragraph also builds on what the reader has learned in the previous paragraphs. That the third paragraph is about the flights of gas *and* of air balloons does not mean that it lacks unity; it is a unified discussion of flight lengths.

Gas balloons swim around in air like a sleeping fish in water, because they weigh about the same as the fluid they're in. A good, big, trans-Atlantic balloon will have 2,000 pounds of vehicle, including gas bag and pilot, taking up about 30 cubic feet (as big as a refrigerator), plus 300 pounds of a "nothing" stuff called helium, which fills 30,000 cubic feet (as big as three houses). Air to fill this 30,030 cubic feet would also weigh 2,300 pounds, so the balloon system averages the same as air, floating in it as part of the wind.

Hot-air balloons use the same size bag filled with hot air instead of helium, kept hot by a boot-sized blowtorch riding just over the pilot's head. Hot air is light, but not as light as helium, so you can't carry as much equipment in a hot-air balloon. You also can't fly as long or as far. Helium will carry a balloon for days (three and a half days is the record), until a lot of gas has leaked out. But a hot-air balloon cools down in minutes, like a house as soon as its heat source runs out of fuel; and today's best fuel (heat-for-weight), propane, lasts only several hours.

A good hot-air flight goes a hundred miles, yet the gas record is 1,897 miles, set by a German in 1914 with the junk (by today's standards) they had then. Unmanned scientific gas balloons have flown half a million miles, staying up more than a year. Japan bombed Oregon in World War II with balloons. Two hot-air balloonists, Tracy Barnes and Malcolm Forbes, have made what they called transcontinental flights, but each was the sum of dozens of end-to-end hops, trailed by pick-up trucks, like throwing a frisbee from Hollywood to Atlantic City.[3]

—David Royce

TOPIC SENTENCES, TOPIC IDEAS

The idea unifying each paragraph may appear as a topic sentence. Topic sentences are especially common, because they are useful, in essays that offer arguments; they are much less common, because they are less useful, in narrative and descriptive essays.

Most commonly the topic sentence is the first sentence in the paragraph, helpfully forecasting what is to come in the rest of the paragraph. But if the paragraph opens with a transitional sentence, the topic sentence is usually the second sentence. Occasionally, however, the topic sentence is the last sentence in

[3] "Moby Balloon," *New York Times Magazine*, 26 May 1974, p. 13.

the paragraph, summarizing the points that the earlier sentences have made, or drawing a generalization based on the earlier details. Least commonly, the topic sentence may appear nowhere in the paragraph, in which case the paragraph has a topic idea—an idea that holds the sentences together although it has not been explicitly stated. Whether explicit or implicit, an idea should unite the sentences of the paragraph.

The following paragraph begins with a topic sentence.

The Marx Brothers' three best films at Paramount—*Monkey Business* (1931), *Horse Feathers* (1932), and *Duck Soup* (1933)—all hurl comic mud at the gleaming marble pillars of the American temple. The target of *Monkey Business* is money and high society, the rich society snobs merely happen to be gangsters who made their money from bootlegging. The target of *Horse Feathers* is the university; knowledge and the pursuit of it are reduced to thievery, bribery, lechery, and foolishness. The target of *Duck Soup* is democracy and government itself; grandiose political ceremonies, governmental bodies, international diplomacy, the law courts, and war are reduced to the absurd. All three films also parody popular "serious" genres— gangster films, college films, and romantic-European-kingdom films. The implication of this spoofing is that the sanctified institution is as hollow and dead as the cinematic cliché; the breezy, chaotic, revolutionary activities of the comic anarchists give society's respectable calcifications a much-deserved comeuppance.[4]

—Gerald Mast

Everything that follows the first sentence amplifies that sentence, first by commenting one by one on the three films named at the outset, and then by speaking of the three films as a group. In short, the writer begins by stating or summarizing his thesis, and he then offers specific evidence to support it.

Here is a paragraph from a descriptive essay; it does not have the obvious orderliness of the previous example, but it still hangs together.

I remember my mother's father, called Granddad, as a small silent man, a cabinetmaker and carpenter with a liking for strong drink. For a time I guess he was the town drunk, and my memories of him are as fogged by shame as his mind was by whiskey. When he was

[4] *The Comic Mind* (New York: Bobbs-Merrill, 1973), pp. 281–82.

working—and he managed to support himself until his death—he was a different man. I remember watching him build a cabinet in our house; his hands were craftsman's hands, marked by his trade. The ends of two fingers were missing, lost in the first power saw brought to the county, when they built a bridge over the North Platte. The nails of the remaining fingers were ridged, horny, discolored, misshapen, not like fingernails but more like the claws of some very old and tough bird. The knuckles had been crushed and mauled until each had its own special shape and size. Every inch of skin was mapped by the building he had done. I can't remember his face and can't forget those hands. When he touched wood those mutilated old hands would turn into something beautiful, as if pure love was flowing from his fingers into the wood.[5]

   —Sharon R. Curtin

A paragraph can make several points, but the points must be related and the nature of the relationship must be indicated so that there is, in effect, a single unifying point to the paragraph. In the example just quoted, we get details about the man's physical appearance and also details about his trade; these two motifs of course are united by the idea that although he was superficially unattractive, when his maimed hands went to work they became beautiful. The next paragraph in that essay describes the grandfather's old age and his death in an automobile accident, the unity of that paragraph being, implicitly: though old and the despair of doctors, he went on living and working until he was violently annihilated. Of course such material could have been worked into the previous paragraph, but the writer felt that the grandfather's old age and death were worth a separate paragraph, balanced against a paragraph on the peculiar beauty he radiated during his working lifetime.

COHERENCE IN PARAGRAPHS

If a paragraph has not only unity but also a reasonable organization or sequence, then we can say it has coherence; its parts fit together.

Exactly how the parts will fit together depends, of course, on exactly what the paragraph is doing. If it is describing a

[5] *Nobody Ever Died of Old Age* (Boston: Little, Brown, 1972), pp. 7–8.

place, it may move from a general view to the significant details—or from some immediately striking details to some less obvious but perhaps more important ones. It may move from near to far, or from far to near; other paragraphs may move from cause to effect, or from effect back to cause, or from past to present. In the following paragraph, written by a student, we move chronologically—from waking at 7:00 A.M., to washing and combing, to readiness for the day's work, and then to a glance at the rest of the day that will undo the 7:00 A.M. clean-up.

I can remember waking at seven to Ma's call. I'd bound out of bed because Ma just didn't allow people to be lazy. She'd grab me and we'd rush to the bathroom for the morning ritual. Bathing, toothbrushing, lotioning, all overseen by her watchful eyes. She didn't let anything go by. No missing behind the ears, no splashing around and pretending to bathe. I bathed and scrubbed and put that lotion on till my whole body was like butter on a warm pan. After inspection it was back to my room and the day's clothes were selected. A bit of tugging and I was dressed. Then she'd sit me down and pull out the big black comb. That comb would glide through my hair and then the braiding would begin. My head would jerk but I never yelled, never even whimpered. Finally I was ready. Ready to start the day and get dirty and spoil all of Ma's work. But she didn't care. She knew you couldn't keep a child from getting dirty but you could teach it to be respectable.

If a paragraph is classifying (dividing a subject into its parts) it may begin by enumerating the parts and go on to study each, perhaps in a climactic order. Or it may make a comparison. (For a discussion of a paragraph that makes a comparison, see pages 37–39.) The only rule that can cover all paragraphs is this: the reader must never feel that he is stumbling as he follows the writer to the end of the paragraph. A paragraph is not a maze; the reader should be able to glide through it in seconds, not minutes.

Transitions

Wagner once said "The art of composition is the art of transition." Transitions contribute to coherence; they establish the connections between your points. Here are some of the most common transitional words and phrases in writing.

1. amplification or likeness: *similarly, likewise, and, also, again, second, third, in addition, furthermore, moreover, finally*
2. emphasis: *chiefly, equally, indeed, even more important*
3. contrast or concession: *but, on the contrary, on the other hand, of course, however, still, doubtless, no doubt, nevertheless, granted that, conversely, although, admittedly*
4. example: *for example, for instance, as an example, specifically, consider as an illustration, that is, such as*
5. consequence or cause and effect: *thus, so, then, it follows, as a result, therefore, hence*
6. restatement: *in short, that is, in effect, in other words*

"Spaghetti," by Vladimir Koziakin

7. place: *in the foreground, further back, in the distance*
8. time: *afterward, next, then, as soon as, later, until, when, finally, last, at last*
9. conclusion: *finally, therefore, thus, to sum up*

Make sure that each sentence in a paragraph is properly related to the preceding and the following sentences. Such obvious transitions as "moreover," "however," "but," "for example," "this tendency," "in the next chapter" are useful, but remember that (1) these transitions should not start every sentence (they can be buried: "Smith, moreover . . ."), and (2) explicit transitions need not appear at all in a sentence, so long as the argument proceeds clearly. The gist of a paragraph might run thus: "Speaking broadly, there were two comic traditions. . . . The first . . . The second . . . The chief difference between them . . . But both traditions . . ."

Consider the following paragraph:

Folklorists are just beginning to look at Africa. A great quantity of folklore materials have been gathered from African countries in the past century and published by missionaries, travelers, administrators, linguists, and anthropologists incidentally to their main pursuits. No fieldworker has devoted himself exclusively or even largely to the recording and analysis of folklore materials, according to a committee of the African Studies Association reporting in 1966 on the state of research in the African arts. Yet Africa is the continent supreme for traditional cultures that nurture folklore. Why this neglect? [6]

—Richard M. Dorson

(Let us pass quickly over the error in agreement in the second sentence, where the singular subject "quantity" is matched with the plural verb "have been." The writer mistakenly thought the subject of the verb was "materials.") The reader gets the point, but the second sentence seems to contradict the first: we are told that folklorists are just beginning to look at Africa, but the next sentence tells of the abundance of collected folklore. An "although" between these sentences would clarify the author's point, especially if the third sentence were hooked on to the second, thus:

[6] "Africa and the Folklorist," *African Folklore*, ed. Richard M. Dorson Bloomington: Indiana University Press, 1972), p. 3.

Folklorists are just beginning to look at Africa. Although a great quantity of folklore materials has been gathered from African countries in the past century by missionaries, travelers, administrators, linguists, and anthropologists incidentally to their main pursuits, no fieldworker has devoted himself . . .

True, this revision gives us an uncomfortably long second sentence. Further revision would help.

The real point of the original passage, though it is smothered, is that although many people have incidentally collected folklore materials in Africa, professional folklorists have not been active there. The contrast ought to be sharpened:

Folklorists are just beginning to look at Africa. True, missionaries, travelers, administrators, linguists, and anthropologists have collected a quantity of folklore materials incidentally to their main pursuits, but folklorists have lagged behind. No fieldworker . . .

In this revision the words that clarify are, of course, the small but important words "true" and "but." The original paragraph is a jigsaw puzzle, missing some tiny but necessary pieces.

Repetition

Coherence may be achieved not only by means of transitional words and phrases but by means of repetition. Words or phrases are repeated, or clear substitutes, such as pronouns and demonstrative adjectives, are provided. Grammatical constructions too can be repeated, the repetitions or parallels linking the sentences (that is, the points) together:

This world taught woman nothing skillful and then said her work was valueless. It permitted her no opinions and said she did not know how to think. It forbade her to speak in public and said the sex had no genius. It robbed her of every vestige of responsibility and then called her weak. It taught her that every pleasure must come as a favor from men, and when to gain it she decked herself in paint and fine feathers as she had been taught to do, it called her vain.[7]

—Carrie Chapman Catt

No one wants to read an entire essay of paragraphs that use repetition so heavily, but an occasional paragraph of this sort

[7] Quoted in the *Boston Globe*.

may be especially effective if it is on a subject that one can rightly be emphatic about. In the next example the repetitions are less emphatic, but again they provide continuity.

Sir Kenneth Clark's *The Nude* is an important book; and, luckily, it is also most readable; but it is not a bedside book. Each sentence needs attention because each sentence is relevant to the whole, and the incorrigible skipper will sometimes find himself obliged to turn back several pages, chapters even, in order to pick up the thread of the argument. Does this sound stiff? The book is not stiff because it is delightfully written. Let the student have no fears; he is not going to be bored for a moment while he reads these 400 pages; he is going to be excited, amused, instructed, provoked, charmed, irritated and surprised.[8]

TRANSITIONS BETWEEN PARAGRAPHS

Something has already been said (pages 63–64) about thin transitional paragraphs. Remember that you probably do not need to devote an entire paragraph to a transition. You can hardly go wrong, though, in making the first sentence of each new paragraph a transition, or perhaps both a transition and a topic sentence.

GROUPS OF PARAGRAPHS

Since a paragraph is, normally, a developed idea, and each developed idea has its place in your overall thesis, as one paragraph follows the next the reader feels he is getting somewhere. Consider the following four consecutive paragraphs. The paragraph preceding the first of these was chiefly concerned with several strategies whereby the Marx Brothers succeeded in making full-length movies, in contrast to the short silent films of a decade earlier. In the first of the following paragraphs, "also" provides the requisite transition.

The Marx Brothers also overcame the problem of the talkies by revealing individual relationships to talk. Groucho talks so much, so rapidly, and so belligerently that talk becomes a kind of weapon. He

[8] *Times Literary Supplement*, 11 Jan. 1957, p. 17.

shoots word bullets at his listeners, rendering them (and the audience) helpless, gasping for breath, trying to grab hold of some argument long enough to make sense of it. But before anyone can grab a verbal handle, Groucho has already moved on to some other topic and implication that seems to follow from his previous one—but doesn't. Groucho's ceaseless talk leads the listener in intellectual circles, swallowing us in a verbal maze, eventually depositing us back at the starting point without knowing where we have been or how we got there. Groucho's "logic" is really the manipulation of pun, homonym, and equivocation. He substitutes the quantity of sound and the illusion of rational connection for the theoretical purpose of talk—logical communication.

Chico's relationship to talk also substitutes sound for sense and the appearance of meaning for meaning. To Chico, "viaduct" sounds like "why a duck," "wire fence" like "why a fence," "shortcut" like "short cake," "sanity clause" like "Santa Claus," "dollars" like "Dallas," "taxes" like "Texas." He alone can puncture Groucho's verbal spirals by stopping the speeding train of words and forcing Groucho to respond to his own erroneous intrusions. Groucho cannot get away with his coy substitution of sound for sense when Chico makes different (but similar) sounds out of the key terms in Groucho's verbal web. Chico's absurd accent (this Italian burlesque would be considered very impolite by later standards) makes him hear Groucho's words as if he, the Italian who speaks pidgin English, were speaking them.

The substitution of sound for sense reaches its perfection in Harpo, who makes only sounds. Harpo substitutes whistling and beeps on his horn for talk. Ironically, he communicates in the films as well as anybody. He communicates especially well with Chico, who understands Harpo better than Groucho does. Chico continually interprets Harpo's noises for Groucho. The irony that a bumbling foreign speaker renders a mute clown's honks, beeps, and whistles into English so it can be understood by the supreme verbal gymnast plays a role in every Marx Brothers film.

Harpo also substitutes the language of the body for speech. In this system of communication, Harpo uses two powerful allies—props and mime. He gives the password ("swordfish") that admits him to a speakeasy by pulling a swordfish out of his pocket. He impersonates Maurice Chevalier by miming a Chevalier song to a phonograph record, produced out of his coat especially for the occasion. Or he orders a shot of Scotch in the speakeasy by snapping into a Highland fling. In these early talkies, talk became one of the comic subjects of the films as well as one of the primary comic devices. As in the early

Chaplin sound films, the Marx Brothers made talk an ally simply by treating it so specially.[9]
—Gerald Mast

A few observations on these paragraphs may be useful. Notice that the first sentence of the first paragraph is, in effect, an introduction to all four paragraphs; because it is too thin to stand by itself, this transition is acceptably attached as a preface to the first paragraph of what is really a unit of four paragraphs. Second, notice that the first paragraph is devoted to Groucho, the second to Chico, and the third and fourth to Harpo. We might think that symmetry requires that Harpo get only one paragraph, like his brothers, but the writer, feeling that each of Harpo's two languages—noises and gestures—is a major point and therefore worth a separate paragraph, rightly allows significance to overrule symmetry. Third, note the simple but adequate transitions at the beginnings of the paragraphs: "Chico's relationship to talk also . . . ," "The substitution of sound for sense reaches its perfection in Harpo," and "Harpo also substitutes the language of the body for speech." Although the repetition of "also" is a trifle mechanical, it serves to let the reader know where he will be going. Finally, notice that this unit discussing the three brothers is arranged climactically; it ends with Harpo, who is said to achieve "perfection" in the matter under discussion. And in this discussion of distorted language, the two paragraphs on Harpo similarly are arranged to form a climax: the second, not the first, gives us the ultimate distortion, language that is not even sound.

INTRODUCTORY PARAGRAPHS

Beginning a long part of one of his long poems, Byron aptly wrote, "Nothing so difficult as a beginning." Almost all writers—professionals as well as amateurs—find that the first paragraphs in their drafts are false starts. Don't worry too much about the opening paragraphs of your draft; you'll almost surely want to revise your opening later anyway, and when writing a first draft you merely need something—almost anything may

[9] *The Comic Mind* (New York: Bobbs-Merrill, 1973), pp. 282–83.

do—to get you going. Though on rereading you will probably find that the first paragraph or two should be replaced, those opening words at least helped you to break the ice. But in your finished paper, the opening cannot be mere throat-clearing. It should be interesting. "Webster says . . . " is not interesting. Nor is a paraphrase of your title ("Anarchism and the Marx Brothers"): "This essay will study the anarchic acts of the Marx Brothers." There is no information about the topic here, at least none beyond what the title already gave, and there is no information about you either, that is, no sense of your response to the topic, such as might be present in, say, "The Marx Brothers are funny, but one often has the feeling that under the fun the violence has serious implications." But in your effort to find your voice and to say something interesting, don't yield to irrelevancy ("*Hamlet* is full of violence" is true, but scarcely relevant to the Marx Brothers) or to the grandiloquence that has wickedly but aptly been called Freshman Omniscience ("Ever since the beginning of time, man has been violent").

Your introductory paragraph will be at least moderately interesting if it gives information, and it will be pleasing if the information provides focus: that is, if it lets the reader know exactly what your topic is, and where you will be going. Remember, when you write, *you* are the teacher; it won't do to begin, "Orwell says he shot the elephant because .·. ." We need at least, "George Orwell, in 'Shooting an Elephant,' says he shot the elephant because . . ." Even better is, "In 'Shooting an Elephant,' George Orwell's uneasy reflections on his service as a policeman in Burma, Orwell suggests that he once shot an elephant because . . . but his final paragraph suggests that we must look for additional reasons."

Let us pursue a little further this business of informative and focused opening sentences. Here are the opening sentences from three essays written by students, on Anne Moody's *Coming of Age in Mississippi*. The book is the autobiography of a black woman, covering her early years with her sharecropper parents, her schooling, and finally her work in the civil rights movement.

The environment that surrounds a person from an early age tends to be a major factor in determining their character.

This is what we call a "zonker" (see pages 176–77), an all-purpose sentence that serves no specific purpose well. Notice also the faulty reference of the pronoun (the plural "their" refers to the singular "a person"), the weaseling of "tends to be a major factor," and the vagueness of "early age" and "environment" and "character." These all warn us that the writer will waste our time.

> It is unfortunate but true that racial or color prejudice shows itself early in the life of a child.

Less pretentious than the first example, but a tedious laboring of the obvious, and annoyingly preachy.

> Anne Moody's autobiography, *Coming of Age in Mississippi,* vividly illustrates how she discovered her black identity.

Surely this is the best of the three openings. Informative and focused, it identifies the book's theme and method, and it offers an evaluation. The essayist has been considerate of her readers: if we are interested in women's autobiographies, life in the South, or black identity we will read on. If we aren't we are grateful to her for letting us off the bus at the first stop.

But of course you can provide interest and focus by other, more indirect means. Among them are:

1. a quotation
2. an anecdote or other short narrative
3. an interesting fact (a statistic, for instance, showing the reader that you know something about your topic)
4. a definition of an important term—but not merely one derived from a desk dictionary
5. a glance at the opposition (disposing of it)
6. a question—but an interesting one, such as "Why do people grow house plants?"

Many excellent opening paragraphs do not use any of these devices, and you need not use any of them if they seem unnatural to you. But the fact is, these devices are widely and successfully used. Here is an example of the second device, an anecdote that makes an effective, indeed an unnerving, introduction to an essay on aging. (More accurately, it is not an opening paragraph—but it could have been one.)

There is an old American folk tale about a wooden bowl. It seems that Grandmother, with her trembling hands, was guilty of occasionally breaking a dish. Her daughter angrily gave her a wooden bowl, and told her that she must eat out of it from now on. The young granddaughter, observing this, asked her mother why Grandmother must eat from a wooden bowl when the rest of the family was given china plates. "Because she is old!" answered her mother. The child thought for a moment and then told her mother, "You must save the wooden bowl when Grandma dies." Her mother asked why, and the child replied, "For when you are old." [10]

—Sharon R. Curtin

The following opening paragraph also is in effect a short narrative, though the point is deliberately obscured—in order to build suspense—until the second paragraph.

For a couple of days after the thing happened, I moved around Los Angeles with an oddly suspended feeling. It was as if I had not known the city before, and the faces on the street that were once merely blank were more personal in their blankness because I was watching them through different eyes, searching out the fugitive among them, or perhaps the victim, and having the feeling that there were lots of both.

I had joined the brotherhood of the victim, a silent membership with high initiation fees. I got robbed and for a while I thought I was going to be killed.[11]

—Charles T. Powers

The fourth strategy, a definition, is fairly common in analytic essays; the essayist first clears the ground by specifying what his topic really is. Here is the beginning of an essay on "primitive" art.

The term "primitive art" has come to be used with at least three distinct meanings. First and most legitimate is its use with reference to the early stages in the development of a particular art, as when one speaks of the Italian primitives. Second is its use to designate works of art executed by persons who have not had formal training in our own art techniques and aesthetic canons. Third is its applica-

---

[10] *Nobody Ever Died of Old Age* (Boston: Little, Brown, 1972), pp. 196–97.
[11] "Say One Word and I'll Cut Your Throat," *Los Angeles Times*, 13 Jan. 1974, sec. 4, p. 1.

tion to the art works of all but a small group of societies which we have chosen to call civilized. The present discussion will deal only with the last.[12]

—Ralph Linton

The author reviews three meanings of the term, and focuses our attention on the relevant one by putting it last.

Here is an effective opening from a chapter on Norman Mailer, by Richard Poirier: "Mailer is an unusually repetitious writer. Nearly all writers of any lasting interest are repetitious." The first sentence, simple though it is, catches our attention by its apparent irreverence; the second, a paradox (that is, an apparent contradiction), gives the first a richer meaning than we had attributed to it. Poirier then goes on to give examples of major writers who are obsessed with certain topics, and he concludes the paragraph with a list of Mailer's obsessions. Such an opening paragraph is a slight variant on a surefire method: you cannot go wrong in suggesting your thesis in your opening paragraph, moving from a rather broad view to a narrower one. This kind of introductory paragraph can be conceived as a funnel, wide at the top and narrowing into what will be the body of the essay. A common version of this kind of paragraph offers some background and concludes with the subject at hand. It may, for example, sketch the past that contrasts with the present. The following paragraph is from an essay on the pictorial effects in modern films.

There are still people who remember when there were no talking pictures, when moving pictures were simply moving pictures. In 1927 the first full-length sound film was made, and sound soon took over. Coffee cups rattled, rain pattered, and people talked and talked and talked. But perhaps film continues to be an essentially visual medium, and we should recognize that films are not dramatic plays frozen on celluloid.

One other kind of introduction is tricky and should be used cautiously. Sometimes an introductory paragraph delicately misleads the audience; the second paragraph reverses the train of

---

[12] " 'Primitive' Art," Preface to Eliot Elisofon, *The Sculpture of Africa* (New York: Frederick A. Praeger, 1958), p. 9.

thought and leads into the main issue. Here is an example by Joseph Wood Krutch, from *"Modernism"* in *Modern Drama*. Only the first part of the second paragraph is given below, but from it you can see what direction Krutch is taking.

One evening in 1892, the first of Oscar Wilde's four successful comedies had in London its first performance. It is said that after the last curtain the audience rose to cheer—and it had good reason to do so. Not in several generations had a new play so sparkled with fresh and copious wit of a curiously original kind.

By now the play itself, *Lady Windermere's Fan*, seems thin and faded. To be successfully revived, as it was a few seasons ago in the United States, it has to be presented as "a period piece"—which means that the audience is invited to laugh at as well as with it. . . .[13]

Here is another example, this one containing the reversal at the end of the opening paragraph.

Time and again I wanted to reach out and shake Peter Fonda and Dennis Hopper, the two motorcyclist heroes of *Easy Rider*, until they stopped their damned-fool pompous poeticizing on the subject of doing your own thing and being your own man. I dislike Fonda as an actor; he lacks humor, affects insufferable sensitivity and always seems to be fulfilling a solemn mission instead of playing a part. I didn't believe in these Honda hoboes as intuitive balladeers of the interstate highways, and I had no intention of accepting them as protagonists in a modern myth about the destruction of innocence. To my astonishment, then, the movie reached out and profoundly shook me.[14]

—Joseph Morgenstern

CONCLUDING PARAGRAPHS

Concluding paragraphs, like opening paragraphs, are especially difficult if only because they are so conspicuous. Fortunately, you are not always obliged to write one. Descriptive essays, for example, may end merely with a final paragraph, not with a paragraph that draws a conclusion. If you are describing a process or mechanism, simply stop when you have finished.

[13] *"Modernism"* in *Modern Drama* (Ithaca, N.Y.: Cornell University Press, 1953), p. 43.
[14] "On the Road," *Newsweek*, 21 July 1969, p. 95.

Just check to see that the last sentence is a good one, clear and vigorous, and stop. In such essays there is usually no need for a crescendo signaling your farewell to the reader. Analytic essays are more likely to need concluding paragraphs, not merely final paragraphs, but even analytic essays, if they are short enough, may end without a formal conclusion. If the last paragraph sets forth the last step of the argument, that may be conclusion enough. Similarly, a short narrative essay, even one that provides meditation on the narrative, need not have a separate concluding paragraph. Consider the following essay, two paragraphs in all.

Out in Akron, Ohio, there is an underground church called Alice's Restaurant, which figures in the most amiable story of the season just past. This group, led by unfrocked priests and unchurched ministers, was doing a deal of earnest good work in a quiet way, all to dramatize and protest the commercialization of Christmas. At shopping centers, for instance, they passed out leaflets calling upon shoppers to limit individual gifts to two-fifty and to devote the overplus to the poor. Then it occurred to one underground churchman, David Bullock by name, to demonstrate the fate that would inevitably befall the Holy Family in a society of heartless abundance. "Joseph and Mary were poor people," Mr. Bullock observed, and he proceeded to devise a scheme that would reveal "what would happen when a poor young couple dressed like Joseph and Mary tried to get a room nearly two thousand years after the birth of Christ." And so it came to pass in those days that Mr. Bullock, in beard and robe, walked out of the cold and darkness of Akron into the lobby of the Downtown Holiday Inn, accompanied by a young woman and a donkey. "I need a room for the night," he told the manager. My wife is heavy with child." He then filled out the registration form, identifying himself as Joseph of Nazareth, travelling with his wife from Judea. Then he waited. The night manager, Mr. Robert Nagel, affably observed that they had come a long way and handed over the key to Room 101. (*Tableau.*)

We picture Mr. Bullock with the key in his hand, his rented donkey lurking behind him, and his faith in human nature crumbling to the ground. To crown his discomfiture, Mr. Nagel offered the wayfarers a free meal. But, alas, in an era of affluence, satiety, like the indiscriminate rain, is apt to descend upon the just and unjust alike. "We weren't very hungry," Mr. Bullock said later, "so I asked him if we could have some drinks." Then he added, "And you know what? He sent them around." For his own part, Mr. Nagel was under no illusions about the financial standing of his new guests. "I knew they couldn't pay," he said. "I mean, a donkey is not a normal form of transportation." One would like to shake him by the hand. We thank Mr. Nagel for adding immeasurably to the merriment of our Christmas, and for his exhibition of that unpredictable, shrewd, and sometimes highly inconvenient human generosity that makes sweeping moral judgments so risky—even for the most earnest of moralists—and makes life so richly interesting for the rest of us.[15]

The first paragraph is almost all narrative; the second, though continuing some part of the narrative, is chiefly the writer's response to it—his reason for sharing it. Of course the final sentence could have been set off as a separate paragraph, but in such isolation it might then have seemed too solemn.

Often, however, a final paragraph is chiefly devoted to drawing a conclusion. With conclusions, as with introductions, try to say something interesting. It is not of the slightest interest to say "Thus we see . . . " and then echo your title and first paragraph. There is some justification for a summary at the end of a long paper because the reader may have half forgotten some of the ideas presented thirty pages earlier, but a paper that can easily be held in the mind needs something different. A good concluding paragraph does more than provide an echo of what the writer has already said. It rounds out the previous discussion, normally with a few sentences that summarize (without the obviousness of "We may now summarize"), but it also may draw an inference that has not previously been expressed. To draw such an inference is not to introduce a new idea—a concluding paragraph is hardly the place for a new idea—but is to see the previous material in a fresh perspective. A good concluding paragraph closes the issue while enriching it. For example, the essay on being assaulted and robbed (the opening paragraphs are quoted on page 77) ends with these two paragraphs:

What do they take when they rob you? Maybe a thousand dollars' worth of stuff. A car. A jar of pennies and small change—the jar, which they would probably end up breaking, worth more than the change inside. A portable radio bought years before at an Army PX. Little things that it takes days to discover are missing.

And what else? The ability to easily enter a darkened apartment or to freely open the door after going out. The worst loss is the sense

---

[15] "Notes and Comment," *The New Yorker*, 10 Jan. 1970, p. 15. Reprinted by permission; © 1970 The New Yorker Magazine, Inc.

of private space, whether it's in your head or your home, and you can never be certain it will not be invaded again.[16]
   —Charles T. Powers

Powers moves from the theft of material objects to the psychological implications of the theft, that is, to a more profound kind of robbery. In a way this is a new topic, but it is, after all, implicit throughout a discussion of assault and robbery and so it enlarges rather than abandons the topic.

We hesitate to offer a do-it-yourself kit for final paragraphs, but the following simple strategies often work:

1. End with a quotation, especially a quotation that amplifies or varies a quotation used in the opening paragraph.
2. End with an allusion, say to a historical or mythological figure or event, putting your topic in a larger framework.
3. End with a glance at the reader—not with a demand that he mount the barricades, but with a suggestion that the next move is his.

If you adopt any of these suggested strategies, do so quietly; avoid the grand finale.

Here are two concluding paragraphs; notice how they wrap things up and at the same time open out by suggesting a larger frame of reference. The first example, from a student's essay on Anthony Burgess' *A Clockwork Orange,* includes quotations from the book and an allusion to a common expression.

Both worlds, youthful anarchy and repressive government, are undesirable. For while "you can't run a country with every chelloveck comporting himself in Alex's manner of the night," there should never be a government with the power to "turn you into something other than a human being . . . with no power of choice any longer." What is frightening is that there is no apparent solution to this futuristic society's dilemma. In fact, with the friendly alliance of Alex and the Minister of the Interior at the end of the book come hints that society may soon enjoy the worst of two worlds.

And here is a concluding paragraph from a student's essay on *Black Elk Speaks,* the life story of an Oglala Sioux holy man.

[16] "Say One Word and I'll Cut Your Throat," *Los Angeles Times,* 13 Jan. 1974, p. 14.

The paragraph includes quotations, and then goes on to suggest that the rest is up to the reader.

"Truth comes into this world with two faces. One is sad with suffering and the other laughs; but it is the same face." The terrible tragedy of the Indian people can never fully be undone. Their "hoop is broken, and there is no center anymore." But perhaps the rising circulation of Black Elk's story will inspire people to look more closely into person-to-person and person-to-nature relationships. Black Elk's message "was given to him for all men and it is true and it is beautiful," but it must be listened to, understood, and acted on.

Every essayist will have to find his own way of ending each essay; the three strategies we suggested a moment ago are common but they are not for you if you don't find them comfortable. And so, rather than ending this section with rules about how to end essays, we suggest how not to end them: Don't merely summarize, don't introduce a totally new point, and don't apologize.

CHAPTER FIVE

EXPOSITION AND DEFINITION

EXPOSITION

The four chief kinds of nonfictional prose are usually said to be exposition, persuasion (or argument), description, and narration. More often than not, however, a single essay combines at least two of these. For example, an expository essay on Zen Buddhism—an essay chiefly concerned with explaining what Zen is—may include a description of a Zen monastery, a narrative of the writer's visit to the monastery, and an argument (that is, a reasoned statement) for the relevance of Zen to us. If the essay is primarily exposition, and most of the writing that most of us do is expository, the descriptive and narrative and persuasive parts will chiefly function to enliven and clarify the explanation of Zen. Similarly, an essay that is primarily an argument for the relevance of Zen to American life may have to sketch the tenets of the creed (exposition) and may tell an anecdote or recount the history of Zen (narration) in order to strengthen the argument.

For the sake of clarity, however, we will talk about relatively pure examples of these four kinds of writing and we will take them up one by one in this and the next two chapters. To talk about them all at once would require the skill of Stephen Leacock's knight, who leaped on his horse and rode madly off in all directions.

The information in a college catalog, telling students how to apply or how to register or how to complete the requirements for a degree, is exposition (from the Latin *exponere*, "to put forth"), a setting-forth of information. It doesn't assume a disagreement, so it doesn't seek to persuade; those paragraphs describing the lovely campus, however, are not exposition but description, offered with the hope of persuading the reader to come. Exposition, in its purest form, seeks only to explain—to expose, we might say—what's what. Exposition may, for example, reveal a process (how to register), or it may reveal the structure of an organization (the purpose and the nature of the college). Of course it often overlaps with description; an account of how a machine works may be considered either exposition or description, depending on whether the emphasis is on the process or the machine's appearance. In fact, description can be considered one kind of exposition, but we will postpone further discussion of this point until the chapter on description.

Here is a short piece, primarily expository. If typed, double-spaced, it would probably be a little more than one page.

IN SEARCH OF THE ELUSIVE PINGO

Canadian scientists are preparing an expedition to the Beaufort Sea to study underwater ice formations that are blocking use of the Northwest Passage as a long-sought commercial route.

The formations, called pingoes, are cones of antediluvian ice, coated with frozen muck, that stick up like fingers from the bottom of the sea to within 45 feet of the surface. They could rip the bottoms of ships, such as supertankers, that ride deep in the water.

The pingoes are an obstacle to exploitation of oil resources and expansion of trade in the Arctic region that were expected to follow the successful pioneer voyage of the S.S. Manhattan through the ice-clogged Northwest Passage five years ago. One tanker ripped open could disrupt the ecological balance of much of the region.

The existence of the pingoes was not known until 1970 when scientists aboard the Canadian scientific ship Hudson, using special sonar equipment to plot the shape of the Beaufort Sea's basin, detected batches of them that the Manhattan was lucky to miss. Since then, oceanographers have charted about 200 pingoes, and there is no telling how many more there are.

Scientists at the United States Geological Survey and the Bedford Institute of Oceanography in Nova Scotia, where the Hudson's expedition originated, have been exploring the origin of the pingoes and seeking in vain ways to neutralize them. Dynamiting has proved ineffective. So scientists from Bedford are going back this summer for another look.[1]

You may not want to learn much more about pingoes, but we hope you found this brief account clear and interesting. We might ask ourselves how the writer sustains our interest: Is the title interesting? What expression in the second paragraph is especially effective? Are the paragraphs given in a reasonable order? Is the final paragraph a satisfactory ending?

Explaining a Process

Let's look at another short piece, this one an explanation of a simple process. It comes from a popular book by a physician.

HOW TO DEAL WITH THE CRYING
Leonard Cammer

If you are a soft, sentimental person you probably cannot stand to see your sick relative cry. It breaks you up. However, where tears serve as a necessary emotional outlet they can be encouraged. In a grief reaction especially, when the person has suffered a loss, crying comes easily and produces a healthy release for pent-up emotion. Momentarily, the tears wash away the depressed feelings.

However, when an exhausting bout of tearfulness continues on and on with extreme agitation, breast beating, and self-abuse, it is time for you to call a halt. Let me show you how to terminate almost any flood of tears by the correct use of a psychologic device.

First, sit directly in front of your relative and say, "Go on crying if you want to, but face me. Look into my eyes." It is a simple fact that no one can sustain crying while gazing straight into another's eyes. If the person does what you ask, his tears will stop. Not right away; he may continue to cry and avert his gaze. Take his hands in yours and again coax him to look at you. You may have to repeat the request several times, but at last he will turn and fix his eyes on you, almost hypnotically. The flow of tears then trickles to an end, and the person may begin to talk about the things that give him mental pain.

Every time you shorten such a spell of crying you stem the waste

---

[1] *New York Times*, 5 May 1974, sec. E, p. 6.

of energy and give the person a chance to preserve his or her stamina in fighting the depression.[2]

Notice that in addition to describing a process, the essay begins by explaining the value of crying and ends by explaining the value of bringing crying to an end. Would the essay be equally good if the first paragraph came last?

Here is another essay, this one a little longer, on a process.

HOW TO GROW AN AVOCADO

To grow an avocado tree indoors, begin with a ripe Florida avocado. (The varieties grown in California, Puerto Rico, and the West Indies can be used, but for some reason they often do not flourish.) The fruit is ripe if the stemmed end yields to the pressure of your thumb. Remove the pit and place it in warm water for about three hours (during the interval you may eat the fruit) and then gently rub off any remaining traces of the fruit and also as much of the paper-thin brown coating as comes easily off the pit. Dry the pit and set it aside for a moment.

Fill a glass almost to the top with warm water. (Remember, the avocado is a tropical tree; cold water harms it.) Next, notice where the base of the pit is (an avocado has a relatively flat base and a relatively tapered top) and insert four toothpicks to half of their length about one-third the way up from the base. If you look down on the avocado from the top, toothpicks are sticking out at what on a clock would be 12:00, 3:00, 6:00, and 9:00. Next, place the avocado in the glass; the base will be in about half an inch of water, but the toothpicks will prevent the pit—or seed, for that is what it is—from sinking to the bottom of the glass. Put the glass in a warm dark place, such as a kitchen closet.

A root may appear at the base within a week, but it is quite usual for nothing to happen for several weeks. Be patient; unless the water turns cloudy, which is a sign that the seed has rotted and must be tossed, out, sooner or later the seed will germinate. During this waiting period, all you can do is keep the water at the proper level. (Reminder: make sure the added water is warm.) In time the root will appear at the base and some time later a pale green shoot will appear at the top. Possibly several shoots will appear, but one will establish itself as the main shoot; ignore the others, which may or may not survive. When the main shoot or stem is about eight

[2] *Up From Depression* (New York: Pocket Books, 1971), p. 102.

inches tall, with a scissors cut off the top four inches so that the top growth will not outstrip the root development. Failure to cut the stem will result in a spindly plant with few leaves. By cutting, you force the stem to send out a new shoot which will grow slowly but which will hold its leaves longer.

When the glass is fairly full of roots (this may be about two weeks after cutting the stem, or as many as six weeks after you prepared the pit), it is time to take it out of the dark and to pot the plant. Use a clay pot about eight and a half inches in diameter. Cover the drainage hole with some pieces of broken pot, and fill the pot to about two-thirds of its height with a mixture of equal parts of good garden soil and sand, mixed with a teaspoon of bone-meal or a couple of tablespoons of dried manure for fertilizer. Remove the toothpicks from the seed, place it on the soil, and then add more of the mixture, until the seed is covered to half of its height. Pour the glass of water over the seed, and then pour an additional glassful of warm water over it. The soil will probably settle; if so, add enough soil to cover the lower half of the seed. Under the pot put a saucer with warm water, and place the saucer and pot in the sunniest place you have.

Water the plant with warm water when the soils appear dry, probably once a day, and be patient. When you cut the main stem you interrupted the plant's growth, and weeks may pass before another stem grows out of the first. But if you water it and give it light, and add plant food about once a month, you are doing all that you can. The main stem—really the trunk of a tree—will in time produce branches that will produce leaves. When leaves develop, you need do nothing except insert a dowel in the pot and loosely tie up any sagging branches. In time you may wish to prune at the top, in order to encourage the lower branches, so that your tree will be bushy rather than spindly. With luck, the tree will flourish; when it is about six feet tall, transplant it to a larger clay pot simply by smashing with a hammer the first pot and then by placing the tree with its ball of roots and earth in a pot prepared just as the first one was. Aside from daily watering (but don't fret if you sometimes miss a day) and occasional fertilizing and pruning, you need do nothing to your tree but enjoy it. But do not spoil your enjoyment by hoping for flowers or fruit; they will never appear.

The organization of this essay is simple but adequate: because it describes a *processus* (Latin *pro* = forward, + *cessus* = movement or step) the essay begins at the beginning and takes the reader through a sequence of steps. This organization is almost inevitable in describing a process; the commonest variation is an opening paragraph that sets forth the goal (here, it might be a description of a flourishing avocado, or a comment on the pleasures of growing things)—but the process itself would still be described chronologically.

DEFINITION

The essay on growing an avocado is, of course, relatively simple because—although avocados are trickier than the essayist admits—there is little to argue about. There is no need, in such an essay, to define "avocado" or even to define "warm" water, and because the process is fairly simple there is no need to clarify it by introducing comparisons to more familiar material. Nor is there a need to explain the purpose of the process.

But many things are not what they sound like: a seedless orange is (according to the citrus industry) an orange with five seeds or less; smoked salmon is not necessarily smoked (it may be salted); plum pudding contains no plums. Asked to define a word, most of us want to take advantage of St. Augustine's ingenious evasion: "I know what it is when you don't ask me." Or we sound like Polonius talking about Hamlet (II.ii.92–94):

> Your noble son is mad.
> Mad call I it, for, to define true madness,
> What is't but to be nothing else but mad?

One way to avoid these pitfalls of definition is to begin with the origin of a word.

Definition by Origin

Sometimes we may know the origin of the word, and the origin may be worth recounting for the light it sheds on the present meaning.

Low Rider. A Los Angeles nickname for ghetto youth. Originally the term was coined to describe the youth who had lowered the bodies of their cars so that they rode low, close to the ground; also implied was the style of driving that these youngsters perfected. Sitting behind the steering wheel and slumped low down in the seat, all that could be seen of them was from their eyes up, which used to be the cool way of driving. When these youthful hipsters

alighted from their vehicles, the term *low rider* stuck with them, evolving to the point where all black ghetto youth—but *never* the soft offspring of the black bourgeoisie—are referred to as low riders.[3]
—Eldridge Cleaver

Or we may know the foreign origins of an English word; pornography, for example, comes from Greek words meaning "writing of prostitutes." A good dictionary provides etymologies (from the Greek, meaning "true word"), and such information about the origin of a word may be interesting and relevant and therefore worth mentioning—but of course a word's present meaning may be far from its origins.

Definition by Synonym

Usually when we are trying to define a word we can come up with at least a single word, a synonym; so we define "helix" by saying "spiral," or "ship" by saying "boat." Definition by synonym, however, doesn't go very far; it equates one word with another, but often no close synonym exists (boat and ship are not close), and in any case such a definition is only a beginning.

Stipulative Definition

You may stipulate (contract for) a particular meaning of a word, as we saw in the passage on "primitive" art (page 77). For instance, if you are writing about Catholics, you may stipulate that in your essay the word refers to all who have been baptized into the Catholic faith. Or you may stipulate that it refers only to those who consider themselves practicing Catholics. As another example, take the expression "third world" people. This term has at least three related but separate meanings:

1. a group of nations, especially in Africa and Asia, that are not aligned with either the Communist or the non-Communist bloc
2. the aggregate of underdeveloped nations of the world
3. the aggregate of minority groups within a larger predominant culture

[3] *Soul on Ice* (New York: Dell Publishing Company, 1968), p. 26.

In fact, a fourth meaning, a variation of the third, seems to be most common in recent American writing: the aggregate of minority groups *other than blacks and Orientals* within the United States. Many discussions of third world people limit themselves to American Indians and to Spanish-speaking people, apparently considering American blacks and Orientals as part of the larger predominant culture. Thus, in an essay you may announce that by "third world" you mean such and such: "In this essay, 'third world' refers not to A and B but to C."

It is entirely legitimate to stipulate or contract for a particular meaning, so long as you don't let other meanings sneak under the umbrella later. Once you have established your meaning, stick to it.

Formal Definition

A formal definition normally takes a term (for instance, "professor") and places it within a class or family ("a teacher") and then goes on to differentiate it from other members of the class ("in a college or university"). Such a definition is sometimes called *inclusive/exclusive* because it includes the word in a relevant category and then excludes other members of that category. Notice, by the way, that such a definition as "A professor is a teacher in a college or university" uses a parallel form—a noun for a noun. Avoid saying "A professor is when you teach . . ." or "Love is where you never have to say you're sorry."

What use can be made of a formal definition? Suppose you want to define "shark." A desk dictionary will give you something like this: "a cartilaginous (as opposed to bony) fish with a body tapering toward each end." Such a definition puts sharks within the family of a type of fish and then goes on to exclude from this type (which happens also to include rays as well as sharks) other members by calling attention to the distinctive shape of the shark's body. But if you are not writing a strictly formal definition you may want to expand it into something like this:

Although the shark and the ray are closely related, being cartilaginous rather than bony fish, the two could scarcely be more different in appearance. The ray, a floppy pancake-like creature, is grotesque but not terrifying; the shark, its tapering body gliding through the water, is perhaps the most beautiful and at the same time the most terrifying sight the sea can offer.

In short, probably in your definition you will want to talk not only about sharks as remote objects but about your sense of them, your response to them.

Longer Definitions

Most of the terms we try to define in college courses will require lengthy definitions. If you are going to say anything of interest about love or machismo or obscenity or freedom or poverty or mother wit you will have to go far beyond a formal definition. If you are writing on a subject you care about, you may find that you will have to write at least several paragraphs until you get to the limits of the word. ("Definition," by the way, is from the Latin *de* "off" and *finis* "end, limit.")

One way of getting toward the limits of the word is to spend some sentences, perhaps a paragraph, on what the word is not. In the paragraph on sharks, half of a sentence was devoted to rays, close to sharks but different. In a more extended definition of a less easily defined topic, more space might be devoted to establishing distinctions. For example, the writer of an essay on gallows humor (briefly defined as humor that domesticates a terrifying situation by making fun of it) might wish to distinguish it from black humor (not the humor of black people, but a brutal or sadistic humor). The superficial similarity of gallows humor to black humor might require the essayist to discuss black humor too in order to make clear the special quality of gallows humor; but of course the discussion of black humor should be clearly subordinated to the main topic lest the essay lose focus. The point of such a strategy is to help the reader see something clearly by holding it against something similar but significantly different. The following extended definition of a proverb follows such a strategy.

A proverb is a concise didactic statement that is widely used in an unchanging form. Among the examples that come to mind are "Look before you leap," "A rolling stone gathers no moss," and "Red sky at night, sailors delight." These, and almost all other proverbs that one can think of, concisely and memorably summarize everyday experience. This everyday experience is usually a

matter of conduct; even "Red sky at night, sailors delight"—
which seems purely descriptive—is followed by "Red sky at morning,
sailors take warning." Most commonly, proverbs advise the hearer
to avoid excess.

We should distinguish proverbs from other concise utterances.
Clichés such as "cool as a cucumber," "last but not least," and "a
sight for sore eyes," though they may be called proverbial phrases,
often do not offer advice implicitly or explicitly. More important,
because clichés are not complete sentences their form changes. He
or she or they can be or are or were "cool as a cucumber." Proverbs
should be distinguished, too, from such conventional utterances as
"Good morning," "Thank you," "Please pass the salt," which are
not didactic.

Closer to proverbs, superficially at least, are epigrams, such as
Oscar Wilde's "A cynic is a man who knows the price of everything
and the value of nothing." Most epigrams are obviously literary;
they usually employ a clever contrast (antithesis) that is rare in
proverbs. And most epigrams, unlike proverbs, are not really
communal property: their authorship is known, and they are not
used by ordinary people in ordinary speech. When used by someone other than the author, they are used by educated speakers or
writers as conscious quotations. In contrast, the speaker of a proverb, though he knows that he did not invent it, rightly feels that
it is part of his own wisdom.

Notice that this extended definition of proverbs begins by including the proverb within a class ("concise didactic statement") and
then proceeds to exclude other members of the class (cliché or
proverbial phrase, conventional utterance, epigram—though
these are not named until the second paragraph) by specifying
that a proverb is "widely used in an unchanging form." The
definition, then, is inclusive and exclusive; it includes the term
to be defined within a class, and it excludes other members of
the class. Notice too that examples are given throughout. If the
examples were omitted, the paragraphs would be less lively and
less clear. But of course, a definition cannot be a mere list of
examples ("a proverb is a saying such as . . ."); generalizations
as well as concrete illustrations are needed.

The definition of a proverb was just that; it was not a focused
essay on proverbs. And it was not an attempt to woo the reader
to be interested in proverbs. It was, like the essay on the avocado, the sort of thing that might be found in a reference book.

If more space had been available, especially if the word were a more elusive one such as "democracy" or "personality" or "feminism," the essay might have had the following structure:

1. statement of the need for a definition
2. survey of the usual definitions (calling attention to their inadequacy)
3. the writer's definition, set forth with illustrative examples, comparisons, and contrasts

Clearly the heart of such an essay is the third part.

Though some essays seek to do nothing more than to define a term, essays with other purposes often include paragraphs defining a word. Here, from a long essay on the recent fad for country music, are some paragraphs defining country music. Notice how this selection moves from a moderately jocose and obviously imprecise definition ("anything that Grandma can hum, whistle, or sing is country") to a list of the subjects of country music and then to a hypothetical example.

What is the fuss all about? Glen George, manager of Kansas City's country radio KCKN, says: "Anything that Grandma can hum, whistle or sing is country." Its traditional message is one of despair, hope, loss, death, the land and, often with cloying sentimentality, love. Country lyrics have always been the cry of the common man. They can, and do give comfort to everyone from sharecroppers and truck-stop waitresses to University of Texas Football Coach Darrell Royal, former Energy Czar John Love, Novelist Kurt Vonnegut Jr. and Operatic Tenor Richard Tucker. Says Moon Mullins, program director of the all-country WINN in Louisville: "If you listen to our station long enough, one of our songs will tell your story."

Cynics like to say that whomever the story belongs to, it will probably deal with trucks, trains, prison, drinking (or moonshine), women misbehaving ("slippin' around" in the country vernacular) or death. The ideal country song might be about a guy who finally gets out of prison, hops a truck home, finds that his wife is slippin' around, gets drunk, and staggers to his doom in front of a high-balling freight.

The music itself, at least as purveyed by many of the superstars of Nashville and Bakersfield, has a vanilla sameness to it that often does not reflect the pain and sorrow of the words. The voices of the singers are often less charged with emotion than their blues and rock counterparts. Most male country stars have deep bass baritones that seem to say: this man sits tall in the saddle. Women stars tend to have bright, unstrained sopranos—or a Lynn Anderson kind of nasal chirpiness—that rule out not only women's lib but any other kind of defiance. In the past, country lyrics have been astonishingly repressive. Blind loyalty to husband, parents, even political leaders has been a common theme. When men have sung about women, the subject (always excepting long-suffering Mother) has often been the pain, not the pleasure.

Today, however, country is taking on a new sound, a new diversity and message as well. Partly that is due to the influence of rock, partly to the visible softening of the once strong accents of American regionalization. Says Kris Kristofferson, 37, the former Rhodes scholar who is now a leader of country's progressive wing: "There's really more honesty and less bullshit in today's music than ever before."[4]

EXERCISES

1. In 300–500 words explain how to do one of the following: a card trick; tell a joke; deliver a baby; change a diaper; change the oil in a car; make bread.

2. In one paragraph define anecdote, partly by comparing it to joke, parable, and short story. Or define riddle, partly by excluding conundrum.

3. Define blues or rock or soul, in less than 250 words.

4. Define guilt, distinguishing it from responsibility, or from shame.

5. Write an expository essay objectively setting forth someone else's views on a topic or limited range of topics. Suggested length: 500 words. Your source for these views should be a published interview. If possible, submit a copy of the interview with your essay. Suggested sources: "A Game of Cosmic Roulette," interview with Jacques Monod (1965 Nobel Prize winner in biology and author of *Chance and Necessity*), the *New York Times,* November 8, 1971, p. 39; Dick Cavett and Christopher Porterfield, *Cavett* (New York: Harcourt Brace Jovanovich, 1974); *Rolling Stone Interviews* (New York: Paperback Library, 1971); Charles Thomas Samuels, *Encountering Directors* (New York: G. P. Putnam's Sons, 1972); and *Writers at Work: The Paris Review Interviews,* ed. Malcolm Cowley (New York: Viking Press, 1958–1968).

---

[4] "Lord, They've Done It All," *Time,* 6 May 1974, pp. 52–53.

CHAPTER SIX

ARGUMENT AND PERSUASION

If you are going to persuade your audience to accept your views, you need to gain and keep its confidence. Unfortunately, confidence is easily lost: for instance, a reader is not likely to trust (and therefore to accept the argument of) a writer who spells the word "arguement." The writer's arguments may be sound, but the reader—reluctant to change his views in any case, and certainly unwilling to ally himself with someone who can't even spell—seizes on this irrelevant error and smugly puts aside the essay, confident that he has nothing to learn.

You must convey to the reader your own competence, not only through technical skills but by (1) your courtesy and (2) your valid reasoning. These two are not entirely separable, as we shall soon see, but for the sake of clarity we can begin by making the distinction.

Courtesy

In persuasive writing—as in almost all writing—you owe it to the reader to be courteous. Being courteous includes taking the trouble to get the right word, to provide interesting examples, and to define crucial terms. We have already talked about definitions on pages 89–95, but a few additional words are appropriate here. If you are arguing that "the sales tax is unfair to the poor," you will probably have to define "unfair" and "poor." What, after all, is a "fair" tax? One that takes account of ability to pay? One that is heavier on luxuries than on necessities? It is legitimate to stipulate a definition (see pages 90–91), but you must then stick to the meaning you stipulate; you cannot quietly use the word in a larger sense than you had contracted for. And be sure to avoid the opposite fault, of using different words to mean the same thing. Don't begin to substitute "fair law" for "reasonable law," or "obscene" for "pornographic"; elegant variation (see page 209) will only cause needless difficulty for the reader.

We can now turn to the more obvious meaning of courtesy in persuasive writing. Don't regard either your reader or your opposition as a fool. When you make a point, make it firmly but quietly; don't shout and don't gloat; and don't use sarcasm. Although desk dictionaries usually define sarcasm as "bitter, caustic irony" or "a kind of satiric wit," if you think of a sarcastic comment that you have heard you will probably agree that "a crude, sneering remark" is a better definition. Lacking the ingenuity or wit of good satire and the wryness or carefully controlled mockery of irony, sarcasm usually relies on gross overstatement and intends simply to humiliate. "Sarcasm" is derived from a Greek word meaning "to tear flesh" or "to bite the lips in rage," altogether an unattractive business. Sarcasm is unfair, for it dismisses an opponent's argument with ridicule rather than with reason; it is also unwise, for it turns the reader against you. Again, think of some occasion when you heard a sarcastic remark, possibly spoken by a teacher to a student who had done outrageously badly on an examination. The teacher may have been right—the student's examination revealed no knowledge of the subject—but a sarcastic remark such as "One point for every minute you spent studying" turns the hearers against the speaker and arouses sympathy for the victim. Wit and irony are acceptable, but sarcasm has no place in persuasive writing.

Reasoning

In persuasive writing you establish your authority chiefly by the force of your argument, or, more exactly, by the force of your interestingly detailed presentation of your argument. An "argument" here is not a wrangle but a reasoned discussion. What separates argument from exposition is this: exposition consists of statements, but in argument some of the statements are offered as *reasons* for other statements. Another way of characterizing the difference is to say that exposition assumes there is no substantial disagreement between informed persons, and argument assumes there is or may be substantial disagreement. But in all of your writing it is useful to assume that you must convince your reader to share your point of view. In a sense, every essay with a thesis, every paragraph with a topic sentence or idea, presents evidence to support it. The evidence may be a series of reasons or, especially in essays on literature, of facts, details, examples, references to the text. Here is the critic William Gass, for example, in a paragraph about William Faulkner. Notice that the first sentence of the paragraph offers two generalizations—the second being the reason ("because") for the first. The rest of the paragraph then goes on to offer supporting details.

Nothing was too mean for his imagination because he did not believe there was any insignificance on earth. A dirt road was worthy of the most elevated consciousness. An old woman or an old mule: he found in them the forms and forces of History itself. To build a house, found a family, lay rails across a state: these were acts an Alexander might have engaged in. The Civil War was War, high water along the river was The Flood, the death of a dog was Sorrow. He managed to give even the mute heart speech, and invest a humble, private, oft-times red-necked life with those epic rhythms and rich sounds which were formerly the hired pomp and commissioned music of emperors and kings.[1]

—William Gass

Let us examine the reasoning process more closely now by considering some obvious errors in reasoning; in logic they are called *fallacies* (from a Latin verb meaning "to deceive"). As Tweedledee says in *Alice through the Looking-Glass*, "If it were so, it would be; but as it isn't, it ain't. That's logic."

---

[1] *New York Review of Books*, 27 June 1974, p. 3.

Common Fallacies

False authority. Don't try to borrow the prestige of authorities who are not authorities on the topic in question—for example, a heart surgeon speaking on politics, or a politician on ecology. However eminent the surgeon and the politician, on these matters they speak merely as persons of eminence, not as persons of expertise. You will only discredit yourself if you think that a surgeon's opinions on redistricting or a politician's opinions on whaling have any special weight. Similarly, some former authorities are no longer authorities, because the problems have changed or because later knowledge has superseded their views. Adam Smith, Jefferson, and Einstein remain men of genius, but their authority to speak on some modern issues even in their fields may be questioned. In short, before you rely on an authority, make sure that the person in question *is* an authority on the topic. Don't assume that every black is an authority on ghetto life; many have never been in a ghetto. Remember the Yiddish proverb: "A goat has a beard, but that doesn't make him a rabbi."

False quotation. If you do quote from an authority, don't misquote. One can argue that the Bible itself says "commit adultery." The words do occur in it, but of course the quotation is taken out of context: the Bible says "Thou shalt not commit adultery." Few writers would offer so outrageous a misquotation, but it is easy to slip into taking from an authority the passages that suit us and neglecting the rest. For example, you may find someone who grants that "there are strong arguments in favor of abolishing the death penalty," but if he goes on to argue that, on balance, the arguments in favor of retaining it seem stronger to him, it is dishonest to quote his words with the implication that he favors abolishing it.

Suppression of evidence. Don't neglect evidence that is contrary to your own argument. To neglect evidence is unfair—and disastrous. You will be found out, and your argument will be dismissed even though it may have some merit. You owe it to yourself and your reader to present all the relevant evidence. Be especially careful not to assume that every question is simply a matter of *either/or*. There may be some truth on both sides. Take the following thesis: "Grades encourage unwholesome competition, and should therefore be abolished." Even if the statement about the evil effect of grading is true, it may not be the whole truth, and therefore it may not follow that grades should be abolished. One might point out that grades do other things too: they may stimulate learning, and they may assist the student by telling him how far he has progressed. One might conclude, on balance, that the fault outweighs the benefits, but one can scarcely hope to be taken seriously if one does not recognize all the facts, or all the supposed facts. Concede to the opposition what is due it, and then outscore the opposition. Any failure to confront the opposing evidence will be noticed; the reader will keep wondering how you can be so foolish as not to see this or that, and soon he will dismiss your argument. Moreover, if you confront the opposition you will almost surely strengthen your own argument. As Edmund Burke said two hundred years ago, "He that wrestles with us strengthens our nerves, and sharpens our skill. Our antagonist is our helper."

Generalization from insufficient evidence. The process of generalizing (inferring a general principle from particular facts) is called *induction;* we study particular cases and then form a generalization. Now, a generalization thus arrived at is only highly probable at best, because there are particulars that have not been encountered. Every cow I have seen has had four legs, but a five-legged cow may exist somewhere. The degree of probability of course varies with the size and representativeness of the sampled particulars. If my first two meals in Tucson are delicious, I may find myself talking about the excellent food there, and I may even slip into saying that all of the restaurants in Tucson serve great food—but if I do say such things I am offering a generalization based on insufficient evidence. This is a gross example, to be sure, but the error can be insidious. Take, for instance, an assertion about student opinion on, say, intercollegiate athletics, based on a careful survey of opinion in the fraternity houses and dormitories. Such a survey leaves out those students who commute, a group that may be different (economically, religiously, and in social outlook) from the surveyed group. Because the surveyed sample is not fully representative, the generalizations drawn from the data may be false. The generalizations may, of course, happen to be true; they may indeed correspond to the views of the commuting students also, but that would be only a lucky accident. In short, when you offer a generalization based on induction, stand back, take another look at your evidence, and decide whether the generalization can be presented as a fact; maybe it's only a probability—or maybe only an opinion.

The genetic fallacy. Don't assume that something can necessarily be explained in terms of its birth or origin. "He wrote the novel to make money, so it can't be any good" is palpable nonsense. The value of the novel need not depend on the initial pressure that motivated the author. If you think the novel is bad, you'll have to offer better evidence. Another example: "Capital punishment arose in days when men sought revenge, so it now ought to be abolished." Again an unconvincing argument; capital punishment may have some present value, for example it may serve as a deterrent to crime. But that's another argument. Be on guard, too, against our nasty tendency to think about people in terms of their origins: Mr. X was born in————, so he is probably untrustworthy or stupid or industrious.

Begging the question and circular reasoning. Don't assume the truth of the point that you should prove. The term "begging the question" is a trifle odd. It means, in effect, "You, like a beggar, are asking me to grant you something at the outset." Examples: "The barbaric death penalty should be abolished" (you should prove, not assert, that it is barbaric); "This senseless language requirement should be dropped," or "The foreign language requirement, because it is valuable, should be retained" (both of these opposed views assume what they should prove). Circular reasoning is usually an extended form of begging the question. What ought to be proved is covertly assumed. Example: "T. S. Eliot is the best twentieth-century poet, because the best critics say so." Who are the best critics? Those who recognize Eliot's supremacy. Circular reasoning, then, normally includes intermediate steps absent from begging the question, but the two fallacies are so closely related that they can be considered one. Another example: "I feel sympathy for him because I identify with him." Despite the "because," no reason is really offered. What follows "because" is merely a restatement, in slightly different words, of what precedes; the shift of words, from "feel sympathy" to "identify with" has misled the writer into thinking he is giving a reason. Other examples: "Students are interested in courses when the subject matter and the method of presentation are interesting"; "There cannot be peace in the Middle East because the Jews and the Arabs will always fight." In short, an assertion that ought to be proved is reasserted as a reason in support of the assertion.

Post hoc ergo propter hoc. Latin: "after this, therefore because of this." Don't assume that because X precedes Y, X must cause Y. Example: "He went to college and came back a pot-head; college corrupted him." He might have taken up pot even if he had not gone to college. Another example: "Since they abolished capital punishment, the crime rate in X has increased." But the implication that the crime rate has increased *because* capital punishment was abolished is not proved; it may have increased for other reasons. One more example: "The riots of the sixties were caused by the permissive child-rearing of the forties." Maybe, but you'll have to demonstrate a causal connection.

Argumentum ad hominem. Here the argument is directed "toward the man," rather than toward the issue. Don't shift from your topic to your opponent. A speaker favors the abolition of capital punishment and his opponent seeks to turn the argument away from the issue and toward the man: "You have a cousin in jail on a murder charge, haven't you?"

Argument from analogy. Don't confuse an analogy with proof. An analogy is an extended comparison between two things; it can be useful in exposition, for it explains the unfamiliar by means of the familiar: "A government is like a ship, and just as a ship has a captain and a crew, so a government has . . ."; "Writing an essay is like building a house; just as an architect must begin with a plan, so the writer must . . ." The usefulness of these comparisons, however, goes only so far. Everything is what it is, and not another thing. A government is not a ship, and a writer is not an architect. Some of what is true about ships may be (roughly) true of governments, and some of what is true about architects may be (again, roughly) true of writers, but there are differences too. We used to hear much of the "domino theory," which argued that the countries of Southeast Asia were like dominoes standing on end one behind the other; if one country toppled into communism the rest would necessarily also topple into communism. An engaging analogy, but apparently not true. And consider the following analogy between a lighthouse and the death penalty:

The death penalty is a warning, just like a lighthouse throwing its beams out to sea. We hear about shipwrecks, but we do not hear about the ships the lighthouse guides safely on their way. We do not have proof of the number of ships it saves, but we do not tear the lighthouse down.[2]

—J. Edgar Hoover

How convincing is it as an argument, that is, as a reason for retaining the death penalty?

False assumption. Beware of such statements as "He goes to Yale, so he must be rich." Possibly the statement is based on faulty induction (the writer knows four Yale men, and all four are rich) but more likely he is just passing on a cliché. The Yale student in question may be on a scholarship, may be struggling to earn the money, or may be backed by parents of modest means who for eighteen years have saved money for his college education. Other examples: "I haven't heard him complain about French 10, so he must be satisfied"; "She's a writer, so she must be well read." A little thought will show how weak such assertions are; they *may* be true, but they may not.

The errors we have discussed are common and are (in this world) unforgivable if they are consciously used. You have a point to make, and you should make it fairly. If it can only be made unfairly, you do an injustice not only to your reader but to yourself; you should try to think about changing your view of the topic. Alas, as George Santayana said, "Nothing requires a rarer intellectual heroism than willingness to see one's equation written out." Difficult, yes; still, you don't want to be like the politician whose speech had a marginal reminder: "Argument weak; shout here."

Logic: Last Words

Probably the chief faults in most persuasive writing are not so much faults of reasoning as they are faults of initial assump-

[2] "Statements in Favor of the Death Penalty," *F.B.I. Law Enforcement Bulletin* 29 (June 1960), quoted in *The Death Penalty in America,* ed. Hugo Adam Bedau (Chicago: Aldine, 1964), p. 131.

tions. We may argue with faultless logic from faulty premises, which are rooted in our tendency to be intolerant of views and prejudices other than our own. We begin with certain cherished ideas, and then we argue from them, seeing only part of a problem or seeing a generality where there is really only an instance. We reason—we have a maddening habit of saying "It stands to reason"—but we won't listen to reason. When it comes to listening, we are like the character in Elizabeth Gaskell's *Cranford* who said, "I'll not listen to reason. Reason always means what someone else has got to say."

Organizing a Persuasive Essay

The word "logic" is from *logos*, Greek for "pattern" or "plan," and though today logic means the science of correct reasoning, one cannot neglect the pattern or plan. As a rough principle, arrange your arguments in order of increasing strength. (Here we pass over the problem of an opening paragraph. For a discussion of opening paragraphs, see pages 74–79.) Now, the danger in following this plan is that you begin with a weak argument; avoid the danger by telling your reader that indeed the first argument is relatively weak (if it is terribly weak, it isn't an argument at all, so scrap it) and that you offer it for the sake of completeness or because it is often given, and immediately assure the reader that far stronger arguments will be given. Face the opposition to this initial argument, grant as much as the opposition deserves, and salvage what is left of the argument. Then proceed to the increasingly strong arguments. As you treat each one, it is usually advisable to state it briefly, to summarize the opposing view, and then to demolish this opposition, thus ending your discussion of each of your own arguments affirmatively. Another way of ensuring an affirmative ending is to begin, after an appropriate introductory paragraph putting the reader straight, by massing, in brief, all the opposing arguments, and then to demolish them one by one.

In short, remember that when you have done your thinking and your rethinking you are not done. You still must turn your thinking into writing, courteously, clearly, concretely. Find the right order, get the right words and provide the right transitions, avoid sarcasm, and enrich your argument with specific examples and perhaps even some narrative—an appropriate anecdote, for instance, or a bit of history.

Persuasion at Work: Four Essays

Following are four persuasive essays for you to consider. The first was written by a student.

AMERICA LAST?

Under the interdepartmental programs, we are offered two areas of concentration in archaeology: classical and Near Eastern archaeology. Course offerings in pre-Columbian cultures are unavailable.

Since adequate provisions have been made for two areas of archaeology, it seems that establishing a concentration in pre-Columbian archaeology is reasonable. It is doubtful that the lack of such a concentration is due to student indifference, to faculty incompetence, or to inadequate facilities. It is due to a tendency to dwell on the magnificence and complexity of Near Eastern and of Greek societies. There can be no denial that these cultures were splendid, but we should study pre-Columbian culture too because we live in the Americas.

Because several very different civilizations (for example, Mayan, Aztec, Zapotec, Olmec) fall under the pre-Columbian label, it is impossible for a college to offer a complete cultural picture. Therefore, in order to gain something of an insight, the focus should be on Mayan civilization, one of the most highly developed cultures in antiquity. The Mayans, like the Egyptians, constructed pyramids honoring sun and moon gods; these pyramids were constructed according to complex astronomical principles. The Mayans equaled and perhaps excelled the Egyptians and Greeks as astronomers, and they were among the greatest of mathematicians. Their development of the calendar is one of their greatest achievements. The Greeks sculpted idealized, orderly, and harmonious figures, and we rightly treasure them. But the Mayans were no less superb as sculptors. Moreover, the Mayan craftsmen created beautiful rings, bracelets, arm bands, and ceremonial headpieces.

Like the Greeks, the Mayans were religious. Basically their culture revolved around the worshipping of a central god, Quetzalcoatl, or Kukulcan, as the Mayans called him. This god taught them laws and customs, but later left them and traveled back across the sea. The influence of Kukulcan is evident in all Mayan art.

Their structure—or rather their lack of structure or disunity—was quite similar to that of the Greeks. The Mayans divided themselves into communities, quarreled constantly with each other, and only united in order to fight an enemy. And, like the Greeks, they were more urban than agricultural.

These comments give only a suggestion of the grandeur of a culture that rivals the Classical and Near Eastern civilizations. But because this culture is not European it has long seemed unimportant to Europeans and to Americans. C. W. Ceram writes in *Gods, Graves, and Scholars,* "It is interesting to note that the first real archaeological institute founded in America—in 1879—for decades concentrated its entire effort on the excavation of the antiquities of Europe and Asia Minor. Even now only a small part of the tremendous sums that American scientific institutions allot for archeological investigations is spent in their own backyards." The neglect of American cultures continues; Gulf Stream College can play some part in setting the balance right.

EXERCISE

1. Jot down the chief arguments offered in "America Last." Do some or all seem convincing to you? Do some need amplification, perhaps with concrete detail?

2. Are the arguments presented in the most effective order? Does the essay summarize opposing arguments and answer them adequately?

3. Is the concluding paragraph persuasive?

PUTTING THE OUTSIDE INSIDE THE FENCE OF LAW
Christopher D. Stone

Los Angeles—The notion of extending legal rights to environmental objects—oceans, rivers, forests—sounds absurd and unthinkable when first encountered. But viewed historically, it is not so. The entire history of the law has been an ever-widening extension in those "things" accorded legal rights, and thus constituted "persons" within the law.

In Roman law the father had *jus vitae necisque*—the power of life and death—over his children. In thirteenth-century England, Jews were treated as men *ferae naturae*, protected by a quasi-forest-law, like the roe and the deer.

Women, particularly married women, only recently were recognized as persons fully capable of holding legal rights.

So, too, it is only through begrudged evolution—that is still in progress—that rights have been accorded the insane, blacks, aliens, fetuses and Indians.

Nor has human form been a prerequisite to holding rights. Ships, still referred to in the feminine gender by courts, have long had an independent legal life, often with striking implications. The world of the lawyer is "peopled" by such inanimate entities as trusts, corporations, joint ventures, municipalities and nation-states.

It is important to remember, too, that throughout legal history each successive extension of rights to some new entity has at first sounded odd or frightening, or laughable. For until the rightless thing receives its rights, we cannot see it as anything but a *thing* for our use; witness how the slave South, its consciousness dulled and reinforced by slave-property law, looked upon the black.

Now, to say that the natural environment should have rights is not to say anything so silly as that no one should ever be allowed to cut down a tree. Human beings have rights, but there are circumstances under which they may suffer the death penalty. Corporations have rights, but they cannot plead the Fifth Amendment. By the same token, to say that the environment should have rights is not to say that it should have every right we can imagine, or even the same rights human beings have.

In general, to recognize the legal rights of the environment would involve allowing nature three distinct benefits it is denied under common law.

The first is standing—the right to have legal actions instituted on its behalf. It is no answer to say that streams and forests cannot speak. Corporations and states cannot speak either. Lawyers speak for them, as they customarily do for ordinary citizens with legal problems.

We could treat natural objects as we do legal incompetents, human beings who have become vegetables. A court simply designates someone the incompetent's guardian with the authority to represent him and manage his affairs.

By analogy, when a friend (presumably one of the established environmental groups) of a natural object perceives it to be endangered, the friend should be able to apply to a court to establish a guardianship. The guardian would thereafter be the legal voice for the voiceless object, instituting actions in its name and appearing before appropriate agencies on its behalf.

Second, when courts make balances of competing interests, as in deciding whether a company that is polluting a stream should have to shut down, it is the competing human interests that they consider exclusively. What does not, but should, weigh in the balance is the damage to the stream itself, to the fish and turtles and "lower" life.

Third, where relief is granted in an environmental case, there is no reason why damages should not go to the benefit of the environment. The natural object's portion would be put into a trust fund to be administered by the object's guardian, to defray the costs of aerating a polluted stream, stocking it with fish and algae, and so on.

It makes more sense than what we are doing now.[3]

EXERCISE

1. Explain Stone's strategy in the first sentence of "Putting the Outside Inside the Fence of Law." Given the next few sentences, does the strategy work?

2. Just beyond the middle of the essay, Stone introduces an analogy. Is the analogy useful? Does Stone fallaciously imply that it proves his point?

3. If Stone's last sentence is not offensively aggressive, what keeps it from being so?

THE RIGHT TO CHOOSE DEATH

O. Ruth Russell

WASHINGTON—Recently 3,500 delegates attended the White House Conference on Aging to discuss the needs and rights of the twenty million Americans who are 65 or over. We have still fresh in our minds the wonderful picture of a man of 95 dancing, but this should not cause us to forget the many who are incapacitated or suffering hopelessly.

One right that apparently was not discussed at the conference is the right to choose death in certain circumstances. Our present laws deny this right.

It is axiomatic that the elderly have a right to live out their lives in dignity. The corollary of this is also true: Each has the right to die in dignity. Today vast numbers are being denied this right.

One of the most potent fears of the aging—both rich and poor—is that they may be subjected to a lingering painful death or that their bodies may go on living after their minds and spirits have ceased, causing an overwhelming burden and grief to their loved ones.

Science has given man a greatly increased power over death. Surely it is time to ask why thousands of dying incurable and senile persons are being kept alive—sometimes by massive blood transfusions, intravenous feeding, artificial respiration and other "heroic" measures—who unmistakably want to die.

The law permits one the right to determine how his earthly possessions are used, and by means of a will to direct what shall be done with them after his death, but the law denies him the right to direct

[3] *New York Times*, 29 Aug. 1974, p. 31.

what happens to him personally in the event he is stricken with a painful incurable illness or condition that renders him helpless and his only remaining wish is that his life be ended.

If a person longs for the relief that only death can provide and he makes a written witnessed statement of his wishes, why should he not be permitted to choose to have the assistance of a physician in mercifully terminating his life? A doctor cannot lawfully grant such a request today.

We must look to the law to enunciate a distinction between a merciful act and a malevolent act. Should not new legislation be enacted that would permit a qualified physician to grant his patient's request for termination of his life, provided that it is done in accordance with, and only in accordance with, legal safeguards to protect each individual's right to live as well as his right to die? Today some doctors admit that they are violating present law in order to grant this wish. Yet, many are unwilling to violate the law or risk being accused of murder. This is especially true if the patient is in a hospital where the action might be discovered and reported.

The subject of euthanasia is still taboo in the United States. Yet it is necessary to recognize openly that death is not always an enemy to be fought with every means known to modern science, and that it is no more a trespass on God's rights to permit an incurable sufferer to choose merciful death than it is to postpone death by dramatic means such as heart transplants. Indeed, one must realize that the function of the medical profession is chiefly one of not leaving the time of death entirely to God. And regarding the sanctity-of-life argument, surely a society that condones death in war of young men who want to live, should be willing to permit the death of an aged person who wants to die.

Many of the most distinguished Protestant theologians in England, the United States and Canada have been in the forefront over the years in advocating the legalization of voluntary euthanasia.

Support would be greater if it had not been for the setback caused by revulsion over the Nazi crimes, some of which were performed by medical doctors who misappropriated the term euthanasia as a cloak for their ruthless killing. We ought not let a rightful abhorrence for what was done by the Nazis obscure the wisdom and compassion underlying present day proposals for euthanasia which would, instead of violating individual human rights, protect and extend them and do so in accord with the best democratic principles, and with legal safeguards.[4]

---

[4] *New York Times*, 14 Feb. 1972, sec. C p. 29.

EXERCISE

1. Professor Russell mentions euthanasia midway in her essay "The Right to Choose Death." Should she have used the term, and defined it, earlier?

2. There is a difference between "passive" euthanasia (allowing people to die by withholding "heroic measures" to keep them alive) and "active" euthanasia (assisting people to die, for example by administering pain-killing drugs to a lethal stage). Does the writer make this distinction clear?

3. Professor Russell says that "thousands of dying incurable and senile persons . . . unmistakably want to die." Is this contention plausible? Are you convinced?

4. The next to the last paragraph cites the support of "distinguished Protestant theologians." Is this, in your opinion, a persuasive use of the "prestige of authorities"?

5. Is the argument in the last paragraph an example of the genetic fallacy?

TOTAL EFFECT AND THE EIGHTH GRADE

Flannery O'Connor

In two recent instances in Georgia, parents have objected to their eighth- and ninth-grade children's reading assignments in modern fiction. This seems to happen with some regularity in cases throughout the country. The unwitting parent picks up his child's book, glances through it, comes upon passages of erotic detail or profanity, and takes off at once to complain to the school board. Sometimes, as in one of the Georgia cases, the teacher is dismissed and hackles rise in liberal circles everywhere.

The two cases in Georgia, which involved Steinbeck's *East of Eden* and John Hersey's *A Bell for Adano*, provoked considerable newspaper comment. One columnist, in commending the enterprise of the teachers, announced that students do not like to read the fusty works of the nineteenth century, that their attention can best be held by novels dealing with the realities of our own time, and that the Bible, too, is full of racy stories.

Mr. Hersey himself addressed a letter to the State School Superintendent in behalf of the teacher who had been dismissed. He pointed out that his book is not scandalous, that it attempts to convey an earnest message about the nature of democracy, and that it falls well within the limits of the principle of "total effect," that principle followed in legal cases by which a book is judged not for isolated parts but by the final effect of the whole book upon the general reader.

I do not want to comment on the merits of these particular cases. What concerns me is what novels ought to be assigned in the eighth and ninth grades as a matter of course, for if these cases indicate anything, they indicate the haphazard way in which fiction is approached in our high schools. Presumably there is a state reading list which contains "safe" books for teachers to assign; after that it is up to the teacher.

English teachers come in Good, Bad, and Indifferent, but too frequently in high schools anyone who can speak English is allowed to teach it. Since several novels can't easily be gathered into one textbook, the fiction that students are assigned depends upon their teacher's knowledge, ability, and taste: variable factors at best. More often than not, the teacher assigns what he thinks will hold the attention and interest of the students. Modern fiction will certainly hold it.

Ours is the first age in history which has asked the child what he would tolerate learning, but that is a part of the problem with which I am not equipped to deal. The devil of Educationism that possesses us is the kind that can be "cast out only by prayer and fasting." No one has yet come along strong enough to do it. In other ages the attention of children was held by Homer and Virgil, among others, but, by the reverse evolutionary process, that is no longer possible; our children are too stupid now to enter the past imaginatively. No one asks the student if algebra pleases him or if he finds it satisfactory that some French verbs are irregular, but if he prefers Hersey to Hawthorne, his taste must prevail.

I would like to put forward the proposition, repugnant to most English teachers, that fiction, if it is going to be taught in the high schools, should be taught as a subject and as a subject with a history. The total effect of a novel depends not only on its innate impact, but upon the experience, literary and otherwise, with which it is approached. No child needs to be assigned Hersey or Steinbeck until he is familiar with a certain amount of the best work of Cooper, Hawthorne, Melville, the early James, and Crane, and he does not need to be assigned these until he has been introduced to some of the better English novelists of the eighteenth and nineteenth centuries.

The fact that these works do not present him with the realities of his own time is all to the good. He is surrounded by the realities of his own time, and he has no perspective whatever from which to view them. Like the college student who wrote in her paper on Lincoln that he went to the movies and got shot, many students go to college unaware that the world was not made yesterday; their studies began with the present and dipped backward occasionally when it seemed necessary or unavoidable.

There is much to be enjoyed in the great British novels of the nineteenth century, much that a good teacher can open up in them for the young student. There is no reason why these novels should be either too simple or too difficult for the eighth grade. For the simple, they offer simple pleasures; for the more precocious, they can be made to yield subtler ones if the teacher is up to it. Let the student discover, after reading the nineteenth-century British novel, that the nineteenth-century American novel is quite different as to its literary characteristics, and he will thereby learn something not only about these individual works but about the sea-change which a new historical situation can effect in a literary form. Let him come to modern fiction with this experience behind him, and he will be better able to see and to deal with the more complicated demands of the best twentieth-century fiction.

Modern fiction often looks simpler than the fiction that preceded it, but in reality it is more complex. A natural evolution has taken place. The author has for the most part absented himself from direct participation in the work and has left the reader to make his own way amid experiences dramatically rendered and symbolically ordered. The modern novelist merges the reader in the experience; he tends to raise the passions he touches upon. If he is a good novelist, he raises them to effect by their order and clarity a new experience—the total effect—which is not in itself sensuous or simply of the moment. Unless the child has had some literary experience before, he is not going to be able to resolve the immediate passions the book arouses into any true, total picture.

It is here the moral problem will arise. It is one thing for a child to read about adultery in the Bible or in *Anna Karenina,* and quite another for him to read about it in most modern fiction. This is not only because in both the former instances adultery is considered a sin, and in the latter, at most, an inconvenience, but because modern writing involves the reader in the action with a new degree of intensity, and literary mores now permit him to be involved in any action a human being can perform.

In our fractured culture, we cannot agree on morals; we cannot even agree that moral matters should come before literary ones when there is a conflict between them. All this is another reason why the high schools would do well to return to their proper business of preparing foundations. Whether in the senior year students should be assigned modern novelists should depend both on their parents' consent and on what they have already read and understood.

The high-school English teacher will be fulfilling his responsibility if he furnishes the student a guided opportunity, through the best writing of the past, to come, in time, to an understanding of the best writing of the present. He will teach literature, not social studies or little lessons in democracy or the customs of many lands.

And if the student finds that this is not to his taste? Well, that is regrettable. Most regrettable. His taste should not be consulted; it is being formed.[5]

EXERCISE

1. Are the first three paragraphs of "Total Effect and the Eighth Grade" irrelevant? Can you justify O'Connor's abrupt dismissal ("I do not want to comment on the merits of these particular cases") of the opposing argument summarized in the second and third paragraphs? How?

2. "English teachers come in Good, Bad, and Indifferent, but too frequently in high schools anyone who can speak English is allowed to teach it." Can you, from your own experience, write one persuasive paragraph supporting this view?

3. Is the tone of the sixth paragraph, beginning "Ours is the first age," sarcastic? If not, how would you characterize it? Do you find it discourteous?

4. Which of O'Connor's arguments might be used to support the rating of movies X, R, PG, and G? Do you support these ratings or oppose them? What other reasons might you add? Write a scratch outline of your argument.

[5] *Mystery and Manners*, ed. Sally and Robert Fitzgerald (New York: Farrar, Straus and Giroux, 1969), pp. 135–40.

CHAPTER SEVEN

DESCRIPTION AND NARRATION

DESCRIPTION

Although much exposition can be called description, here we will specify that description represents in words our sensory impressions, usually of a place, a person, or an object. In much descriptive writing visual imagery dominates, but descriptions that depend only on the sense of sight are often impoverished. Look at Saul Bellow's two paragraphs describing Leventhal (pages 11–12), and note the passages that describe sense impressions other than sight.

Describing People

In real life we seldom observe people at dead rest; we see them in action; we form our impressions of them from how they move, what they do. Good descriptions, then, frequently show us a person performing some action, a particularly revealing action, or a characteristic one. If, for example, you want to suggest a person's height and weight, it's much more interesting to show him maneuvering through a subway turnstile, perhaps laden with packages, than to say, "He was only five feet four but weighed 185 pounds" or "he was short and stocky." Here is Maya Angelou describing Mr. Freeman, a man who lived for a while with her mother.

Mr. Freeman moved gracefully, like a big brown bear, and seldom spoke to us. He simply waited for Mother and put his whole self into the waiting. He never read the paper or patted his foot to radio. He waited. That was all.

If she came home before we went to bed, we saw the man come alive. He would start out of the big chair, like a man coming out of sleep, smiling. I would remember then that a few seconds before, I had heard a car door slam; then Mother's footsteps would signal from the concrete walk. When her key rattled the door, Mr. Freeman would have already asked his habitual question, "Hey, Bibbi, have a good time?"

His query would hang in the air while she sprang over to peck him on the lips. Then she turned to Bailey and me with the lipstick kisses. "Haven't you finished your homework?" If we had and were just reading—"O.K., say your prayers and go to bed." If we hadn't— "Then go to your room and finish . . . then say your prayers and go to bed."

Mr. Freeman's smile never grew, it stayed at the same intensity. Sometimes Mother would go over and sit on his lap and the grin on his face looked as if it would stay there forever.[1]

—Maya Angelou

Notice how animated this description is, how filled not only with Mr. Freeman's physical presence but also with his mysterious inner life. We have a portrait of Mother, too, reflected in Mr. Freeman's waiting, his concentration on the slam of her car door, her footsteps, her key rattling, and, most of all, in his smile. More subtly and more pervasively, the description is animated by our identification with the observer, the small child watching the man who waits so intently for the woman who is her mother.

Describing Places

Like any other piece of good writing, a good description has a good organization. The most obvious structures are from left to right, from bottom to top, from near to far, from general to particular. Obvious, but not contemptible. Walt Whitman

---

[1] *I Know Why the Caged Bird Sings* (New York: Random House, 1970), p. 59.

didn't scorn such a simple organization in his short poem
called "A Farm Picture."

> Through the ample open door of the peaceful country barn,
> A sunlit pasture field with cattle and horses feeding,
> And haze and vista, and the far horizon fading away.

Our descriptions will be longer (but not necessarily better),
and they may slightly vary the basic pattern. One might, for
example, describe the Brooklyn Bridge as it is seen at a distance,
then move a little closer, describing the texture as well as the
outline, and then move from bottom to top. Finally, one might
back away, ending with words that evoke the opening paragraph, leaving the reader with a richer understanding of this
splendid distant monument. But of course the organization need
not be so apparent. In fact, it ought not to be apparent; it ought
to be unobtrusive, not so much seen as sensed.

Good descriptions of places, like good descriptions of people,
are seldom static. (As readers we tend to skip the static ones.)
The writer shows us not simply a place, but something happening there. And again, our attention is likely to be captured by
our identification with the observer or narrator. Here are two
descriptions of buildings on fire. The first is by a student trying
her hand at description for the first time. The second is by a
professional writer.

The thick, heavy smoke, that could be seen for miles, filled the blue
July sky. Firemen frantically battled the blaze that engulfed Hempstead High School, while a crowd of people sadly looked on. Eyes
slowly filled up with tears as the reality of having no school to go
to started to sink in. Students that had once downed everything that
the high school stood for and did, began to realize how much they
cared for their school. But it was too late, it was going up in smoke.

We were on the porch only a short time when I heard a lot of
hollering coming from toward the field. The hollering and crying got
louder and louder. I could hear Mama's voice over all the rest. It
seemed like all the people in the field were running to our house. I
ran to the edge of the porch to watch them top the hill. Daddy was
leading the running crowd and Mama was right behind him.
"Lord have mercy, my children is in that house!" Mama was
screaming. "Hurry, Diddly!" she cried to Daddy. I turned around and
saw big clouds of smoke booming out of the front door and shooting

out of cracks everywhere. "There, Essie Mae is on the porch," Mama said. "Hurry, Diddly! Get Adline outta that house!" I looked back at Adline. I couldn't hardly see her for the smoke.

George Lee was standing in the yard like he didn't know what to do. As Mama them got closer, he ran into the house. My first thought was that he would be burned up. I'd often hoped he would get killed, but I guess I didn't really want him to die after all. I ran inside after him but he came running out again, knocking me down as he passed and leaving me lying face down in the burning room. I jumped up quickly and scrambled out after him. He had the water bucket in his hands. I thought he was going to try to put out the fire. Instead he placed the bucket on the edge of the porch and picked up Adline in his arms.

Moments later Daddy was on the porch. He ran straight into the burning house with three other men right behind him. They opened the large wooden windows to let some of the smoke out and began ripping the paper from the walls before the wood caught on fire. Mama and two other women raked it into the fireplace with sticks, broom handles, and everything else available. Everyone was coughing because of all the smoke.[2]

—Anne Moody

What can we learn from the professional writer? First notice her patience with detail, the concreteness of the passage. Where the student is content with "Firemen frantically battled the blaze that engulfed Hempstead High School," Anne Moody shows us individuals and exactly what each does. Look again at the final paragraph:

Moments later Daddy was on the porch. He ran straight into the burning house with three other men right behind him. They opened the large wooden windows to let some of the smoke out and began ripping the paper from the walls before the wood caught on fire. Mama and two other women raked it into the fireplace with sticks, broom handles, and anything else available. Everyone was coughing because of all the smoke.

Where the student generalizes the reaction of the observers, "Eyes slowly filled up with tears" and "Students . . . began to realize how much they cared for their school," in Moody's passage Mama screams, "Lord have mercy, my children is in that house!"

[2] *Coming of Age in Mississippi* (New York: Dial Press, 1968), p. 5.

But most important, in the professional sample, the writer establishes the observer's physical position. At the beginning she is on the porch, looking toward the field. It is only when she hears her mother scream that she turns around and sees the smoke. And notice that she *does have to turn,* and the writer has the patience to tell us "I turned around and saw . . ." We could, if we wished to, place the position of the observer, exactly, throughout the action as if we were blocking a scene in a play. By contrast notice that there is no real observer in the student's description. If there were, he would first have to be miles away from the scene and looking up into the sky to see the smoke. Then, in the second sentence he would be across the street, watching the firemen. By the third sentence he'd be closer still, not close to the fire but close to the other observers. In fact, he'd have to be inside their heads to know what they were thinking. As readers we sense this lack of focus; we have no one to identify with. Though we may find the passage moderately interesting, it will not engage us and we will soon forget it.

Another technique we can learn from professional writers and natural story tellers is illustrated by this passage from *Black Elk Speaks.* Black Elk, an Oglala Sioux holy man, is describing the Battle of Little Bighorn (1876).

The valley went darker with dust and smoke, and there were only shadows and a big noise of many cries and hoofs and guns. On the left of where I was I could hear the shod hoofs of the soldiers' horses going back into the brush and there was shooting everywhere. Then the hoofs came out of the brush, and I came out and was in among men and horses weaving in and out and going upstream, and everybody was yelling, "Hurry! Hurry!" The soldiers were running upstream and we were all mixed there in the twilight and the great noise. I did not see much; but once I saw a Lakota charge at a soldier who stayed behind and fought and was a very brave man. The Lakota took the soldier's horse by the bridle, but the soldier killed him with a six-shooter. I was small and could not crowd in to where the soldiers were, so I did not kill anybody. There were so many ahead of me, and it was all dark and mixed up.[3]

—Black Elk

[3] Quoted in John G. Neihardt, *Black Elk Speaks* (Lincoln: University of Nebraska Press, 1972), p. 113.

Black Elk was an old man when he told this story. How old would you guess he was at the time it happened? How do you know? What is the secret here of writing good description?

Much of the following essay is descriptive, but the description is combined with evaluation: the Rayburn Building is a bad building. That is, the description is offered from a particular point of view; it argues for a conclusion.

THE RAYBURN BUILDING

Ada Louise Huxtable

It is moving time on Capitol Hill for 169 Congressmen eligible for space in the new Rayburn House Office Building. The structure's three-room suites complete with refrigerators and safes are being raffled off to applicants who may have a view of the Capitol dome or an interior court, depending on seniority. Even seniority, however, does not give any legislator a door leading from his office, or his aide's office, to his working staff without passage through a waiting room full of constituents and special pleaders. To correct this small planning error would add $200,000 to costs already estimated at anywhere from $86 million to $122 million for the expensive and controversial building.

Some Congressmen are moving in reluctantly. Representative Thomas L. Ashley, Democrat of Ohio, for one, rejected his office on sight. But he is making the move anyway this week because his present quarters are too small. "This layout could paralyze us," he said during his inspection tour. "It's an ugly building." Mr. Ashley is not alone. The professional architectural press has been bitterly critical as construction progressed. (The building has taken seven years and $22 million more to complete than originally estimated largely as the result of expensive miscalculations; change orders have reached 300 per cent over Government average; bid estimates on contracts have been as much as $45 million off.) There have been accusations of secret planning, pork barrel commissions and possible misuse of public funds. The fact that the general contractor was Matthew J. McCloskey, Democrat party stalwart of Philadelphia, has not escaped notice. But the storm swirls uselessly around a behemoth that is obviously here to stay. Architecturally, the Rayburn Building is a national disaster. Its defects range from profligate mishandling of 50 acres of space to elephantine esthetic banality at record costs. The costs are now being investigated by the General Accounting Office.

Equal to the question of costs, however, is the question of what

Congress and the capital have received for the investment. It is quite possible that this is the worst building for the most money in the history of the construction art. It stuns by sheer mass and boring bulk. Only 15 per cent of its space is devoted to the offices and hearing rooms for which it was erected. Forty-two per cent of the floor area is used for parking. Endless corridors have been likened to *Last Year at Marienbad*. Stylistically, it is the apotheosis of humdrum.

It is hard to label the building, but it might be called Corrupt Classic. Its empty aridity and degraded classical details are vulgarization without drama, and to be both dull and vulgar may be an achievement of sorts.

The structure's chief "design features" are hollow exercises in sham grandeur. A supercolossal exterior expanse of stolid, Mussolini-style pomp is embellished with sculpture that would be the apogee of art in the Soviet Union, where overscaled muscles and expressions of empty solemnity are still admired. A monumental entrance at second floor level is reached by pretentious steps that will never be used. The real entrance, on the ground floor just below, abandons false dignity for no dignity at all. The formal marble front with its blank, machine-stamped look sits on a gargantuan base of informal, random-cut granite of obviously miscalculated proportions, an effect comparable to combining a top hat with blue jeans. Groups of columns meant to dress up the drab, flat façade not only fail to suggest that columns are traditionally supporting members, but they also terminate incongruously on balconies that appear to support the columns— a neat combination of structural illogic and stylistic flimflam.

Inside, a pedestrian statue of Sam Rayburn presents the seat of its pants to entering visitors.[4] It faces a huge landscaped central court that is an artless cliché. Embracing Mr. Sam is another cliché, a two-story curved double stair fated to be not only useless but graceless. In the hearing rooms, coarse, lifeless classical cornices and moldings are joined to stock modern acoustic ceilings and panel lighting for a state of esthetic warfare tempered only by their matching mediocrity. This model comes in red, green, gold and blue. Behind the scenes, the classic false front is abandoned and working sub-committee rooms use ordinary partitions and fittings of the lowest commercial common denominator. Throughout the building, the design level is consistent: whatever is not hack is heavy-handed.

---

[4] Turned around after this article appeared—the rewards of architectural criticism.

For $100 million, give or take a few million (the cost of New York's mammoth Pan Am Building) the gentlemen of the House have got a sterile, stock plan of singularly insensitive design and detailing that was moribund more than half a century ago. Even the basic functional requirements have been insufficiently studied. The making of useful and beautiful public spaces with the power to inspire and symbolize as well as to serve—the timeless aim of architecture and one that is mandatory for Washington—is conspicuously absent.

The Rayburn Building is the third solid gold turkey in a row to come out of the office of the Architect of the Capitol, J. George Stewart, who is not an architect, but who picks them for Congress. For this one he selected Harbeson, Hough, Livingston & Larson of Philadelphia. He is also responsible for the ill-advised remodeling of the Capitol's East Front and the construction of the new Senate Office Building. There are no controls or reviews for Mr. Stewart's work, and none for the House committee that authorized the Rayburn Building's construction and appropriations, generally behind closed doors.

An old architectural saying has it that there's no point in crying over spilled marble. Seven million pounds of it have been poured onto Capitol Hill in this latest Congressional building venture, and there is nothing quite as invulnerable as a really monumental mistake. The Rayburn Building's ultimate claim to fame may well be that it is the biggest star-spangled architectural blunder of our time.[5]

EXERCISE

Write an essay of 500–1000 words describing and evaluating a college building.

One picture may be worth a thousand words, but there are times when we want to use words to talk about pictures. In the following essay, a student describes an advertisement and then comments on its latent message.

ADMAN'S ATLANTA

Centered in the top third of the page is a three-line, deep black headline: "Atlanta's suburban style of urban living." The first A is the only capital letter, there is a period after living, and the letters

---

[5] *New York Times*, 30 March 1965, p. 32.

are the Roman script of a regular typewriter. A round picture in black and white with a diameter the size of half the page is separated from the heading by three blocks of copy and a very small black and white rectangular picture. Each photo has a caption under it. In the round picture a beautifully gnarled tree casts its shadow over the driveway and cobblestone sidewalks that front two clean-lined, white apartment buildings at right angles to each other. In the break between the buildings a lamp of five white globes contrasts with dark trees behind it. A well-dressed businessman and businesswoman walk in the sun in front of the building on the left; at the entrance of the other building another suited man climbs into a new-looking compact car. In the other photo Atlanta's skyline glows pale in a flawless afternoon sky behind a mass of trees that covers the bottom two-thirds of the shot. The copy tells of the joys of living in Atlanta, explaining that life there combines the best of the city with the best of the suburb.

In attempting to persuade the reader that "Atlanta's style of living" is worth finding out about (by writing to the Atlanta Chamber of Commerce), the creators of the ad have used several techniques to associate living in Atlanta with business and with luxury; in short, with the common idea of success.

First to catch the reader's eye is the dark solid heading. The forceful deep black print is softened by its curved, but simple, design. Compact but not crowded, these words add up to a plain positive statement with a modestly assertive period at the end.

This business-like handling shows also in the picture centered below. It depicts clean white modern buildings lived in by purposeful people who are apparently going about a normal day in their successful lives. The dominance of the foreground tree and other trees in the background complement the buildings, preventing any appearance of harshness. A sense of gentleness and luxury is augmented by the blurred round border that makes the picture seem to be surrounded by sunlight. The sun is important in this picture, and also in the rectangular picture to the left. In both, the sun heightens the contrast between the clean brightness of the buildings and the luxurious darkness of the trees, producing an atmosphere of happy leisure.

Lest leisure seem to be merely idleness, any emptiness created by the word "suburban" is immediately filled by the word "urban." The copy emphasizes both the convenience of living "close in"—that is, being near "necessities and pleasures: schools, shopping, churches, cultural activities . . ."—and the flexibility of being able to live in the city "in almost any manner you choose," be it some kind of urban apartment or a home of your own. Life in Atlanta is urban but

Atlanta's suburban style of urban living.

In Atlanta you can live close in and still be close to wooded green. This blending of the urban and suburban makes Atlanta one of the most attractive and convenient big cities you'll find. And you can live here in almost any manner you choose. Up in a high-rise. In a formal town house. In a garden apartment with pool and tennis courts. Or amidst a rolling lawn and garden of your own.

And no matter which you choose, you're never far from the necessities and pleasures: schools, shopping, churches, cultural activities, entertainment, and of course your office. Find out about Atlanta's style of living. Contact: Paul Miller, Atlanta Chamber of Commerce, 1314 Commerce Building, Atlanta, Ga. 30303, 404—521-0845

TREES IN ATLANTA REACH INTO THE HEART OF DOWNTOWN.

TREES SURROUND LUXURY APARTMENTS ON PEACHTREE ROAD, 10 MINUTES FROM DOWNTOWN.

"close to the wooded green." This idea is brought out not only in the copy, but emphasized in the pictures by beginning both captions with the word "trees."

This advertisement creates a favorable impression of city living, counteracting many readers' associations of a city with dirt, smog, and crowds. It indirectly advertises the "good life" of a prosperous businessman, be it in "a formal town house" or with "a rolling lawn and garden of your own." It also advertises middle-class values, beginning with religion and ending with business: "churches, cultural activities, entertainment, and of course your office."

EXERCISES

1. Describe a person by showing him or her performing some action that takes less than five minutes. From the description we should be able to infer some of the following: height, weight, age, sex, occupation, economic or educational background. You may find it helpful to look at the passage by Saul Bellow on pages 11–12.

2. Describe a room by showing something happening in it.

3. Study an advertisement and describe it accurately. Put into words the implications about the product and the assumptions about the reader that you find in the advertisement. Include a copy of the advertisement with your essay.

4. Choose a current or recent political cartoon to describe and analyze. In one paragraph, your first, describe the drawing (including any words in it) thoroughly enough so that someone who has not seen it can visualize or even draw it fairly accurately. In a second paragraph explain the political message. Don't inject your own opinion; present the cartoonist's point objectively. Submit a copy of the cartoon with your essay. Be sure to choose a cartoon of sufficient complexity to make the analysis worthwhile.

NARRATION

Usually we think of narrative writing as the art of the novelist or short story writer, but narratives need not be fictional. Biography and autobiography, for example, are narratives. Moreover, narrative passages may appear in writings that as a whole are not themselves narratives. For instance, expository and persuasive essays may include narratives—perhaps anecdotes or brief sketches of historical occurrences that may serve to clarify the essayist's point. Indeed, narrative may be considered one species of exposition—an exposition of what happened. Nevertheless, here we shall follow tradition in regarding narrative as a form distinct from exposition.

Essentially a narrative tells a story, true or fictional. It is chiefly concerned with events in past time (what happened at the Battle of Little Bighorn), but it often includes exposition (the causes of the battle, the deployment of the forces) and description (the terrain, the combatants). The organization is normally chronological, though fairly often it begins at the end, for a dramatic opening, and then presents the earlier parts of the story in chronological order.

In the following passage, describing a teacher's visit to a prison, the narrative is infused with personal comment.

POETRY CLASS AT NORFOLK PRISON
Sayre P. Sheldon

Driving to Norfolk is pleasant on a May afternoon with tulips and trees in blossom on suburban lawns but something from the morning newspaper is bothering me: a convicted felon named Spiro Agnew got a standing ovation in a theatre the other night. Add to that the million dollars he is getting for his book. Now on my car radio comes the news of a bill to cut down the prison furlough program. The senator sponsoring the bill is interviewed; he says permissive treatment of convicts must be stopped. The bill has been passed on a voice vote by the same Legislature which refuses to take guns away from its citizens.

Wondering if the news has already spread through the prison, I sign in at the gate-house, writing "no" where it says "Have you ever committed a felony?", have my books checked, pass through the metal detector and, after a short wait, get an escort to walk across the prison yard.

The grass has produced dandelions since last week and a noisy volley-ball game is in progress behind one of the units; the place looks more like a small, run-down, rural college than usual.

One of my students catches up with us and the furlough issue recedes as he tells me about his paper on Auden's poem "The Shield of Achilles." As we near the brick school building, some men call down from the classroom windows—windows that we keep open all winter to let out some of the torrent of state-provided steam heat. Inside, now unescorted, I hurry up the stairs to our shabby classroom, with its varnished wood walls, brown linoleum floor, and combined smell of chalk and Lysol so reassuringly like old public school rooms everywhere.

More men gradually arrive until we have moved the heavy oak chairs with writing arms into a circle of nine or 10 and Harry reads the first poem, "My Life Had Stood A Loaded Gun." He explains that he never liked poetry except Shakespeare's until he read Emily Dickinson and others agree that she is one of the best. Bill sees a new meaning to this poem; his explanation gets quite lengthy when he brings in Emerson, Thoreau and Transcendentalism but everyone listens just as politely as they do when I talk too much.

We are off for two hours of intense far-ranging discussion, interrupted continually by men leaving to see lawyers, called to a visit over the booming loudspeaker, or coming in late from one of their innumerable committee meetings. We are talking about sound (the assignment for today), finding different kinds of rhyme and alliteration in poems like "We Real Cool," relating poetic terms to music, trying to decide whether man has an instinct for harmony and variation.

Richard reads "Kubla Khan" majestically and Malik is reminded of Shelley's "Ozymandias" which brings up the idea of man's smallness in time and space. I ask why poets write so continually about time—thoughtless question to ask of men "doing time." As usual, my blunder is tactfully overlooked and talk rushes along until my own time is up; all women have to be out of Norfolk by 4 o'clock. Regretfully, I gather up my books and papers and say goodbye until next week.

I go out with the afternoon shift, everyone chattering about weekend plans. Getting out is faster than getting in; automatic metal doors clang heavily behind me and the guard barely glances at my books. I pull my car out of the lot, away from the high cement walls, and head back to Boston. School buses are dropping off kids in Medfield, fathers back from work are getting out lawn mowers, and if I turn on the radio, I might catch some news about the furlough bill and will certainly get the latest on Watergate.[6]

The next passage is Malcolm X's narrative of how he evaded the draft during World War II. Two terms may need explanation: the classification 4-F was given to persons thought to be

---

[6] *Boston Globe*, 22 May 1974.

unsuited for military service; "Greetings" was the opening word in the notice from the draft board, telling the recipient to report for a mental and physical examination.

In those days only three things in the world scared me: jail, a job, and the Army. I had about ten days before I was to show up at the induction center. I went right to work. The Army Intelligence soldiers, those black spies in civilian clothes, hung around in Harlem with their ears open for the white man downtown. I knew exactly where to start dropping the word. I started noising around that I was frantic to join . . . the Japanese Army.

When I sensed that I had the ears of the spies, I would talk and act high and crazy. A lot of Harlem hustlers actually had reached that state—as I would later. It was inevitable when one had gone long enough on heavier and heavier narcotics, and under the steadily tightening vise of the hustling life. I'd snatch out and read my Greetings aloud, to make certain they heard who I was, and when I'd report downtown. (This was probably the only time my real name was ever heard in Harlem in those days.)

The day I went down there, I costumed like an actor. With my wild zoot suit I wore the yellow knob-toe shoes, and I frizzled my hair up into a reddish bush of conk.

I went in, skipping and tipping, and I thrust my tattered Greetings at that reception desk's white soldier—"Crazy-o, daddy-o, get me moving. I can't wait to get in that brown—," very likely that soldier hasn't recovered from me yet.

They had their wire on me from uptown, all right. But they still put me through the line. In that big starting room were forty or fifty other prospective inductees. The room had fallen vacuum-quiet, with me running my mouth a mile a minute, talking nothing but slang. I was going to fight on all fronts: I was going to be a general, man, before I got done—such talk as that.

Most of them were white, of course. The tender-looking ones appeared ready to run from me. Some others had that vinegary "worst kind of nigger" look. And a few were amused, seeing me as the "Harlem jigaboo" archetype.

Also amused were some of the room's ten or twelve Negroes. But the stony-faced rest of them looked as if they were ready to sign up to go off killing somebody—they would have liked to start with me.

The line moved along. Pretty soon, stripped to my shorts, I was making my eager-to-join comments in the medical examination rooms —and everybody in the white coats that I saw had 4-F in his eyes.

I stayed in the line longer than I expected, before they siphoned me off. One of the white coats accompanied me around a turning hall-way: I knew we were on the way to a headshrinker—the Army psychiatrist.

The receptionist there was a Negro nurse. I remember she was in her early twenties, and not bad to look at. She was one of those Negro "firsts."

Negroes know what I'm talking about. Back then, the white man during the war was so pressed for personnel that he began letting some Negroes put down their buckets and mops and dust rags and use a pencil, or sit at some desk, or hold some twenty-five-cent title. You couldn't read the Negro press for the big pictures of smug black "firsts."

Somebody was inside with the psychiatrist. I didn't even have to put on any act for this black girl; she was already sick of me.

When, finally, a buzz came at her desk, she didn't send me, *she* went in. I knew what she was doing, she was going to make clear, in advance, what she thought of me. This is still one of the black man's big troubles today. So many of those so-called "upper class" Negroes are so busy trying to impress on the white man that they are "different from those others" that they can't see they are only helping the white man to keep his low opinion of *all* Negroes.

And then, with her prestige in the clear, she came out and nodded to me to go in.

I must say this for that psychiatrist. He tried to be objective and professional in his manner. He sat there and doodled with his blue pencil on a tablet, listening to me spiel to him for three or four minutes before he got a word in.

His tack was quiet questions, to get at why I was so anxious. I didn't rush him; I circled and hedged, watching him closely, to let him think he was pulling what he wanted out of me. I kept jerking around, backward, as though somebody might be listening. I knew I was going to send him back to the books to figure what kind of a case I was.

Suddenly, I sprang up and peeped under both doors, the one I'd entered and another that probably was a closet. And then I bent and whispered fast in his ear. "Daddy-o, now you and me, we're from up North here, so don't you tell nobody. . . . I want to get sent down South. Organize them nigger soldiers, you dig? Steal us some guns, and kill up crackers!"

That psychiatrist's blue pencil dropped, and his professional man-ner fell off in all directions. He stared at me as if I were a snake's egg hatching, fumbling for his red pencil. I knew I had him. I was going back out past Miss First when he said, "That will be all."

A 4-F card came to me in the mail, and I never heard from the Army any more, and never bothered to ask why I was rejected.[7]

—Malcolm X

The passage not only tells a story, or a history, but includes social comment. Would it be equally interesting if the social comment were omitted? In what ways is the last sentence like the last sentence of a joke?

[7] Malcolm X with Alex Haley, *The Autobiography of Malcolm X* (New York: Grove Press, 1964), pp. 104–07.

CHAPTER EIGHT

THE RESEARCH PAPER

WHAT RESEARCH IS

Because a research paper requires its writer to collect the available evidence—usually including the opinions of earlier investigators—one sometimes hears that a research paper, unlike a critical essay, is not the expression of personal opinion. But such a view is unjust both to criticism and to research. A critical essay is not a mere expression of personal opinion; if it is any good it offers evidence that supports the opinions and it thus persuades the reader of their objective rightness. And a research paper, in the final analysis, is largely personal, because the author continuously uses his own judgment to evaluate the evidence, deciding what is relevant and convincing. A research paper is not the mere presentation of what a dozen scholars have already said about a topic; it is a thoughtful evaluation of the available evidence, and so it is, finally, an expression of what the author thinks the evidence adds up to.

Research can be a tedious and frustrating business; there are hours spent reading books and articles that prove to be irrelevant, there are contradictory pieces of evidence, and there is never enough time. Research, in short, is not a procedure that is attractive to everyone. The poet William Butler Yeats, though an indefatigable worker on projects that interested him, engagingly expressed an indifference to the obligation that confronts every researcher: to look carefully at all of the available evidence. Running over the possible reasons why Jonathan Swift did not marry (that he had syphilis, for instance, or that he feared he would transmit a hereditary madness) Yeats says, "Mr. Shane Leslie thinks that Swift's relation to Vanessa was not platonic, and that whenever his letters speak of a cup of coffee they mean the sexual act; whether the letters seem to bear him out I do not know, for those letters bore me." [1]

Though research sometimes requires one to read boring works, those who engage in it feel, at least at times, an exhilaration, a sense of triumph at having studied a problem thoroughly and at having arrived at conclusions that at least for the moment seem objective and irrefutable. Later perhaps new evidence will turn up that will require a new conclusion, but until that time, one may reasonably feel that one knows *something*.

PRIMARY AND SECONDARY MATERIALS

The materials of most research can be conveniently divided into two sorts, primary and secondary. The primary materials or sources are the real subject of study, the secondary materials are critical and historical accounts already written about these primary materials. For example, if you want to know whether Shakespeare's attitude toward Julius Caesar was highly traditional or highly original, or a little of each, you would read *Julius Caesar*, other Elizabethan writings about Caesar, and Roman writings known to the Elizabethans, and you would also read secondary material such as modern books on Shakespeare and on Elizabethan attitudes toward Rome and toward monarchs. The line between these two kinds of sources, of course, is not always clear. For example, if you are concerned with the degree to which Joyce's *Portrait of the Artist as a Young Man* is autobiographical, primary materials include not only *A Portrait* and Joyce's letters, but perhaps also his brother Stanislaus' diary and autobiography. Although the diary and autobiography might be considered secondary sources—certainly a scholarly biography about Joyce or his brother would be a secondary source—because Stanislaus' books are more or less

---

[1] *Variorum Edition of the Plays of Yeats*, ed. Russell K. Alspach (New York: Macmillan, 1966), p. 966.

contemporary with your subject they can reasonably be called primary sources.

FROM SUBJECT TO THESIS

First, a subject. No subject is unsuited. Perhaps sports, war, art, dreams, food. As G. K. Chesterton said, "There is no such thing on earth as an uninteresting subject; the only thing that can exist is an uninterested person." Research can be done on almost anything that interests you, though of course (1) materials on current events may be extremely difficult to get hold of, since crucial documents may not yet be in print and you may not have access to the people involved, and (2) materials on some subjects may be unavailable to you because they are in languages you can't read or in publications that your library doesn't have. So you probably won't try to work on the stuff of today's headlines, and (because almost nothing in English has been written on it) you won't try to work on the use of perspective in Oriental painting. But no subject is too trivial for study: Newton, according to legend, wondered why an apple fell to the ground.

You cannot, however, write a research paper on subjects as broad as sports, war, art, dreams, food. You have to focus on a much smaller area within such a subject. Let's talk about food. You might want to study the dietary laws of the Jews, the food of American Indians before the white man came, the consumption of whale meat, subsidies to hog farmers, or legislation governing the purity of food. Your own interests will guide you to the topic—the part of the broad subject—that you wish to explore.

But of course, though you have an interest in one of these narrower topics, you don't know a great deal about it; that's one of the reasons you are going to do research on it. Let's say that you happened to read or hear about Ralph Nader's stomach-turning essay on frankfurters (*New Republic*, 18 March 1972, pages 12–13), in which Nader reports that although today's frankfurters contain only 11.7 percent protein (the rest is water, salt, spices, and preservatives), they contain a substantial dose of sodium nitrate to inhibit the growth of bacteria and to keep the meat from turning gray.

Assuming that your appetite for research on food continues, you decide that you want to know something more about additives, that is, substances (such as sodium nitrate) added to preserve desirable properties—color, flavor, freshness—or to suppress undesirable properties. You want to do some reading, and you must now find the articles and books. Of course, as you do the reading, your focus may shift a little; you may stay with frankfurters, you may shift to the potentially dangerous effects, in various foods, of sodium nitrate, or to the proven harmful effect of cyclamate (a sweetener on the market from 1951 until it was banned in 1970), or you may concentrate on so-called "enriched bread," which is first robbed of many nutrients by refining and bleaching the flour and is then enriched by the synthetic addition of some of the nutrients. Exactly what you will focus on you may not know until you do some more reading. But how do you find the relevant material?

FINDING THE MATERIAL

You may happen already to know of some relevant material that you have been intending to read, but if you are at a loss where to begin, consult the card catalog of your library and consult the appropriate guides to articles in journals.

The Card Catalog

The card catalog has cards arranged alphabetically not only by author and by title but also by subject.[2] It probably won't have an entry for "frankfurter," but it will have an entry for "food," followed by cards listing books on this topic. And on the "food" card will be a note telling you of relevant entries to consult. In fact, even before you look at the catalog you can

[2] A note on using the card catalog. (1) Under the *author's name*, books are arranged in this order: first, collected works; next, single works; next, books about the author. Note that authors whose names begin *Mc* or *Mac* are all listed as though spelled *Mac*. (2) *Subject headings* are alphabetized word by word, thus "Folk Songs" precedes "Folklore." After the subject heading, books are listed alphabetically by author's last name. (3) Under *titles*, omit *A, An, The* and their foreign equivalents when looking up a title. Words that would normally be abbreviated are spelled out: *Doctor Zhivago, Mister Roberts, Saint Joan.*

```
FOOD

    see also

COOKERY
DIET
DIETARIES
FARM PRODUCE
FRUIT
GASTRONOMY
GRAIN
MARKETS
MEAT
NUTRITION
POULTRY
                              ●        see next card
```

know what subject-entries it contains by checking one of two books: *Sears List of Subject Headings* (for libraries that use the Dewey Decimal System of arranging books) and *Subject Headings Used in the Dictionary Catalogs of the Library of Congress*, 7th edition. (Because most academic libraries use the Library of Congress system, the second of these is probably the book you'll use.) If you look for "Food" in *Subject Headings*, you will find two pages of listings, including cross references such as "*sa* [= see also] Animal Food." Among the subject entries that sound relevant are Bacteriology, Food Contamination, and Preservation.

At this stage, two options are available. Having checked the card catalog and written down the relevant data (author, title, call number), you can begin to scan the books, or you can postpone looking at the books until you have found some relevant articles in periodicals. For the moment, let's postpone the periodicals.

Put a bunch of books in front of you, and choose one as an introduction. How do you choose one from half a dozen? Partly by its size—choose a thin one—and partly by its quality. Roughly speaking, it should be among the more recent publications, and it should strike you as fair. A pamphlet published by a meat-packers association is desirably thin but you have a hunch that it may be biased. Roger John Williams' *Nutrition in a Nutshell* is published by a well-known commercial press (Doubleday), and it is only 171 pages, but because it was published in 1962 it may not reflect current food chemistry. Though it is rather big (260 pages), Michael Jacobson's *Eater's Digest: The Consumer's Factbook of Food Additives* (New York: Doubleday, 1972) probably is about right. At this stage it is acceptable to trust one's hunches—you are only going to scan the book, not buy it or even read it—but you may want to look up some book reviews to assure yourself that the book has merit. There are three especially useful indexes to book reviews: *Book Review Digest* (1905–), *Book Review Index* (1965–), *Index to Book Reviews in the Humanities* (1960–). If the book is older than 1965, obviously the second of these indexes will be of no use; and if your topic is additives to food, the third, indexing only books in the humanities, will be of no use. You find some reviews, look them up, and draw some conclusions about the merit of the book in question. Of course you cannot assume that every review is fair, but a book that on the whole gets good reviews is probably at least good enough for a start.

By quickly reading such a book (take few or no notes at this stage) you will probably get an overview of your topic, and you will see exactly what part of the topic you wish to pursue.

Indexes to Periodicals

An enormous amount is published in magazines and scholarly journals; you cannot start thumbing through them at random, but fortunately there are indexes to them. More than one hundred of the more familiar magazines—such as *Atlantic, Ebony, Nation, Scientific American, Sports Illustrated, Time*—are indexed in the *Reader's Guide to Periodical Literature* (1900–). Many of the less popular, more scholarly journals—for example, quarterlies published by learned societies—are indexed in *Social Sciences and Humanities Index* (1965–). Before 1965 it was known as *International Index* (1907–64). The names of the periodicals indexed in these volumes are printed at the front of the volumes. Both of these invaluable indexes include subject-headings as well as entries alphabetically by author. If you know that you are looking for a piece by Ralph Nader, look it up under Nader. But if you don't know the author, look under the subject. For example, if you look up "additives" in the *Reader's Guide* you will find: "Additives. See Food additives," and so you next turn to "Food additives," where you will find a listing (by author) of the relevant articles. You will also find, under "Food," a note referring you to other subject-entries that may be relevant, for example "Food, Organic," and "Food adulteration."

```
FOOD additives
   Food additives. G. O. Kermode. il Sci Am
      226:15-21 bibliog(p 126) Mr '72
   Food flavoring additives, how safe? B. T.
      Hunter. Consumer Bull 55:14-15 O '72
   Hysteria about food additives. T. Alexander.
      il Fortune 85:62-5+ Mr '72
   Regular family meal: aargh! C. McCarthy.
      Sat R 55:5-6+ S 2 '72
   Royal crown battles the additive bans. il
      Bus W p60+ Mr 25 '72
   Will added nutrients really help? D. Callo-
      way. il McCalls 99:36 F '72
      See also
   Carrageenan
   Diethyl pyrocarbonate
   Monosodium glutamate
   Sodium nitrite
```

A third index that you are likely to use is the *New York Times Index* (covering the years from 1851 to the present). This index, enabling you to locate articles that were published in the *Times,* is especially useful if you are working on a recent public event.

The three indexes just mentioned (along with the three indexes to book reviews) are the ones you are most likely to use, but here are some others that may be valuable, depending on what your topic is:

Applied Science and Technology Index (1958–); formerly *Industrial Arts Index* (1913–57)

Art Index (1929–)

Biological and Agricultural Index (1964–); before 1964 it was known as *Agricultural Index* (1942–64)

Biography Index (1947–)

Dramatic Index (1909–49)

Education Index (1929–)

Monthly Catalog of United Sates Government Publications (1895–)

Music Index (1949–)

Poole's Index for Periodical Literature (1802–1907)

Public Affairs Information Service Bulletin (1915–)

United Nations Documents Index (1950–)

Whichever indexes you use, begin with the most recent years and work your way back. If you collect the titles of articles published in the last five years you will probably have as much as you can read. These articles will probably incorporate the significant points of earlier writings. But of course it depends on the topic; you may have to—and want to—go back fifty or more years before you find a useful body of material.

Caution: Indexes drastically abbreviate the titles of the periodicals. Before you put the indexes back on the shelf, be sure to check the key to the abbreviations, so that you know the full titles of the periodicals you are looking for.

Other Guides to Published Material

There is a large number of reference books—not only general dictionaries and encyclopedias but dictionaries of technical words, encyclopedias of special fields, and also books devoted to telling you where to find material in special fields. Examples: Helen J. Poulton, *The Historian's Handbook: A Descriptive Guide to Reference Works* (1972); Elizabeth Miller and Mary Fisher, eds., *The Negro in America: A Bibliography*, rev. ed. (1970); Bernard Klein and Daniel Icolari, eds., *Reference Encyclopedia of the American Indian*, 2d ed. (1971). The best guide to such guides—a book telling you about such books—is Constance M. Winchell, *Guide to Reference Books*, 8th edition, with three paperbound supplements, the last of which (published in 1972) includes books published through 1970. There are also guides to all of these guides: reference librarians. If you don't know where to turn to find something, turn to the librarian.

TAKING BIBLIOGRAPHIC NOTES

Practice and theory differ. In theory, one should write down each citation (whether a book or an article) on a separate three-by-five index card, giving complete information. Our own practice at the start of any research is more shoddy. Instead of carefully recording all of this information from the card catalog (for a book that may be lost) or from an index to periodicals (for a periodical that may not be in the library) we usually jot down the citations of books on a sheet of paper, and of

TX
553.83
J23

Jacobson, Michael F.
<u>Eater's Digest</u>. New York: 1972.

Zwerdling, Daniel. "Death for
Dinner," <u>The New York Review</u>,
21, No. 1 (21 Feb. 1974), 22-24.

---

articles on another sheet. Then we see how much of this material is available. When we actually get hold of the material, we make out a card, as illustrated. True, we sometimes regret our attempted shortcut if we later find that on the sheet we forgot to write the year of the periodical and we must now hunt through indexes again to locate it. We recall the wisdom of the Chinese proverb. "It is foolish to go to bed early to save the candle if the result is twins," but we have never been able to resist taking a shortcut at the start.

READING AND TAKING NOTES

As you read, you will of course find references to other publications and you will jot these down so that you can look at them later. It may turn out, for example, that a major article was published twenty years ago, and that most commentary is a series of footnotes to this piece. You will have to look at it, of course, even though common sense had initially suggested (incorrectly, it seems) that the article is out of date.

Our own practice in reading an article or a chapter of a book is to read it through, *not* taking notes. By the time you reach the end, you may find it isn't noteworthy. Or you may find a useful summary near the end that will contain most of what you can get from the piece. Or you will find that, having a sense of the whole, you can now quickly reread the piece and take notes on the chief points.

When you take notes use four-by-six-inch cards, and write on one side only; material on the back of a card is usually neglected when you come to write the paper. Use four-by-six cards because the smaller cards, suitable for bibliographic notes, do not provide enough space for your summaries of useful material. Here is a guide to note-taking:

1. We suggest summaries rather than paraphrases (that is, abridgments rather than restatements which in fact may be as long or longer than the original) because there is rarely any point to paraphrasing; generally speaking, either quote exactly (and put the passage in quotation marks, with a notation of the source, including the page number or numbers) or summarize, reducing a page or even an entire article or chapter of a book to a single four-by-six card. Even when you summarize, indicate your source (including the page numbers) on the card, so that you can give appropriate credit in your paper.

2. Of course in your summary you will sometimes quote a phrase or a sentence—putting it in quotation marks—but quote sparingly. You are not doing stenography; rather you are assimilating knowledge and you are thinking, and so for the most

part your source should be digested rather than engorged whole. Probably most of your direct quotations will be effectively stated passages or crucial passages or both. In your finished paper these quotations will provide authority and emphasis.

3. If you quote but omit some material within the quotation, be sure to indicate the omission by three spaced periods, as explained on page 229.

4. *Never* copy a passage by changing an occasional word, under the impression that you are thereby putting it into your own words. Notes of this sort may find their way into your paper, your reader will sense a style other than your own, and suspicions of plagiarism may follow.

5. In the upper corner of each note card, write a brief key—for example "effect on infants' blood"—so that later you can tell at a glance what is on the card. The sample card shown here summarizes a few pages; notice that it includes a short quotation and records the source. The source is not given in full bibliographic form because the full form is recorded on a bibliography card.

As you work, especially if you are working on a literary or historical topic, you'll of course find yourself returning again and again to the primary materials—and you'll probably find

---

Verrett, pp. 152-54   botulism argument
                                     search for substitute

P. 152 Industry and gov't approved nitrite as color-fixer. Now shifting ground, saying it prevents botulism. Verrett points out "legal snag": new approval needed for new use. (Thus public hearing and unwanted attention.)

P. 154 ". . . the industry-USDA-FDA coalition seems firm in its position that there is no substitute for nitrate, now or ever. Their posture is misdirected at defending nitrites, devising ways to keep it in food rather than ways to get it out."

    Verrett and Carper, _Eating May Be Hazardous_

to your surprise that a good deal of the secondary material is unconvincing or even wrong, despite the fact that it is printed in a handsome book. One of the things we learn from research is that not everything in print is true; one of the pleasures we get from research results from this discovery.

WRITING THE PAPER

There remains the difficult job of writing up your findings, usually in 2000–3000 words (eight to twelve double-spaced typed pages). Beyond referring you to the rest of this book, we can offer only five further pieces of advice.

1. Begin by rereading your note cards, sorting them into packets by topic. Put together what belongs together. After sorting and resorting, you will have a kind of first draft without writing a draft. From these packets, you can make a first outline.

2. When you write your first draft, leave lots of space at the top and bottom of each page so that you can add material, which will be circled and connected by arrows to the proper place.

3. Write or type your quotations, even in the first draft, exactly as you want them to appear in the final version. Short quotations (less than three lines of poetry or less than five lines of prose) are run into your own text, in quotation marks, but longer quotations are set off (triple space before them and after them), slightly indented, and are *not* enclosed in quotation marks.

4. Include, right in the body of the draft, all of the relevant citations (later these will become footnotes), so that when you come to revise you don't have to start hunting through your notes to find who said what, and where. You can, for the moment, enclose these citations within diagonal lines, or within double parentheses—anything at all to remind you that they will be your footnotes.

5. Beware of the compulsion to include every note card in your essay. You have taken all these notes, and there is a strong temptation to use them all. But, truth to tell, in hindsight many are useless. Beware of simply telling the reader, "A says . . . B says . . . C says. . . ." When you write a research paper, you are not merely setting the table with other

people's dinnerware; you are cooking the meal. You must have a point, an opinion, a thesis; you are working toward a conclusion, and the reader should always feel he is moving toward that conclusion (by means of your thoughtful evaluation of the evidence) rather than reading an anthology of commentary on the topic.

You must persuade the reader of the validity of your opinion, and you do this by (a) letting the reader see that you know what of significance has been written on the topic; (b) letting the reader hear the best representatives of the chief current opinions, whom you will correct or confirm; and (c) advancing your opinion, by offering generalizations supported by concrete details. And so, because you have a focus, we should get things like: "There are three common views on. . . . The first two are represented by A and B; the third, and by far the most reasonable, is C's view that . . ." or "A argues . . . but . . ." or "Although the third view, C's, is not conclusive, still . . ." or "Moreover, C's point can be strengthened when we consider a piece of evidence that he does not make use of . . ." All of this, of course, is fleshed out with careful summaries and with effective quotations (footnoted as explained on pages 230–38) and with judicious analyses of your own, so that by the end of the paper the reader not only has read a neatly typed paper (see pages 225–26), but he also is persuaded that under your guidance he has seen the evidence, heard the arguments justly summarized, and reached a sound conclusion. He may not become a better person but he is better informed.

A bibliography or list of works consulted (see pages 238–40) is usually appended to the research paper, so that the reader may easily look further into the primary and secondary material if he wishes. But if you have done your job well, the reader will be content to leave things where you left them, grateful that you have set things straight.

SAMPLE RESEARCH PAPER

Here is a sample research paper. This essay is preceded by a thesis statement and an outline, helpful but not obligatory additions.

Nitrites: Cancer for Many, Money for Few

by

Jacob Alexander

English 1B

Mr. McCabe

April 30, 1975

Thesis

Sodium nitrite and sodium nitrate, added to cured meats and smoked
fish as a color fixative, combine in meat and in the stomach to form a
powerful carcinogen (cancer-producing substance). This fact puts the
profit motive of the food industry and the health of the American public
squarely into opposition, and thus far the government regulatory agencies
are supporting the food industry.

Outline

I. Sodium nitrite and nitrate can be poison.

   A. Nitrites combine with blood to form a pink pigment which does not
      carry oxygen.

   B. They have a number of other ominous side-effects.

II. Nitrites combine with amines to form nitrosamines, among the most
    potent carcinogens known.

   A. Nitrites are likely to combine with amines in the human stomach
      to form nitrosamines.

   B. Animals of all kinds, fed nitrites and amines, develop cancer
      in various parts of their bodies.

   C. Nitrosamines are sometimes present in nitrited food even before
      we ingest it.

III. Why are nitrites used in food?

   A. Nitrites are traditionally used as color fixers.

   B. Producers argue that they are also preservatives.

IV. Why does the government allow nitrites?

   A. Nitrites and nitrates have a very long history of use.

   B. Government regulatory mechanisms are full of loopholes.

      1. Delaney Clause in Food Additive Amendment (1958) does not
         apply.

      2. FDA controls fish; USDA controls meats.

      3. Both depend on industry-oriented NAS.

C. The agencies defend themselves.

    1. They find fault with the experiments.

    2. They claim nitrites prevent botulism.

    3. They claim that there is a "no-effect" level of use for carcinogens, though doctors disagree.

V. American government is serving the food industry rather than the people.

    A. Food industry's enormous profits enable them to bring pressure to bear on regulatory agencies.

    B. Hazy patriotic optimism contributes to inaction.

VI. Stop eating nitrated fish and meat.

Americans eat between three thousand and ten thousand additives in
their food today, most of them untested[1] and many of them known to be
dangerous. Of these, nitrites are among the most hazardous of all. In
this country, ham, bacon, corned beef, salami, bologna, lox, and other
cold cuts and smoked fish almost invariably contain sodium nitrite (or
sodium nitrate, which readily converts to nitrite in the human body). In
fact, one-third of the federally inspected meat and fish we consume--more
than seven billion pounds of it every year--contains this chemical.[2]

To begin with, nitrite is just plain poison in amounts only slightly
greater than those allowed in cured meats. Jacqueline Verrett, who worked
for the Food and Drug Administration (FDA) for fifteen years, and
Jean Carper list in their book, Eating May Be Hazardous to Your Health,
recent instances of people poisoned by accidental overdoses.

> In Buffalo, New York, six persons were hospitalized with
> "cardiovascular collapse" after they ate blood sausage which
> contained excessive amounts of nitrites. . . . In New Jersey,
> two persons died and many others were critically poisoned after
> eating fish illegally loaded with nitrites. In New Orleans,
> ten youngsters between the ages of one and a half and five
> became seriously ill . . . after eating wieners or bologna
> overnitrited by a local meat-processing firm; one wiener that
> was obtained later from the plant was found to contain a
> whopping 6,570 parts per million of nitrate, whereas the
> federal limitation is 200 parts per million. In Florida, a
> three-year-old boy died after eating hot dogs with three times
> greater nitrite concentration than the government allows.[3]

The chemical has the unusual and difficult-to-replace quality of
keeping meat a fresh-looking pink throughout the cooking, curing, and

[1] Daniel Zwerdling, "Food Pollution," Ramparts, 9, No. 11
(June 1971), 34.

[2] Michael F. Jacobson, Eater's Digest (New York: Doubleday, 1972),
p. 169.

[3] (New York: Simon and Schuster, 1974), pp. 138-39.

storage process. The nitrous acid from the nitrite combines with the hemoglobin in the blood of the meat, fixing its red color so that the meat does not turn the tired brown or gray natural to cured meats.

Unfortunately, it does much the same thing in humans. Although most of the nitrite passes through the body unchanged, a small amount is released into the bloodstream. This combines with the hemoglobin in the blood to form a pigment called methomoglobin, which cannot carry oxygen. If enough oxygen is incapacitated, a person dies. The allowable amount of nitrite in a quarter pound of meat can incapacitate between 1.4 and 5.7 percent of the hemoglobin in an average-sized adult.[4] When 10 to 20 percent is incapacitated, a victim discolors and has difficulty breathing.[5] One of the problems with nitrite poisoning is that infants under a year, because of the quantity and makeup of their blood, are especially suscep-tible to it.

If the consumer of nitrite is not acutely poisoned, his blood soon returns to normal and this particular danger passes; the chemical, however, has long-term effects. Nitrite can cause headaches in people who are especially sensitive to it, an upsetting symptom in light of the fact that in rats who ate it regularly for a period of time it has produced lasting "epileptic-like" changes in the brain--abnormalities which showed up when the rats were fed only a little more than an American fond of cured meats might eat.[6] Experiments with chickens, cattle, sheep, and rats have shown that nitrite, when administered for several days, inhibits the ability of the liver to store vitamin A and carotene.[7] And, finally,

[4] Verrett and Carper, pp. 138-39.

[5] Jacobson, p. 166.

[6] Harrison Wellford, Sowing the Wind (New York: Bantam, 1973), p. 173.

[7] Beatrice Trum Hunter, Fact/Book on Food Additives and Your Health (New Canaan, Conn.: Keats, 1972), p. 90.

Nobel laureate Joshua Lederberg points out that, in microorganisms, nitrite
enters the DNA. "If it does the same thing in humans," he says, "it will
cause mutant genes." Geneticist Bruce Ames adds, "If out of one million
people, one person's genes are mutant, that's a serious problem. . . . If
we're filling ourselves now with mutant genes, they're going to be around
for generations."[8]

By far the most alarming characteristic of nitrite, however, is that
in test tubes, in meats themselves, in animal stomachs, and in human
stomachs--wherever a mildly acidic solution is present--it can and does
combine with amines to form nitrosamines. And nitrosamines are carcinogens. They cause cancer. Even the food industry and the agencies responsible for allowing the use of nitrite in foods admit that nitrosamines
cause cancer. Those people who have studied them feel, in fact, that they
are among the surest and most deadly of all the carcinogens currently
recognized.

Now it is important to note that nitrite _alone_, when fed to rats on
an otherwise controlled diet, does not induce cancer. It must first combine with amines to form nitrosamines. Considering, however, that the
human stomach has the kind of acidic solution in which amines and nitrites
readily combine, and considering as well that amines are present in beer,
wine, cereals, tea, fish, cigarette smoke, and a long list of drugs including antihistamines, tranquilizers, and even oral contraceptives, it
is hardly surprising to find that nitrosamines have been found in human
stomachs.

When animals are fed amines in combination with nitrite, they develop
cancer with a statistical consistency that is frightening, even to scientists. Verrett and Carper report that William Lijinsky, a scientist at
Oak Ridge National Laboratory who has been studying the effects of nitrite

[8] Zwerdling, pp. 34-35.

in food since 1961, after feeding animals 250 parts per million (ppm) of nitrites and amines--an amount comparable to what some Americans are taking in today--

> found malignant tumors in 100 percent of the test animals within six months, and he thinks they all will be dead in the next three months. "Unheard of," he says. . . . "You'd usually expect to find 50 percent at the most. And the cancers are all over the place--in the brain, lung, pancreas, stomach, liver, adrenals, intestines. We open up the animals and they are a bloody mess.[9]

> [He] believes that nitrosamines, because of their incredible versatility in inciting cancer, may be the key to an explanation of the mass production of cancer in seemingly dissimilar populations. In other words, nitrosamines may be a common factor in cancer that has been haunting us all these years.[10]

Lijinsky also claims that nitrites "seem to be most effective in eliciting tumors when they are applied in small doses over a long period, rather than as large single doses."[11]

Verrett and Carper list still more damning evidence. Nitrosamines have caused cancer in rats, hamsters, mice, guinea pigs, dogs, and monkeys. It has been proven that nitrosamines of over a hundred kinds cause cancer. Nitrosamines have been shown to pass through the placenta from the mother to cause cancer in the offspring. Even the lowest levels of nitrosamines ever tested have produced cancer in animals. When animals are fed nitrite and amines separately over a period of time, they develop cancers of the same kind and at the same frequency as animals fed the corresponding nitrosamines already formed. In a part of South Africa where the people drink a locally distilled liquor containing a high concentration of nitrosamines, there is an "extraordinarily high incidence

[9] P. 136.

[10] P. 142

[11] Statement of Dr. William Lijinsky, Eppely Institute, Univ. of Nebraska, before the Intergovernmental Relations Subcommittee of the Committee on Government Operations, U.S. House of Representatives, 16 March 1971, quoted in Wellford, p. 172.

of human esophageal cancer." Finally, Verrett and Carper quote Lijinsky again:

> We have evidence that while the amount of carcinogen might not build up, the effect in the animal body does build up. In other words, the more carcinogen you are exposed to, the more cells are damaged and the more likely you are to develop a tumor within your lifetime. So I feel no amount of a nitrosamine can be ignored.[12]

Nitrosamines even form _in_ food, before it reaches the table. According to Verrett and Carper,

> In February 1972 the Agriculture Department and the FDA detected nitrosamines in eight samples of processed meat taken from packing plants and retail stores. Nitrosamines at levels of eleven to forty-eight parts per billion were found in dried beef and cured pork, at five parts per billion in ham, and at eighty parts per billion in hot dogs. More alarmingly, four bacon samples--all different brands--that when raw yielded no nitrosamines revealed up to 106 parts per billion of nitrosamines _after cooking_. In November 1972 the FDA revealed that further experiments had found high levels of a cancer-causing nitrosamine--up to 108 parts per billion--in four other brands of bacon that had been pan-fried, proving that nitrosamines are widespread in cooked bacon. . . . The FDA also found nitrosamines in smoked chub and salmon at levels up to twenty-six parts per billion.[13]

As if this were not enough, Beatrice Trum Hunter claims that "some nitrosamines, in Cantonese dried fish, were capable of inducing cancer by a single dose."[14]

The question, then, is why nitrite continues to be used in a third of the meat Americans consume. Although nitrite adds a small amount to flavor, it is used primarily for cosmetic purposes, and is, in fact, legally sanctioned _only_ as a color fixative. United States meat processors, however, are allowed to use up to twenty times as much nitrite as is needed to fix color.

[12] Pp. 143-46.

[13] Pp. 146-47.

[14] P. 93.

Recently, as controversy over nitrite has accelerated, food producers are arguing that nitrite also prevents the growth of botulinum, an argument to which the public is particularly susceptible because of a number of recent botulism scares. Michael Jacobson explains the preservative action of nitrite:

> Nitrite makes botulinum spores sensitive to heat. When foods are treated with nitrite and then heated, any botulinum spores that may be present are killed. In the absence of nitrite, spores can be inactivated only at temperatures that ruin the meat products. . . . Nitrite's preservative action is particularly important in foods that are not cooked after they leave the factory, such as ham, because these offer an oxygen-free environment, the kind in which botulinum can grow. The toxin does not pose a danger in foods that are always well cooked, such as bacon, because the toxin would be destroyed in cooking. Laboratory studies demonstrate clearly that nitrite can kill botulinum, but whether it actually does in commercially processed meat is now being questioned. Frequently, the levels used may be too low to do anything but contribute to the color.[15]

It seems unlikely that sodium nitrite is really necessary as a preservative. After extensive hearings in 1971, a congressional subcommittee concluded it was not, except possibly in a few cases like that of canned ham.[16] Bratwurst and breakfast sausage are manufactured now without nitrite because they don't need to be colored pink; bacon is always cooked thoroughly enough to kill off any botulinum spores present; and the Maple Crest Sausage Company has been distributing frozen nitrite-free hot dogs, salami, and bologna to health food stores since 1966 without poisoning anyone. Certainly there are other ways of dealing with botulism. High or low temperature prevents botulism. What nitrite undoubtedly does lower, however, is the level of care and sanitation necessary in handling meat.

The use of nitrite in smoked fish is particularly frivolous. If the

[15] P. 165.

[16] Verrett and Carper, p. 138.

fish is heated to 180° for thirty minutes, as it is supposed to be by law, and then distributed with adequate refrigeration, there should be no need for nitrite. The fish industry has appealed to the government with the argument that it should be allowed to use nitrite in more products precisely because some plants do not possess the facilities to process fish at properly high temperatures. Furthermore, the government exercises little control over nitrite in fish. In 1969, three out of six food packaging firms surveyed were putting dangerously high levels of nitrite into their fish, yet only in the most extreme case did the FDA confiscate the fish.[17]

Clearly, the use of nitrite adds immeasurably to the profit-making potential of the meat industry, but why does the federal government allow this health hazard in our food--that same government which stands firmly behind the message that "Americans . . . are blessed with better food at lower costs than anyone in any other country," a message William Robbins calls the "big lie"?[18]

In the first place, nitrite and nitrate have been used for so long that it is hard for lawmakers to get past their instinctive reaction, "But that's the way we've always done it." Indeed, the Romans used saltpeter, a nitrate, to keep meat and, as early as 1899, scientists discovered that the nitrate breaks down into nitrite and that it is the nitrite which actually preserves the red color in meats.[19] Thus, by the time the U.S. Department of Agriculture and the Food and Drug Administration got into the business of regulating food, they tended to accept nitrite and nitrate as givens. For example, the tolerance level of

[17] Verrett and Carper, pp. 149-50.

[18] William Robbins, The American Food Scandal (New York: Morrow, 1974), p. 2.

[19] Jacobson, pp. 164-65.

nitrite set by these agencies is based, not on experiment, but on the level found, in 1925, to be the maximum level usually found in cured ham. Following this government standard, a representative of the fish industry, petitioning to use nitrite, claimed that "no extensive reports of investigations to establish safety are required in view of the long history in common use and the previously accepted safety of these curing agents in the production of meat and fish products within the already established tolerances."[20]

A second reason for the inadequacy of regulation is that government mechanisms for protecting the consumer are full of curious loopholes. In 1958 Congress passed the Food Additive Amendment, including the Delaney Clause which clearly states that additives should be banned if they induce cancer in laboratory animals. Unfortunately, however, the amendment does not apply to additives that were in use before it was passed, so, since nitrite and nitrate had already been in use for a long time, they were automatically included on the list of chemicals "Generally Recognized as Safe." To complicate matters further, nitrite in meat is regulated by the USDA, while nitrite in fish is under the jurisdiction of the FDA. And these agencies generally leave it to industry--the profit-maker--to determine whether or not an additive is safe. The final irony in this long list of governmental errors is that the FDA depends heavily, for "independent" research and advice, on the food committees of the National Academy of Sciences, which Daniel Zwerdling claims are "like a Who's Who of the food and chemical industry."[21]

Nevertheless, as they have come under fire in recent years on the subject of nitrite and nitrate, the FDA and the USDA have found it necessary to give reasons for their continued sanction of these chemicals.

[20] Verrett and Carper, p. 148.

[21] P. 34.

First, they find fault with the experiments done to date. According to the USDA, for example,

> The Department was aware that under certain conditions, nitrites do interact with secondary amines to form nitrosamines and that some nitrosamines are carcinogenic. However, knowledge in this area was limited and analytical methods available to study the possibility of nitrosamine formation in meat food products containing the permissible amounts of sodium nitrate lacked the necessary accuracy and reliability to give conclusive results.[22]

Despite the Delaney Clause, moreover, the FDA points out, "Man is the most important experimental animal and nitrites have not been linked to cancer in all the years that man has been eating the chemical."[23] This is an almost foolproof argument, since cancer usually shows up only after its inception, and it is extremely difficult to trace it to any source. And certainly it is unlikely that any sizeable group will offer to serve as guinea pigs for nitrite experiments. In evaluating this argument, it is significant that humans are generally _more_ susceptible to chemical damage than animals--ten times more so than rats, for example.[24] Following through on its own logic, however, since nitrite has indeed been proven to cause cancer in dogs, the FDA has dutifully and responsibly banned its use in dog food.

The industry's second argument is that nitrite prevents botulism. However, the USDA regulations approve the use of nitrate and nitrite _only_ as color fixers. If they are being used as preservatives, this is a new use and comes squarely under the auspices of the Delaney Clause, which would have them banned outright because they cause cancer in animals.

[22] Verrett and Carper, p. 152.

[23] Regulation of Food Additives and Medicated Animal Feeds, Hearings, Intergovernmental Relations Subcommittee, Committee on Government Operations, U.S. House of Representatives (March 1971), pp. 215 ff., quoted in Wellford, p. 179.

[24] Verrett and Carper, p. 59.

The last argument is that small enough doses of carcinogens are not dangerous. Dr. Leo Friedman, director of the FDA's Division of Toxicology, puts it this way:

> . . . there is always a threshold level below which the substance does not exert any physiologically significant effect. . . . The design of a safety evaluation study is to determine a level at which there is no demonstrable effect. This level, when divided by a suitable safety factor, is then considered to be a safe level, in that there is a practical certainty that no harm will result from the use of the substance at that level.[25]

The medical community does not agree. The Surgeon General's committee stated in 1970, "The principle of a zero tolerance for carcinogenic exposures should be retained in all areas of legislation presently covered by it and should be extended to cover other exposures as well."[26] Hughes Ryser stated in the New England Journal of Medicine: ". . . weak carcinogenic exposures have irreversible and additive effects and cannot be dismissed lightly as standing 'below a threshold of action.' " He also commented that, until the carcinogens are removed from the environment, "efforts must continue to educate populations and government about their presence."[27] Even with this, the FDA Commissioner, Charles Edwards, strenuously disagrees: "We can't deluge the public with scare items based on our suspicions. . . . The pendulum swings too far in most cases, and consumers tend to boycott a product . . . even though we might feel that continued use within certain limits is entirely justified."[28]

Something has gone wrong. The issue is one of what we eat. It makes no sense at all to eat a substance until it is proven to be poison. Even

[25] Memorandum from Dr. Leo Friedman to Dr. Virgil Wodicka, 17 Dec. 1971, quoted in Wellford, p. 180.

[26] Wellford, p. 181.

[27] "Chemical Carcinogenesis," 285, No. 13 (23 Sept. 1971), 721-34, quoted in Wellford, p. 181.

[28] Wellford, p. 18.

a starving man is reluctant to eat mushrooms unless he knows what he's doing. Nitrite is banned altogether in Norway, and forbidden in fish in Canada. European allowances are generally lower than ours, and even the Germans make their "wursts" without nitrite.

One is forced to a radical conclusion. The American government is, in this instance, clearly serving the interests of the industry rather than the people. The fact is that the food industry is willing to spend millions every year to make sure the regulatory agencies act in ways that please them. Each time an additive is banned, the food industry finds itself in the spotlight. It feels an implicit threat to all its other additives, and ultimately to the immense profits Daniel Zwerdling describes:

> This marvelous chemical additive technology has earned $500 million a year for the drug companies . . . and it has given the food manufacturers enormous control over the mass market. Additives like preservatives enable food that might normally spoil in a few days or a week to endure unchanged for weeks, months, or even years. A few central manufacturers can saturate supermarket shelves across the country with their products because there's no chance the food will spoil. Companies can buy raw ingredients when they're cheap, produce and stockpile vast quantities of the processed result, then withhold the products from the market for months, hoping to manipulate prices upward and make a windfall.[29]

Under pressure from the food industry, and probably influenced as well by a sincere, if hazy, patriotic optimism, the FDA issued a fact sheet in May 1967, stating unequivocally that our soil is not being poisoned by fertilizers, that pesticide residues are entirely safe, that our soil is the "envy of every nation," and that food processing is a "modern marvel because the natural value of the food is not lost in the process." It concludes, "Today's scientific knowledge, working through good laws to protect consumers, assures the safety and wholesomeness of every component

[29] "Death for Dinner," The New York Review, 21, No. 1 (21 Feb. 1974), 22.

of our food supply."[30] The FDA's continuing support for nitrite allowances, despite increasing evidence that nitrite is lethal, indicates that
the FDA has not removed its rose-colored glasses.

Until the FDA and other regulatory agencies begin to see clearly, the
American consumer has little choice other than to give up eating the
nitrited cured meats and smoked fish on the market today.

[30] _Regulation of Food Additives_, pp. 215 ff., quoted in Wellford,
p. 179.

Works Cited

Hunter, Beatrice Trum. *Fact/Book on Food Additives and Your Health*.
    New Canaan, Conn.: Keats, 1972.

Jacobson, Michael F. *Eater's Digest*. New York: Doubleday, 1972.

Robbins, William. *The American Food Scandal*. New York: Morrow, 1974.

Verrett, Jacqueline, and Jean Carper. *Eating May Be Hazardous to Your
    Health*. New York: Simon and Schuster, 1974.

Wellford, Harrison. *Sowing the Wind*. New York: Bantam, 1973.

Zwerdling, Daniel. "Death for Dinner." *The New York Review*, 21, No. 1
    (21 Feb. 1974), 22-24.

_____. "Food Pollution." *Ramparts*, 9, No. 11 (June 1971), 31-37, 53-54.

A NOTE ON THE USE OF COMPUTERS IN RESEARCH AND WRITING

We've all become familiar in recent years with computers and their seemingly limitless uses: from guiding space vehicles to computing a day's business receipts. When you make an airline reservation, cash a check at a bank, or register as a student in college, the chances are that a computer has assisted (or impeded) you in reserving your air space, checking your balance, or electing your courses. Computers are also being used increasingly in research and writing.

Computers are used in research in at least two ways. First, computer services available at some libraries help scholars to generate bibliographies and refine research problems. If you are interested in food additives, for example, and your library subscribes to *Medline* (a computer based system operated by the National Library of Medicine), a specially trained librarian can help you to retrieve a printed list of relevant articles published in some 1200 journals of biology, medicine, and related sciences within the last three years. If, after receiving a printout of, say, 1500 references, you decide your topic is too broad, you can, again with the assistance of the specialist and the computer, progressively narrow your search to a more compassable topic, perhaps the carcinogenic effects of nitrites in cured meat and fish. In about an hour and a half then—an hour with the computer specialist learning to translate your research problem into the language of the system, and half an hour at the terminal in conversation with the computer—you will not only have retrieved a comprehensive and up-to-date list of articles, you will have retrieved it far more quickly and have stored it more efficiently (with less tedium and less bulk) than you could have using conventional library materials: catalogs, bound indexes, and notecards.

Second, computers are frequently used where research projects require statistical analyses, mathematical computations, or simulated experiments. With access to a computer and knowledge of its language you might, for example, use, modify, or devise a computer program to analyze election data, calculate the weight of a star, or simulate the air flow over an airplane wing.

When you come to write a report, a computer with a text editing program can further assist you. You will again have to invest some time learning to use it, but if you are doing a substantial piece of work—a thesis, for example—you might find your time well spent. With a text editing program—which functions something like a smart typewriter with a faultless memory—you can compose, revise, and edit your writing and then make copies of the finished essay, all on the same machine. You can, for example, start by typing a rough draft, then delete whole paragraphs or sections of them, and continue by adding new material. When you want to check your revisions, you can request a clean copy of any part of your text. If you discover that you have misspelled a word a dozen times, you can with one command to the computer, correct the error every place it appears. When you have the final version of your essay stored, you can request as many copies as you want and, with a sophisticated program, your computer will present them to you correctly paged, footnotes in place, left and right margins adjusted, and all neatly typed.

Computer facilities vary greatly from place to place; those we describe here—automated bibliographic searches and mathematical, scientific, and text editing programs—are only examples of some of the current uses of computers in research and writing. It's unlikely therefore that these particular facilities are all available to you now. Even if they are available, they may not prove useful for any work you are now doing, and even if they're useful, the chances are they'll cost more than you want to spend. (That hour and a half with Medline and the specialist, for example, currently costs about $17.00.) Nevertheless, computers and their applications are proliferating, as computers become not only more powerful and more versatile, but also smaller and cheaper; and we expect them to be more commonly available within the next few years. If any facilities are available to you now, then, we suggest you find out about them and acquire some computer literacy, even if you must take a course, invent a project, or apply for a grant to do it. Look in your college catalog to see what opportunities exist, and ask your instructors and the reference librarian. Sometimes even where computer facilities exist, it takes some persistence to find out about them.

CHAPTER NINE

SPECIAL ASSIGNMENTS

WRITING AN EXPLICATION

An explication (literally, unfolding or spreading out) is a commentary, usually line by line, on what is going on in a poem or in a short passage of prose. An explication is not concerned with the writer's life or times, nor is it a paraphrase, a rewording—though it may include paraphrase; it is a commentary revealing your sense of the meaning of the work. To this end it calls attention, as it proceeds, to the implications of words, the function of rhymes, the shifts in point of view, the development of contrasts, and any other contributions to the meaning.

Take, for example, the short poem by William Butler Yeats that opens this book:

THE BALLOON OF THE MIND

Hands, do what you're bid:
Bring the balloon of the mind
That bellies and drags in the wind
Into its narrow shed.[1]

If we are familiar with the work of Yeats we might remember

---

[1] *Variorum Edition of the Poems of W. B. Yeats*, ed. Peter Allt and Russell K. Alspach (New York: Macmillan, 1957), p. 358.

that in a prose work, *Reveries over Childhood and Youth*, Yeats already had used the figure of a balloon (dirigible) to represent mental activity: "My thoughts were a great excitement, but when I tried to do anything with them, it was like trying to pack a balloon into a shed in a high wind." But because explication usually confronts the work itself, without relating it to biography, we can pass over this interesting anticipation and confine ourselves to the poem's four lines.

Yeats's "Balloon of the Mind" is about poetry, specifically about the difficulty of getting one's floating thoughts down into lines on the page. The first line, a short, stern, heavily stressed command to the speaker's hands, implies by its impatient tone that these hands will be disobedient or inept or careless if not watched closely: the poor bumbling body so often fails to achieve the goals of the mind. The bluntness of the command in the first line is emphasized by the fact that all of the subsequent lines are longer. Furthermore, the first line is a grammatically complete sentence, whereas the thought of line 2 spills over into the subsequent lines, implying the difficulty of fitting ideas into confining spaces. Lines 2 and 3 amplify the metaphor already stated in the title (a thought is an airy but unwieldy balloon) and they also contain a second command, "Bring." Alliteration ties this command, "Bring," to the earlier "bid"; it also ties both of these verbs to their object, "balloon," and to the verb that most effectively describes the balloon, "bellies." In comparison with the peremptory first line of the poem, lines 2 and 3 themselves seem almost swollen, bellying and dragging, an effect aided by using adjacent unstressed syllables ("of the," "[bell]ies and," "in the") and by using an eye rhyme ("mind" and "wind") rather than an exact rhyme. And then comes the short last line: the cumbersome balloon—here, the idea that is to be packed into the stanza —almost before we could expect it, is successfully lodged in its "narrow shed." Aside from the relatively colorless "into," the only words of more than one syllable in the poem are "narrow," "balloon," and "bellies," and all three of them emphasize the difficulty of the task. But after "narrow" (the word itself almost looks long and narrow, in this context like a hangar) we get the simplicity of the monosyllable "shed," and the difficult job is done, the thought is safely packed away, the poem is completed—but again with an off rhyme ("bid" and "shed"), for neatness can go only so far when hands and the mind and a balloon are involved.

Because the language of a literary work is denser (richer in associations or connotations) than the language of discursive prose such as this paragraph, explication is much concerned with bringing to the surface the meanings that are in the words but that may not be immediately apparent. Explication, in short, seeks to make explicit the implicit.

The reader of an explication needs to see the text. Since the explicated text is usually short, it is advisable to quote the entire text. You can quote it, complete, at the outset, or you can quote the first unit (for example, a stanza) and then explicate the unit, and then quote the next unit, and so on. If the poem or passage of prose is longer than, say, six lines, it is advisable to number each line at the right for easy reference.

WRITING A BOOK REVIEW

Because a book review is usually about a newly published work, the reviewer normally assumes that his readers will be unfamiliar with the book. The reviewer takes it as his job to acquaint the reader with the book, its contents and its value, and to help him decide whether or not he wishes to read it. Since most reviews are brief (500–1500 words), appearing as they do in newspapers and magazines, they cannot, like explications comment on everything. On the other hand they cannot, like analyses, focus on one aspect of the writing; they attempt in some way to cover the book. Reviews, then, usually contain more summary and more evaluation than explications or analyses. Nevertheless the reviewer must approach his task analytically if he is to accomplish it in the relatively small space allotted to him. And he must, to be convincing, support his opinions by quotations, examples, and specific references to the text so that the reader may think and feel the way the reviewer thinks and feels.

A review commonly has a structure something like this:

1. an opening paragraph giving the reader some idea of the nature and scope of the work and establishing the tone of the review (more about tone in a moment)
2. a paragraph or two of plot summary if the book is a novel; some summary of the contents if it is not
3. a paragraph on the theme, purpose, idea, or vision embodied in the book
4. a paragraph or two on the strengths, if any

5. a paragraph or two on the weaknesses, if any
6. a concluding paragraph in which the reviewer delivers the point he has to make

Tone, as we suggest elsewhere in this book (see pages 286–87) usually refers to the writer's attitude toward his subject, readers, and self. The tone of a review is therefore somewhat dependent on the publication in which it will appear. A review in *Scientific American* will have a different tone from one in *Ms.* Since you have not been commissioned to write your review and are essentially playing a game, you must *imagine* your reader. It's a reasonable idea to imagine that your classmates are your readers, forgetting of course that they may be reviewing the same book you are. (It's a very bad idea to imagine that your teacher is your reader.) And it's always productive to treat both your reader and your subject with respect. This does not mean you need to be solemn or boring; on the contrary, the best way to show your respect for your reader is to write something you would be interested in reading yourself.

Here is a published book review. Although some reviews are untitled, this one has a title; unless your instructor tells you otherwise, give your review a title. (Finding your title will help you, in revising your review, to see if you have focused your essay.)

FAMILY MAN

Wampeters, Foma, & Granfalloons: Opinions by Kurt Vonnegut, Jr.

(Delacorte Press; $8.95)

Readers of Vonnegut's novels will like these essays, speeches, reviews and an interview. But those who think his fiction thin, unformed and full of cheap tickles will find these essays just that.

Vonnegut seems an honest man, which is admirable enough these days. Yet honesty leaves him confessing many sad things. When he was confronted with a list of his publications, for instance, he "felt like a person who was creepily alive, still, and justly accused of petty crime." He says he has tried to "tell the truth plonkingly." That is, the writing trades "allow mediocre people who are patient and industrious to revise their stupidity, to edit themselves into something like intelligence." He goes on: "my career astonishes me. How could anybody have come this far with so little information, with such garbled ideas of what other writers have said?" He was the 98-pound weakling to whom a high school coach once awarded a Charles Atlas course. He remembers his family's maid reading to him from a book called *More Heart Throbs*—and he thinks that she contributed to the "almost intolerable sentimentality about everything" he's written.

There have of course been other contributions to that sentimentality. His mother committed suicide. As a POW he survived the fire-bombing of Dresden. The University of Chicago gave him his happiest day when they accepted him as a graduate student in anthropology—but then they rejected his thesis. To his own three children, his sister's early death from cancer added three more lives for him to father. And so he had a large family there on Cape Cod in his struggling days of what he calls "sleazo" paperbacks and short stories, when no one was reviewing him and, it seemed, not very many were reading him either.

Now, when people are reading him by the millions, he still has a feel for families, and especially for the fathering of families. He admires the Biafran extended families who obviated government welfare programs during much of that land's short life. And he yearns for a return to the 19th-century family structure as a sort of not-so-voluntary group. His next novel will even propose assigned families: the government will provide the same middle name—Chromium or Daffodil—to random groups of 20,000 persons, and these people will all rely on each other, just like cousins supposedly used to do. If he's thinking a lot about families these days, the father-family axis is still all the more telling as the sustenance of his style. Which is to say that his writing has a modern paternalism to it—that of a father who would like also to be a buddy. Or, of a buddy who would also like to be a father.

That is, Vonnegut is a sneaky moralist. He admires the simplicity and untextured responses of the young, just as they admire his reductiveness and his untextured precepts. He speaks to an audience which has not been compromised by the corruptions and conventions of getting on. And he hankers for an age that has not suffered the same fate. His analogies, therefore, are to the 19th century. Since the 19th century will not return, his plots are into the vague future. And so on.

The phrases *and so on* and *so it goes* are so essential to Vonnegut that even though his critics have complained that such expressions are irking, he's not about to excise them. He can't. The world is full of binary and-so-ons for him: people whose lives are compromised and those whose lives are not; bad officers and nice enlisted men; innocent scientists who cause harm, and cynical scientists who hate the destruction to which they inevitably contribute; smart people and dumb people; happy people and lonely people; and so it goes. People who are caught in this world, and those with the liberated perspective of having lived in space, and so on. People who are substantial and those who are not: the somebodies and the nothings; those who are the "merest wisp of an implication" and those who slip back into Nothing, and so it goes. He's not trying to be vague. Rather he's emphasizing how eternally the world is a simple place which we overcome or in which we are overcome. And so on.

The world is not that sort of place: not so clean nor well-lighted. It is messy, in fact, and most of us keep on going during and after being overcome by the dirt and the dark. Vonnegut knows that, and his life shows it if his writing does not. His taste shows it too. That he admires George Orwell and raves over Hunter Thompson tells us much about his own work. Orwell punctured duplicity with angry clarity and had the presence to keep it up all alone. Thompson overwhelms duplicity with manic rage. But Vonnegut has neither the clarity nor the rage of the authors he respects. Instead he has the professional's ability to send back a cable. He says, "I come to work every morning and I see what words come out of the typewriter. I feel like a copyboy whose job is to tear off stories from the teletype machine and deliver them to an editor." Creepily, plonkingly, he's still alive. This is the feeling of an honest man who is hoping at best for the merest wisp of an implication, for a whisper rebuking his silence and the silence around him: Billy Pilgrim wandering in snowdrifts, muttering. Still it would surely be great fun to drive across country with him, or share a bottle with him, or have him for a father. And, because he believes in all the right things even if loosely and only tepidly, he already is a brother.[2]

—W. T. Lhamon, Jr.

EXERCISE

1. Characterize or describe the tone of Lhamon's review.

2. Write a one-sentence summary of each paragraph. Your list of sentences should resemble an outline. (See the paragraph outline on page 57.)

3. How well does your outline correspond with the structure we say reviews commonly have? (See pages 163–64.)

[2] *The New Republic*, 1 June 1974, pp. 27–28.

4. If there are discrepancies between what we have said about reviews and the review by Lhamon, can you offer a reasonable explanation for these discrepancies? Or would you argue that we revise our discussion, or that we choose a different review as an example?

5. Write a brief argument (two or three paragraphs) defending your answer to question 4.

TAKING ESSAY EXAMINATIONS

What Examinations Are

An examination not only measures learning and thinking but stimulates them. Even so humble an examination as a short-answer quiz—chiefly a device to coerce the student to do the assigned reading—is a sort of push designed to move the student forward. Of course internal motivation is far superior to external, but even such crude external motivation as a quiz can have a beneficial effect. Students know this; indeed they often seek external compulsion, choosing a course "Because I want to know something about it, and I know that I won't do the reading on my own." (Teachers often teach a new course for the same reason; we want to become knowledgeable about, say, the Theater of the Absurd, and we know that despite our lofty intentions we may not seriously confront the subject unless we are under the pressure of facing a class.) In short, however ignoble it sounds, examinations force the student to acquire learning and then to convert learning into thinking. Sometimes it is not until preparing for the final examination that the student—rereading the chief texts and classroom notes—sees what the course was really about; until this late stage, the trees obscure the forest, but now, as the student reviews and sorts things out, a pattern emerges. The experience of reviewing and then of writing an examination, though fretful, can be highly exciting as connections are made and ideas take on life. Such discoveries about the whole subject matter of a course can almost never be made by writing critical essays on topics of one's own construction, for such topics rarely require a view of the whole. Furthermore, most of us are more likely to make imaginative leaps when trying to answer questions that other people pose to us, than when we are trying to answer questions we pose to ourselves. And although questions posed by others cause anxiety, when they have been confronted and responded to on an examination the student often makes yet another discovery—a self-discovery, a sudden and satisfying awareness of powers one didn't know one had.

Writing Essay Answers

Here are five obvious but important practical suggestions:

1. Take a moment to jot down, as a sort of outline or source of further inspiration, a few ideas that strike you after you have thought a little about the question. You may at the outset realize there are, say, three points you want to make, and unless you jot these down, you may spend all the allotted time on one point.

2. Answer the question. If you are asked to compare two characters, compare them; don't just write two character sketches. Take seriously such words as "compare," " evaluate," and "summarize."

3. You can often get a good start merely by turning the question into an affirmation, for example by turning "In what ways is the poetry of Ginsberg influenced by Whitman?" into "The poetry of Ginsberg is influenced by Whitman in at least . . . ways."

4. Don't waste time summarizing at length what you have read unless asked to do so—but of course occasionally you may have to give a brief summary in order to support a point. The instructor wants to see that you can *use* your reading, not merely that you have done the reading.

5. Be concrete. Illustrate your arguments with facts—names, dates, and quotations if possible.

Beyond these general suggestions, we can best talk about essay examinations by looking at specific types of questions.

Questions on Literature

The five most common sorts of questions encountered in literature examinations are:

1. a passage to explicate
2. a historical question, such as "Trace T. S. Eliot's religious development," "Trace the development of Shakespeare's

conception of the tragic hero," "How is Frost's nature poetry indebted to Emerson's thinking?"

3. a critical quotation to be evaluated
4. a wild question such as "What would Dickens think of Vonnegut's *Cat's Cradle?*" or "What would Macbeth do if he were in Hamlet's position?"
5. a comparison, such as "Compare the dramatic monologues of Browning with those of T. S. Eliot"

A few remarks on each of these types may be helpful.

For a discussion of how to write an explication, see pages 161–63. As a short rule, look carefully at the tone (speaker's attitude toward self, subject, and audience) and at the implications of the words (the connotations or associations) and see if there is a pattern of imagery. For example, religious language ("adore," "saint") in a secular love poem may define the nature of the lover and of the beloved. Remember, *an explication is not a paraphrase* (a putting into other words) but an attempt to show the relations of the parts, especially by calling attention to implications. Organization of such an essay is rarely a problem, since most explications begin with the first line and go on to the last.

A good essay on a historical question will offer a nice combination of argument and evidence; the thesis will be supported by concrete details (names, dates, perhaps even brief quotations). A discussion of Eliot's movement toward the Church of England cannot be convincing if it does not specify certain works as representative of Eliot in certain years. If you are asked to relate a writer or a body of work to an earlier writer or period, list the chief characteristics of the earlier writer or of the period and then show *specifically* how the material you are discussing is related to these characteristics. And if you can quote some relevant lines from the works, your reader will feel that you know not only titles and stock phrases but also the works themselves.

If you are asked to evaluate a critical quotation, read it carefully and in your answer take account of *all* of the quotation. If the critic has said, "Eliot in his plays always . . . but in his poems rarely . . ." you will have to write about both the plays and the poems; it will not be enough to talk only about the plays (unless, of course, the instructions on the examination ask you to take only as much of the quotation as you wish). Watch especially for words like "always," "for the most part," "never"; that is, although the passage may on the whole approach the truth, you may feel that some important qualifications are needed. This is not being picky; true thinking involves making subtle distinctions, yielding assent only so far and no further. And, again, be sure to give concrete details, supporting your argument with evidence.

Curiously, a wild question such as "What would Dickens think of *Cat's Cradle?*" or "What would Macbeth do in Hamlet's position?" usually produces tame answers: a half dozen ideas about Dickens or Macbeth are neatly applied to Vonnegut or Hamlet, and the gross incompatibilities are thus revealed. But, as the previous paragraph suggests, it may be necessary to do more than to set up bold and obvious oppositions. The interest in such a question and in the answer to it may largely be in the degree to which superficially different figures *resemble* each other in some important ways. And remember that the wildness of the question does not mean that all answers are equally acceptable; as usual, a good answer will be supported by concrete detail.

Comparisons are discussed on pages 37–42. Because comparisons are especially difficult to write, be sure to take a few moments to jot down a sort of outline so that you can know where you will be going. A comparison of Browning's and Eliot's monologues might treat three poems by each, devoting alternate paragraphs to one author; or it might first treat one author's poems and then turn to the other. But if it adopts this second strategy, the essay may break into two parts. You can guard against this weakness by announcing at the outset that you will treat the authors separately, then by reminding your reader during your treatment of the first author that certain points will be picked up when you get to the second author, and again by briefly reminding your reader during the second part of the essay of certain points already made.

Questions on the Social Sciences

The techniques students develop in answering questions on literature may be transferred to examinations in the social sciences. A political science student, for example, can describe through explication the implicit tone or attitude in some of the landmark decisions of the Supreme Court. Similarly, the student of history who has learned to write an essay with a good combination of argument and evidence will not simply present a list of facts unconnected by some central thesis, and the student who is able to evaluate a critical quotation or to compare literary works can also evaluate and compare documents in all the social sciences. Answers to wild questions (number 4, above) can be as effective or as trite in the social sciences as in literature. "You are the British ambassador in Petrograd in November 1918. Write a report to your government about the Bolshevik revolution of that month" is to some instructors and students an absurd question but to others it is an interesting and effective way of ascertaining whether a student has not only absorbed the facts of an event but has also learned how to interpret it.

Questions on the Physical Sciences and Mathematics

Although the answer to an examination question in the physical sciences usually requires a mathematical computation, a few sentences may be useful in explaining the general plan of the computation, the assumptions involved, and sometimes the results.

It is particularly valuable to set down at the outset in a brief statement, probably a single sentence, your plan for solving the problem posed by the examination question. The statement is equivalent to the topic sentence of a paragraph. For instance, if the examination question is "What is the time required for an object to fall from the orbit of the moon to the earth?" the statement of your plan might be: "The time can be obtained by integration from Newton's law of motion, taking account of the increasing gravitational force as the object approaches the earth." Explicitly setting down your plan in words is useful first in clarifying your thought: is the plan a complete one leading to the desired answer? Do I know what I need to know to implement the plan? If your plan doesn't make sense you can junk it right away before wasting more time on it.

The statement of plan is useful also in communicating with

the instructor. Your plan of solution, although valid, may be a surprise to the instructor. (He or she may have expected a solution to the problem posed above starting from Kepler's laws without any integration.) When this is so the instructor will need your explanation to become oriented to your plan, and to properly assess its merits. Then if you botch the subsequent computation or can't remember how the gravitational force varies with the distance you will still have demonstrated that you have some comprehension of the problem. If on the other hand you present an erroneous computation without any explanation, the instructor will see nothing but chaos in your effort.

Further opportunities to use words will occur when you make assumptions or simplifications: "I assume the body is released with zero velocity and accordingly set $b = 0$," or "The third term is negligible and I drop it."

Finally, the results of your computation should be summarized or interpreted in words to answer the question asked. "The object will fall to the earth in five days." (The correct answer, for those who are curious.) Or, if you arrive at the end of your computation and of the examination hour and find you have a preposterous result, you can still exit gracefully (and increase your partial credit) with an explanation: "The answer of 53 days is clearly erroneous since the fall time of an object from the moon's orbit must be less than the 7 days required for the moon to travel a quarter orbit."

2. REVISING

The friends that have it I do wrong
When ever I remake a song,
Should know what issue is at stake:
It is myself that I remake.

—William Butler Yeats

CHAPTER TEN

REVISING FOR CONCISENESS

. . . excess is the common substitute for energy.
—Marianne Moore

All writers who want to keep the attention and confidence of their readers revise for conciseness. The general rule is to say everything relevant in as few words as possible. The conclusion of the Supreme Court's decision in *Brown* v. *the Board of Education of Topeka*, for example—"Separate educational facilities are inherently unequal"—says it all in six words.

The time to begin revising for conciseness is when you have an acceptable first draft in hand—something that pretty much covers your topic and comes reasonably close to saying what you believe about it. As you go over it, study each sentence to see what, without loss of meaning or emphasis, can be deleted. (Delete by crossing out, not erasing; this saves time, and keeps a record of something you may want to reintroduce.) Read each paragraph, preferably aloud, to see if each sentence supports the topic sentence or idea and clarifies the point you are making. Leave in the concrete and specific details and examples that support your ideas (you may in fact be adding them) but cut out all the deadwood that chokes them: extra words, empty or pretentious phrases, weak qualifiers, redundancies, negative constructions, wordy uses of the verb *to be*, and other extra verbs and verb phrases. We'll discuss these problems in the next pages, but first we offer some examples of sentences that cannot be improved upon; they're so awful there's nothing to do but

DOONESBURY   **by Garry Trudeau**

cross them out and start over. Zonker, in Garry Trudeau's cartoon, is a master of what we call Instant Prose (stuff that sounds like the real thing, but isn't).

INSTANT PROSE (ZONKERS)

Here are some examples of Instant Prose from students' essays:

> Frequently a chapter title in a book reveals to the reader the main point that the author desires to bring out during the course of the chapter.

We could try revising this, cutting the twenty-seven words down to seven:

> A chapter's title often reveals its thesis.

But why bother? Unless the title is an exception, is the point worth making?

> The two poems are basically similar in many ways, yet they have their significant differences.

True; all poems are both similar to and different from other poems. Start over with your next sentence, perhaps something like: "The two poems, superficially similar in rough paraphrase, are strikingly different in diction and theme."

> Although the essay is simple in plot, the theme encompasses many vital concepts of emotional make-up.

> Following a transcendental vein, the nostalgia in the poem takes on a spiritual quality.

Pure zonkers. Not even the writers of these sentences now know what they mean.

Writing Instant Prose is an acquired habit, like smoking cigarettes or watching *Star Trek;* fortunately it's easier to kick. It often begins in high school, sometimes earlier, when the victim is assigned a ten-page paper, or is told that a paragraph *must* contain at least three sentences, or that a thesis is stated in the introduction, elaborated in the body of the essay, and repeated in the conclusion. If the instructions appear arbitrary, and the student is bored or intimidated by them, his response is likely to be, like Zonker's, meaningless and mechanical. He forgets, or never learns, the true purpose of writing—the discovery and communication of ideas, attitudes, and judgments—and concentrates instead on the word count: stuffing sentences, padding paragraphs, stretching and repeating points, and adding flourishes. Rewarded by a satisfactory grade, he repeats the performance, and in time, through practice, develops some fluency in spilling out words without thought or commitment, and almost without effort. Such a student enters, as Zonker would say, the college of his choice, feeling somehow inauthentic, perhaps even aware that he doesn't really mean what he writes: symptoms of habitual use of, or addiction to, Instant Prose.

How to Avoid Instant Prose

1. Trust yourself. Writing Instant Prose is not only a habit; it's a form of alienation. If you habitually write zonkers you probably don't think of what you write as your own but as something you produce on demand for someone else. (Clearly Zonker is writing for that unreasonable authority, the teacher, whose mysterious whims and insatiable appetite for words he must somehow satisfy.) Breaking the habit begins with recognizing it, and then acknowledging the possibility that you can take yourself and your work seriously. It means learning to respect your ideas and experiences (unlearning the passive habits that got you through childhood) and determining that when you write you'll write what you mean—nothing more, nothing less. This involves taking some risks, of course; habits offer some security or they would have no grip on us. Moreover, we all have moments when we doubt that our ideas are worth taking

seriously. Keep writing honestly anyway. The self-doubts will pass; accomplishing something—writing one clear sentence—can help make them pass.

2. Distrust your first draft. Learn to recognize Instant Prose Additives when they crop up in your writing, and in what you read. And you *will* find them in what you read—in textbooks and in academic journals, notoriously.

Here's an example from a recent book on contemporary theater: "One of the principal and most persistent sources of error that tends to bedevil a considerable proportion of contemporary literary analysis is the assumption that the writer's creative process is a wholly conscious and purposive type of activity." Notice all the extra stuff in the sentence: "principal and most persistent," "tends to bedevil," "considerable proportion," "type of activity." Cleared of deadwood the sentence might read: "The assumption that the writer's creative process is wholly conscious and purposive bedevils much contemporary criticism."

3. Acquire a new habit, Revising for Conciseness, along with a pair of scissors, a pot of glue, and a wastebasket.

REVISING FOR CONCISENESS
Extra Words and Empty Words

Extra words should, by definition, be eliminated; vague, empty, or pretentious words and phrases may be replaced by specific and direct language.

wordy However, it must be remembered that Ruth's marriage could have positive effects on Naomi's situation.

concise Ruth's marriage, however, will also provide security for Naomi.

In the second version, the unnecessary "it must be remembered that" has been eliminated; for the vague "positive effects" and "situation," specific words communicating a precise point have been substituted. The revision, though briefer, says more.

wordy In high school, where I had the opportunity for three years of working with the student government, I realized how significantly a person's enthusiasm could be destroyed merely by the attitudes of his superiors.

concise In high school, during three years on the student council, I saw students' enthusiasm destroyed by insecure teachers and cynical administrators.

Again, the revised sentence gives more information in fewer words. How?

wordy The economic situation of Miss Moody was also a crucial factor in the formation of her character.

concise Anne Moody's poverty also helped form her character.

"Economic situation" is evasive for poverty; "crucial factor" is pretentious. Both are Instant Prose.

wordy It creates a better motivation of learning when students can design their own programs involving education. This way students' interests can be focused on.

concise Motivation improves when students design their own programs, focused on their own interests.

Now try revising this wordy sentence:

Perhaps they basically distrusted our capacity to judge correctly.

Notice how, in the preceding sentences, the following words crop up: "basically," "significant," "situation," "factor," "involving," "effect." These words have legitimate uses, but are often no more than Instant Prose Additives. Cross them out whenever you can. Similar words to watch out for: "aspect," "facet," "fundamental," "manner," "nature," "type," "ultimate," "utilization," "viable," "virtually," "vital." If they make your writing "sound good" don't hesitate—cross them out at once.

Weak Intensifiers and Qualifiers

Words like "very," "quite," "rather," "completely," "definitely," and "so" can usually be struck from a sentence without loss. (Paradoxically, sentences are often more emphatic without intensifiers.) Try reading the following sentences both with and without the bracketed words:

At that time I was [very] idealistic.
We found the proposal [quite] feasible.
The remark, though unkind, was [entirely] accurate.
It was a [rather] fatuous statement.

What she did next was [completely] inexcusable.
The first line [definitely] establishes that the father had been drinking.

Always avoid using intensifiers with "unique." Either something is unique—the only one of its kind—or it is not. It can't be very, quite, so, pretty, or fairly unique.

Circumlocutions

Roundabout ways of saying things enervate your prose and tire your reader. Notice how each circumlocution in the first column is matched by a concise expression in the second.

I came to the realization that	I realized that
She is of the opinion that	She thinks that
The quotation is supportive of	The quotation supports
Concerning the matter of	About
During the course of	During
For the period of a week	For a week
In the event that	If
In the process of	During, while
Regardless of the fact that	Although
Due to the fact that	Because
Inasmuch as	Since
If the case was such that	If
It is often the case that	Often
In all cases	Always
I made contact with	I called, saw, phoned, wrote
At that point in time	Then
At this point in time	Now

Wordy Beginnings

Vague, empty words and phrases clog the beginnings of some sentences. They're like elaborate wind-ups before the pitch.

wordy   By analyzing carefully the last lines in this stanza, you find the connections between the loose ends of the poem.

concise   The last lines of the stanza connect the loose ends of the poem.

wordy   What the cartoonist is illustrating and trying to get across is the greed of the oil producers.

concise   The cartoon illustrates the greed of the oil producers.

wordy   Dealing with the crucial issue of the year, the editorial is expressing ironical disbelief in any possible solution to the Middle East crisis.

concise   The editorial ironically expresses disbelief in the proposed solutions to the Middle East crisis.

wordy   In Langston Hughes' case, he "was saved from sin" when he was going on thirteen.

concise   Langston Hughes "was saved from sin" when he was going on thirteen.

wordy   In the last stanza is the conclusion (as usual) and it tells of the termination of the dance.

concise   The last stanza concludes with the end of the dance.

wordy   In opposition to the situation of the younger son is that of the elder who remained in his father's house, working hard and handling his inheritance wisely.

concise   The elder son, by contrast, remained in his father's house, worked hard, and handled his inheritance wisely.

Notice in the above examples that when the deadwood is cleared from the beginning of the sentence, the subject appears early, and the main verb appears close to it:

The last lines . . . connect . . .
The cartoon illustrates . . .
The editorial . . . expresses . . .
Langston Hughes "was saved" . . .
The last stanza concludes . . .
The elder son . . . remained . . .

Locating the right noun for the subject, and the right verb for the predicate, is the key to revising sentences with wordy beginnings. Try revising the following sentence:

The way that Mabel reacts toward her brother is a fine representation of her nature.

Empty Conclusions

Often a sentence that begins well has an empty conclusion. The words go on but the sentence seems to stand still; if it's not revised, it requires another sentence to explain it. A short sentence is not necessarily concise.

empty   "Those Winter Sundays" is composed so that a reader can feel what the poet was saying. (How is it composed? What is he saying?)

concise   "Those Winter Sundays" describes the speaker's anger as a child, and his remorse as an adult.

empty   In both Orwell's and Baldwin's essays the feeling of white supremacy is very important. (Why is white supremacy important?)

concise   Both Orwell and Baldwin trace the insidious consequences of white supremacy.

empty   Being the only white girl among about ten black girls was quite a learning experience. (What did she learn?)

concise   As the only white girl among about ten black girls I began to understand the experiences of isolation, helplessness, and rage regularly reported by minority students.

Wordy Uses of the Verbs "To Be," "To Have," and "To Make"

Notice that in the preceding unrevised sentences a form of the verb *to be* introduces the empty conclusion. In each revision, the right verb added and generated substance. In the following sentences, substitutions for the verb *to be* both invigorate and shorten otherwise substantial sentences.

wordy   The scene is taking place at night, in front of the capitol building.

concise   The scene takes place at night, in front of the capitol building.

wordy   In this shoeshining and early rising there are indications of church attendance.

concise   The early rising and shoeshining indicate church attendance.

wordy   The words "flashing," "rushing," "plunging," and "tossing" are suggestive of excitement.

concise   The words, "flashing," "rushing," "plunging," and "tossing" suggest excitement.

The rule is, whenever you can, replace

1. a form of the verb *to be* and a participle ("is taking")
2. a form of the verb *to be* and a noun ("are indications")
3. a form of the verb *to be* and an adjective ("are suggestive")

with a verb ("takes," "indicate," "suggest"). Sentences with the verbs *to have* and *to make* can similarly be reduced:

wordy   The Friar has knowledge that Juliet is alive.
concise The Friar knows that Juliet is alive.

wordy   The stanzas make a vivid contrast between Heaven and Hell.
concise The stanzas vividly contrast Heaven and Hell.

Like all rules, this one has exceptions. We don't list them here; you'll discover them by listening to your sentences.

Redundancy

This term, derived from a Latin word meaning "overflowing, overlapping," refers to unnecessary repetition in the expression of ideas. Unlike repetition, which often provides emphasis or coherence (for example, "government of the people, by the people, for the people") redundancy can always be eliminated.

redundant Any student could randomly sit anywhere. (If the stu-, dents could sit anywhere, the seating was random.)
concise   Students could sit anywhere.
       We chose our seats at random.

redundant I have no justification with which to excuse myself.
concise   I have no justification for my action.
       I can't justify my action.
       I have no excuse for my action.
       I can't excuse my action.

redundant In the orthodox Cuban culture, the surface of the female role seemed degrading. (Perhaps this sentence means what it says. More probably "surface" and "seemed" are redundant.)
concise   In the orthodox Cuban culture, the female role seemed degrading.
       In the orthodox Cuban culture, the female role was superficially degrading.

redundant In "Araby" the boy feels alienated emotionally from his family.
concise   In "Araby" the boy feels alienated from his family.

Try eliminating redundancy from the following sentence:

Marriage in some form has long existed since prehistoric times.

Many phrases in common use are *redundant:* Watch for phrases like these when you revise:

round in shape   resulting effect
purple in color   close proximity
poetic in nature   connected together
tall in stature   prove conclusively
autobiography of her life must necessarily
basic fundamentals   very unique
true fact   very universal
free gift   the reason why is because

Negative Constructions

Negative constructions are often not only wordy but pretentious.

wordy   Housing for married students is not unworthy of consideration.

concise Housing for married students is worthy of consideration.

"See what I mean? You're never sure just where you stand with them."
Drawing by Ross; © *1971 The New Yorker Magazine, Inc.*

better The trustees should earmark funds for married students' housing. (Probably what the author meant)

wordy After reading the second paragraph you aren't left with an immediate reaction as to how the story will end.

concise The first two paragraphs create suspense.

wordy There aren't too many persons one can find to share one's misery with.

concise Few persons will share one's misery.

The following example from a syndicated column is not untypical:

> Although it is not reasonably to be expected that someone who fought his way up to the Presidency is less than a largely political animal and sometimes a beast, it is better not to know—really— exactly what his private conversations were composed of.

The Golden Rule of writing is "Write for others as you would have them write for you" not "Write for others in a manner not unreasonably dissimilar to the manner in which you would have them write for you." (But see the discussion of *not . . . un-* on page 276 for effective use of the negative.)

Extra Predicates

Some sentences use more verbs than they need. Often clauses can be reduced to phrases, or phrases to single words.

wordy The lawyer was moved by pity and he became gloomy.
concise The lawyer, moved by pity, became gloomy.

wordy At top left of the cartoon are the two remaining devils who are standing around looking at him with their pitchforks in their hands.

concise At top left of the cartoon the remaining two devils stand, looking at him, pitchforks in their hands.

wordy George Orwell is the pen name of Eric Blair, who was an English writer.

concise George Orwell is the pen name of Eric Blair, an English writer.

wordy The Book of Ruth was probably written in the fifth century B.C. It was a time when women were in a definite subordinate position to men.

concise The Book of Ruth was probably written in the fifth century B.C. when women were clearly subordinate to men.

Watch particularly for sentences beginning with "it is," "this is," "there are." (Again, wordy uses of the verb *to be*.)

wordy It is frequently considered that *Hamlet* is Shakespeare's most puzzling play.

concise *Hamlet* is frequently considered Shakespeare's most puzzling play.

wordy This is a quotation from Black Elk's autobiography which discloses his prophetic powers.

concise This quotation from Black Elk's autobiography discloses his prophetic powers.

Try revising the following sentence:

There are many writers who believe that writing can't be taught.

SOME CONCLUDING REMARKS

We spoke earlier about how students learn to write Instant Prose and acquire other wordy habits—by writing what they think the teacher has asked for. We haven't forgotten that teachers assign papers of a certain length in college too. What do you do when you've been asked to produce a ten-page paper and after diligent writing and revising you find you've said everything relevant to your topic in seven and a half pages? Our advice is, hand it in. We can't remember ever counting the words or pages of a substantial, interesting essay; we assume that our colleagues elsewhere are equally reasonable and equally overworked. If we're wrong, tell us about it—in writing, and in the fewest possible words.

CHAPTER ELEVEN

REVISING FOR CLARITY

CLARITY

We have seen new realities created by the advance of physics. But this chain of creation can be traced back far beyond the starting point of physics. One of the most primitive concepts is that of an object. The concepts of a tree, a horse, any material body, are creations gained on the basis of experience, though the impressions from which they arise are primitive in comparison with the world of physical phenomena. A cat teasing a mouse also creates, by thought, its own primitive reality. The fact that the cat reacts in a similar way toward any mouse it meets shows that it forms concepts and theories which are its guide through its own world of sense impressions.[1]

—Albert Einstein and Leopold Infeld

Skills constitute the manipulative techniques of human goal attainment and control in relation to the physical world, so far as artifacts or machines especially designed as tools do not yet supplement them. Truly human skills are guided by organized and codified *knowledge* of both the things to be manipulated and the human capacities that are used to manipulate them. Such knowledge is an aspect of cultural-level symbolic processes, and, like other aspects to be discussed presently, requires the capacities of the human central nervous system,

---

[1] *The Evolution of Physics* (New York: Simon & Schuster, 1942), pp. 310–11.

particularly the brain. This organic system is clearly essential to all of the symbolic processes; as we well know, the human brain is far superior to the brain of any other species.[2]

—Talcott Parsons

Why is the first passage easier to understand than the second?

Both passages discuss the relationship between the brain and the physical world it attempts to understand. The first passage, by Einstein and Infeld is, if anything, more complex both in what it asserts and in what it suggests than the second, by Parsons. Both passages explain that the brain organizes sense impressions. But Einstein and Infeld further explain that the history of physics can be understood as an extension of the simplest sort of organization, such as we all make in distinguishing a tree from a horse, or such as even a cat makes in teasing a mouse. Parsons only promises that "other aspects" will "be discussed presently." How many of us are eager for those next pages?

Good writing is clear, not because it presents simple ideas, but because it presents ideas in the simplest form the subject permits. A clear analysis doesn't reduce a complex problem to a simple one; it breaks it down into its simple, comprehensible parts and discusses them, one by one, in a logical order. A clear paragraph explains one of these parts coherently, thoroughly, and in language as simple and as particular as the reader's understanding requires and the context allows. Where Parsons writes of "organized and codified *knowledge* of . . . the things to be manipulated," Einstein and Infeld write simply of the concept of an object. And even "object," a simple but general word, is further clarified by the specific, familiar examples, "tree" and "horse." Parsons writes of "the manipulative techniques of . . . goal attainment and control in relation to the physical world, so far as artifacts or machines especially designed as tools do not yet supplement them." Einstein and Infeld show us a cat teasing a mouse.

Notice also the clear organization of Einstein and Infeld's paragraph. The first sentence, clearly transitional, refers to the

---

[2] *Societies: Evolutionary and Comparative Perspectives* (Englewood Cliffs, N.J.: Prentice-Hall, 1966), p. 31.

advance of physics traced in the preceding pages. The next sentence introduced by "But" reverses our direction: we are now going to look not at an advance, but at primitive beginnings. And the following sentences, to the end of the paragraph, fulfill that promise. We move back to primitive human concepts, clarified by examples, and finally to the still more primitive example of the cat. Parsons' paragraph is also organized, but the route is much more difficult to follow.

Why do people write obscurely? Walter Kaufman, in an introduction to Martin Buber's *I and Thou,* says "Men love jargon. It is so palpable, tangible, visible, audible; it makes so obvious what one has learned; it satisfies the craving for results. It is impressive for the uninitiated. It makes one feel that one belongs. Jargon divides men into Us and Them."

Maybe. (For our definition of jargon, see page 195.) Surely some students learn to write obscurely by trying to imitate the style of their teachers or textbooks. The imitation may spring from genuine admiration of these authorities, mixed perhaps with an understandable wish to be one of Us (the authorities) not Them (the dolts). Or students may feel that a string of technical-sounding words is what the teacher expects. If this thought has crossed your mind, we can't say you're entirely wrong. Learning a new discipline often involves acquiring a specialized vocabulary. But we add the following cautions: (1) What teachers expect is that your writing show thought and make sense. They are likely to be frustrated by the question, "Do you want me to use critical terms in this paper?" (2) If you try to use technical terms appropriate to one field when you write about another, you are likely to write nonsense. Don't write "He was paranoid" if you mean only that he was easily offended. (3) When you do write for specialists in a particular field use technical terms precisely. Don't write in an art paper, "I was looking at a print of Van Gogh's 'Sunflowers' " if you mean "I was looking at a reproduction of Van Gogh's 'Sunflowers.' " (4) No matter what you are writing, don't become so enamored of technical words that you can't write a sentence without peppering it with "viable," "interface," "death-symbol," "parameter," "feedback," and so on.

But to return to the question, "Why do people write obscurely?"—we'd like to offer a second answer to Kaufman's

"Men love jargon." It's difficult to write clearly.[3] Authorities may be unintelligible not because they want to tax you with unnecessary difficulties, but because they don't know how to avoid them. In our era, when we sometimes seem to be drowning in a flood of print, few persons who write know how to write well. If you have ever tried to assemble a mechanical toy or to thread an unfamiliar sewing machine by following the "easy instructions," you know that the simplest kind of expository writing, giving instructions, can foil the writers most eager for your good will (that is, those who want you to use their products). Few instructions, unfortunately, are as unambiguous as "Go to jail. Go directly to jail. Do not pass Go. Do not collect $200."

You can, though, learn to write clearly, by learning to recognize common sources of obscurity in writing and by consciously revising your own work. We offer, to begin with, three general rules:

1. Use the simplest, most exact, most specific language your subject allows.
2. Put together what belongs together, in the essay, in the paragraph, and in the sentence.
3. Keep your reader in mind, particularly when you revise.

Now for more specific advice, and examples—the cats and mice of revising for clarity.

CLARITY AND EXACTNESS:
USING THE RIGHT WORD
Denotation

Be sure the word you choose has the right denotation (explicit meaning). Did you mean sarcastic or ironic? Fatalistic or pessimistic? Disinterested or uninterested? Biannual or semiannual? If you're not sure, check the dictionary. You'll find some of the most commonly misused words discussed in Chapter 16. Here are examples of a few others.

---

[3] Our first draft of this sentence read "Writing clearly is difficult." Can you see why we changed it?

Daru faces a dilemma between his humane feelings and his conceptions of justice. (Strictly speaking, a dilemma requires a choice between two equally unattractive alternatives. "Conflict" would be a better word here.)

However, as time dragged on, exercising seemed to lose its charisma. (What is charisma? Why is it inexact here?)

Ms. Wu's research contains many symptoms of depression which became evident during the reading period. (Was Ms. Wu depressed by her research? We hope not. Probably she described or listed the symptoms.)

Connotation

Be sure the word you choose has the right connotation (association, implication).

Boston politics has always upheld the reputation of being especially crooked. ("Upheld" inappropriately suggests that Boston has proudly, maintained its reputation. "Has always had" would be appropriate here, but pale. "Deserved" would, in this context, be ironic, implying—accurately—the writer's scorn.)

Driving down Main Street, I was struck by the peaceful aura of the eighteenth-century white wooden houses, the evenly spaced elms screening them from the traffic. ("Charmed" by a peaceful aura, maybe, or "lulled." But not "struck.")

New Orleans, notorious for its good jazz and good food . . . (Is "notorious" the word here? or "famous?")

Sunday, Feb. 9. Another lingering day at Wellesley. (In this entry from a student's journal, "lingering" strikes us as right. What does "lingering" imply about Sundays at Wellesley that "long" would not?)

Note that many words have social, political, or sexist overtones. We read for example of the "children" of the rich, but the "offspring" of the poor. What is implied by the distinction? Consider the differences in connotation in each of the following series:

1. friend, boyfriend, young man, lover (What age is the speaker?)
2. dine, eat (What was on the menu? Who set the table?)
3. spinster, bachelor (Which term is likely to be considered an insult?)

4. underdeveloped nations, developing nations, emerging nations (Which does your college catalog list a course in?)
5. terrorist, guerrilla, commando, freedom fighter (Where in the Mideast would you place each?)
6. an inaccurate account, an inoperative statement, a lie

Quotation Marks as Apologies

When you have used words with exact meanings (denotations) and appropriate associations (connotations) for your purpose, don't apologize for them by putting quotation marks around them. If the words "copped a plea," "ripped off" or "kids" suit you better than "plea-bargained," "stolen," or "children," use them. If they are inappropriate, don't put them in quotation marks; find the right words.

Being Specific

In writing descriptions, catch the richness, complexity, and uniqueness of things. Suppose, for example, you are describing a scene from your childhood, a setting you loved. There was, in particular, a certain tree . . . And you write: "Near the water there was a big tree that was rather impressive." Most of us would produce something like that sentence. Here is the sentence Ernesto Galarza wrote in *Barrio Boy:*

> On the edge of the pond, at the far side, there was an enormous walnut tree, standing like an open umbrella whose ribs extended halfway across the still water of the pool.[4]

We probably could not have come up with the metaphor of the umbrella because we wouldn't have seen the similarity. (As Aristotle observed, the gift for making metaphors distinguishes the poet from the rest of us.) But we can all train ourselves to be accurate observers and reporters. For "the water" (general) we can *specify* "pond"; for "near" we can say how near, "on the edge of the pond," and add the specific location, "at the far side"; for "tree" we can give the *species*, "walnut tree"; and for "big" we can provide a picture, its branches "extended halfway across" the pond: it was, in fact, "enormous."

[4](New York: Ballantine Books, 1972), p. 10.

Galarza does not need to add, as we did, limply that the tree "was rather impressive." The tree he describes *is* impressive. That he accurately remembered it persuades us that he was impressed, without his having to tell us he was. A good general rule: Show, don't tell. Be as specific as you can be in all forms of exposition too. Take the time, when you revise, to find the exact word to replace vague, woolly phrases or clichés.

vague	The clown's part in *Othello* is very small.
specific	The clown appears in only two scenes in *Othello*.
	The clown in *Othello* speaks only thirty lines.
	(Notice the substitution of the verb "appears" or "speaks" for the frequently debilitating "is." And in place of the weak intensifier "very" we have specific details to tell us how small the role is.)
vague	He feels uncomfortable at the whole situation. (Many feelings are uncomfortable. Which one does he feel? What's the situation?)
specific	He feels guilty for having distrusted his father.
vague	The passage reveals a somewhat calculating aspect behind Antigone's noble motives. ("A somewhat calculating aspect" is vague—and wordy—for "calculation." Or did the writer mean "shrewdness"? What differences in connotation are there between "shrewd" and "calculating"?)
vague	She uses simplicity in her style of writing. (Do we know, exactly, what simplicity in style means?)
specific	She uses familiar words, normal word order, and conversational phrasing.
vague cliché	Then she criticized students for living in an ivory tower. (Did she criticize them for being detached or secluded? For social irresponsibility or studiousness?)
specific	Then she criticized students for being socially irresponsible.

Using Examples

In addition to exact words and specific details, illustrative examples make for clear writing. Einstein and Infeld, in the passage quoted on page 187, use as an example of a primitive concept a cat teasing not only its first mouse, but "any mouse it meets." Here are two paragraphs which clarify their topic sentences through examples; the first is again from *Barrio Boy*.

In Jalco people spoke in two languages—Spanish and with gestures. These signs were made with the face or hands or a combination of both. If you bent one arm and tapped the elbow with the other hand, it meant "He is stingy." When you sawed one arm across the other you were saying that someone you knew played the fiddle terribly. To say that a man was a tippler you made a set of cow's horns with the little finger and the thumb of one hand, bending the three middle fingers to the palm and pointing the thumb at your mouth. And if you wanted to indicate, without saying so for the sake of politeness, that a mutual acquaintance was daffy, you tapped three times on your forehead with your middle finger.[5]

—Ernesto Galarza

In the next paragraph, Northrop Frye, writing about the perception of rhythm, illustrates his point:

Ideally, our literary education should begin, not with prose, but with such things as "this little pig went to market"—with verse rhythm reinforced by physical assault. The infant who gets bounced on somebody's knee to the rhythm of "Ride a cock horse" does not need a footnote telling him that Banbury Cross is twenty miles northeast of Oxford. He does not need the information that "cross" and "horse" make (at least in the pronunciation he is most likely to hear) not a rhyme but an assonance. . . . All he needs is to get bounced.[6]

Frye does not say our literary education should begin with "simple rhymes" or with "verse popular with children." He says "with such things as 'this little pig went to market,' " and then he goes on to add "Ride a cock horse." We know exactly what he means. Notice, too, that we do not need a third example. Be detailed, but know when to stop.

Your reader is likely to be brighter and more demanding than Lady Pliant, who in a seventeenth-century play says to a would-be seducer, "You are very alluring—and say so many fine Things, and nothing is so moving to me as a fine Thing." "Fine

---

[5] P. 19.
[6] *The Well-Tempered Critic* (Bloomington: Indiana University Press, 1963), p. 25.

Things," of course, are what is wanted, but only exact words and apt illustrations will convince an intelligent reader that he is hearing fine things.

Now look at a paragraph from a freshman's essay whose thesis is that rage can be a useful mechanism for effecting change. Compare the paragraph with the same paragraph, revised. Note the specific ways, sentence by sentence, the student revised for clarity.

In my high school we had little say in the learning processes that were used. The subjects that we were required to take were irrelevant. One had to take them to earn enough points to graduate. Some of the teachers were sympathetic to our problem. They would tell us about when they were young, how they tried to oppose their school system. But when they were young it was a long time ago, for most of them. The principal would call assemblies to speak on the subject. They were entitled, "The Value of an Education" or "Get a Good Education to Have a Bright Future." The titles were not inviting. They had nothing to do with our plight. Most students never came to any agreements with the principal because most of his thoughts and views seemed old and outdated.

Here is the revised version:

In my high school we had little say about our curriculum. We were required, for example, to choose either American or European History to earn enough points for graduation. We wanted, but were at first refused, the option of Black History. Some of our teachers were sympathetic with us; one told me about her fight opposing the penmanship course required in her school. Nor was the principal totally indifferent—he called assemblies. I remember one talk he gave called "The Value of an Education in Today's World," and another, "Get a Good Education to Have a Bright Future." I don't recall hearing about a Black History course in either talk. Once, he invited a group of us to meet with him in his office, but we didn't reach any agreement. He solemnly showed us an American History text (not the one we used) that had a whole chapter devoted to Black History.

Jargon and Technical Language

Jargon is the unnecessary, inappropriate, or inexact use of technical or specialized language. Look at this passage:

DODGERS KEEP PERFECT RECORD
IN KNOCKING OUT SOUTHPAWS

NEW YORK (AP)—The Brooklyn Dodgers didn't win the first World Series game yesterday, but they got a measure of comfort in that they maintained one of their season records.

No left-hander went the distance in beating them the past season. Six lefties got the decision but none was around at the end.

New York hurler Whitey Ford made No. 7, but he, too, went the way of the other southpaws . . . empty consolation, to be sure, in view of the Yanks' 6–5 victory in the World Series opener.[7]

Consider the diction of this news story: "went the distance," "lefties," "got the decision," "around at the end," "hurler," "southpaws," "made No. 7." Do you understand the individual words? Most of them, probably. Do you know what the item is about? Some of us do, some don't. Is it written in technical language, or jargon?

The answer depends, as we define jargon, on where the story appeared, and for whom it was intended. Because it appeared on the sports page of a newspaper, we would classify the diction as technical language, not jargon. Properly used, technical language communicates information concisely and clearly, and can, as it does here, create a comfortable bond between reader and writer. Both are having fun. If the same story appeared on the front page of the newspaper, we would classify the language as jargon because it would baffle the general reader.

If the baseball story makes perfect sense to you, try explaining it in nontechnical language to someone to whom it does not. And while you're at it, can you explain why baseball fans are particularly interested in left-handed pitchers—in other words, what makes the statistic here a statistic? Why are baseball fans so interested in statistics anyway—more interested, say, than football or hockey fans? Is it because baseball is intrinsically boring?

Let's move quickly to another example:

For many years Boston parents have tried to improve the public schools. But any input the parents might have desired has been stifled by the Boston School Committee.

[7] *The Michigan Daily*, 29 Sept. 1955, p. 3.

What does "input" mean in this sentence? Is the term used as technical language here, or jargon? (And by the way, how would you go about stifling an input?)

A student wrote the passage just quoted. But recently in Dallas, parents of children in kindergarten through third grade received a twenty-eight page manual written by a professional educator to help them decipher their children's report cards. The title of the manual: *Terminal Behavioral Objectives for Continuous Progression Modules in Early Childhood Education.* Terminal objectives, it seems, means goals. What does the rest mean? If you were one of the parents, would you expect much help from the manual?

Here's a film critic discussing the movie *Last Tango in Paris:*

> The failure of the relationship between Paul and Jeanne is a function of the demands placed on the psyche by bourgeois society, and it is the family as mediator of psychological and social repression which provides the dialectic of Bertolucci's film.[8]

Perhaps some film criticism should be x-rated?

And finally, a deliberate parody. A. P. Herbert in his book *What a Word!* tells us how a social scientist might write a familiar Biblical command:

> In connection with my co-citizens, a general standard of mutual good will and reciprocal non-aggression is obviously incumbent upon me.

What is the command? (See Leviticus xix. 18.)

In general, when you write for nonspecialists, avoid technical terms; if you must use them, define them. If you use a technical term when writing for specialists, be sure you know its precise meaning. But whenever you can, even among specialists, use plain English.

Clichés

Clichés (literally, in French, molds from which type is cast) are trite expressions, mechanically—that is, mindlessly—produced. Since they are available without thought they are great

---

[8] Joan Mellen, *Women and Their Sexuality in the New Film* (New York: Horizon Press, 1974).

Instant Prose Additives (see page 179). Writers who use them are usually surprised to be criticized: they find the phrases attractive, and may even think them exact. (Phrases become clichés precisely because they have wide appeal and therefore wide use.) But clichés, by their very nature, cannot communicate the uniqueness of your thoughts. Furthermore, because they come

"You're right as rain. It's the dawn of history, and there are no clichés as yet. I'll drink to that!"

Drawing by Handelsman; © 1972 *The New Yorker Magazine, Inc.*

instantly to mind, they tend to block the specific detail or exact expression that will let the reader know what precisely is in your mind. When, in revising, you strike out a cliché, you force yourself to do the work of writing clearly. The following examples are full of clichés:

> Finally, the long awaited day arrived. Up bright and early . . .
>
> She peered at me with suspicion; then a faint smile crossed her face.

Other examples:

fatal flaw	short but sweet
budding genius	few and far between
slowly but surely	D-day arrived
little did I know	sigh of relief
the big moment	last but not least

In attempting to avoid clichés, however, don't go to the other extreme of wildly original, super-vivid writing—" 'well then, say something to her,' he roared, his whole countenance gnarled in rage." It's often better to simply say, "he said." (Anyone who intends to write dialogue should memorize Ring Lardner's intentionally funny line, " 'Shut up!' he explained.") Note also that such common expressions as "How are you?" "Please pass the salt," and "So long" are not clichés; they make no claim to be colorful.

Mixed Metaphors

Ordinary speech abounds with metaphors (implied comparisons). We speak or write of the foot of a mountain, the germ (seed) of an idea, the root of a problem. Metaphors so deeply embedded in the language that they no longer evoke pictures in our minds are called *dead metaphors*. Ordinarily, they offer us, as writers, no problems: we need neither seek them nor avoid them; they are simply there. (Notice, for example, "embedded" two sentences back.) Such metaphors become problems when we unwittingly call them back to life. Howard Nemerov observes: "That these metaphors may be not dead but only sleeping, or that they may arise from the grave and walk in our sentences, is something that has troubled everyone who has ever tried to write plain expository prose. . . ."

Dead metaphors are most likely to haunt us when they are embodied in clichés. Since we use clichés without attention to what they literally say or point to, we are unlikely to be aware of the dead metaphors buried in them. But when we attach one cliché to another, we may raise the metaphors from the grave. The result is likely to be a mixed metaphor; the effect is almost always absurd.

> Water seeks its own level whichever way you want to slice it.
>
> Traditional liberal education has run out of gas and educational soup kitchens are moving into the vacuum.
>
> The low ebb has been reached and hopefully it's turned the corner.
>
> Her energy, drained through a stream of red tape, led only to closed doors.
>
> We no longer ask for whom the bell tolls but simply chalk it up as one less mouth to feed.

As Joe E. Lewis observed, "Show me a man who builds castles in the air and I'll show you a crazy architect." Unless you're sure that you've hit on an original and accurate comparison, leave metaphor-making to poets and comedians.

Passive or active voice?

1. I baked the bread. (Active voice)
2. The bread was baked by me. (Passive voice)
3. The bread will be baked. (Passive voice)

Although it is the verb that is in the active or the passive voice, notice that the words "active" and "passive" describe the subjects of the sentences. That is, in the first sentence the verb "baked" is in the active voice; the subject "I" acts. In the second and third sentences the verbs "was baked" and "will be baked" are in the passive voice; the subject "bread" is acted upon. Notice also the following points:

1. The *voice* of the verb is distinct from its *tense*. Don't confuse the passive voice with the past tense. (Compare sentences 2 and 3.)
2. The passive voice uses more words than the active voice. (Compare sentences 1 and 2.)
3. A sentence with a verb in the passive voice may leave the doer of the action unidentified. (See sentence 3.)

Finally, notice that in each of the three sentences the emphasis is different.

In revising, take a good look at each sentence in which you have used the passive voice. If the passive voice clarifies your meaning, retain it; if it obscures your meaning, change it. More often than not, the passive voice obscures meaning.

obscure   The revolver given Daru by the gendarme is left in the desk drawer. (Left by whom? Since the writer was arguing in this paragraph that Daru—in Camus' story "The Guest"—treated his prisoner like a guest, the passive voice here obscures the point.)

clear   Daru leaves the gendarme's revolver in the desk drawer.

obscure   In the Parable of the Prodigal Son, the older son is expected to receive his father's favor. (Read the Parable, pages 34–35. You'll see that a clear analysis must say who expects the older son to receive his father's favor.)

clear   In the Parable of the Prodigal Son, the older son expects to receive his father's favor.
In the Parable of the Prodigal Son, the reader expects the older son to receive his father's favor.

obscure   Daru serves tea and the Arab is offered some. (Confusing shift from the active voice "serves" to the passive voice "is offered")

clear   Daru serves tea and offers the Arab some.

appropriate   For over fifty years *Moby Dick* was neglected. ("Was neglected" suggests that the novel was neglected by almost everyone. The passive voice catches the passivity of the response. Changing the sentence to "For over fifty years few readers read *Moby Dick*" would make "readers" the subject of the sentence, but the true subject is— as in the original—*Moby Dick*.)

Euphemisms

Euphemisms are words substituted for other words thought to be offensive. In deodorant advertisements there are no armpits, only "underarms" which may "perspire," but not sweat, and even then they don't smell. A parent reading a report card is likely to learn not that his child got an F in conduct, but that she "experiences difficulty exercising self-control: (a) verbally (b) physically." And where do old people go? To Sun City, "a retirement community for senior citizens."

Euphemisms are used for two reasons: to avoid giving offense, and, sometimes unconsciously, to disguise fear and animosity. We do not advise you to write or speak discourteously; we do advise you, though, to use euphemisms consciously and sparingly, when tact recommends them. It's customary in a condolence letter to avoid the word death, and, depending both on your own feelings and those of the bereaved, you may wish to follow that custom. But there's no reason on earth to write "Hamlet passes on." You should be aware, however, that some people find euphemisms themselves offensive. There may be more comfort for your friend in "I'm sorry about his death" or even in "too bad about your old lady," than in "I regret to hear of your loss." And speaking of old ladies, there is one in Philadelphia, Margaret Kuhn, who would probably prefer to be called a woman than a lady, and certainly prefers "old" to "senior"—because "Old," she says, "is the right word. . . . I think we should wear our gray hair, wrinkles, and crumbling joints as badges of distinction. After all, we worked damn hard to get them." She has organized a militant group called the Gray Panthers to fight agism.

In revising, replace needless euphemisms with plain words. Your writing will be sharper, and you might, in examining and confronting them, free yourself of a mindless habit, an unconscious prejudice, or an irrational fear.

A Digression on Public Lying

> Mr. Wilson   How do you know that, Mr. Chairman?
> Senator Ervin   Because I can understand the English language. It is my mother tongue.
>
> —From the Senate hearings on Watergate

There is a kind of lying which, in the words of Walker Gibson, we may call *public lying*. Its rules are to avoid substance, direct answers, and plain words. Its tendency is to subvert the English language. It employs and invents euphemisms, but the public liar intends to protect not his listeners, but himself and his friends, and he misleads and deceives consciously. Public lying was not invented during the Vietnam War or the Watergate hearings. (In 1946 George Orwell had already written the definitive essay on it, "Politics and the English Language.") Nor did it cease with the return of American prisoners, or with the resignation of our thirty-seventh president. But the war and the hearings produced some classic examples, from which we select a few.

The war, of course, was not a war, but a "conflict" or an "era" which has been succeeded by "peace." "Our side" never attacked "the other side," we made "protective reaction raids"; we didn't invade, we "incursed." We didn't bomb villages, we "pacified" them; peasants were not herded into concentration

"This is not a stickup."
Drawing by C. Barsotti; © *1974 The New Yorker Magazine, Inc.*

camps, but "relocated." We didn't spray the countryside with poisons, destroying forests, endangering or killing plant, animal, and human life, we "practiced vegetation control."

"In the interests of national security" some buildings and rooms ("the White House," "the Oval Office") hired not burglars but "electronic surveillance experts" who didn't bug, spy, break and enter, or steal, but "performed intelligence-gathering operations"—all according to "a game plan" designed to ensure "deniability."

There is a Gresham's law in rhetoric as there is in economics: bad language drives out good. Bad language is contagious; learn to detect the symptoms: use of vague words for clear words; use of sentences or phrases where words suffice; evasive use of the passive voice; and outright lying.

CLARITY AND COHERENCE

Writing a coherent essay is hard work; it requires mastery of a subject and skill in presenting it; it always takes a lot of time. Writing a coherent paragraph often takes more fussing and patching than you expect, but once you have the hang of it, it's relatively easy and pleasant. Writing a coherent sentence requires only that you stay awake until you get to the end of it. We all do nod sometimes, even over our own prose. But if you make it a practice to read your work over several times, at least once aloud, you give yourself a chance to spot the incoherent sentence before your reader does, and to revise it. Once you see that a sentence is incoherent, it's usually easy to recast it.

Cats Are Dogs

In some sentences a form of the verb *to be* asserts that one thing is in a class with another. Passover is a Jewish holiday. Dartmouth is a college. But would anyone not talking in his sleep say "Dartmouth is a Jewish holiday"? Are cats dogs? Students did write the following sentences:

incoherent   X. J. Kennedy's poem "Nothing in Heaven Functions as it Ought" is a contrast between Heaven and Hell. (As soon as you ask yourself the question "Is a poem a contrast?" you have, by bringing the two words close together, isolated the problem. A poem may be a sonnet, an epic, an ode—but not a contrast. The writer was trying to say what the poem does, not what it is. Substitute the right verb for "is.")

coherent   X. J. Kennedy's poem "Nothing in Heaven Functions as it Ought" contrasts Heaven and Hell.

incoherent   Besides, he tells himself, a matchmaker is an old Jewish custom. (Is a matchmaker a custom?)

coherent   Besides, he tells himself, consulting a matchmaker is an old Jewish custom.

Try revising the following:

The essay is also an insight into imperialism.

In a related problem, one part of the sentence doesn't know what the other is doing:

incoherent   Ruth's devotion to Naomi is rewarded by marrying Boaz. (Can devotion marry Boaz?)

coherent   Ruth's marriage to Boaz rewards her devotion to Naomi.

incoherent   He demonstrates many human frailties, such as the influence of others' opinions upon one's actions. (Is influence a frailty? How might this sentence be revised?)

Modifiers

A modifier should appear close to the word it modifies (that is, describes or qualifies). If it seems to modify the wrong word, it is called *misplaced*. Misplaced modifiers are often unintentionally funny. The judo parlor that advertised "For $20 learn basic methods of protecting yourself from an experienced instructor" probably attracted more amused readers than paying customers. If the modifier is ambiguous, that is, if it can be applied equally to more than one term, it is sometimes called a *squinting* modifier. If the term it should modify appears nowhere in the sentence, the modifier is called *dangling*.

Misplaced Modifiers

misplaced   Orwell shot the elephant under pressured circumstances. (Orwell was under pressure, not the elephant. Put the modifier near what it modifies.)

revised	Orwell, under pressure, shot the elephant.
misplaced	Orwell lost his individual right to protect the elephant as part of the imperialistic system. (The elephant was not part of the system; Orwell was.)
revised	As part of the imperialistic system, Orwell lost his right to protect the elephant.
misplaced	Amos Wilder has been called back to teach at Harvard Divinity School after ten years retirement due to a colleague's illness. (Did Wilder retire for ten years because a colleague was ill? Revise the sentence.)

Sometimes other parts of sentences are misplaced:

misplaced	We learn from the examples of our parents who we are. (The sentence appears to say we are our parents.)
revised	We learn who we are from the examples of our parents.
misplaced	It is up to the students to revise the scheme, not the administrators. (We all know you can't revise administrators. Revise the sentence.)
revised	It is up to the students, not the administrators, to revise the scheme.

Squinting Modifiers

squinting	Being with Jennifer more and more enrages me. (Is the writer spending more time with Jennifer, or is he more enraged? Probably more enraged.)
revised	Being with Jennifer enrages me more and more.
squinting	Writing clearly is difficult. (The sentence may be talking about writing—it's clearly difficult to write—or about writing clearly—it's difficult to write clearly.)
squinting	Students only may use this elevator. (Does "only" modify students? If so, no one else may use the elevator. Or does it modify elevator? If so, students may use no other elevator.)
revised	Only students may use this elevator. Students may use only this elevator.

Note: the word "only" often squints. In general, put "only" immediately before the word or phrase it modifies. Often it appears too early in the sentence. (See page 277.)

Dangling Modifiers

dangling   Being small, his ear scraped against the belt when his father stumbled. (The writer meant that the boy was small, not the ear. But the boy is not in the sentence.)

  revised   Because the boy was small his ear scraped against the belt when his father stumbled.
Being small, the boy scraped his ear against the belt when his father stumbled.

dangling   A meticulously organized person, his suitcase could be tucked under an airplane seat. (How would you revise the sentence?)

The general rule: when you revise sentences, put together what belongs together.

Reference of Pronouns

A pronoun is used in place of a noun. Because the noun usually precedes the pronoun, the noun to which the pronoun refers is called the antecedent (Latin: "going before"). For example; "When *Sheriff Johnson* was on a horse, *he* was a big man." But the noun can follow the pronoun, as in "When *he* was on a horse, *Sheriff Johnson* was a big man."

Be sure that whenever possible a pronoun has a clear reference. Sometimes it isn't possible: "it" is commonly used with an unspecified reference, as in "It's hot today," and "Hurry up please, it's time"; and there can be no reference for interrogative pronouns: "What's bothering you?" and "Who's on first?"

Vague References

  vague   Apparently, they fight physically and it can become rather brutal. ("It" doubtless refers to fight, but fight in this sentence is the verb, not an antecedent noun.)

  clear   Their fights are apparently physical, and sometimes brutal.

  vague   I was born in Colon, the second largest city in the Republic of Panama. Despite this, Colon is still an undeveloped town. (*This* has no specific antecedent. It appears to refer to the writer's having been born in Colon.)

  clear   Although Colon, where I was born, is the second largest city in Panama, it remains undeveloped.
(On "this," see also page 280.)

Try revising the following sentence:

They're only applying to medical school because it's a well-paid profession.

Shift in Pronouns

This common error is easily corrected.

In many instances the child was expected to follow the profession of *your* father. (Expected to follow the profession of whose father, *yours* or *his?*)

Having a tutor, *you* can get constant personal encouragement and advice that will help *me* budget *my* time. (If *you* have a tutor will that help *me?*)

Revise the following sentence:

Schools bring people of the same age together and teach you how to get along with each other.

Ambiguous Reference of Pronouns

A pronoun normally refers to the first appropriate noun or pronoun preceding it. Same-sex pronouns and nouns, like dogs, often get into scraps.

ambiguous	Her mother died when she was eighteen. (Who was eighteen, the mother or the daughter?)
clear	Her mother died when Mabel was eighteen.
	Her mother died at the age of eighteen. (Note the absence of ambiguity in "*His* mother died when he was eighteen.")
ambiguous	Daru learns that he must take an Arab to jail against his will. (This comment on Camus' "The Guest" is confusing. Both Daru and the Arab are male. The writer of the sentence meant that Daru learns *he* must act against *his* will.)
clear	Daru learns that he must, against his will, take an Arab to jail.

The general rule: put together what belongs together.

Repetition and Variation

Don't be afraid to repeat a word if it is the best word. The following paragraph repeats "interesting," "paradox," "Salinger," "What makes," and "book"; notice also "feel" and "feeling." Repetition, a device necessary for continuity and clarity, holds the paragraph together.

The reception given to *Franny and Zooey* in America has illustrated again the interesting paradox of Salinger's reputation there; great public enthusiasm, of the *Time* magazine and Best Seller List kind, accompanied by a repressive coolness in the critical journals. What makes this a paradox is that the book's themes are among the most ambitiously highbrow, and its craftsmanship most uncompromisingly virtuoso. What makes it an interesting one is that those who are most patronising about the book are those who most resemble its characters; people whose ideas and language in their best moments resemble Zooey's. But they feel they ought not to enjoy the book. There is a very strong feeling in American literary circles that Salinger and love of Salinger must be discouraged.[9]

—Martin Green

Use pronouns, when their reference is clear, as substitutes for nouns. Notice Green's use of pronouns; notice also his substitution of "the book," for "*Franny and Zooey*," and then "its" for "the book's." Substitutions which neither confuse nor distract keep a paragraph from sounding like a broken phonograph record.

Avoid the mistake of Elegant Variation. A fear of repetition sometimes leads students to write first, for example, of "Salinger," then of "the writer," then of "our author." Such variations strike the reader as silly. They can, moreover, be confusing: Does "the writer" mean "Salinger," or the person writing about him? Substitute "he" for "Salinger" if "he" is clear and sounds better. Otherwise, repeat "Salinger."

Don't repeat a word if it is being used in two different senses.

confusing	Green's theme focuses on the theme of the book. (The first "theme" means "essay"; the second means "underlying idea" or "motif.")
clear	Green's essay focuses on the theme of the book.
confusing	Caesar's character is complex. The comic characters too have some complexity. (The first "character" means "personality"; the second means "persons" or "figures in the play.")

[9] *Re-appraisals: Some Commonsense Readings in American Literature* (New York: W. W. Norton, 1965), p. 197.

clear Caesar is complex; the comic characters too have some complexity.

Eliminate words repeated unnecessarily. Use of words like "surely," "in all probability," "it is noteworthy" may become habitual. If they don't help your reader to follow your thoughts, they are Instant Prose Additives. Cross them out.

In general, when you revise, decide if a word should be repeated, varied, or eliminated, by testing sentences and paragraphs for both sound and sense.

Euphony

The word is from the Greek, "sweet voice," and though you need not aim at sweetness, try to avoid cacophony, or "harsh voice." Avoid awkward repetitions of sound, as in "The story is marked by a remarkable mystery," and "This is seen in the scene in which . . ." Such echoes call attention to themselves, getting in the way of the points you are making. When you revise, tune out irrelevant sound effects.

Not all sound effects are irrelevant; some contribute meaning. James Baldwin, in his essay "Stranger in the Village," argues that the American racial experience has permanently altered black and white relationships throughout the world. His concluding sentence is, "This world is white no longer, and it will never be white again." As the sentence opens, the repetition of sounds in "*w*orld is *w*hite," binds the two words together, but the idea that they are permanently bound is swiftly denied by the more emphatic repetition of sounds in "*n*o," "*n*ever," "agai*n*," as the sentence closes. Or take another example: "America, Love It or Leave It." If it read "America, Love it or Emigrate," would the bumper sticker still imply, as clearly and menacingly, that there are only two choices, and for the patriot only one?

Transitions

Repetition holds a paragraph together by providing continuity and clarity. Transitions such as "next," "on the other hand," and "therefore" also provide continuity and clarity. Because we discuss transitions at length on pages 68–71, in our chapter on paragraphs, we here only remind you to make certain that the relation between one sentence and the next, and one paragraph and the next, is clear. Often it will be clear without an explicit transition: "He was desperately unhappy. He quit school." But do not take too much for granted; relationships between sentences may not be as clear to the reader as they are to you. You know what you are talking about; he doesn't. After reading the passage the reader may see, in retrospect, that you have just given an example, or a piece of contrary evidence, or an amplification, but readers like to know in advance where they are going; brief transitions such as "for example," "but," "finally" (readers are keenly interested in knowing when they are getting near the end) are enormously helpful.

CLARITY AND SENTENCE STRUCTURE

Make the structure of your sentence reflect the structure of your thought.

When you write you attempt to convey ideas from your mind to another. Sentences are not only your vehicle, but your reader's map; they should not only express your thoughts, but also reflect your arrangement of them, and indicate the direction of your argument. This is not as formidable as it sounds. If you keep your reader in mind, remembering that you are explaining something to someone who understands it less well than you, you will almost automatically not only say what you think but show how you think.

Almost automatically. In revising, read your work as if you were not the writer of it, but your intended reader. If you reach a bump or snag, where the shape of your thought, or the direction of it, isn't clear, revise your sentence structure. Three general rules help:

1. Put main ideas in main (independent) clauses.
2. Subordinate the less important elements in the sentence to the more important.
3. Put parallel ideas in parallel constructions.

The time to consult these rules consciously is not while you write, but while you revise.

The first two rules are amplified in the next chapter, Revising for Emphasis. Clarity and emphasis are closely related, as the following discussion of parallel construction makes evident.

Parallel Construction

Use parallel constructions to clarify relationships—to emphasize similarities, for instance, and to define differences.

> Those who make peaceful revolution impossible will make violent revolution inevitable.
> —John F. Kennedy

> I divorce myself from my feelings and immerse myself in my obligations.
> —From a student journal

> She drew a line between respect, which we were expected to show, and fear, which we were not.[10]
> —Ernesto Galarza

In revising, put parallel ideas in parallel constructions.

awkward
: The dormitory rules needed revision, a smoking area was a necessity, and a generally more active role for the school in social affairs were all significant to her.

parallel
: She recommended that the school revise its dormitory rules, provide a smoking area for girls, and organize more social activities.

awkward
: Most Chinese parents disapprove of interracial dating or they just do not permit it.

parallel
: Most Chinese parents disapprove of interracial dating, and many forbid it.

awkward
: He was aware of the injustices inflicted on the Burmese, recalled in images of wretched prisons and the torture of prisoners.

parellel
: He was aware of the injustices inflicted on the Burmese, recalled in images of wretched prisons and tortured prisoners.

---

[10] *Barrio Boy*, p. 18.

Parallel Forms

In parallel constructions, use parallel forms: check the consistency of articles, prepositions, and conjunctions.

LOVE POEM
Robert Bly

When we are in love, we love the grass,
And the barns, and the lightpoles,
And the small mainstreets abandoned all night.[11]

Suppose we change "Love Poem" by omitting a conjunction or an article here and there:

When we are in love, we love the grass,
Barns, and lightpoles,
And the small mainstreets abandoned all night.

We've changed the rhythm, of course, but what difference does that make? Not much. We still get the point: the lover loves all the world. But in the original poem, the syntax of the sentence, the consistent repetition of "and the . . ." "and the . . ." makes us feel, without our thinking about it, that when we are in love we love the world, everything in it, equally. The list could extend infinitely, and everything in it would give us identical pleasure. In our altered version, we sacrifice this unspoken assurance. We bump a little, and stumble. As readers, without consciously being aware of it, we wonder if there's some distinction being made, some qualification we've missed. We still get the point of the poem, but don't feel it the same way.

To sum up:

A pupil once asked Artur Schnabel [the noted pianist] whether it was better to play in time or to play as one feels; his characteristic mordant reply was another question: "Why not feel in time?" [12]

—David Hamilton

---

[11] "Silence in the Snowy Fields" (Middletown, Conn.: Wesleyan University Press, 1962), p. 41.
[12] *The New Yorker*, 1 April 1974, p. 100.

CHAPTER TWELVE

REVISING FOR EMPHASIS

EMPHASIS

In revising for conciseness and clarity we begin to discover what we were largely unaware of in the early stages of writing: what in our topic most concerns us and precisely why it interests us. That moment of discovery (or several discrete moments) yields more pleasure than any other in writing. From there on we work, sometimes as if inspired, to make our special angle of vision seem as inevitable to our readers as it is to us. Now as we tighten sentences or expand them, as we shift the position of a word or a paragraph, or as we subordinate a less important idea to a more important one, we are assigning relative value and weight to each of our statements. The expression of value and weight is what is meant by emphasis.

AVOIDING FALSE EMPHASIS

Inexperienced writers may *try* to achieve emphasis as Queen Victoria did, by a style consisting *almost entirely* of italics and exclamation marks!!! Or they may spice their prose with clichés ("little did I realize") or with a liberal sprinkling of intensifiers ("really beautiful," "definitely significant," and so on). But these devices, unconvincing to readers, are abandoned by experienced writers. Emphasis is more securely achieved by exploiting the possibilities of position, of brevity and length, of repetition, and of subordination.

Emphasis by Position

First, let us see how a single word may be emphasized. If a word appears in an unusual position it gains emphasis, as in "Admirable is the view from the river." The normal order, of course, would be "The view from the river is admirable." But this device is tricky; a word in an unusual position often seems ludicrous, the writer fatuous.

A word may also be emphasized by being set off. Compare "A glittering eye appeared at the window" with "An eye, glittering, appeared at the window." Again, of course, the word is in an abnormal position, but here it is further emphasized by the pause before and after it. And, again, the device may backfire. Still, as you reread your work, you may see that an important word or phrase should be given this sort of emphasis.

Let us now consider a less strained sort of emphasis by position. The beginning and the end of a sentence or a paragraph are emphatic positions; of these two positions, the end is usually the more emphatic. Here is a sentence that properly moves to an emphatic end:

> Having been ill-treated by Hamlet and having lost her father, Ophelia goes mad.

If the halves are reversed, the sentence peters out:

> Ophelia goes mad because she has been ill-treated by Hamlet and she has lost her father.

Still, even this version is better than the shapeless

> Having been ill-treated by Hamlet, Ophelia goes mad, partly too because she has lost her father.

The important point, that she goes mad, is dissipated in the last version by the lame addition of words about her father. In short, avoid anticlimaxes.

anticlimactic   Besides not owning themselves women also could not own property.

    emphatic   Women could not own property; in fact, they did not own themselves.

In students' writing, the commonest anticlimaxes are weak qualifiers ("in my opinion," "it seems to me," "in general") tacked
on to interesting statements.

anticlimactic   Poodles are smart but they are no smarter than pigs,
I have read.

   emphatic   Poodles are smart, but I have read that they are no
smarter than pigs.

The rule: try to bury dull qualifiers in the middle of the sentence.

Emphasis by Brevity and Length: Short and Long Sentences

How long should a sentence be? One recalls Lincoln's remark
to a heckler who asked him how long a man's legs should be:
"Long enough to reach the ground." No rules about length can
be given, but be careful not to bore your reader with a succession of short sentences (say, under ten words) and be careful
not to tax your reader with a monstrously long sentence. Victor
Hugo's sentence in *Les Misérables* containing 823 words punctuated by ninety-three commas, fifty-one semicolons, and four
dashes, is not a good model for beginners.

Consider this succession of short sentences:

The purpose of the refrain is twofold. First, it divides the song into
stanzas. Second, it reinforces the theme of the song.

These sentences are clear, but since the points are simple the
reader feels he is addressed as though he were a kindergarten
child. There is too much emphasis (too many heavy pauses) on
too little. The reader can take all three sentences at once:

The purpose of the refrain is twofold: it divides the song into
stanzas and it reinforces the theme.

The three simple sentences have been turned into one compound
sentence, allowing the reader to keep going for a while.

Sometimes, however, the choppiness of a succession of short
sentences is effective. Look at this description of the efforts by
which George Jackson, in prison, resisted efforts to destroy his
spirit:

He trains himself to sleep only three hours a night. He studies
Swahili, Chinese, Arabic and Spanish. He does pushups to control

his sexual urge and to train his body. Sometimes he does a thousand a day. He eats only one meal a day. And, always, he is reading and thinking.[1]

—Julius Lester

That the author is capable of writing longer, more complicated sentences is evident in the next paragraph: "Yet, when his contact with the outside world is extended beyond his family to include Angela Davis, Joan, a woman who works with the Soledad defense committee, and his attorney, he is able to find within himself feelings of love and tenderness." Can we account for the success of the passage describing Jackson's prison routine? First, the short sentences, with their repeated commonplace form (subject, verb, object) in some degree imitate their subject: they are almost monotonously disciplined, almost as regular as the pushups the confined Jackson does. Later, when Jackson makes contact with Angela Davis and others, the long sentence helps to suggest the expansion of his world. Second, the brevity of the sentences suggests their enormous importance, certainly to Jackson and to Julius Lester and, Lester hopes, to the reader.

Keep in mind this principle: *any one sentence in your essay is roughly equal to any other sentence.* If a sentence is short, it must be relatively weighty. A lot is packed into a little. Less is more. (The chief exceptions are transitional sentences such as, "Now for the second point.") Consider the following passage:

It happened that in September of 1933 Lord Rutherford, at the British Association meeting, made some remark about atomic energy never becoming real. Leo Szilard was the kind of scientist, perhaps just the kind of good-humored, cranky man, who disliked any statement that contained the word "never," particularly when made by a distinguished colleague. So he set his mind to think about the problem.[2]

—J. Bronowski

The first two sentences are relatively long (twenty-three words and thirty-one words); the third is relatively short (ten words),

---

[1] *New York Times Book Review*, 20 Nov. 1970, pp. 12–14.
[2] *The Ascent of Man* (Boston: Little, Brown, 1974), p. 368.

and its brevity—its weight or density—emphasizes Szilard's no-nonsense attitude.

Emphasis by Repetition

Don't be afraid to repeat a word if it is important. The repetition will add emphasis. Notice in these lucid sentences by Helen Gardner the effective repetition of "end" and "beginning."

Othello has this in common with the tragedy of fortune, that the end in no way blots out from the imagination the glory of the beginning. But the end here does not merely by its darkness throw up into relief the brightness that was. On the contrary, beginning and end chime against each other. In both the value of life and love is affirmed.[3]

The substitution of "conclusion" or "last scene" for the second "end" would be worse than pointless; it would destroy Miss Gardner's point that there is *identity* or correspondence between beginning and end.

Emphasis by Subordination

Before we can discuss the use of subordination for emphasis, we must first talk about what a sentence is, and about five kinds of sentences.

If there is an adequate definition of a sentence, we haven't found it. Perhaps the best definition is not the old one, "a complete thought," but "a word or group of words that the hearer takes to be complete." This definition includes such utterances as "Who?" and "Help!" and "Never!" and "Maybe." These expressions are understood as complete, whereas "I am going to the" cannot possibly be regarded as a complete thought.

Usually a sentence names someone or something (this is the subject) and it tells us something about the subject (this is the predicate); that is, it "predicates" something about the subject. Let us look at five kinds of sentences: simple, compound, complex, compound-complex, and sentence fragments.

[3] *The Noble Moor* (New York: Oxford University Press, 1956), p. 203.

A *simple sentence* has one predicate, here italicized:

Shakespeare *died.*
Shakespeare and Jonson *were contemporaries.*

The subject can be elaborated ("Shakespeare and Jonson, England's chief Renaissance dramatists, were contemporaries"), or the predicate can be elaborated ("Shakespeare and Jonson were contemporaries in the Renaissance England of Queen Elizabeth"); but the sentence remains technically a simple sentence, consisting of only one main (independent) clause with no dependent (subordinate) clause.

A *compound sentence* has two or more main clauses, each containing a subject and a predicate. It is, then, two or more simple sentences connected by a coordinating conjunction (*and, but, for, nor, or, yet*) or by *not only . . . but also* or by a semicolon or colon or, rarely, a comma.

Shakespeare died in 1616, and Jonson died in 1637.
Shakespeare died in 1616; Jonson died twenty-one years later.

A *complex sentence* has one main (independent) clause and one or more subordinate (dependent) clauses. Here the main clause is italicized.

Although Shakespeare died, *England survived.*

Jonson did not write a commemorative poem when Shakespeare died.

The parts not italicized are subordinate or dependent because they cannot stand as sentences by themselves.

A *compound-complex sentence* has two or more main clauses (here italicized) and one or more subordinate clauses.

In 1616 Shakespeare died and *his wife inherited the second-best bed* because he willed it to her.

We will return to subordination, but let us first look at the fifth kind of sentence, the sentence fragment.

A *sentence fragment* does not fit the usual definition of a sentence but the thought is often clear and complete enough. Intentional fragments are common in advertisements:

Made of imported walnut. For your pleasure. At finer stores.

More native than the Limbo. More exciting than the beat of a steel drum. Tia Maria. Jamaica's haunting liqueur.

And yet another example, this one not from an advertisement but from an essay on firewood:

> Piles of it. Right off the sidewalk. Split from small logs of oak or ash or maple. Split. Split again.[4]
> —John McPhee

All these examples strike us as pretentious in their obviously studied efforts at understatement. Words are hoarded, as though there is much in little, and as though to talk more fully would demean the speaker and would desecrate the subject. A few words, and then a profound silence. Here less is not more; it is too much. The trouble with these fragmentary sentences is not that they don't convey complete thoughts but that they attract too much attention to themselves; they turn our minds too emphatically to their writers, and conjure up images of unpleasantly self-satisfied oracles.

Here, however, is a passage, from a student's essay, where the fragmentary sentences seem satisfactory to us:

> The film has been playing to sellout audiences. Even though the acting is inept. Even though the sound is poorly synchronized. Even though the plot is incoherent.

If this passage is successful, isn't it partly successful because the emphasis is controlled? The author is dissatisfied, and by means of sentence fragments she conveys a moderately engaging weariness and a gentle exasperation. And of course we see that if the first three periods were changed to commas we would have an orthodox complex sentence.

Having surveyed the kinds of sentences, we can at last talk about the use of subordination. Subordination often helps to avoid monotony and to attain brevity, but chiefly it helps to give appropriate emphasis.

Make sure that the level of subordination is appropriate to the logical importance of the detail. Make the less important element subordinate to the more important. In the following example the first clause, summarizing the writer's previous sen-

---

[4] "A Reporter at Large (Firewood)," *The New Yorker*, 25 March 1974 p. 81.

tences, is a subordinate or dependent clause; the new material is made emphatic by being put into two independent clauses:

> As soon as the Irish Literary Theatre was assured of a nationalist backing, it started to dissociate itself from any political aim, and the long struggle with the public began.

The second and third clauses in this sentence, linked by "and," are coordinate—that is, of equal importance.

Probably most of the sentences that you read and write are complex sentences: an independent clause and one or more subordinate clauses. Whatever is outside of the independent clause is subordinate, less important. Consider this sentence:

> Aided by Miss Horniman's money, Yeats dreamed of a poetic drama.

The writer puts Yeats's dream in the independent clause, subordinating the relatively unimportant Miss Horniman. Had the writer wished to give Miss Horniman more prominence, the passage might have run:

> Yeats dreamed of a poetic drama, and that dream was subsidized by Miss Horniman.

Here Miss Horniman at least stands in an independent clause, linked to the previous independent clause by *and*. Notice, however, that even in the revision Miss Horniman is less prominent than Yeats because the subject of the second independent clause is still Yeats's dream—"that dream." If the writer had wanted to emphasize her and to diminish Yeats, he might have written:

> While Yeats dreamed of a poetic drama, Miss Horniman provided the means by which the dream might be realized.

In short, though simple sentences and compound sentences have their place, they make everything of equal importance. Since everything is not of equal importance, you must often write complex and compound-complex sentences, subordinating some things to other things.

Having made the point that subordination reduces monotony and conveys appropriate emphasis, we must reiterate that there are times when a succession of simple or compound sentences is effective, as in the passage on pages 216–17 describing George Jackson.

EXERCISE

Here is one way to test your grasp of the relationship of independent and subordinate elements in a sentence. This *haiku* (a Japanese poetic form) consists of one sentence which can be written as prose: "After weeks of watching the roof leak, I fixed it tonight by moving a single board."

HITCH HAIKU
Gary Snyder

After weeks of watching the roof leak
    I fixed it tonight
by moving a single board.[5]

1. Identify the independent clause and the subordinate elements in the poem.

2. The "I" in the poem's sentence does or has done three things. Write three simple sentences, each expressing one of the actions.

3. Write one sentence in which all three of the poem's actions are expressed, but put in the independent clause one of the two actions that appear in a subordinate element in the poem.

4. Compare your sentence with the poem's. Both sentences should be clear. How do they vary in emphasis?

5. Optional: Compare the original sentence written as poetry and written as prose.

[5] *The Back Country* (New York: New Directions, 1968), p. 25.

3. EDITING

No iron can stab the heart
with such force as a period
put just at the right place.

—Isaac Babel

MANUSCRIPT FORM

To edit a manuscript is to refine it for others to read. When your essay at last says what you want to say, you are ready to get it into good physical shape, into an edited manuscript.

SOME REMARKS ABOUT MANUSCRIPT FORM

Basic Manuscript Form

Much of what follows is nothing more than common sense. Unless your instructor specifies something different, you can adopt these principles as a guide.

1. Use 8½-by-11-inch paper of good weight. Keep as lightweight a carbon copy as you wish, but hand in a sturdy original.

2. Write on one side of the page only. If you typewrite, double-space, typing with a reasonably fresh ribbon. If you submit a handwritten copy, use lined paper and write, in ink, on every other line if the lines are closely spaced.

3. Put your name and class or course number in the upper left-hand corner of the first page. It is a good idea to put your name in the upper left corner of each page so the instructor can easily reassemble your essay if somehow a page gets detached in his briefcase.

4. Center the title of your essay about two inches from the top of the first page. Capitalize the first letter of the first and

last words of your title, and capitalize the first letter of all the other words except articles, conjunctions, and prepositions, thus:

```
The Diabolic and Celestial Images in The Scarlet Letter
```

Notice that your title is neither underlined nor enclosed in quotation marks (though of course if, as here, it includes material that would normally be italicized or in quotation marks that material continues to be so written).

5. Begin the essay an inch or two below the title. If your instructor prefers a title page, begin the essay on the next page.

6. Leave an adequate margin—an inch or an inch and a half—at top, bottom, and sides.

7. Number the pages consecutively, using arabic numerals in the upper right-hand corner. A title page is not numbered; the page that follows it is page 1.

8. Fasten the pages of your paper with a paper clip in the upper lefthand corner. Stiff binders are unnecessary; indeed, they are a nuisance to the instructor, adding bulk and making it awkward to write annotations.

Corrections in the Final Copy

Your extensive revisions should have been made in your drafts, but minor last-minute revisions may be made on the finished copy. Proofreading may catch some typographical errors, and you may notice some small weaknesses. For example, you may notice in the final copy an error in agreement between subject and verb, as in "The insistent demands for drastic reform has disappeared from most of the nation's campuses." The subject is "demands" and so the verb should be plural, "have" rather than "has." (The error of making a verb widely separated from its subject agree, incorrectly, with the immediately preceding noun is common, and should be watched for.) You need not retype the page, or even erase. You can make corrections with the following proofreader's symbols.

Changes in wording may be made by crossing through words and rewriting just above them:

```
                                           have
The insistent demands for drastic reform has disappeared from most of

the nation's campuses.
```

Additions should be made above the line, with a caret below the line at the appropriate place:

> The insistent demands for drastic reform have disappeared ⟨*from*⟩ most of the
>
> nation's campuses.

Transpositions of letters may be made thus:

> The insistent dem⟨an⟩ds for drastic reform have disappeared from most of
>
> the nation's campuses.

Deletions are indicated by a horizontal line through the word or words to be deleted. Delete a single letter by drawing a vertical or diagonal line through it.

> The insistent demands for drastic reform ~~reform~~ have disappeared from
>
> most of the nation's campuse/s.

Separation of words accidentally run together is indicated by a vertical line, *closure* by a curved line connecting the things to be closed up.

> The insistent|demands for drastic reform have disappeared f⁀rom most of
>
> the nation's campuses.

Paragraphing may be indicated by the symbol ¶ before the word that is to begin the new paragraph.

> The insistent demands for drastic reform have disappeared from most of
>
> the nation's campuses. ¶Another sign that the country's

QUOTATIONS AND QUOTATION MARKS

Quotations from the material you are writing about are indispensable. They not only let the reader know what you are talking about; they give the reader the material you are responding to, thus letting him share your responses.

Here are some mechanical matters:

1. Distinguish between short and long quotations, and treat each appropriately. Short quotations (usually defined as less than three lines of poetry or five lines of prose) are enclosed within quotation marks and run into the text (rather than set off, without quotation marks).

LeRoi Jones's "Preface to a Twenty Volume Suicide Note" ends with a glimpse of the speaker's daughter peeking into her "clasped hands," either playfully or madly.

Pope's Essay on Criticism begins informally with a contraction, but the couplets nevertheless have an authoritative ring: " 'Tis hard to say, if greater want of skill / Appear in writing or in judging ill."

Notice that in the second example a slash (diagonal line, virgule) is used to indicate the end of a line of verse other than the last line quoted. The slash is, of course, not used if the poetry is set off, indented, and printed as verse, thus:

Pope's Essay on Criticism begins informally with a contraction, but the couplets nevertheless have an authoritative ring:

> 'Tis hard to say, if greater want of skill
> Appear in writing or in judging ill;
> But of the two less dangerous is the offense
> To tire our patience than mislead our sense.

Material that is set off (usually three or more lines of verse, five or more lines of prose) is not enclosed within quotation marks. To set it off, triple-space before and after the quotation and single-space the quotation. (Some manuals of style call for double-spacing, some for indenting prose quotations. But whichever procedure you adopt, be consistent.) Be sparing in your use of long quotations. Use quotations as evidence, not as padding. Do not bore the reader with material that can be effectively reduced either by paraphrase or by cutting. If you cut, indicate ellipses as explained below under 3.

2. The quotation must fit grammatically into your sentence.

incorrect   Near the end of the play Othello says that he "have done the state some service."

correct   Near the end of the play Othello says that he has "done the state some service."

Don't try to introduce a long quotation (say, more than a complete sentence) into the middle of one of your own sentences. It is almost impossible for the reader to come out of the quotation and to pick up the thread of your own sentence. It is better to lead into the long quotation with "Jones says . . . "

and then, after the quotation, to begin a new sentence of your own.

3. The quotation must be exact. Any material that you add must be in square brackets, thus:

> When Pope says that Belinda is "the rival of his [i.e., the sun's] beams," he uses comic hyperbole.
>
> Stephen Dedalus sees the ball as a "greasy leather orb [that] flew like a heavy bird through the grey light."

If you wish to omit material from within a quotation, indicate the ellipsis by three spaced periods. If a sentence ends in an omission, add a closed-up period and then three spaced periods to indicate the omission. The following example is based on a quotation from the sentences immediately above this one:

> The manual says that "if you . . . omit material from within a quotation, you must indicate the ellipsis. . . . If a sentence ends in an omission, add a closed-up period and then three spaced periods. . . ."

Notice that although material preceded "If you," periods are not needed to indicate the omission because "If you" began a sentence in the original. Customarily initial and terminal omissions are indicated only when they are part of the sentence you are quoting. Even such omissions need not be indicated when the quoted material is obviously incomplete—when, for instance, it is a word or phrase. (See the first example in this section, which quotes Pope's phrase "the rival of his beams.") Notice, too, that although quotations must be given word for word, the initial capitalization can be adapted, as here where "If" is reduced to "if."

When a line or more of verse is omitted from a passage that is set off, the three spaced periods are printed on a separate line.

4. Identify the speaker or writer of the quotation, so that the reader is not left with a sense of uncertainty. Usually this identification precedes the quoted material (e.g., "Smith says . . .") in accordance with the principle of letting the reader know where he is going, but occasionally it may follow the quo-

tation, especially if it will provide something of a pleasant surprise. For example, in a discussion of T. S. Eliot's poetry, you might quote a hostile comment on one of the poems and then reveal that Eliot himself was the speaker.

5. Commas and periods go inside of the quotation marks; other marks of punctuation (e.g., semicolons, colons, and dashes) go outside. Question marks and exclamation points go inside if they are part of the quotation, outside if they are your own.

Amanda ironically says to her daughter, "How old are you, Laura?" Is

it possible to fail to hear Laura's weariness in her reply, "Mother,

you know my age"?

6. Use *single* quotation marks for material contained within a quotation that itself is within quotation marks, thus:

T. S. Eliot says, "Mr. Richards observes that 'poetry is capable of

saving us.' "

7. Use quotation marks around titles of short works, that is, for titles of chapters in books and for stories, essays, and poems that might not be published by themselves. Titles of unpublished works, even book-length dissertations, are also enclosed in quotation marks. Use quotation marks also for titles of paintings and statues. But use italics—indicated by underlining—for titles of books, that is, novels, periodicals, collections of essays, and long poems such as *The Rime of the Ancient Mariner* and *Paradise Lost*. Use italics also for film titles and for the names of planes, ships, and trains. An exception is the Bible and the names of books of the Bible, such as Revelation, which are neither italicized nor enclosed within quotation marks. To cite a book of the Bible with chapter and verse, give the name of the book, then a space, then a small roman numeral for the chapter, a period, and an arabic numeral (*not* preceded by a space) for the verse, thus: Exodus xx.14–15. Standard abbreviations for the books of the Bible (for example, "Chron.") are permissible.

FOOTNOTES

Kinds of Footnotes

Footnotes are of two sorts: (1) they may give the sources of quotations, facts, and opinions used; or (2) they may give additional comment that would interrupt the flow of the argument in the body of the paper. This second type perhaps requires amplification. A writer may wish to indicate that he is familiar with an opinion contrary to the one he is offering, but he may not wish to digress upon it during the course of his argument. A footnote lets him refer to it and indicate why he is not considering it. Or a footnote may contain full statistical data that support his point but that would seem unnecessarily detailed and even tedious in the body of the paper.

What to Footnote

Honesty requires that you acknowledge your indebtedness for material, not only when you quote directly from a work, but also when you appropriate an idea that is not common knowledge. Not to acknowledge such borrowing is plagiarism. If in doubt as to whether or not to give credit in a footnote, give credit. But you ought to develop a sense of what is considered common knowledge. Definitions in a dictionary can be considered common knowledge, and so there is no need to say "According to Webster, a novel is . . ." (That's weak in three ways: it's unnecessary, it's uninteresting, and it's unclear, since "Webster" appears in the titles of several dictionaries, some good and some bad.) Similarly, the date of Freud's death can be considered common knowledge. Few can give it when asked, but it can be found out from innumerable sources, and no one need get the credit for providing you with the date. The idea that Hamlet delays is also a matter of common knowledge. But if you are impressed by So-and-so's argument that Claudius has been much maligned, you should give credit to So-and-so. Again, if you simply *know*, from your reading of Freud, that Freud was interested in literature, you need not cite a specific source for an assertion to that effect, but if you know only because some commentator on Freud said so, and you have no idea whether the fact is well-known or not, you should give credit to the source that gave you the information. Not to give credit—for ideas as well as for quoted words—is to plagiarize.

Reducing the Number of Footnotes

Keep the number of footnotes down to an honest minimum, partly by including the documentation within the body of the paper where reasonable and partly by not cluttering up the bottoms of the pages with references to material that is common knowledge. If you give frequent quotations from one book— for example, *Black Elk Speaks* or a play by Shakespeare— specify which edition you are using in the footnote to the first quotation and then mention that all subsequent quotations from the work are from that edition. After each subsequent quotation, put parentheses including the page number or—a more useful procedure when you are quoting plays—act, scene, and line (III.ii.178); if you are quoting from various plays, be sure to include the title of the play in the parentheses. If the quotation is run into the text, close the quotation, give the parenthetic material, and then add the final period.

> The idea that a tragic hero has exhausted all of his life's possibilities is revealed in Macbeth, when Malcolm says, "Macbeth / Is ripe for shaking" (IV.iii.237-38).

> Artists have painted pretty pictures of Custer just before his death, standing gorgeous against the sun, but we have Black Elk's word that "it was all dark and mixed up" (Black Elk Speaks, p. 113).

If the quotation is set off, end the quotation with a period (unless what follows in your essay is a continuation of a sentence, of which the quotation is a part), double-space, and below the last words of the quotation add the parenthetic material. This parenthetic identification, in the body of the paper, does everything that a footnote would do.

The second kind of footnote, which gives additional commentary, should be used sparingly. There are times when supporting details may be appropriately relegated to a footnote, but if the thing is worth saying, it is usually worth saying in the body of the paper. Don't get into the habit of affixing either trivia or miniature essays to the bottom of each page of your essay.

Footnote Numbers and Position

Number the notes consecutively throughout the essay or chapter. Although some instructors allow students to group all of the notes at the rear of the essay, most instructors—

and surely all readers—believe that the best place for a footnote is at the foot of the appropriate page. If in your draft you type all your footnotes, when typing your final copy you can easily gauge how much space the footnotes for any given page will require. Micrometric carbon paper (carbon paper with a protruding margin which bears the line numbers from 64, at the top, down to 1, at the bottom) is a great help.

Footnote Style

The principles discussed here are commonly observed in writing about the humanities. But some of the sciences and social sciences use different principles; it is therefore advisable to ask your instructors if they have strong ideas about footnote style.

To indicate that there is a footnote, put a raised arabic numeral (without a period and without parentheses) after the final punctuation of the sentence, unless clarity requires it earlier. (In a sentence about Albee, Beckett, and Cocteau you may need a footnote for each and a corresponding numeral after each name instead of one at the end of the sentence, but usually a single reference at the end will do. The single footnote might explain that Albee says such and such in his book entitled ————, Beckett says such and such in his book entitled ————, and Cocteau says such and such in his book entitled ————.) At the bottom of the page triple-space before giving the first footnote. Then indent five spaces, raise the typewriter carriage half a line, and type the arabic numeral. Lower the carriage to the regular position and type the footnote, single-spacing it. If it runs more than one line, the subsequent lines are flush with the left margin, but each new note begins with an indentation of five spaces. Each note begins with an indented, raised numeral, then a capital letter, and ends with a period or other terminal punctuation. Double-space between footnotes.

First Reference to a Book

Here is a typical first reference to a book:

[1] Curtis F. Brown, *Ingrid Bergman* (New York: Pyramid, 1973), p. 55.

Notice that you give the author's name as it appears on the
title page, *first name first*. You need not give the subtitle, but
if you give it, put a colon between the title and the subtitle
and underline the subtitle. The name of the city (without the
state or country) is usually enough, but if the city is not well
known, or may be confused with another city of the same
name (Cambridge, England, and Cambridge, Massachusetts) the
state or country is added. The name of the publisher (here,
Pyramid Publications) may be shortened. The conventional
abbreviation for page is "p." and for pages is "pp." (*not* "pg."
and "pgs."). If you give the author's name in the body of the
page—for example, in such a sentence as "Curtis F. Brown says
that Bergman . . ."—do not repeat the name in the footnote.
Merely begin with the title. If the author's name and the title
have both been given in the body ("Curtis F. Brown, in *Ingrid
Bergman,* says . . ."), repeat neither the name nor the title.
Begin with the opening of the parenthesis before the place of
publication, thus:

[1] (New York: Pyramid, 1973), p. 55

For a book in one volume, by one author, revised edition:

[2] X. J. Kennedy, <u>An Introduction to Poetry</u>, 3d ed. (Boston:
Little, Brown, 1974), p. 41.

For a book in one volume, by one author, later reprint:

[3] D. H. Lawrence, <u>Studies in Classic American Literature</u> (1923;
rpt. Garden City, N.Y.: Doubleday, 1953), pp. 87-88.

For a book in more than one volume (notice that the volume
number is given in roman numerals, the page number in arabic
numerals, and abbreviations such as "vol." and "p." are *not*
used):

[4] Frank Freidel, <u>Franklin D. Roosevelt: Launching the New Deal</u>
(Boston: Little, Brown, 1973), IV, 197-201.

For a book by more than one author (if there are too many authors to list, give the full name of the first author and add *et
al.,* the Latin abbreviation for "and others"):

[5] Carl Bernstein and Bob Woodward, <u>All the President's Men</u> (New
York: Simon and Schuster, 1974), pp. 163-72.

For an edited or translated book:

⁶ The <u>Letters</u> of <u>John</u> <u>Keats</u>, <u>1814</u>-<u>1821</u>, ed. Hyder Edward Rollins (Cambridge, Mass.: Harvard Univ. Press, 1958), II, 129.

⁷ Paul Ginestier, <u>The Poet</u> and <u>the Machine</u>, trans. Martin B. Friedman (Chapel Hill: Univ. of North Carolina Press, 1961), p. 28.

⁸ Albert Gilman and Roger Brown, "Personality and Style in Concord," in <u>Transcendentalism</u> and <u>Its Legacy</u>, ed. Myron Simon and Thornton H. Parsons (Ann Arbor: Univ. of Michigan Press, 1966), pp. 103-104.

As note 8 indicates, when you are quoting from an essay in an edited book, you begin with the essayist(s) and the essay, then go on to give the title of the book and the name of the editor(s).

First Reference to a Journal

Footnote 9 is for a journal (here, volume 43) paginated consecutively throughout the year; footnote 10 is for a journal that paginates each issue separately. A journal paginated separately requires the month or week or day as well as the year. Current practice favors omitting the volume number for popular weeklies (see footnote 11) and for newspapers, in which case the full date is given without parentheses.

⁹ John Demos, "The American Family in Past Time," <u>American Scholar</u>, 43 (Summer 1974), 423-24.

¹⁰ Hortense J. Spillers, "Martin Luther King and the Style of the Black Sermon," <u>The Black Scholar</u>, 3, No. 1 (September 1971), 15.

¹¹ Bernard McCabe, "Taking Dickens Seriously," <u>Commonweal</u>, 14 May 1965, p. 245.

The author's name and the title of the article are given as they appear in the journal (*first name first*), the title of the article in quotation marks and the title of the journal underlined (to indicate italics). Until recently the volume number, before the date, was given with capital roman numerals, the page or pages with arabic numerals, but current practice uses arabic numerals for both the volume and the page or pages. Notice that when a volume number is given, as in notes 9 and 10, the page number is *not* preceded by "p." or "pp."

If a *book review* has a title, the review may be treated as an article. If, however, the title is merely that of the book reviewed, or even if the review has a title but for clarity you wish to indicate that it is a review, the following form is commonly used:

[12] N. R. McWilliams, review of Kate Millett, <u>Sexual Politics</u> (Garden City, N.Y.: Doubleday, 1970), <u>Commonweal</u>, 2 Oct. 1970, p. 25.

Subsequent References

If you quote a second or third or fourth time from a work and you do not wish to incorporate the reference within your text, use a short form in your footnote. The most versatile short form is simply the author's last name and the page number, thus:

[13] Lawrence, p. 34.

You can even dispense with the author's name if you have mentioned it in the sentence to which the footnote is keyed. That is, if you have said "Lawrence goes on to say . . . ," the footnote need only be:

[14] P. 34.

If, however, you have made reference to more than one work by the author, you must indicate by a short title which work you are referring to, thus:

[15] Lawrence, <u>Studies</u>, p. 34.

Or, if your sentence mentions that you are quoting Lawrence, the footnote may be:

[16] <u>Studies</u>, p. 34.

If you have said something like "Lawrence, in *Studies in Classic American Literature*, argues . . . ," the reference may be merely:

[17] P. 34.

In short, a subsequent reference should be as brief as clarity allows. The form "ibid." (for *ibidem*, in the same place), indicating that the material being footnoted comes from the same place as the material of the previous footnote, is no longer preferred for second references. "Op. cit." (for *opere citato*, in the work cited) and "loc. cit." (for *loco citato*, in the place cited) have almost disappeared. Identification by author, or by author and short title if necessary, is preferable, with "ibid." used only immediately after such a subsequent reference, and never when it would fall as the first footnote on a page. A reminder: as page 232 suggests, if you are going to quote frequently from one source, it will be best to say in your first reference to this source that subsequent quotations from this work will be indicated by parentheses within the body of the paper.

References to Introductions and to Reprinted Essays

You may want to footnote some material that is printed along with a reprint of a work of literature. If, for example, you use Robert B. Heilman's edition of Shakespeare's *The Taming of the Shrew*, and you say "Robert B. Heilman points out . . . ," your footnote will look like this:

[18] Introd. to William Shakespeare, The Taming of the Shrew (New York: New American Library, 1966), p. xxv.

Heilman's edition of the play includes, as a sort of appendix, several previously published commentaries. If you want to quote from one of them, the monstrous footnote to the quotation might run:

[19] Maynard Mack, "Engagement and Detachment in Shakespeare's Plays," in Essays on Shakespeare and Elizabethan Drama in Honor of Hardin Craig, ed. Richard Hosley (Columbia: Univ. of Missouri Press, 1962), rpt. in William Shakespeare, The Taming of the Shrew, ed. Robert B. Heilman (New York: New American Library, 1966), p. 213.

(You learned from Heilman's credit-note the title, editor, etc., of the book in which Mack's essay originally appeared.)

Secondhand References

If you are quoting, say, Sir Arthur Pickard-Cambridge, but have derived the quotation not from his book, *Dithyramb, Tragedy and Comedy*, but from a book or article that quotes from his book, your footnote should indicate both the place where you found it and (if possible) the place where the original passage appears.

<blockquote>
[20] Sir Arthur Pickard-Cambridge, <u>Dithyramb</u>, <u>Tragedy</u> <u>and</u> <u>Comedy</u> (Oxford: 1927), p. 243, quoted in Katherine Lever, <u>The</u> <u>Art</u> <u>of</u> <u>Greek</u> <u>Comedy</u> (London: Methuen, 1956), p. 57.
</blockquote>

In this example, Lever's book is what you read. If her book had mentioned the publisher of Pickard-Cambridge's book, you would have included that too. Another example, this one from a journal which quoted from Charles Reich's *The Greening of America:*

<blockquote>
[21] Charles A. Reich, <u>The</u> <u>Greening</u> <u>of</u> <u>America</u>, quoted in Carl H. Madden, "The Greening of Economics," <u>Virginia</u> <u>Quarterly</u> <u>Review</u>, 50 (Spring 1974), 161.
</blockquote>

In this example, Madden's article is what you read. If Madden had given the place, publisher, date, and page of Reich's book, you would have included all that material in your footnote; but he didn't, so you give only as much as you can.

Footnoting Interviews, Lectures, Letters

<blockquote>
[22] Interview with Rose Moss, novelist, Wellesley College, Wellesley, Mass., 1 March 1975.
</blockquote>

<blockquote>
[23] Howard Saretta, "Buying College Athletes," lecture delivered at Atlantic College, Hudson, N.Y., 3 March 1975.
</blockquote>

<blockquote>
[24] Information in a letter to the author, from William Takayanagi of Atlantic College, Hudson, N.Y., 28 February 1975.
</blockquote>

BIBLIOGRAPHY

A bibliography is a list of the works cited in the piece of writing or, less often, a list of all of the relevant writing. (There is rarely much point in the second sort; if you haven't made use of a particular book or article, why list it?) Normally a bibliography is given only in a long manuscript such as a research paper or a book, but instructors may require a bibliography even for a short paper if they wish to see at a glance the material that the student has used. In this case, a heading such as "Works Consulted" or "Works Cited" is less pretentious than "Bibliography."

Because a bibliography is arranged alphabetically by author, the author's last name is given first. If a work is by more than one author, it is given under the first author's name; his last name is given first, but the other author's or authors' names follow the normal order of first name first. (See the entry under "Wimsatt" below.) Anonymous works are sometimes grouped at the beginning, arranged alphabetically under the first word of the title (or the second word, if the first word is an article), but the recent tendency has been to list them at the appropriate alphabetical place, giving the initial article, if any, but alphabetizing under the next word. Thus, an anonymous article entitled "A View of Freud" would retain the "A" but would be alphabetized under V.

In addition to giving the last name first, a bibliographic entry differs from a footnote in putting a period after the author's name; in putting a period after the title of a book and after the number of volumes if more than one; and in not enclosing in parentheses the place and date of publication of a book. And, of course, a bibliographic entry does not include page references for books, though it includes the page numbers that an essay in a book or in a journal spans. Begin flush with the left-hand margin; if the entry runs over the line, indent the subsequent lines of the entry five spaces. Double-space between entries. Below are a few samples.

Aries, Philippe. <u>Western Attitudes Toward Death</u>: <u>From the Middle Ages to the Present</u>, trans. Patricia M. Ranum. Baltimore: Johns Hopkins Univ. Press, 1974.

Bush, Douglas. "Wordsworth: A Minority Report," in <u>Wordsworth</u>: <u>Centenary Studies</u>, ed. Gilbert T. Dunklin. Princeton: Princeton Univ. Press, 1951, pp. 3-22.

Frye, Northrop. <u>Fables of Identity</u>: <u>Studies in Poetic Mythology</u>. New York: Harcourt, 1963.

_____. <u>Fools of Time</u>: <u>Studies in Shakespearian Tragedy</u>. Toronto: Univ. of Toronto Press, 1967.

The horizontal line indicates that the author is the same as in the previous item; multiple titles by one author are arranged alphabetically, as here where *Fables* precedes *Fools*.

Gogol, Nikolai. <u>Dead Souls</u>, trans. Andrew MacAndrew. New York: New American Library, 1961.

Lame Deer, John Fire, and Richard Erdoes. <u>Lame Deer</u>: <u>Seeker of Visions</u>: <u>The Life of a Sioux Medicine Man</u>. New York: Simon and Schuster, 1972.

Lang, Andrew. "Ballads," <u>Encyclopaedia</u> <u>Britannica</u>, 11th ed., III, 264-67.

MacCaffrey, Isabel Gamble. Introd. to John Milton, <u>Samson</u> <u>Agonistes</u> <u>and the</u> <u>Shorter</u> <u>Poems</u>. New York: New American Library, 1966.

This last entry suggests that the student made use of the introduction, rather than the main body, of the book; if the body of the book were used, the book would be alphabetized under M for Milton, and the form would resemble that of the next item, with "ed. Isabel Gamble MacCaffrey" following the title.

Pope, Alexander. <u>The</u> <u>Correspondence</u> <u>of</u> <u>Alexander</u> <u>Pope</u>, ed. George Sherburn. 5 vols. Oxford: Clarendon, 1956.

Reynolds, Lloyd G. "Making a Living in China," <u>Yale</u> <u>Review</u>, 53 (June 1974), 481-97.

Valdez, Luis, and Stan Steiner, eds. <u>Aztlan</u>, <u>An</u> <u>Anthology</u> <u>of</u> <u>Mexican</u> <u>American</u> <u>Literature</u>. New York: Knopf, 1972.

This entry is an anthology, edited by Valdez and Steiner; an anthology may be entered under the editor's name or under its title. See below, *Victorian Poetry*.

Vendler, Helen. Review of <u>Essays</u> <u>on</u> <u>Style</u>, ed. Roger Fowler. <u>Essays</u> <u>in</u> <u>Criticism</u>, 16 (1966), 457-63.

<u>Victorian</u> <u>Poetry</u> <u>and</u> <u>Poetics</u>, 2nd ed., ed. Walter E. Houghton and G. Robert Stange. Boston: Houghton Mifflin, 1968.

Wimsatt, W. K., Jr., and Cleanth Brooks. <u>Literary</u> <u>Criticism</u>: <u>A</u> <u>Short</u> <u>History</u>. New York: Knopf, 1957.

CHAPTER FOURTEEN

PUNCTUATION

Speakers can raise or lower the volume or pitch of their voices; they can speak a phrase slowly and distinctly and then (making a parenthetical remark, perhaps) quicken the pace. They can wave their arms, pound a table, or pause meaningfully. But writers, physically isolated from their audience, have only paper and ink to work with. Nevertheless, they can embody some of the tones and gestures of speech—in the patterns of their written sentences, and in the dots, hooks, and dashes of punctuation that clarify those patterns.

Punctuation clarifies, first of all, by removing or reducing ambiguity. Consider the following sentence:

He arrived late for the rehearsal didn't end until midnight.

Almost surely you stumbled in the middle of the sentence, thinking that it was about someone arriving tardily at a rehearsal, and then, since what followed made no sense, you probably went back and mentally added the comma (by pausing) at the necessary place:

He arrived late, for the rehearsal didn't end until midnight.

Punctuation helps to keep the reader on the right path. And the path is your train of thought. If your punctuation is faulty, you unintentionally point the reader off your path and toward dead end streets and quagmires. Let's look at an example.

Once more, with feeling.
Once more with feeling.

Is there a difference between these two sentences or do they have identical meanings? Well, if punctuation is not just ink on paper, the first sentence means something like "Let's do it again, but this time do it with feeling," while the second sentence means "The last performance had feeling, and so let's do it once more, keeping the feeling."

Even when punctuation is not the key to meaning, it usually helps your meaning to get across neatly. Consider the following sentences:

> There are two kinds of feminism—one is the growing struggle of women to understand and change the shape of their lives and the other is a narrow ideology whose adherents are anxious to clear away whatever does not conform to their view.

This is clear enough, but by changing the punctuation it can be sharpened. Because a dash usually indicates an abrupt interruption—it usually precedes a sort of afterthought—a colon would be better. The colon, usually the signal of an amplification of what precedes it, here would suggest that the two classifications are not impromptu thoughts but carefully considered ones. Second, and more important, in the original version the two classifications are run together without any intervening punctuation, but since the point is that the two are utterly different, it is advisable to separate them by inserting a comma or a semicolon, indicating a pause. A comma before "and the other" would do, but probably a semicolon is preferable because it is a heavier pause, thereby making the separation clearer. Here is the sentence, revised:

> There are two kinds of feminism: one is the growing struggle of women to understand and change the shape of their lives; the other is a narrow ideology whose adherents are anxious to clear away whatever does not conform to their view.

The right punctuation enables the reader to move easily through the sentence.

Now, although punctuation helps a reader to move through a sentence, it must be admitted that some of the rules of punctuation do not contribute to meaning or greatly facilitate reading.

For example, in American usage a period never comes immediately after quotation marks; it precedes quotation marks, thus:

He said, "Put the period inside the quotation marks."

If you put the period after the closing quotation mark, the meaning remains the same, but you also are informing your reader that you don't know the relevant convention. Since a misspelled word or a misplaced period often gives the impression of laziness, ignorance, or incompetence, why not generate as little friction as possible by learning the chief conventions.

THE PERIOD

1. Periods are used to mark the ends of sentences (or intentional sentence fragments) other than questions and exclamations.

A sentence normally ends with a period.
He said, "I'll pass."
Yes.
Once more, with feeling.

But a sentence within a sentence is punctuated according to the needs of the longer sentence. Notice, in the following example, that periods are *not* used after "pass" or directly after "said."

"I'll pass," he said (he meant he hoped he would).

If a sentence ends with a quotation, the period goes *inside* the quotation marks unless parenthetic material follows the quotation.

Brutus says, "Antony is but a limb of Caesar."
Brutus says, "Antony is but a limb of Caesar" (*Julius Caesar*, II.i.165).

2. Periods are used with abbreviations of titles and terms of reference:

Dr., Mr., Mrs., Ms.
p., pp. (for "page" and "pages"), i.e., e.g., etc.

But when the capitalized initial letters of the words naming an organization are used in place of the full name, the periods are commonly omitted:

CBS, CORE, IBM, NBA, UCLA, UNICEF, USAF

3. Periods are also used to separate chapter from verse in the Bible.

Genesis iii.2, Mark vi.10

For further details on references to the Bible, see page 230.

THE COLON

The colon has three chief uses: to introduce a list or series of examples; to introduce an amplification of what precedes the colon; and to introduce a quotation (though a quotation can be introduced by other means). A less important use is in the indication of time.

1. The colon may introduce a list or series.

She excelled in sports: swimming, tennis, hockey, gymnastics, and wrestling.

2. As a formal introduction to an amplification, the colon is almost equivalent to "namely," or "that is." What is on one side of the colon more or less equals what is on the other side.

She explained her fondness for wrestling: she did it to shock her parents.

The forces which in China created a central government were absent in Japan: farming had to be on a small scale, there was no need for extensive canal works, and a standing army was not required to protect the country from foreign invaders.

Many of the best of the Civil War photographs must be read as the fossils of earlier events: The caissons with their mud-encrusted wheels, the dead on the field, the empty landscapes, all speak of deeds already past.[1]

—John Szarkowski

Notice in this last example that the writer uses a capital letter after the colon; the usage is acceptable when a complete sentence

[1] *Looking at Photographs* (New York: Museum of Modern Art, 1973), p. 28.

follows the colon, as long as that style is followed consistently throughout a paper. But most students find it easier to use lower-case letters after colons, the prevalent style in writing today.

3. The colon, like the comma, may be used to introduce a quotation; it is more formal than the comma, setting off the quotation to a geater degree.

> The black sculptor Ed Wilson tells his students: "Malcolm X is my brother, Martin Luther King is my brother, Eldridge Cleaver is my brother! But Michelangelo is my grandfather!"[2]
>
> —Albert E. Elsen

4. A colon is used to separate the hour from the minutes when the time is given in figures.

> 9:15, 12:00

Colons (like semicolons) go outside of closing quotation marks.

> "There is no such thing as a free lunch": the truth of these words is confirmed every day.

THE SEMICOLON

Typographically a semicolon is part comma, part period, and it does indeed function as a strong comma or as a weak period. (It can never function as a colon.)

1. As a strong comma, the semicolon can be used as follows:

> Only in countries touching on the Mediterranean has the nude been at home; and even there its meaning was often forgotten.[3]

> In the greatest age of painting, the nude inspired the greatest works; and even when it ceased to be a compulsive subject it held its position as an academic exercise and a demonstration of mastery.

As a strong comma, it can be used to separate a series of phrases or clauses with internal commas.

> He had a car, which he hadn't paid for; a wife, whom he didn't love; and a father, who was unemployed.

---

[2] *Purposes of Art*, 3rd ed. (New York: Holt, Rinehart & Winston, 1972), p. 466.

[3] Review of Kenneth Clark, *The Nude, Times Literary Supplement*, 11 Jan. 1957, p. 10.

But:

He had a car, a wife, and a father.

2. As a weak period, the semicolon joins independent statements that the writer wishes to bring together more closely than a period allows.

He wrote essays, stories, and poems but he wasn't satisfied; he tried to make a film, but the film also displeased him.

All the windows seemed to be in the wrong places; it was a house designed to hold the darkness.[4]
—Sharon R. Curtin

The catacombs were not underground churches where Christians secretly worshiped; they were burial chambers connected by long passages, and they were well known to official Rome.

He never complained; he knew it wouldn't do any good.

With short clauses, such as those in the last example, a comma could be used, but some purists would object.

Use a semicolon also before a conjunctive adverb (that is, a transitional word such as *also, consequently, furthermore, however, moreover, nevertheless, therefore*) connecting independent clauses, and put a comma after the conjunctive adverb.

His hair was black and wavy; however, it was false.

Semicolons (like colons) go outside of closing quotation marks.

He said, "I do"; and he walked away.

THE COMMA

A comma (from a Greek word meaning "to cut") indicates a relatively slight pause within a sentence. If after checking the rules you are still uncertain of whether or not to use a comma in a given sentence, read the sentence aloud and see if it sounds better with or without a pause, and then add or omit the comma. In typing, always follow a comma with a space.

1. Independent clauses (unless short) joined by a coordinating

[4] *Nobody Ever Died of Old Age* (Boston: Little, Brown, 1972), p. 9.

conjunction *(and, or, nor, but, for, yet, still)* take a comma before the conjunction.

> Most students see at least a few football games, and many go to every game of the season.
>
> Most students seem to have an intuitive sense of when to use a comma, but in fact the "intuition" is the result of long training.
>
> He dieted but he continued to gain weight.

In the last example the comma is omitted because the introductory clause is short.

A *run-on sentence* or a *comma splice* results when a comma is mistakenly placed between two independent clauses without a coordinating conjunction. (A period or semicolon is needed.)

> He dieted by eating only oranges, his wife thought it was a bad idea.

But such a construction can be acceptable and effective if the clauses are balanced or contrasted:

> He dieted, he lost weight, he grew careless, he got fat again.

A passage in Churchill's address to the House of Commons, given on 4 June 1940, is famous:

> We shall fight on the beaches, we shall fight on the landing grounds, we shall fight in the fields and in the streets, we shall fight in the hills; we shall never surrender.

As a rule of thumb, don't write run-on sentences unless you are sure that a period or semicolon would introduce too heavy a pause.

2. An introductory subordinate clause or long phrase is usually followed by a comma.

> Having revised his manuscript for the third time, he went to bed.
> In order to demonstrate his point, the instructor stood on his head.

If the introductory subordinate clause or phrase is short, say four words or less, the comma may be omitted, provided no ambiguity results from the omission.

> Having left he soon forgot.

But compare this last example with the following:

> Having left, the instructor soon forgot.

If the comma is omitted, the sentence is misread. Where are commas needed in the following sentences?

Instead of discussing the book he wrote a summary.
When Shakespeare wrote comedies were already popular.
While he ate his poodle would sit by the table.
As we age small things become killers.

3. A subordinate clause or long modifying phrase tacked on as an afterthought is usually preceded by a comma.

I have decided not to be nostalgic about the 1920's, despite the hoopla over *The Great Gatsby*.

Buster Keaton fell down a flight of stairs without busting, thereby gaining his nickname from Harry Houdini.

By the end of 1973 Hank Aaron had 713 home runs, only one less than Babe Ruth's record.

With afterthoughts, the comma may be omitted if there is a clear sequence of cause and effect, signaled by *because, for, so,* etc. Compare the two following examples:

In 1601 Shakespeare wrote *Hamlet*, probably his best-known play.
In 1601 Shakespeare wrote *Hamlet* because revenge tragedy was in demand.

4. A pair of commas can serve as a pair of unobtrusive parentheses. Be sure not to omit the first comma.

Doctors, I think, have an insufficient knowledge of acupuncture.

The earliest known paintings of Christ, dating from the third century, are found in the catacombs outside of Rome.

Medicare and Medicaid, the chief sources of federal support for patients in nursing homes, are frequently confused.

Under this heading we can include sentences in which conjunctive adverbs (such as *also, besides, consequently, however, likewise, nevertheless, therefore*) link a statement to a previous one. These transition words are set off between a pair of commas.

His hair, however, was stringy.

When these words begin a sentence, the comma is optional. Notice that the presence of such a word as "however" is not always a safeguard against a comma fault; if the word occurs between two independent clauses, you need a semicolon before it and a comma after it.

His hair was black and wavy; however, it was false.

5. Use a comma to set off a nonrestrictive modifier. A nonrestrictive modifier, as the following examples will make clear, is a sort of parenthetical addition; it gives supplementary information but it can be omitted without changing the subject. A restrictive modifier, however, is not supplementary but essential; if a restrictive modifier is omitted, the subject becomes much larger. In Dorothy Parker's celebrated poem "Men seldom make passes At girls who wear glasses,"[5] "who wear glasses" is a restrictive modifier, narrowing or restricting the subject down from "girls" to a particular group of girls. Here is a nonrestrictive modifier:

> For the majority of immigrants, who have no knowledge of English, language is the chief problem.

Now a restrictive modifier:

> For the majority of immigrants who have no knowledge of English, language is the chief problem.

The first version says—in addition to its obvious message that language is the chief problem—that the majority of immigrants have no knowledge of English. The second version makes no such assertion; it talks not about the majority of immigrants but only about a more restricted group—those immigrants who have no knowledge of English.

Other examples:

> Shakespeare's shortest tragedy, *Macbeth*, is one of his greatest plays.

In this sentence, "*Macbeth*" is nonrestrictive because the subject is already as restricted as possible; Shakespeare can have written only one "shortest tragedy." But compare

> Shakespeare's tragedy *Macbeth* is one of his greatest plays.

with the misleadingly punctuated sentence,

> Shakespeare's tragedy, *Macbeth*, is one of his greatest plays.

The first of these is restrictive, narrowing or restricting the subject "tragedy" down to one particular tragedy, and so it rightly

[5] "News Item," in *Not So Deep as a Well* (New York: Viking Press, 1936), p. 70.

does not separate the modifier from the subject by a comma. The second, punctuated so that it is nonrestrictive, falsely implies that *Macbeth* is Shakespeare's only tragedy. Here is an example of a nonrestrictive modifier correctly punctuated:

> Women, who constitute 51.3 percent of the population and 53 percent of the electorate, constitute only 2.5 percent of the House of Representatives and 1 percent of the Senate.

6. Use a comma to set off direct discourse.

> "It's a total failure," he said.
> He said, "It's a total failure."

But do not use a comma for indirect discourse.

> He said that it is a total failure.
> He said it is a total failure.

7. Words, phrases, and clauses in series take a comma after each item, though the comma between the last two items may be omitted if there is no ambiguity.

> Photography is a matter of eyes, intuition, and intellect.[6]
> —John Szarkowski

> He wrote plays, poems, and stories.
> He wrote plays, sang songs, and danced jigs.
> He wrote a wise, witty, humane book.

But adjectives in a series may cause difficulty. The next two examples correctly omit the commas.

> a funny silent film
> a famous French professor

In each of these last two examples, the adjective immediately before the noun forms with the noun a compound that is modified by the earlier adjective. That is, the adjectives are not a coordinate series (what is funny is not simply a film but a silent film, what is famous is not simply a professor but a French professor) and so commas are not used. Compare:

> a famous French professor
> a famous, arrogant French professor

[6] *Looking at Photographs*, p. 84.

In the second example, only "famous" and "arrogant" form a coordinate series. If in doubt, see if you can replace the commas with "and"; if you can, the commas are correct. In the example given, you could insert "and" between "famous" and "arrogant," but not between "famous" and "French."

Commas are not needed if all the members of the series are connected by conjunctions.

He ate steak for breakfast and lunch and supper.

8. Use a comma to set off "yes" and "no."

Yes, he could take Freshman English at ten o'clock.

9. Use a comma to set off words of address.

Look, Bill, take Freshman English at ten o'clock.

10. Use a comma to separate a geographical location within another geographical location.

He was born in Brooklyn, New York, in 1895.

11. Use a comma to set off the year from the month or day.

He was born on June 10, 1957. (No comma is needed if you use the form "10 June 1957.")

12. Use a comma to separate a name from degree or titles that follow it.

He signed all his letters with John Smith, Ph.D.

If a comma is required with parenthetic material, it follows the parenthesis.

Because Japan was secure from invasion (even the Mongols were beaten back), her history is unusually self-contained.

The only time a comma may precede a parenthesis is when parentheses surround a digit or letter used to enumerate a series.

Questions usually fall into one of three categories: (1) true-false, (2) multiple choice, (3) essay.

A comma always goes inside of closing quotation marks unless the quotation is followed by a parenthesis.

"Sayonara," he said.
"Sayonara" (Japanese for goodbye), he said.

THE DASH

A dash—made by typing two hyphens, with no space before, between, or after—indicates an abrupt break or pause. Overuse of the dash gives writing an unpleasantly explosive quality.

1. The material within dashes may be, in a sense, parenthetic, though the dashes indicate that it is less dispensable than is parenthetic material.

The bathroom—that private place—has rarely been the subject of scholarly study.

The Great Wall of China forms a continuous line over 1400 miles long—the distance from New York to Kansas City—running from Peking to the edge of the mountains of Central Asia.

The old try to survive by cutting corners—eating less, giving up small pleasures like tobacco and movies, doing without warm clothes—and pay the price of ill-health and a shortened life-span.[7]
—Sharon R. Curtin

Notice that when two dashes are used, if the material within them is deleted the remainder still forms a grammatical sentence.

2. A dash can serve, somewhat like a colon, as a pause before a series. It is more casual than a colon.

The earliest Shinto holy places were natural objects—trees, boulders, mountains, islands.

Each of the brothers had his distinct comic style—Groucho's double-talk, Chico's artfully stupid malapropisms, Harpo's horseplay.[8]
—Gerald Mast

Especially in this last example, where the series is elaborated, a colon could have been used, but it would have been more formal; here the dash is more appropriate to the subject.

A dash is never used next to a comma or a period. When used with closing quotation marks it goes inside if it is part of the quotation, outside if it is not.

[7] *Nobody Ever Died of Old Age*, p. 55.
[8] *The Comic Mind* (Indianapolis, Ind.: Bobbs-Merrill, 1973), p. 282.

PARENTHESES

1. Parentheses subordinate material; what is in parentheses is almost a casual aside, less essential than similar material set off in commas, less vigorously spoken than similar material set off in dashes.

> While guest curator for the Whitney (he has since returned to the Denver Art Museum), Feder assembled a magnificent collection of masks, totems, paintings, clothing, and beadwork.

Two cautions: avoid an abundance of these interruptions, and avoid a long parenthesis within a sentence (you are now reading a simple example of this annoying but common habit of writers who have trouble sticking to the point) because the reader will lose track of the main sentence.

2. Use parentheses to enclose digits or letters in a list that is given in running text.

> The exhibition included (1) decorative screens, (2) ceramics, (3) ink paintings, (4) kimonos.

3. Do not confuse parentheses with square brackets, which are used around material you add to a quotation. See page 229.

4. For the use of parentheses in footnotes, see pages 234–37.

The example under rule number 2, of parentheses enclosing digits or letters in a list given in running text, is the rare exception to the rule that within a sentence, punctuation other than quotation marks never immediately precedes an opening parenthesis. Notice that in the example under rule number 1, the comma which normally would have followed "Whitney" had there not been a parenthesis follows instead the closing parenthesis. If an entire sentence is in parentheses, put the final punctuation (period, question mark, or exclamation mark) inside the closing parenthesis.

QUOTATION MARKS

1. Use quotation marks to attribute words to a speaker or writer. (Long quotations that are set off do not take quotation marks. See page 228.) If your quotation includes a passage that was enclosed in quotation marks, alter these inner quotation marks to single quotation marks.

According to Professor Hugo, "The male dragon in Chinese art has deep-set eyes, the female has bulging eyes, but as one Chinese scholar put it, 'This is a matter of interest only to dragons.' "

British quotation marks are just the reverse: single for ordinary quotations, double for inner quotations. If you are setting off a long passage that includes such quotation marks, change them to the American form.

2. Use quotation marks to indicate the title of a painting or a statue or a written work that is less than book-length—for example, an essay, chapter, short story, or poem of less than, say, twenty pages. Titles of book-length works, such as long poems, novels, plays, movies, are underlined, indicating italics. Names of ships, planes, and trains are also italicized.

3. Use quotation marks to identify a word or term to which you wish to call special attention. (But italics, indicated by underlining, may be used instead of quotation marks.)

By "comedy" I mean not only a funny play, but any play that ends happily.

4. Do *not* use quotation marks to enclose slang or a term that you fear is low; use the term or don't use it, but don't hedge by putting it in quotation marks, as in these examples.

"Streaking" was first popularized by Lady Godiva.
Because of "red tape" it took three years.
At last I was able to "land" a good job.

In all three of these sentences the writer is signaling his uneasiness; in neither the first nor the second is there any cause for uneasiness, but probably the third should be rewritten to get rid of the cliché.

Be sparing, too, in using quotation marks to convey sarcasm, as in

These "poets" are mere dispensers of fantasies.

Sarcasm is usually a poor form of argument, best avoided. But of course there are borderline cases when you many want to convey your dissatisfaction with a word used by others.

African sculpture has a long continuous tradition, but this tradition has been jeopardized recently by the introduction of "civilization" to Africa.

Perhaps the quotation marks here are acceptable, because the writer's distaste has not yet become a sneer and because he is, in effect, quoting. But why not change "civilization" to "western culture," omitting the quotation marks?

Commas and periods go inside closing quotation marks except when the quotation marks are followed by parentheses, in which case they follow the closing parenthesis. Colons, semicolons, and footnote numbers go outside of the closing quotation marks. Question marks and exclamation points go inside if they are part of the quotation, outside if they are not.

> While Thelma Todd rows the canoe, Groucho listens to her chatter, looks at a duck swimming near the canoe, and asks, "Did that come out of you or the duck?"

> What is funny about Groucho saying, "Whatever it is, I'm against it"?

ITALICS

Italic type is indicated by underlining.

1. Use italics for the names of planes, ships, and trains, and for the titles of book-length works: plays, long poems, movies, magazines, and all other books except the Bible and books of the Bible. But essays, short poems, short stories, chapters, and titles of paintings and statues are given in quotation marks.

2. As suggested on page 214, use italics only sparingly for emphasis. Sometimes, however, this method of indicating your tone of voice is exactly right.

> In 1911 Jacques Henri Lartigue was not merely as unprejudiced as a child; he *was* a child.[9]
> —John Szarkowski

3. Use italics for foreign words that have not become a part of the English language.

> Acupuncture aims to affect the *ch'i,* a sort of vital spirit which circulates through the bodily organs.

---

[9] *Looking at Photographs,* p. 66.

But:

> He ate a pizza.
> She behaved like a prima donna.
> Avoid clichés.

4. You may use italics in place of quotation marks to identify a word or term to which you wish to call special attention.

> Claude Lévi-Strauss tells us that one of the great purposes of art is that of *miniaturization*. He points out that most works of art are miniatures, being smaller (and therefore more easily understood) than the objects they represent.

CAPITAL LETTERS

Certain obvious conventions—the use of a capital for the first word in a sentence, for proper nouns, and for words derived from proper nouns (such as pro-French)—need not be discussed here.

1. Titles of works in English are usually given according to the following formula. Use a capital for the first letter of the first word, for the first letter of the last word, and for the first letter of all other words that are not articles, conjunctions, or prepositions. The article preceding the name of a newspaper or a magazine, however, is not capitalized unless, of course, it is the first word of your sentence.

> *The Merchant of Venice*
> *A Midsummer Night's Dream*
> *Up and Out*
> "The Short Happy Life of Francis Macomber"
> the *New York Times*

2. Use a capital for a quoted sentence within a sentence, but not for a quoted phrase (unless it is at the beginning of the sentence) and not for indirect discourse.

> He said, "You can even fool some of the people all of the time."
> He said you can fool some people "all of the time."
> He said that you can even fool some of the people all of the time.

3. Use a capital for a rank or title preceding a proper name or for a title substituting for a proper name.

She said she was Dr. Perez.
He told President Ford that the Vice President was away.

But:

Why would anyone wish to be president?
Washington was the first president.

4. Use a capital when the noun designating a family relationship is used as a substitute for a proper noun.

If Mother is busy, ask Tim.
Because my mother was busy, I asked Tim.

5. Formal geographical locations (but not mere points on the compass) are capitalized.

North America, Southeast Asia, the Far East

In the Southwest, rain sometimes evaporates before touching the ground.
The wind came from the north.
Czechoslovakia is adjoined on the north by East Germany.

Do *not* capitalize the names of the seasons.

THE HYPHEN

The hyphen has five uses, all drawing on the etymology of the word *hyphen*, which comes from the Greek for "in one," "together."

1. Use a hyphen to divide certain prefixes from root words. *All-* and *ex-* and *self-* are the most common of these ("all-powerful," "ex-wife," "self-made"), but note that even these prefixes are not always followed by a hyphen. If in doubt, check a dictionary. Prefixes before proper names are always followed by a hyphen:

anti-Semite, pro-Roosevelt, un-American

Prefixes ending in *i* are hyphenated before a word beginning with *i*:

anti-intellectual, semi-intelligible

A hyphen is normally used to break up a triple consonant resulting from the addition of a prefix:

ill-lit, all-loving

2. Use a hyphen to tie compound adjectives into a single visual unit:

out-of-date theory, twenty-three books, long-term loan
eighteenth- and nineteenth-century novels

The sea-tossed raft was a common nineteenth-century symbol of man's tragic condition.

But if a compound modifier follows the modified term, it is usually not hyphenated, thus:

The theory was out of date.

3. Use a hyphen to join some compound nouns:

Scholar-teacher, philosopher-poet

4. Use a hyphen to divide a word at the end of a line. Because words may be divided only as indicated by a dictionary, it is easier to end the line with the last complete word you can type than to keep reaching for a dictionary. But here are some principles governing the division of words at the end of a line:

a. Never hyphenate words of one syllable, such as "called," "doubt," "right," "through."
b. Never hyphenate so that a single letter stands alone—"a-bout," "hair-y."
c. If a word already has a hyphen, divide it at the hyphen: anti-intellectual, semi-intelligible
d. Divide prefixes and suffixes from the root: mis-spell, pro-vide, drunken-ness, walk-ing
e. Divide between syllables. If you aren't sure of the proper syllabification, check a dictionary.

5. Use a hyphen to indicate a span of dates or page numbers.

1957-79, pp. 162-68

THE APOSTROPHE

Use an apostrophe to indicate the possessive, to indicate a contraction, and for certain unusual plurals.

1. The possessive. The most common way to indicate the possessive of a singular noun is to add an apostrophe and then an *s*.

a dog's life, a week's work
a mouse's tail, Keats's poems

But many authorities suggest that for a proper noun of more than one syllable which ends in s or another sibilant (-cks, -x, -z), it is better to add only an apostrophe:

Jesus' parables, Sophocles' plays, Chavez' ideas

When in doubt, say the name aloud and notice if you are adding an s. If you are adding an s when you say it, add an apostrophe and an s when you write it.

Pronouns do not take an apostrophe.

his book, its fur ("it's fur" is short for "it is fur")
The book is hers, not ours.
The book is theirs.

For plurals ending in s, add only an apostrophe to indicate the possessive:

the boys' father, the Smiths' house, the Joneses' car

If the plural does not end in s, add an apostrophe and an s.

women's clothing, mice's eyes

Don't try to form the possessive of the title of a work (for example, of a play, a book, or a film): Write "the imagery in *The Merchant of Venice*" rather than "*The Merchant of Venice's* imagery." Using an apostrophe gets you into the problem of whether or not to italicize the s; similarly, if you use an apostrophe for a work normally enclosed in quotation marks, you can't put the apostrophe and the s after the quotation marks, but you can't put them inside either. And the work really can't possess anything anyway—the imagery, or whatever else, is the author's.

2. Contractions. Use an apostrophe to indicate the omitted letters or numbers in contractions.

She won't.
It's time to go.
the class of '79

3. Unusual plurals. Use an apostrophe to make plurals of words that do not usually have a plural, and to make the plurals of digits and letters.

His speech was full of if's and and's and but's.
Ph.D.'s don't know everything.
Mind your p's and q's.
I got two A's and two B's.
He makes his 4's in two ways.
the 1920's

But if the number is written out, it does not take an apostrophe:

In the envelope were two tens and two fives.
She is in her twenties.

ABBREVIATIONS

In general, avoid abbreviations except in footnotes and except for certain common ones listed below. Abundant use of abbreviations makes an essay sound like a series of newspaper headlines. Usually "United States" is better than "U.S." and "the Soviet Union" better than "U.S.S.R."

1. Abbreviations, with the first letter capitalized, are used before a name.

Dr. Bellini, Ms. Smith, St. Thomas

But:

The doctor took her temperature and ten dollars.

2. Degrees that follow a name are abbreviated:

B.A., D.D.S., M.D., Ph.D.

3. Other acceptable abbreviations include:

A.D., B.C., a.m., p.m., e.g., i.e.

(By the way, "i.e." means "that is"; "e.g." means "for example." The two ought not to be confused. See pages 274 and 272.)

4. The name of an agency or institution (for instance, the Committee on Racial Equality; International Business Machines; Southern Methodist University) may be abbreviated by using the initial letters, capitalized and usually without periods (e.g., "CORE"), but it is advisable to give the name in full when first mentioning it (not everyone knows that "AARP" means "American Association of Retired Persons," for instance), and to use the abbreviation in subsequent references.

NUMBERS

1. Write them out if they are less than three words; otherwise, use figures.

sixteen, seventy-two, ten thousand
10,200; 10,200,000

Always write out round millions and billions, to avoid a string of zeroes.

a hundred and ten million

Some handbooks say that because a figure cannot be capitalized, if a number begins a sentence it should always be written out.

2. Use figures in dates, addresses, decimals, percentages, page numbers, and hours followed by "a.m." or "p.m."

February 29, 1900; .06 percent; 6 percent; 8:16 a.m.

But hours unmodified by minutes are usually written out, and followed by "o'clock."

Executions in England regularly took place at eight o'clock.

3. To make the plural of figures (but not of numbers written out) use an apostrophe.

three 6's, two tens

Use an apostrophe to indicate omitted figures.

class of '79

But use a hyphen to indicate a span.

1975-79, pp. 162-68

CHAPTER FIFTEEN

SPELLING

Life would be easier if a sound were always represented by the same letter. Some modern European languages come close to this principle, but English is not among them. This is not the place to explain why English spelling is so erratic, but it may be consoling to know that the trouble goes back at least to the Norman French Conquest of England in 1066; after the Conquest, French scribes spelled English words more or less as though the words were French. Moreover, though pronunciation kept changing, spelling became relatively fixed, so that even in Shakespeare's time spelling often reflected a pronunciation that had long been abandoned. And today the spelling of many words still reflects the long-lost medieval pronunciation. The silent *e* in *life*, and the silent consonants in *knight* and *through*, for example, were pronounced in Chaucer's day.

But medieval pronunciation accounts for only some of our spellings. There are many other reasons for the oddities: the *b* in *debt* is there, for example, only because scholars mistakenly thought the word came into English through the Latin *debitum*. Most rules for spelling, then, must immediately be modified with lists of exceptions. Even the most famous,

I before *e* except after *c*
Or when sounded as *a*
In *neighbor* and *sleigh*,

has more exceptions than cheery handbooks admit. Always *ei* after *c*? What about *ancient, efficient,* and *sufficient*? Oh, but in these words the *c* is pronounced *sh,* an easy enough exception to keep in mind. But how can we explain *financier*? And of words where a *c* does not precede the letters in question, does the rule *ie* really govern all those not "sounded as *a* / In *neighbor* and *sleigh*"? How about *either, neither, leisure, seize, sheik, weird*?

Instead of offering rules with menacing lists of exceptions, we offer a single list of words commonly misspelled in college writing. And here are three suggestions:

1. Read the list, mark any words whose spelling surprises you, and make a conscientious effort to memorize them.
2. Keep a dictionary at hand, and consult it while you are editing your work.
3. Make a list of words you misspell, and write them over and over until the correct spellings become automatic.

abridgment
absence
accessible
accidentally
accommodate
achievement
acknowledgment
acquire
across
actually
address
adjacent
adolescence
adolescent
advice (noun)
advise (verb)
aggravate
aggressive
aging
alcohol
allege
all right
a lot
already

alter (to change)
altogether
analysis
analyze
apparent
appreciate
arctic
argument
assassin
assistance
assistant
athlete
attendance
balloon
beggar
beginner
believe
bourgeois
bourgeoisie
Britain
bureau
bureaucracy
burglar
business

calendar
capital (noun: seat
    of government,
    money; adjective:
    chief)
capitol (building)
category
ceiling
cemetery
changeable
chief
choose (distinguish
    from past
    tense, chose)
chosen
commit
committee
comparative
competent
complement (noun:
    that which com-
    pletes; verb: to
    complete)
compliment (praise)

conferred
congratulate
conscience
conscious
consistent
controlled
controversy
coolly
corollary
counterfeit
criticism
curiosity
deceive
decision
defendant
definite
deity
dependent
description
desirable
despair
desperate
develop
development
dilemma
disappear
disappoint
disastrous
divide
divine
eighth
embarrass
envelop (verb)
envelope (noun)
environment
equipped
equivalent
especially
essence
exaggerate
exceed
excellence
excellent
exhilarate

existence
experience
explanation
familiar
fascinate
fiend
fiery
foreign
foreword (preface)
forty
fourth
friend
gauge
genealogy
goddess
government
grammar
grievance
guarantee
height
heroes
hoping
hypocrisy
imagination
immediately
impel
incidentally
incredible
independence
independent
indispensable
insistence
insistent
intelligent
interest
interpretation
interrupt
irrelevant
irresistible
judgment
led (past tense of
    "to lead")
leisure
license

loneliness
loose (adjective)
lose (verb)
losing
maneuver
marriage
mathematics
medicine
misspell
necessary
necessity
niece
ninety
noticeable
occasion
occasionally
occur
occurred
omit
omitted
original
parallel
pastime
peaceable
performance
permanent
persistent
playwright
possession
practically
precede
predominant
preferred
prejudice
prevalent
principal (adjec-
    tive: foremost;
    noun: chief)
principle (noun:
    rule)
privilege
probably
procedure
proceed

prominent
prophecy (noun)
prophesy (verb)
pursue
quantity
realize
really
receipt
receiving
recommend
referring
relevance
relevant
relieve
remembrance
repentance
repetition
resistance
rhyme
rhythm
sacrifice

secretary
seize
sense
separate
shining
shriek
siege
similar
solely
specimen
sponsor
stationary (still)
stationery (paper)
strength
subtlety
subtly
succeed
supersede
surprise
syllable
temperament

tendency
theories
therefore
thorough
tragedy
transferred
tried
truly
unnecessary
useful
usually
various
vengeance
villain
weird
wholly
who's (who is)
whose (possessive
  pronoun)
withhold
writing

CHAPTER SIXTEEN

USAGE

Some things are said or written and some are not. More precisely, anything can be said or written, but only some things are acceptable to the ears and minds of many readers. "I don't know nothing about it" has been said and will be said again, but many readers who encounter this expression might judge the speaker as uneducated—and immediately tune out.

Although such a double negative today is not acceptable, it used to be: Chaucer's courteous Knight never spoke no baseness, and Shakespeare's courtly Mercutio, in *Romeo and Juliet*, "will not budge for no man." But things have changed; what was acceptable in the Middle Ages and the Renaissance (for example, emptying chamber pots into the gutter) is not always acceptable now. And some of what was once unacceptable has become acceptable. At the beginning of the twentieth century, grammarians suggested that one cannot use "drive" in speaking of a car; one drives (forces into motion) an ox, or even a person ("He drove her to distraction") but not a machine. Some seventy years of usage, however, have erased all objections.

This chapter presents a list of expressions that, although commonly used, still set many teeth on edge. Seventy years from now some of these expressions may be as acceptable as "drive a car"; but we are writing for today, and we might as well try to hold today's readers by following today's taste. If our essays are thoughtful, they will provide enough challenges to the reader; we should not arouse additional antagonism by using constructions that will allow the reader to brush us off as ignoramuses.

You may not be familiar with some of the abuses in the following list; if so, our citing them will not instruct you, but may entertain you.

a, an Either is acceptable before an initial *h* that is pronounced (for example, in *hundred*), but *an* may sound affected, and so it is better to use *a*, as in "a hamburger." Before a silent *h*, always use *an*, as in "an hour."

above Try to avoid writing "for the above reasons," "in view of the above," "as above," etc. These expressions sound unpleasantly legalistic. Substitute *therefore* or some such word.

academics The only acceptable meanings of this word are "members of an institution of higher learning," and "persons who are academic in background or outlook." Avoid using it to mean "academic subjects," as in "A student should pay attention not only to academics but also to recreation."

accept, except *Accept* means "to receive with consent." *Except* means "to exclude" or "excluding."

affect, effect *Affect* is usually a verb, meaning (1) "to influence, to produce an effect, to impress," (2) "to pretend, to put on," as in "He affected an English accent." Psychologists use it as a noun for "feeling," e.g., "The patient experienced no affect." *Effect*, as a verb, means "to bring about" ("The workers effected the rescue in less than an hour"). As a noun, *effect* means "result" ("The effect was negligible").

aggravate "To worsen, to increase for the worse," as in "Smoking aggravated the irritation." Although it is widely used to mean "annoy" ("He aggravated me") many readers are annoyed by such a use.

all ready, already *All ready* means "everything is ready." *Already* means "by this time."

all right, alright The first of these is the preferable spelling; for some readers the first is the only acceptable spelling.

allusion, illusion An allusion is an implied or indirect reference. "As Lincoln says" is a reference to Lincoln, but a phrase quoted from the Gettysburg Address constitutes an allusion to Lincoln. The student who, in a demonstration at Berkeley, carried a placard saying "I am a human being—please do not fold, spindle, or mutilate," referred to himself and alluded to a computer card. *Allusion* has nothing to do with *illusion* (a deception). Note the spelling (especially the second *i*) in *disillusioned* (left without illusions, disenchanted).

a lot Two words (not *alot*).

amount, number *Amount* refers to bulk or quantity: "A small amount of gas was still in the tank." Use *number*, not *amount*, to refer to separate (countable) units: "A large number of people heard the lecture" (not "a large amount of people"). Similarly, "an amount of money," but "a number of dollars."

analyzation Unacceptable; use *analysis*.

and/or Acceptable, but a legalism and unpleasant-sounding. Often *or* by itself will do, as in "students who know Latin or Italian." When *or* is not enough ("The script was written by Groucho and/or Harpo") it is better to recast ("The script was written by Groucho or Harpo, or both").

ante, anti *Ante* means "before" (*antebellum*, "before the Civil War"); *anti* means "against" (*antivivisectionist*). Hyphenate *anti* before capitals (*anti-Semitism*) and before *i* (*anti-intellectual*).

anthology, collection Because an anthology is a collection of writings by several authors, one cannot speak of "an anthology of poems by Robert Frost"; one can speak of a "collection of poems by Robert Frost."

a number of Requires a plural verb: "A number of women are presidents of corporations." But when *number* is preceded by *the* it requires a singular verb: "The number of women who are presidents is small." (The plural noun after *number* of course may require a plural verb, but *the number* itself remains singular.)

anxious Best reserved for uses that suggest anxiety ("He was anxious before the examination"), though some authorities now accept it in the sense of "eager" ("He was anxious to serve the community").

anybody An indefinite pronoun, written as one word; if two words (*any body*), you mean any corpse ("Several people died in the fire, but the police cannot identify any body").

any more Written as two words.

anyone One word, unless you mean "any one thing," as in "Here are three books; you may take any one."

area of Like *field of* and *topic of* (the field of literature, the topic of politics), *area of* can usually be deleted. "The area of literature" equals "literature."

around Avoid using *around* in place of *about:* "He wrote it in about three hours."

as, like *As* is a conjunction; use it in forming comparisons, to introduce clauses:

You can learn to write, as you can learn to swim.
Huck speaks the truth as he sees it.
He is as tall as I.

In "He is as tall as I," notice that the verb "am" is implied and that the pronoun "I" is its subject:

He is as tall as I (am).

As can also introduce a clause in which both the verb and the subject are implied. Notice that the following two sentences mean different things (the words in parentheses are implied).

Rose distrusts him as much as I (do).
Rose distrusts him as much as (she distrusts) me.

Like is a preposition; use it to introduce prepositional phrases:

He looks like me.
Like Hamlet, Laertes too has lost a father.
She thinks like a lawyer.

Writers who are fearful of incorrectly using *like* resort to cumbersome evasions: "He eats in the same manner that a pig eats." But there's nothing wrong with "He eats like a pig."

as of now Best deleted, or replaced by *now*. Not "As of now I don't smoke" but "Now I don't smoke" or "I don't smoke now" or "I don't smoke."

aspect Literally, "a view from a particular point," but it has come to mean "topic," as in "There are several aspects to be considered." Try to get a sharper word; for example, "There are several problems to be considered," or "There are several consequences to be considered."

as such Often meaningless, as in "Tragedy as such evokes pity."

as to Usually *about* is preferable. Not "I know nothing as to the charges," but "I know nothing about the charges."

beside, besides *Beside* means "at the side of." Because *besides* can mean either "in addition to" or "other than," it is ambiguous. Conservative readers hold that "Something besides TB caused his death" means something in addition to TB (not merely other than TB); it is best, then, to use *in addition to* or *other than*.

between Only English teachers who have had a course in Middle English are likely to know that it comes from *by twain*. And only English teachers and editors are likely to object to its use (and to call for *among*) when more than two are concerned, as in "among the three of us."

Between, a preposition, takes an object ("between you and me"); only people who mistakenly think that *me* is vulgar say "between you and I."

biannually, bimonthly, biweekly Every two years, every two months, every two weeks (*not* twice a year, etc.). Twice a year is *semiannually*. Because *biannually*, *bimonthly*, and *biweekly* are commonly misunderstood, it is best to avoid them and to say "every two . . ."

Black, black Although one sometimes sees the word capitalized when it refers to race, most publishers use a lower case letter, making it consistent with *white*, which is never capitalized.

compare, contrast To compare is to note likenesses or differences: "Compare a motorcycle with a bicycle." To contrast is to emphasize differences.

complement, compliment *Complement* as a noun means "that which completes; as a verb, "to fill out, to complete." *Compliment* as a noun is an expression of praise; as a verb it means "to offer praise."

comprise "To include, contain, consist of": "The university comprises two colleges and a medical school" (not "is comprised of"). Conservative authorities hold that "to be comprised of" is always incorrect.

concept Should often be deleted. For "The concept of the sales tax is regressive" write "The sales tax is regressive."

continual, continuous Conservative authorities hold that *continuous* means "uninterrupted," as in "It rained continuously for six hours"; *continually* means "repeated often, recurring at short intervals," as in "For a year he continually wrote letters to her."

criteria Plural of *criterion*, hence it is always incorrect to speak of "a criteria."

data Plural of *datum*. Although some social scientists speak of "this data," "these data" is preferable: "These data are puzzling." Because the singular, *datum*, is rare and sounds odd, it is best to substitute *fact* or *figure* for *datum*.

definitely Omit this word as an intensifier. See pages 179–80.

different from Prefer it to *different than*, unless you are convinced that in a specific sentence *different from* sounds terribly wrong, as in "These two books are more different than I had expected." (In this example, *more*, not *different*, governs *than*.)

dilemma A situation requiring a choice between equally undesirable alternatives; not every difficulty or plight or predicament is a dilemma. Not "Her dilemma was that she had nowhere to go," but "Her dilemma was whether to go out or to stay home: one was frightening, the other was embarrassing." And note the spelling (two *m*'s, no *n*).

disinterested Though the word is often used to mean "indifferent," "unconcerned," "uninterested," reserve it to mean "impartial": "A judge should be disinterested."

due to Some people, holding that *due to* cannot modify a verb, tolerate it only when it modifies a noun or pronoun ("His failure was due to illness") and insist that it cannot begin a sentence ("Due to illness, he failed"). In fact, however, daily usage accepts both. But because it almost always sounds stiff, try to substitute *because of*, or *through*.

due to the fact that Wordy for *because*.

each Although many authorities hold that *each*, as a subject, is singular, even when followed by *them* ("Each of them is satisfactory") some authorities accept and even favor the plural ("Each of them are satisfactory"). When *each* is in apposition with a plural subject, the verb must be plural: "They each have a book"; "We each are trying." *Each* has no genitive form; you cannot say "Each's opinion is acceptable."

effect See *affect*.

e.g. Abbreviation for *exempli gratia*, meaning "for example." It is thus different from *i.e.* (an abbreviation for *id est*, meaning "that is"). E.g. (not italicized) introduces an example; i.e. (also not italicized) introduces a definition. Because these two abbreviations of Latin words are often confused, it may be preferable to avoid them and use their English equivalents.

enthuse Objectionable to many readers. For "He enthused," say "He was enthusiastic." Use *enthuse* only in the sense of "to be excessively enthusiastic," "to gush."

et cetera, etc. Latin for "and other things"; if you mean "and other people," you need *et al.*, short for *et alii*. Because *etc.* is vague, its use is usually inadvisable. Not "He studied mathematics, etc." but "He studied mathematics, history, economics, and French." Or, if the list is long, cut it by saying something a little more informative than *etc.*—for example, "He studied mathematics, history, and other liberal arts subjects." Confine *etc.* (and most other abbreviations, including *et al.*) to footnotes, and even in footnotes try to avoid it.

everybody, everyone These take a singular verb ("Everybody is here"), and a pronoun referring to them is usually singular ("Everybody thinks his problems are suitable topics of conversation"), but use a plural pronoun if the singular would seem unnatural ("Everybody was there, weren't they?").

exists Often unnecessary and a sign of wordiness. Not "The problem that exists here is" but "The problem here is."

expound Usually pretentious for *explain* or *say*. To expound is to give a methodical explanation, especially of theological or philosophical matters.

facet Literally "little face," especially one of the surfaces of a gem. Don't use it (and don't use *aspect* or *factor* either) to mean "part" or "topic." It is most acceptable when, close to its literal meaning, it suggests a new appearance, as when a gem is turned: "Another facet appears when we see this law from the taxpayer's point of view."

factor Strictly speaking, a factor helps to produce a result, but students commonly use it in the sense of "point": "Another factor to be studied is . . ." Used with the sense of "point" it usually sounds pretentious and dull: "The possibility of plagiarism is a factor that must be considered" simply adds

up to "The possibility of plagiarism must be considered."
Factor is almost never the precise word: "the factors behind
Gatsby's actions" are, more precisely, "Gatsby's motives."

farther, further Some purists claim that *farther* always refers to
distance and *further* to time ("The gymnasium is farther than
the library"; "Let us think further about this"). But many
people substitute *further* for *farther:* "I walked further than
that."

fatalistic, pessimistic *Fatalistic* means "characterized by the belief that all events are predetermined and therefore inevitable"; *pessimistic,* "characterized by the belief that the world
is evil," or, less gloomily, "expecting the worst."

fewer, less See *less.*

field of See *area of.*

firstly, secondly Acceptable, but it is better to use *first, second.*

former, latter These words are acceptable but often cumbersome,
because they force the reader to reread earlier material in
order to locate what *the former* and *the latter* refer to. The
expressions are legitimately used in order to avoid repeating
lengthy terms. If you are talking about an easily repeated
subject, however—say, Lincoln and Nixon—don't hesitate to
replace *the former* and *the latter* with their names. The repetition will clarify rather than bore.

his or her Legally the male pronoun in most legislation includes
females, thus making unnecessary the awkward *his or her.*
But in other writing the implicit male chauvinism of *his* may
be more offensive than the awkwardness of *his or her.* Do
what you can to avoid the dilemma. Sometimes you can use
the plural *their:* "Students are expected to hand in their
papers on Monday" (instead of "The student is expected to
hand in his or her paper on Monday"). Or eliminate the possessive: "The student must hand in a paper on Monday."

hopefully Commonly used to mean "I hope" or "It is hoped"
("Hopefully, the rain will stop soon"), but it is best to avoid
what some consider a dangling modifier. Confine it to its
adverbial use, meaning "in a hopeful manner": "Hopefully
he uttered a prayer."

however It is preferable not to begin a sentence with *however*
unless it is an adverb meaning "to whatever extent or degree,"
as in "However hard he studied, he couldn't remember ir-

regular verbs." When *however* is a conjunctive adverb, put it later in the sentence, between commas: "He failed the examination, however, and didn't graduate." (Not "However, he failed the examination and didn't graduate." If you want to begin a sentence with a sharp contrast, use *but* or *nevertheless*. Note too that you cannot link independent clauses with a *however* preceded by a comma; you need a semicolon ("He tried; however, he failed"). Even here, however, *but* is usually preferable, without a semicolon.

i.e. Latin for *id est*, "that is." The English words are preferable to the Latin abbreviation. On the distinction between *i.e.* and *e.g.*, see *e.g.*

immanent, imminent *Immanent*, "remaining within, intrinsic"; *imminent*, "likely to occur soon, impending."

imply, infer The writer or speaker implies (suggests); the perceiver infers (draws a conclusion): "Karl Marx implied that . . . but his modern disciples infer from his writings that *;* . ." Although *infer* is widely used for *imply*, preserve the distinction.

individual Avoid using the word to mean only "person": "He was a generous individual." But it is precise when it implicitly makes a contrast with a group: "In a money-mad society, he was a generous individual; "Although the faculty did not take a stand on this issue, faculty members as individuals spoke out."

in regard to, with regard to Often wordy for *about, concerning,* or *on,* and sometimes even these words are unnecessary. Compare: "He knew a great deal in regard to jazz"; "He knew a great deal about jazz." Compare: "Hemingway's story is often misunderstood with regard to Robert Wilson's treatment of Margot Macomber"; "In Hemingway's story, Robert Wilson's treatment of Margot Macomber is often misunderstood."

instances Instead of *in many instances* use *often*. Strictly speaking an instance is not an object or incident in itself but one offered as an example. Thus "another instance of his failure to do his duty" (not "In three instances he failed to do his duty").

irregardless Unacceptable; use *regardless*.

it is Usually this expression needlessly delays the subject: "It is unlikely that many students will attend the lecture" could just as well be "Few students are likely to attend the lecture."

its, it's The first is a possessive pronoun ("The flock lost its leader"); the second is a contraction of *it is* ("It's a wise father that knows his child").

kind of Singular, as in "This kind of motorcycle is expensive." If you are really talking about more than one kind, use *kinds* and be sure the demonstrative pronoun and the verb are plural: "These kinds of motorcycles are expensive."

latter See under *former*.

lay, lie *To lay* means "to put, to set, to cause to rest." It takes an object: "May I lay the coats on the table?" The past tense and the participle are *laid*: "I laid the coats on the table"; "I have laid the coats on the table." *To lie* means "to recline," and it does not take an object: "When I am tired I lie down." The past tense is *lay*, the participle is *lain*: "Yesterday I lay down"; "I have lain down hundreds of times without wishing to get up."

lend, loan The usual verb is *lend*: "Lend me a pen." The past tense and the participle are both *lent*. *Loan* is a noun: "This isn't a gift, it's a loan." But, curiously, *loan* as a verb is acceptable in past forms: "I loaned him my bicycle." In its present form ("I often loan money") it is used chiefly by bankers.

less, fewer *Less* (as an adjective) refers to bulk amounts (also called mass nouns): less milk, less money, less time. *Fewer* refers to separate (countable) items: fewer glasses of milk, fewer dollars, fewer hours.

like, as See under *as*.

literally It means "strictly in accord with the primary meaning; not metaphorically." It is not a mere intensive. "He was literally dead" means that he was a corpse; if he was merely exhausted, *literally* won't do. You cannot be "literally stewed" (except by cannibals),, "literally tickled pink," or "literally head over heels in love."

majority Usually singular ("the majority rules") but if followed by a plural noun a plural verb is acceptable: "An overwhelming majority of congressmen have kept their opinions to themselves."

me The right word in such expressions as "between you and me" and "They gave it to John and me." It is the object of verbs and of prepositions. In fact, *me* rather than *I* is the usual form after any verb, including the verb *to be*; "It is me" is nothing to be ashamed of.

medium, media *Medium* is singular, *media* is plural: "TV is the medium to which most children are most exposed. Other media include film, radio, and publishing." It follows, then, that *mass media* takes a plural verb: "The mass media exert an enormous influence."

most Although it is acceptable in speech to say "most everyone," "most anybody," it is preferable in writing to use "almost everyone," "almost anybody." But of course: "Most students passed."

nature You can usually delete "the nature of," as in "The nature of my contribution is not political but psychological."

needless to say The reader may well wonder why you go on to say it. Of course this expression is used to let the reader know that he is probably familiar with what comes next, but usually *of course* will better serve as this sign.

Negro Capitalized, whether a noun or an adjective, though *white* is not. In recent years *Negro* has been replaced by *black*.

nobody, no one, none *Nobody* and *no one* are singular, requiring a singular verb ("Nobody believes this," "No one knows"); but they can be referred to by a plural pronoun: "Nobody believes this, do they?" "No one knows, do they?" *None*, though it comes from *no one*, almost always requires a plural verb when it refers to people ("Of the ten people present, none are freshmen") and a singular verb when it refers to things ("Of the five assigned books, none is worth reading").

not . . . un- Such an expression as "not unfamiliar" is useful only if it conveys something different from the affirmative. Compare the frostiness of "I am not unfamiliar with your methods" with "I am familiar with your methods." If the negative has no evident advantage, use the affirmative. See pages 184–85.

notorious Widely and unfavorably known; not merely famous, but famous for some discreditable trait or deed.

of Be careful not to use it when *have* is required. Not "He might of died in the woods," but "He might have died in the woods." Note that what we often hear as "would've" or "should've" is "would have" or "should have," *not* "would of" or "should of."

off of Use *off* or *from*: "Take it off the table"; "He jumped from the bridge."

one British usage accepts the shift from *one* to *he* in "One begins to die the moment he is born," but American usage prefers "One begins to die the moment one is born." A shift from *one* to *you* ("One begins to dies the moment you are born") is unacceptable. As a pronoun, *one* can be useful in impersonal statements, but don't use it as a disguise for yourself ("One objects to Smith's argument"). Try to avoid *one;* one *one* usually leads to another, resulting in a sentence that, in James Thurber's words, "sounds like a trombone solo"[1] ("If one takes oneself too seriously, one begins to . . .").

one of Takes a plural noun, and if this is followed by a clause, the preferred verb is plural: "one of those students who are," "one of those who feel." In such an expression as "one out of a hundred," the following verb may be singular or plural ("One out of a hundred is," "One out of a hundred are").

only Be careful where you put it. The classic textbook example points out that in the sentence "I hit him in the eye," *only* can be inserted in seven places (beginning in front of *I* and ending after *eye*) with at least six different meanings. Try to put it just before the expression it qualifies. Thus, not "Presidential aides are only responsible to one man," but "Presidential aides are responsible to only one man" (or "to one man only"). See page 206.

per Usually it sounds needlessly technical ("twice per hour") or disturbingly impersonal ("as per your request"). Preferable: "twice an hour," "according to your request" (or "as you requested," "in accordance with your request").

per se Latin for "by itself." Usually sounds legalistic or pedantic, as in "Meter per se has an effect."

pessimistic See *fatalistic*.

phase Often used to mean "appearance" or "stage," but unnecessary and vague. Strictly, a phase is one of the recurring appearances of something that goes through a cycle of changes in appearance; try to preserve that meaning.

---

[1] *The Owl in the Attic* (New York: Harper & Bros., 1931), p. 122.

phenomenon, phenomena The plural is *phenomena;* thus, "these phenomena" but "this phenomenon."

plus Unattractive and imprecise as a noun ("His experience was a plus") and equally unattractive as a substitute for *moreover* ("The examination was easy, plus I had studied") or as a substitute for *and* ("I studied the introduction plus the first chapter").

politics Preferably singular ("Ethnic politics has been a strong force for a century") but a plural verb is acceptable.

preventative, preventive Both are acceptable but the second form is the form now used by writers on medicine ("preventive medicine"); *preventative* therefore has come to seem amateurish.

protagonist Literally, the first actor, and, by extension, the chief actor. It is odd, therefore, to speak of "the protagonists" in a single literary work or occurrence. Note also that the prefix is *proto*, "first," not the prefix *pro*, "for"; it does *not* mean one who strives for something.

quite Usually a word to delete, along with *definitely, pretty, rather,* and *very.* See pages 179–80. *Quite* used to mean "completely" ("I quite understand") but it has come also to mean "to a considerable degree," and so it is ambiguous as well as vague.

quotation, quote The first is a noun, the second a verb. "I will quote Churchill" is fine, but not "these quotes from Churchill" And remember, you may quote one of Hamlet's speeches, but Hamlet does not quote them; he says them.

rather Avoid use with strong adjectives. "Rather intelligent" makes sense, but "rather tremendous" does not. "Rather brilliant" probably means "bright"; "rather terrifying" probably means "frightening," "rather unique" probably means "unusual." Get the right adjective, not *rather* and the wrong adjective.

sarcasm Heavy, malicious sneering ("Oh, you're really a great friend, aren't you?" addressed to someone who won't lend the speaker ten dollars). If the apparent praise, which really communicates dispraise, is at all clever, conveying, say, a delicate mockery or wryness, it is irony, not sarcasm. The passages by Szarkowski on pages 287–88 are ironic, not sarcastic.

seem Properly it suggests a suspicion that appearances may be deceptive: "He seems honest (but . . .)." Don't say "The book seems to lack focus" if you believe it does lack focus.

shall, will, should, would The old principle held that in the first person *shall* is the future indicative of *to be* and *should* the conditional ("I shall go," "We should like to be asked"); and that *will* and *would* are the forms for the second and third persons. When the forms are reversed ("I will go," "Government of the people . . . shall not perish from the earth"), determination is expressed. But today almost nobody adheres to these principles. Indeed, *shall* (except in questions) sounds stilted to many ears.

simplistic Means "falsely simplified by ignoring complications." Do not confuse it with *simplified*, whose meanings include "reduced to essentials" and "clarified."

since Traditional objections to *since*, in the sense of "because," have all but vanished. Note, however, that when *since* is ambiguous and may also refer to time ("Since he joined the navy, she found another boyfriend") it is better to say *because* or *after*.

split infinitives The infinitive is the verb form that merely names the action, without indicating when or by whom performed ("walk," rather than "walked" or "I walk"). Grammarians, however, developed the idea that the infinitive was "to walk," and they held that one cannot separate or split the two words: "to quickly walk." But James Thurber says this idea is "of a piece with the sentimental and outworn notion that it is always wrong to strike a lady."[2] Notice, however, that often the inserted word can be deleted ("to really understand is "to understand"), and that if many words are inserted between *to* and the verb, the reader may get lost ("to quickly and in the remaining few pages before examining the next question conclude").

stanza See under *verse*.

that, which, who Many pages have been written on these words; opinions differ, but you will offend no one if you observe the following principles. (1) Use *that* in restrictive (that is, limiting) clauses: "The rocking chair that creaks is on the porch." (2) Use *which* in non-restrictive (in effect, paren-

[2] *The Owl in the Attic*, p. 110.

thetic) clauses: "The rocking chair, which creaks, is on the porch." (See pages 249–50.) The difference between these two sentences is this: in the first, one rocking chair is singled out from several—the one that creaks; in the second, the fact that the rocking chair creaks is simply tossed in, and is not added for the purpose of identifying the one chair out of several. (3) Use *who* for people, in restrictive and in nonrestrictive clauses: "The men who were playing poker ignored the women"; "The men, who were playing poker, ignored the women." But note that often *that, which,* and *who* can be omitted: "The creaky rocking chair is on the porch"; "The men, playing poker, ignored the women." In general, omit these words if the sentence remains clear. See pages 185–86.

the fact that Usually wordy. "Because of the fact that boys played female roles in Elizabethan drama" can be reduced to "because boys played female roles in Elizabethan drama."

the idea that Usually dull and wordy. Not "The idea that we grow old is frightening," but "That we grow old is frightening," or (probably better) "Growing old is frightening."

the reason . . . is because Usually *because* is enough (not "The reason they fail is because they don't study," but simply "They fail because they don't study"). Similarly, *the reason why* can usually be reduced to *why*. Notice, too, that because *reason* is a noun, it cannot neatly govern a *because* clause: not "The reason for his absence is because he was sick," but "The reason for his absence was illness."

this Often refers vaguely to "what I have been saying." Does it refer to the previous sentence, the previous paragraph, the previous page? Try to modify it by being specific: "this last point," "This clue gave the police all they needed."

thusly Unacceptable; *thus* is an adverb and needs no adverbial ending.

till, until Both are acceptable, but *until* is preferable because *till*—though common in speech—looks literary in print. The following are *not* acceptable: *til, 'til, 'till.*

topic of See *area of.*

toward, towards Both are standard English; *toward* is more common in the United States, *towards* in Great Britain.

type Often colloquial (and unacceptable in most writing) for *type of,* as in "this type teacher." But *type of* is not especially pleasing either. Better to write "this kind of teacher." And avoid using *type* as a suffix: "essay-type examinations" are essay examinations; "natural-type ice cream" is natural ice cream. Sneaky manufacturers make "Italian-type cheese," implying that their domestic cheese is imported and at the same time protecting themselves against charges of misrepresentation.

unique The only one of its kind. Someone or something cannot be "rather unique" or "very unique" or "somewhat unique," any more than a woman can be somewhat pregnant.

usage Don't use *usage* where *use* will do, as in "Here Vonnegut completes his usage of dark images." *Usage* properly implies a customary practice that has created a standard: "Usage has eroded the difference between 'shall' and 'will.' "

use of The use of *use of* is usually unnecessary. "Through the use of setting he conveys a sense of foreboding" may read "The setting conveys" or "His setting conveys."

utilize, utilization Often inflated for *use* and *using*, as in "The infirmary has noted that it is freshmen who have most utilized the counseling service."

verbal Often used where *oral* would be more exact. *Verbal* simply means "expressed in words," and thus a verbal agreement may be either written or spoken. If you mean spoken, call it an oral agreement.

verse, stanza, A *verse* is a single line of a poem; a stanza is a group of lines, commonly bound by a rhyme scheme. But in speaking or writing about songs, usage sanctions *verse* for *stanza*, as in "Second verse, same as the first."

very See pages 179–80.

viable A term from physiology, meaning "capable of living" (for example, referring to a fetus at a stage of its development). Now pretentiously used and overused, especially by politicians and journalists, to mean "workable," as in "a viable presidency." Avoid it.

we If you mean *I*, say *I*. Not "The first fairy tale we heard" but the first fairy tale I heard." (But of course *we* is appropriate in some statements: "We have all heard fairy tales"; "If we look closely at the evidence, we can agree that . . .") The rule: don't use *we* as a disguise for *I*. See page 23.

which Often can be deleted. "Students are required to fill out scholarship applications which are lengthy" can be written "Students are required to fill out lengthy scholarship applications." Another example: "*The Tempest*, which is Shakespeare's last play, was written in 1611"; "*The Tempest*, Shakespeare's last play, was written in 1611," or "Shakespeare wrote his last play, *The Tempest*, in 1611." For the distinction between *which* and *that*, see the entry on *that*.

while Best used in a temporal sense: "While I was speaking, he kept looking at his watch." While it is not wrong to use it in a nontemporal sense (as in this sentence), it is preferable to replace it with *although* when possible. And do not use it if you mean *and*: "Freshmen take English 1–2, while sophomores take English 10–11" (substitute *and* for *while*).

who, whom Strictly speaking, *who* must be used for subjects, even when they look like objects: "He guessed who would be chosen." (Here *who* is the subject of the clause "who would be chosen.") *Whom* must be used for the objects of a verb, verbal (gerund, participle), or preposition: "Whom did he choose?"; "Whom do you want me to choose?"; "To whom did he show it?" We may feel stuffy in writing "Whom did he choose?" or "Whom are you talking about?" but to use *who* is certain to annoy some readers. Often you can avoid the dilemma by re-writing: "Who was chosen?"; "Who is the topic of conversation?" See also the entry on *that*.

whom, whomever The objective forms. They are often incorrectly used as the subject of a clause. "Open the class to whomever wants to take it" is incorrect. The object of *to* is not *whomever* but is the entire clause—"whoever wants to take it"—and of course *whoever* is the subject of *wants*.

who's, whose The first is a contraction of *who is* ("I'm everybody who's nobody"). The second is a possessive pronoun: "Whose book is it?" "I know whose it is."

would "I would think that" is the same as "I think that."

your, you're The first is a possessive pronoun ("your book"); the second is a contraction of *you are* ("You're mistaken").

4. ACQUIRING STYLE AND FLUENCY

Two monks were arguing about a flag. One said: "The flag is moving."

The other said: "The wind is moving."

The sixth patriarch happened to be passing by. He told them: "Not the wind, not the flag: mind is moving."

—Paul Reps

CHAPTER SEVENTEEN

DEFINING STYLE

STYLE

> The style is the man.
>
> —Buffon

The word *style* comes from the Latin *stilus*, a Roman writing instrument. Even in Roman times *stilus* had acquired a figurative sense, still retained when we say a writer has a fluent style. The word appropriate to the instrument is transferred to the writer's choice of words and arrangement of words into sentences. But is it simply the choice and arrangement of words we comment on when we speak of a writer's style, or are we also commenting on the writer himself? Don't we feel that a piece of writing, whether it's on Civil War photographs or on genetics and intelligence, is also about the writer? His writing, after all, sets forth his views of his topic, his perceptions and responses to something he has thought about, his evidence and his conclusions; he has, from the start, from his choice of a topic, revealed that he found it worth thinking about. His essay, in attempting to persuade us to think as he does, reveals not only how and what he thinks, but what he values. There is no escape from this revelation of personality, not even objectivity. As Remy de Gourmont has said, "To be impersonal is to be personal in a special kind of way. . . . The objective is one of the forms of the subjective."

When we write about things "out there," our writing always reveals the form and likeness of our minds, just as every work of art reveals the creator as well as the ostensible subject. A portrait painting, for example, is not only about the sitter; it is about the artist's perceptions of the sitter, hence the saying that every portrait is a self-portrait. A student's essay similarly, if it is truly written, is not exclusively about *"La Causa* and the New Chicana"; it is also about June Ojeda's perceptions and responses to both racism and sexism.

Style is not simply a flower here and some gilding there; it pervades the whole work. Rembrandt's style, or Walt Disney's, let us say, consists in part of features recurring throughout a single work and from one work to the next: angular or curved lines, hard or soft edges, strong or gentle contrasts, and so on. Pictures of a seated woman by each of the two artists are utterly different, and if we have seen a few works by each, we can readily identify who did which one. Each artist leaves his finger-prints, so to speak, all over his work; the writer leaves his voiceprint.

STYLE AND TONE

> The style is the man. Rather say the
> style is the way the man takes himself.
>
> —Robert Frost

Suppose we take a page of handwriting, or even a signature. We need not believe that graphology is an exact science to believe that the shape of the ink-lines on paper (apart from the meaning of the words) often tells us something about the writer. We look at a large, ornate signature and we sense that the writer is confident; or we look at a tiny signature written with the finest of pens, and we wonder why anyone is so self-effacing.

More surely than handwriting, the writer's style reveals, chief among his other perceptions and responses, his attitude toward himself (as Frost's addition to Buffon's epigram suggests), toward his reader, and toward his subject. The writer's attitudes are reflected in what is usually called tone. It is difficult to distinguish between style and tone, but we can try. Most discussions of style concentrate on what might be thought of as ornament: figurative language ("a sea of troubles"), inversion ("A leader he is not"), repetition and parallelism ("government of the people, by the people, and for the people"), balance and antithesis ("It was the best of times, it was the worst of times"). Indeed, for centuries style has been called "the dress of thought," implying that the thought is something separate from the expression; the thought, in this view, is dressed up in stylistic devices. But in most of the writing that we read with interest and pleasure the stylistic devices seem not to be ornamental and occasional but integral and pervasive. When we talk about, say, wit, sincerity, tentativeness, self-assurance, aggressiveness, objectivity, we can say we are talking about style, but we should recognize that style is now not a matter of ornamental devices but of devices that enable us to hear the unified yet appropriately varied tone of the writer's voice. To take a brief example: the famous English translation of Caesar's report of a victory, "I came, I saw, I conquered," might be paraphrased thus: "After getting to the scene of the battle I studied the situation. Then I devised a strategy that won the battle." But the brevity and the parallelism of the original, as well as the alliteration (*c*ame, *c*onquered) convey tight-lipped self-assurance—convey, that is, the tone which reveals Caesar to us.

Here, for example, is a short paragraph from John Szarkowski's *Looking at Photographs*. Szarkowski is writing about one of Alexander Gardner's photographs of a dead Confederate sharpshooter.

Among the pictures that Gardner made himself is the one reproduced here. Like many Civil War photographs, it showed that the dead of both sides looked very much the same. The pictures of earlier wars had not made this clear.[1]

Try, in a word or two, to characterize the tone (attitude, as we sense it in the inflection of the voice) of the first sentence.

---

[1] *Looking at Photographs* (New York: Museum of Modern Art, 1973), p. 26.

Next, the tone of the second, and then of the third. Suppose the second and third sentences had been written thus:

> It showed that the dead of both sides looked very much the same. This is made clear in Civil War photographs, but not in pictures of earlier wars.

How has the tone changed? What word can you find to characterize the tone of the whole, as Szarkowski wrote it?

Now another passage from Szarkowski's book:

> Jacob A. Riis was a newspaper reporter by occupation and a social reformer by inclination. He was a photographer rather briefly and apparently rather casually; it seems beyond doubt that he considered photography a useful but subservient tool for his work as reporter and reformer. It is clear that he had no interest in "artistic" photography, and equally clear that the artistic photographers of his time had no interest in him.[2]

Do you find traces of Szarkowski's fingerprints—or, better, voiceprint—here?

Finally, a longer passage by the same writer. After you read it, again try to verbalize the resemblances—the qualities that allow us to speak of the writer's tone.

> There are several possible explanations for the fact that women have been more important to photography than their numbers alone would warrant. One explanation might be the fact that photography has never had licensing laws or trade unions, by means of which women might have been effectively discriminated against. A second reason might be the fact that the specialized technical preparation for photography need not be enormously demanding, so that the medium has been open to those unable to spend long years in formal study.
>
> A third possible reason could be that women have a greater natural talent for photography than men do. Discretion (or cowardice) suggests that this hypothesis is best not pursued, since a freely speculative exploration of it might take unpredictable and indefensible lines. One might for example consider the idea that the art of photography is in its nature receptive, or passive, thus suggesting that women are also.[3]

[2] *Looking at Photographs*, p. 48.
[3] *Looking at Photographs*, p. 52.

STYLE AND LEVELS OF USAGE

Although the dividing lines cannot always be drawn easily, tradition recognizes three levels: formal, informal, and vulgar or popular, though sometimes "popular" is used to designate a level between informal and vulgar. In textbooks, the most obvious purpose of discussions of these levels has been to dislodge older, more rigid ideas about "good" and "bad" or "correct" and "incorrect" English, and to replace them with the more flexible and more accurate standard of appropriateness. The labels formal and informal (we can for the moment drop vulgar, since few essays are written in it) attempt to describe the choices a writer makes under particular circumstances, rather than to prescribe those he ought to make under all circumstances. The choices, often unconscious, include those of vocabulary, sentence structure, and tone.

Formal writing, found mostly in scholarly articles, textbooks, ceremonial speeches, and scientific reports, assumes an audience, not only generally well-educated but also with special knowledge of or interest in the writer's subject. The writer can therefore use a wide vocabulary (including words and references that in another context would be pretentious or obscure) and sentence patterns that demand close attention. A noted figure, say a respected literary critic, examining an influential book and addressing the world of thoughtful readers, may use a formal style, as Lionel Trilling does here in a criticism of V. L. Parrington's *Main Currents in American Literature*. Trilling assumes an attentive reader, capable of holding in mind a long sentence.

To throw out Poe because he cannot be conveniently fitted into a theory of American culture, to speak of him as a biological sport and as a mind apart from the main current, to find his gloom to be merely personal and eccentric, "only the atrabilious wretchedness of a dipsomaniac," as Hawthorne's was "no more than the skeptical questioning of life by a nature that knew no fierce storms," to judge Melville's response to American life to be less noble than that of Bryant or of Greeley, to speak of Henry James as an escapist, as an artist similar to Whistler, a man characteristically afraid of stress—this is not merely to be mistaken in aesthetic judgment; rather it is to examine without attention and from the point of view of a limited and essentially arrogant conception of reality the documents which are in some respects the most suggestive testimony to what America was and is, and of course to get no answer from them.[4]

—Lionel Trilling

Notice that in Trilling's sentence the structure is this: "To throw . . . to speak . . . to find . . . to judge . . . to speak," and we still do not have an independent clause. Two-thirds of the way through, with "this is not merely to be mistaken," the previous words come into focus, but the meaning is still incomplete. To do such-and-such "is not merely to be mistaken," but what *is* it to be? At last we are told: "It is to examine without attention . . . and . . . to get no answer. . . ."

A formal sentence need not be long. Here is a fairly short formal sentence by W. H. Auden: "Owing to its superior power as a mnemonic, verse is superior to prose as a medium for didactic instruction." In another frame of mind Auden might have written something less formal, along these lines: "Because it stays more easily in the memory, verse is better than prose for teaching." This revision of Auden's sentence can be called informal, but it is high on the scale, the language of an educated man writing courteously to an audience he conceives of as his peers. It is the level of almost all serious writing about literature. A low informal version might be: "Poetry sticks in the mind better than prose; so if you want to teach something, poetry is better." This is the language any of us might use in our more casual moments; it is almost never the language used in writing to our peers.

Finding the Appropriate Level

Despite their outwardly democratic and permissive air, discussions of levels of usage generally try to steer students away from using embarrassingly colloquial or low language in their compositions. We find ourselves taking a different tack. The actual practice of writers has shifted in recent years: the writing of scholars is moving toward informality, the writing of students toward formality and pretentiousness.

What is appropriate in writing, as in dress, is subject to

[4] *The Liberal Imagination* (New York: Viking Press, 1950). p. 21.

change, and the change recently has been to greater informality in both. Students who attend classes, concerts, and even their own weddings in blue jeans might experiment with similar freedom in writing college essays, and work toward a style that feels comfortable and natural to them. Developing a natural style, writing at an appropriate level, does take work. Consider, for example, the following opening paragraph from a student's theme:

> The college experience is traumatic, often because one must adjust not only to new academic horizons and new friends but also to the new physical environment constituted by the college and by the community surrounding it. One might think that, coming from a city only sixty miles from Wellesley, I would be exempt from this aspect of adaptation. However, this assumption has proven to be false.

Traumatic? Academic horizons? Constituted? Exempt from this aspect of adaptation? Assumption . . . proven to be false? There's nothing wrong with the language here—that is, nothing ungrammatical—but the paragraph has a hollow ring, a tone of insincerity, because the diction and syntax—the writer's level of usage—so ill-suit the theme which the student developed: a personal and spirited defense of the writer's lower-middle-class industrial home town, whose liveliness, friendliness, and above all, informality, she emphatically prefers to the aloofness of suburban Wellesley.

By contrast, in a review of *Soledad Brother—The Prison Letters of George Jackson*, another student described Jackson's style as "clear, simple, expressive, and together." The word "together," though technically incorrect (an adverb, here used as an adjective) strikes us, in context, as exactly right. And, when later in the essay we read "Surviving on glasses of water, crumbs of bread, deep concentration, daily push-ups, and cigarettes, Jackson shouts to the black world to wake up: get off your knees and start kicking asses because 'God helps those who help themselves,' " we feel that the deliberately inconsistent use of the formal series of parallels with the colloquial or vulgar "kicking asses" exactly expresses both Jackson's discipline and rage, and the writer's empathy with them.

In most of your college writing you are addressing people like yourself; use a language that you would like to read, neither stuffy nor aggressively colloquial. Probably it will stand somewhere in between the levels of "aspects of adaptation" and "kicking asses."

TONE: FOUR EXAMPLES

This chapter has suggested that style is largely a matter of *tone*. Since tone is usually associated with the spoken language, it may be useful to look at some paragraphs that were spoken before they were printed. Three of the four excerpts in this section were originally spoken. The first is the opening paragraph of a talk given by Professor Talcott Parsons in Germany, on the centenary of the birth of the German sociologist Max Weber. The second passage comprises the first three paragraphs of Norman Mailer's speech accepting a literary prize. (You might compare Parsons' and Mailer's attitudes toward themselves and their audience.) The third passage, by Alfred North Whitehead, was, like the first two, originally part of a talk. The fourth, by Pauline Kael, is the beginning of an essay on the tedium of most modern films.

After you read these four pieces, ask yourself if the writer is clear, inspires confidence, and is worth hearing more from.

It is indeed both an honor and a challenge to be invited to participate in this most significant occasion, the observance of the one hundredth anniversary of the birth of Max Weber. It is also a great pleasure to revisit the University of Heidelberg, though not quite for the first time, just short of forty years after my enrollment here as a student in 1925. This was too late to know Max Weber in person, but of course his intellectual influence was all-pervasive in the Heidelberg of that time, constituting the one primary point of reference about which all theoretical and much empirical discussion in the social and cultural fields revolved. I was also privileged to know his gracious and highly intelligent widow, Marianne Weber, in particular to attend a number of her famous "sociological teas" on Sunday afternoons. It was an extraordinarily stimulating intellectual environment, participation in which was one of the most important factors in determining my whole intellectual and professional career.[5]

—Talcott Parsons

[5] "Evaluation and Objectivity in Social Science," *Sociological Theory and Modern Society* (New York: Free Press, 1967), p. 80.

On Monday when queried by Mr. Raymont of the *Times* about my reaction to winning one of the National Book Awards, I was sufficiently ungracious to say, "There's something obscene about a middle-aged man who wins an award. Prizes are for the young and the old." Writers are notoriously double- and triple-layered—like color film they have their yellow base, their blue-green, their slice of sensitivity to red. Who knows what was meant? It could have been bitterness, or the growl of a curmudgeon kicking at the edge of his pleasure.

At any rate, standing on this podium, your speaker is here to state that he likes prizes, honors, and awards and will accept them. He will accept them. The honorable Jean-Paul Sartre, an author it is impossible not to esteem, refused the Nobel Prize a few years ago with the remark—let this approximate his words—that he wished the bourgeoisie to know him as Jean-Paul Sartre, not Jean-Paul Sartre, Nobel Prize Winner. Respectful of his integrity, one could nonetheless disagree with his decision. The most bourgeois elements in French society had been speaking of him for years as Jean-Paul Sartre, perverted existentialist, and would continue to do so. How much better for the final subtleties of their brain if they had been obliged instead to think of him as Jean-Paul Sartre, perverted existentialist *and* Nobel Prize Winner. An entrance might have been made into the complexity of his vision. It might have introduced that bourgeoisie to the vertiginous schizophrenia of the modern condition, a clifflike species of cultural dislocation.

We are a savagely mechanical society poised upon the lip, no, the main of a spiritual revolution which will wash the psychic roots of every national institution out to sea. We are on the brink of dreams and disasters. We are entering a world in which the value systems of the stoutest ego will spin like a turning table, the assertions of the inner voice go caroming through vales of electronic rock.[6]

—Norman Mailer

Style, in its finest sense, is the last acquirement of the educated mind; it is also the most useful. It pervades the whole being. The administrator with a sense for style hates waste; the engineer with a sense for style economizes his material; the artisan with a sense for style prefers good work. Style is the ultimate morality of mind. . . . With style the end is attained without side issues, without raising undesirable inflammations. With style you attain your end and nothing but your end. With style the effect of your activity is calculable, and foresight is the last gift of gods to men. With style your power is

[6] *Existential Errands* (Boston: Little, Brown, 1972), pp. 254–55.

increased, for your mind is not distracted with irrelevancies, and you are more likely to attain your object.[7]

—Alfred North Whitehead

Early this year, the most successful of the large-circulation magazines for teen-age girls took a two-page spread in the *Times* for an "interview" with its editor-in-chief, and after the now ritual bulling (Question: "You work with young people—what is your view of today's generation?" Answer: "My faith in them is enormous. They make a sincere attempt at being totally honest, at sharing. They're happily frank about their experiences. They're the most idealistic generation in history. . . . When you consider the vast problems confronting us, their optimism and activism is truly inspirational"), and after the obeisance to the new myths ("They are the best-educated and most aware generation in history"), the ad finally got to the come-on. Question: "Is it true that your readers don't differentiate between your ads and your editorials?" Answer: "Yes, that's true. Our readers are very impressionable, not yet cynical about advertising . . . eager to learn . . . to believe." The frightening thing is, it probably is true that the teen-agers don't differentiate between the ads and the editorials, and true in a much more complex sense than the delicately calculated Madison Avenue-ese of the editor's pitch to advertisers indicates. Television is blurring the distinction for all of us; we don't know what we're reacting to anymore, and, beyond that, it's becoming just about impossible to sort out the con from the truth because a successful con makes its lies come true.[8]

—Pauline Kael

[7] *The Aims of Education* (New York: New American Library, 1949), p. 24.
[8] "Numbing the Audience," *Deeper into Movies* (Boston: Little, Brown, 1973), p. 145.

CHAPTER EIGHTEEN

ACQUIRING STYLE

> Draw lines, young man,
> draw many lines.
>
> —Old Ingres to the
> young Degas

In the preceding pages on style we said that your writing reveals not only where you stand (your topic) and how you think (the structure of your argument) but who you are and how you take yourself (your tone). To follow our argument to its limit, we might say that everything in this book—including rules on the comma (where you breathe)—is about style. We do. What more is there to say?

CLARITY AND TEXTURE

First, a distinction Aristotle makes between two parts of style: that which gives *clarity*, and that which gives *texture*. Exact words, concrete illustrations of abstractions, conventional punctuation, and so forth—matters we have treated in some detail in the sections on revising and editing—make for clarity. On the whole, this part of style is inconspicuous when present; when absent the effect ranges from mildly distracting to ruinous. Clarity is the foundation of style. It can be achieved by anyone willing to make the effort.

Among the things that give texture, or individuality, are effective repetition, variety in sentence structure, wordplay, and so forth. This second group of devices, on the whole more noticeable, makes the reader aware of the writer's particular voice.

These devices can be learned too, but seldom by effort alone. In fact playfulness helps here more than doggedness. Students who work at this part of style usually enjoy hanging around words. At the same time, they're likely to feel that when they put words on paper, even in a causal letter to a friend, they're putting themselves on the line. Serious, as most people are about games they really care about, but not solemn, they'll come to recognize the rules of play in John Holmes's advice to young poets: "You must believe that your feelings and your words for your feelings are important. . . . That they are unique is a fact; that you believe they are unique is necessary."[1]

A REPERTORY OF STYLES

We make a second distinction: between style as one perceives it from the written word, and style as the writer experiences it. The first is static: it's fixed in writing or print; we can point to it, discuss it, analyze it. The second, the writer's experience of his own style, changes as the writer changes. In his essay "Why I Write" George Orwell said, "I find that by the time you have perfected any style of writing, you have always outgrown it."[2] An exaggeration that deposits a truth. The essay concludes, however, "Looking back through my work, I see that it is invariably where I lacked a *political* purpose that I wrote lifeless books and was betrayed into purple passages, sentences without meaning, decorative adjectives and humbug generally."[3] A suggestion surely, that through trial and error, and with maturity, a writer comes to a sense of self, a true style, not static and not constantly changing, but achieved.

Undergraduates seldom know what purpose, in Orwell's sense, they will have. You may be inclined toward some subjects and against others, you may have decided on a career—many times. But if your education is worth anything like the money and time invested in it, your ideas and feelings will change more rapidly in the next few years than ever before in your memory, and perhaps more than they ever will again. Be glad of the confusion you're in; it's a vital sign. Reach out for new experiences to as-

---

[1] *Writing Poetry* (Boston. *The Writer* Magazine, 1960), p. 54.
[2] *A Collection of Essays* (Garden City, N.Y.: Doubleday, 1957), pp. 319–20.
[3] *A Collection of Essays*, p. 320.

similate; make whatever connections you can from your reading to your inner life, reaching back into your past and forward into your future. And keep writing: "Draw lines . . . draw many lines."

To keep pace with your changing ideas—and here is our main point—you'll need to acquire not one style, but a repertory of styles, a store of writing habits on which you can draw as the need arises.

ORIGINALITY AND IMITATION

Finally, a paradox: one starts to acquire an individual style by studying and imitating the style of others. The paradox isn't limited to writing. Stylists in all fields begin as apprentices. The young ball player imitates the movements of Reggie Jackson, the potter joins a workshop in California to study under Marguerite Wildenhain, the chess player hangs around the park or club watching the old pros, then finds a book which probably begins with Roy Lopez' opening. The would-be writer may be lucky enough to have a teacher, one he can imitate; more likely he will, in W. H. Auden's words, "serve his apprenticeship in the library."[4]

The following section offers some ways to study, imitate, and re-create what you find in books: other writer's voices.

PRACTICE IN ACQUIRING STYLE

Benjamin Franklin's Exercise

Benjamin Franklin says in his *Autobiography*, "Prose writing has been of great use to me in the course of my life, and was a principal means of my advancement,"[5] and reveals how he acquired his ability in it. (He had just abandoned, at about the age of eleven, his ambition to be a great poet—after his father told him that "verse-makers were generally beggars.")

About this time I met with an odd volume of the *Spectator*. It was the third. I had never before seen any of them. I bought it, read it over and over, and was much delighted with it. I thought the writing

---

[4] *The Dyer's Hand* (New York: Random House, 1962), p. 37.
[5] *Benjamin Franklin's Autobiography and Selected Writings* (New York: Holt, Rinehart and Winston, 1965), p. 12.

excellent, and wished, if possible, to imitate it. With that view I took some of the papers, and making short hints of the sentiment in each sentence, laid them by a few days, and then, without looking at the book, tried to complete the papers again by expressing each sentiment at length, and as fully as it had been expressed before, in any suitable words that should come to hand. Then I compared my *Spectator* with the original, discovered some of my faults, and corrected them.[6]

A few pages later Franklin confides, with characteristic understatement (which he learned, he thought, by imitating Socrates), "I sometimes had the pleasure of fancying that in certain particulars of small import I had been lucky enough to improve the method or the language."[7]

EXERCISE

1. Outline, in a list of brief notes, Franklin's exercise.
2. Choose a passage of current prose writing whose style you admire and follow Franklin's method. (Don't forget the last step: where you've improved on your model, congratulate yourself with becoming modesty.)

Franklin's method is a good way not only to acquire style, but to master material you're studying for an examination. But you'll need another skill to write the examination—the ability to summarize.

Writing Summaries

A summary is a compressed version of a piece of writing. It gives the gist of the original writer's argument or narrative, stripped of illustrative or descriptive materials, dialogue, or extensive quotations. A summary is usually said to be about one-third the length of the original. The rule is arbitrary, but useful; anything longer can probably be further condensed. But there are times when a shorter summary suits your purpose. In writing a letter to the editor you may summarize the view you're opposing in a sentence or two. In reviewing a book, you may summarize its contents in one or two paragraphs.

---

[6] *Benjamin Franklin's Autobiography*, p. 13.
[7] *Benjamin Franklin's Autobiography*, p. 14.

In summaries of about one-third the length of the original, one usually follows the organization of the original. Sometimes, though, a re-organization allows for greater condensation or clarity. If, for example, the writer begins with an anecdote, or a setting forth of the evidence, and only states the essay's thesis in its conclusion, it may be economical to reverse the order: first a summary of the argument, then a summary of the evidence. Summaries may also use the key terms and expressions of the original. But, since it should be clear from your work that you are summarizing someone else's, there is little need for quotation marks or such expressions as "she says," "she then goes on to prove," and so forth. Transitions, though, are useful. Remember that a summary of someone else's writing is a sample of your own writing; it should be clear and coherent.

On pages 34–35 you'll find the Parable of the Prodigal Son, and on page 35 a summary of it; another briefer summary appears in the essay on pages 36–37. Notice that it's customary in writing summaries to use the present tense (though that rule too can be altered to suit your purpose).

In the following example from *Scientific American*, the first paragraph summarizes an article previously published by *Scientific American;* the second and third paragraphs summarize an article from the *Harvard Educational Review*.

HYPERACTIVITY AND DRUGS

At times almost all children are unduly fidgety, noisy, disruptive or generally difficult to handle, but clearly some are more so than others; hyperkinesis, or hyperactivity, is recognized as a distinct syndrome. For some years it has been considered a specific "disease," and it has been treated by the administration of amphetamines and other stimulant drugs. The effect of the drugs is often dramatic, with the children quieting down, paying attention to their schoolwork and in some cases doing better in school. Although many psychiatrists have felt that the stimulants are not getting at the causes of a hyperactive child's disturbance, drug therapy has seemed at least to interrupt the characteristic record of failure in school and to make it possible to treat a child by other methods (see "Hyperactive Children," by Mark A. Stewart; *Scientific American*, April, 1970).

The practice and concept of drug therapy for hyperkinesis has been strongly criticized by Lester Grinspoon of the Harvard Medical School and Susan B. Singer, then of the Massachusetts Mental Health Center, in an article in the *Harvard Educational Review*. They base their article on an intensive review of the literature on hyperactivity and its treatment. They conclude that there is no justification for "the supposition that [the behavioral syndrome] is the result of a specific disorder of the central nervous system," and they question whether behavior that may stem from many different causes can be treated rationally by one type of drug. It has been assumed, they point out, that the apparent calming effect of stimulants on hyperactive children is a paradoxical effect, indicating that such children are physiologically different from other people; that assumption in turn reinforces the idea that the drug therapy is appropriate for them. In fact, the effect may not be paradoxical at all. Many studies have shown that increased attention and better performance are normal results of treatment with stimulants. The children may be reacting just like an adult who finds he can work better if he takes Benzedrine or Ritalin or some other stimulant.

Grinspoon and Singer estimate that some 200,000 children are now given stimulants routinely, and they consider it "impossible to believe" that all of them suffer from organic brain damage or chemical deficiencies. They suggest that the syndrome should be treated as a social problem, not a physical disease.[8]

Practice in writing summaries helps to improve your style because it requires of you a more thorough understanding of someone else's writing than you would have had from merely reading it. In organizing your own summary you are studying not only what the passage says but how the writer thinks. If his organization is clear, you learn by imitating it; if unclear, you learn by improving it. In condensing the material you get practice in the precise use of key terms, and of course, in writing concisely.

EXERCISES

1. Choose a good current editorial and summarize it in about one-third its number of words.

2. Using the outline of "Columbo Knows the Butler Didn't Do It" (page 59) and the essay itself (pages 47–49), write a summary of the essay.

3. If your library subscribes to *Scientific American* and the *Harvard*

---

[8] *Scientific American*, July 1974, p. 47.

Educational Review, compare the summaries in the brief article above with the original articles. Analyze and evaluate the summaries.

Paraphrasing

A summary is always much shorter than the original; a paraphrase is often a bit longer. To paraphrase a sentence, replace each word or phrase in it with one of your own. (Articles, pronouns, and conjunctions need not be replaced.) Your sentence should say substantially what the original says, but in your own words, and in a fluent, natural style. Consider the following sentence by W. H. Auden, and the paraphrase which follows it:

> Owing to its superior power as a mnemonic, verse is superior to prose as a medium for didactic instruction.[9]
>   —W. H. Auden

> Because it is more easily memorized and can be retained in the mind for a longer time, poetry is better than prose for teaching moral lessons.

Paraphrasing is useful for several reasons. First, paraphrasing helps you to increase your vocabulary. (Many students say that a limited vocabulary is their chief source of difficulty in writing.) You may know, for example, that "didactic" means "intended for instruction, or instructive." But why then does Auden say "didactic instruction"? Are the words redundant, or is Auden stipulating a kind of instruction? Your dictionary, which may list "tending to teach a moral lesson" as one of three or four meanings of didactic, will help you understand Auden's sentence. But notice, first, that you'll have to choose the appropriate definition, and second, that you won't be able to insert that definition as is into your sentence. To paraphrase "didactic instruction" you'll have to put "didactic" in your own words. (If you look up "mnemonic" you'll find an even more complex puzzle resolved in our paraphrase.) Paraphrasing, then, expands your vocabulary because to paraphrase accurately and gracefully you must actively understand the use of an unfamiliar word, not simply memorize a synonym for it.

[9] *The Dyer's Hand,* p. 26.

Paraphrasing also helps you to focus your attention on what you read. If you want, for example, to become a better reader of poetry, the best way is to *pay attention,* and the best way of paying attention is to try paraphrasing a line whose meaning escapes you. So too with understanding art history or economics or any specialized study. If you come across a difficult passage, don't just stare at it, paraphrase it. (If you don't have time to stop and puzzle through a sentence that is not entirely clear to you, you can always make time to jot it down on a three-by-five card. As Stanislav Andreski says, "Paper is patient."[10])

Finally, in paraphrasing, you are observing closely and actively the way another mind works. You are, in effect, serving as an apprentice stylist. (Some masters, of course, are not worth serving or emulating. Be discriminating.)

EXERCISE

Try paraphrasing the following sentences:

Generally speaking and to a varying extent, scientists follow their temperaments in their choice of problems.[11]

—Charles Hermite

To commit violent and unjust acts, it is not enough for a government to have the will or even the power; the habits, ideas, and passions of the time must lend themselves to their committal.[12]

—Alexis de Tocqueville

The most intolerable people are provincial celebrities.[13]

—Anton Chekhov

A distinction must be made between my uncle's capricious brutality and my aunt's punishments and repressions, which seem to have been dictated to her by her conscience.[14]

—Mary McCarthy

Consciousness reigns but doesn't govern.[15]

—Paul Valery

[10] *Social Sciences and Sorcery* (London: André Deutsch, 1972).
[11] Quoted in W. H. Auden, *A Certain World* (New York: Viking Press, 1970), p. 335.
[12] Quoted in Auden, *A Certain World,* p. 208.
[13] Quoted in Auden, *A Certain World,* p. 43.
[14] *Memories of a Catholic Girlhood* (New York: Berkley Publishing Corp., 1963), p. 63.
[15] Quoted in Auden, *A Certain World,* p. 260.

The more extensive your acquaintance is with the works of those who have excelled, the more extensive will be your powers of invention, and what may appear still more like a paradox, the more original will be your composition.[16]

—Sir Joshua Reynolds

To express is to impress.

—Aristotle

Imitating the Cumulative Sentence

When you write, you make a point, not by subtracting as though you sharpened a pencil, but by adding. When you put one word after another, your statement should be more precise the more you add. If the result is otherwise, you have added the wrong thing, or you have added more than was needed.[17]

—John Erskine

In *Notes Toward a New Rhetoric* Francis Christensen cites Erskine's "principle" and argues that "the cumulative sentence" best fulfills it.[18] The cumulative sentence makes a statement in the main clause; the rest of the sentence consists of modifiers *added* to make the meaning of the statement more precise. The cumulative sentence adds *texture* to writing because as the writer adds modifiers he is examining his impressions, summarized in the main clause. At the same time he reveals to the reader how those impressions impinged on his mind. Here are some of Christensen's examples:

He dipped his hands in the bichloride solution and shook them, a quick shake, fingers down, like the fingers of a pianist above the keys.[19]

—Sinclair Lewis

The jockeys sat bowed and relaxed, moving a little at the waist with the movement of their horses.[20]

—Katherine Anne Porter

[16] *Longinus' "On the Sublime" and Sir Joshua Reynolds' "Discourses on Art,"* introd. Elder Olson (Chicago: Packard and Co., 1945), p. 105.
[17] Quoted in Francis Christensen, *Notes Toward a New Rhetoric* (New York: Harper and Row, 1967), p. 24.
[18] Pp. 24–25.
[19] P. 8.
[20] P. 10.

The Texan turned to the nearest gatepost and climbed to the top of it, his alternate thighs thick and bulging in the tight trousers, the butt of the pistol catching and losing the sun in pearly gleams.[21]

—William Faulkner

George was coming down in the telemark position, kneeling, one leg forward and bent, the other trailing, his sticks hanging like some insect's thin legs, kicking up puffs of snow, and finally the whole kneeling, trailing figure coming around in a beautiful right curve like points of light, all in a wild cloud of snow.[22]

—Ernest Hemingway

EXERCISE

Try writing a cumulative sentence. First, re-read Christensen's sample sentences out loud. Then, during a second reading, try to sense the similarities in structure. For the next few days train yourself to observe people closely, the way they walk, move, gesture, smile, speak. Take notes when you can. Then, after reading the sentences again, try writing one. Either imitate one of the sentences closely, word by word (substituting your own words) or start with your subject, imitating the structure you have detected or have simply absorbed.

Transformations

If you take a proverb, an epigram, or any interesting, suggestive sentence and change it enough to make it say something else, something on *your* mind, you have a transformation. To cite a famous example, G. K. Chesterton transformed

If a thing is worth doing it is worth doing well

to

If a thing is worth doing it is worth doing badly.

A student transformed

We must be as clear as our natural reticence allows us to be

to

We must be as outspoken as our adversaries would forbid us to be.

[21] P. 10.
[22] P. 10.

EXERCISE

What can you make of one or more of the following?

When a poor man eats a chicken, one of them is sick.

—Yiddish proverb

In a real sense one could say that Maxwell was to Faraday what Newton was to Galileo and Kepler.

—Jeremy Bernstein

You can't step into the same river twice.

—Heraclitus

Mañana es otro día.

—Proverb

Finding Poems

Finding poems is a variation of the language game called acquiring style. It amuses the student who enjoys hanging around words but who is tired of writing, tired of pulling words out of his mind and making them shape up—weary too, very weary, of reading "fine things." Still, he hungers for print, consuming the words on the cereal box along with the cereal, reading last week's classified ads when he has nothing to sell, no money to buy. What can be made of such an affliction? A poem.

Here are X. J. Kennedy's directions for finding a poem.

In a newspaper, magazine, catalogue, textbook, or advertising throwaway, find a sentence or passage that (with a little artistic manipulation on your part) shows promise of becoming a poem. Copy it into lines like poetry, being careful to place what seem to be the most interesting words at the ends of lines to give them greatest emphasis. According to the rules of found poetry you may excerpt, delete, repeat, and rearrange elements but not add anything.[23]

Here are some examples of "found poems." The first was found by Jack S. Margolis in the Watergate transcripts; he published it in *The Poetry of Richard Milhous Nixon*.

---

[23] *An Introduction to Poetry*, 3rd ed. (Boston: Little, Brown, 1974), p. 170.

AND ALL THOSE OTHERS
I'm the President
Of the country—
And I'm going
To get on with it
And meet
Italians
and
Germans,
And all those others.[24]

Here is a passage from a textbook, followed by the poem a student found in it:

> A symbol, then, is an image so loaded with significance that it is not simply literal, and it does not simply stand for something else; it is both itself *and* something else that it richly suggests, a kind of manifestation of something too complex or too elusive to be otherwise revealed.[25]

SYMBOLISM
    An image
so loaded with
    significance
that it is not
    simply literal,
and it does not
    simply stand
for
    something else;
it is both
    itself
and
    something else
that it
    richly suggests,
a kind of
    manifestation

---

[24] *The Poetry of Richard Milhous Nixon* (Los Angeles: Cliff House Books, 1974).

[25] Sylvan Barnet, Morton Berman, and William Burto, *An Introduction to Literature*, 5th ed. (Boston: Little, Brown and Company, 1973), pp. 397–98.

of
    something
    too complex
or
    too elusive
to be
    otherwise revealed,
is a
    symbol.

Finally, a poem found by a student in an advertisement in *Newsweek*:[26]

Winchester model 101
made for hands
that know the difference
There's more
than meets the eye
to any fine
shotgun

EXERCISE

1. Find a poem.
2. Explain in one sentence (a) how finding poems might help you acquire style or (b) why such an exercise is a waste of time.

[26] 12 April 1972, p. 43.

CHAPTER NINETEEN

ACQUIRING FLUENCY

Nulla dies sine linea.
No day without a line.

KEEPING A JOURNAL

As the instruction in this book raises your consciousness about language and the way you use it, it may make you too conscious of what you say, or too self-critical to say anything. We hope not. But to guard against hyperconsciousness, or as an antidote to it, practice writing daily: keep a journal. The word *journal* derives from the Latin *dies* (day) and *diurnalis* (daily), which became *journal* (daily) in medieval French. Keep a journal: *nulla dies sine linea.*

Writing in a journal keeps your writing loose, fluent. It helps you to overcome the fear of writing most people have, and it gives you a chance to practice skills you are acquiring. As we said at the start, writing is a physical act, and to keep in trim, you should practice daily. (Or, to be honest, as close to daily as you can manage.) Keeping a journal then is practical; for many students it is, from the start, enjoyable.

If keeping a journal is an assignment in your composition course, your instructor may ask you to write in a loose-leaf notebook—so that pages may be turned in occasionally, and the instructor won't have to stagger home with twenty or thirty notebooks. If you're keeping a journal strictly for your own use, write with, and on, whatever materials feel comfortable: pen, pencil, typewriter; loose sheets, bound notebook, or whatever. (Dr. William Carlos Williams often wrote poems on pre-scription blanks.)

When to write? Any time; ten to fifteen minutes a day. Some people find it helpful to establish a regular time of day for writing, just before they go to sleep, for example. Habits can be helpful; but not all of us can or should lead well-regulated lives. Suit yourself.

How long is an entry? An entry may be a few words, a line or two, a few pages. There's no special length, but keep writing for at least the minimum recommended time.

Write freely. Don't correct or revise, don't worry about spell-ing, vocabulary, punctuation. Use whatever language, idiom, voice you wish. If you have a "home language"—black or Puerto Rican, for example—write entries in it. It's a good way to keep in touch with yourself, and the friends and family you've tem-porarily left. You *can* go home again; you can, that is, if you don't leave college an educated zombie.

As for content, write about anything that comes to mind. But don't confuse a journal with a diary. A diary mentions things that have happened ("Concert at 8, with J. and R."); a journal reflects on the happenings. A diary lists appointments; a journal records events, but gives some sense of why they were meaning-ful. Think of your journal as a record of your life now, which you might read with pleasure some years from now when many of the rich details of your daily experience would otherwise be buried in your memory. Still, it's probably better to write "Had a peanut butter sandwich for lunch" than to write nothing.

Write down your thoughts, feelings, impressions, responses, dreams, memories. May Sarton once said "The senses are the keys to the past." If you have a strong sensory memory of something—the mixed smell of salt water, sand, and machinery oil, for example—try to describe it in words, and then to track it down. You may find a buried scene from your childhood that you can rescue from your memory by a train of associations. If you keep tracking, and writing, you may discover why that scene is important to you still.

Jot down reactions, ideas, feelings about something you are reading, something you may want to use later, in an essay. Did you stop reading and start daydreaming? What is the link between the text and your daydream? If you write it down, you may be able to cut down on the daydreaming, or at least make something out of it.

Practice writing descriptions; short, medium, long; of persons, places, things; literal, figurative, or impressionistic. (When writing about real people observe one caution: use fictitious names.)

When you have nothing to say, write anyway. Practice writing summaries, paraphrases, transformations (see pages 298–303, 304–05). Or copy out a passage of someone else's writing. If you can, explain why you find it attractive, why you want to remember it.

If you're too preoccupied to write because there's a decision you must make, and can't make, start writing. List all the reasons for following a course of action; then all the reasons against it.

Here, to prime the pump, are some examples of journal entries. Some are by professional writers, others by students. You'll find nothing remarkable in many of these entries (except honesty) and perhaps you'll discover in yourself the assurance that you can do as well or better.

SOME JOURNAL ENTRIES
BY PROFESSIONAL WRITERS

My aunt had an eye that went through and through you like a needle. She was endowed, she said, "with the fatal gift of penetration." She disgusted everybody because she knew them too well.

The things taught in colleges and schools are not an education, but the means of education.

A sleeping child gives me the impression of a traveler in a very far country.

This filthy enactment [The Fugitive Slave Law] was made in the nineteenth century, by people who could read and write. I will not obey it, by God.[1]

—Ralph Waldo Emerson

August A sudden idea of the relationship between "lovers." We are neither male nor female. We are a compound of both. I choose the male who will develop and expand the male in me; he chooses me to expand the female in him. Being made whole. . . . And why

[1] *The Heart of Emerson's Journals*, ed. Bliss Perry (Boston: Houghton Mifflin, 1926), pp. 59, 51, 56, 256.

I choose *one* man for this rather than many is for safety. We bind ourselves within a ring and that ring is as it were a wall against the outside world. It is our refuge, our shelter. Here the tricks of life will not be played. Here is *safety* for us to *grow. Why, I talk like a child.*[2]

—Katherine Mansfield

You hear a lot of jazz about Soul Food. Take chitterlings: the ghetto blacks eat them from necessity while the black bourgeoisie has turned it into a mocking slogan. Eating chitterlings is like going slumming to them. Now that they have the price of a steak here they come prattling about Soul Food. The people in the ghetto want steaks. *Beef Steaks.* I wish I had the power to see to it that the bourgeoisie really *did* have to make it on Soul Food.[3]

—Eldridge Cleaver

Wanted: a dog that neither barks nor bites, eats broken glass and shits diamonds.[4]

—Goethe

SOME JOURNAL ENTRIES BY STUDENTS

Helpless! I remember when I used to stand on a kitchen chair with both my arms raised in the air so that my grandmother could dress me for school. I was so spoiled that the only muscles I moved were in my mouth. Those were the days when breakfast tasted good.

The Rat: "You gap-legged, sky-scraping, knock-kneed, pot-bellied, flat-chested, slack-behind, wooly-headed hollow sculpture of a man!" . . . I died laughing!

As orange as the top of a ladybug seen flying in the southwest corner of 36 Elm St., Sioux City, Iowa, June 12, 1957.

I divorce myself from my feelings and immerse myself in my obligations.

It is difficult to believe that not understanding a physics problem isn't the worst problem in the world.

[2] *Journal of Katherine Mansfield,* ed. J. Middleton Murry (New York: Alfred A. Knopf, 1927), p. 191.

[3] *Soul on Ice* (New York: Dell Publishing Co., 1968), p. 29.

[4] Quoted in W. H. Auden, *A Certain World* (New York: Viking Press, 1970), p. 118.

The rain can be heard on the roof and I feel a steady sprinkling through the open window. Trucks are loading and unloading down in the courtyard. Cars beeping as they turn the blind corner. Distraction . . .

The trees swish outside, the curtains inside. . . .

Anticipating something is like falling off a cliff and never reaching the bottom.

63RD STREET RAP

What happening? Ain't nothing to it. What's going on at the Woods? Everything is Everything. Been to any sets lately? Yeah it was on 64th street last night. We partied back. Wish I could have made it. Well times will get better they can't get no worse. Right On! Right On!

Translation:

Hello. How are you. I am fine. What activities are taking place at your high school named Englewood. There are many exciting activities taking place at my high school. Have you attended any parties recently. Yes I attended a party on 64th street last night. We had a very nice time. I wish I could have attended the party also. Well you will probably be fortunate enough to attend the next party, there is no logical reason for you not to. That is correct, that is correct.

It seems that much of my daily writing consists of unresolved questions to which I am still seeking answers. Every answer that I do find serves to ask more questions. Finding answers to my questions creates such a feeling of accomplishment within me that I feel as though I could burst with happiness. However questions that remain unresolved for any length of time begin to puzzle me more and more. I find myself thinking about them at the oddest and most inconvenient times . . . sitting in French class. . . .

LAST WORDS

A rich patron once gave money to the painter Chu Ta, asking him to paint a picture of a fish. Three years later, when he still had not received the painting, the patron went to Chu Ta's house to ask why the picture was not done. Chu Ta did not answer, but dipped a brush in ink and with a few strokes drew a splendid fish. "If it is so easy," asked the patron, "why didn't you give me the picture three years ago?" Again Chu Ta did not answer. Instead, he opened the door of a large cabinet. Thousands of pictures of fish tumbled out.

INDEX

315

TO THE STUDENT

As publishers, we realize that one way to improve education is to improve textbooks. We also realize that you, the student, largely determine the success or failure of textbooks. Although it is the instructor who assigns them, it is the student who buys and uses them. If enough of you don't like a particular book and make your feelings known, the chances are your instructor will not assign it again.

Usually only instructors are asked about the quality of a textbook; their opinions alone are considered as revisions are planned or as new books are developed. Now Little, Brown would like to ask you about *Barnet & Stubbs's Practical Guide to Writing:* how you liked or disliked it; why it was interesting or dull; if it taught you anything. Would you please fill in this form and return it to us at: Little, Brown and Co., College Division, 34 Beacon Street, Boston, Mass. 02106. This is your chance to directly affect the publication of future textbooks.

School: _____

Course title: _____

Instructor's name: _____

Other books required: _____

1. Did you like the book? _____

2. **Content:** Was it too easy? _____

    Was it too difficult? _____

Did you read it all? _____

Which chapters were most useful? _____
_____

Which chapters were least useful? _____
_____

3. **Format:** Did you like the cover design? _____
   Did you like the organization of the contents? _____
4. Were the exercises useful? _____
   How might they be changed? _____
   _____

   _____

5. Did you like the examples? _____
   How might they be improved? _____
   _____

6. Do you feel the professor should continue to assign this book next
   year? _____
7. Will you keep this book for your library? _____
8. Please add any comments or suggestions. _____
   _____

   _____

   _____

   _____

9. May we quote you in our promotion efforts for this book?
   _____yes_____no

_____   _____
date   signature

_____
address

In 1958 Congress passed the Food Additive Amendment, including the Dela-
ney Clause, which clearly states that additives should be banned if they
induce cancer in laboratory animals. Unfortunately, however, the amendment does not apply to additives that were in use before it was passed,
so, since nitrite and nitrate had already been in use for a long time,
they were automatically included on the list of chemicals "Generally
Recognized as Safe." To complicate matters further, nitrite in meat is
regulated by the USDA, while nitrite in fish is under the jurisdiction
of the FDA. And these agencies generally leave it to industry—the
profit-maker—to determine whether or not an additive is safe. The final irony in this long list of governmental errors is that the FDA depends heavily, for "independent" research and advice, on the food committees of the National Academy of Sciences, which Daniel Zwerdling
claims are "like a Who's Who of the food and chemical industry" (Verrett
and Carper 34).

Nevertheless, as they have come under fire in recent years on the
subject of nitrite and nitrate, the FDA and the USDA have found it necessary to give reasons for their continued sanction of these chemicals.
First, they find fault with the experiments done to date. According to
the USDA, for example,

> The Department was aware that under certain conditions, ni-
> trites do interact with secondary amines to form nitrosamines
> and that some nitrosamines are carcinogenic. However, knowl-
> edge in this area was limited and analytical methods available
> to study the possibility of nitrosamine formation in meat food
> products containing the permissible amount of sodium nitrate
> lacked the necessary accuracy and reliability to give conclu-
> sive results (Verrett and Carper 152).

Despite the Delaney Clause, moreover, the FDA points out, "Man is the most important experimental animal and nitrites have not been linked to cancer in all the years that man has been eating the chemical" (qtd. in Wellford 179). This is an almost foolproof argument, since cancer usually shows up only after its inception, and it is extremely difficult to trace it to any source. And certainly it is unlikely that any sizable group will offer to serve as guinea pigs for nitrite experiments. In evaluating this argument, it is significant that humans are generally more susceptible to chemical damage than animals—ten times more so than rats, for example (Verrett and Carper 59). Following through on its own logic, however, since nitrite has indeed been proven to cause cancer in dogs, the FDA has dutifully and responsibly banned its use in dog food.

The industry's second argument is that nitrite prevents botulism. However, the USDA regulations approve the use of nitrite and nitrate only as color fixers. If they are being used as preservatives, this is a new use and comes squarely under the auspices of the Delaney Clause, which would have them banned outright because they cause cancer in animals.

The last argument is that small enough doses of carcinogens are not dangerous. Dr. Leo Friedman, director of the FDA's Division of Toxicology, puts it this way:

> . . . There is always a threshold level below which the substance does not exert any physiologically significant effect. . . . The design of a safety evaluation study is to determine a level at which there is no demonstrable effect. This level, when divided by a suitable safety factor, is then considered to be a safe level, in that there is a practical

certainty that no harm will result from the use of the sub-

stance at that level.   (Qtd. in Wellford 180)

The medical community does not agree. The Surgeon General's committee

stated in 1970, "The principle of a zero tolerance for carcinogenic ex-

posures should be retained in all areas of legislation presently covered

by it and should be extended to cover other exposures as well" (Wellford

181). Hughes Ryser stated in the New England Journal of Medicine:

". . . weak carcinogenic exposures have irreversible and additive ef-

fects and cannot be dismissed lightly as standing 'below a threshold of

action.'" He also commented that, until the carcinogens are removed

from the environment, "efforts must continue to educate populations and

government about their presence" (qtd. in Wellford 181). Even with

this, the FDA Commissioner, Charles Edwards, strenuously disagrees: "We

can't deluge the public with scare items based on our suspicions. . . .

The pendulum swings too far in most cases, and consumers tend to boycott

a product . . . even though we might feel that continued use within cer-

tain limits is entirely justified" (qtd. in Wellford 18).

Something has gone wrong. The issue is one of what we eat. It

makes no sense at all to eat a substance until it is proven to be poi-

son. Even a starving man is reluctant to eat mushrooms unless he knows

what he's doing. Nitrite is banned altogether in Norway, and forbidden

in fish in Canada. European allowances are generally lower than

ours, and even the Germans make their "wursts" without nitrite.

One is forced to a radical conclusion. The American government is,

in this instance, clearly serving the interests of the industry rather

than the people. The fact is that the food industry is willing to spend

millions every year to make sure the regulatory agencies act in ways

that please them. Each time an additive is banned, the food industry

finds itself in the spotlight. It feels an implicit threat to all its other additives, and ultimately to the immense profits Daniel Zwerdling

describes:

> This marvelous chemical additive technology has earned $500
> million a year for the drug companies . . . and it has given
> the food manufacturers enormous control over the mass market.
> Additives like preservatives enable food that might normally
> spoil in a few days or a week to endure unchanged for weeks,
> months, or even years. A few central manufacturers can satu-
> rate supermarket shelves across the country with their prod-
> ucts because there's no chance the food will spoil. Companies
> can buy raw ingredients when they're cheap, produce and stock-
> pile vast quantities of the processed result, then withhold
> the products from the market for months, hoping to manipulate
> prices upward and make a windfall. (22)

Under pressure from the food industry, and probably influenced as

well by a sincere, if hazy, patriotic optimism, the FDA issued a fact

sheet in May 1967, stating unequivocally that our soil is not being poi-

soned by fertilizers, that pesticide residues are entirely safe, that

our soil is the "envy of every nation," and that food processing is a

"modern marvel because the natural value of the food is not lost in the

process." It concludes, "Today's scientific knowledge, working through

good laws to protect consumers, assures the safety and wholesomeness of

every component of our food supply." The FDA's continuing support for

nitrite allowances, despite increasing evidence that nitrite is lethal,

indicates that the FDA has not removed its rose-colored glasses.

A recent extended discussion, The Health Effects of Nitrate, Ni-

trite and N-Nitroso Compounds, issued in 1981 under the auspices of the

National Academy of Sciences, offers no new information but by saying

that nitrites in cured meats may be no more harmful than those in vege-

tables, baked goods, and cereals, it seems to suggest that cured meats
may be less dangerous than has been thought. Still, as Marian Burros
pointed out in the New York Times, many specialists feel that The Health
Effects offers no new evidence. And in fact, an even more recent study
by a committee organized by the National Academy of Science strongly implies (Assembly 12) that the government should develop a safe alternate
to nitrites.

Until the FDA and other regulatory agencies begin to see clearly,
then, the American consumer has little choice other than to give up eating the nitrited cured meats and smoked fish on the market today. If we
do so, we will be following the practice of Dr. William Lijinsky, a biologist who has studied the problem for fifteen years. "I don't touch
any of that stuff when I know nitrite has been added" (qtd. in Sheraton
18).

Modern Language Form

Works Cited

Assembly of Life Science. <u>Alternatives to the Current Use of Nitrite in Food</u>. Washington: National Academy Press, 1982.

Hunter, Beatrice Trum. <u>Fact/Book on Food Additives and Your Health</u>. New Canaan, Conn.: Keats, 1972.

Jacobson, Michael F. <u>Eater's Digest</u>. Washington: Center for Science in the Public Interest, 1982.

Robbins, William. <u>The American Food Scandal</u>. New York: Morrow, 1974.

Sheraton, Mimi. "Take Away the Preservatives, and How Do Meats Taste?" <u>New York Times</u>, 13 June 1985, p. 26.

Verrett, Jacqueline, and Jean Carper. <u>Eating May Be Hazardous to Your Health</u>. New York: Simon and Schuster, 1974.

Wellford, Harrison. <u>Sowing the Wind</u>. New York: Bantam, 1973.

Zwerdling, Daniel. "Death for Dinner." <u>The New York Review</u>, 21, No. 1 (21 Feb. 1974), 22–24.

————. "Food Pollution." <u>Ramparts</u>, 9, No. 11 (June 1971), 31–37, 53–54.

Beyond the Institution:

The Effects of Labeling on Ex—Mental Patients

by

Lisa Temple

May 17, 1985

Writing 125 S

When mental health professionals decide that an individual is mentally ill and should be hospitalized, the public usually agrees with
this judgment. However, when the same professionals determine that a
person is no longer mentally ill and has the competence and the right to
return to normal society, the public does not generally defer to their
decision. Instead, they continue to view the individual under the con-
straints of his previous label. Thus, they see the ex-mental patient
through the bias of a label which is no longer professionally accurate
and which places the former patient at a disadvantage in most, if not
all, aspects of social integration into the community.

Those social psychologists and others who subscribe to "Labeling
Theory" hold that a label does not merely describe a condition; rather,
a label helps to produce behavior appropriate to the label. That is,
persons who are labeled deviants may, because of the label, behave in
the expected way. If we accept this theory, there is reason to doubt the
widely accepted assumption that social control is a preventative response to deviance. Rather, it can be maintained, this cause-and-effect
relationship is in reality reversed; social control causes deviance. According to labeling theorists, when rule breakers are labeled and forced
to adopt society's view of themselves as deviant, they begin to act in a
manner that conforms to the stereotype commonly associated with this label. Scheff makes this point when he states that ". . . among residual
rule breakers, labeling is the single most important cause of careers of
residual deviance" (Scheff, 1966, pp. 92-93). In short, supporters of
labeling theory claim that societal efforts to control deviance not only
fail to effectively reduce deviance but actually increase it.

The potential effects of labeling can be placed into three distinct
categories: 1) the creation of deviance, 2) the stabilization of deviant
behavior, and 3) the consequences of a label in relation to other areas

of an individual's life, such as employment, friendships, family relations, and mate selection (Link, 1982). It is the third category which
most affects ex-mental patients as they attempt to reenter conventional
society while confronting the effects of their past label on their immediate community, family, and employer.

An important consideration for ex-mental patients is how they are
viewed by the community in which they live. Jones and Cochrane of the
University of Birmingham found in an experiment (1981) that a stereotype
of mental illness exists and that the stereotype is a reasonably accurate impression of the behavior of the mentally ill. Most people believe
that mental patients are excessively introverted and are given to rapid,
unprovoked mood swings from one emotional extreme to the other. This
stereotype closely resembles the behavior of psychiatric patients described in objective studies.

According to labeling theory, this close relationship between stereotype and reality occurs because the cultural stereotype of mental illness acts as a "self-fulfilling prophecy." That is, others react toward
the potential patient in a way that leads him or her to fulfill the expected role, which in turn reinforces the original label. This reaction
and counterreaction become a cycle which can lead to the point where alternative roles are no longer available to the prospective patient;
adopting the role of a mentally ill person may become the only possible
way the person can cope with the label. As Jones's and Cochrane's study
shows, the general population has a negative attitude toward the mentally ill, and mental patients' attitudes concerning themselves reflect
those of the public.

Another experiment, done by Phillips (1966), demonstrates the effect a label can have on "attitudinal social distance," which is a measure of rejection. In this study, several short descriptions of various
individuals were given to subjects, and psychiatric hospitalization was

mentioned in some of the descriptions to measure the amount of rejection provoked by the label psychiatric hospitalization suggested. Various questions were asked about the individuals described in each vignette, ranging from questions about the desirability of having the person as a neighbor, of working with him, and of the degree to which one should discourage one's children from marrying him. The results showed that a person with a label is very likely to have more difficulty finding a job, friends, a marriage partner, and a place to live than would a person without a label, even if both have exactly the same mental characteristics. Thus it seems that a label has a substantial effect upon the individual it concerns.

It follows, then, that many of us also hold a certain stereotypical attitude toward mental patients after they have left the institution and that this public attitude has an effect on the self-concept and behavior of the ex-mental patient. The relationship between label and self-concept is demonstrated quite effectively in an experiment by Farina et al. (1968). The purpose of this experiment was to show that a label can have a great effect, even when the label in question has no factual basis. In this study, unacquainted male college students were paired randomly. Each member of the pair was led to believe that the other was told that the former was in some way deviant. The results showed that merely believing that one is viewed as stigmatized can influence a person's behavior; the labeled individual is likely to become less confident and thus less capable of adequately fulfilling normal expectations. This failure in turn leads to rejection by the other individuals and to increased feeling of stigmatization.

Another study (Stensrud and Stensrud, 1980) was performed specifically to determine whether the stigma attached to a person who once received psychiatric hospitalization persists over time, even after the

individual has shown that he has successfully reintegrated into the society and that the stigma is inappropriate. In this experiment subjects
were asked to rate several unknown persons on amount of internal control
versus tendency to be controlled by chance and "powerful others." In the
study a successful individual who was described as having once experienced depression, and as having sought treatment as a psychiatric in-
patient was evaluated by subjects as possessing less internal control
than an equally successful person who had experienced depression, but
who hadn't sought treatment, even though both had current personal histories that were considered very successful. In other words, a person
who had been a psychiatric patient but who had since then stabilized his
disability and successfully integrated himself into the culture was
still perceived as mentally ill by others. This finding supports the hypothesis that once the label of mental illness is attached to an individual, all future interactions with others are influenced by this label. Regardless of the person's current status, a previous label
continues to influence how others perceive the person.

Family is another sphere of the ex-mental patient's life that is
affected by a previous label. Although relatives are closer to the former patient, they do not necessarily place less stigma on the patient's
label than does the rest of society. This was shown in a study by Vannicelli et al. (1980), in which the relatives of schizophrenic patients
fostered attitudes that were more similar to those prevalent in their
own social class than to those held by mental health professionals. Like
other members of society, relatives of ex-mental patients tend to associate this label with strong negative connotations. Although one study
(Hollingshead and Redlich, 1958) showed a technical difference in the
attitudes of family members in differing social classes — higher class
relatives were more likely to experience shame and guilt while lower

class relatives felt more resentment and fear toward the former patient
— all of these attitudes are very clearly negative ones.

Similarly, several other experiments have shown that ". . . the
stigma of mental illness is reflected in the shame and rejection experienced by patients [as well as] . . . the sensitivity and embarrassment
experienced by close friends and family" (Nuehring, 1979, p. 626; Freeman and Simmons, 1963; Siassi et al., 1973; Yarrow et al., 1955). One
experiment in particular (Nuehring, 1979) concentrated on feelings of
stigma among discharged state mental hospital patients as well as the
stigmatizing attitudes held by family and close friends toward these ex-
patients. Nuehring discovered that a stigma is not, to any great degree,
a result of patients' social characteristics, environment, or function-
ing. Instead, there are two specific dependent variables which affect
feelings of stigma and stigmatizing attitudes: the patient's degree of
depression and the degree to which he is seen as a burden to his "significant others."

This study suggests that ex-patients who feel relatively more depressed are more likely to experience stigma, perhaps because feeling
depressed and feeling stigmatized are negatively reinforcing. The study
also suggests that former patients who receive aftercare are thought of
as a burden, especially if they are depressed, or show a lack of anxiety, or are male. It seems possible that these cases are considered more
stigmatizing because they are individuals who failed in fulfilling society's norms to an even greater extent than did other ex-mental patients.
All mental patients are usually considered deviant, but former mental
patients who receive treatment may be more stigmatized than other ex-patients because, although living in the outside community, they are still
receiving treatment. Male ex-patients may be more stigmatized than female ex-patients simply because, in our society, males are typically
thought of as the stronger and less emotional of the two sexes; thus,

male ex-patients seem to stray more from the norm and are more likely to be stigmatized. In addition, the ex-patients most likely to be seen as burdens by family and friends are those who seek high degrees of social interaction. This seems to imply that the more integrated into a community a former patient tries to become, the more unfavorably he is looked upon by the community.

The ex-mental patient's previous label also affects his chances of finding and keeping a job. According to Link (1982), there are two major ways in which former mental patients are harmed in the world of work. One of these is through direct discrimination by employers. As documented in a study done by Olshansky et al. (1958), employers openly admit that they would prefer not to hire former mental patients. Furthermore, it has been shown that ". . . employers are less friendly in an interview situation and rate the applicant's chance of getting the job significantly lower when he reveals a history of mental illness" (Farina and Felner, 1973, p. 270). In fact, individuals with a history of mental hospitalization are automatically prohibited in many states from pursuing certain careers such as firefighter, teacher, or police officer (Ennis and Siegal, 1973). In addition, former mental patients can be refused privileges to which others have access, such as a driver's license, which defacto excludes them from certain jobs. Thus a label, as well as being a source of direct discrimination, can indirectly affect a person's ability to find a job. In other words, a label such as that of the ex-mental patient increases one's chances of being unemployed and decreases one's chances of obtaining a well-paying job.

In addition to increasing discrimination, the label of the former mental patient in another way negatively affects chances of employment. This concerns the ". . . mechanisms which operate through the individual's expectations of rejection" (Link, 1982, p. 204). Even before treat-

ment, most patients fear rejection because of their own beliefs about
mental illness and their knowledge of the public's attitude. During
treatment, the "mortification process" (Goffman, 1961) strengthens the
fears of patients, who come to believe that they need certain restrictions and thus deserve to be regarded negatively. This fear of rejection
then becomes a self-fulfilling prophecy. Ex-patients act more defen-
sively, less confidently, or totally avoid threatening contact because
they fear and expect rejection. The ex-patient internalizes this negative view and begins to think of himself as ". . . totally ineffective
. . . [or as a hopeless case"] (Link, 1982, p. 204). As a result, these
former mental patients appear to prospective employers as unconfident
and incompetent.

In summary, the previous label of the ex-mental patient negatively
affects the former patient's life. Specifically, this label increases
environmental stresses such as unemployment and rejection by family and
friends, reduces the individual's access to social supports, and produces a tentativeness and lack of confidence which greatly weaken the
person's usual means of coping. Moreover, these effects are exactly
those which have been found by environmentally oriented researchers to
be of most importance in the origins of mental illness. It is entirely
possible then, that a previous psychiatric label plays a significant
role in the maintenance of mental disorder (Link, 1982). Any attempt to
improve the plight of the ex-mental patient, therefore, must include educational programs not only for ex-patients but also for the community
in which they live. Before former mental patients can be expected to in-
tegrate successfully into society, there must first be a significant and
necessary change in society's view of these individuals.

References

Bord, R. (1971) Rejection of the Mentally Ill: Continuities and
Further Developments. Social Problems, 18, 496–509.

Cumming, E., and Cumming, J. (1957). Closed Ranks: An Experiment in
Mental Health. Cambridge: Harvard.

Ennis, B., and Siegal, L. (1973). The Rights of Mental Patients. New
York: Avon.

Farina, A., Allen, J., and Saul, B. (1968). The Role of the
Stigmatized in Affecting Social Relationships. Journal of
Personality, 36, 169–82.

Freeman, H., and Simmons, O. (1963). The Mental Patient Comes Home.
New York: Wiley.

Goffman, E. (1961). Asylums. Garden City, New York: Doubleday.

Hollingshead, H., and Redlich, F. (1958). Social Change and Mental
Illness. New York: Wiley.

Jones, L., and Cochrane, R. (1981). Stereotypes of Mental Illness: A
Test of the Labeling Hypothesis. International Journal of Social
Psychiatry, 27, 99–107.

Link, B. (1982). Mental Patient Status, Work, and Income: An
Examination of the Effects of a Psychiatric Label. American
Sociological Review, 47, 202–15.

Nuehring, E. M. (1979). Stigma and State Hospital Patients. American
Journal of Orthopsychiatry, 49, 626–33.

Nunnally, J. (1961). Popular Conceptions of Mental Health: Their
Development and Change. New York: Holt.

Olshansky, S., Grob, S., and Malmud, I. T. (1958). Employers'
Attitudes and Practices in the Hiring of Ex-Mental Patients.
Mental Hygiene, 42, 391–401.

Phillips, D. (1966). Public Identification and Acceptance of the Mentally Ill. <u>American Journal of Public Health</u>, <u>56</u>, 755–63.

Scheff, T. (1966). <u>Being Mentally Ill: A Sociological Theory</u>. Chicago: Aldine.

Siassi, I., Spiro, H., and Crocetti, G. (1973). The Social Acceptance of the Ex-Mental Patient. <u>Community Mental Health Journal</u>, 233–43.

Star, S. (1955). <u>The Public's Ideas About Mental Illness</u>. Chicago: National Opinion Research Center.

Stensrud, R., and Stensrud, K. (1980). Attitudes Toward Successful Individuals with and without Histories of Psychiatric Hospitalization. <u>Psychological Reports</u>, <u>47</u>, 495–498.

Vannicelli, M., Washburn, S. L., and Scheff, B. J. (1980). Family Attitudes Toward Mental Illness: Immutable with Respect to Time, Treatment Setting, and Outcome. <u>American Journal of Orthopsychiatry</u>, <u>50</u>, 151–55.

Yarrow, M., Clausen, J., and Robbins, P. (1955). The Social Meaning of Mental Illness. <u>Journal of Social Issues</u>, <u>11</u>, 33–48.

A NOTE ON THE USE OF COMPUTERS IN RESEARCH AND WRITING

We've all become familiar in recent years with computers and their seemingly limitless uses: from guiding space vehicles to computing a day's business receipts. When you make an airline reservation, cash a check at a bank, or register as a student in college, the chances are that a computer has assisted (or impeded) you in reserving your air space, checking your balance, or electing your courses. Computers are also being used increasingly in research and writing.

Computers are used in research in at least two ways. First, computer services available at some libraries help scholars to generate bibliographies and refine research problems. If, for example, you are interested in the possibility that some food additives cause cancer, and if your library subscribes to Bibliographic Retrieval Services (a database that provides bibliographies and abstracts from more than fifty databases in business, the social sciences, the physical sciences, and the life sciences), you will log into BRS and instruct the computer to search databases under such headings as *cancer, nitrites,* and *food additives* in order to find articles concerned with your specific topic. If you merely search for *food additives* you will find that one database alone, *Medline* (a computer-based system operated by the National Library of Medicine), can provide some 1500 references for the last three years. Such a search is far too broad for your purposes. It is important, then, to formulate the right group of key words — they are called *descriptors* — so that the computer will make a narrow search and will produce only the most relevant articles. A computer librarian will help you to formulate the terminology. The computer will then inform you of the number of articles with your descriptors in each database, and you can then instruct the computer to list the titles. Although the hourly cost of the service is fairly high, if you have carefully planned your search, the search with the computer will probably take only a few minutes.

If a title sounds relevant, you can then ask the computer to print the full citation (author, journal, pages, date) and a summary of about fifty words (called an abstract). When you have read the

*"Please, Daddy. I don't want to learn to use a computer.
I want to learn to play the violin."*

Drawing by Weber; © 1984 The New Yorker Magazine, Inc.

abstract, you have a pretty clear idea of whether or not you should go on to read the article itself. Some, but not all, of the articles will themselves be available on the computer, and in a minute or two you can have an entire article put onto your disk, which you can read later at your leisure. Thus, you pay only for the time of the search and for the time it takes to copy the article, not for the much longer time it will take to read from your disk. But note that although the abstracts of many articles are on line, only some of these articles are themselves on line; for those that are not, you will have to read the journal in the library.

Computers are frequently used not only for bibliographic searches but also for statistical analyses, mathematical computations, or simulated experiments. With access to a computer and knowledge of its language, you might, for example, use, modify, or devise a computer program to analyze election data, calculate the weight of a star, or simulate the air flow over an airplane wing.

When you come to write a report, a computer with a text-editing program can further assist you, as we pointed out in chapter 1. You will again have to invest some time learning to use it, but you will find your time well spent. With a text-editing program, or word processor — which functions something like a smart typewriter with a faultless memory — you can compose, revise, and edit your writing and then make copies of the finished essay, all on the same machine. You can, for example, start by typing a rough draft, then delete whole paragraphs or sections, and continue by adding new material. When you want to check your revisions, you can request a clean copy of any part of your text. If you discover that you have misspelled a word a dozen times, you can, with one command to the computer, correct the error every place it appears. When you have the final version of your essay stored in the computer's memory, you can request as many copies as you want; and, with a sophisticated program, your computer will present them to you correctly paged, footnotes in place, left and right margins adjusted, and all neatly typed.

Computer facilities vary greatly from place to place; those we describe here — automated bibliographic searches and mathematical, scientific, and text-editing programs — are only examples of some of the current uses of computers in research and writing. It's unlikely therefore that all of these particular facilities are available to you now. Even if they all are available, they may not prove useful for any·work you are now doing, and even if they're useful, they might cost more than you want to spend. Nevertheless, computers and their applications are proliferating, as computers become not only more powerful and more versatile, but also smaller and cheaper; and every year they are more commonly available. If any facilities are available to you now, then, we suggest you find out about them and acquire some computer literacy, even if you must take a course, invent a project, or apply for a grant to do it. Look in your college catalog to see what opportunities exist, and ask your instructors and the reference librarian. Sometimes even where computer facilities exist, it takes some persistence to find out about them.

EXERCISES

1. If you have trouble finding material in the library, don't hesitate to ask a librarian for assistance. But you will soon learn to solve many of the commonest problems yourself. Here are a few.

   a. You want to do some research for a paper on Mexican immigrants in the United States. You look in the card catalog and find only one card, reprinted below. How can you find other books on the subject?

   ```
           The Mexican immigrant.

   JV      Gamio, Manuel, 1883-1960, comp.
   6798       The Mexican immigrant.  New York,
   .M6     Arno Press, 1969.
   G28        xiii, 288 p. map. 22 cm.  (The
   1969    American immigration collection)
              Reprint of the 1931 ed.
              1.United States--Emigration and
           immigration. 2.Mexico--Emigration and
           immigration. 3.Mexicans in the United
           States. I.T.




   RG77-115225  r                   69-18778
   JV6798.M6G28  1969                   301.453/72/
   ```

   b. You want to do a paper on Richard Wright's short stories, and the catalog lists several relevant books, but when you check the stacks you find none of these books is on the shelf. What do you do, short of abandoning the topic or going to another library?
   c. You are looking for a book by David McCord, called *Far and Few*. You look under the author's name, but find that a card for "Mbunda (Bantu tribe)" is followed not by a card for McCord but by a card for "Mchedishvili, Georgii." You next look for the book by its title; you find a card for an author named "Faral," and you assume that *Far and Few* should be the next card or so, but in fact the next card is for an author named "Fararo, T. J." Yet you know that the library has McCord's *Far and Few*. Where did you go wrong?
   d. You need reviews of a film released a few months ago. There are no books on this film, and the *Readers' Guide* lists nothing under the film's title. What do you do?

e. You find references to *CQ Weekly Report,* the *Department of State Bulletin,* and the *Journal of the American Oriental Society,* but these journals don't seem to be listed alphabetically in the periodical file. Still, you have heard that the library does have them. How can that be?

f. You are looking for an issue of a journal published a few months ago. It is not on the shelf with the current issues, and it is not on the shelf with the bound volumes. Where is it?

g. You want to write a paper on bilingual education, or, more exactly, on bilingual education of Mexican Americans. What do you look for in the card catalog? And what periodical indexes do you consult?

h. You want to know if juvenile delinquency in the Soviet Union increased during the 1970's, but you can't find anything on the topic. What do you do?

2. Using the MLA form, list the following items in Works Cited.

a. A book entitled *Areas of Challenge for Soviet Foreign Policy,* with an introduction by Adam B. Ulam. The book, published in 1985 by the Indiana University Press, in Bloomington, is written by three authors: Gerrit W. Gong, Angela E. Stent, and Rebecca V. Strode. Write *two* entries for Works Cited, the first entry indicating that you referred only to Ulam's introduction, the second entry indicating that you referred to material written by the three authors of the book.

b. *Journal of Political and Military Strategy* paginates its issues continuously; the second issue takes up where the first issue leaves off. The issues of 1984 constitute volume 12. Issue number 2 (the fall issue) contains an article that runs from page 229 to page 241. The article, written by James Burke, is entitled "Patriotism and the All-Volunteer Force."

c. *International Security* begins the pagination of each issue with page 1. The issues of 1985 constitute volume 9. Issue number 4 (the spring issue) contains an article that runs from page 79 to page 98. The article, written by Klaus Knorr, is entitled "Controlling Nuclear War."

d. On page 64 of the book you are now holding in your hand you will find an essay by Jeff Greenfield. How would you list the essay in Works Cited?

3. Go to your library and prepare entries for Works Cited for each of the following:
   a. A signed article in a recent issue of a journal devoted to some aspect of psychology.
   b. A signed article in a newspaper.
   c. A signed article in a recent issue of *Time*.
   d. An unsigned article in a recent issue of *Newsweek*.
   e. An unsigned article from the Macropaedia portion of *Encyclopaedia Britannica*.
   f. A signed article from the Micropaedia portion of *Encyclopaedia Britannica*.
   g. a catalog from your college.
   h. a book (one of your textbooks will do) written by one author.

11
Special Assignments, Special Forms

WRITING AN EXPLICATION

An explication (literally, unfolding or spreading out) is a commentary, usually line by line, on what is going on in a poem or in a short passage of prose. An explication is not concerned with the writer's life or times, nor is it a paraphrase, a rewording — though it may include paraphrase; it is a commentary revealing your sense of the meaning of the work. To this end it calls attention, as it proceeds, to the implications of words, the function of rhymes, the shifts in point of view, the development of contrasts, and any other contributions to the meaning.

Take, for example, the short poem by William Butler Yeats that opens this book, "The Balloon of the Mind":

Hands, do what you're bid:
Bring the balloon of the mind
That bellies and drags in the wind
Into its narrow shed.

Now, if we have done research on the work of Yeats we may remember that in an autobiography, *Reveries over Childhood and Youth,* Yeats already had used the figure of a balloon (dirigible) to represent mental activity: "My thoughts were a great excitement, but when I tried to do anything with them, it was like trying to pack a balloon into a shed in a high wind." But because explication usually confronts the work itself, without relating it to biography, we can pass over this interesting anticipation and confine ourselves to the poem's four lines. Here is the final version of an explication that went through several drafts after many readings (some aloud) of the poem. After reading this explication do not chastise yourself for not seeing all the subtleties when you read the poem. The writer herself did not see them all during the first, or even the fifth, reading. Notice that among the topics discussed are the tone (of the first line), the lengths of the lines, and the effect of patterns of sound, including rhythm, rhyme, and alliteration.

Yeats's "Balloon of the Mind" is about poetry, specifically about the difficulty of getting one's floating thoughts down into lines on the page. The first line, a short, stern, heavily stressed command to the speaker's hands, implies by its impatient tone that these hands will be disobedient or inept or careless if not watched closely: the poor bumbling body so often fails to achieve the goals of the mind. The bluntness of the command in the first line ("Hands, do what you're bid") is emphasized by the fact that it has fewer syllables than each of the subsequent lines. Furthermore, the first line is a grammatically complete sentence, whereas the thought of line 2 spills over into the subsequent lines, implying the difficulty of fitting ideas into confining spaces. Lines 2 and 3 amplify the metaphor already stated in the title (a thought is an airy but unwieldy balloon) and they also contain a second command: "Bring." Alliteration ties this command, "Bring," to the earlier "bid"; it also ties both of these verbs to their object, "balloon," and to the verb that most effectively describes the balloon, "bellies." In comparison with the peremptory first line of the poem, lines 2 and 3 themselves seem almost swollen, bellying and dragging, an effect aided by using adjacent unstressed syllables ("of the," "[bell]ies and," "in the") and by using an eye-rhyme ("mind" and "wind") rather than an exact rhyme. And then comes the short last line: almost before we could expect it, the cumbersome balloon — here, the idea that is to be packed into the stanza — is successfully lodged in its "narrow shed." Aside from the relatively colorless "into," the only words of more than one syllable in the poem are "narrow," "balloon," and "bellies," and all three of them emphasize the difficulty of the task. But after "narrow" (the word itself almost looks long and narrow, in this context like a hangar) we get the simplicity of the monosyllable "shed," and the difficult job is done, the thought is safely packed away, the poem is completed — but again with an off rhyme ("bid" and "shed"), for neatness can go only so far when hands and the mind and a balloon are involved.

Because the language of a literary work is denser (richer in associations or connotations) than the language of discursive prose, such as this paragraph, explication is concerned with bringing to the surface the meanings that are in the words but may not be immediately apparent. Explication, in short, seeks to make explicit the implicit.

The reader of an explication needs to see the text. Since the explicated text is usually short, it is advisable to quote the entire text. You can quote it, complete, at the outset, or you can quote the first unit (for example, a stanza) and then explicate the unit, and then quote the next unit and explicate it, and so on. If the poem or passage of prose is longer than, say, six lines, it is advisable to number each line at the right for easy reference.

WRITING A BOOK REVIEW

Because book reviews in newspapers or magazines are usually about a newly published work, reviewers normally assume that their readers will be unfamiliar with the book. Reviewers take it as their job to acquaint readers with the book, its contents and its value, and to help them decide whether or not they wish to read it. Since most reviews are brief (500–1500 words) they cannot, like explications, comment on everything. On the other hand they cannot, like analyses, focus on one aspect of the writing; they usually attempt in some way to cover the book. Reviews, then, usually contain more summary and more evaluation than explications or analyses. Nevertheless, reviewers must approach the task analytically if they are to accomplish it in the relatively small space allotted. And if they are to be convincing, they must support their opinion by quotations (usually indispensable), examples, and specific references to the text so that readers may think and feel the way the reviewer thinks and feels.

A review commonly has a structure something like this:

1. an opening paragraph that names the author and the title, gives the reader some idea of the nature and scope of the work (a children's book; a book for the general reader; a book for specialists), and establishes the tone of the review (more about tone in a moment)
2. a paragraph or two of plot summary if the book is a novel; some summary of the contents if it is not
3. a paragraph on the theme, purpose, idea, or vision embodied in the book, perhaps within the context of related works
4. a paragraph or two on the strengths, if any (for instance, the book fulfills its purpose)
5. a paragraph or two on the weaknesses, if any
6. a concluding paragraph in which the reviewer delivers his or her point — but the point in some degree has probably been implied from the beginning, because the concluding paragraph is a culmination rather than a surprise.

Tone, as we suggest elsewhere in this book (see pages 507–15), usually refers to the writer's attitude toward the subject, the readers, and the writer's self. The tone of a review is therefore somewhat dependent on the publication in which it will appear. A review in *Scientific American* will have a different tone from one in *Ms.* Since you have not been commissioned to write your review and are essentially playing a game, you must *imagine* your reader. It's a reasonable idea to imagine that your classmates are your readers, forgetting of course that they may be reviewing the same book you are. (It's a very bad idea to imagine that your teacher is your reader.) And it's always productive to treat both your reader and your subject with respect. This does not mean you need to be solemn or boring; on the contrary, the best way to show your respect for your reader is to write something you would be interested in reading yourself.

Here is a book review, from *The New York Times*. Although some reviews are untitled, this one has a title; unless your instructor tells you otherwise, give your review a title. (Finding your title will help you to see if you have focused your essay.)

The Tough Got Going

SIGNIFICANT SISTERS
The Grassroots of Active Feminism:
1839-1939
By Margaret Forster

By Carole Klein

A poem by Marge Piercy, called "Rough Times," begins:

We are trying to live
as if we were an experiment
conducted by the future.

The eight women whose lives form *Significant Sisters* were selected for the ways in which their separately courageous breaks with tradition set the future of feminism in motion. Having decided that feminist history can be divided into eight areas of changed experience, Margaret Forster provides narrative biographies of the women responsible for starting each change that has taken place.

Some of these British and American pioneers are familiar to us, such as Margaret Sanger, who made birth control a feminist issue, and Emma Goldman, who served as a bridge between feminist ideologies of the 19th and late 20th centuries. Some other sisters are relatively unknown, and I for one am indebted to Miss Forster for bringing them to my attention. I confess to having scarcely heard, for example, of Caroline Norton. A bitterly unhappy marriage gave her, a well-connected woman and popular writer, the impetus to fight for the reform of English marriage and divorce laws — laws which had made married women powerless chattels, completely at their husbands' mercy. In another sphere of experience, education, we find Emily Davies, who challenged the entrenched belief that education for British girls should be shorter and softer than for boys, and eventually established Girton College for women at Cambridge University in 1873.

What is particularly provocative in this history is how different these women were from each other in temperament and ideology. By no means were all even purposefully advancing a feminist cause as they fought their separate battles. Indeed, Elizabeth Blackwell, the first woman doctor, born in Britain, educated there and in the United States, was decidedly unsympathetic to organized feminism. She saw her own ambitions as atypical, her success due to special gifts. Other women, she thought, should devote themselves to life's highest calling — being good wives and mothers. Of course, as Miss Forster points out, by establishing the principle that gender doesn't rule out professional achievement, Elizabeth Blackwell was in fact a feminist, indeed one who made immense contributions to feminist history.

I must note here that Miss Forster appears to be a bit insensitive to the feminist commitments of many contemporary women physicians. After discussing Blackwell's hope that future female doctors would devote themselves to humanizing medicine, paying particular attention to the medical problems of women, Miss Forster writes: "There are no measurable signs that the entry of women into the medical profession has significantly humanized it. No broad changes exist for the better which are the result of female medical action." Such categorical dismissal seems to ignore the various and well-organized advances female doctors continue to make by, for example, demystifying the physician's role, helping women to participate in their own health care, and in making childbirth a far less clinical and isolating affair. For the most part, however, Miss Forster seems to be quite clear-eyed about her subjects and their legacies, neither romanticizing motives nor being unduly critical of what, from a modern perspective, might seem contradictory or naïve behavior.

Margaret Forster has written two biographies, one a highly acclaimed study of Thackeray. She is also the author of 12 novels, among them the sprightly "Georgy Girl." Her substantial research for *Significant Sisters* draws on diaries, private and published papers and autobiographies. But in constructing her profiles from these historical sources, she employs the novelist's tools of evocative language and skillful rendering of character, story and theme.

Perhaps the most persistent theme in these pages is the conflict between being feminine and feminist. Marriage and motherhood, even love and sex, more often than not eroded a woman's strength. Miss Forster does not believe this conflict is over. Many women still fear that a separate self will be submerged in the roles of wife and mother. But she suggests that in the arc of feminist history we are headed towards a time when such integration really will be possible. As a result of reading this engaging book, we shall certainly know which ancestral sisters to thank when that time arrives.

QUESTIONS

1. Characterize or describe the tone of Klein's review.
2. Write a one-sentence summary of each paragraph. Your list of sentences should resemble an outline. (See the paragraph outline on page 78.)
3. How well does your outline correspond with the structure we say reviews commonly have? (See page 392.)
4. If there are discrepancies between what we have said about reviews and the review by Klein, can you offer a reasonable explanation for these discrepancies? Or would you argue that we revise our discussion, or that we choose a different review as an example?
5. Write a brief argument (one or two paragraphs) defending your answer to question 4.

WRITING OTHER REVIEWS

Our suggestions for writing a book review, with obvious modifications, can serve as guidelines for other reviews you may be assigned or choose to write: of a play, a movie, a concert, or other performance. Again, it is the reviewer's job to acquaint readers, real or imagined, with a performance they are assumed to be unfamiliar with (although in fact reviews are often read by readers who want to see their own judgments confirmed, or their small talk improved). And again, you must adopt an appropriate tone, suggesting both your own expert knowledge of your topic and your respect for your readers' intelligence and taste. Your best preparation for writing a review is to read reviews in publications you trust, consciously noting what you find informative, interesting, and persuasive. Then, if you are covering a live event, you'll find it useful to ask to see in advance the promotional material usually in the hands of the organization sponsoring the event.

You'll want to be skeptical of some of the rave reviews you'll find quoted (and of course you mustn't use them in your own review without acknowledging their sources), but you may well find biographical and other background information that will prepare you for the performance and make notetaking easier. And you must go prepared to take notes — often in the dark — and allow yourself sufficient time immediately after the event to type or rewrite them legibly.

Reviewing a record or tape obviously has some advantages. You can listen to it many times, you may have access to the score or lyrics and previous recordings, and you can choose your own time and place for listening. Or perhaps the relaxed and witty style of the review we print below just makes it seem easier. The review was written by a student for a college newspaper.

Jimmy Buffett Is Going Coconuts?!

Pat Bellanca

This is what Jimmy Buffett used to do: sail around the Caribbean with his friends, smoke a lot of pot, drink a lot of tequila, write some songs — and every year or so return (rather unwillingly, he would have had us believe) to the mainland to record an album, tour the country and make some money so that he could afford to keep his sailboat running and himself pleasantly numbed to the realities of humdrum, everyday American existence.

Romantically melancholy escapism is the theme that Buffett has consistently examined, espoused and re-examined in all of the albums he has released since he first achieved a kind of pop stardom with "Margaritaville," the single from his 1977 album *Changes in Latitudes, Changes in Attitudes.* In that album he developed a formula that worked commercially.

In his most recent effort, *Coconut Telegraph,* released several weeks ago, he reworks an extremely watered-down version of the formula into yet another of his silly celebrations of sailing, smoking and drinking with fellow "expatriated Americans." But now, in keeping with his absorption into the mainstream of pop music, he writes noticeably less about smoking, drinking and wandering than he did before. It sounds like he's raising a family.

Coconut Telegraph is a cleanly produced country-rock-pop album which, despite Buffett's latest change in attitude, almost entirely consists of musical and thematic clones of songs he has previously recorded.

There is the song about the escapades of the businessman in the islands: "The Weather Is Here, Wish You Were Beautiful," which was recycled from "American Friend," a track from *Son of a Son of a Sailor,* Buffett's seventh album. There's the gee-I-kinda-wish-I-could-go-home song, "Incommunicado," this year's model of "Miss You So Badly" from *Changes.* And there's the campy crooner song, "Stars Fell on Alabama" (a 1934 Parish/Perkins song, actually one of the brighter moments on the album), reminiscent of "Pencil Thin Moustache" which Buffett wrote for his 1974 album, *Living and Dying in 3/4 Time.*

With *Coconut Telegraph,* Buffett has completed his transformation from a cult songwriter of nutty hippie anthems (check out "God's Own Drunk" and "The Great Filling Station Hold-up" on two of his earlier albums) to an unambitious, unfunny middle of the middle of the road pop craftsman. In the year which Christopher Cross walked away with multiple Grammy Awards, it's hardly surprising.

In "Growing Older But Not Up" Buffett tells us, "My metabolic rate is pleasantly stuck/So let the winds of change blow over my head . . ." And that's probably the best summation of the attitude behind the album. It's entirely pleasant.

The combined effect of the ever-present congas, steel drums, acoustic guitars, unobtrusive strings and effortlessly wailing harmonica is pleasantly mellow. The song about Buffett's daughter, "Little Miss Magic," is pleasantly sentimental without being overly gooey. The hooks are pleasantly "catchy," particularly in "The Weather Is Here, Wish You Were Beautiful," a single from the album which seems to be getting a fair amount of airplay on WEEI-FM. Even the photo of the star on the cover of the album is pleasantly unassuming — he is wearing topsiders, chinos and an off-white crew-neck.

Of course, all of this is about as relevant and meaningful as sitting in a wad of bubblegum, but if one could prevent oneself from becoming bored and irritated by the unrelieved "pleasantness" of *Coconut Telegraph,* one might find it — a-hem — enjoyable.

QUESTIONS

1. Characterize the writer's tone. It is appropriate to her material and her audience? Explain.
2. On the basis of this review, would you buy *Coconut Telegraph*? If you didn't have to pay for the record, would you be interested, because of the review, in listening to it? Explain why, or why not.
3. If you saw this writer's byline in your newspaper would you read the article? Explain.
4. Write a review of a current album. Or, attend a concert and review it. In a note appended to your review, define your intended audience.

WRITING AN ESSAY BASED ON AN INTERVIEW

We have all been treated to the television interview with (and perhaps by) a celebrity: Question: "Which fight was the toughest that you have ever lost?" Answer: "Uh, well, Howard, that's a tough question." Question: "When did you have your first sexual experience?" Answer: "Oh, Barbara, I knew you'd ask me that!" And we've read similarly inspiring transcriptions in popular magazines (while standing in the checkout line at a supermarket). But the interview is also an important tool of social science research and serious journalism. Sociologists and psychologists regularly use interviews, and biographers and historians often rely heavily on interviews when they write about recent events. Interviews with poets and fiction writers in literary magazines help us to learn not only about the writers and their work but also about the craft of poetry or fiction. For the apprentice writer, interviews provide excellent sources for interesting expository essays about the person being interviewed or about issues and ideas.

A college campus is an ideal place to practice interviewing. Faculties are composed of experts in a variety of fields and distinguished visitors are a regular part of extracurricular life. In the next few pages, we'll offer some advice on conducting interviews and writing essays based on them. If you take our advice, you'll acquire a skill you may well put to further, more specialized use in social science courses; at the same time you'll be developing skill in asking questions and shaping materials relevant to all research and writing.

Before we list the steps for you to follow, we offer two examples, essays based largely on interviews. First read "The Einstein of Happiness." Then answer the questions that follow it.

The Einstein of Happiness

By Patricia Freeman

If the truth be known, being a professor of happiness is no picnic. People deride your research, trivialize your interests — then badger you for the secret of eternal bliss. Nevertheless, Allen Parducci, fifty-seven-year-old professor of psychology at UCLA, has been exploring the fabric of human felicity for over forty years.

Parducci became a happiness scholar because of his father, a stern architectural sculptor in Grosse Pointe, Michigan, who voiced a vexing conviction that "things balance out" between happiness and woe — or, as Mark Twain put it, "Every man is a suffering machine and a happiness machine combined, and for every happiness turned out in one department, the other stands ready to modify it with a sorrow or pain." Young Parducci, wondering why he ought to bother getting out of bed in the morning if that were true, set out to debunk the theory.

He conducted his research everywhere. He quizzed his college roommates as to the completeness of their contentment. He grilled his fellow sailors during World War II: "As the ship rolled back and forth and they retched, I'd ask them, 'How happy are you now? Are you really unhappy?'"

Eventually he received a graduate degree in psychology from Berkeley, where he could finally study the phenomenon scientifically. Today, he is known around the world for his work in "the relativism of absolute judgments" — a fancy phrase meaning that how we evaluate a thing depends on what we compare it to. (Though his work was an outgrowth of his search for the answers to human happiness, hardly anybody in academia has applied it that way). To back up his ideas, he devised several studies to show that judgments of all kinds depend on the context in which they are made.

For one study, he gave a "test" of moral judgments to college students, who were asked to assign each item in a list of behaviors a ranking of from "1 — not particularly bad or wrong" to "5 — extremely evil." Half of the students were given a list of comparatively mild acts of wrongdoing, including such items as "cheating at solitaire," "wearing shorts on the street where it is illegal" and "stealing towels from a hotel room." The other half were given a much nastier list, including such acts as "selling to a hospital milk from diseased cattle." Both lists contained six of the same items. The crucial feature of the test was that the students were to judge the items according to their own personal values and not to judge them in comparison to one another. Nonetheless, the experiment showed that students' moral judgments depended on how the list was "skewed" — the six acts appearing on both lists were rated more leniently by students who judged them in the context of the nasty list than by those who encountered them on the mild list. "Poisoning a neighbor's barking dog," for example, got a rather harsh score of 4.19 when it appeared along with "playing poker on a Sunday" and a less disapproving 3.65 when it came just after "murdering your mother without justification or provocation."

According to the same principle, which Parducci calls a "negatively skewed distribution," our judgments of personal satisfaction depend on how often we experience the things we deem most satisfying. To demonstrate this, he devised a study in which two groups of students selected cards from two different decks and won money based on the value assigned to each card. One group played with cards marked from 1 cent to 21 cents, with the higher values predominating, and the other groups with cards marked from 7 cents to 27 cents, with low sums predominating. Every player won the same total of money for the series, but group one, which garnered its winnings primarily from the higher end of the scale, reported themselves happier with their winnings.

What does all of this mean for us? It means, Parducci says, that just as the cardplayers were happiest when most of their winnings were close to the maximum that could be earned, we will likely be most satisfied if our lives are arranged so that the best of what we experience happens more frequently. The happy person, who finds "zest, fun and joy in life," says Parducci, is one for whom "the things he's experiencing are high relative to his standards." And conversely, the unhappy person — whose life is marked by "terror, anxiety and misery" — sets inappropriate standards for himself, often comparing his life to an impossible ideal.

Parducci will venture a few tips on living the happy life, but only with prodding. If we want to be happy, he says, we ought not to live in the future, thinking that we'd be happy if only we could double our income, marry this person or get that job; instead we should learn to delight in what we have and look forward to things that happen every day. Above all, we should let go of what's impossible.

"We all know people who have had a great love affair break up and their friends say, 'Get it out of your head,' but they can't. But if they could, in effect, drop that relationship out of their context altogether, then the best of their experience with someone new would seem good and wonderful. They could experience the same high even with a lesser person."

The happiest person Parducci has ever known (though he doesn't think he's particularly good at telling whether people are happy or not) was a woman who died of cancer in her mid-thirties. "The six months before she died was like a party every night," he recalls. "Her friends would come over, her ex-husbands would visit, and everybody would have a great time. I asked her, 'Joanne, how do you feel about death?' and she said, 'I know I could die any time, but I'm very happy.'" Joanne was married approximately five times if you count both legal and informal spouses. "She'd meet these men anybody would say she shouldn't marry," Parducci says, "and it would be disastrous. She'd see virtues in people that no one else could see. It seemed that she was living in a dream world. I would have said, looking at her life, that she should see things the way they are. But sometimes I think some people are just born to be happy."

Most Americans, in fact, say that they are happy. According to national polls the average citizen gives himself a happiness rating of seven on a scale of one to ten. Parducci gives himself a six, a rating he believes actually makes him significantly more sanguine than most Americans. "People's reports of their own happiness show an astonishing positive bias," he says. He thinks people make themselves out to be happier than they really are because "there's the implication that there's something wrong with you if you can't somehow arrange your life to be satisfying."

In fact, unhappiness seems to be a national personality trait. "The success credo of American business is that you're supposed to always be setting higher standards," Parducci says. "And in setting inappropriately high standards, we can't help but doom ourselves to unhappiness. Society is pyramidal. There's only one position at the top, and if everyone is pushing toward that one position, the great majority must inevitably fall by the wayside." But still we push our children to aim for medical school or sports superstardom.

Does Parducci hope, in some small way, to make the world a happier place to live? "I'm very skeptical about the possibility of doing that," he says. Still, there are those who would make him into a guru of good cheer. But, unlike Leo Buscaglia, psychologist to the masses and a fixture on the best-seller lists, Parducci is uninterested in providing road maps to felicity and pointers to pleasure. "I've been approached by several literary agents," he says. "There's always a pressure toward self-help. You know, 'The Ten Rules for Happiness.' But if it were that simple, it would have been discovered by now."

People tell him that he could make a fortune if only he would become at least a bit of a happiness hawker. "I ask myself, if lightning struck in that way, if I made a million dollars, would I be happier? But friends of mine who have made that kind of money say that it hasn't made them happy," he says.

Even though Parducci says he'd like to be "more happy," in the end there's something he considers more important — and that is, "being good." He will readily declare that religion — particularly Christianity — has fostered unhappiness by holding up an ideal of goodness that is impossible to live up to. Still, he says, "I think there are rules that people ought to follow, rules that may be difficult. Suppose Mephistopheles came and said, 'If you kill a few people I'll make you very happy.' I hope I would be strong enough to turn him down. I don't want to be identified with the 'me first' psychology that says we're all out for ourselves."

If he can't make people happier and he doesn't consider happiness the most important thing in the world anyway, why does Parducci press on with his work? "There's a satisfaction," he submits, "in just understanding things. We can understand how the planets move around the sun, though we can't affect them. We get satisfaction out of understanding happiness, even though we can't do much about it."

QUESTIONS

1. What homework do you think Patricia Freeman did in preparation for the interview?
2. List the questions Freeman might have posed to elicit the information in each paragraph or group of paragraphs. Were there

any paragraphs for which you had difficulty imagining questions? Can you explain why? (Or, what information do you suppose did not come from Professor Parducci's own words? Who or what do you imagine to be the source of this information?)

3. Through much of the article we hear Parducci's voice, either paraphrased or directly quoted. Where do we hear the interviewer's voice as well?

4. Suppose you had begun with only the information that Allen Parducci is a professor of psychology at an American University. What library sources might tell you his age, education, major field of interest, publications, and current academic post? (See if you can find this information in your own library.)

Now read the second article and answer the questions following it.

Ethnobotanists Race Against Time to Save Useful Plants
Eileen Garred

Although a white lab coat hangs from a bookshelf in his cramped office and an IBM personal computer sits on a nearby table, these are not the tools Mark Plotkin prefers to use. As an ethnobotanist, Plotkin has spent months in the tropical forests of South America, bringing along newspapers and moth balls to press and preserve plant specimens he then hauls back to the Botanical Museum at Harvard.

In annual visits over the past eight years, Plotkin has been patiently cultivating the trust of tribal medicine men in the Suriname jungle in order to learn how the native people use forest plants in their cultures. It is a race against time and the steadily increasing influences of civilization.

Tropical forests the world over are shrinking as deforestation escalates and development spurred by rapid population growth reaches further into the jungle. The Amazon region alone contains approximately 80,000 species of plants, a vast resource of living organisms, many of which are yet unknown to science. Plants of great potential value for medical, agricultural, and industrial uses are vanishing even before they are identified.

Perhaps more important, knowledge about plants long used by native Indians for beneficial purposes is dying out with the witch doctors. "Within one generation after civilization arrives, aboriginal peoples will forget most of their plant lore," predicts Richard Schultes, Director of the Botanical Museum.

The Westerners who arrive to build roads or preach the Gospel also bring with them Western medicines. "Our medicines are effective, cheap, and easy to get," Schultes adds. "The natives are not going to run through the forest to look for a leaf their ancestors used to alleviate sickness if they don't have to."

Few of the witch doctors today have young apprentices from the tribe because visiting missionaries have strongly discouraged shamanism. The last of the medicine men in the tribes must be coaxed to reveal their secrets to a new breed of botanist like Plotkin.

Last year, for example, Plotkin returned from Suriname with a small tree limb called *doubredwa*. The South American Indians scrape the bark into rum and claim the resulting drink is a powerful male aphrodisiac. "The world doesn't need more people," explains Plotkin. "What it needs is a treatment for impotence — and there it is in a woody vine from the Amazon."

Curare, a native arrow poison, has been used for a number of years in hospitals as an anesthetic and muscle relaxant during surgery. Another plant poison that stupefies fish and forces them to the water's surface where they are easy targets for spearfishers is the basis for the pesticide rotenone. Because it is biodegradable, rotenone is widely used in the United States.

Fruit from a common Amazonian palm produces oil that is very similar to olive oil, and the fruit from still another species is extremely rich in vitamins C and A.

"The so-called 'wonder drugs,' including penicillin, cortisone, and reserpine, that have revolutionized the practice of medicine came from plants that had some use in primitive societies that called the attention of a chemist to the plant," says Schultes.

According to Schultes, tribes of the northwest Amazon utilize just under 2000 different plant species for "medicinal" purposes. "In these plants there is a tremendous storehouse of new chemicals," he explains. "In the hands of a chemist, a naturally occurring chemical can be changed to form the basis of many new semi-synthetic chemicals. So if you find in a plant one useful chemical, you are finding literally hundreds that chemists can make using that natural structure as a base. How can chemists hope to procure and analyze 80,000 species of plants?

"One shortcut for the chemist is to concentrate on the plants that native peoples by trial and error over thousands of years have found to have some biological activity," he says.

Although it often takes two decades or more of research from discovery of a plant to a packaged drug, ethnobotanists who provide chemists with the material must work quickly since the varieties of jungle plants and the numbers of medicine men who know how to identify and use them are disappearing at an alarming rate.

As a defined field of study, ethnobotany is more than a century old, but it has received greater attention only in recent years. Schultes, a pioneer in the field, lived and worked in Colombia and Peru from 1941 to 1954. During that time, he collected 24,000 plants and filled dozens of field notebooks, which he is still trying to put into publishable form.

"We call this work an 'ethnobotanical salvage operation,'" says Plotkin, "which just means that we are documenting the plants the Indians use and the ways in which they use them." The U.S. Division of the World Wildlife Fund is sponsoring Plotkin's work at the Harvard Botanical Museum. As part of the Tropical South American Conservation and Ethnobotany Project, Plotkin has compiled a catalog of more than 1000 useful plant species, which includes Latin and vernacular names, data on distribution, aboriginal use, chemical composition and economic potential. Previously, much of this information was widely scattered and not available to botanists, conservationists and development planners.

Plotkin, whose initial interest in the beneficial uses of plants was cultivated by Schultes, is now primarily concerned with tying ethnobotany to conservation. Money, he says, is the bottom line. In fighting for preservation of the Amazon's tropical forest with its large reserve of natural resources, Plotkin aims to put conservation in economic terms.

"The ill-planned development in the tropics by local governments and transnational corporations is causing serious damage," he says. "But you can't tell Brazil, a country with the largest foreign debt in the world, 'Don't cut down the forest because you've got the cutest little monkey living there.' You have to explain that plant A is worth 'x' number of dollars and plant B, if you manage it right, will be worth 'y' number of dollars.

"You have to convince the government that it is worth more as a forest than as an agricultural area, which is probably going to fail anyway over the long term. Until you can put it in concrete economic terms, it's just talk."

As an example, Plotkin points to the irony that Brazil imports $20 million worth of olive oil a year, although there are millions of the palm trees that produce a similar edible oil within its borders.

One of the most common trees in the Amazon, the *buriti* palm, has a multitude of uses discovered by the Indians. Its fruit is rich in vitamins, an extract from the stem can be used to make bread, the fibers can be used to make twine, houses are built from its wood, and it grows only in swampy areas that could not otherwise be used for agriculture. However, says Plotkin, the Brazilian government has yet to step in to look for high yielding strains of the *buriti,* or "tap into what is a potential gold mine" by putting it into plantations.

"Conservation works best if it's in that country's self-interest," says Plotkin. "Ethnobotany" — the study of the use of plants by native peoples who have intimate knowledge of forests and the useful products they contain — "is really in the forefront of international conservation efforts."

"For thousands of years, aboriginal peoples have been living with and depending on the native vegetation. Now civilization is destroying that knowledge," says Schultes. "Much more endangered than any species is the knowledge about plant lore. If we don't pick it up now, we'll never get it."

QUESTIONS

1. Is the article primarily about Plotkin or about Schultes? If neither, what is it about?
2. What is ethnobotany? Where in the article is it defined? Should Garred have defined it earlier? Why or why not?
3. Garred is on the editorial staff of the *Harvard Gazette,* a weekly devoted to news of the Harvard community. How do you suppose Garred came upon her story? Reconstruct the steps she probably took to research her article.
4. From what office or offices at your institution might you learn of an activity of more than usual interest engaged in by a faculty member, an administrator, a student, an alumnus, or a trustee? (Check your college catalog and directory for possible leads.)

As these two essays illustrate, writers use interviews in writing about people, and they also use interviews in writing about issues. For either purpose, an interview produces, and the writer reproduces, more than information. By skillful selection of the most interesting remarks for quotation and by reporting gestures and settings, the writer allows us to experience both the writer's and the speaker's interest in the topic under discussion.

Here are some steps to follow in conducting an interview and writing an essay based on it.

1. *Finding a subject for an interview.* As with all writing projects, the best place to start is with your own interests. If you are taking a course from a particularly interesting professor, you might end your search, and begin your research, there. Or, you might use an interview as a way of investigating a department you're thinking of majoring in. Your college catalog lists the names of all faculty members, by department. Scan the list in the department that interests you and begin to ask questions of upperclassmen. Then, with a name or two in mind, check your library for appropriate biographical reference works. *Directory of American Scholars* contains the most names of academicians, but also check various Who's Who volumes. In addition to *Who's Who in America,* you'll also find such works as *Who's Who in the West,* (and similar titles for the East, South, Southwest, and Midwest), *Who's Who Among Black Americans, Who's Who in Religion, Who's Who of American Women.* In addition, the circulation desk or the research librarian may have a list of current publications by faculty members. In some libraries, current publications by faculty and alumni are on display. Department secretaries are good sources of information not only about the special interests of the faculty, but also about guest speakers scheduled by the department in the near future. Investigate the athletic department if you're interested in sports; or the departments of music, art, and drama, for the names of resident or visiting performing artists. Other sources of newsworthy personalities or events: the publicity office, the president's office, the college newspaper. All are potential sources for information about recent awards, or achievements, or upcoming events that may lead you to a subject for an interview, and a good story.

2. *Preliminary homework.* Find out as much as you can about your potential interviewee's work, from the sources we mentioned above. If the subject of your interview is a faculty member, ask the department secretary if you may see a copy of that person's vita (pronounced vee-ta). Many departments have these brief biographical sketches on file for publicity purposes. The vita will list, among other things, publications and current research interests.

3. *Requesting the interview.* In making your request, don't hesitate to mention that you are fulfilling an assignment, but also make evident your own interest in the person's work or area of expertise. (Showing that you already know something about the work, that you've done some preliminary homework, is persuasive evidence of your interest.) Request the interview, preferably in writing, at least a week in advance, and ask for ample time (probably an hour to an hour and a half) for a thorough interview.

4. *Preparing thoroughly.* If your subject is a writer, read and take notes on the publications that most interest you. Read book reviews, if available; read reviews of performances if your subject is a performing artist. As you read, write out the questions that occur to you. As you work on them, try to phrase your questions so that they require more than a yes or no answer. A "why" or "how" question is likely to be productive, but don't be afraid of a general question such as "Tell me something about. . . ."

Revise your questions and put them in a reasonable order. Work on an opening question that you think your subject will find both easy and interesting to answer. "How did you get interested in . . ." is often a good start. Type your questions or write them boldly so that you will find them easy to refer to.

Think about how you will record the interview. Although a tape recorder may seem like a good idea, there are good reasons not to rely on one. First of all, your subject may be made uneasy by its presence and freeze up. Second, the recorder (or the operator) may malfunction, leaving you with a partial record, or nothing at all. Third, even if all goes well, when you prepare to write you will face a mass of material, some of it inaudible, and all of it daunting to transcribe. If, despite these warnings, you decide (with your subject's permission) to tape, expect to take notes anyway. It's the only way you can be sure you will have a record of what was important to you out of all that was said. Think beforehand, then, of how you will take notes, and if you can manage to, practice by interviewing a friend. You'll probably find that you'll want to devise some system of shorthand, perhaps no more than using initials for names that frequently recur, dropping the vowels in words that you transcribe — whatever assists you to write quickly but legibly. But don't think that you must transcribe every word. Be prepared to do a lot more listening than writing.

5. *Presenting yourself for the interview.* Dress appropriately, bring your prepared questions and a notebook or pad for your notes, and appear on time.

6. *Conducting the interview.* At the start of the interview, try to engage briefly in conversation, without taking notes, to put your subject at ease. Even important people can be shy. Remembering that will help keep you at ease, too. If you want to use a tape recorder, ask your subject's permission, and if it is granted, ask where the microphone may be conveniently placed. As the interview proceeds, keep your purpose in mind. Are you trying to gain information about an issue or topic, or are you trying to get a portrait of a personality? Listen attentively to your subject's answers and be prepared to follow up with your own responses and spontaneous questions. Here is where your thorough preparation will pay off. A good interview develops like a conversation. Keep in mind that your prepared questions, however essential, are not sacred. At the same time don't hesitate to steer your subject, courteously, from apparent irrelevancies (what one reporter calls "sawdust") to something that interests you more. "I'd like to hear a little more about . . ." you can say. Or, "Would you mind telling me about how you . . ." It's also perfectly acceptable to ask your subject to repeat a remark so that you can record it accurately, and if you don't understand something, don't be afraid to admit it. Experts are accustomed to knowing more than others do and are particularly happy to explain even the most elementary parts of their lore to an interested listener.

7. *Concluding the interview.* Near the end of the time you have agreed upon, ask your subject if he or she wishes to add any material, or to clarify something said earlier. Express your thanks and, at the appointed time, leave promptly.

8. *Preparing to write.* As soon as possible after the interview, review your notes, amplify them with details you wish to remem-

ber but might have failed to record, and type them up. You might have discovered during the interview, or you might see now, that there is something more that you want to read by or about your subject. Track it down and take further notes.

9. *Writing the essay.* In writing your first draft, think about your audience. Unless a better idea occurs to you, consider your college newspaper or magazine, or a local newspaper, as the place you hope to publish your story. Write with the readers of that publication in mind. Thinking of your readers will help you to be clear; for instance, to identify names that have come up in the interview but which may be unfamiliar to your readers. As with other writing, begin your draft with any idea that strikes you, and write at a fast clip until you have exhausted your material (or yourself). When you revise, remember to keep your audience in mind; your material should, as it unfolds, tell a coherent and interesting story. Interviews, like conversations, tend to be delightfully circular or disorderly. But an essay, like a story, should reveal its contents in a sequence that captures and holds attention. If you've done a thorough job of interviewing you may find that you have more notes than you can resonably incorporate without disrupting the flow of your story. Don't be tempted to plug them in anyway. If they're really interesting, save them, perhaps by copying them into your journal; if not, chuck them out. (For a wretched example of a story that ends with a detail the writer couldn't bear to let go, see "Fish Eats Brazilian Fisherman," page 103.)

In introducing direct quotations from your source, choose those that are particularly characteristic, or vivid, or memorable. Paraphrase or summarize the rest of what is usable. Although the focus of your essay is almost surely the person you interviewed, it is your story, and most of it should be in your own words. Even though you must keep yourself in the background, your writing will gain in interest if your reader hears your voice as well as your subject's.

You might want to use a particularly good quotation for your conclusion. (Notice that both essays we've chosen as examples conclude this way.) Now make sure that you have an attractive opening paragraph. Identifying the subject of your interview and describing the setting is one way to begin. (Again, look at the sample essays.) Give your essay an attractive title. Before you prepare your final draft, read your essay aloud. You're almost certain to catch phrases you can improve, and places where a transition will help your reader to follow you without effort. Check your quotations for accuracy; check with your subject any quotations or other details you're in doubt about. Type your final draft, then edit and proofread carefully.

10. *Going public.* Make two copies of your finished essay, one for the person you interviewed, one for yourself. The original is for your instructor; hand it in on time.

EXERCISE

Write an essay based on an interview. You needn't be limited in your choice of subject by the examples we've given. A very old person, a recent immigrant, the owner or manager of an interesting store or business, a veteran of the Vietnam war, a gardener, are only a few of the possibilities. If you can manage to do so, include a few photographs of your subject, with appropriate captions.

TAKING ESSAY EXAMINATIONS

What Examinations Are

An examination not only measures learning and thinking but stimulates them. Even so humble an examination as a short-answer quiz — chiefly a device to coerce the student to do the assigned reading — is a sort of push designed to move the student forward. Of course internal motivation is far superior to external, but even such crude external motivation as a quiz can have a beneficial effect. Students know this; indeed they often seek external compulsion, choosing a course "because I want to know something about it, and I know that I won't do the reading on my own." (Teachers often teach a new course for the same reason; we want to become knowledgeable about, say, the theater of the absurd, and we know that despite our lofty intentions we may not seriously confront the subject unless we are under the pressure of facing a class.) In short, however ignoble it sounds, examinations force the student to acquire learning and then to convert learning into thinking.

Sometimes it is not until preparing for the final examination that the student — rereading the chief texts and classroom notes — sees what the course was really about; until this late stage, the trees obscured the forest, but now, as the student reviews and sorts things out, a pattern emerges. The experience of reviewing and then of writing an examination, though fretful, can be highly exciting as connections are made and ideas take on life. Such discoveries about the whole subject matter of a course can almost never be made by writing critical essays on topics of one's own construction, for such topics rarely require a view of the whole. Furthermore, most of us are more likely to make imaginative leaps when trying to answer questions that other people pose to us, than when we are trying to answer questions we pose to ourselves. And although questions posed by others cause anxiety, when they have been confronted and responded to on an examination students often make yet another discovery — a self-discovery, a sudden and satisfying awareness of powers they didn't know they had.

Writing Essay Answers

We assume that before the examination you have read the assigned material, made notes in the margins of your books, made summaries of the reading and of the classroom comments, reviewed all of this material, and had a decent night's sleep. Now you are facing the examination sheet.

Here are eight obvious but important practical suggestions.

1. Take a moment to jot down, as a kind of outline or source of further inspiration, a few ideas that strike you after you have thought a little about the question. You may at the outset realize there are three points you want to make: unless you jot these down — three key words will do — you may spend all the allotted time on only one.

2. Don't bother to copy the question in the examination booklet, but if you have been given a choice of questions do indicate the question number, or write a word or two that will serve as a cue to the reader.

3. Answer the question. Consider this question: "Fromm and Lorenz try to explain aggression. Compare their theories, and discuss the extent to which they assist us in understanding the Arab-Israeli conflict." Notice that you must compare — not just summarize — two theories, and that you must also evaluate their relevance to a particular conflict. In short, take seriously such words as *compare, define, evaluate,* and *summarize.* And don't waste time generalizing about aggression; again, answer the question.

4. You can often get a good start merely by turning the question into an affirmation, for example by turning "In what ways is the poetry of Ginsberg influenced by Whitman?" into "The poetry of Ginsberg is influenced by Whitman in at least . . . ways."

5. Don't waste time summarizing at length what you have read, unless asked to do so — but of course occasionally you may have to give a brief summary in order to support a point. The instructor wants to see that you can *use* your reading, not merely that you have done the reading.

6. Budget your time. Do not spend more time on a question than the allotted time.

7. Be concrete. Illustrate your arguments with facts — names, dates, and quotations if possible.

8. Leave space for last minute additions. Either skip a page between essays, or write only on the right-hand pages so that on rereading you can add material at the appropriate place on the left-hand pages.

Beyond these general suggestions, we can best talk about essay examinations by looking at specific types of questions.

Questions on Literature

The five most common sorts of questions encountered in literature examinations are

1. a passage to explicate
2. a historical question, such as "Trace T. S. Eliot's religious development," "Trace the development of Shakespeare's conception of the tragic hero," or "How is Frost's nature poetry indebted to Emerson's thinking?"
3. a critical quotation to be evaluated

4. a comparison, such as "Compare the dramatic monologues of Browning with those of T. S. Eliot"
5. a wild question, such as "What would Dickens think of Vonnegut's *Cat's Cradle*?" or "What would Macbeth do if he were in Hamlet's position?"

A few remarks on each of these types may be helpful:

1. For a discussion of how to write an explication, see pages 389–91. As a short rule, look carefully at the tone (speaker's attitude toward self, subject, and audience) and at the implications of the words (the connotations or associations), and see if there is a pattern of imagery. For example, religious language ("adore," "saint") in a secular love poem may define the nature of the lover and of the beloved. Remember, *an explication is not a paraphrase* (a putting into other words) but an attempt to show the relations of the parts, especially by calling attention to implications. Organization of such an essay is rarely a problem, since most explications begin with the first line and go on to the last.

2. A good essay on a historical question will offer a nice combination of argument and evidence; the thesis will be supported by concrete details (names, dates, perhaps even brief quotations). A discussion of Eliot's movement toward the Church of England cannot be convincing if it does not specify certain works as representative of Eliot in certain years. If you are asked to relate a writer or a body of work to an earlier writer or period, list the chief characteristics of the earlier writer or the period and then show *specifically* how the material you are discussing is related to these characteristics. And if you can quote some relevant lines from the works, your reader will feel that you know not only titles and stock phrases but also the works themselves.

3. If you are asked to evaluate a critical quotation, read it carefully and in your answer take account of *all* of the quotation. If the critic has said, "Eliot in his plays always . . . but in his poems rarely . . ." you will have to write about both the plays and the poems; it will not be enough to talk only about the plays (unless, of course, the instructions on the examination ask you to take only as much of the quotation as you wish). Watch especially for words like "always," "for the most part," "never"; although the passage may on the whole approach the truth, you may feel that some important qualifications are needed. This is not being

picky; true thinking involves making subtle distinctions, yielding assent only so far and no further. And, again, be sure to give concrete details, supporting your argument with evidence.

4. Comparisons are discussed on pages 45–52. Because comparisons are especially difficult to write, be sure to take a few moments to jot down a sort of outline so that you can know where you will be going. A comparison of Browning's and Eliot's monologues might treat three poems by each, devoting alternate paragraphs to one author; or it might first treat one author's poems and then turn to the other. But if it adopts this second strategy, the essay may break into two parts. You can guard against this weakness by announcing at the outset that you will treat the authors separately, then by reminding your reader during your treatment of the first author that certain points will be picked up when you get to the second author, and again by briefly reminding your reader during the second part of the essay of certain points already made.

5. Curiously, a wild question such as "What would Dickens think of *Cat's Cradle*?" or "What would Macbeth do in Hamlet's position?" usually produces tame answers: a half dozen ideas about Dickens or Macbeth are neatly applied to Vonnegut or Hamlet, and the gross incompatibilities are thus revealed. But, as the previous paragraph suggests, it may be necessary to do more than to set up bold and obvious oppositions. The interest in such a question and in the answer to it may largely be in the degree to which superficially different figures *resemble* each other in some important ways. And remember that the wildness of the question does not mean that all answers are equally acceptable; as usual, a good answer will be supported by concrete details.

Questions on the Social Sciences

First, an obvious statement: courses in the social sciences almost always require lots of reading. Do the reading when it is assigned, rather than try to do it the night before the examination. Second, when confronted with long reading assignments, you probably will read more efficiently if you scan the table of contents of a book to see the layout of the material, and then read the first and last chapters, where the authors usually summarize their theses.

Books and articles on history, psychology, and sociology are not whodunits; there is nothing improper about knowing at the start how it will all turn out. Indeed, if at the start you have a clear grasp of the author's thesis, you may have the pleasure of catching the author perpetrating the crime of arguing from insufficient evidence. The beginning and the end of an article in a journal also may offer summaries that will assist you to read the article with relative ease. But only a reading of the entire work (perhaps with a little skimming) will offer you all of the facts and — no less important — the fully developed view or approach that the instructor believes is essential to an understanding of the course.

The techniques students develop in answering questions on literature may be transferred to examinations in the social sciences. A political science student, for example, can describe through explication the implicit tone or attitude in some of the landmark decisions of the Supreme Court. Similarly, the student of history who has learned to write an essay with a good combination of argument and evidence will not simply offer generalizations or present a list of facts unconnected by some central thesis, but will use relevant facts to support a thesis. The student who is able to evaluate a critical quotation or to compare literary works can also evaluate and compare documents in all the social sciences. Answers to wild questions can be as effective or as trite in the social sciences as in literature. "You are the British ambassador in Petrograd in November 1918. Write a report to your government about the Bolshevik revolution of that month" is to some instructors and students an absurd question but to others it is an interesting and effective way of ascertaining whether a student has not only absorbed the facts of an event but has also learned how to interpret them.

Questions on the Physical Sciences and Mathematics

Although the answer to an examination question in the physical sciences usually requires a mathematical computation, a few sentences may be useful in explaining the general plan of the computation, the assumptions involved, and sometimes the results.

It is particularly valuable to set down at the outset in a brief statement, probably a single sentence, your plan for solving the problem posed by the examination question. The statement is equivalent to the topic sentence of a paragraph. For instance, if the examination question is "What is the time required for an object to fall from the orbit of the moon to the earth?" the statement of your plan might be: "The time required for an object to fall from the orbit of the moon to the earth can be obtained by integration from Newton's law of motion, taking account of the increasing gravitational force as the object approaches the earth." Explicitly setting down your plan in words is useful first in clarifying your thought: is the plan a complete one leading to the desired answer? Do I know what I need to know to implement the plan? If your plan doesn't make sense you can junk it right away before wasting more time on it.

The statement of plan is useful also in communicating with the instructor. Your plan of solution, although valid, may be a surprise to the instructor. (She may have expected a solution to the problem posed above starting from Kepler's laws without any integration.) When this is so, the instructor will need your explanation to become oriented to your plan, and to properly assess its merits. Then if you botch the subsequent computation or can't remember how the gravitational force varies with the distance you will still have demonstrated that you have some comprehension of the problem. If on the other hand you present an erroneous computation without any explanation, the instructor will see nothing but chaos in your effort.

Further opportunities to use words will occur when you make assumptions or simplifications: "I assume the body is released with zero velocity and accordingly set $b = 0$," or "The third term is negligible and I drop it."

Finally, the results of your computation should be summarized or interpreted in words to answer the question asked. "The object will fall to the earth in five days." (The correct answer, for those who are curious.) Or, if you arrive at the end of your computation and of the examination hour and find you have a preposterous result, you can still exit gracefully (and increase your partial credit) with an explanation: "The answer of 53 days is clearly erroneous since the fall time of an object from the moon's orbit must be less than the 7 days required for the moon to travel a quarter orbit."

WRITING RÉSUMÉS, LETTERS FOR JOBS, AND APPLICATIONS FOR GRADUATE AND PROFESSIONAL PROGRAMS

In writing for a job, you need to send not only a letter but also a résumé (French for summary). The letter will be addressed to a specific person and may be an application for a specific job, but the résumé should give as full a picture of you as is possible to give in one page.

The Résumé

Make every effort to keep your résumé down to one page, so that the reader can get the whole picture — education, experience, interests, and so forth — at a single glance. You need not include any statement about race, religion, weight, sex, marital status, or age, but if you think such information may be to your advantage, include it. Several formats are acceptable, but on page 421 we illustrate the most common. Notice that information in each category is given in *reverse chronological order* — the most recent experience first.

After your name, address, and telephone number (if you live at a college, give your home number as well as your local number, with dates of residence, so that you can be reached during vacations), give a "job objective" *if* you know exactly what you are looking for. Examples:

```
Entry-level sales position with a firm that provides opportunity to meet
people who work with computer systems

Editorial work with publisher of social science textbooks

To work in customer relations in a department store, to continue my edu-
cation part time, and eventually to assume a managerial position
```

You may, of course, want to prepare two or even three résumés, varying the job objective in order to suit different kinds of potential employers.

If you can't state a job objective, begin with either "Education" or with "Work Experience," whichever seems stronger to you. The point, of course, is to begin with your chief credentials.

Notice that under "Work Experience" you do not simply list names of employers, or even titles of jobs; you also specify the kind of work done, the responsibilities fulfilled. Thus, if you worked at a ski shop you might say:

```
sales; assisted buyer at spring ski show
```

If you were a sports medicine intern at the Lahey Clinic, you might add

```
administered prescribed treatment for physical therapy outpatients
```

If honesty allows, use such words as "administered," "developed," "initiated," "installed," "operated," "responsible for," "supervised," "advanced to," and "promoted to."

Similarly, under "Education" you should not only give the reader a sense of the program you studied but should also specify any academic awards, including scholarships, that you received.

The heading called "Personal Interests" (or "Personal Data") gives you an additional chance to convey what sort of person you are. Don't hesitate to list hobbies; hobbies often suggest important traits. For example, if you are an amateur magician, you probably are at ease with audiences, and if you are a Go player (Go is a sort of Japanese chess) you probably like to solve problems. But if you have a collection of snakes, keep that information to yourself unless you are applying for a job in a pet store or on a snake farm.

The last heading in a résumé usually is "References." Before you list a name (with an address and telephone number, of course), be sure to get permission; if the person seems cool when you ask if you may give his or her name, find someone else. In fact, since you don't want a lukewarm letter, don't simply ask people if you may list their names as references. Rather, ask if they feel that they know you and your work well enough to write a helpful recommendation. If you state the matter this way, someone who otherwise might write a dutiful but unenthusiastic (and therefore unhelpful and perhaps even damaging) letter can gracefully decline, saying that you ought to turn to someone else who knows you better.

Be sure, also, to allow the letter writer ample time to write a thoughtful, unhurried letter. Ten days is a minimum; two weeks is better. And provide what help you can — a transcript, a résumé, a draft of your letter applying for a job, and possibly copies of course papers that you had submitted.

After you have drafted and typed your résumé, show it to a couple of friends and, if possible, to someone who has had experience in reading résumés. Revise it in the light of their suggestions. In typing the final copy, keep an eye on the design: don't crowd your material into the upper two-thirds of the sheet. Make sure that there are no typographical errors (a prospective employer will take a typo as evidence that you are careless) and no spelling errors (widely, though mistakenly, thought to be a sign of stupidity). If you were a resident adviser in a dormitory, don't say you were a resident adviser in a dormatory. (If you don't get the point, look again at the last word in the previous sentence.) Finally, take the résumé to a photocopy shop or an offset printer and have it reproduced on 8½-by-11-inch paper. Never use carbon, thermofax, or mimeographed copies.

The Covering Letter

Employers, even if they are philanthropic institutions such as churches, schools, and museums, are not engaged in philanthropy when they hire employees. They are looking to get rather than to give; that is, they are looking for people who can be useful to them. Your letter of application, therefore, must indicate what you can contribute.

Unlike your résumé, your letter should be an original, not a copy. Address it to a specific person, not to "Dear Sir," "Dear Sir or Madam," "Director of Personnel," or "To Whom It May Concern." A vague address means that you haven't bothered to make a telephone call to find out the name of the person to whom you

[SAMPLE RÉSUMÉ]

Howard Saretta

School Address   Home Address
(until 16 May 1986)   (after 17 May 1986)
Buckminster Hall, #202   38 Barker's Road
Redding College   Somerville, MA 02150
Woodmere, MA 02156   (617) 352-6650
(617) 864-2964

JOB OBJECTIVE   Marketing or advertising trainee

EDUCATION

1982-86   Redding College, Woodmere, MA
                        Degree: BA (expected in June 1986)
                        Major: Business administration
                        Minor: English

1978-82   Somerville High School

WORK EXPERIENCE

Summer 1985   Acting Assistant Manager, O'Neill's Sports Cen-
                          ter, Medford, MA. Responsible for checking
                          inventory, dealing with retail customers, as-
                          sisting buyers

Summer 1984   Salesclerk, O'Neill's Sports Center

1982-84   Part-time work in shipping office of Blackston's
                          Department Store. Processed orders. Respon-
                          sible for insuring valuable parcels.

EXTRACURRI-CULAR   Undergraduate Senate, Redding College (1984-85)
ACTIVITIES   Debating Society, Redding College (1983-85; Vice
                          President, 1985)
                        Drama Club, Somerville High School (1982)

PERSONAL INTERESTS   Drama, photography, crossword puzzles

REFERENCES   Academic References:
                          Office of Student Placement
                          Redding College
                          Woodmere, MA. 02156

                       Mr. Bert Williams
                          O'Neill's Sports Center
                          200 Main Street
                          Medford, MA 02155

are writing. And be sure to spell the name correctly; a misspelling (Bergman for Bergmann) will be taken as a sign of carelessness. Getting the right name, and spelling it right, shows that you have done at least a little homework; it suggests that you are conscientious, and that you know something about the institution that you are seeking to join. If you are aware of an opening in a particular department, it usually is best to send your letter and résumé to the head of the department rather than to the personnel office. Probably the head will routinely route your material to Personnel, but possibly he or she will scan it, notice something of interest, and may at least scrawl "looks good" at the top of the letter before sending it on to Personnel.

Try to keep the letter down to one page; since your résumé will accompany the letter, there is no need to repeat much of the information given in the résumé. But there is no harm in stating your job objective early in the letter even though it is also in the résumé. Similarly, you can mention your strongest point (possibly your academic major, or possibly some experience on the job) in the letter as well as in the résumé. Encountering this information near the outset, the reader of the letter may feel that you are indeed the person that the company is looking for. If someone already working for the company suggested that you write — and has given you permission to use his or her name — it's not a bad idea to begin by saying, "John Doe has suggested that I write to you. . . ." If Doe is respected, your letter will get extra attention, especially because the reader will assume that Doe is endorsing your candidacy.

The gist of the letter should suggest, if possible, that you are especially interested in this job and in this company. For instance, if you are writing to a small company you may indicate that you are especially interested because you will have the opportunity to work in several departments and thus be able to get a sense of the overall activities of the company. On the other hand, if your interests are fairly specialized and you are writing to a large company, you may want to indicate that you prefer such a company because it can use all of your time in a single sort of activity. If you are writing for a particular job — let's say for one that has been advertised — say so. The implication in the letter should be that you believe the company can use you, perhaps because you have the necessary experience, or, if experience is lacking, because you have the necessary brains and interest. Notice the "you believe" in the previous sentence. You letter should be affirmative, but it should not be arrogant. Statements such as "I am fully qualified to do . . ." and "I am expert at . . ." will probably turn most readers off. It's better to say something like "My experience as an assistant manager at Pizza Hut taught me to be patient with customers and to make demands on myself," or "The manager of Pizza Hut has recommended me for the position of night manager, but I have decided to . . . ."

When you read and reread your draft, try to imagine what sort of person it reveals. It ought to reveal someone diligent and competent, but not a braggart and not a clown (unless you are applying for a job as a clown). It's difficult, of course, to avoid bragging and yet at the same time to convey the impression that it's to the employer's self-interest to invite you for an interview, but it can be done. If your letter is clear and direct, and if it suggests that the job and the company are just the sort of thing you are keenly interested in, you will have a chance.

Let's assume the letter is one page long, probably with three or four paragraphs so that it can be read easily. The last paragraph usually includes a polite request for an interview. Show your draft of the letter to a friend or two, to an instructor, and if possible to an employer, with an eye toward revising it, and then type up your final version on 8½-by-11-inch paper. (Smaller, personal stationery — especially with fancy lettering or with a flower in a corner — will not do.) Single-space all of the writing, but double-space between units — for instance, between the date and the name of the recipient — and double-space between paragraphs, as in the example on page 424. Be sure to check the spelling and the typing; it's not a bad idea to ask a friend to do a second check.

If you do get an interview, and you feel after the interview that you are still interested in the job, write a followup letter. In this letter, reaffirm your interest, include any information that you wish you had mentioned during the interview, and thank the interviewer for having given you the opportunity to present yourself.

[SAMPLE LETTER APPLYING FOR A JOB]

29 Cleveland Street
Waltham, MA 02254
20 May, 1986

Mr. William C. Bliss, Personnel Director
Conway Products, Inc.
17 Main Street
Worcester, MA 01610

Dear Mr. Bliss:

Dr. Helen Stone, who serves as a writing consultant to Conway Products and who is one of my professors at Hewson College, has suggested that I write to you about the possibility of a position in the junior management training program at Conway. I will graduate from Hewson, with a major in English, in May 1986, and will then be available for full-time work.

In the second term of my junior year I served as an aide in the Writing Program, assisting freshmen whose native language was not English to improve their writing. I am now an assistant supervisor in this program, guiding ten other upperclass students in their work with freshmen. I am also the assistant advertising manager of <u>The Observer</u>, the college's weekly newspaper, with special responsibility for generating new accounts. I enjoy working with others and meeting challenges, and these activities have given me experience in dealing with people and in responding to minor crises. Certainly the challenge (successfully met) to double our advertising revenue was a stimulant. I believe that my background would enable me, after training in the management program, to work effectively at Conway Products.

I enclose a résumé so that you may have a more detailed idea of my interests and my qualifications. I can be reached at 628-5000, and I can arrange my schedule so that I will be available for an interview at almost any time.

Sincerely yours,

Doris Cursor

Doris Cursor

EXERCISE

Clip out an advertisement for a job that is of some interest to you, and write a letter of application. (For the purposes of this exercise, assume that you are in your last year of schooling; thus, you can invent reasonable accomplishments for yourself.) Hand in a copy of the advertisement with your letter.

Applying to Graduate and Professional Programs

Our comments on writing a letter applying for a job are applicable to writing for admission to a graduate or professional program. Most programs receive far more applicants — even qualified applicants — than they can admit, and so they admit only those applicants who seem able to make a contribution because they are especially strong. A person who seeks admission to the law school at New York University "because my wife has just taken a job in New York" is revealing not strength but naivete.

Carefully study the catalog to see if you have any special strengths that will suit the program, and if you do, call attention to them. For instance, if you have had a course or two in folklore and are applying to do graduate work in English in a department that is especially strong in folklore, you might want to indicate that one of the reasons you are applying is the chance to do more work in this field. If you speak Spanish, call attention to this strength, which equips you to study Hispanic folklore. Similarly, if you have had some teaching experience, and you notice that the department awards teaching assistantships to first-year students, mention your experience and perhaps specify the name of the professor who supervised your work. If an alumnus of the program is one of the persons who is recommending you, be sure to mention this point, and indicate (if true) that Professor X's comments on the program have suggested to you that it is a program in which you would especially like to participate, perhaps because the program emphasizes interdisciplinary studies, or because it is small, or because it is innovative, or whatever.

Finding out about programs by studying catalogs and by talking to people who have been through the programs is not merely a way of writing an application that will help to get you accepted; it is a way of finding the program that will in fact best suit you.

PART TWO
Revising

The friends that have it I do wrong
When ever I remake a song,
Should know what issue is at stake:
It is myself that I remake.
— WILLIAM BUTLER YEATS

A NOTE ON REVISING

The following pages on revising deal with relatively small-scale revisions, touching up or polishing an essay that the writer believes has already reached (or come close to reaching) an acceptable shape.

This sort of revision, however, is necessarily preceded by another sort, revision that alters the proportions of an essay or that, for example, rearranges the sequence of the arguments supporting (or opposing) capital punishment in order to present the case more clearly and more effectively. Thus, a writer who in the first draft gave three arguments supporting a position might in the second draft decide to put the third argument first, perhaps because it is the easiest to grasp (or the most commonly held, or the most widely misunderstood). And in the process of reorganizing the material a fourth idea may even come to mind, which will require even further reorganization of the material. We have tried to deal with large-scale revision earlier in the book, for instance in our comments on outlining and on organizing various kinds of writing.

If you write on a word processor, you can shift passages of text merely by tapping some keys on the keyboard. If you don't use a word processor, you can at first get away with circling passages and attaching arrows to them, indicating where the passages are to be inserted, or attaching labels such as "add to end of second parag. on p. 4," but pretty soon you will have to start using scissors and paste or Scotch tape so that you can see if your essay really does proceed coherently. Assuming that it does seem to have a coherent structure, you are then ready to make the sorts of further revisions that we discuss below.

What follows here, then, is a discussion of revisions of what a writer hopes is a fairly late draft. But (bad news) it of course doesn't always work out that way. In the process of touching up—for example in the attempt to clarify a sentence by changing a vague word—you may find that the entire paragraph is out of place, or needs rethinking, or is irrelevant, and so you have to go back to the drawing board.

Still (good news), writers usually find that they can make most of their large-scale revisions in their second or third drafts, and there comes a time when they can concentrate their attention chiefly on fine tuning. And it is to this sort of revision that we now turn, cautioning you that if, as you work on the details, you see the need for more extensive revision, well, you'll just have to do something about it. The process of writing cannot be as compartmentalized as a textbook.

12
Revising for Conciseness

Excess is the common substitute for energy.
— MARIANNE MOORE

All writers who want to keep the attention and confidence of their readers revise for conciseness. The general rule is to say everything relevant in as few words as possible. The conclusion of the Supreme Court's decision in *Brown* v. *The Board of Education of Topeka*, for example — "Separate educational facilities are inherently unequal" — says it all in six words.

The writers of the following sentences talk too much; they bore us because they don't make every word count.

> There are two pine trees which grow behind this house.
>
> On his left shoulder is a small figure standing. He is about the size of the doctor's head.
>
> The judge is seated behind the bench and he is wearing a judicial robe.

Compare those three sentences with these revisions:

> Two pine trees grow behind this house.
>
> On his left shoulder stands a small figure, about the size of the doctor's head.
>
> The judge, wearing a robe, sits behind the bench.

We will soon discuss in some detail the chief patterns of wordiness, but here it is enough to say that if you prefer the revisions you already have a commendable taste for conciseness. What does your taste tell you to do with the following sentences?

> A black streak covers the bottom half. It appears to have been painted with a single stroke of a large brush.

The time to begin revising for conciseness is when you think you have an acceptable draft in hand — something that pretty much covers your topic and comes reasonably close to saying what you believe about it. As you go over it, study each sentence to see what, without loss of meaning or emphasis, can be deleted. (Delete by crossing out, not erasing; this saves time, and keeps a record of something you may want to reintroduce.) Read each paragraph, preferably aloud, to see if each sentence supports the topic sentence or idea and clarifies the point you are making. Leave in the concrete and specific details and examples that support your ideas (you may in fact be adding more) but cut out all the deadwood that chokes them: extra words, empty or pretentious phrases, weak qualifiers, redundancies, negative constructions, wordy uses of the verb *to be*, and other extra verbs and verb phrases. We'll discuss these problems in the next pages, but first we offer some examples of sentences that cannot be improved upon; they're so awful there's nothing to do but cross them out and start over. Zonker, in Garry Trudeau's cartoon, is a master of what we call Instant Prose (stuff that sounds like the real thing, but isn't).

INSTANT PROSE (ZONKERS)

Here are some examples of Instant Prose from students' essays:

> Frequently a chapter title in a book reveals to the reader the main point that the author desires to bring out during the course of the chapter.

We could try revising this, cutting the twenty-seven words down to seven:

> A chapter's title often reveals its thesis.

[Handwritten margin notes: "What can be deleted" and "recd out loud"]

DOONESBURY
by Garry Trudeau

But why bother? Unless the title is an exception, is the point worth making?

The two poems are basically similar in many ways, yet they have their significant differences.

True; all poems are both similar to and different from other poems. Start over with your next sentence, perhaps something like: "The two poems, superficially similar in rough paraphrase, are strikingly different in diction."

> Although the essay is simple in plot, the theme encompasses many vital concepts of emotional makeup.
>
> Following a transcendental vein, the nostalgia in the poem takes on a spiritual quality.
>
> Cassell only presents a particular situation concerning the issue, and with clear descriptions and a certain style sets up an interesting article.

Pure zonkers. Not even the writers of these sentences now know what they mean.

Writing Instant Prose is an acquired habit, like smoking cigarettes or watching soap operas; fortunately it's easier to kick. It often begins in high school, sometimes earlier, when the victim is assigned a ten-page paper, or is told that a paragraph *must* contain at least three sentences, or that a thesis is stated in the introduction to an essay, elaborated in the body, and repeated in the conclusion. If the instructions appear arbitrary, and the student is bored or intimidated by them, the response is likely to be, like Zonker's, meaningless and mechanical. Such students forget, or never learn, the true purpose of writing — the discovery and communication of ideas, attitudes, and judgments. They concentrate instead on the word count: stuffing sentences, padding paragraphs, stretching and repeating points, and adding flourishes. Rewarded by a satisfactory grade, they repeat the performance, and in time, through practice, develop some fluency in spilling out words without thought or commitment, and almost without effort. Such students enter, as Zonker would say, the college of their choice, feeling somehow inauthentic, perhaps even aware that they don't really mean what they write: symptoms of habitual use of, or addiction to, Instant Prose.

How to Avoid Instant Prose

1. Trust yourself. Writing Instant Prose is not only a habit; it's a form of alienation. If you habitually write zonkers you probably don't think of what you write as your own but as something

you produce on demand for someone else. (Clearly Zonker is writing for that unreasonable authority, the teacher, whose mysterious whims and insatiable appetite for words he must somehow satisfy.) Breaking the habit begins with recognizing it, and then acknowledging the possibility that you can take yourself and your work seriously. It means learning to respect your ideas and experiences (unlearning the passive habits that got you through childhood) and determining that when you write you'll write what you mean — nothing more, nothing less. This involves taking some risks, of course; habits offer some security or they would have no grip on us. Moreover, we all have moments when we doubt that our ideas are worth taking seriously. Keep writing honestly anyway. The self-doubts will pass; accomplishing something — writing one clear sentence — can help make them pass.

2. Distrust your first draft. Learn to recognize Instant Prose Additives when they crop up in your writing, and in what you read. And you *will* find them in what you read — in textbooks and in academic journals, notoriously.

Here's an example from a recent book on contemporary theater:

> One of the principal and most persistent sources of error that tends to bedevil a considerable proportion of contemporary literary analysis is the assumption that the writer's creative process is a wholly conscious and purposive type of activity.

Notice all the extra stuff in the sentence: "principal and most persistent," "tends to bedevil," "considerable proportion," "type of activity." Cleared of deadwood the sentence might read: "The assumption that the writer's creative process is wholly conscious bedevils much contemporary criticism."

3. Acquire two things: a new habit, Revising for Conciseness; and what Isaac Singer calls "the writer's best friend," a wastebasket.

REVISING FOR CONCISENESS

Extra Words and Empty Words

Extra words should, by definition, be eliminated; vague, empty, or pretentious words and phrases may be replaced by specific and direct language.

Wordy

However, it must be remembered that Ruth's marriage could have positive effects on Naomi's situation.

Concise

Ruth's marriage, however, will also provide security for Naomi.

In the second version, the unnecessary "it must be remembered that" has been eliminated; for the vague "positive effects" and "situation," specific words communicating a precise point have been substituted. The revision, though briefer, says more.

Wordy

In high school, where I had the opportunity for three years of working with the student government, I realized how significantly a person's enthusiasm could be destroyed merely by the attitudes of his superiors.

Concise

In high school, during three years on the student council, I saw students' enthusiasm destroyed by insecure teachers and cynical administrators.

Again, the revised sentence gives more information in fewer words. How?

Wordy

The economic situation of Miss Moody was also a crucial factor in the formation of her character.

Concise

Anne Moody's poverty also helped to form her character.

"Economic situation" is evasive for poverty; "crucial factor" is pretentious. Both are Instant Prose.

Wordy

It creates a better motivation of learning when students can design their own programs involving education. This way students' interests can be focused on.

Concise

Motivation improves when students design their own programs, focused on their own interests.

Now revise the following wordy sentences:

1. Perhaps they basically distrusted our capacity to judge correctly.
2. The use of setting is also a major factor in conveying a terrifying type atmosphere.

Notice how, in the examples provided, the following words *watch* crop up: "basically," "significant," "situation," "factor," "involv-*for* ing," "effect," "type." These words have legitimate uses, but are *these words* often no more than Instant Prose Additives. Cross them out when-ever you can. Similar words to watch out for: *aspect, facet, funda-mental, manner, nature, ultimate, utilization, viable, virtually, vital.* If they make your writing sound good, don't hesitate — cross them out at once.

Weak Intensifiers and Qualifiers

Words like *very, quite, rather, completely, definitely,* and *so* can usually be struck from a sentence without loss. Paradoxically, sentences are often more emphatic without intensifiers. Try read-ing the following sentences both with and without the bracketed words:

At that time I was [very] idealistic.
We found the proposal [quite] feasible.
The remark, though unkind, was [entirely] accurate.
It was a [rather] fatuous statement.
The scene was [extremely] typical.
Both films deal with disasters [virtually] beyond our control.
The death scene is [truly] grotesque.
What she did next was [completely] inexcusable.
The first line [definitely] establishes that the father had been drink-ing.

Always avoid using intensifiers with *unique.* Either something is unique — the only one of its kind — or it is not. It can't be very, quite, so, pretty, or fairly unique.

Circumlocutions

Roundabout ways of saying things enervate your prose and tire your reader. Notice how each circumlocution in the first col-umn is matched by a concise expression in the second.

I came to the realization that	I realized that
She is of the opinion that	She thinks that
The quotation is supportive of	The quotation supports
Concerning the matter of	About
During the course of	During
For the period of a week	For a week
In the event that	If
In the process of	During, while
Regardless of the fact that	Although
Due to the fact that	Because
For the simple reason that	Because
The fact that	That
Inasmuch as	Since
If the case was such that	If
It is often the case that	Often
In all cases	Always
I made contact with	I called, saw, phoned, wrote
At that point in time	Then
At this point in time	Now

Now revise this sentence:

These movies have a large degree of popularity for the simple reason that they give the viewers insight in many cases.

Wordy Beginnings

Vague, empty words and phrases clog the beginnings of some sentences. They're like elaborate windups before the pitch.

1. *Wordy*

By analyzing carefully the last lines in this stanza, you find the connections between the loose ends of the poem.

Concise

The last lines of the stanza connect the loose ends of the poem.

2. *Wordy*

What the cartoonist is illustrating and trying to get across is the greed of the oil producers.

Concise

The cartoon illustrates the greed of the oil producers.

3. *Wordy*

Dealing with the crucial issue of the year, the editorial is expressing ironical disbelief in any possible solution to the Middle East crisis.

Concise

The editorial ironically expresses disbelief in the proposed solutions to the Middle East crisis.

4. *Wordy*

In the last stanza is the conclusion (as usual) and it tells of the termination of the dance.

Concise

The last stanza concludes with the end of the dance.

5. *Wordy*

In opposition to the situation of the younger son is that of the elder who remained in his father's house, working hard and handling his inheritance wisely.

Concise

The elder son, by contrast, remained in his father's house, worked hard, and handled his inheritance wisely.

Notice in the above examples that when the deadwood is cleared from the beginning of the sentence, the subject appears early, and the main verb appears close to it:

1. The last lines . . . connect . . .
2. The cartoon illustrates . . .
3. The editorial . . . expresses . . .
4. The last stanza concludes . . .
5. The elder son . . . remained . . .

Locating the right noun for the subject, and the right verb for the predicate, is the key to revising sentences with wordy beginnings. Try revising the following sentences:

1. The way that Mabel reacts toward her brother is a fine representation of her nature.
2. In Langston Hughes's case he was "saved from sin" when he was going on thirteen.

Empty Conclusions

Often a sentence that begins well has an empty conclusion. The words go on but the sentence seems to stand still; if it's not revised, it requires another sentence to explain it. A short sentence is not necessarily concise.

1. *Empty*

"Those Winter Sundays" is composed so that a reader can feel what the poet was saying. (How is it composed? What is he saying?)

Concise

"Those Winter Sundays" describes the speaker's anger as a child, and his remorse as an adult.

2. *Empty*

In both Orwell's and Baldwin's essays the feeling of white supremacy is very important. (Why is white supremacy important?)

Concise

Both Orwell and Baldwin trace the insidious consequences of white supremacy.

3. *Empty*

Being the only white girl among about ten black girls was quite a learning experience. (What did she learn?)

Concise

As the only white girl among about ten black girls, I began to understand the experiences of isolation, helplessness, and rage regularly reported by minority students.

Wordy Uses of the Verbs "To Be," "To Have," and "To Make"

Notice that in the preceding unrevised sentences a form of the verb *to be* introduces the empty conclusion: "*was* saying," "*is* very important," "*was* quite a learning experience." In each revision, the right verb added and generated substance. In the following sentences, substitutions for the verb *to be* both invigorate and shorten otherwise substantial sentences.

1. *Wordy*

The scene is taking place at night, in front of the capitol building.

Concise

The scene takes place at night, in front of the capitol building.

2. *Wordy*

In this shoeshining and early rising there are indications of church attendance.

Concise

The early rising and shoeshining indicate church attendance.

3. *Wordy*

The words "flashing," "rushing," "plunging," and "tossing" are suggestive of excitement.

Concise

The words "flashing," "rushing," "plunging," and "tossing" suggest excitement.

The rule is, whenever you can, replace a form of the verb *to be* with a stronger verb.

To Be	*Strong Verb*
1. and a participle ("is taking")	1. takes
2. and a noun ("are indications")	2. indicate
3. and an adjective ("are suggestive")	3. suggest

Try revising the following sentence:

The rising price of sugar is representative of the spiraling cost of all goods.

Sentences with the verbs *to have* and *to make* can similarly be reduced:

1. *Wordy*

The Friar has knowledge that Juliet is alive.

Concise

The Friar knows that Juliet is alive.

2. *Wordy*

The stanzas make a vivid contrast between Heaven and Hell.

Concise

The stanzas vividly contrast Heaven and Hell.

Like all rules, this one has exceptions. We don't list them here; you'll discover them by listening to your sentences.

Redundancy

This term, derived from a Latin word meaning "overflowing, overlapping," refers to unnecessary repetition in the expression of ideas. "Future plans," after all, are only plans, and "to glide smoothly" or "to scurry rapidly" is only to glide or to scurry. Unlike repetition, which often provides emphasis or coherence (for example, "government of the people, by the people, for the people"), redundancy can always be eliminated.

1. *Redundant*

Any student could randomly sit anywhere. (If the students could sit anywhere, the seating was random.)

Concise

Students could sit anywhere.
Students chose their seats at random.

2. *Redundant*

I have no justification with which to excuse myself.

Concise

I have no justification for my action.
I can't justify my action.
I have no excuse for my action.
I can't excuse my action.

3. *Redundant*

In the orthodox Cuban culture, the surface of the female role seemed degrading. (Perhaps this sentence means what it says. More probably "surface" and "seemed" are redundant.)

Concise

In the orthodox Cuban culture, the female role seemed degrading.
In the orthodox Cuban culture, the female role was superficially degrading.

4. *Redundant*

In "Araby" the boy feels alienated emotionally from his family.

Concise

In "Araby" the boy feels alienated from his family.

Try eliminating redundancy from the following sentences:

1. The reason why she hesitates is because she is afraid.
2. Marriage in some form has long existed since prehistoric times.

What words can be crossed out of the following phrases?

1. throughout the entire article
2. her attitude of indifference
3. a conservative type suit
4. all the different tasks besides teaching
5. his own personal opinion
6. elements common to both of them
7. emotions and feelings
8. shared together
9. falsely padded expense accounts
10. alleged suspect

Many phrases in common use are redundant. For example, there is no need to write "blare noisily," since the meaning of the adverb "noisily" is already in the verb "blare." Watch for phrases like these when you revise:

round in shape	resulting effect
purple in color	close proximity
poetic in nature	connected together
tall in stature	prove conclusively
autobiography of her life	must necessarily
basic fundamentals	very unique
true fact	very universal
free gift	the reason why is because

Negative Constructions

Negative constructions are often wordy and sometimes pretentious.

1. *Wordy*

Housing for married students is *not unworthy of* consideration.

Concise

Housing for married students is worthy of consideration.

Better

The trustees should earmark funds for married students' housing. (Probably what the author meant)

2. *Wordy*

After reading the second paragraph *you aren't left with* an immediate reaction as to how the story will end.

Concise

The first two paragraphs create suspense.

The following example from a syndicated column is not untypical:

> Although it is not reasonably to be expected that someone who fought his way up to the Presidency is less than a largely political animal and sometimes a beast, it is better not to know — really — exactly what his private conversations were composed of.

The Golden Rule of writing is "Write for others as you would have them write to you," not "Write for others in a manner not unreasonably dissimilar to the manner in which you would have them write for you." (But see the discussion of *not . . . un-* on page 731 for effective use of the negative.)

Extra Sentences, Extra Clauses: Subordination

Sentences are sometimes wordy because ideas are given more elaborate grammatical constructions than they need. In revising, these constructions can be grammatically subordinated, or reduced. Two sentences, for example, may be reduced to one, or a clause may be reduced to a phrase.

1. *Wordy*

The Book of Ruth was probably written in the fifth century B.C. It was a time when women were considered the property of men.

Concise

The Book of Ruth was probably written in the fifth century B.C., when women were considered the property of men.

"See what I mean? You're never sure just where you stand with them."

Drawing by Rossi; © 1971 The New Yorker Magazine, Inc.

2. *Wordy*

The first group was the largest. This group was seated in the center of the dining hall.

Concise

The first group, the largest, was seated in the center of the dining hall.

3. *Wordy*

The colonists were upset over the tax on tea and they took action against it.

Concise

The colonists, upset over the tax on tea, took action against it.

Watch particularly for clauses beginning with *who, which,* and *that.* Often they can be shortened.

1. *Wordy*

George Orwell is the pen name of Eric Blair, who was an English writer.

Concise

George Orwell is the pen name of Eric Blair, an English writer.

2. *Wordy*

They are seated at a table which is covered with a patched and tattered cloth.

Concise

They are seated at a table, covered with a patched and tattered cloth.

3. *Wordy*

There is one feature that is grossly out of proportion.

Concise

One feature is grossly out of proportion.

Also watch for sentences and clauses beginning with *it is, this is, there are*. (Again, wordy uses of the verb *to be*.) These expressions often lead to a *which* or a *that*, but even when they don't they may be wordy.

1. *Wordy*

The trail brings us to the timberline. This is the point where the trees become stunted from lack of oxygen.

Concise

The trail brings us to the timberline, the point where the trees become stunted from lack of oxygen.

2. *Wordy*

This is a quotation from Black Elk's autobiography which discloses his prophetic powers.

Concise

This quotation from Black Elk's autobiography discloses his prophetic powers.

3. *Wordy*

It is frequently considered that *Hamlet* is Shakespeare's most puzzling play.

Concise

Hamlet is frequently considered Shakespeare's most puzzling play.

4. *Wordy*

In Notman's photograph of Buffalo Bill and Sitting Bull there are definite contrasts between the two figures.

Concise

Notman's photograph of Buffalo Bill and Sitting Bull contrasts the two figures.

Try revising the following sentences:

1. There are many writers who believe that writing can't be taught.
2. Always take more clothes than you think you will need. This is so that you will be prepared for the weather no matter what it is.
3. This is an indication that the child has a relationship with his teacher which is very respectful.

(For further discussion of subordination see pages 496–500. On *which* clauses, see also page 739.)

SOME CONCLUDING REMARKS

We spoke earlier about how students learn to write Instant Prose and acquire other wordy habits — by writing what they think the teacher has asked for. We haven't forgotten that teachers assign papers of a certain length in college too. But the length given is not an arbitrary limit that must be reached — the teacher who asks for a five-page or twenty-page paper is probably trying to tell you the degree of elaboration expected on the assignment. Such, apparently, was the intention of William Randolph Hearst, the newspaper publisher, who cabled an astronomer, "Is there life on Mars? Cable reply 1000 words." The astronomer's reply was, "Nobody knows," repeated five hundred times.

What do you do when you've been asked to produce a ten-page paper and after diligent writing and revising you find you've said everything relevant to your topic in seven and a half pages? Our advice is, hand it in. We can't remember ever counting the words or pages of a substantial, interesting essay; we assume that our colleagues elsewhere are equally reasonable and equally overworked. If we're wrong, tell us about it — in writing, and in the fewest possible words.

EXERCISE

First identify the fault or faults that make the following sentences wordy, and then revise them for conciseness.

1. There were quite a number of contrasts that White made between the city school and the country school which was of a casual nature all throughout.
2. The study of political topics involves a careful researching of the many components of the particular field.
3. Virtually the most significant feature of any field involving science is the vital nature of the technical facilities, the fundamental factor of all research.
4. Like a large majority of American people, I, too, have seen the popular disaster films.
5. Something which makes this type of film popular (disaster) is the kind of subconscious aspect of "Can man overcome this problem?" Horror films, on the other hand, produce the aspects of whether or not man can make amends for his mistakes.
6. The average American becomes disappointed and downtrodden due to the fact that he can't help himself and is at the mercy of inflation and unemployment.
7. Some relationships have split up because of the simple fear of having an abnormal child, while perhaps there might have been other alternatives for these couples.
8. Reading has always been a fascinating and exciting pastime for me for as long as I can remember.
9. This cartoon appeared in the 17 September 1979 issue of *Newsweek*. This political cartoon was originally taken from the *Tulsa Tribune*. The cartoonist is Simpson.
10. Only once in the first two sentences does the author make reference to the first person.
11. The length of the sentences are similar in moderation and in structural clarity.
12. The magnitude of student satisfaction with the program ranged from total hatred to enthusiastic approval.
13. Taking a look at the facial expressions of the man and the woman in both pictures one can see a difference in mood.

14. One drawing is done in watercolor and the other is done in chalk which is a revision of the watercolor.
15. The dialogue places the role of the two gods on a believable basis.
16. Senseless crimes such as murder and muggings are committed on a daily basis.
17. One must specify that the current disco craze which is so very popular today is not considered to be black music.
18. The two major aspects behind the development of a performer are technique and musicianship.
19. I remember my first desire to smoke cigarettes as I watched my father smoke. My father often sat in his favorite easy chair idly smoking cigarettes.
20. Christopher Stone's article "Putting the Outside Inside the Fence of Law" is concerning the legal rights of the environment. He comments on the legal rights of other inanimate entities which seem to be acceptable. Just as these entities are represented, so should the environment be represented.

13
Revising for Clarity

"Here's to plain speaking and clear understanding."
— Sidney Greenstreet, The Maltese Falcon

CLARITY

We have seen new realities created by the advance of physics. But this chain of creation can be traced back far beyond the starting point of physics. One of the most primitive concepts is that of an object. The concepts of a tree, a horse, any material body, are creations gained on the basis of experience, though the impressions from which they arise are primitive in comparison with the world of physical phenomena. A cat teasing a mouse also creates, by thought, its own primitive reality. The fact that the cat reacts in a similar way toward any mouse it meets shows that it forms concepts and theories which are its guide through its own world of sense impressions.

— Albert Einstein and Leopold Infeld

Skills constitute the manipulative techniques of human goal attainment and control in relation to the physical world, so far as artifacts or machines especially designed as tools do not yet supplement them. Truly human skills are guided by organized and codified *knowledge* of both the things to be manipulated and the human capacities that are used to manipulate them. Such knowledge is an aspect of cultural-level symbolic processes, and, like other aspects to be discussed presently, requires the capacities of the human central nervous system, particularly the brain. This organic system is clearly essential to all of the symbolic processes; as we well know, the human brain is far superior to the brain of any other species.

— Talcott Parsons

Why is the first passage easier to understand than the second?

Both passages discuss the relationship between the brain and the physical world it attempts to understand. The first passage, by Einstein and Infeld, is, if anything, more complex both in what it asserts and in what it suggests than the second, by Parsons. Both passages explain that the brain organizes sense impressions. But Einstein and Infeld further explain that the history of physics can be understood as an extension of the simplest sort of organization, such as we all make in distinguishing a tree from a horse, or such as even a cat makes in teasing a mouse. Parsons only promises that "other aspects" will "be discussed presently." How many of us are eager for those next pages?

Good writing is clear, not because it presents simple ideas, but because it presents ideas in the simplest form the subject permits. A clear analysis doesn't reduce a complex problem to a simple one; it breaks it down into its simple, comprehensible parts and discusses them, one by one, in a logical order. A clear paragraph explains one of these parts coherently, thoroughly, and in language as simple and as particular as the reader's understanding requires and the context allows. Where Parsons writes of "organized and codified *knowledge* of . . . the things to be manipulated," Einstein and Infeld write simply of the concept of an object. And even "object," a simple but general word, is further clarified by the specific, familiar examples, "tree" and "horse." Parsons writes of "the manipulative techniques of . . . goal attainment and control in relation to the physical world, so far as artifacts or machines especially designed as tools do not yet supplement them." Einstein and Infeld show us a cat teasing a mouse.

Notice also the clear organization of Einstein and Infeld's paragraph. The first sentence, clearly transitional, refers to the advance of physics traced in the preceding pages. The next sentence, introduced by "But," reverses our direction: we are now going to look not at an advance, but at primitive beginnings. And the following sentences, to the end of the paragraph, fulfill that promise. We move back to primitive human concepts, clarified by examples, and finally to the still more primitive example of the cat. Parsons's paragraph is also organized, but the route is much more difficult to follow.

Why do people write obscurely? Walter Kaufmann, in an introduction to Martin Buber's *I and Thou*, says "Men love jargon. It is so palpable, tangible, visible, audible; it makes so obvious what one has learned; it satisfies the craving for results. It is impressive for the uninitiated. It makes one feel that one belongs. Jargon divides men into Us and Them."

Maybe. (For our definition of jargon, see pages 462–64.) Surely some students learn to write obscurely by trying to imitate the style of their teachers or textbooks. The imitation may spring from genuine admiration for these authorities, mixed perhaps with an understandable wish to be one of Us (the authorities) not one of Them (the dolts). Or students may feel that a string of technical-sounding words is what the teacher expects. If this thought has crossed your mind, we can't say you're entirely wrong. Learning a new discipline often involves acquiring a specialized vocabulary. But we add the following cautions:

1. What teachers expect is that your writing show thought and make sense. They are likely to be puzzled by the question "Do you want me to use technical terms in this paper?"

2. If you try to use technical terms appropriate to one field when you write about another, you are likely to write nonsense. Don't write "the machine was viable" if you mean only that it worked.

3. When you do write for specialists in a particular field use technical terms precisely. Don't write in an art history paper "This print of Van Gogh's *Sunflowers*" if you mean "This reproduction of Van Gogh's *Sunflowers*."

4. No matter what you are writing, don't become so enamored of technical words that you can't write a sentence without peppering it with *input, interface, death-symbol, parameter, feedback,* and so on.

But to return to the question, "Why do people write obscurely?" — we'd like to offer a second answer to Kaufmann's

"Men love jargon." It's difficult to write clearly.[1] Authorities may be unintelligible not because they want to tax you with unnecessary difficulties, but because they don't know how to avoid them. In our era, when we sometimes seem to be drowning in a flood of print, few persons who write know how to write well. If you have ever tried to assemble a mechanical toy or to thread an unfamiliar sewing machine by following the "easy instructions," you know that the simplest kind of expository writing, giving instructions, can foil the writers most eager for your goodwill (that is, those who want you to use their products). Few instructions, unfortunately, are as unambiguous as "Go to jail. Go directly to jail. Do not pass Go. Do not collect $200."

You can, though, learn to write clearly, by learning to recognize common sources of obscurity in writing and by consciously revising your own work. We offer, to begin with, three general rules:

1. Use the simplest, most exact, most specific language your subject allows.
2. Put together what belongs together, in the essay, in the paragraph, and in the sentence.
3. Keep your reader in mind, particularly when you revise.

Now for more specific advice, and examples — the cats and mice of revising for clarity.

CLARITY AND EXACTNESS: USING THE RIGHT WORD

Denotation

Be sure the word you choose has the right *denotation* (explicit meaning). Did you mean sarcastic or ironic? Fatalistic or pessimistic? Disinterested or uninterested? Biannual or semiannual? Enforce or reinforce? Use or usage? If you're not sure, check the dictionary.

---

[1] Our first draft of this sentence read "Writing clearly is difficult." Can you see why we changed it?

You'll find some of the most commonly misused words discussed in Chapter 21. Here are examples of a few others.

1. Daru faces a dilemma between his humane feelings and his conceptions of justice. (Strictly speaking, a dilemma requires a choice between two equally unattractive alternatives. "Conflict" would be a better word here.)
2. However, as time dragged on, exercising seemed to lose its charisma. (What is charisma? Why is it inexact here?)
3. Ms. Wu's research contains many symptoms of depression which became evident during the reading period. (Was Ms. Wu depressed by her research? We hope not. Probably she described or listed the symptoms.)
4. When I run I don't allow myself to stop until I have reached my destiny. (Which word is inexact?)

A related error is the use of one part of speech for another part. Politicians and sociologists seem especially fond of using, for instance, "impact" as a verb, but few have equalled former Secretary of State Alexander Haig, who regularly began his answers with "Let me context that for you." Such talk sounds silly; hearers don't quite know if the speaker is being pretentious or is just ignorant, but they do know that they are confused. A journalist nicely spoofed Haig's unnerving way of talking, and although Haig is gone, the way of talking, and writing, persists:

> Haig, in congressional hearings before his confirmatory, paradoxed his auditioners by abnormalling his responds so that verbs were nouned, nouns verbed and adjectives adverbised. He techniqued a new way to vocabulary his thoughts so as to informationally uncertain anybody listening about what he had actually implicated.

This is good fun, but avoid nouning verbs and verbing nouns unless you want to evoke smiles.

Connotation

Be sure the word you choose has the right *connotation* (association, implication). As Mark Twain said, the difference between the right word and the almost right word is the difference between lightning and the lightning bug.

Positive [handwritten]

1. Boston politics has always upheld the reputation of being especially crooked. ("Upheld" inappropriately suggests that Boston has proudly maintained its reputation. "Has always had" would be appropriate here, but pale. "Deserved" would, in this context, be ironic, implying — accurately — the writer's scorn.)
2. This book, unlike many other novels, lacks tedious descriptive passages. ("Lacks" implies a deficiency. How would you revise the sentence?) *ok for flashy style* [handwritten]
3. New Orleans, notorious for its good jazz and good food. . . . (Is "notorious" the word here? or "famous"?)
4. Sunday, Feb. 9. Another lingering day at Wellesley. (In this entry from a student's journal, "lingering" strikes us as right. What does "lingering" imply about Sundays at Wellesley that "long" would not?)

Because words have connotations, most writing — even when it pretends to be objective — conveys attitudes as well as facts. Consider, for example, this passage by Jessica Mitford, describing part of the procedure used today for embalming:

> A long, hollow needle attached to a tube . . . is jabbed into the abdomen, poked around the entrails and chest cavity, the contents of which are pumped out. . . .

In a way this passage accurately describes part of the procedure, but it also, of course, records Mitford's contempt for the procedure. Suppose she wanted to be more respectful — suppose, for example, she were an undertaker writing an explanatory pamphlet. Instead of the needle being "jabbed" it would be "inserted," and instead of being "poked around the entrails" it would be "guided around the viscera," and the contents would not be "pumped out" but would be "drained." Mitford's words would be the wrong words for an undertaker explaining embalming to apprentices or to the general public, but, given her purpose, they are exactly the right ones because they convey her attitude with great clarity. *Same actions, how it is looked at* [handwritten]

Note too that many words have social, political, or sexist overtones. We read for example of the *children* of the rich, but the *offspring* of the poor. What is implied by the distinction? Consider the differences in connotation in each of the following series:

1. friend, boyfriend, young man, lover (What age is the speaker?)
2. dine, eat (What was on the menu? Who set the table?)

"I'm not quite clear on this, Fulton. Are you moaning about your prerequisites, your requisites, or your perquisites?"

Drawing by Richter; © 1976 The New Yorker Magazine, Inc.

3. spinster, bachelor (Which term is likely to be considered an insult?)
4. underdeveloped nations, developing nations, emerging nations
5. preference, bias, prejudice,
6. upbringing, conditioning, brainwashing
7. message from our sponsor, commercial, ad, plug
8. intelligence gathering, espionage, spying
9. emigrate, defect, seek asylum
10. anti-abortion, pro-life; pro-abortion, pro-choice

Quotation Marks as Apologies

When you have used words with exact meanings (denotations) and appropriate associations (connotations) for your purpose, <u>don't apologize</u> for them <u>by putting</u> quotation <u>marks around</u> them. If the words *copped a plea, ripped off,* or *kids* suit you better than *plea-bargained, stolen,* or *children,* use them. If they are inappropriate, don't put them in quotation marks; find the right words.

Being Specific

In writing <u>descriptions</u>, <u>catch</u> the <u>richness</u>, <u>complexity</u>, and <u>uniqueness of things.</u> Suppose, for example, you are describing a scene from your childhood, a setting you loved. There was, in particular, a certain tree . . . and you write: "Near the water there was a big tree that was rather impressive." Most of us would produce something like that sentence. Here is the sentence Ernesto Galarza wrote in *Barrio Boy*:

> On the edge of the pond, at the far side, there was an enormous walnut tree, standing like an open umbrella whose ribs extended halfway across the still water of the pool.

We probably could not have come up with the metaphor of the umbrella because we wouldn't have seen the similarity. (As Aristotle observed, the <u>gift for making metaphors</u> distinguishes the poet from the rest of us.) But we can all train ourselves to be accurate observers and reporters. For "the water" (general) we can *specify* "pond"; for "near" we can say how near, "on the edge of the pond," and add the specific location, "at the far side"; for "tree" we can give the *species*, "walnut tree"; and for "big" we can provide a picture, its branches "extended halfway across" the pond: it was, in fact, "enormous."

Galarza does not need to add limply, as we did, that the tree "was rather impressive." The tree he describes *is* impressive. That he accurately remembered it persuades us that he was impressed, without his having to tell us he was. For writing descriptions, a good general rule is: show, don't tell.

Be as specific as you can be in <u>all forms of</u> exposition too. Take the time, when you revise, to find the exact word to replace vague, woolly phrases or clichés. (In the following examples we have had to guess or invent what the writer meant.)

1. *Vague*

The clown's part in *Othello* is very small.

Specific

The clown appears in only two scenes in *Othello*.
The clown in *Othello* speaks only thirty lines.
(Notice the substitution of the verb "appears" or "speaks" for the frequently debilitating "is." And in place of the weak intensifier "very" we have specific details to tell us how small the role is.)

2. *Vague*

He feels uncomfortable at the whole situation. (Many feelings are uncomfortable. Which one does he feel? What's the situation?)

Specific

He feels guilty for having distrusted his father.

3. *Vague*

The passage reveals a somewhat calculating aspect behind Antigone's noble motives. ("A somewhat calculating aspect" is vague — and wordy — for "calculation." Or did the writer mean "shrewdness"? What differences in connotation are there between "shrewd" and "calculating"?)

4. *Vague*

She uses simplicity in her style of writing. (Do we know, exactly, what simplicity in style means?)

Specific

She uses familiar words, normal word order, and conversational phrasing.

5. *Vague Cliché*

Then she criticized students for living in an ivory tower. (Did she criticize them for being detached or secluded? For social irresponsibility or studiousness?)

Specific

Then she criticized students for being socially irresponsible.

Using Examples

In addition to exact words and specific details, illustrative examples make for clear writing. Einstein and Infeld, in the passage quoted on page 450, use as an example of a primitive concept a cat teasing not only its first mouse, but "any mouse it meets." Here are two paragraphs which clarify their topic sentences through examples; the first is again from *Barrio Boy*.

> In Jalco people spoke in two languages — Spanish and with gestures. These signs were made with the face or hands or a combination of both. If you bent one arm and tapped the elbow with the other hand, it meant "He is stingy." When you sawed one arm across the other you were saying that someone you knew played the fiddle terribly. To say that a man was a tippler you made a set of cow's horns with the little finger and the thumb of one hand, bending the three middle fingers to the palm and pointing the thumb at your mouth. And if you wanted to indicate, without saying so for the sake of politeness, that a mutual acquaintance was daffy, you tapped three times on your forehead with your middle finger.
>
> — Ernesto Galarza

In the next paragraph, Northrop Frye, writing about the perception of rhythm, illustrates his point:

> Ideally, our literary education should begin, not with prose, but with such things as "this little pig went to market" — with verse rhythm reinforced by physical assault. The infant who gets bounced on somebody's knee to the rhythm of "Ride a cock horse" does not need a footnote telling him that Banbury Cross is twenty miles northeast of Oxford. He does not need the information that "cross" and "horse" make (at least in the pronunciation he is most likely to hear) not a rhyme but an assonance. . . . All he needs is to get bounced.

Frye does not say our literary education should begin with "simple rhymes" or with "verse popular with children." He says "with such things as 'this little pig went to market,'" and then he goes on to add "Ride a cock horse." We know exactly what he means. Notice, too, that we do not need a third example. Be detailed, but know when to stop.

Your reader is likely to be brighter and more demanding than Lady Pliant, who in a seventeenth-century play says to a would-be seducer, "You are very alluring — and say so many fine Things, and nothing is so moving to me as a fine Thing." "Fine Things," of course, are what is wanted, but only exact words and apt illustrations will convince intelligent readers that they are hearing fine things.

Now look at a paragraph from a student's essay whose thesis is that rage can be a useful mechanism for effecting change. Then compare the left hand paragraph with the same paragraph, revised, at the right. Note the specific ways, sentence by sentence, the student revised for clarity.

In my high school we had little say in the learning processes that were used. The subjects that we were required to take were irrelevant. One had to take them to earn enough points to graduate. Some of the teachers were sympathetic to our problem. They would tell us about when they were young, how they tried to oppose their school system. But when they were young it was a long time ago, for most of them. The principal would call assemblies to speak on the subject. They were entitled, "The Value of an Education" or "Get a Good Education to Have a Bright Future." The titles were not inviting. They had nothing to do with our plight. Most students never came to any agreements with the principal because most of his thoughts and views seemed old and outdated.

In my high school we had little say about our curriculum. We were required, for example, to choose either American or European History to earn enough points for graduation. We wanted, but were at first refused, the option of Black History. Some of our teachers were sympathetic with us; one told me about her fight opposing the penmanship course required in her school. Nor was the principal totally indifferent — he called assemblies. I remember one talk he gave called "The Value of an Education in Today's World," and another, "Get a Good Education to Have a Bright Future." I don't recall hearing about a Black History course in either talk. Once, he invited a group of us to meet with him in his office, but we didn't reach any agreement. He solemnly showed us an American History text (not the one we used) that had a whole chapter devoted to Black History.

Using Analogies

In the revised essay that we have just quoted, the writer clarified his point about the academic program by citing specific examples, for instance by mentioning a particular course (Black History) that the students wanted to study. But sometimes the topic is such that examples of this sort cannot be given, and the writer may be forced to clarify the topic by giving an analogy, that is by giving an extended comparison which makes the unfamiliar more familiar. Earlier, on page 199, we illustrated analogy with this example: "A government is like a ship, and just as a ship has a captain and a crew, so a government . . ." Or one can construct an analogy between the mind and the body: as the body is fed with food, so the mind is fed with ideas. The mind's diet, one might explain, must be taken at appropriate intervals, in proper amounts, and it must be balanced.

In an effort to explain the part that law plays in settling disputes, K. N. Llewellyn sets forth an analogy, comparing the law to an umpire in a game:

> Strikes are called and fought through and settled. Often some phases of them reach the courts. Often none do. Almost never does the main question in a strike occupy a court. But perhaps the case of the strike is as good as any to bring out the part that law does play. Law (in the person of judges, police and sheriffs) does lay down rules within which strike and lockout and struggle of employer and employee are to be worked out. "Rules" of the game: no beating, no shooting, no intimidation, no blacklisting. Does it follow that these rules of the game are always observed? It does not. The games are few in number in which the rules are *always* observed. But what is vital is to see that the law official functions somewhat like an umpire in *attempting to see* that they are. Somewhat like an umpire, but not wholly. Like an umpire in that he does not always see the breach of the rules. Like an umpire in that at times he is severely partial to one side, or stubborn, or ignorant, or ill tempered. Like an umpire, at least on the criminal side, in that he reaches in to decide and control on his own motion. But on the civil side, on the side of private law, less like an umpire in this: that he does not reach in on his own motion, but waits to be called upon. Always, however, and on both civil and criminal sides, like an umpire, I repeat, in that when acting he tries in the main, and in the main with some success, to insist that the rules of the game shall be abided by; in that he takes the rules of the game in the main not from his own inner consciousness, but from existing practice, and again in the main from authoritative sources (which in the case of the law are largely statutes and the decisions of the courts). Like an umpire finally in that his decision is made only after the event, and that play is held up while he is making it, and that he is cursed roundly by the losing party and gets little enough thanks from the winner.

Notice, by the way, that Llewellyn is not taken in by his own analogy. That is, he realizes that the comparison goes only so far and no further. As we said in our earlier discussion of analogy, an analogy cannot prove anything, it can only hope to clarify. After all, the relation between employer and striker is *not* a game; there are essential differences between a strike and a baseball game. Still, the relationship between (on the one hand) employer, striker, and law and (on the other hand) rival teams and the umpire can be clarified or made easy and familiar through the comparison. As Sigmund Freud said, "Analogies prove nothing, but they can make one feel at home." If, then, you are trying to clarify a point, consider the possibility that an analogy, in which you compare the unfamiliar with the familiar, will help your reader to see what you are getting at.

Jargon and Technical Language

Jargon is the unnecessary, inappropriate, or inexact use of technical or specialized language. Look at this passage:

Dodgers Keep Perfect Record in Knocking Out Southpaws

NEW YORK (AP) — The Brooklyn Dodgers didn't win the first World Series game yesterday, but they got a measure of comfort in that they maintained one of their season records.

No left-hander went the distance in beating them the past season. Six lefties got the decision but none was around at the end.

New York hurler Whitey Ford made No. 7, but he, too, went the way of the other southpaws . . . empty consolation, to be sure, in view of the Yanks' 6–5 victory in the World Series opener.

Consider the diction of this sports story: "went the distance," "lefties," "got the decision," "around at the end," "hurler," "southpaws," "opener," "made No. 7." Do you understand the individual words? Most of them, probably. Do you know what the item is about? Some of us do, some don't. Is it written in technical language, or jargon?

The answer depends, as we define jargon, on where the story appeared, and for whom it was intended. Because it appeared on the sports page of a newspaper, we would classify the diction as technical language, not jargon. Properly used, technical language communicates information concisely and clearly, and can, as it does here, create a comfortable bond between reader and writer. Both are having fun. If the same story appeared on the front page of the newspaper, we would classify the language as jargon because it would baffle the general reader.

If the baseball story makes perfect sense to you, as an exercise, try to explain it in nontechnical language to someone who does not understand it. And while you're at it, can you explain why baseball fans are particularly interested in left-handed pitchers — in other words, what makes the statistic here a statistic? Why are baseball fans so interested in statistics anyway — more interested, say, than football or hockey fans? Is it because baseball is intrinsically boring?

Let's move quickly to another example:

> For many years Boston parents have tried to improve the public schools. But any input the parents might have desired has been stifled by the Boston School Committee.

What does "input" mean in this sentence? Is the term used as technical language here, or jargon? (And by the way, how would you go about stifling an input?)

A student wrote the passage just quoted. But recently in Dallas, parents of children in kindergarten through third grade received a twenty-eight page manual written by a professional educator to help them decipher their children's report cards. The title of the manual: *Terminal Behavioral Objectives for Continuous Progression Modules in Early Childhood Education*. Terminal objectives, it seems, means goals. What does the rest mean? If you were one of the parents, would you expect much help from the manual?

Here's a film critic discussing the movie *Last Tango in Paris*:

> The failure of the relationship between Paul and Jeanne is a function of the demands placed on the psyche by bourgeois society, and it is the family as mediator of psychological and social repression which provides the dialectic of Bertolucci's film.

Perhaps some film criticism should be x-rated?

And finally, a deliberate parody. A. P. Herbert in his book *What a Word!* tells us how a social scientist might write a familiar Biblical command:

"With you, I think I've found a maximization of experience."

Drawing by Donald Reilly; © 1978. The New Yorker Magazine, Inc.

In connection with my co-citizens, a general standard of mutual good will and reciprocal non-aggression is obviously incumbent upon me.

What is the command? (See Leviticus xix.18.)

In general, when you write for nonspecialists, avoid technical terms; if you must use them, define them. If you use a technical term when writing for specialists, be sure you know its precise meaning. But whenever you can, even among specialists, use plain English.

Clichés

Clichés (literally, in French, molds from which type is cast) are trite expressions, mechanically — that is, mindlessly — produced. Since they are available without thought they are great Instant Prose Additives (see pages 432–34). Writers who use them are usually surprised to be criticized: they find the phrases attractive, and may even think them exact. (Phrases become clichés precisely because they have wide appeal and therefore wide use.) But clichés, by their very nature, cannot communicate the uniqueness of your thoughts. Furthermore, because they come instantly to mind, they tend to block the specific detail or exact expression that will let the reader know what precisely is in your mind. When, in revising, you strike out a cliché, you force yourself to do the work of writing clearly. The following examples are full of clichés:

Finally, the long awaited day arrived. Up bright and early. . . .

She peered at me with suspicion; then a faint smile crossed her face.

Other examples:

first and foremost	time honored
the acid test	bustled to and fro
fatal flaw	short but sweet
budding genius	few and far between
slowly but surely	D-day arrived
little did I know	sigh of relief
the big moment	last but not least

In attempting to avoid clichés, however, don't go to the other extreme of wildly original, super-vivid writing — "'Well then, say something to her,' he roared, his whole countenance gnarled in rage." It's often better to simply say, "he said." (Anyone who intends to write dialogue should memorize Ring Lardner's intentionally funny line, "Shut up!' he explained.") Note also that such common expressions as "How are you?" "Please pass the salt," and "So long" are not clichés; they make no claim to be colorful.

Metaphors and Mixed Metaphors

Ordinary speech abounds with metaphors (implied comparisons). We speak or write of the foot of a mountain, the germ (seed) of an idea, the root of a problem. Metaphors so deeply embedded in the language that they no longer evoke pictures in our minds are called *dead metaphors.* Ordinarily, they offer us, as writers, no problems: we need neither seek them nor avoid them; they are simply there. (Notice, for example, "embedded" two sentences back.) Such metaphors become problems, however,

*"You're right as rain. It's the dawn of history,
and there are no clichés as yet. I'll drink to that."*

Drawing by Handelsman; © 1972 The New Yorker Magazine, Inc.

when we unwittingly call them back to life. Howard Nemerov observes: "That these metaphors may be not dead but only sleeping, or that they may arise from the grave and walk in our sentences, is something that has troubled everyone who has ever tried to write plain expository prose. . . ."

Dead metaphors are most likely to haunt us when they are embodied in clichés. Since we use clichés without attention to what they literally say or point to, we are unlikely to be aware of the dead metaphors buried in them. But when we attach one cliché to another, we may raise the metaphors from the grave. The result is likely to be a mixed metaphor; the effect is almost always absurd.

Water seeks its own level whichever way you want to slice it.

Traditional liberal education has run out of gas and educational soup kitchens are moving into the vacuum.

The low ebb has been reached and hopefully it's turned the corner.

Her energy, drained through a stream of red tape, led only to closed doors.

We no longer ask for whom the bell tolls but simply chalk it up as one less mouth to feed.

As Joe E. Lewis observed, "Show me a man who builds castles in the air and I'll show you a crazy architect."

Fresh metaphors, on the other hand, imaginatively combine accurate observations. They are not prefabricated ideas; they are a means of discovering or inventing new ideas. They enlarge thought and enliven prose. Here are two examples from students' journals:

I have some sort of sporadic restlessness in me, like the pen on a polygraph machine. It moves along in curves, then suddenly shoots up, blowing a bubble in my throat, making my chest taut, forcing me to move around. It becomes almost unbearable and then suddenly it will plunge, leaving something that feels like a smooth orange wave.

Time is like wrapping papers. It wraps memories, decorates them with sentiment. No matter (almost) what's inside, it's remembered as a beautiful piece of past time. That's why I even miss my high school years, which were filled with tiredness, boredom, confusion. . . .

And here is a passage from an essay in which a student analyzes the style of a story he found boring:

Every sentence yawns, stretches, shifts from side to side, and then quietly dozes off. . . .

Experiment with metaphors, let them surface in the early drafts of your essays and in your journals, and by all means, introduce original and accurate comparisons in your essays. But leave the mixed metaphors to politicians and comedians.

Euphemisms

Euphemisms are words substituted for other words thought to be offensive. In deodorant advertisements there are no armpits, only *underarms*, which may *perspire*, but not sweat, and even then they don't smell. A parent reading a report card is likely to learn not that his child got an F in conduct, but that she "experiences difficulty exercising self-control: (a) verbally (b) physically." And where do old people go? To Sun City, "a retirement community for senior citizens."

Euphemisms are used for two reasons: to avoid giving offense, and, sometimes unconsciously, to disguise fear or animosity. We do not advise you to write or speak discourteously; we do advise you, though, to use euphemisms consciously and sparingly, when tact recommends them. It's customary in a condolence letter to avoid the word "*death*," and, depending both on your own feelings and those of the bereaved, you may wish to follow that custom. But there's no reason on earth to write "Hamlet passes on." You should be aware, moreover, that some people find euphemisms themselves offensive. There may be more comfort for your friend in "I'm sorry about his death" than in "I regret to hear of your loss." And Margaret Kuhn argues that the word "old" is preferable to "senior." "Old," she says "is the right word. . . . I think we should wear our gray hair, wrinkles, and crumbling joints as badges of distinction. After all, we worked damn hard to get them." She has organized a militant group called the Gray Panthers to fight agism.

In revising, replace needless euphemisms with plain words. Your writing will be sharper, and you might, in examining and confronting them, free yourself of a mindless habit, an unconscious prejudice, or an irrational fear.

A Digression on Public Lying

There is a kind of lying which, in the words of Walker Gibson, we may call *public lying*. Its rules are to avoid substance, direct answers, and plain words. Its tendency is to subvert the English language. It employs and invents euphemisms, but the public liar intends to protect not his listeners, but himself and his friends, and he misleads and deceives consciously. Public lying was not invented during the Vietnam War (in 1946 George Orwell had already written the definitive essay on it, "Politics and the English Language"). But the war produced some classic examples, from which we select a few.

The war, of course, was not a war, but a "conflict" or an "era." "Our side" never attacked "the other side," we made "protective reaction raids"; we didn't invade, we "incursed." We didn't bomb villages, we "pacified" them; peasants were not herded into concentration camps, but "relocated." We didn't spray the countryside with poisons, destroying forests, endangering or killing plant, animal, and human life, we "practiced vegetation control." When American intelligence agents drowned a spy they referred to their action as "termination with extreme prejudice."

More recently, it was disclosed that the CIA published a manual for insurgents in Nicaragua instructing that "It is possible to neutralize carefully selected and planned targets, such as court judges, police and state security officials, etc." And the State Department now substitutes for the word "killing," in reports on human rights, "unlawful or arbitrary deprivation of life." A national committee of English teachers gave the State Department its 1984 Doublespeak Award for that.

There is a Gresham's law in rhetoric as there is in economics: bad language drives out good. Bad language is contagious; learn to detect the symptoms: use of vague words for clear words; use of sentences or phrases where words suffice; evasive use of the passive voice; and outright lying.

Passive or Active Voice?

1. I baked the bread. (Active voice)
2. The bread was baked by me. (Passive voice)
3. The bread will be baked. (Passive voice)

Although it is the verb that is in the active or the passive voice, notice that the words *active* and *passive* describe the subjects of the sentences. That is, in the first sentence the verb "baked" is in the active voice; the subject "I" acts. In the second and third sentences the verbs "was baked" and "will be baked" are in the

Feiffer

passive voice; the subject "bread" is acted upon. Notice also the following points:

a. The *voice* of the verb is distinct from its *tense*. Don't confuse the passive voice with the past tense. (Sentence 2 above happens to be in the past tense, but 3 is not; both 2 and 3 are in the passive voice.)

b. The passive voice uses more words than the active voice. (Compare sentences 1 and 2.)

c. A sentence with a verb in the passive voice may leave the doer of the action unidentified. (See sentence 3.)

d. Finally, notice that in each of the three sentences the emphasis is different.

In revising, take a good look at each sentence in which you have used the passive voice. If the passive clarifies your meaning, retain it; if it obscures your meaning, change it. More often than not, the passive voice obscures meaning.

1. *Obscure*

The revolver given Daru by the gendarme is left in the desk drawer. (Left by whom? The passive voice here obscures the point.)

Clear

Daru leaves the gendarme's revolver in the desk drawer.

2. *Obscure*

Daru serves tea and the Arab is offered some. (Confusing shift from the active voice "serves" to the passive voice "is offered.")

Clear

Daru serves tea and offers the Arab some.

3. *Appropriate*

For over fifty years *Moby-Dick* was neglected. ("Was neglected" suggests that the novel was neglected by almost everyone. The passive voice catches the passivity of the response. Changing the sentence to "For over fifty years few readers read *Moby-Dick*" would make "readers" the subject of the sentence, but the true subject is — as in the original — *Moby-Dick*.)

Finally, avoid what has been called the Academic Passive: "In this essay it has been shown that. . . ." This cumbersome form used to be common in academic writing (to convey scientific objectivity) but *I* is usually preferable to such stuffiness.

The Writer's "I"

It is seldom necessary in writing an essay (even on a personal experience) to repeat "I think that" or "in my opinion." Your reader knows that what you write is your opinion. Nor is it necessary, if you've done your job well, to apologize. "After reading the story over several times I'm not really sure what it is about, but. . . ." Write about something you are reasonably sure of. Occasionally, though, when there is a real problem in the text, for example the probable date of the Book of Ruth, it is not only permissible to disclose doubts and to reveal tentative conclusions; it may be necessary to do so.

Note also that there is no reason to avoid the pronoun *I* when you are in fact writing about yourself. Attempts to avoid *I* ("this writer," "we," expressions in the passive voice such as "it has been said above" and "it was seen") are noticeably awkward and distracting. And sometimes you may want to focus on your subjective response to a topic in order to clarify a point. The following opening paragraph of a movie review provides an example:

> I take the chance of writing about Bergman's *Persona* so long after its showing because this seems to me a movie there's no hurry about. It will be with us a long time, just as it has been on my mind for a long time. Right now, when I am perhaps still under its spell, it seems to me Bergman's masterpiece, but I can't imagine ever thinking it less than one of the great movies. This of course is opinion; what I know for certain is that *Persona* is also one of the most difficult movies I will ever see; and I am afraid that in this case there is a direct connection between difficulty and value. It isn't only that *Persona* is no harder than it has to be; its peculiar haunting power, its spell, and its value come directly from the fact that it's so hard to get a firm grasp on.
>
> — Robert Garis

Students who have been taught not to begin sentences with *I* often produce sentences that are eerily passive even when the verbs are in the active voice. For example:

1. Two reasons are important to my active participation in dance.
2. The name of the program that I was in is the Health Careers Summer Program.
3. An eager curiosity overcame my previous feeling of fear to make me feel better.

But doesn't it make more sense to say:

1. I dance for two reasons.
2. I was enrolled in the Health Careers Summer Program.
3. My curiosity aroused, I was no longer afraid.

A good rule: make the agent of the action the subject of the sentence. A practical suggestion: to avoid a boring series of sentences all beginning with *I*, subordinate for conciseness and emphasis. (See pages 444–47 and 496–500.)

CLARITY AND COHERENCE

Writing a coherent essay is hard work; it requires mastery of a subject and skill in presenting it; it always takes a lot of time.

Writing a coherent paragraph often takes more fussing and patching than you expect, but once you have the hang of it, it's relatively easy and pleasant. Writing a coherent sentence requires only that you stay awake until you get to the end of it. We all do nod sometimes, even over our own prose. But if you make it a practice to read your work over several times, at least once aloud, you give yourself a chance to spot the incoherent sentence before your reader does, and to revise it. Once you see that a sentence is incoherent, it's usually easy to recast it.

Cats Are Dogs

In some sentences a form of the verb *to be* asserts that one thing is in a class with another. Passover is a Jewish holiday. Dartmouth is a college. But would anyone not talking in his sleep say "Dartmouth is a Jewish Holiday"? Are cats dogs? Students did write the following sentences:

1. *Incoherent*

X. J. Kennedy's poem "Nothing in Heaven Functions as It Ought" is a contrast between Heaven and Hell. (As soon as you ask yourself the question "Is a poem a contrast?" you have, by bringing the two words close together, isolated the problem. A poem may be a sonnet, an epic, an ode — but not a contrast. The writer was trying to say what the poem does, not what it is.)

Coherent

X. J. Kennedy's poem "Nothing in Heaven Functions as It Ought" contrasts Heaven and Hell.

2. *Incoherent*

Besides, he tells himself, a matchmaker is an old Jewish custom. (Is a matchmaker a custom?)

Coherent

Besides, he tells himself, consulting a matchmaker is an old Jewish custom.

Try revising the following:

The essay is also an insight into imperialism.

In a related problem, one part of the sentence doesn't know what the other is doing:

1. *Incoherent*

Ruth's devotion to Naomi is rewarded by marrying Boaz. (Does devotion marry Boaz?)

Coherent

Ruth's marriage to Boaz rewards her devotion to Naomi.

2. *Incoherent*

He demonstrates many human frailties, such as the influence of others' opinions upon one's actions. (Is influence a frailty? How might this sentence be revised?)

False Series

If you were given a shopping list that mentioned apples, fruit, and pears, you would be puzzled and possibly irritated by the inclusion of "fruit." Don't puzzle or irritate your reader. Analyze sentences containing items in a series to be sure that the items are of the same order of generality. For example:

False Series

His job exposed him to the "dirty work" of the British and to the evils of imperialism. ("The 'dirty work' of the British" is a *specific* example of the more *general* "evils of imperialism." The false series makes the sentence incoherent.)

Revised

His job, by exposing him to the "dirty work" of the British, brought him to understand the evils of imperialism.

In the following sentence, which item in the series makes the sentence incoherent?

Why should one man, no matter how important, be exempt from investigation, arrest, trial, and law enforcing tactics?

Modifiers

A modifier should appear close to the word it modifies (that is, describes or qualifies). Three kinds of faulty modifiers are common: misplaced, squinting, and dangling.

MISPLACED MODIFIERS

If the modifier seems to modify the wrong word, it is called *misplaced*. Misplaced modifiers are often unintentionally funny. The judo parlor that advertised "For $20 learn basic methods of protecting yourself from an experienced instructor" probably attracted more amused readers than paying customers.

1. *Misplaced*

Orwell shot the elephant under pressured circumstances. (Orwell was under pressure, not the elephant. Put the modifier near what it modifies.)

Revised

Orwell, under pressure, shot the elephant.

2. *Misplaced*

Orwell lost his individual right to protect the elephant as part of the imperialistic system. (The elephant was not part of the system; Orwell was.)

Revised

As part of the imperialistic system, Orwell lost his right to protect the elephant.

3. *Misplaced*

Amos Wilder has been called back to teach at Harvard Divinity School after ten years retirement due to a colleague's illness. (Did Wilder retire for ten years because a colleague was ill? Revise the sentence.)

Revise the following:

1. Sitting Bull and William Cody stand side by side, each supporting a rifle placed between them with one hand.
2. Complete with footnotes the author has provided her readers with some background information.

Sometimes other parts of sentences are misplaced:

1. *Misplaced*

We learn from the examples of our parents who we are. (The sentence appears to say we are our parents.)

Revised

We learn who we are from the examples of our parents.

2. *Misplaced*

It is up to the students to revise the scheme, not the administrators. (We all know you can't revise administrators. Revise the sentence.)

SQUINTING MODIFIERS

If the modifier is ambiguous, that is, if it can be applied equally to more than one term, it is sometimes called a *squinting modifier*: it seems to look forward, and it seems to look backward.

1. *Squinting*

Being with Jennifer more and more enrages me. (Is the writer spending more time with Jennifer, or is he more enraged? Probably more enraged.)

Revised

Being with Jennifer enrages me more and more.

2. *Squinting*

Writing clearly is difficult. (The sentence may be talking about writing — it's clearly difficult to write — or about writing clearly — it's difficult to write clearly.)

3. *Squinting*

Students only may use this elevator. (Does "only" modify students? If so, no one else may use the elevator. Or does it modify elevator? If so, students may use no other elevator.)

Revised

Only students may use this elevator.
Students may use only this elevator.

Note: the word *only* often squints. In general, put *only* immediately before the word or phrase it modifies. Often it appears too early in the sentence. (See page 733.)

DANGLING MODIFIERS

If the term it should modify appears nowhere in the sentence, the modifier is called *dangling*.

1. *Dangling*

Being small, his ear scraped against the belt when his father stumbled. (The writer meant that the boy was small, not the ear. But the boy is not in the sentence.)

Revised

Because the boy was small his ear scraped against the belt when his father stumbled.

Being small, the boy scraped his ear against the belt when his father stumbled.

2. *Dangling*

A meticulously organized person, his suitcase could be tucked under an airplane seat. (How would you revise the sentence?)

The general rule: *when you revise sentences, put together what belongs together.*

Reference of Pronouns

A pronoun is used in place of a noun. Because the noun usually precedes the pronoun, the noun to which the pronoun refers is called the antecedent (Latin: "going before"). For example: in "When Sheriff Johnson was on a horse, he was a big man" the noun, "Sheriff Johnson," precedes the pronoun, "he." But the noun can also follow the pronoun, as in "When he was on a horse, Sheriff Johnson was a big man."

Be sure that whenever possible a pronoun has a clear reference. Sometimes it isn't possible: *it* is commonly used with an unspecified reference, as in "It's hot today," and "Hurry up please, it's time"; and there can be no reference for interrogative pronouns: "What's bothering you?" and "Who's on first?" But otherwise always be sure that you've made clear what noun the pronoun is standing for.

VAGUE REFERENCES

1. *Vague*

Apparently, they fight physically and it can become rather brutal. ("It" doubtless refers to "fight," but "fight" in this sentence is the verb, not an antecedent noun.)

Clear

Their fights are apparently physical, and sometimes brutal.

2. *Vague*

I was born in Colon, the second largest city in the Republic of Panama. Despite this, Colon is still an undeveloped town. ("This" has no specific antecedent. It appears to refer to the writer's having been born in Colon.)

Clear

Although Colon, where I was born, is the second largest city in Panama, it remains undeveloped.
(On *this,* see also page 000.)

Revise the following sentence:

They're applying to medical school because it's a well-paid profession.

SHIFT IN PRONOUNS

This common error is easily corrected.

1. In many instances the child was expected to follow the profession of your father. (Expected to follow the profession of whose father, "yours" or "his"?)
2. Having a tutor, you can get constant personal encouragement and advice that will help me budget my time. (If "you" have a tutor will that help "me"?)
3. If one smokes, you should at least ask permission before you light up. (If "one" smokes, why should "you" ask permission? But here the change to "If one smokes, one should at least ask permission before one lights up," though correct, sounds inappropriately formal. Omit a "one": "If one smokes, one should at least ask permission before lighting up." Or forget about "one" and use "you" throughout the sentence.)

Revise the following sentences:

1. Schools bring people of the same age together and teach you how to get along with each other.
2. If asked why you went to a mixer, one might say they were simply curious.

AMBIGUOUS REFERENCE OF PRONOUNS

A pronoun normally refers to the first appropriate noun or pronoun preceding it. Same-sex pronouns and nouns, like dogs, often get into scraps.

1. *Ambiguous*

Her mother died when she was eighteen. (Who was eighteen, the mother or the daughter?)

Clear

Her mother died when Mabel was eighteen.
Her mother died at the age of eighteen. (Note the absence of ambiguity in "His mother died when he was eighteen.")

2. *Ambiguous*

Daru learns that he must take an Arab to jail against his will. (Both Daru and the Arab are male. The writer of the sentence meant that Daru learns he must act against his will.)

Clear

Daru learns that he must, against his will, take an Arab to jail.

The general rule: *put together what belongs together.*

Agreement

NOUN AND PRONOUN

Everyone knows that a singular noun requires a singular pronoun, and a plural noun requires a plural pronoun, but writers sometimes slip.

1. *Faulty*

A dog can easily tell if people are afraid of them.

Correct

A dog can easily tell if people are afraid of it.

2. *Faulty*

Every student feels that Wellesley expects them to do their best.

Correct

Every student feels that Wellesley expects her to do her best.

Each, everybody, nobody, no one, and *none* are especially troublesome. See the entries on these words in the glossary.

SUBJECT AND VERB

A singular subject requires a singular verb, a plural subject a plural verb.

Faulty

Horror films bring to light a subconscious fear and shows a character who succeeds in coping with it.

Correct

Horror films bring to light a subconscious fear and show a character who succeeds in coping with it.

The student who wrote "shows" instead of "show" thought that the subject of the verb was "fear," but the subject really is "Horror films," a plural.

Faulty

The manager, as well as the pitcher and the catcher, were fined.

Correct

The manager, as well as the pitcher and the catcher, was fined.

If the sentence had been "The manager and the pitcher . . . ," the subject would have been plural and the required verb would be "were," but in the sentence as it is given, "as well as" (like *in addition to, with,* and *together with*) does *not* add a subject to a subject and thereby make a plural subject. "As well as" merely indicates that what is said about the manager applies to the pitcher and the catcher.

Revise the following:

About mid-morning during Spanish class the sound of jeeps were heard.

Sometimes a sentence that is grammatically correct may nevertheless sound awkward:

One of its most noticeable features is the lounges.

Because the subject is "one," the verb must be singular, "is," but "is" sounds odd when it precedes the plural "lounges." The solution: revise the sentence.

Among the most noticeable features are the lounges.

Repetition and Variation

1. Don't be afraid to repeat a word if it is the best word. The following paragraph repeats "interesting," "paradox," "Salinger," "What makes," and "book"; notice also "feel" and "feeling." Repetition, a device necessary for continuity and clarity, holds the paragraph together.

> The reception given to *Franny and Zooey* in America has illustrated again the interesting paradox of Salinger's reputation there: great public enthusiasm, of the *Time* magazine and Best Seller List kind, accompanied by a repressive coolness in the critical journals. What makes this a paradox is that the book's themes are among the most ambitiously highbrow, and its craftsmanship most uncompromisingly virtuoso. What makes it an interesting one is that those who are most patronizing about the book are those who most resemble its characters: people whose ideas and language in their best moments resemble Zooey's. But they feel they ought not to enjoy the book. There is a very strong feeling in American literary circles that Salinger and love of Salinger must be discouraged.
>
> — Martin Green

2. Use pronouns, when their reference is clear, as substitutes for nouns. Notice Green's use of pronouns; notice also his substitution of "the book," for *"Franny and Zooey,"* and then "its" for "the book's." Substitutions that neither confuse nor distract keep a paragraph from sounding like a broken phonograph record.

3. Do not, however, confuse the substitutions we have just spoken of with the fault called Elegant Variation. A groundless fear of repetition sometimes leads students to write first, for example, of "Salinger," then of "the writer," then of "our author." Such variations strike the reader as silly. They can, moreover, be confusing. Does "the writer" mean "Salinger," or the person writing about him? Substitute "he" for "Salinger" if "he" is clear and sounds better. Otherwise, repeat "Salinger."

4. But don't repeat a word if it is being used in two different senses.

1. *Confusing*

Green's theme focuses on the theme of the book. (The first "theme" means "essay"; the second means "underlying idea" or "motif.")

Clear

Green's essay focuses on the theme of the book.

2. *Confusing*

Caesar's character is complex. The comic characters, however, are simple. (The first "character" means "personality"; the second means "persons" or "figures in the play.")

Clear

Caesar is complex; the comic characters, however, are simple.

5. Finally, eliminate words repeated unnecessarily. Use of words like *surely, in all probability, it is noteworthy* may become habitual. If they don't help your reader to follow your thoughts, they are Instant Prose Additives. Cross them out.

In general, when you revise, decide if a word should be repeated, varied, or eliminated, by testing sentences and paragraphs for both sound and sense.

Euphony

The word is from the Greek, "sweet voice," and though you need not aim at sweetness, try to avoid cacophony, or "harsh voice." Avoid distracting repetitions of sound, as in "The story is marked by a remarkable mystery," and "This is seen in the scene in which. . . ." Such echoes call attention to themselves, getting in the way of the points you are making. When you revise, tune out irrelevant sound effects.

Not all sound effects are irrelevant; some contribute meaning. James Baldwin, in his essay "Stranger in the Village," argues that the American racial experience has permanently altered black and white relationships throughout the world. His concluding sentence is "This world is white no longer, and it will never be white again." As the sentence opens, the repetition of sounds in "*w*orld is *w*hite" binds the two words together, but the idea that they are permanently bound is swiftly denied by the most emphatic repetition of sounds in "*no*," "*never*," "*again*," as the sentence closes. Or take another example: "America, Love It or Leave It." If it read "America, Love It or Emigrate," would the bumper sticker still imply, as clearly and menacingly, that there are only two choices, and for the patriot only one?

Transitions

Repetition holds a paragraph together by providing continuity and clarity. Transitions such as *next, on the other hand,* and *therefore* also provide continuity and clarity. Because we discuss transitions at length on pages 94–97, in our chapter on paragraphs, we here only remind you to make certain that the relation between one sentence and the next, and one paragraph and the next, is clear. Often it will be clear without an explicit transition: "She was desperately unhappy. She quit school." But do not take too much for granted; relationships between sentences may not be as clear to your readers as they are to you. You know what you are talking about; they don't. After reading the passage readers may see, in retrospect, that you have just given an example, or a piece of contrary evidence, or an amplification, but readers like to know in advance where they are going; brief transitions such as *for example, but, finally* (readers are keenly interested in knowing when they are getting near the end) are enormously helpful.

CLARITY AND SENTENCE STRUCTURE: PARALLELISM

Make the structure of your sentence reflect the structure of your thought. This is not as formidable as it sounds. If you keep your reader in mind, remembering that you are explaining something to someone who understands it less well than you, you will almost automatically not only say *what* you think but show *how* you think.

Almost automatically. In revising, read your work as if you were not the writer of it, but your intended reader. If you reach a bump or snag, where the shape or direction of your thought isn't clear, revise your sentence structure. Three general rules help:

1. Put main ideas in main (independent) clauses.
2. Subordinate the less important elements in the sentence to the more important.
3. Put parallel ideas and details in parallel constructions.

The time to consult these rules consciously is not while you write, but while you revise. (The first two rules are amplified in the next chapter, "Revising for Emphasis." Clarity and emphasis are closely related, as the following discussion of parallel construction makes evident.)

Consider the following sentence and the revision:

Awkward

He liked eating and to sleep.

Parallel

He liked to eat and to sleep.

In the first version, "eating" and "to sleep" are not grammatically parallel; the difference in grammatical form blurs the writer's point that there is a similarity. Use parallel constructions to clarify relationships — for instance to emphasize similarities or to define differences.

I divorce myself from my feelings and immerse myself in my obligations.

— From a student journal

She drew a line between respect, which we were expected to show, and fear, which we were not.

— Ernesto Galarza

I will not accept if nominated and will not serve if elected.

— William Tecumseh Sherman

Fascist art glorifies surrender; it exalts mindlessness; it glamorizes death.

— Susan Sontag

In the following examples, the parallel construction is printed in italic type.

1. *Awkward*

The dormitory rules needed revision, a smoking area was a necessity, and a generally more active role for the school in social affairs were all significant to her.

Parallel

She recommended that the school *revise* its dormitory rules, *provide* a smoking area, and *organize* more social activities.

2. *Awkward*

Most Chinese parents disapprove of interracial dating or they just do not permit it.

Parallel

Most Chinese parents *disapprove* of interracial dating, and many *forbid* it.

Revise the following sentence:

The rogallo glider is recommended for beginners because it is easy to assemble, to maintain, and it is portable.

In parallel constructions, be sure to check the consistency of articles, prepositions, and conjunctions. For example, "He wrote papers on a play by Shakespeare, a novel by Dickens, and a story by Oates," *not* "He wrote papers on a play by Shakespeare, a novel of Dickens, and a story by Oates." The shift from "by" to "of " and back to "by" serves no purpose and is merely distracting.

Let's study this matter a little more, using a short poem as our text.

Love Poem

Robert Bly

───────────────────────────────

When we are in love, we love the grass,
And the barns, and the lightpoles,
And the small mainstreets abandoned all night.

───────────────────────────────

Suppose we change "Love Poem" by omitting a conjunction or an article here and there:

When we are in love, we love the grass,
Barns, and lightpoles,
And the small mainstreets abandoned all night.

We've changed the rhythm, of course, but we still get the point: the lover loves all the world. In the original poem, however, the syntax of the sentence, the consistent repetition of "and the . . ." "and the . . ." makes us feel, without our thinking about it, that when we are in love we love the world, everything in it, equally. The list could extend infinitely, and everything in it would give us identical pleasure. In our altered version, we sacrifice this unspoken assurance. We bump a little, and stumble. As readers, without consciously being aware of it, we wonder if there's some distinction being made, some qualification we've missed. We still get the point of the poem, but we don't feel it the same way.

To sum up:

> A pupil once asked Arthur Schnabel [the noted pianist] whether it was better to play in time or to play as one feels; his characteristic mordant reply was another question: "Why not feel in time?"
>
> — David Hamilton

EXERCISES

1. In the following sentences, underline phrases in which you find the passive voice. Recast the sentences, using the active voice:

   a. The phrases in which the passive voice is found should be underlined.
   b. The active voice should be used.
   c. In the letter from Mrs. Mike advice was sought regarding her problem with her tenant.
   d. The egg is guarded, watched over, and even hatched by the male penguin.
   e. After the Industrial Revolution, the workers' daylight hours were spent in factories.
   f. Tyler found that sexual stereotyping was reinforced in the kindergarten: the girls were encouraged to play with dolls and the boys with Mack trucks.
   g. Insufficient evidence was given in the report to prove her hypothesis that reading problems originate in peer relationships.

2. Revise the following sentences to eliminate faults in modifiers:

   a. At the age of ten years, my family moved to Zierenberg, West Germany.
   b. Without knowing the reason, my father's cheeks became red with embarrassment.

c. Buffalo Bill became friends with Sitting Bull while performing together in the Wild West Show.

d. During a drought, annual plants will succumb without help.

e. Looking out from my window, the sky was inky black.

f. Mr. Karajan conducted the orchestra three times during the week-end before returning to his home in the Alps to the delight of the audience.

g. "Some of it is sitting down with the most powerful single person in the free world." (John Glenn, alluding to President Reagan)

3. In the following sentences, locate the errors in agreement and correct them.

a. Locate the error and correct them.

b. One must strive hard to reach their goal.

c. I would recommend the book to anyone who wants to improve their writing.

d. Her collection of antique toys fill the house.

4. Recast the following sentences, using parallel constructions to express parallel ideas:

a. Jacoby's aim in writing is to disgrace the passively committed and opposition to feminism.

b. The boys segregated themselves less, the girls showed broader career interests, and unromantic, cross-sex relationships were achieved.

c. The study shows parents and educators that it is important to change and it can be done.

d. I do believe that there should be equality between men and women: equal pay for equal work; everybody should have an equal chance to attain whatever goals they may have set for themselves; and everybody should share the same responsibilities toward society.

5. Identify the specific faults that make the following sentences unclear, then revise each sentence for clarity. (Note that you will often have to invent what the writer thought he or she had said.)

a. Actually, she was aging, and quite average in other respects.

b. If technology cannot sort out its plusses and minuses, and work to improve them, man must.

c. Brooks stresses the farm workers' strenuous way of life and the fact that they have the bare necessities of life.

d. Instead of movable furniture, built-in ledges extend into the center of the room to be used as tables or to sit on.

e. The issue has been saved for my final argument because it is controversial.

f. I am neither indifferent nor fond of children.

g. When the students heard that their proposal was rejected a meeting was called.

h. A viable library is the cornerstone of any college campus.

i. Her main fault was that she was somewhat lacking in decision-making capabilities.

j. After industrialization a swarm of immigrants came bantering to our shores.

k. Each group felt there was very personal rapport and thus very candid feedback resulted.

l. He can tolerate crowding and pollution and seems disinterested or ignorant of these dangers.

m. The wooden door occupies the majority of the stone wall.

n. Yale students frequently write to Ann Landers telling her fictional stories of their so-called troubles as a childish prank.

o. At my grandmother's house vegetables were only served because meat was forbidden.

p. My firm stand seemed to melt a little.

q. The conclusion leaves the conflict neatly tied in smooth knots.

r. The paragraph reeks of blandness.

6. The following sentences, published in *AIDE*, a magazine put out by an insurance company, were written to the company by various policyholders. The trouble is that the writers mean one thing but their sentences say another. Make each sentence clearly say what the writer means.

a. The other car collided with mine without giving warning of its intentions.

b. I collided with a stationary truck coming the other way.

c. The guy was all over the road; I had to swerve a number of times before I hit him.

d. I pulled away from the side of the road, glanced at my mother-in-law, and headed over the embankment.

e. In my attempt to kill a fly, I drove into a telephone pole.

f. I had been driving for forty years when I fell asleep at the wheel and had the accident.

g. To avoid hitting the bumper of the car in front, I struck the pedestrian.

h. The pedestrian had no idea which direction to run, so I ran over him.

i. The indirect cause of this accident was a little guy in a small car with a big mouth.

7. In 1983, while conflicting reports were being broadcast about an invasion of Grenada by U.S. troops, Admiral Wesley L. McDonald, in the Pentagon, answered a reporter's question thus: "We were not micromanaging Grenada intelligencewise until about that time frame." Bruce Felknor, director of yearbooks for the *Encyclopaedia Britannica,* says that he was "inspired" by that answer to translate "a small selection of earlier admirals' heroic prose for the edification, indeed enjoyment, of our young." Below we list Felknor's translations and, in parentheses, the names of the admirals, the battles, and the dates of their heroic prose. What were the original words?

a. "Combatwise, the time frame is upcoming." (John Paul Jones, off the English coast, September 23, 1779)

b. "Area accessed in combat mode; mission finished." (Oliver Hazard Perry, after the Battle of Lake Erie, September 10, 1813)

c. "Disregard anticipated structural damage. Continue as programmed." (David Farragut, Mobile Bay, August 5, 1864)

d. "Implementation of aggressive action approved; time frame to be selected by fire control officer." (George Dewey, Manila Bay, May 1, 1898)

8. Translate the following euphemisms into plain English:

a. micromanaging Grenada intelligencewise

b. revenue enhancement

c. atmospheric deposition of anthropogenically derived acidic substances

d. resize our operations to the level of profitable opportunities (spoken by a business executive)

e. reconcentrate (or redeploy) our forces

14
Revising
for
Emphasis

In revising for conciseness and clarity we begin to discover what we may have been largely unaware of in the early stages of writing: what in our topic most concerns us and precisely why it interests us. That moment of discovery (or those several discrete moments) yields more pleasure than any other in writing. From there on we work, sometimes as if inspired, to make our special angle of vision seem as inevitable to our readers as it is to us. Now as we tighten sentences or expand them, as we shift the position of a word or a paragraph, or as we subordinate a less important idea to a more important one, we are assigning relative value and weight to each of our statements. The expression of value and weight is what is meant by emphasis.

Inexperienced writers may *try* to achieve emphasis as Queen Victoria did, by a style consisting *almost entirely* of italics and — dashes — and — exclamation marks!!! Or they may spice their prose with clichés ("little did I realize," "believe it or not") or with a liberal sprinkling of intensifiers ("really beautiful," "definitely significant," and so on). But experienced writers abandon these unconvincing devices. Emphasis is more securely achieved by exploiting the possibilities of position, of brevity and length, of repetition, and of subordination.

EMPHASIS BY POSITION

First, let's see how a word or phrase may be emphasized. If it appears in an unusual position it gains emphasis, as in "This course he liked." Because in English the object of the verb usually comes after the verb (as in "He liked this course"), the object is emphasized if it appears first. But this device is tricky; words in an unusual position often seem ludicrous, the writer fatuous: "A mounted Indian toward the forest raced."

Let's now consider a less strained sort of emphasis by position. The beginning and the end of a sentence or a paragraph are emphatic positions; of these two positions, the end is usually the more emphatic. What comes last is what stays most in the mind. Compare these two sentences:

> The essay is brief but informative.
> The essay is informative but brief.

The first sentence leaves the reader with the impression that the essay, despite its brevity, is worth looking at. The second, however, ends more negatively, leaving the reader with the impression that the essay is so brief that its value is fairly slight. Because the emphasis in each sentence is different, the two sentences say different things.

It usually makes sense, then, to put the important point near the end, lest the sentence become anticlimactic. Here is a sentence that properly moves to an emphatic end:

> Although I could not read its six hundred pages in one sitting, I never willingly put it down.

If the halves are reversed the sentence trails off:

> I never willingly put it down, although I could not read its six hundred pages in one sitting.

This second version straggles away from the real point — that the book was interesting.

Anticlimactic
Besides not owning themselves women also could not own property.

Emphatic

Women could not own property; in fact, they did not own themselves.

The commonest anticlimaxes are caused by weak qualifiers (*in my opinion, it seems to me, in general, etc.*) tacked on to interesting statements. Weak qualifiers usually can be omitted. Even useful ones rarely deserve an emphatic position.

Anticlimactic

Poodles are smart but they are no smarter than pigs, I have read.

Emphatic

Poodles are smart, but I have read that they are not smarter than pigs.   ← state sources

The rule: try to bury dull but necessary qualifiers in the middle of the sentence.

EMPHASIS BY BREVITY AND LENGTH: SHORT AND LONG SENTENCES

How long should a sentence be? One recalls Lincoln's remark to a heckler who asked him how long a man's legs should be: "Long enough to reach the ground." No rules about length can be given, but be careful not to bore your reader with a succession of short sentences (say, under ten words) and be careful not to tax your reader with a monstrously long sentence. Victor Hugo's sentence in *Les Misérables* containing 823 words punctuated by ninety-three commas, fifty-one semicolons, and four dashes, is not a good model for beginners.

Consider this succession of short sentences:

The purpose of the refrain is twofold. First, it divides the song into stanzas. Second, it reinforces the theme of the song.

These sentences are clear, but since the points are simple, readers may feel they are being addressed as if they were children. There is too much emphasis (too many heavy pauses) on too little. The reader can take all three sentences at once:

The purpose of the refrain is twofold: it divides the song into stanzas and it reinforces the theme.

The three simple sentences have been turned into one compound sentence, allowing the reader to keep going for a while.

Now compare another group of sentences with a revision.

Hockey is by far the fastest moving team sport in America. The skaters are constantly on the go. They move at high speeds. The action rarely stops.

These four sentences, instead of suggesting motion, needlessly stop us. Here is a revision:

Hockey is by far the fastest moving team sport in America. The skaters, constantly on the go, move at high speeds, and the action rarely stops.

By combining the second, third, and fourth sentences, the reader, like the players, is kept on the go.

Next, a longer example that would be thoroughly delightful if parts of it were less choppy.

Conceit

At my high school graduation we had two speakers. One was a member of our class, and the other was a faculty member. The student speaker's name was Alva Reed. The faculty speaker's name was Mr. Williams. The following conversation took place after the graduation ceremony. Parents, relatives, faculty, and friends were all outside the gymnasium congratulating the class of 1979. Alva was surrounded by her friends, her parents, and some faculty members who were congratulating her on her speech. Not standing far from her was Mr. Williams with somewhat the same crowd.

"Alva dear, you were wonderful!"

"Thanks Mom. I sure was scared though; I'm glad it's over."

At that moment, walking towards Alva were her grandparents. They both were wearing big smiles on their faces. Her grandfather said rather loudly, "That was a good speech dear. Nicely done, nicely done." Walking past them at that moment was Mr. Williams.

> He stuck his head into their circle and replied, "Thank you," and walked away.

The first four sentences seem to be written in spurts. They can easily be combined and improved thus:

> At my high school graduation we had two speakers. One was a member of our class, Alva Reed, and the other was a faculty member, Mr. Williams.

If we think that even this version, two sentences instead of four, is a little choppy, we can rewrite it into a single sentence:

> At my high school graduation we had two speakers, Alva Reed, a member of our class, and Mr. Williams, a faculty member.

or:

> The two speakers at my high school graduation were Alva Reed, a member of our class, and Mr. Williams, a faculty member.

The rest of the piece is less choppy, but reread it and see if you don't discover some other sentences that should be combined. Revise them.

Sometimes, however, the choppiness of a succession of short sentences is effective. Look at this description of the methods by which George Jackson, in prison, resisted efforts to destroy his spirit:

> He trains himself to sleep only three hours a night. He studies Swahili, Chinese, Arabic and Spanish. He does pushups to control his sexual urge and to train his body. Sometimes he does a thousand a day. He eats only one meal a day. And, always, he is reading and thinking.
>
> — Julius Lester

That the author is capable of writing longer, more complicated sentences is evident in the next paragraph:

> Yet, when his contact with the outside world is extended beyond his family to include Angela Davis, Joan, a woman who works with the Soledad defense committee, and his attorney, he is able to find within himself feelings of love and tenderness.

Can we account for the success of the passage describing Jackson's prison routine? First, the short sentences, with their repeated commonplace form (subject, verb, object) in some degree imitate Jackson's experience: they are almost monotonously disciplined, almost as regular as the pushups the confined Jackson does. Later, when Jackson makes contact with Angela Davis and others, the long sentence helps to suggest the expansion of his world. Second, the brevity of the sentences suggests their enormous importance, certainly to Jackson and to Julius Lester and, Lester hopes, to the reader.

Keep in mind this principle: *any one sentence in your essay is roughly equal to any other sentence.* If a sentence is short, it must be relatively weighty. A lot is packed into a little. Less is more. (The chief exceptions are transitional sentences such as, "Now for the second point.") Consider the following passage:

> It happened that in September of 1933 Lord Rutherford, at the British Association meeting, made some remark about atomic energy never becoming real. Leo Szilard was the kind of scientist, perhaps just the kind of good-humored, cranky man, who disliked any statement that contained the word "never," particularly when made by a distinguished colleague. So he set his mind to think about the problem.
>
> — Jacob Bronowski

The first two sentences are relatively long (twenty-three words and thirty-one words); the third is relatively short (ten words), and its brevity — its weight or density — emphasizes Szilard's no-nonsense attitude.

EMPHASIS BY REPETITION — *related to parallel construction*

Don't be afraid to repeat a word if it is important. The repetition will add emphasis. Notice in these lucid sentences by Helen Gardner the effective repetition of "end" and "beginning."

> *Othello* has this in common with the tragedy of fortune, that the end in no way blots out from the imagination the glory of the beginning. But the end here does not merely by its darkness throw up into relief the brightness that was. On the contrary, beginning

passive voice, but
— is an abstract

and end chime against each other. In both the value of life and love
is affirmed. ·

The substitution of "conclusion" or "last scene" for the second
"end" would be worse than pointless; it would destroy Miss Gardner's point that there is *identity* or correspondence between beginning and end.

EMPHASIS BY SUBORDINATION

Five Kinds of Sentences

Before we can discuss the use of subordination for emphasis,
we must first talk about what a sentence is, and about five kinds
of sentences.

If there is an adequate definition of a sentence, we haven't
found it. Perhaps the best definition is not the old one, "a complete
thought," but "a word or group of words that the reader takes to
be complete." This definition includes such utterances as "Who?"
and "Help!" and "Never!" and "Maybe." Now, in speaking,
"While he was walking down the street" may be taken as a complete thought, if it answers the question "When did the car hit
him?" In writing, however, it would be a sentence fragment that
probably should be altered to, say, "While he was walking down
the street he was hit by a car." We will discuss intentional fragments
on pages 497–98 and ways to correct unintentional fragments on
pages 000–00. But first we should take a closer look at complete
sentences.

Usually a sentence names someone or something (this is the
subject) and it tells us something about the subject (this is the
predicate); that is, it "predicates" something about the subject. Let
us look at five kinds of sentences: simple, compound, complex,
compound–complex, and sentence fragments.

1. A *simple sentence* has one predicate, here italicized:

Shakespeare *died.*
Shakespeare and Jonson *were contemporaries.*

The subject can be elaborated ("Shakespeare and Jonson, England's
chief Renaissance dramatists, were contemporaries"), or the pred-

icate can be elaborated ("Shakespeare and Jonson were contemporaries in the Renaissance England of Queen Elizabeth"); but the sentence remains technically a simple sentence, consisting of only one main (independent) clause with no dependent (subordinate) clause.

2. A *compound sentence* has two or more main clauses, each containing a subject and a predicate. It is, then, two or more simple sentences connected by a coordinating conjunction (*and, but, for, nor, or, yet*) or by *not only . . . but also*, or by a semicolon or colon or, rarely, by a comma.

> Shakespeare died in 1616, and Jonson died in 1637. *received more emphasis,*
> Shakespeare not only wrote plays, but he also acted in them.
> Shakespeare died in 1616; Jonson died twenty-one years later.

3. A *complex sentence* has one main (independent) clause and one or more subordinate (dependent) clauses. Here the main clause is italicized.

> Although Shakespeare died, *England survived.* *main clause*
> *Jonson did not write a commemorative poem* when Shakespeare died. *subordinate*

The parts not italicized are subordinate or dependent because they cannot stand as sentences by themselves.

4. A *compound-complex sentence* has two or more main clauses (here italicized) and one or more subordinate clauses.

> *In 1616 Shakespeare died* and *his wife inherited the second-best bed* because he willed it to her.

Each of the two italicized passages could stand by itself as a sentence, but "because he willed it to her" could not (except as the answer to a question). Each italicized passage, then, is a main (independent) clause, and "because he willed it to her" is a subordinate (dependent) clause.

We will return to subordination, but let us first look at the fifth kind of sentence, the sentence fragment.

5. A *sentence fragment* does not fit the usual definition of a sentence, but when the fragment is intended the thought is often clear and complete enough. Intentional fragments are common in advertisements:

> Made of imported walnut. For your pleasure. At finer stores.

> More native than the Limbo. More exciting than the beat of a steel drum. Tia Maria. Jamaica's haunting liqueur.

And yet another example, this one not from an advertisement but from an essay on firewood:

> Piles of it. Right off the sidewalk. Split from small logs of oak or ash or maple. Split. Split again.
>
> — John McPhee

All these examples strike us as pretentious in their obviously studied efforts at understatement. Words are hoarded, as though there is much in little, and as though to talk more fully would demean the speaker and would desecrate the subject. A few words, and then a profound silence. Here less is not more; it is too much. The trouble with these fragmentary sentences is not that they don't convey complete thoughts but that they attract too much attention to themselves; they turn our minds too emphatically to their writers, and conjure up images of unpleasantly self-satisfied oracles.

Here, however, is a passage from a student's essay, where the fragmentary sentences seem satisfactory to us. The passage begins with a simple sentence, and then gives three fragmentary sentences.

```
    The film has been playing to sellout audiences. Even though the
acting is inept. Even though the sound is poorly synchronized. Even
though the plot is incoherent.
```

If this passage is successful, it is because the emphasis is controlled. The author is dissatisfied, and by means of parallel fragments (each beginning with the same words) she conveys a moderately engaging weariness and a gentle exasperation.

Then, too, we see that if the first three periods were changed to commas we would have an orthodox complex sentence. In short, because the fragments are effective we find them acceptable.

For ways to correct ineffective or unacceptable fragments, see pages 497–98.

Subordination

Having surveyed the kinds of sentences, we can at last talk about using subordination to give appropriate emphasis.

<u>Make sure that</u> the <u>less important element is subordinate to</u> the <u>more important</u>. In the following example the first clause, summarizing the writer's previous sentences, is a subordinate or dependent clause; the new material is made emphatic by being put into two independent clauses, italicized here:

> As soon as the Irish Literary Theatre was assured of a nationalist backing, *it started to dissociate itself from any political aim,* and *the long struggle with the public began.*

The second and third clauses in this sentence, linked by "and," are coordinate — that is, of equal importance.

Probably most of the sentences that you read and write are complex sentences: an independent clause and one or more subordinate clauses. Whatever is outside of the independent clause is subordinate, less important. Consider this sentence:

> When Miss Horniman provided money, Yeats dreamed of a poetic drama.

The writer puts Yeats's dream in the independent clause, subordinating the relatively unimportant Miss Horniman. Miss Horniman and her money are of some importance, of course, or they would not have been mentioned, but they are *less* important than Yeats's dream. (Notice, by the way, that emphasis by subordination often works along with emphasis by position. Here the independent clause comes *after* the subordinate clause; the writer appropriately put the more important material in the more emphatic position.) Had the writer wished to give Miss Horniman more prominence, the passage might have run:

> Yeats dreamed of a poetic drama, and Miss Horniman subsidized that dream.

Here Miss Horniman at least stands in an independent clause, linked to the previous independent clause by "and." The two clauses, and the two people, are now of approximately equal importance. If the writer had wanted to emphasize Miss Horniman and to deemphasize Yeats, she might have written:

> While Yeats dreamed of a poetic drama, Miss Horniman provided the money.

Here Yeats is reduced to the subordinate clause, and Miss Horniman is given the dignity of the only independent clause. (And again notice that the important point is also in the emphatic position, near the end of the sentence. A sentence is likely to sprawl if an independent clause comes first, followed by a long subordinate clause of lesser importance, such as the sentence you are now reading. See the discussion of emphasis by position on pages 491–92.)

In short, though simple sentences and compound sentences have their place, they make everything of equal importance. Since everything is not of equal importance, you must often write complex and compound-complex sentences, subordinating some things to other things. Look again at the first four sentences of "Conceit" (page 493), and at the suggested revisions.

Having made the point that subordination reduces monotony and conveys appropriate emphasis, we must again say that there are times when a succession of simple or compound sentences is effective, as in the passage on page 494 describing George Jackson. As a rough rule, however, don't write more than two consecutive simple sentences unless you know what you are doing.

EXERCISES

1. Here is one way to test your grasp of the relationship of independent and subordinate elements in a sentence. This *haiku* (a Japanese poetic form) consists of one sentence that can be written as prose: "After weeks of watching the roof leak, I fixed it tonight by moving a single board."

Hitch Haiku

Gary Snyder

After weeks of watching the roof leak
   I fixed it tonight
by moving a single board.

   a. Identify the underlined independent clause and the subordinate elements in the poem.

   b. The "I" in the poem's sentence does or has done three things. Write three simple sentences, each expressing one of the actions.

   c. Write one sentence in which all three of the poem's actions are expressed, but put in the independent clause one of the two actions that appear in a subordinate element in the poem.

   d. Compare your sentence with the poem's. Both sentences should be clear. How do they vary in emphasis?

   e. Optional: Compare the original sentence written as poetry and written as prose.

2. First identify the fault or faults that make the following sentences unemphatic, and then revise them for emphasis.

   a. He lists some of the rights given to humans and things and both admits and accounts for the oddity of his proposal well by citing examples.

   b. Rights for women, blacks and the insane were granted though many couldn't see the value in it and so now our environment should be granted rights even though it takes some getting used to the idea.

   c. Thus Creon's pride forces Antigone's death which drives his son to suicide and then his wife.

   d. Stock breeding will give the same result as population evolution, defenders of positive eugenics claim.

   e. The family today lacks the close relationship it had before the industrial age, for example.

   f. The woman's face is distraught, her hair is unkempt, and her dress is rumpled.

   g. There is probably no human being who would enjoy being eaten by a shark.

3. Analyze the ways of achieving emphasis in the following passage by Theodore Roosevelt on Grand Canyon.

> In Grand Canyon Arizona has a natural wonder which, so far as I know, is in kind absolutely unparalleled throughout the rest of the world. . . . Leave it as it is. You cannot improve upon it. The ages have been at work on it, and man can only mar it. What you can do is to keep it for your children, your children's children, and for all those who come after you as one of the great sights which every American, if he can travel at all, should see.

PART THREE
Acquiring Style and Fluency

Two monks were arguing about a flag. One said: "The flag is moving."

The other said: "The wind is moving."

The sixth patriarch happened to be passing by. He told them: "Not the wind, not the flag: mind is moving."

— ZEN ANECDOTE

15
Defining Style

Style is not simply a flower here and some gilding there; it pervades the whole work. Van Gogh's style, or Walt Disney's, let us say, consists in part of features recurring throughout a single work and from one work to the next: angular or curved lines, hard or soft edges, strong or gentle contrasts, and so on. Pictures of a seated woman by each of the two artists are utterly different, and if we have seen a few works by each, we can readily identify who did which one. Artists leave their fingerprints, so to speak, all over their work; writers leave their voiceprints.

The word *style* comes from the Latin *stilus,* a Roman writing instrument. Even in Roman times *stilus* had acquired a figurative sense, referring not only to the instrument but also to the writer's choice of words and arrangement of words into sentences. But is it simply the choice and arrangement of words we comment on when we speak of a writer's style, or are we also commenting on the writer's mind? Don't we feel that a piece of writing, whether it's on Civil War photographs or on genetics and intelligence, is also about the writer? The writing, after all, sets forth the writer's views of his or her topic. It sets forth perceptions and responses to something the writer has thought about. The writer has, from the start, from the choice of a topic, revealed that he or she found it worth thinking about. The essay, in attempting to persuade us to think as the writer does, reveals not only how and what the writer thinks, but what he or she values.

When we write about things "out there," our writing always reveals the form and likeness of our minds, just as every work of art reveals the creator as well as the ostensible subject. A portrait painting, for example, is not only about the sitter; it is about the artist's perceptions of the sitter, hence the saying that every portrait is a self-portrait. Even photographs are as much about the photographer as they are about the subject. Richard Avedon said of his portraits of famous people, "They are all pictures of me, of the way I feel about the people I photograph." A student's essay similarly, if it is truly written, is not exclusively about "*La Causa* and the New Chicana"; it is also about her perceptions and responses to both racism and sexism.

Still, a useful distinction can be made between the author and the speaker of an essay. The flesh-and-blood author creates, through words, a particular speaker or voice or (to use the term common in literary criticism) persona. The persona is the author in a role adopted for a specific audience. When Abraham Lincoln wrote, he sometimes did so in the persona of the commander in chief of the Union Army, but he sometimes did so in the very different persona of the simple man from Springfield, Illinois. The persona is a mask put on for a performance (*persona* is the Latin word for mask). If mask suggests insincerity, we should remember that whenever we speak or write we do so in a specific role — as friend, or parent, or teacher, or applicant for a job, or whatever. Although Lincoln was a husband, a father, a politician, a president, and many other things, when he wrote a letter to his son, the persona (or, we might say, personality) is that of the father, not that of the commander in chief. The distinction between the writer (who necessarily fills many roles) and the persona who writes or speaks a given work is especially useful in talking about satire, because the satirist often invents a mouthpiece very different from himself or herself. The satirist — say Jonathan Swift — may be strongly opposed to a view, but the persona (the invented essayist) may favor the view; the reader must perceive that the real writer is ridiculing the invented essayist.

STYLE AND TONE

The style is the man. Rather say the
style is the way the man takes himself.
— ROBERT FROST

Suppose we take a page of handwriting, or even a signature.
We need not believe that graphology is an exact science to believe
that the shape of the ink-lines on paper (apart from the meaning
of the words) often tells us something about the writer. We look
at a large, ornate signature, and we sense that the writer is confident; we look at a tiny signature written with the finest of pens,
and we wonder why anyone is so self-effacing.

More surely than handwriting, the writer's style reveals,
among other things, his attitude toward the self (as Frost's addition
to Buffon's epigram suggests), toward the reader, and toward the
subject. The writer's attitudes are reflected in what is usually called
tone. It is difficult to distinguish between style and tone, but we
can try. Most discussions of style concentrate on what might be
thought of as ornament: figurative language ("a sea of troubles"),
inversion ("A leader he is not"), repetition and parallelism ("government of the people, by the people, for the people"), balance
and antithesis ("It was the best of times, it was the worst of times").
Indeed, for centuries style has been called "the dress of thought,"
implying that the thought is something separate from the expression; the thought, in this view, is dressed up in stylistic devices.
But in most of the writing that we read with interest and pleasure
the stylistic devices are not ornamental and occasional but integral
and pervasive. When we talk about wit, sincerity, tentativeness,
self-assurance, aggressiveness, objectivity, and so forth, we can say
we are talking about style, but we should recognize that style now
is not a matter of ornamental devices that dress up some idea, but
part of the idea itself. And "the idea itself" includes the writer's
unified yet appropriately varied tone of voice.

To take a brief example: the famous English translation of
Caesar's report of a victory, "I came, I saw, I conquered," might
be paraphrased thus: "After getting to the scene of the battle I
studied the situation. Then I devised a strategy that won the battle." But this paraphrase loses much of Caesar's message; the brevity and the parallelism of the famous version, as well as the allit-

eration (*c*ame, *c*onquered), convey tight-lipped self-assurance — convey, that is, the tone that reveals Caesar to us. And this tone is a large part of Caesar's message. Caesar is really telling us not only about what he did, but about what sort of person he is. He is perceptive, decisive, and effective. The three actions, Caesar in effect tells us, are (for a man like Caesar) one. (The Latin original is even more tight-lipped and more unified by alliteration: *veni, vidi, vici.*)

Let's look now at a longer sentence, the opening sentence of Lewis Thomas's essay called "On Natural Death":

> There are so many new books about dying that there are now special shelves set aside for them in bookstores, along with the health-diet and home-repair paperbacks and the sex manuals.

This sentence could have ended where the comma is placed: the words after "bookstores" are, it might seem, not important. One can scarcely argue that by specifying some kinds of "special shelves" Thomas clarifies an otherwise difficult or obscure concept. What, then, do these additional words do? They tell us nothing about death and almost nothing about bookshops, but they tell us a great deal about Thomas's *attitude* toward the new books on death. He suggests that such books are faddish and perhaps (like "the sex manuals") vulgar. After all, if he had merely wanted to call up a fairly concrete image of a well-stocked bookstore he could have said "along with books on politics and the environment," or some such thing. His next sentence runs:

> Some of them are so packed with detailed information and step-by-step instructions for performing the function you'd think this was a new sort of skill which all of us are now required to learn.

Why "you'd think" instead of, say, "one might believe"? Thomas uses a colloquial form, and a very simple verb, because he wants to convey to us his common-sense, homely, down-to-earth view that these books are a bit pretentious — a pretentiousness conveyed in his use of the words "performing the function," words that might come from the books themselves. In short, when we read Thomas's paragraph we are learning as much about Thomas as we are about books on dying. We are hearing a voice, perceiving an attitude, and we want to keep reading, not only because we are interested in death but also because Thomas has managed to make us interested in Thomas, a thoughtful but unpretentious fellow, the sort of fellow Holden Caulfield might want to talk to.

Now listen to a short paragraph from John Szarkowski's *Looking at Photographs*. Szarkowski is writing about one of Alexander Gardner's photographs of a dead Confederate sharpshooter.

> Among the pictures that Gardner made himself is the one reproduced here. Like many Civil War photographs, it showed that the dead of both sides looked very much the same. The pictures of earlier wars had not made this clear.

Try, in a word or two, to characterize the tone (the attitude, as we sense it in the inflection of the voice) of the first sentence. Next, the tone of the second, and then of the third. Suppose the second and third sentences had been written thus:

> It showed that the dead of both sides looked very much the same. This is made clear in Civil War photographs, but not in pictures of earlier wars.

How has the tone changed? What word can you find to characterize the tone of the whole, as Szarkowski wrote it?

Now another passage from Szarkowski's book:

> Jacob A. Riis was a newspaper reporter by occupation and a social reformer by inclination. He was a photographer rather briefly and apparently rather casually; it seems beyond doubt that he considered photography a useful but subservient tool for his work as reporter and reformer. It is clear that he had no interest in "artistic" photography, and equally clear that the artistic photographers of his time had no interest in him.

Do you find traces of Szarkowski's voiceprint here?

Finally, a longer passage by the same writer. After you read it, try to verbalize the resemblances between this and the other passages — the qualities that allow us to speak of the writer's tone.

> There are several possible explanations for the fact that women have been more important to photography than their numbers alone would warrant. One explanation might be the fact that photography has never had licensing laws or trade unions, by means of which women might have been effectively discriminated against. A second reason might be the fact that the specialized technical preparation for photography need not be enormously demanding, so that the

medium has been open to those unable to spend long years in formal study.

A third possible reason could be that women have a greater natural talent for photography than men do. Discretion (or cowardice) suggests that this hypothesis is best not pursued, since a freely speculative exploration of it might take unpredictable and indefensible lines. One might for example consider the idea that the art of photography is in its nature receptive, or passive, thus suggesting that women are also.

STYLE AND LEVELS OF USAGE

Although the dividing lines between levels of usage cannot always be drawn easily, tradition recognizes three: *formal, informal,* and *popular* or *vulgar.* Sometimes *popular* is used to designate a level between informal and vulgar. (*Vulgar* here doesn't mean dirty words; rather, it refers to the speech characteristic of uneducated people, speech that uses such expressions as *ain't, nohow,* and *he don't.*)

Formal writing, found mostly in scholarly articles, textbooks, ceremonial speeches, and scientific reports, assumes an audience not only generally well educated but also with special knowledge of or interest in the writer's subject. The writer can therefore use a wide vocabulary (including words and references that in another context would be pretentious or obscure) and sentence patterns that demand close attention. A noted figure, say a respected literary critic, examining an influential book and addressing the world of thoughtful readers, may use a formal style, as Lionel Trilling does here in a criticism of V. L. Parrington's *Main Currents in American Literature.* Trilling assumes an attentive reader, capable of holding in mind a long sentence.

> To throw out Poe because he cannot be conveniently fitted into a theory of American culture, to speak of him as a biological sport and as a mind apart from the main current, to find his gloom to be merely personal and eccentric, "only the atrabilious wretchedness of a dipsomaniac," as Hawthorne's was "no more than the skeptical questioning of life by a nature that knew no fierce storms," to judge Melville's response to American life to be less noble than that of Bryant or of Greeley, to speak of Henry James as an escapist, as an

artist similar to Whistler, a man characteristically afraid of stress —
this is not merely to be mistaken in aesthetic judgment; rather it is
to examine without attention and from the point of view of a limited
and essentially arrogant conception of reality the documents which
are in some respects the most suggestive testimony to what America
was and is, and of course to get no answer from them.

— Lionel Trilling

Now, although "to throw out" is fairly informal, as opposed to,
say, "to dismiss," the sentence as a whole is formal. Notice the
structure: "To throw . . . to speak . . . to find . . . to judge . . .
to speak," and we still do not have an independent clause. Two-
thirds of the way through, with "this is not merely to be mistaken," the previous words come into focus, but the meaning is
still incomplete. To do such-and-such "is not merely to be mistaken," but what *is* it to be? At last we are told: "it is to examine
without attention . . . and . . . to get no answer. . . ."

A formal sentence need not be long. Here is a fairly short
formal sentence by W. H. Auden:

Owing to its superior power as a mnemonic, verse is superior to
prose as a medium for didactic instruction.

In another frame of mind Auden might have written something
less formal, along these lines:

Because it stays more easily in the memory, verse is better than
prose for teaching.

This revision of Auden's sentence can be called informal, but it is
high on the scale, the language of an educated man writing courteously to an audience he conceives of as his peers. It is the level
of almost all serious writing about literature. A low informal
version might be:

Poetry sticks in the mind better than prose; so if you want to teach
something, poetry is better.

This is the language any of us might use in conversation; it is
almost never the language used in writing to our peers.

In textbooks, the most obvious purpose of discussions of
levels has been to dislodge older, more rigid ideas about "good"
and "bad" or "correct" and "incorrect" English, and to replace
them with the more flexible and more accurate standard of appro-

priateness. The labels *formal* and *informal* (we can for the moment drop *vulgar,* since few essays are written in it) attempt to describe the choices that writers make under particular circumstances, rather than to prescribe those they ought to make under all circumstances. The choices, often unconscious, include those of vocabulary, sentence structure, and tone.

Finding the Appropriate Level

What is appropriate in writing, as in dress, is subject to change, and the change recently has been to greater informality in both. Students who attend classes, concerts, and even their own weddings in blue jeans might experiment with similar freedom in writing college essays, and work toward a style that feels comfortable and natural to them. Developing a natural style, writing at an appropriate level, does take work. Consider, for example, the following opening paragraph from a student's theme:

> The college experience is traumatic, often because one must adjust not only to new academic horizons and new friends but also to the new physical environment constituted by the college and by the community surrounding it. One might think that, coming from a city only sixty miles from Wellesley, I would be exempt from this aspect of adaptation. However, this assumption has proven to be false.

"Traumatic"? "Academic horizons"? "Constituted"? "Exempt from this aspect of adaptation"? "Assumption . . . proven to be false"? There's nothing wrong with the language here, that is, nothing ungrammatical. But the paragraph has a hollow ring, a tone of insincerity, because the diction and syntax — the writer's level of usage — so ill suit the theme: a personal and spirited defense of the writer's lower-middle-class industrial home town, whose liveliness, friendliness, and above all, informality, she emphatically prefers to the aloofness of suburban Wellesley.

By contrast, in a review of *Soledad Brother — The Prison Letters of George Jackson,* another student described Jackson's style as "clear, simple, expressive, and together." The word "together," though technically incorrect (an adverb, here used as an adjective), strikes us, in context, as exactly right. And, when later in the essay we read "Surviving on glasses of water, crumbs of bread, deep concentration, daily push-ups, and cigarettes, Jackson shouts to the black world to wake up: get off your knees and start kicking asses," we feel that the deliberately inconsistent use of the formal series of parallels with the colloquial or vulgar "kicking asses" exactly expresses both Jackson's discipline and rage, and the writer's empathy with them.

In most of your college writing you are addressing people like yourself; use a language that you would like to read, neither stuffy nor aggressively colloquial. Probably it will stand somewhere in between the levels of "aspects of adaptation" and "kicking asses."

Tone: Four Examples

The first two excerpts are the opening paragraphs of two speeches. The third, though not an opening paragraph, is also from a speech. The fourth, by Pauline Kael, is the beginning of an essay on the tedium of most modern films.

1. It is indeed both an honor and a challenge to be invited to participate in this most significant occasion, the observance of the one hundredth anniversary of the birth of Max Weber. It is also a great pleasure to revisit the University of Heidelberg, though not quite for the first time, just short of forty years after my enrollment here as a student in 1925. This was too late to know Max Weber in person, but of course his intellectual influence was all-pervasive in the Heidelberg of that time, constituting the one primary point of reference about which all theoretical and much empirical discussion in the social and cultural fields revolved. I was also privileged to know his gracious and highly intelligent widow, Marianne Weber, in particular to attend a number of her famous "sociological teas" on Sunday afternoons. It was an extraordinarily stimulating intellectual environment, participation in which was one of the most important factors in determining my whole intellectual and professional career.

   — Talcott Parsons

2. It has been suggested that I discuss what it is like to be a poet these days (the only days in which my opinion could possibly be useful), or, if that is immodest, what it is like to write poetry, what one thinks about the art, what its relation is to

the life we supposedly live these days, and so on. This is a fascinatingly large range in which to wander, and I shall be interested to find out what I do think. I hope you will be interested, too. But I must advise you that this will not be a coherently organized essay running in a smooth and logical progression from question to conclusion. Nor will the views expressed necessarily be consistent. I have consulted with my selves, and come up, as usual, with a number of fragmentary notions, many of them aphoristic in expression, and I believe I will do best simply to put these before you without much in the way of explanation or connective tissue.

— Howard Nemerov

3. Style, in its finest sense, is the last acquirement of the educated mind; it is also the most useful. It pervades the whole being. The administrator with a sense for style hates waste; the engineer with a sense for style economizes his material; the artisan with a sense for style prefers good work. Style is the ultimate morality of mind. . . . With style the end is attained without side issues, without raising undesirable inflammations. With style you attain your end and nothing but your end. With style the effect of your activity is calculable, and foresight is the last gift of gods to men. With style your power is increased, for your mind is not distracted with irrelevancies, and you are more likely to attain your object.

— Alfred North Whitehead

4. Early this year, the most successful of the large-circulation magazines for teen-age girls took a two-page spread in the *Times* for an "interview" with its editor-in-chief, and after the now ritual bulling (Question: "You work with young people — what is your view of today's generation?" Answer: "My faith in them is enormous. They make a sincere attempt at being totally honest, at sharing. They're happily frank about their experiences. They're the most idealistic generation in history. . . . When you consider the vast problems confronting us, their optimism and activism is truly inspirational"), and after the obeisance to the new myths ("They are the best-educated and most aware generation in history"), the ad finally got to the come-on. Question: "Is it true that your readers don't differentiate between your ads and your editorials?" Answer: "Yes, that's true. Our readers are very impressionable, not yet cynical about advertising . . . eager to learn . . . to believe." The frightening thing is, it probably is true that the

teen-agers don't differentiate between the ads and the editorials, and true in a much more complex sense than the delicately calculated Madison Avenue-ese of the editor's pitch to advertisers indicates. Television is blurring the distinction for all of us; we don't know what we're reacting to anymore, and, beyond that, it's becoming just about impossible to sort out the con from the truth because a successful con makes its lies come true.

— Pauline Kael

EXERCISES

1. What is Parsons's attitude toward himself? Exactly how do you know?
2. What is Nemerov's attitude toward himself, and how do you know?
3. Suppose that the first sentence of Whitehead's passage began thus: "I want to point out to you today that style may be regarded not only as the last acquirement of what I consider the mind that has been well educated, but it is also the most useful, I definitely believe." What is lost?
4. Do you think that Pauline Kael knows what she is talking about? Why?
5. Read a political speech (you can find lots of examples in a periodical called *Vital Speeches*), and in a paragraph analyze the speaker's attitude toward himself or herself. In another paragraph analyze his or her attitude toward the audience.

A RANGE OF STYLES

Professions for Women[1]

Virginia Woolf

When your secretary invited me to come here, she told me that your Society is concerned with the employment of women and she

[1] This essay was originally a talk delivered in 1931 to the Women's Service League.

suggested that I might tell you something about my own professional experiences. It is true I am a woman; it is true I am employed;
but what professional experiences have I had? It is difficult to say.
My profession is literature; and in that profession there are fewer
experiences for women than in any other, with the exception of the
stage — fewer, I mean, that are peculiar to women. For the road
was cut many years ago — by Fanny Burney, by Aphra Behn, by
Harriet Martineau, by Jane Austen, by George Eliot — many famous women, and many more unknown and forgotten, have been
before me, making the path smooth, and regulating my steps. Thus,
when I came to write, there were very few material obstacles in my
way. Writing was a reputable and harmless occupation. The family
peace was not broken by the scratching of a pen. No demand was
made upon the family purse. For ten and sixpence one can buy
paper enough to write all the plays of Shakespeare — if one has a
mind that way. Pianos and models, Paris, Vienna and Berlin, masters and mistresses, are not needed by a writer. The cheapness of
writing paper is, of course, the reason why women have succeeded
as writers before they have succeeded in the other professions.

But to tell you my story — it is a simple one. You have only
got to figure to yourselves a girl in a bedroom with a pen in her
hand. She had only to move that pen from left to right — from ten
o'clock to one. Then it occurred to her to do what is simple and
cheap enough after all — to slip a few of those pages into an
envelope, fix a penny stamp in the corner, and drop the envelope
into the red box at the corner. It was thus that I became a journalist;
and my effort was rewarded on the first day of the following month
— a very glorious day it was for me — by a letter from an editor
containing a check for one pound ten shillings and sixpence. But to
show you how little I deserve to be called a professional woman,
how little I know of the struggles and difficulties of such lives, I
have to admit that instead of spending that sum upon bread and
butter, rent, shoes and stockings, or butcher's bills, I went out and
bought a cat — a beautiful cat, a Persian cat, which very soon
involved me in bitter disputes with my neighbors.

What could be easier than to write articles and to buy Persian
cats with the profits? But wait a moment. Articles have to be about
something. Mine, I seem to remember, was about a novel by a
famous man. And while I was writing this review, I discovered that
if I were going to review books I should need to do battle with a
certain phantom. And the phantom was a woman, and when I came
to know her better I called her after the heroine of a famous poem,

The Angel in the House. It was she who used to come between me and my paper when I was writing reviews. It was she who bothered me and wasted my time and so tormented me that at last I killed her. You who come of a younger and happier generation may not have heard of her — you may not know what I mean by the Angel in the House. I will describe her as shortly as I can. She was intensely sympathetic. She was immensely charming. She was utterly unselfish. She excelled in the difficult arts of family life. She sacrificed herself daily. If there was chicken, she took the leg; if there was a draught she sat in it — in short she was so constituted that she never had a mind or a wish of her own, but preferred to sympathize always with the minds and wishes of others. Above all — I need not say it — she was pure. Her purity was supposed to be her chief beauty — her blushes, her great grace. In those days — the last of Queen Victoria — every house had its Angel. And when I came to write I encountered her with the very first words. The shadow of her wings fell on my page; I heard the rustling of her skirts in the room. Directly, that is to say, I took my pen in hand to review that novel by a famous man, she slipped behind me and whispered: "My dear, you are a young woman. You are writing about a book that has been written by a man. Be sympathetic; be tender; flatter; deceive; use all the arts and wiles of our sex. Never let anybody guess that you have a mind of your own. Above all, be pure." And she made as if to guide my pen. I now record the one act for which I take some credit to myself, though the credit rightly belongs to some excellent ancestors of mine who left me a certain sum of money — shall we say five hundred pounds a year? — so that it was not necessary for me to depend solely on charm for my living. I turned upon her and caught her by the throat. I did my best to kill her. My excuse, if I were to be had up in a court of law, would be that I acted in self-defense. Had I not killed her she would have killed me. She would have plucked the heart out of my writing. For, as I found, directly I put pen to paper, you cannot review even a novel without having a mind of your own, without expressing what you think to be the truth about human relations, morality, sex. And all these questions, according to the Angel in the House, cannot be dealt with freely and openly by women; they must charm, they must conciliate, they must — to put it bluntly — tell lies if they are to succeed. Thus, whenever I felt the shadow of her wing or the radiance of her halo upon my page, I took up the inkpot and flung it at her. She died hard. Her fictitious nature was of great assistance to her. It is far harder to kill a phantom than a reality.

She was always creeping back when I thought I had despatched her. Though I flatter myself that I killed her in the end, the struggle was severe; it took much time that had better have been spent upon learning Greek grammar; or in roaming the world in search of adventures. But it was a real experience; it was an experience that was bound to befall all women writers at that time. Killing the Angel in the House was part of the occupation of a woman writer.

But to continue my story. The Angel was dead; what then remained? You may say that what remained was a simple and common object — a young woman in a bedroom with an inkpot. In other words, now that she had rid herself of falsehood, that young woman had only to be herself. Ah, but what is "herself"? I mean, what is a woman? I assure you, I do not know. I do not believe that you know. I do not believe that anybody can know until she has expressed herself in all the arts and professions open to human skill. That indeed is one of the reasons why I have come here — out of respect for you, who are in process of showing us by your experiments what a woman is, who are in process of providing us, by your failures and successes, with that extremely important piece of information.

But to continue the story of my professional experiences. I made one pound ten and six by my first review; and I bought a Persian cat with the proceeds. Then I grew ambitious. A Persian cat is all very well, I said; but a Persian cat is not enough. I must have a motor car. And it was thus that I became a novelist — for it is a very strange thing that people will give you a motor car if you will tell them a story. It is a still stranger thing that there is nothing so delightful in the world as telling stories. It is far pleasanter than writing reviews of famous novels. And yet, if I am to obey your secretary and tell you my professional experiences as a novelist, I must tell you about a very strange experience that befell me as a novelist. And to understand it you must try first to imagine a novelist's state of mind. I hope I am not giving away professional secrets if I say that a novelist's chief desire is to be as unconscious as possible. He has to induce in himself a state of perpetual lethargy. He wants life to proceed with the utmost quiet and regularity. He wants to see the same faces, to read the same books, to do the same things day after day, month after month, while he is writing, so that nothing may break the illusion in which he is living — so that nothing may disturb or disquiet the mysterious nosings about, feelings round, darts, dashes and sudden discoveries of that very shy and illusive spirit, the imagination. I suspect that this state is the same both for men and women. Be that as it may, I want you to imagine me writing a novel in a state of trance. I want you to figure to yourselves a girl sitting with a pen in her hand, which for minutes, and indeed for hours, she never dips into the inkpot. The image that comes to my mind when I think of this girl is the image of a fisherman lying sunk in dreams on the verge of a deep lake with a rod held out over the water. She was letting her imagination sweep unchecked round every rock and cranny of the world that lies submerged in the depths of our unconscious being. Now came the experience, the experience that I believe to be far commoner with women writers than with men. The line raced through the girl's fingers. Her imagination had rushed away. It had sought the pools, the depths, the dark places where the largest fish slumber. And then there was a smash. There was an explosion. There was foam and confusion. The imagination had dashed itself against something hard. The girl was roused from her dream. She was indeed in a state of the most acute and difficult distress. To speak without figure she had thought of something, something about the body, about the passions which it was unfitting for her as a woman to say. Men, her reason told her, would be shocked. The consciousness of what men will say of a woman who speaks the truth about her passions had roused her from her artist's state of unconsciousness. She could write no more. This I believe to be a very common experience with women writers — they are impeded by the extreme conventionality of the other sex. For though men sensibly allow themselves great freedom in these respects, I doubt that they realize or can control the extreme severity with which they condemn such freedom in women.

These then were two very genuine experiences of my own. These were two of the adventures of my professional life. The first — killing the Angel in the House — I think I solved. She died. But the second, telling the truth about my own experiences as a body, I do not think I solved. I doubt that any woman has solved it yet. The obstacles against her are still immensely powerful — and yet they are very difficult to define. Outwardly, what is simpler than to write books? Outwardly, what obstacles are there for a woman rather than for a man? Inwardly, I think, the case is very different; she has still many ghosts to fight, many prejudices to overcome. Indeed it will be a long time still, I think, before a woman can sit down to write a book without finding a phantom to be slain, a rock to be dashed against. And if this is so in literature, the freest of all professions for women, how is it in the new professions which you are now for the first time entering?

Those are the questions that I should like, had I time, to ask you. And indeed, if I have laid stress upon these professional experiences of mine, it is because I believe that they are, though in different forms, yours also. Even when the path is nominally open — when there is nothing to prevent a woman from being a doctor, a lawyer, a civil servant — there are many phantoms and obstacles, as I believe, looming in her way. To discuss and define them is I think of great value and importance; for thus only can the labor be shared, the difficulties be solved. But besides this, it is necessary also to discuss the ends and the aims for which we are fighting, for which we are doing battle with these formidable obstacles. Those aims cannot be taken for granted; they must be perpetually questioned and examined. The whole position, as I see it — here in this hall surrounded by women practising for the first time in history I know not how many different professions — is one of extraordinary interest and importance. You have won rooms of your own in the house hitherto exclusively owned by men. You are able, though not without great labor and effort, to pay the rent. You are earning your five hundred pounds a year. But this freedom is only a beginning; the room is your own, but it is still bare. It has to be furnished; it has to be decorated; it has to be shared. How are you going to furnish it, how are you going to decorate it? With whom are you going to share it, and upon what terms? These, I think, are questions of the utmost importance and interest. For the first time in history you are able to ask them; for the first time you are able to decide for yourselves what the answers should be. Willingly would I stay and discuss those questions and answers — but not tonight. My time is up; and I must cease.

QUESTIONS

1. The first two paragraphs seem to describe the ease with which women enter writing as a profession. What difficulties or obstacles for women do these paragraphs imply?
2. Try to characterize Woolf's tone, especially her attitude toward her subject and herself, in the first paragraph.
3. What do you think Woolf means when she says (page 517), "It is far harder to kill a phantom than a reality"?
4. Woolf conjectures (page 519) that she has not solved the prob-

lem of "telling the truth about my own experiences as a body."
Is there any reason to believe that today a woman has more
difficulty than a man in telling the truth about the experiences
of the body?

5. In her final paragraph, Woolf suggests that phantoms as well
as obstacles impede women from becoming doctors and lawyers. What might some of these phantoms be?

6. This essay is highly metaphoric. Speaking roughly (or, rather,
as precisely as possible), what is the meaning of the metaphor
of "rooms" in the final paragraph? What does Woolf mean
when she says, "The room is your own, but it is still bare. . . .
With whom are you going to share it, and upon what terms?"

7. Evaluate the last two sentences. Are they too abrupt and mechanical? Or do they provide a fitting conclusion to the speech?

Beer Can

John Updike

This seems to be an era of gratuitous inventions and negative
improvements. Consider the beer can. It was beautiful — as beautiful as the clothespin, as inevitable as the wine bottle, as dignified
and reassuring as the fire hydrant. A tranquil cylinder of delightfully
resonant metal, it could be opened in an instant, requiring only the
application of a handy gadget freely dispensed by every grocer. Who
can forget the small, symmetrical thrill of those two triangular
punctures, the dainty *pffff*, the little crest of suds that foamed eagerly
in the exultation of release? Now we are given, instead, a top
beetling with an ugly, shmoo-shaped "tab," which, after fiercely
resisting the tugging, bleeding fingers of the thirsty man, threatens
his lips with a dangerous and hideous hole. However, we have
discovered a way to thwart Progress, usually so unthwartable. *Turn
the beer can upside down and open the bottom.* The bottom is still the
way the top used to be. True, this operation gives the beer an
unsettling jolt, and the sight of a consistently inverted beer can
might make people edgy, not to say queasy. But the latter difficulty
could be eliminated if manufacturers would design cans that looked
the same whichever end was up, like playing cards. What we need
is Progress with an escape hatch.

QUESTIONS

1. What is the tone of the first sentence? What effect is gained by following this relatively long sentence with a short one? What would be lost or gained if Updike had written, instead of "Consider the beer can," "Think of a beer can"?
2. Do you intend to use a can opener on the bottom of a beer can?

The Iks

Lewis Thomas

The small tribe of Iks, formerly nomadic hunters and gatherers in the mountain valleys of northern Uganda, have become celebrities, literary symbols for the ultimate fate of disheartened, heartless mankind at large. Two disastrously conclusive things happened to them: the government decided to have a national park, so they were compelled by law to give up hunting in the valleys and become farmers on poor hillside soil, and then they were visited for two years by an anthropologist who detested them and wrote a book about them.

The message of the book is that the Iks have transformed themselves into an irreversibly disagreeable collection of unattached, brutish creatures, totally selfish and loveless, in response to the dismantling of their traditional culture. Moreover, this is what the rest of us are like in our inner selves, and we will all turn into Iks when the structure of our society comes all unhinged.

The argument rests, of course, on certain assumptions about the core of human beings, and is necessarily speculative. You have to agree in advance that man is fundamentally a bad lot, out for himself alone, displaying such graces as affection and compassion only as learned habits. If you take this view, the story of the Iks can be used to confirm it. These people seem to be living together, clustered in small, dense villages, but they are really solitary, unrelated individuals with no evident use for each other. They talk, but only to make ill-tempered demands and cold refusals. They share nothing. They never sing. They turn the children out to forage as soon as they can walk, and desert the elders to starve whenever they can, and the foraging children snatch food from the mouths of the helpless elders. It is a mean society.

They breed without love or even casual regard. They defecate on each other's doorsteps. They watch their neighbors for signs of misfortune, and only then do they laugh. In the book they do a lot of laughing, having so much bad luck. Several times they even laughed at the anthropologist, who found this especially repellent (one senses, between the lines, that the scholar is not himself the world's luckiest man). Worse, they took him into the family, snatched his food, defecated on his doorstep, and hooted dislike at him. They gave him two bad years.

It is a depressing book. If, as he suggests, there is only Ikness at the center of each of us, our sole hope for hanging on to the name of humanity will be in endlessly mending the structure of our society, and it is changing so quickly and completely that we may never find the threads in time. Meanwhile, left to ourselves alone, solitary, we will become the same joyless, zestless, untouching lone animals.

But this may be too narrow a view. For one thing, the Iks are extraordinary. They are absolutely astonishing, in fact. The anthropologist has never seen people like them anywhere, nor have I. You'd think, if they were simply examples of the common essence of mankind, they'd seem more recognizable. Instead, they are bizarre, anomalous. I have known my share of peculiar, difficult, nervous, grabby people, but I've never encountered any genuinely, consistently detestable human beings in all my life. The Iks sound more like abnormalities, maladies.

I cannot accept it. I do not believe that the Iks are representative of isolated, revealed man, unobscured by social habits. I believe their behavior is something extra, something laid on. This unremitting, compulsive repellence is a kind of complicated ritual. They must have learned to act this way; they copied it, somehow.

I have a theory, then. The Iks have gone crazy.

The solitary Ik, isolated in the ruins of an exploded culture, has built a new defense for himself. If you live in an unworkable society you can make up one of your own, and this is what the Iks have done. Each Ik has become a group, a one-man tribe on its own, a constituency.

Now everything falls into place. This is why they do seem, after all, vaguely familiar to all of us. We've seen them before. This is precisely the way groups of one size or another, ranging from committees to nations, behave. It is, of course, this aspect of humanity that has lagged behind the rest of evolution, and this is why the Ik seems so primitive. In his absolute selfishness, his incapacity to give anything away, no matter what, he is a successful committee. When he stands at the door of his hut, shouting insults at his neighbors in a loud harangue, he is city addressing another city.

Cities have all the Ik characteristics. They defecate on doorsteps, in rivers and lakes, their own or anyone else's. They leave rubbish. They detest all neighboring cities, give nothing away. They even build institutions for deserting elders out of sight.

Nations are the most Iklike of all. No wonder the Iks seem familiar. For total greed, rapacity, heartlessness, and irresponsibility there is nothing to match a nation. Nations, by law, are solitary, self-centered, withdrawn into themselves. There is no such thing as affection between nations, and certainly no nation ever loved another. They bawl insults from their doorsteps, defecate into whole oceans, snatch all the food, survive by detestation, take joy in the bad luck of others, celebrate the death of others, live for the death of others.

That's it, and I shall stop worrying about the book. It does not signify that man is a sparse, inhuman thing at his center. He's all right. It only says what we've always known and never had enough time to worry about, that we haven't yet learned how to stay human when assembled in masses. The Ik, in his despair, is acting out this failure, and perhaps we should pay closer attention. Nations have themselves become too frightening to think about, but we might learn some things by watching these people.

QUESTIONS

1. Find the grim joke in the first paragraph.
2. Suppose that "of course" were omitted from the first sentence of the third paragraph. Would anything significant be lost? Suppose in the second sentence of the third paragraph, instead of "You have to agree," Thomas had written "One has to agree." What would be gained or lost?
3. In the third and fourth paragraphs, what is the effect of repeating the structure of subject and verb: "They talk . . .," "They share . . .," "They never sing," "They turn . . .," "They breed . . .," and so on?
4. Point to a few colloquial expressions, and to a few notably informal sentences. Do you find them inappropriate to a discussion of a serious topic?

5. What is Thomas's attitude toward the anthropologist and his book? Cite some passages that convey his attitude, and explain how they convey it, or how they attempt to persuade us to share it.

My Wood

E. M. Forster

A few years ago I wrote a book which dealt in part with the difficulties of the English in India. Feeling that they would have had no difficulties in India themselves, the Americans read the book freely. The more they read it the better it made them feel, and a cheque to the author was the result. I bought a wood with the cheque. It is not a large wood — it contains scarcely any trees, and it is intersected, blast it, by a public footpath. Still, it is the first property that I have owned, so it is right that other people should participate in my shame, and should ask themselves, in accents that will vary in horror, this very important question: What is the effect of property upon the character? Don't let's touch economics; the effect of private ownership upon the community as a whole is another question — a more important question, perhaps, but another one. Let's keep to psychology. If you own things, what's their effect on you? What's the effect on me of my wood?

In the first place, it makes me feel heavy. Property does have this effect. Property produces men of weight, and it was a man of weight who failed to get into the Kingdom of Heaven. He was not wicked, that unfortunate millionaire in the parable, he was only stout; he stuck out in front, not to mention behind, and as he wedged himself this way and that in the crystalline entrance and bruised his well-fed flanks, he saw beneath him a comparatively slim camel passing through the eye of a needle and being woven into the robe of God. The Gospels all through couple stoutness and slowness. They point out what is perfectly obvious, yet seldom realized: that if you have a lot of things you cannot move about a lot, that furniture requires dusting, dusters require servants, servants require insurance stamps, and the whole tangle of them makes you think twice before you accept an invitation to dinner or go for a bathe in the Jordan. Sometimes the Gospels proceed further and say with Tolstoy that property is sinful; they approach the difficult ground of asceticism here, where I cannot follow them. But as to the immediate effects of property on people, they just show straightforward logic. It produces men of weight. Men of weight cannot, by definition, move like the lightning from the East unto the West, and the ascent of a fourteen-stone bishop into a pulpit is thus the exact antithesis of the coming of the Son of Man. My wood makes me feel heavy.

In the second place, it makes me feel it ought to be larger.

The other day I heard a twig snap in it. I was annoyed at first, for I thought that someone was blackberrying, and depreciating the value of the undergrowth. On coming nearer, I saw it was not a man who had trodden on the twig and snapped it, but a bird, and I felt pleased. My bird. The bird was not equally pleased. Ignoring the relation between us, it took fright as soon as it saw the shape of my face, and flew straight over the boundary hedge into a field, the property of Mrs. Henessy, where it sat down with a loud squawk. It had become Mrs. Henessy's bird. Something seemed grossly amiss here, something that would not have occurred had the wood been larger. I could not afford to buy Mrs. Henessy out, I dared not murder her, and limitations of this sort beset me on every side. Ahab did not want that vineyard — he only needed it to round off his property, preparatory to plotting a new curve — and all the land around my wood has become necessary to me in order to round off the wood. A boundary protects. But — poor little thing — the boundary ought in its turn to be protected. Noises on the edge of it. Children throw stones. A little more, and then a little more, until we reach the sea. Happy Canute! Happier Alexander! And after all, why should even the world be the limit of possession? A rocket containing a Union Jack, will, it is hoped, be shortly fired at the moon. Mars. Sirius. Beyond which . . . But these immensities ended by saddening me. I could not suppose that my wood was the destined nucleus of universal dominion — it is so very small and contains no mineral wealth beyond the blackberries. Nor was I comforted when Mrs. Henessy's bird took alarm for the second time and flew clean away from us all, under the belief that it belonged to itself.

In the third place, property makes its owner feel that he ought to do something to it. Yet he isn't sure what. A restlessness comes over him, a vague sense that he has a personality to express — the same sense which, without any vagueness, leads the artist to an act of creation. Sometimes I think I will cut down such trees as remain in the wood, at other times I want to fill up the gaps between them with new trees. Both impulses are pretentious and empty. They are not honest movements towards money-making or beauty. They spring from a foolish desire to express myself and from an inability to enjoy what I have got. Creation, property, enjoyment form a sinister trinity in the human mind. Creation and enjoyment are both very very good, yet they are often unattainable without a material basis, and at such moments property pushes itself in as a substitute, saying, "Accept me instead — I'm good enough for all three." It is not enough. It is, as Shakespeare said of lust, "The expense of spirit in a waste of shame": it is "Before, a joy proposed; behind, a dream." Yet we don't know how to shun it. It is forced on us by our economic system as the alternative to starvation. It is also forced on us by an internal defect in the soul, by the feeling that in property may lie the germs of self-development and of exquisite or heroic deeds. Our life on earth is, and ought to be, material and carnal. But we have not yet learned to manage our materialism and carnality properly; they are still entangled with the desire for ownership, where (in the words of Dante) "Possession is one with loss."

And this brings us to our fourth and final point: the blackberries.

Blackberries are not plentiful in this meagre grove, but they are easily seen from the public footpath which traverses it, and all too easily gathered. Foxgloves, too — people will pull up the foxgloves, and ladies of an educational tendency even grub for toadstools to show them on the Monday in class. Other ladies, less educated, roll down the bracken in the arms of their gentlemen friends. There is paper, there are tins. Pray, does my wood belong to me or doesn't it? And, if it does, should I not own it best by allowing no one else to walk there? There is a wood near Lyme Regis, also cursed by a public footpath, where the owner has not hesitated on this point. He has built high stone walls each side of the path, and has spanned it by bridges, so that the public circulate like termites while he gorges on the blackberries unseen. He really does own his wood, this able chap. Dives in Hell did pretty well, but the gulf dividing him from Lazarus could be traversed by vision, and nothing traverses it here.[1] And perhaps I shall come to this in

---

[1] Editors' note: According to Christ's parable in Luke xvi. 19–26, the rich man (unnamed, but traditionally known as Dives), at whose gate the poor man Lazarus had begged, was sent to hell, from where he could see Lazarus in heaven.

time. I shall wall in and fence out until I really taste the sweets of property. Enormously stout, endlessly avaricious, pseudo-creative, intensely selfish, I shall wear upon my forehead the quadruple crown of possession until those nasty Bolshies come and take it off again and thrust me aside into the outer darkness.

QUESTION

Much of the strength of the essay is in its concrete presentation of generalities. Note, for example, that the essay is called "My Wood," but we might say that the general idea of the essay is "The Effect of Property on Owners." Forster gives four effects, chiefly through concrete statements. What are they? Put these four effects in four general statements.

16
Acquiring Style

Draw lines, young man,
 draw many lines
— OLD INGRES TO THE
 YOUNG DEGAS

In the preceding pages on style we said that your writing reveals not only where you stand (your topic) and how you think (the structure of your argument), but also who you are and how you take yourself (your tone). To follow our argument to its limit, we might say that everything in this book — including rules on the comma (where you breathe) — is about style. We do. What more is there to say?

CLARITY AND TEXTURE

First, a distinction Aristotle makes between two parts of style: that which gives *clarity,* and that which gives *texture.* Exact words, concrete illustrations of abstractions, conventional punctuation, and so forth — matters we treat in some detail in the sections on revising and editing — make for clarity. On the whole, this part of style is inconspicuous when present; when absent the effect ranges from mildly distracting to ruinous. Clarity is the foundation of style. It can be achieved by anyone willing to make the effort.

Among the things that give texture, or individuality, are effective repetition, variety in sentence structure, wordplay, and so forth. This second group of devices, on the whole more no-ticeable, makes the reader aware of the writer's particular voice. These devices can be learned too, but seldom by effort alone. In fact playfulness helps here more than doggedness. Students who work at this part of style usually enjoy hanging around words. At the same time, they're likely to feel that when they put words on paper, even in a casual letter to a friend, they're putting themselves on the line. Serious, as most people are about games they really care about, but not solemn, they'll come to recognize the rules of play in John Holmes's advice to young poets: "You must believe that your feelings and your words for your feelings are impor-tant. . . . That they are unique is a fact; that you believe they are unique is necessary."

A REPERTORY OF STYLES

We make a second distinction: between style as the reader perceives it from the written word, and style as the writer expe-riences it. The first is static: it's fixed in writing or print; we can point to it, discuss it, analyze it. The second, the writer's experi-ence of his or her own style, changes as the writer changes. In his essay "Why I Write" George Orwell said, "I find that by the time you have perfected any style of writing, you have always outgrown it." An exaggeration that deposits a truth. The essay concludes, however, "Looking back through my work, I see that it is invar-iably where I lacked a *political* purpose that I wrote lifeless books and was betrayed into purple passages, sentences without meaning, decorative adjectives and humbug generally." A suggestion surely, that through trial and error, and with maturity, a writer comes to a sense of self, a true style, not static and not constantly changing, but achieved.

Undergraduates seldom know what purpose, in Orwell's sense, they will have. You may be inclined toward some subjects and against others, you may have decided on a career — many times. But if your education is worth anything like the money and time invested in it, your ideas and feelings will change more rapidly in the next few years than ever before in your memory, and perhaps more than they ever will again. Make use of the confusion you're in. Reach out for new experiences to assimilate; make whatever connections you can from your reading to your inner life, reaching back into your past and forward into your future. And keep writing: "Draw lines . . . draw many lines."

To keep pace with your changing ideas — and here is our main point — you'll need to acquire not one style, but a repertory of styles, a store of writing habits on which you can draw as the need arises.

ORIGINALITY AND IMITATION

Finally, a paradox: one starts to acquire an individual style by studying and imitating the style of others. The paradox isn't limited to writing. Stylists in all fields begin as apprentices. The young ball player imitates the movements of Reggie Jackson, the potter joins a workshop in California to study under Marguerite Wildenhain, the chess player hangs around the park or club watching the old pros, then finds a book that probably recommends beginning with Ruy Lopez's opening. When Michelangelo was an apprentice he copied works by his predecessors; when Millet was young he copied works by Michelangelo; when Van Gogh was young he copied works by Millet. The would-be writer may be lucky enough to have a teacher, one he can imitate; more likely he will, in W. H. Auden's words, "serve his apprenticeship in the library."

PRACTICE IN ACQUIRING STYLE

Benjamin Franklin's Exercise

Benjamin Franklin says in his *Autobiography,* "Prose writing has been of great use to me in the course of my life, and was a principal means of my advancement," and he reveals how he acquired his ability in it. (He had just abandoned, at about the age of eleven, his ambition to be a great poet — after his father told him that "verse-makers were generally beggars.")

> About this time I met with an odd volume of the *Spectator*. It was the third. I had never before seen any of them. I bought it,

read it over and over, and was much delighted with it. I thought the writing excellent, and wished, if possible, to imitate it. With that view I took some of the papers, and making short hints of the sentiment in each sentence, laid them by a few days, and then, without looking at the book, tried to complete the papers again by expressing each sentiment at length, and as fully as it had been expressed before, in any suitable words that should come to hand. Then I compared my *Spectator* with the original, discovered some of my faults, and corrected them.

A few pages later Franklin confides, with characteristic understatement (which he learned, he thought, by imitating Socrates), "I sometimes had the pleasure of fancying that in certain particulars of small import I had been lucky enough to improve the method or the language."

EXERCISES

1. Outline, in a list of brief notes, Franklin's exercise.
2. Choose a passage of current prose writing whose style you admire and follow Franklin's method. (Don't forget the last step: where you've improved on your model, congratulate yourself with becoming modesty.)

Paraphrasing

Do not confuse a paraphrase with a summary.

A summary is always much shorter than the original; a paraphrase is often a bit longer. To paraphrase a sentence, replace each word or phrase in it with one of your own. (Articles, pronouns, and conjunctions need not be replaced.) Your sentence should say substantially what the original says, but in your own words, and in a fluent, natural style. Consider the following sentence by W. H. Auden, and the paraphrase that follows it:

> Owing to its superior power as a mnemonic, verse is superior to prose as a medium for didactic instruction.
>
> — W. H. Auden

Because it is more easily memorized and can be retained in the mind for a longer time, poetry is better than prose for teaching moral lessons.

Paraphrasing is useful for several reasons. First, paraphrasing helps you to increase your vocabulary. (Many students say that a limited vocabulary is their chief source of difficulty in writing.) You may know, for example, that "didactic" means "intended for instruction, or instructive." But why then does Auden say "didactic instruction"? Are the words redundant, or is Auden stipulating a kind of instruction? Your dictionary, which may list "tending to teach a moral lesson" as one of three or four meanings of didactic, will help you understand Auden's sentence. But notice, first, that you'll have to choose the appropriate definition, and second, that you won't be able to insert that definition as is into your sentence. To paraphrase "didactic instruction" you'll have to put "didactic" in your own words. (If you look up "mnemonic" you'll find an even more complex puzzle resolved in our paraphrase.) Paraphrasing, then, expands your vocabulary because to paraphrase accurately and gracefully you must actively understand the use of an unfamiliar word, not simply memorize a synonym for it.

Paraphrasing also helps you to focus your attention on what you read. If you want, for example, to become a better reader of poetry, the best way is to *pay attention,* and the best way of paying attention is to try paraphrasing a line whose meaning escapes you. So too with understanding art history or economics or any specialized study. If you come across a difficult passage, don't just stare at it, paraphrase it. (If you don't have time to stop and puzzle through a sentence that is not entirely clear to you, you can always make time to jot it down on a three-by-five card. As Stanislav Andreski says, "Paper is patient.")

Finally, in paraphrasing, you are observing closely and actively the way another mind works. You are, in effect, serving as an apprentice stylist. (Some masters, of course, are not worth serving or emulating. Be discriminating.)

EXERCISE

Try paraphrasing the following sentences:

> Generally speaking and to a varying extent, scientists follow their temperaments in their choice of problems.
>
> — Charles Hermite

> To commit violent and unjust acts, it is not enough for a government to have the will or even the power; the habits, ideas, and passions of the time must lend themselves to their committal.
>
> — Alexis de Tocqueville

> The most intolerable people are provincial celebrities.
>
> — Anton Chekhov

> A distinction must be made between my uncle's capricious brutality and my aunt's punishments and repressions, which seem to have been dictated to her by her conscience.
>
> — Mary McCarthy

> Consciousness reigns but doesn't govern.
>
> — Paul Valéry

> The more extensive your acquaintance is with the works of those who have excelled, the more extensive will be your powers of invention, and what may appear still more like a paradox, the more original will be your composition.
>
> — Sir Joshua Reynolds

> The fashion wears out more apparel than the man.
>
> — William Shakespeare

> What is expressed is impressed.
>
> — Aristotle

> All the road to heaven is heaven.
>
> — Saint Teresa of Avila

> When the shoe fits, the foot is forgotten.
>
> — Chuang Tzu

Imitating the Cumulative Sentence

When you write, you make a point, not by subtracting as though you sharpened a pencil, but by adding. When you put one word after another, your statement should be more precise the more you add. If the result is otherwise, you have added the wrong thing, or you have added more than was needed.

— John Erskine

In *Notes Toward a New Rhetoric* Francis Christensen cites "Erskine's principle" and argues that "the cumulative sentence" best fulfills it. The cumulative sentence makes a statement in the main clause; the rest of the sentence consists of modifiers *added* to make the meaning of the statement more precise. The cumulative sentence adds *texture* to writing because as the writer adds modifiers he is examining his impressions, summarized in the main clause. At the same time he reveals to the reader how those impressions impinged on his mind. Here are some of Christensen's examples:

He dipped his hands in the bichloride solution and shook them, a quick shake, fingers down, like the fingers of a pianist above the keys.

— Sinclair Lewis

The jockeys sat bowed and relaxed, moving a little at the waist with the movement of their horses.

— Katherine Anne Porter

The Texan turned to the nearest gatepost and climbed to the top of it, his alternate thighs thick and bulging in the tight trousers, the butt of the pistol catching and losing the sun in pearly gleams.

— William Faulkner

George was coming down in the telemark position, kneeling, one leg forward and bent, the other trailing, his sticks hanging like some insect's thin legs, kicking up puffs of snow, and finally the whole kneeling, trailing figure coming around in a beautiful right curve like points of light, all in a wild cloud of snow.

— Ernest Hemingway

EXERCISE

Try writing a cumulative sentence. First, reread Christensen's sample sentences out loud. Then, during a second reading, try to sense the similarities in structure. For the next few days train yourself to observe people closely, the way they walk, move, gesture, smile, speak. Take notes when you can. Then, after reading the sentences again, try writing one. Either imitate one of the sentences closely, word by word (substituting your own words) or start with your subject, imitating the structure you have detected or have simply absorbed.

Transformations

If you take a proverb, an epigram, or any interesting, suggestive sentence and change it enough to make it say something else, something on *your* mind, you have a transformation. To cite a famous example, G. K. Chesterton transformed

If a thing is worth doing it is worth doing well

to

If a thing is worth doing it is worth doing badly.

Professor Marion Levy transformed Leo Durocher's

Nice guys finish last

to

Last guys don't finish nice.

A student transformed Marianne Moore's

We must be as clear as our natural reticence allows us to be

to

We must be as outspoken as our adversaries would forbid us to be.

EXERCISE

How can you transform one or more of the following?

When a poor man eats a chicken, one of them is sick.
— Yiddish proverb

The Battle of Waterloo was won on the playing fields of Eton.
— Attributed to the Duke of Wellington

You can't step into the same river twice.

— Heraclitus

Mañana es otro día.

— Proverb

Finding Poems

Finding poems is a variation of the language game called acquiring style. It amuses the student who enjoys hanging around words but who is tired of writing, tired of pulling words out of his mind and making them shape up — weary too, very weary, of reading "fine things." Still, he hungers for print, consuming the words on the cereal box along with the cereal, reading last week's classified ads when he has nothing to sell, no money to buy. What can be made of such an affliction? A poem.

Here are X. J. Kennedy's directions for finding a poem.

> In a newspaper, magazine, catalogue, textbook, or advertising throwaway, find a sentence or passage that (with a little artistic manipulation on your part) shows promise of becoming a poem. Copy it into lines like poetry, being careful to place what seem to be the most interesting words at the ends of lines to give them greatest emphasis. According to the rules of found poetry you may excerpt, delete, repeat, and rearrange elements but not add anything.

Here are some examples of "found poems." The first, "And All Those Others," was found by Jack S. Margolis in the Watergate transcripts; he published it in *The Poetry of Richard Milhous Nixon.*

I'm the President
Of the country —
And I'm going
To get on with it
  And meet
  Italians
  and
  Germans,
And all those others.

Here is a passage from a textbook, followed by the poem, "Symbolism," a student found in it:

A symbol, then, is an image so loaded with significance that it is not simply literal, and it does not simply stand for something else; it is both itself *and* something else that it richly suggests, a kind of manifestation of something too complex or too elusive to be otherwise revealed.

An image
so loaded with
  significance
that it is not
  simply literal,
and it does not
  simply stand
for
  something else;
it is both
  itself
and
  something else
that it
  richly suggests,
a kind of
  manifestation
of
  something
  too complex
or
  too elusive
to be
  otherwise revealed,
is a
  symbol.

Finally, a poem found by a student in an advertisement in *Newsweek:*

Winchester model 101
made for hands
that know the difference
There's more
than meets the eye
to any fine
shotgun

EXERCISES

1. Find a poem.
2. Explain in one sentence (a) how finding poems might help you acquire style or (b) why such an exercise is a waste of time.

17

Acquiring Fluency

Nulla dies sine linea.
No day without a line.

KEEPING A JOURNAL

Sometimes our efforts to improve our writing make us too conscious of what we say, or too self-critical to say anything. To guard against hyperconsciousness, or as an antidote to it, practice writing daily: keep a journal. The word *journal* derives from the Latin *dies* ("day") and *diurnalis* ("daily"), which became *journal* ("daily") in medieval French. Keep a journal: *nulla dies sine linea.*

Writing in a journal keeps your writing loose, fluent. It helps you to overcome the fear of writing most people have, and it gives you a chance to practice skills you are acquiring. As we said at the start, writing is a physical act, and to keep in trim, you should practice daily. (Or, to be honest, as close to daily as you can manage.) Keeping a journal then is practical; for many students it is, from the start, enjoyable.

Writing a journal also gets you into the habit of jotting down ideas, and one idea leads to another. Some of these ideas, perhaps especially those that record your responses to your reading, may well turn up later in more formal papers that you write.

If keeping a journal is an assignment in your composition course, your instructor may ask you to write in a loose-leaf notebook — so that pages may be turned in occasionally, and the instructor won't have to stagger home with twenty or thirty notebooks. If you're keeping a journal strictly for your own use, write with, and on, whatever materials feel comfortable: pen, pencil, typewriter; loose sheets, bound notebook, or whatever. (Dr. William Carlos Williams often wrote poems on prescription blanks.)

When to write? Any time; ten to fifteen minutes a day. Some people find it helpful to establish a regular time of day for writing, just before they go to sleep, for example. Habits can be helpful; but not all of us can or should lead well-regulated lives. Suit yourself.

How long is an entry? An entry may be a few words, a line or two, a few pages. There's no special length, but keep writing for at least the minimum recommended time.

Write freely. Don't correct or revise, don't worry about spelling, vocabulary, punctuation. Use whatever language, idiom, voice you wish. If you have a "home language" — Black English, for example — write entries in it. It's a good way to keep in touch with yourself, and the friends and family you've temporarily left. You *can* go home again; you can, that is, if you don't leave college an educated zombie.

As for content, write about anything that comes to mind. But don't confuse a journal with a diary. A diary mentions things that have happened ("Concert at 8, with J. and R."); a journal reflects on the happenings. A diary lists appointments; a journal records events, but gives some sense of why they were meaningful. Think of your journal as a record of your life now, which you might read with pleasure some years from now when many of the rich details of your daily experience would otherwise be buried in your memory. Still, it's probably better to write "Had a peanut butter sandwich for lunch" than to write nothing.

Write down your thoughts, feelings, impressions, responses, dreams, memories. May Sarton once said, "The senses are the keys to the past." If you have a strong sensory memory of something — the mixed smell of saltwater, sand, and machinery oil, for example — try to describe it in words, and then to track it down. You may find a buried scene from your childhood that you can rescue from your memory by a train of associations. If you keep tracking, and writing, you may discover why that scene is important to you still. But don't be afraid to embroider the truth a little, or to understate it. As Santayana observed, "Sometimes we have to change the truth in order to remember it."

Jot down reactions, ideas, feelings about something you are reading, something you may want to use later, in an essay. Did you stop reading and start daydreaming? What is the link between the text and your daydream? If you write it down, you may be able to cut down on the daydreaming, or, better still, make something out of it.

Practice writing descriptions: short, medium, long; of persons, places, things; literal, figurative, or impressionistic. Try cross-cutting from one description of a scene or an experience to another that might illuminate it. (When writing about real people observe one caution: use fictitious names.)

When you have nothing to say, write anyway. Practice writing paraphrases and transformations (see pages 532–34 and 536). Or copy out a passage of someone else's writing. If you can, explain why you find it attractive, why you want to remember it.

If you're too preoccupied to write because there's a decision you must make, and can't make, start writing. List all the reasons for following a course of action; then all the reasons against it.

Here, to prime the pump, are some examples of journal entries. Some are by professional writers, others by students. You'll find nothing remarkable in many of these entries (except honesty) and perhaps you'll discover in yourself the assurance that you can do as well or better.

SOME JOURNAL ENTRIES BY PUBLISHED WRITERS

You hear a lot of jazz about Soul Food. Take chitterlings: the ghetto blacks eat them from necessity while the black bourgeoisie has turned it into a mocking slogan. Eating chitterlings is like going slumming to them. Now that they have the price of a steak here they come prattling about Soul Food. The people in the ghetto want steaks. *Beef Steaks.* I wish I had the power to see to it that the bourgeoisie really *did* have to make it on Soul Food.

— Eldridge Cleaver

August A sudden idea of the relationship between "lovers." We are neither male nor female. We are a compound of both. I choose the male who will develop and expand the male in me; he chooses me to expand the female in him. Being made whole. . . . And why I choose *one* man for this rather than many is for safety. We bind ourselves within a ring and that ring is as it were a wall against the outside world. It is our refuge, our shelter. Here the tricks of life will not be played. Here is *safety* for us to *grow*. *Why, I talk like a child.*

— Katherine Mansfield

Wanted: a dog that neither barks nor bites, eats broken glass and shits diamonds.

— Goethe

The difficulty about all this dying is that you can't tell a fellow anything about it, so where does the fun come in?

— Alice James

With Brett to a nearby "movie," perhaps a little worse than the usual average of mediocrity. Yet why is it that I can be emotionally moved at the most vapid climax, the while I intellectually deride the whole false and mushy mess? It is of course but the awakening of memories by some act or gesture related to the past, — some unrealized hope is returned, a lost thread is for the moment woven into reality. However, the absurdity of my Jekyll and Hyde situation, with my mouth in a grin and my throat choked, and this from viewing some quite preposterous melodrama, ridiculously conceived, acted by imbeciles, presented for bovine clodhoppers, brings the question am I infantile? senile? maudlin? or also beef-witted? With a superlative stretch of the neck I answer these questions, "No!" — yet feeling uneasy over the sureness of my self-estimation. Better to wink at my weakness than to discover it a truth!

— Edward Weston

The man who would be stupid enough to defend the present economic order would be ass enough to do nothing for it.

Disorderly thinking should be as unwelcome in polite society as disorderly conduct. In fact, it *is* disorderly conduct.

On the sands of Ogunquit I saw a sandpiper, one of whose legs was lamed, rest on its wings as a man would on a pair of crutches.

— Lewis Mumford

It is so many years before one can believe enough in what one feels even to know what the feeling is.

For some months now I have lived with my own youth and childhood, not always writing indeed but thinking of it almost every day, and I am sorrowful and disturbed. It is not that I have accomplished too few of my plans, for I am not ambitious; but when I think of all the books I have read, and of the wise words I have heard spoken, and of the anxiety I have given to parents and grandparents, and of the hopes that I have had, all life weighed in the scales of my own life seems to me a preparation for something that never happens.

— William Butler Yeats

From *The Journals of Sylvia Plath*

Sylvia Plath[1]

I am jealous of those who think more deeply, who write better, who draw better, who ski better, who look better, who love better, who live better than I. I am sitting at my desk looking out at a bright antiseptic January day, with an icy wind whipping the sky into a white-and-blue froth. I can see Hopkins House, and the hairy black trees; I can see a girl bicycling along the gray road. I can see the sunlight slanting diagonally across the desk, catching on the iridescent filaments of nylon in the stockings I hung over the curtain rod to dry. I think I am worthwhile just because I have optical nerves and can try to put down what they perceive. What a fool!

The dialogue between my Writing and my Life is always in danger of becoming a slithering shifting of responsibility, of evasive rationalizing: in other words: I justified the mess I made of life by saying I'd give it order, form, beauty, writing about it; I justified my writing by saying it would be published, give me life (and prestige to life). Now, you have to begin somewhere, and it might as well be with life; a belief in me, with my limitations, and a strong punchy determination to fight to overcome [them] one by one: like languages, to learn French, ignore Italian (a sloppy knowledge of 3 languages is dilettantism) and revive German again, to build each solid. To build all solid.

---

[1] Sylvia Plath wrote these entries in her journal when she was an undergraduate at Smith College (1950–55) and the holder of a Fulbright grant at Newnham College (1955–57).

April 1. Program: to win friends and influence people.
· *Don't drink much* — (remember misfortunes w. Iko after St. John's party, Hamish — 2 dates, *St. Botolph's* party and London night); stay sober.
· *Be chaste* and don't throw self at people (c.f. David Buck, Mallory, Iko, Hamish, Ted, Tony Gray) — in spite of rumor and M. Boddy, let no one verify this term the flaws of last.
· *Be friendly and more subdued* — if necessary, smog of "mystery woman," quiet, nice, slightly bewildered at colored scandals. Refuse ease of Sally Bowles act.
· *Work on inner life to enrich* — concentrate on work for Krook — writing (stories, poems, articles for *Monitor* — sketches) — *French daily.*
· *Don't blab too much* — listen more; sympathize and "understand" people.
· *Keep troubles to self.*
· Bear mean gossip and snubbing and pass beyond it — be nice and positive to all.
· *Don't criticize anybody* to anyone else — misquoting is like a telephone game.
· Don't date either Gary or Hamish — be nice but *not too enthusiastic* to Keith et al.
Be stoic when necessary and *write* — you have seen a lot, felt deeply, and your problems are universal enough to be made meaningful — WRITE.

April 18. Now the forces are gathering still against me, and my dearest grandmother, who took care of me all my life while Mother worked, is dying very very slowly and bravely of cancer and she has not even been able to have intravenous feeding for six weeks but is living on her body, which will be all sublimed away, and then only she may die. My mother is working, teaching, cooking, driving, shoveling snow from blizzards, growing thin in the terror of her slow sorrow. I had hoped to make her strong and healthy, and now she may be too weak herself after this slow death, like my father's slow long death, to come to me. And I am here, futile, cut off from the ritual of family love and neighborhood and from giving strength and love to my dear brave grandmother's dying whom I loved above thought. And my mother will go, and there is the terror of having no parents, no older seasoned beings, to advise and love me in this world.

*The Pillow Book
of Sei Shōnagon*[1]

Hateful Things

One is in a hurry to leave, but one's visitor keeps chattering away. If it is someone of no importance, one can get rid of him by saying, "You must tell me all about it next time"; but, should it be the sort of visitor whose presence commands one's best behavior, the situation is hateful indeed.

One finds that a hair has got caught in the stone on which one is rubbing one's inkstick, or again that gravel is lodged in the inkstick, making a nasty, grating sound.

One is just about to be told some interesting piece of news when a baby starts crying.

A flight of crows circle about with loud caws.

An admirer has come on a clandestine visit, but a dog catches sight of him and starts barking. One feels like killing the beast.

One has gone to bed and is about to doze off when a mosquito appears, announcing himself in a reedy voice. One can actually feel the wind made by his wings and, slight though it is, one finds it hateful in the extreme.

One is telling a story about old times when someone breaks in with a little detail that he happens to know, implying that one's own version is inaccurate — disgusting behavior!

Very hateful is a mouse that scurries all over the place.

Some children have called at one's house. One makes a great fuss of them and gives them toys to play with. The children become accustomed to this treatment and start to come regularly, forcing their way into one's inner rooms and scattering one's furnishings and possessions. Hateful!

A man with whom one is having an affair keeps singing the praises of some woman he used to know. Even if it is a thing of the past, this can be very annoying. How much more so if he is

---

[1] Perhaps the most marvelous of all journals is the one kept about a thousand years ago by Sei Shōnagon, a Japanese woman who served for some ten years as lady-in-waiting to an empress. Presumably she wrote most of these entries before going to bed, hence the title: *The Pillow Book of Sei Shōnagon*. We give a few selections, translated by Ivan Morris.

still seeing the woman! (Yet sometimes I find that it is not as unpleasant as all that.)

A lover who is leaving at dawn announces that he has to find his fan and his paper. "I know I put them somewhere last night," he says. Since it is pitch dark, he gropes about the room, bumping into the furniture and muttering, "Strange! Where on earth can they be?" Finally he discovers the objects. He thrusts the paper into the breast of his robe with a great rustling sound; then he snaps open his fan and busily fans away with it. Only now is he ready to take his leave. What charmless behavior! "Hateful" is an understatement.

Equally disagreeable is the man who, when leaving in the middle of the night, takes care to fasten the cord of his headdress. This is quite unnecessary; he could perfectly well put it gently on his head without tying the cord. And why must he spend time adjusting his cloak or hunting costume? Does he really think someone may see him at this time of night and criticize him for not being impeccably dressed?

A good lover will behave as elegantly at dawn as at any other time. He drags himself out of bed with a look of dismay on his face. The lady urges him on: "Come, my friend, it's getting light. You don't want anyone to find you here." He gives a deep sigh, as if to say that the night has not been nearly long enough and that it is agony to leave. Once up, he does not instantly pull on his trousers. Instead he comes close to the lady and whispers whatever was left unsaid during the night. Even when he is dressed, he still lingers, vaguely pretending to be fastening his sash.

Presently he raises the lattice, and the two lovers stand together by the side door while he tells her how he dreads the coming day, which will keep them apart; then he slips away. The lady watches him go, and this moment of parting will remain among her most charming memories.

Indeed, one's attachment to a man depends largely on the elegance of his leave-taking. When he jumps out of bed, scurries about the room, tightly fastens his trouser-sash, rolls up the sleeves of his Court cloak, overrobe, or hunting costume, stuffs his belongings into the breast of his robe and then briskly secures the outer sash — one really begins to hate him.

Rare Things

People who live together and still manage to behave with reserve towards each other. However much these people may try to hide their weaknesses, they usually fail.

To avoid getting ink stains on the notebook into which one is copying stories, poems, or the like. If it is a very fine notebook, one takes the greatest care not to make a blot; yet somehow one never seems to succeed.

One has given some silk to the fuller and, when he sends it back, it is so beautiful that one cries out in admiration.

Enviable People

One has been learning a sacred text by heart; but, though one has gone over the same passage again and again, one still recites it haltingly and keeps on forgetting words. Meanwhile one hears other people, not only clerics (for whom it is natural) but ordinary men and women, reciting such passages without the slightest effort, and one wonders when one will ever be able to come up to their standard.

When one is ill in bed and hears people walking about, laughing loudly and chatting away as if they did not have a care in the world, how enviable they seem!

SOME JOURNAL ENTRIES BY STUDENTS

Helpless! I remember when I used to stand on a kitchen chair with both my arms raised in the air so that my grandmother could dress me for school. I was so spoiled that the only muscles I moved were in my mouth. Those were the days when breakfast tasted good.

The Rat: "You gap-legged, sky-scraping, knock-kneed, pot-bellied, flat-chested, slack-behind, wooly-headed hollow sculpture of a man!" . . . I died laughing!

I divorce myself from my feelings and immerse myself in my obligations.

It is difficult to believe that not understanding a physics problem isn't the worst problem in the world.

The rain can be heard on the roof and I feel a steady sprinkling through the open window. Trucks are loading and unloading down in the courtyard. Cars beeping as they turn the blind corner. Distraction . . .

The trees swish outside, the curtains inside. . . .

Anticipating something is like falling off a cliff and never reaching the bottom.

Old people have been following me all my life. . . . And at times scaring me out of my wits. When I was a very young child, one of my mother's best friends was an old crone named Bettina. . . . A witch-like figure dressed (always) in black with a pointed nose and chin. She had startling blue eyes that pierced one's being and a voice that cackled and shrieked in Italian. She filled the air with ethnic gossip and snide attacks on the marital behavior of her daughter, deriding her treatment of her son-in-law of whom she was extremely fond. My mother would smile and nod, all the while cooking, a major occupation of her life.

Subject — Echoes from My Childhood
Topic — Kitchen Memories

"Teruko-san! How come you don't understand what I am saying to you!! How come you are repeating these errors so many times!! One! Two! Three! Go!!" My arms, hands, fingers and even my brain are frozen. Tears are running down my cheek. My both hands are sitting on the keyboard frighteningly. Silence. I hear my heart, beating thump thump thump. With a deep sigh, Mrs. Ikebuchi closes the page of a score which is blackened with fingering numbers, circles and crosses. Without saying any words, she leaves the room, and goes to the kitchen. The lesson is over. I sigh and wipe off my tears with the back of my hands, pick up the scores, go to the living room and sit on the tatami-floor stiffly. "By the way Teruko-san, did you see my gardenia? It is so beautiful! Come! come and see it!" She comes out from the kitchen with a big round black lacquer tray with tea and cookies on it. She puts the tray on the table and walks out to the garden to the gardenia bush. "Isn't this pretty?" "Yes." "Isn't this a nice smell?" "Yes." Mrs. Ikebuchi walks back to the living room and I follow her three steps behind and sit on the tatami-floor stiffly again. Mrs. Ikebuchi pours tea and asks me merrily, "How much sugar do you want? how much cream do you want? which cookie do you want? rabbit? elephant? or duck?" I answer politely, "two sugars, please? (it is cube sugar), that's enough, thank you (for cream). May I have a rabbit?" "Oh you like the rabbit! Good! By the way do you know the story about the rabbit? Ah — what was it? Ah, Peter Rabbit!" Her story is going on and on and on. Meanwhile I finish my tea and cookie. "Well, Teruko-san, see you next Monday." I stand up, my legs are numb from sitting on the tatami-floor, and start to walk slowly, my toes are tickling. I pick up my scores and bow and say "Thank you very much." Walk out the sliding door. Release! I skip home.

My roommate is going to get engaged. I can sense it, I expect it, and I'm scared. Our reading of "The Story of an Hour" and "The Secret Woman" made me think about her. The marriages described in those two stories were sad and the wives had lost part of themselves. They had lost their independence, their ambition, their identities. I don't want this to happen to my friend. She values her freedom, she's ambitious, and she's going to achieve great things if she has the chance. I hope she waits.

Running back to the dorm, I took a deep breath of air and for perhaps the first time in my life I noticed the special smell of winter. The air was very still, and the sky was an odd color gray. It was as if the air held some kind of secret message. Walking along, I picked a piece of bark off a tree and knew that its rough texture would somehow have to be incorporated in my art project. Suddenly, I understood the message.

When God created Friday, Mankind discovered Hope.

63rd Street Rap: What's happening? Ain't nothing to it. What's going on at the Woods? Everything is Everything. Been to any sets lately? Yeah it was on 64th street last night. We partied back. Wish I could have made it. Well times will get better they can't get no worse. Right On! Right On!

Translation: Hello. How are you. I am fine. What activities are taking place at your high school named Englewood? There are many exciting activities taking place at my high school. Have you attended any parties recently? Yes I attended a party on 64th street last night. We had a very nice time. I wish I could have attended the party also. Well you will probably be fortunate enough to attend the next party, there is no logical reason for you not to. That is correct, that is correct.

School begins at 8:40 and ends at 2:00 the next morning. What did you say about revising for conciseness?

It seems that much of my daily writing consists of unresolved questions to which I am still seeking answers. Every answer that I do find serves to ask more questions. Finding answers to my questions creates such a feeling of accomplishment within me that I feel as though I could burst with happiness. However questions that remain unresolved for any length of time begin to puzzle me more and more. I find myself thinking about them at the oddest and most inconvenient times . . . sitting in French class. . . .

PART FOUR
Additional Readings

The Flag
Russell Baker

At various times when young, I was prepared to crack skulls, kill and die for Old Glory. I never wholly agreed with the LOVE IT OR LEAVE IT bumper stickers, which held that everybody who didn't love the flag ought to be thrown out of the country, but I wouldn't have minded seeing them beaten up. In fact, I saw a man come very close to being beaten up at a baseball park one day because he didn't stand when they raised the flag in the opening ceremonies, and I joined the mob screaming for him to get to his feet like an American if he didn't want lumps all over his noodle. He stood up, all right. I was then thirteen, and a Boy Scout, and I knew you never let the flag touch the ground, or threw it out with the trash when it got dirty (you burned it), or put up with disrespect for it at the baseball park.

At eighteen, I longed to die for it. When World War II ended in 1945 before I could reach the combat zone, I moped for months about being deprived of the chance to go down in flames under the guns of a Mitsubishi Zero. There was never much doubt that I would go down in flames if given the opportunity, for my competence as a pilot was such that I could barely remember to lower the plane's landing gear before trying to set it down on a runway.

I had even visualized my death. It was splendid. Dead, I would be standing perhaps 4,000 feet up in the sky. (Everybody knew that heroes floated in those days.) Erect and dashing, surrounded by beautiful cumulus clouds, I would look just as good as ever, except for being slightly transparent. And I would smile, devil-may-care, at the camera — oh, there would be cameras there — and the American flag would unfurl behind me across 500 miles of glorious American sky, and back behind the cumulus clouds the Marine Band would be playing "The Stars and Stripes Forever," but not too fast.

Then I would look down at June Allyson and the kids, who had a gold star in the window and brave smiles shining through their tears, and I would give them a salute and one of those brave, wistful Errol Flynn grins, then turn and mount to Paradise, becoming more transparent with each step so the audience could get a great view of the flag waving over the heavenly pastures.

Okay, so it owes a lot to Louis B. Mayer in his rococo period. I couldn't help that. At eighteen, a man's imagination is too busy with sex to have much energy left for fancy embellishments of patriotic ecstasy. In the words of a popular song of the period, there was a star-spangled banner waving somewhere in The Great Beyond, and only Uncle Sam's brave heroes got to go there. I was ready to make the trip.

All this was a long time ago, and, asinine though it now may seem, I confess it here to illustrate the singularly masculine pleasures to be enjoyed in devoted service to the Stars and Stripes. Not long ago I felt a twinge of the old fire when I saw an unkempt lout on a ferryboat with a flag sewed in the crotch of his jeans. Something in me wanted to throw him overboard, but I didn't since he was a big muscular devil and the flag had already suffered so many worse indignities anyhow, having been pinned in politicians' lapels, pasted on cars to promote gasoline sales and used to sanctify the professional sports industry as the soul of patriotism even while the team owners were instructing their athletes in how to dodge the draft.

For a moment, though, I felt some of the old masculine excitement kicked up by the flag in the adrenal glands. It's a man's flag, all right. No doubt about that. Oh, it may be a scoundrel's flag, too, and a drummer's flag, and a fraud's flag, and a thief's flag. But first and foremost, it is a man's flag.

Except for decorating purposes — it looks marvelous on old New England houses — I cannot see much in it to appeal to women. Its pleasures, in fact, seem so exclusively masculine and its sanctity so unassailable by feminist iconoclasts that it may prove to be America's only enduring, uncrushable male sex symbol.

Observe that in my patriotic death fantasy, the starring role is not June Allyson's, but mine. As defender of the flag, I am able to leave a humdrum job, put June and the kids with all their humdrum problems behind me, travel the world with a great bunch of guys, do exciting things with powerful flying machines, and, fetchingly uniformed, strut exotic saloons on my nights off.

In the end, I walk off with all the glory and the big scene.

And what does June get? Poor June. She gets to sit home with the kids the rest of her life dusting my photograph and trying to pay the bills, with occasional days off to visit the grave.

No wonder the male pulse pounds with pleasure when the Stars and Stripes comes fluttering down the avenue with the band smashing out those great noises. Where was Mrs. Teddy Roosevelt when Teddy was carrying it up San Juan Hill? What was Mrs. Lincoln doing when Abe was holding it aloft for the Union? What was Martha up to while George Washington was carrying it across the

Delaware? Nothing, you may be sure, that was one-tenth as absorbing as what their husbands were doing.

Consider some of the typical masculine activities associated with Old Glory: Dressing up in medals. Whipping cowards, slackers and traitors within an inch of their miserable lives. Conquering Mount Suribachi. Walking on the moon. Rescuing the wagon train. Being surrounded by the whole German Army and being asked to surrender and saying, "You can tell Schicklgruber my answer is 'Nuts.'" In brief, having a wonderful time. With the boys.

Yes, surely the American flag is the ultimate male sex symbol. Men flaunt it, wave it, punch noses for it, strut with it, fight for it, kill for it, die for it.

And women —? Well, when do you see a woman with the flag? Most commonly when she is wearing black and has just received it, neatly folded, from coffin of husband or son. Later, she may wear it to march in the Veterans Day parade, widows' division.

Male pleasures and woman's sorrow — it sounds like the old definition of sex. Yet these are the immemorial connotations of the flag, and women, having shed the whalebone girdle and stamped out the stag bar, nevertheless accept it, ostensibly at least, with the same emotional devotion that men accord it.

There are good reasons, of course, why they may be reluctant to pursue logic to its final step and say, "To hell with the flag, too." In the first place, it would almost certainly do them no good. Men hold all the political trumps in this matter. When little girls first toddle off to school, does anyone tell them the facts of life when they stand to salute the flag? Does anyone say, "You are now saluting the proud standard of the greatest men's club on earth?" You bet your chewing gum nobody tells them that. If anyone did, there would be a joint session of Congress presided over by the President of the United States to investigate the entire school system of the United States of America.

What little girls have drilled into them is that the flag stands for one nation indivisible, with liberty and justice for all. A few years ago, the men of the Congress, responding to pressure from the American Legion (all men) and parsons (mostly all men), all of whom sensed perhaps that women were not as gullible as they used to be, revised the Pledge of Allegiance with words intimating that it would be ungodly not to respect the flag. The "one nation indivisible" became "one nation *under God,* indivisible," and another loophole for skeptics was sealed off. The women's movement may be brave, but it will not go far taking on national indivisibility, liberty, justice and God, all in one fight. If they tried it, a lot of us men would feel perfectly justified in raising lumps on their lovely noodles.

Philosophically speaking, the masculinity of the American flag is entirely appropriate. America, after all, is not a motherland — many places still are — but a fatherland, which is to say a vast nation-state of disparate people scattered over great distances, but held together by a belligerent, loyalty-to-the-death devotion to some highly abstract political ideas. Since these ideas are too complex to be easily grasped, statesmen have given us the flag and told us it sums up all these noble ideas that make us a country.

Fatherland being an aggressive kind of state, the ideas it embodies must be defended, protected and propagated, often in blood. Since the flag is understood to represent these ideas, in a kind of tricolor shorthand, we emote, fight, bleed and rejoice in the name of the flag.

Before fatherland there was something that might be called motherland. It still exists here and there. In the fifties, when Washington was looking for undiscovered Asiatic terrain to save from un-American ideologies, somebody stumbled into an area called Laos, a place so remote from American consciousness that few had ever heard its name pronounced. (For the longest time, Lyndon Johnson, then Democratic leader of the Senate, referred to it as "Low Ass.") Federal inspectors sent to Laos returned with astounding information. Most of the people living there were utterly unaware that they were living in a country. Almost none of them knew the country they were living in was called Laos. All they knew was that they lived where they had been born and where their ancestors were buried.

What Washington had discovered, of course, was an old-fashioned motherland, a society where people's loyalties ran to the place of their birth. It was a Pentagon nightmare. Here were these people, perfectly happy with their home turf and their ancestors' graves, and they had to be put into shape to die for their country, and they didn't even know they had a country to die for. They didn't even have a flag to die for. And yet, they were content!

The point is that a country is only an idea and a fairly modern one at that. Life would still be going on if nobody had ever thought of it, and would probably be a good deal more restful. No flags. Not much in the way of armies. No sharing of exciting group emotions with millions of other people ready to do or die for

national honor. And so forth. Very restful, and possibly very primitive, and almost surely very nasty on occasion, although possibly
not as nasty as occasions often become when countries disagree.

I hear my colleagues in masculinity protesting, "What? No
country? No flag? But there would be nothing noble to defend, to
fight for, to die for, in the meantime having a hell of a good time
doing all those fun male things in the name of!"

Women may protest, too. I imagine some feminists may object
to the suggestion that fatherland's need for prideful, warlike and
aggressive citizens to keep the flag flying leaves women pretty much
out of things. Those who hold that sexual roles are a simple matter
of social conditioning may contend that the flag can offer the same
rollicking pleasures to both sexes once baby girls are trained as
thoroughly as baby boys in being prideful, warlike and aggressive.

I think there may be something in this, having seen those
harridans who gather outside freshly desegregated schools to wave
the American flag and terrify children. The question is whether
women really want to start conditioning girl babies for this hitherto
largely masculine sort of behavior, or spend their energies trying to
decondition it out of the American man.

In any case, I have no quarrel with these women. Living in a
fatherland, they have tough problems, and if they want to join the
boys in the flag sports, it's okay with me. The only thing is, if they
are going to get a chance, too, to go up to Paradise with the Marine
Band playing "The Stars and Stripes Forever" back behind the
cumulus clouds, I don't want to be stuck with the role of sitting
home dusting their photographs the rest of my life after the big
scene is ended.

QUESTIONS

1. Baker's first five paragraphs are devoted to his childhood and
   adolescence. On what attitudes does he focus our attention? Do
   you think that his attitudes during those years were exceptional,
   or was he pretty much like other male adolescents?
2. How does Baker make it clear in the first five paragraphs,
   where he is describing his youthful ideals, that these *were* youthful ideals, ideals he no longer holds?
3. After saying that the flag "is a man's flag," Baker reminds us
   that we don't associate it with Mrs. Teddy Roosevelt, Mrs.
   Lincoln, or Martha Washington. But let's say that Baker's wife,
   reading his manuscript, reminded him of the tradition that

Betsy Ross ("with a single snip of her scissors") cut the five-pointed star for the flag. Using Baker's style, write the paragraph that Baker might then have been tempted (or pressured) to add.

4. How is Baker's last sentence connected to the rest of the essay? Why is the sentence amusing?

5. Baker is kidding around, and the essay amuses, but one can argue that it is also serious. Make the case.

6. If someone, having skimmed Baker's essay, were to charge that Baker is unpatriotic, how (on the basis of this essay) would you defend him from that charge?

7. In a paragraph, explain, for someone who has not read this essay, what Baker means by calling the American flag "the ultimate male sex symbol."

Stranger in the Village

James Baldwin

From all available evidence no black man had ever set foot in this tiny Swiss village before I came. I was told before arriving that I would probably be a "sight" for the village; I took this to mean that people of my complexion were rarely seen in Switzerland, and also that city people are always something of a "sight" outside of the city. It did not occur to me — possibly because I am an American — that there could be people anywhere who had never seen a Negro.

It is a fact that cannot be explained on the basis of the inaccessibility of the village. The village is very high, but it is only four hours from Milan and three hours from Lausanne. It is true that it is virtually unknown. Few people making plans for a holiday would elect to come here. On the other hand, the villagers are able, presumably, to come and go as they please — which they do: to another town at the foot of the mountain, with a population of approximately five thousand, the nearest place to see a movie or go to the bank. In the village there is no movie house, no bank, no library, no theater; very few radios, one jeep, one station wagon; and at the moment, one typewriter, mine, an invention which the woman next door to me here had never seen. There are about six hundred people living here, all Catholic — I conclude this from the fact that the Catholic church is open all year round, whereas the Protestant chapel, set off on a hill a little removed from the village, is open only in the summertime when the tourists arrive. There are four or five hotels, all closed now, and four or five *bistros*,[1] of which, however, only two do any business during the winter. These two do not do a great deal, for life in the village seems to end around nine or ten o'clock. There are a few stores, butcher, baker, *épicerie*,[2] a hardware store, and a money-changer — who cannot change travelers' checks, but must send them down to the bank, an operation which takes two or three days. There is something called the *Ballet Haus,* closed in the winter and used for God knows what, certainly not ballet, during the summer. There seems to be only one schoolhouse in the village, and this for the quite young children; I suppose this to mean that their older brothers and sisters at some point descend from these mountains in order to complete their education — possibly, again, to the town just below. The landscape is absolutely forbidding, mountains towering on all four sides, ice and snow as far as the eye can reach. In this white wilderness, men and women and children move all day, carrying washing, wood, buckets of milk or water, sometimes skiing on Sunday afternoons. All week long boys and young men are to be seen shoveling snow off the rooftops, or dragging wood down from the forest in sleds.

The village's only real attraction, which explains the tourist season, is the hot spring water. A disquietingly high proportion of these tourists are cripples, or semi-cripples, who come year after year — from other parts of Switzerland, usually — to take the waters. This lends the village, at the height of the season, a rather terrifying air of sanctity, as though it were a lesser Lourdes. There is often something beautiful, there is always something awful, in the spectacle of a person who has lost one of his faculties, a faculty he never questioned until it was gone, and who struggles to recover it. Yet people remain people, on crutches or indeed on deathbeds; and wherever I passed, the first summer I was here, among the native villagers or among the lame, a wind passed with me — of astonishment, curiosity, amusement, and outrage. That first summer I stayed two weeks and never intended to return. But I did return in the winter, to work; the village offers, obviously, no distractions whatever and has the further advantage of being ex-

---

[1] Editors' note: French for "taverns" or "bars."
[2] Editors' note: French for "grocery," but more properly translated as "grocer" in this context.

tremely cheap. Now it is winter again, a year later, and I am here again. Everyone in the village knows my name, though they scarcely ever use it, knows that I come from America — though, this, apparently, they will never really believe: black men come from Africa — and everyone knows that I am the friend of the son of a woman who was born here, and that I am staying in their chalet. But I remain as much a stranger today as I was the first day I arrived, and the children shout *Neger! Neger!* as I walk along the streets.

It must be admitted that in the beginning I was far too shocked to have any real reaction. In so far as I reacted at all, I reacted by trying to be pleasant — it being a great part of the American Negro's education (long before he goes to school) that he must make people "like" him. This smile-and-the-world-smiles-with-you routine worked about as well in this situation as it had in the situation for which it was designed, which is to say that it did not work at all. No one, after all, can be liked whose human weight and complexity cannot be, or has not been, admitted. My smile was simply another unheard-of phenomenon which allowed them to see my teeth — they did not, really, see my smile and I began to think that, should I take to snarling, no one would notice any difference. All of the physical characteristics of the Negro which had caused me, in America, a very different and almost forgotten pain were nothing less than miraculous — or infernal — in the eyes of the village people. Some thought my hair was the color of tar, that it had the texture of wire, or the texture of cotton. It was jocularly suggested that I might let it all grow long and make myself a winter coat. If I sat in the sun for more than five minutes some daring creature was certain to come along and gingerly put his fingers on my hair, as though he were afraid of an electric shock, or put his hand on my hand, astonished that the color did not rub off. In all of this, in which it must be conceded there was the charm of genuine wonder and in which there was certainly no element of intentional unkindness, there was yet no suggestion that I was human: I was simply a living wonder.

I knew that they did not mean to be unkind, and I know it now; it is necessary, nevertheless, for me to repeat this to myself each time that I walk out of the chalet. The children who shout *Neger!* have no way of knowing the echoes this sound raises in me. They are brimming with good humor and the more daring swell with pride when I stop to speak with them. Just the same, there are days when I cannot pause and smile, when I have no heart to play with them; when, indeed, I mutter sourly to myself, exactly as I muttered on the streets of a city these children have never seen, when I was no bigger than these children are now: *Your* mother *was a nigger.* Joyce is right about history being a nightmare — but it may be the nightmare from which no one *can* awaken. People are trapped in history and history is trapped in them.

There is a custom in the village — I am told it is repeated in many villages — of "buying" African natives for the purpose of converting them to Christianity. There stands in the church all year round a small box with a slot for money, decorated with a black figure, and into this box the villagers drop their francs. During the *carnaval* which precedes Lent, two village children have their faces blackened — out of which bloodless darkness their blue eyes shine like ice — and fantastic horsehair wigs are placed on their blond heads; thus disguised, they solicit among the villagers for money for the missionaries in Africa. Between the box in the church and the blackened children, the village "bought" last year six or eight African natives. This was reported to me with pride by the wife of one of the *bistro* owners and I was careful to express astonishment and pleasure at the solicitude shown by the village for the souls of black folks. The *bistro* owner's wife beamed with a pleasure far more genuine than my own and seemed to feel that I might now breathe more easily concerning the souls of at least six of my kinsmen.

I tried not to think of these so lately baptised kinsmen, of the price paid for them, or the peculiar price they themselves would pay, and said nothing about my father, who having taken his own conversion too literally never, at bottom, forgave the white world (which he described as heathen) for having saddled him with a Christ in whom, to judge at least from their treatment of him, they themselves no longer believed. I thought of white men arriving for the first time in an African village, strangers there, as I am a stranger here, and tried to imagine the astounded populace touching their hair and marveling at the color of their skin. But there is a great difference between being the first white man to be seen by Africans and being the first black man to be seen by whites. The white man takes the astonishment as tribute, for he arrives to conquer and to convert the natives, whose inferiority in relation to himself is not even to be questioned; whereas I, without a thought of conquest, find myself among a people whose culture controls me, has even, in a sense, created me, people who have cost me more in anguish and rage than they will ever know, who yet do not even know of my existence. The astonishment with which I might have greeted them, should they have stumbled into my African village a few hundred years ago, might have rejoiced their hearts. But the astonishment with which they greet me today can only poison mine.

And this is so despite everything I may do to feel differently, despite my friendly conversations with the *bistro* owner's wife, despite their three-year-old son who has at last become my friend, despite the *saluts* and *bonsoirs* which I exchange with people as I walk, despite the fact that I know that no individual can be taken to task for what history is doing, or has done. I say that the culture of these people controls me — but they can scarcely be held responsible for European culture. America comes out of Europe, but these people have never seen America, nor have most of them seen more of Europe than the hamlet at the foot of their mountain. Yet they move with an authority which I shall never have; and they regard me, quite rightly, not only as a stranger in their village but as a suspect latecomer, bearing no credentials, to everything they have — however unconsciously — inherited.

For this village, even were it incomparably more remote and incredibly more primitive, is the West, the West onto which I have been so strangely grafted. These people cannot be, from the point of view of power, strangers anywhere in the world; they have made the modern world, in effect, even if they do not know it. The most illiterate among them is related, in a way that I am not, to Dante, Shakespeare, Michelangelo, Aeschylus, Da Vinci, Rembrandt, and Racine; the cathedral at Chartres says something to them which it cannot say to me, as indeed would New York's Empire State Building, should anyone here ever see it. Out of their hymns and dances come Beethoven and Bach. Go back a few centuries and they are in their full glory — but I am in Africa, watching the conquerors arrive.

The rage of the disesteemed is personally fruitless, but it is also absolutely inevitable; this rage, so generally discounted, so little understood even among the people whose daily bread it is, is one of the things that makes history. Rage can only with difficulty, and never entirely, be brought under the domination of the intelligence and is therefore not susceptible to any arguments whatever. This is a fact which ordinary representatives of the *Herrenvolk*,[3] having never felt this rage and being unable to imagine, quite fail to understand. Also, rage cannot be hidden, it can only be dissembled. This dissembling deludes the thoughtless, and strengthens rage and

---

[3] Editors' note: German for "master race."

adds, to rage, contempt. There are, no doubt, as many ways of coping with the resulting complex of tensions as there are black men in the world, but no black man can hope ever to be entirely liberated from this internal warfare — rage, dissembling, and contempt having inevitably accompanied his first realization of the power of white men. What is crucial here is that, since white men represent in the black man's world so heavy a weight, white men have for black men a reality which is reciprocal; and hence all black men have toward all white men an attitude which is designed, really, either to rob the white man of the jewel of his naiveté, or else to make it cost him dear.

The black man insists, by whatever means he finds at his disposal, that the white man cease to regard him as an exotic rarity and recognize him as a human being. This is a very charged and difficult moment, for there is a great deal of will power involved in the white man's naïveté. Most people are not naturally reflective any more than they are naturally malicious, and the white man prefers to keep the black man at a certain human remove because it is easier for him thus to preserve his simplicity and avoid being called to account for crimes committed by his forefathers, or his neighbors. He is inescapably aware, nevertheless, that he is in a better position in the world than black men are, nor can he quite put to death the suspicion that he is hated by black men therefore. He does not wish to be hated, neither does he wish to change places, and at this point in his uneasiness he can scarcely avoid having recourse to those legends which white men have created about black men, the most usual effect of which is that the white man finds himself enmeshed, so to speak, in his own language which describes hell, as well as the attributes which lead one to hell, as being as black as night.

Every legend, moreover, contains its residuum of truth, and the root function of language is to control the universe by describing it. It is of quite considerable significance that black men remain, in the imagination, and in overwhelming numbers in fact, beyond the disciplines of salvation; and this despite the fact that the West has been "buying" African natives for centuries. There is, I should hazard, an instantaneous necessity to be divorced from this so visibly unsaved stranger, in whose heart, moreover, one cannot guess what dreams of vengeance are being nourished; and, at the same time, there are few things on earth more attractive than the idea of the unspeakable liberty which is allowed the unredeemed. When, beneath the black mask, a human being begins to make himself felt one cannot escape a certain awful wonder as to what kind of human being it is. What one's imagination makes of other people is dictated, of course, by the laws of one's own personality and it is one of the ironies of black-white relations that, by means of what the white man imagines the black man to be, the black man is enabled to know who the white man is.

I have said, for example, that I am as much a stranger in this village today as I was the first summer I arrived, but this is not quite true. The villagers wonder less about the texture of my hair than they did then, and wonder rather more about me. And the fact that their wonder now exists on another level is reflected in their attitudes and in their eyes. There are the children who make those delightful, hilarious, sometimes astonishingly grave overtures of friendship in the unpredictable fashion of children; other children, having been taught that the devil is a black man, scream in genuine anguish as I approach. Some of the older women never pass without a friendly greeting, never pass, indeed, if it seems that they will be able to engage me in conversation; other women look down or look away or rather contemptuously smirk. Some of the men drink with me and suggest that I learn how to ski — partly, I gather, because they cannot imagine what I would look like on skis — and want to know if I am married, and ask questions about my *métier*.[4] But some of the men have accused *le sale negre*[5] — behind my back — of stealing wood and there is already in the eyes of some of them that peculiar, intent paranoiac malevolence which one sometimes surprises in the eyes of American white men when, out walking with their Sunday girl, they see a Negro male approach.

There is a dreadful abyss between the streets of this village and the streets of the city in which I was born, between the children who shout *Neger!* today and those who shouted *Nigger!* yesterday — the abyss is experience, the American experience. The syllable hurled behind me today expresses, above all, wonder: I am a stranger here. But I am not a stranger in America and the same syllable riding on the American air expresses the war my presence has occasioned in the American soul.

For this village brings home to me this fact: that there was a day, and not really a very distant day, when Americans were scarcely Americans at all but discontented Europeans, facing a great unconquered continent and strolling, say, into a marketplace and seeing

[4] Editors' note: French for "profession."
[5] Editors' note: French for "the dirty black man."

black men for the first time. The shock this spectacle afforded is suggested, surely, by the promptness with which they decided that these black men were not really men but cattle. It is true that the necessity on the part of the settlers of the New World of reconciling their moral assumptions with the fact — and the necessity — of slavery enhanced immensely the charm of this idea, and it is also true that this idea expresses, with a truly American bluntness, the attitude which to varying extents all masters have had toward all slaves.

But between all former slaves and slave-owners and the drama which begins for Americans over three hundred years ago at Jamestown, there are at least two differences to be observed. The American Negro slave could not suppose, for one thing, as slaves in past epochs had supposed and often done, that he would ever be able to wrest the power from his master's hands. This was a supposition which the modern era, which was to bring about such vast changes in the aims and dimensions of power, put to death; it only begins, in unprecedented fashion, and with dreadful implications, to be resurrected today. But even had this supposition persisted with undiminished force, the American Negro slave could not have used it to lend his condition dignity, for the reason that this supposition rests on another: that the slave in exile yet remains related to his past, has some means — if only in memory — of revering and sustaining the forms of his former life, is able, in short, to maintain his identity.

This was not the case with the American Negro slave. He is unique among the black men of the world in that his past was taken from him, almost literally, at one blow. One wonders what on earth the first slave found to say to the first dark child he bore. I am told that there are Haitians able to trace their ancestry back to African kings, but any American Negro wishing to go back so far will find his journey through time abruptly arrested by the signature on the bill of sale which served as the entrance paper for his ancestor. At the time — to say nothing of the circumstances — of the enslavement of the captive black man who was to become the American Negro, there was not the remotest possibility that he would ever take power from his master's hands. There was no reason to suppose that his situation would ever change, nor was there, shortly, anything to indicate that his situation had ever been different. It was his necessity, in the words of E. Franklin Frazier, to find a "motive for living under American culture or die." The identity of the American Negro comes out of this extreme situation, and the evolution of this identity was a source of the most intolerable anxiety in the minds and the lives of his masters.

For the history of the American Negro is unique also in this: that the question of his humanity, and of his rights therefore as a human being, became a burning one for several generations of Americans, so burning a question that it ultimately became one of those used to divide the nation. It is out of this argument that the venom of the epithet *Nigger!* is derived. It is an argument which Europe has never had, and hence Europe quite sincerely fails to understand how or why the argument arose in the first place, why its effects are frequently disastrous and always so unpredictable, why it refuses until today to be entirely settled. Europe's black possessions remained — and do remain — in Europe's colonies, at which remove they represented no threat whatever to European identity. If they posed any problem at all for the European conscience, it was a problem which remained comfortingly abstract: in effect, the black man, as a *man,* did not exist for Europe. But in America, even as a slave, he was an inescapable part of the general social fabric and no American could escape having an attitude toward him. Americans attempt until today to make an abstraction of the Negro, but the very nature of these abstractions reveals the tremendous effects the presence of the Negro has had on the American character.

When one considers the history of the Negro in America it is of the greatest importance to recognize that the moral beliefs of a person, or a people, are never really as tenuous as life — which is not moral — very often causes them to appear; these create for them a frame of reference and a necessary hope, the hope being that when life has done its worst they will be enabled to rise above themselves and to triumph over life. Life would scarcely be bearable if this hope did not exist. Again, even when the worst has been said, to betray a belief is not by any means to have put oneself beyond its power; the betrayal of a belief is not the same thing as ceasing to believe. If this were not so there would be no moral standards in the world at all. Yet one must also recognize that morality is based on ideas and that all ideas are dangerous — dangerous because ideas can only lead to action and where the action leads no man can say. And dangerous in this respect: that confronted with the impossibility of remaining faithful to one's beliefs, and the equal impossibility of becoming free of them, one can be driven to the most inhuman excesses. The ideas on which American beliefs are based are not, though Americans often seem to think so, ideas which originated in America. They came out of Europe. And the establishment of democracy on the American continent was scarcely as radical a break with the past as was the necessity, which Americans faced, of broadening this concept to include black men.

This was, literally, a hard necessity. It was impossible, for one thing, for Americans to abandon their beliefs, not only because these beliefs alone seemed able to justify the sacrifices they had endured and the blood that they had spilled, but also because these beliefs afforded them their only bulwark against a moral chaos as absolute as the physical chaos of the continent it was their destiny to conquer. But in the situation in which Americans found themselves, these beliefs threatened an idea, which, whether or not one likes to think so, is the very warp and woof of the heritage of the West, the idea of white supremacy.

Americans have made themselves notorious by the shrillness and the brutality with which they have insisted on this idea, but they did not invent it; and it has escaped the world's notice that those very excesses of which Americans have been guilty imply a certain, unprecedented uneasiness over the idea's life and power, if not, indeed, the idea's validity. The idea of white supremacy rests simply on the fact that white men are the creators of civilization (the present civilization, which is the only one that matters; all previous civilizations are simply "contributions" to our own) and are therefore civilization's guardians and defenders. Thus it was impossible for Americans to accept the black man as one of themselves, for to do so was to jeopardize their status as white men. But not so to accept him was to deny his human reality, his human weight and complexity, and the strain of denying the overwhelmingly undeniable forced Americans into rationalizations so fantastic that they approached the pathological.

At the root of the American Negro problem is the necessity of the American white man to find a way of living with the Negro in order to be able to live with himself. And the history of this problem can be reduced to the means used by Americans — lynch law and law, segregation and legal acceptance, terrorization and concession — either to come to terms with this necessity, or to find a way around it, or (most usually) to find a way of doing both these things at once. The resulting spectacle, at once foolish and dreadful, led someone to make the quite accurate observation that "the Negro-in-America is a form of insanity which overtakes white men."

In this long battle, a battle by no means finished, the unforeseeable effects of which will be felt by many future generations, the white man's motive was the protection of his identity; the black man was motivated by the need to establish an identity. And despite the terrorization which the Negro in America endured and endures sporadically until today, despite the cruel and totally inescapable ambivalence of his status in his country, the battle for his identity has long ago been won. He is not a visitor to the West, but a citizen there, an American; as American as the Americans who despise him, the Americans who fear him, the Americans who love him — the Americans who became less than themselves, or rose to be greater than themselves by virtue of the fact that the challenge he represented was inescapable. He is perhaps the only black man in the world whose relationship to white men is more terrible, more subtle, and more meaningful than the relationship of bitter possessed to uncertain possessors. His survival depended, and his development depends, on his ability to turn his peculiar status in the Western world to his own advantage and, it may be, to the very great advantage of that world. It remains for him to fashion out of his experience that which will give him sustenance, and a voice.

The cathedral at Chartres, I have said, says something to the people of this village which it cannot say to me; but it is important to understand that this cathedral says something to me which it cannot say to them. Perhaps they are struck by the power of the spires, the glory of the windows; but they have known God, after all, longer than I have known him, and in a different way, and I am terrified by the slippery bottomless well to be found in the crypt, down which heretics were hurled to death, and by the obscene, inescapable gargoyles jutting out of the stone and seeming to say that God and the devil can never be divorced. I doubt that the villagers think of the devil when they face a cathedral because they have never been identified with the devil. But I must accept the status which myth, if nothing else, gives me in the West before I can hope to change the myth.

Yet, if the American Negro has arrived at his identity by virtue of the absoluteness of his estrangement from his past, American white men still nourish the illusion that there is some means of recovering the Eruopean innocence, of returning to a state in which black men do not exist. This is one of the greatest errors Americans can make. The identity they fought so hard to protect has, by virtue of that battle, undergone a change: Americans are as unlike any other white people in the world as it is possible to be. I do not think, for example, that it is too much to suggest that the American vision of the world — which allows so little reality, generally speaking, for any of the darker forces in human life, which tends until today to paint moral issues in glaring black and white — owes a great deal to the battle waged by Americans to maintain between themselves and black men a human separation which could not be bridged. It is only now beginning to be borne in on us — very faintly, it must be admitted, very slowly, and very much against our will — that this vision of the world is dangerously inaccurate, and perfectly useless. For it protects our moral high-mindedness at the terrible expense of weakening our grasp of reality. People who shut their eyes to reality simply invite their own destruction, and anyone who insists on remaining in a state of innocence long after that innocence is dead turns himself into a monster.

The time has come to realize that the interracial drama acted out on the American continent has not only created a new black man, it has created a new white man, too. No road whatever will lead Americans back to the simplicity of this European village where white men still have the luxury of looking on me as a stranger. I am not, really, a stranger any longer for any American alive. One of the things that distinguishes Americans from other people is that no other people has ever been so deeply involved in the lives of black men, and vice versa. This fact, faced, with all its implications, it can be seen that the history of the American Negro problem is not merely shameful, it is also something of an achievement. For even when the worst has been said, it must also be added that the perpetual challenge posed by this problem was always, somehow, perpetually met. It is precisely this black-white experience which may prove of indispensable value to us in the world we face today. This world is white no longer, and it will never be white again.

QUESTIONS

1. Why does Baldwin establish at the beginning of the essay, and at some length, the Swiss village's isolation?
2. Explain in your own words the chief differences, according to Baldwin, between the experience of a white man arriving as a stranger in an African village, and a black man arriving as a stranger in a white village.
3. Baldwin's densely packed, highly allusive sentences often require close study. Try to paraphrase (that is, rewrite in your words) or to explain the meaning of the following sentences (page 564):

    a. "For this village, even were it incomparably more remote and incredibly more primitive, is the West, the West onto which I have been so strangely grafted."

    b. "The rage of the disesteemed is personally fruitless, but it is also absolutely inevitable; this rage, so generally discounted, so little understood even among the people whose daily bread it is, is one of the things that makes history."

4. Why, according to Baldwin, have whites created legends about blacks? What legends does Baldwin refer to in this essay?

5. On page 568 Baldwin refers to American beliefs that were threatened by the idea of white supremacy. What were those beliefs?

6. Baldwin wrote "Stranger in the Village" in the early 1950s. Does his conclusion still ring true? Explain.

How to Get Things Done

Robert Benchley

A great many people have come up to me and asked me how I manage to get so much work done and still keep looking so dissipated. My answer is "Don't you wish you knew?" and a pretty good answer it is, too, when you consider that nine times out of ten I didn't hear the original question.

But the fact remains that hundreds of thousands of people throughout the country are wondering how I have time to do all my painting, engineering, writing and philanthropic work when, according to the rotogravure sections and society notes I spend all my time riding to hounds, going to fancy-dress balls disguised as Louis XIV or spelling out GREETINGS TO CALIFORNIA in formation with three thousand Los Angeles school children. "All work and all play," they say.

The secret of my incredible energy and efficiency in getting work done is a simple one. I have based it very deliberately on a well-known psychological principle and have refined it so that it is now almost *too* refined. I shall have to begin coarsening it up again pretty soon.

The psychological principle is this: anyone can do any amount of work, provided it isn't the work he is *supposed* to be doing at that moment.

Let us see how this works out in practice. Let us say that I have five things which have to be done before the end of the week: (1) a basketful of letters to be answered, some of them dating from October 1928, (2) some bookshelves to be put up and arranged with books (3) a hair-cut to get (4) a pile of scientific magazines to go through and clip (I am collecting all references to tropical fish that I can find, with the idea of some day buying myself one) and (5) an article to write for this paper.

Now. With these five tasks staring me in the face on Monday morning, it is little wonder that I go right back to bed as soon as I have had breakfast, in order to store up health and strength for the almost superhuman expenditure of energy that is to come. *Mens sana in corpore sano*[1] is my motto, and, not even to be funny, am I going to make believe that I don't know what the Latin means. I feel that the least that I can do is to treat my body right when it has to supply fuel for an insatiable mind like mine.

As I lie in bed on Monday morning storing up strength, I make out a schedule. "What do I have to do first?" I ask myself. Well, those letters really should be answered and the pile of scientific magazines should be clipped. And here is where my secret process comes in. Instead of putting them first on the list of things which have to be done, I put them last. I practice a little deception on myself and say: "First you must write that article for the newspaper." I even say this out loud (being careful that nobody hears me, otherwise they would *keep* me in bed) and try to fool myself into really believing that I must do the article that day and that the other things can wait. I sometimes go so far in this self-deception as to make out a list in pencil, with "No. 1. Newspaper article" underlined in red. (The underlining in red is rather difficult, as there is never a red pencil on the table beside the bed, unless I have taken one to bed with me on Sunday night.)

Then, when everything is lined up, I bound out of bed and have lunch. I find that a good, heavy lunch, with some sort of glutinous dessert, is good preparation for the day's work as it keeps one from getting nervous and excitable. We workers must keep cool and calm, otherwise we would just throw away our time in jumping about and fidgeting.

---

[1] Editors' note: Latin for "A sound mind in a sound body."

I then seat myself at my desk with my typewriter before me and sharpen five pencils. (The sharp pencils are for poking holes in the desk-blotter, and a pencil has to be pretty sharp to do that. I find that I can't get more than six holes out of one pencil.) Following this I say to myself (again out loud, if it is practical), "Now, old man! Get at this article!"

Gradually the scheme begins to work. My eye catches the pile of magazines, which I have artfully placed on a near-by table beforehand. I write my name and address at the top of the sheet of paper in the typewriter and then sink back. The magazines being within reach (also part of the plot) I look to see if anyone is watching me and get one off the top of the pile. Hello, what's this! In the very first one is an article by Dr. William Beebe, illustrated by horrifying photographs! Pushing my chair away from my desk, I am soon hard at work clipping.

One of the interesting things about the Argyopelius, or "Silver Hatchet" fish, I find, is that it has eyes in its wrists. I would have been sufficiently surprised just to find out that a fish had wrists, but to learn that it has eyes in them is a discovery so astounding that I am hardly able to cut out the picture. What a lot one learns simply by thumbing through the illustrated weeklies! It is hard work, though, and many a weaker spirit would give it up half-done, but when there is something else of "more importance" to be finished (you see, I still keep up the deception, letting myself go on thinking that the newspaper article is of more importance) no work is too hard or too onerous to keep one busy.

Thus, before the afternoon is half over, I have gone through the scientific magazines and have a neat pile of clippings (including one of a Viper Fish which I wish you could see. You would die laughing). Then it is back to the grind of the newspaper article.

This time I get as far as the title, which I write down with considerable satisfaction until I find that I have misspelled one word terribly, so that the whole sheet of paper has to come out and a fresh one be inserted. As I am doing this, my eye catches the basket of letters.

Now, if there is one thing that I hate to do (and there is, you may be sure) it is to write letters. But somehow, with the magazine article before me waiting to be done, I am seized with an epistolary fervor which amounts to a craving, and I slyly sneak the first of the unanswered letters out of the basket. I figure out in my mind that I will get more into the swing of writing the article if I practice a little on a few letters. This first one, anyway, I really must answer.

True, it is from a friend in Antwerp asking me to look him up when I am in Europe in the summer of 1929, so he can't actually be watching the incoming boats for an answer, but I owe something to politeness after all. So instead of putting a fresh sheet of copy-paper into the typewriter, I slip in one of my handsome bits of personal stationery and dash off a note to my friend in Antwerp. Then, being well in the letter-writing mood, I clean up the entire batch. I feel a little guilty about the article, but the pile of freshly stamped envelopes and the neat bundle of clippings on tropical fish do much to salve my conscience. Tomorrow I will do the article, and no fooling this time either.

When tomorrow comes I am up with one of the older and more sluggish larks. A fresh sheet of copy-paper in the machine, and my name and address neatly printed at the top, and all before eleven A. M.! "A human dynamo" is the name I think up for myself. I have decided to write something about snake-charming and am already more than satisfied with the title "These Snake-Charming People." But, in order to write about snake-charming, one has to know a little about its history, and where should one go to find history but to a book? Maybe in that pile of books in the corner is one on snake-charming! Nobody could point the finger of scorn at me if I went over to those books for the avowed purpose of research work for the matter at hand. No writer could be supposed to carry all that information in his head.

So, with a perfectly clear conscience, I leave my desk for a few minutes and begin glancing over the titles of the books. Of course, it is difficult to find any book, much less one on snake-charming, in a pile which has been standing in the corner for weeks. What really is needed is for them to be on a shelf where their titles will be visible at a glance. And there is the shelf, standing beside the pile of books! It seems almost like a divine command written in the sky: "If you want to finish that article, first put up the shelf and arrange the books on it!" Nothing could be clearer or more logical.

In order to put up the shelf, the laws of physics have decreed that there must be nails, a hammer and some sort of brackets to hold it up on the wall. You can't just wet a shelf with your tongue and stick it up. And, as there are no nails or brackets in the house (or, if there are, they are probably hidden somewhere) the next thing to do is put on my hat and go out to buy them. Much as it disturbs me to put off the actual start of the article, I feel that I am doing only what is in the line of duty to put on my hat and go out to buy nails and brackets. And, as I put on my hat, I realize to my chagrin that I need a hair-cut badly. I can kill two birds with one stone, or at least with two, and stop in at the barber's on the way back. I will feel all the more like writing after a turn in the fresh air. Any doctor would tell me that.

So in a few hours I return, spick and span and smelling of lilac, bearing nails, brackets, the evening papers and some crackers and peanut butter. Then it's ho! for a quick snack and a glance through the evening papers (there might be something in them which would alter what I was going to write about snake-charming) and in no time at all the shelf is up, slightly crooked but up, and the books are arranged in a neat row in alphabetical order and all ready for almost instantaneous reference. There does not happen to be one on snake-charming among them, but there is a very interesting one containing some Hogarth prints and one which will bear even closer inspection dealing with the growth of the Motion Picture, illustrated with "stills" from famous productions. A really remarkable industry, the motion-pictures. I might want to write an article on it sometime. Not today, probably, for it is six o'clock and there is still the one on snake-charming to finish up first. Tomorrow morning sharp! Yes, *sir!*

And so, you see, in two days I have done four of the things I had to do, simply by making believe that it was the fifth that I *must* do. And the next day, I fix up something else, like taking down the bookshelf and putting it somewhere else, that I *have* to do, and then I get the fifth one done.

The only trouble is that, at this rate, I will soon run out of things to do, and will be forced to get at that newspaper article the first thing Monday morning.

QUESTIONS

1. In the first sentence, what did you expect after the words "looking so"? Why didn't Benchley say what you expected?
2. On page 573 Benchley claims that he is deliberately practicing self-deception when he lists writing an article as the first thing he must do, and that "the other things can wait." How do we know that he is being ironic — that writing the article really is the most urgent task? Write a 500-word essay, due Monday, explaining your answer (or answer the next question).
3. Why did you turn to this question?
4. Write an essay setting down in meticulous detail everything

you do when you go about writing an essay. Play it straight, but don't be surprised if it comes out sounding like a spoof.

Joey: A "Mechanical Boy"
Bruno Bettelheim

Joey, when we began our work with him, was a mechanical boy. He functioned as if by remote control, run by machines of his own powerfully creative fantasy. Not only did he himself believe that he was a machine but, more remarkably, he created this impression in others. Even while he performed actions that are intrinsically human, they never appeared to be other than machine-started and executed. On the other hand, when the machine was not working we had to concentrate on recollecting his presence, for he seemed not to exist. A human body that functions as if it were a machine and a machine that duplicates human functions are equally fascinating and frightening. Perhaps they are so uncanny because they remind us that the human body can operate without a human spirit, that body can exist without soul. And Joey was a child who had been robbed of his humanity.

Not every child who possesses a fantasy world is possessed by it. Normal children may retreat into realms of imaginary glory or magic powers, but they are easily recalled from these excursions. Disturbed children are not always able to make the return trip; they remain withdrawn, prisoners of the inner world of delusion and fantasy. In many ways Joey presented a classic example of this state of infantile autism.

At the Sonia Shankman Orthogenic School of the University of Chicago it is our function to provide a therapeutic environment in which such children may start life over again. I have previously described the rehabilitation of another of our patients ("Schizophrenic Art: A Case Study"; *Scientific American,* April 1952). This time I shall concentrate upon the illness, rather than the treatment. In any age, when the individual has escaped into a delusional world, he has usually fashioned it from bits and pieces of the world at hand. Joey, in his time and world, chose the machine and froze himself in its image. His story has a general relevance to the understanding of emotional development in a machine age.

Joey's delusion is not uncommon among schizophrenic children today. He wanted to be rid of his unbearable humanity, to become completely automatic. He so nearly succeeded in attaining this goal that he could almost convince others, as well as himself, of his mechanical character. The descriptions of autistic children in the literature take for their point of departure and comparison the normal or abnormal human being. To do justice to Joey I would have to compare him simultaneously to a most inept infant and a highly complex piece of machinery. Often we had to force ourselves by a conscious act of will to realize that Joey was a child. Again and again his acting-out of his delusions froze our own ability to respond as human beings.

During Joey's first weeks with us we would watch absorbedly as this at once fragile-looking and imperious nine-year-old went about his mechanical existence. Entering the dining room, for example, he would string an imaginary wire from his "energy source" — an imaginary electric outlet — to the table. There he "insulated" himself with paper napkins and finally plugged himself in. Only then could Joey eat, for he firmly believed that the "current" ran his ingestive apparatus. So skillful was the pantomime that one had to look twice to be sure there was neither wire not outlet nor plug. Children and members of our staff spontaneously avoided stepping on the "wires" for fear of interrupting what seemed the source of his very life.

For long periods of time, when his "machinery" was idle, he would sit so quietly that he would disappear from the focus of the most conscientious observation. Yet in the next moment he might be "working" and the center of our captivated attention. Many times a day he would turn himself on and shift noisily through a sequence of higher and higher gears until he "exploded," screaming "Crash, crash!" and hurling items from his ever-present apparatus — radio tubes, light bulbs, even motors or, lacking these, any handy breakable object. (Joey had an astonishing knack for snatching bulbs and tubes unobserved.) As soon as the object thrown had shattered, he would cease his screaming and wild jumping and retire to mute, motionless nonexistence.

Our maids, inured to difficult children, were exceptionally attentive to Joey; they were apparently moved by his extreme infantile fragility, so strangely coupled with megalomaniacal superiority. Occasionally some of the apparatus he fixed to his bed to "live him" during his sleep would fall down in disarray. This machinery he contrived from masking tape, cardboard, wire and other paraphernalia. Usually the maids would pick up such things and leave them on a table for the children to find, or disregard them entirely. But Joey's machine they carefully restored: "Joey must have the carburetor so he can breathe." Similarly they were on the alert to pick up and preserve the motors that ran him during the day and the exhaust pipes through which he exhaled.

How had Joey become a human machine? From intensive interviews with his parents we learned that the process had begun even before birth. Schizophrenia often results from parental rejection, sometimes combined ambivalently with love. Joey, on the other hand, had been completely ignored.

"I never knew I was pregnant," his mother said, meaning that she had already excluded Joey from her consciousness. His birth, she said, "did not make any difference." Joey's father, a rootless draftee in the wartime civilian army, was equally unready for parenthood. So, of course, are many young couples. Fortunately most such parents lose their indifference upon the baby's birth. But not Joey's parents. "I did not want to see or nurse him," his mother declared. "I had no feeling of actual dislike — I simply didn't want to take care of him." For the first three months of his life Joey "cried most of the time." A colicky baby, he was kept on a rigid four-hour feeding schedule, was not touched unless necessary and was never cuddled or played with. The mother, preoccupied with herself, usually left Joey alone in the crib or playpen during the day. The father discharged his frustrations by punishing Joey when the child cried at night.

Soon the father left for overseas duty, and the mother took Joey, now a year and a half old, to live with her at her parents' home. On his arrival the grandparents noticed that ominous changes had occurred in the child. Strong and healthy at birth, he had become frail and irritable; a responsive baby, he had become remote and inaccessible. When he began to master speech, he talked only to himself. At an early date he became preoccupied with machinery, including an old electric fan which he could take apart and put together again with surprising deftness.

Joey's mother impressed us with a fey quality that expressed her insecurity, her detachment from the world and her low physical vitality. We were struck especially by her total indifference as she talked about Joey. This seemed much more remarkable than the actual mistakes she made in handling him. Certainly he was left to cry for hours when hungry, because she fed him on a rigid schedule; he was toilet-trained with great rigidity so that he would give no trouble. These things happen to many children. But Joey's existence never registered with his mother. In her recollections he was fused at one moment with one event or person; at another, with something or somebody else. When she told us about his birth and infancy, it was as if she were talking about some vague acquaintance, and soon her thoughts would wander off to another person or to herself.

When Joey was not yet four, his nursery school suggested that he enter a special school for disturbed children. At the new school his autism was immediately recognized. During his three years there he experienced a slow improvement. Unfortunately a subsequent two years in a parochial school destroyed this progress. He began to develop compulsive defenses, which he called his "preventions." He could not drink, for example, except through elaborate piping systems built of straws. Liquids had to be "pumped" into him, in his fantasy, or he could not suck. Eventually his behavior became so upsetting that he could not be kept in the parochial school. At home things did not improve. Three months before entering the Orthogenic School he made a serious attempt at suicide.

To us Joey's pathological behavior seemed the external expression of an overwhelming effort to remain almost nonexistent as a person. For weeks Joey's only reply when addressed was "Bam." Unless he thus neutralized whatever we said, there would be an explosion, for Joey plainly wished to close off every form of contact not mediated by machinery. Even when he was bathed he rocked back and forth with mute, engine-like regularity, flooding the bathroom. If he stopped rocking, he did this like a machine too; suddenly he went completely rigid. Only once, after months of being lifted from his bath and carried to bed, did a small expression of puzzled pleasure appear on his face as he said very softly: "They even carry you to your bed here."

For a long time after he began to talk he would never refer to anyone by name, but only as "that person" or "the little person" or "the big person." He was unable to designate by its true name anything to which he attached feelings. Nor could he name his anxieties except through neologisms or word contaminations. For a long time he spoke about "master paintings" and "a master painting room" (i.e., masturbating and masturbating room). One of his machines, the "criticizer," prevented him from "saying words which have unpleasant feelings." Yet he gave personal names to the tubes and motors in his collection of machinery. Moreover, these dead things had feelings; the tubes bled when hurt and sometimes got sick. He consistently maintained this reversal between animate and inanimate objects.

In Joey's machine world everything, on pain of instant destruction, obeyed inhibitory laws much more stringent than those of physics. When we came to know him better, it was plain that in his moments of silent withdrawal, with his machine switched off, Joey was absorbed in pondering the compulsive laws of his private universe. His preoccupation with machinery made it difficult to establish even practical contacts with him. If he wanted to do something with a counselor, such as play with a toy that had caught his vague attention, he could not do so: "I'd like this very much, but first I have to turn off the machine." But by the time he had fulfilled all the requirements of his preventions, he had lost interest. When a toy was offered to him, he could not touch it because his motors and his tubes did not leave him a hand free. Even certain colors were dangerous and had to be strictly avoided in toys and clothing, because "some colors turn off the current, and I can't touch them because I can't live without the current."

Joey was convinced that machines were better than people. Once when he bumped into one of the pipes on our jungle gym he kicked it so violently that his teacher had to restrain him to keep him from injuring himself. When she explained that the pipe was much harder than his foot, Joey replied: "That proves it. Machines are better than the body. They don't break; they're much harder and stronger." If he lost or forgot something, it merely proved that his brain ought to be thrown away and replaced by machinery. If he spilled something, his arm should be broken and twisted off because it did not work properly. When his head or arm failed to work as it should, he tried to punish it by hitting it. Even Joey's feelings were mechanical. Much later in his therapy, when he had formed a timid attachment to another child and had been rebuffed, Joey cried: "He broke my feelings."

Gradually we began to understand what had seemed to be contradictory in Joey's behavior — why he held onto the motors and tubes, then suddenly destroyed them in a fury, then set out immediately and urgently to equip himself with new and larger tubes. Joey had created these machines to run his body and mind because it was too painful to be human. But again and again he became dissatisfied with their failure to meet his need and rebellious at the way they frustrated his will. In a recurrent frenzy he "exploded" his light bulbs and tubes, and for a moment became a human being — for one crowning instant he came alive. But as soon as he had asserted his dominance through the self-created explosion, he felt his life ebbing away. To keep on existing he had immediately to restore his machines and replenish the electricity that supplied his life energy.

What deep-seated fears and needs underlay Joey's delusional system? We were long in finding out, for Joey's preventions effectively concealed the secret of his autistic behavior. In the meantime we dealt with his peripheral problems one by one.

During his first year with us Joey's most trying problem was toilet behavior. This surprised us, for Joey's personality was not "anal" in the Freudian sense; his original personality damage had antedated the period of his toilet-training. Rigid and early toilet-training, however, had certainly contributed to his anxieties. It was our effort to help Joey with this problem that led to his first recognition of us as human beings.

Going to the toilet, like everything else in Joey's life, was surrounded by elaborate preventions. We had to accompany him; he had to take off all his clothes; he could only squat, not sit, on the toilet seat; he had to touch the wall with one hand, in which he also clutched frantically the vacuum tubes that powered his elimination. He was terrified lest his whole body be sucked down.

To counteract this fear we gave him a metal wastebasket in lieu of a toilet. Eventually, when eliminating into the wastebasket, he no longer needed to take off all his clothes, nor to hold on to the wall. He still needed the tubes and motors which, he believed, moved his bowels for him. But here again the all-important machinery was itself a source of new terrors. In Joey's world the gadgets had to move their bowels, too. He was terribly concerned that they should, but since they were so much more powerful than men, he was also terrified that if his tubes moved their bowels, their feces would fill all of space and leave him no room to live. He was thus always caught in some fearful contradiction.

Our readiness to accept his toilet habits, which obviously entailed some hardship for his counselors, gave Joey the confidence to express his obsessions in drawings. Drawing these fantasies was a first step toward letting us in, however distantly, to what concerned him most deeply. It was the first step in a year-long process of externalizing his anal preoccupations. As a result he began seeing feces everywhere; the whole world became to him a mire of excrement. At the same time he began to eliminate freely wherever he happened to be. But with this release from his infantile imprisonment in compulsive rules, the toilet and the whole process of elimination became less dangerous. Thus far it had been beyond Joey's comprehension that anybody could possibly move his bowels without mechanical aid. Now Joey took a further step forward; defecation became the first physiological process he could perform without the help of vacuum tubes. It must not be thought that he was proud of this ability. Taking pride in an achievement presupposes that one accomplishes it of one's own free will. He still did not feel himself an autonomous person who could do things on his own. To Joey defecation still seemed enslaved to some incomprehensible but utterly binding cosmic law, perhaps the law his parents had imposed on him when he was being toilet-trained.

It was not simply that his parents had subjected him to rigid, early training. Many children are so trained. But in most cases the parents have a deep emotional investment in the child's performance. The child's response in turn makes training an occasion for interaction between them and for the building of genuine relationships. Joey's parents had no emotional investment in him. His obedience gave them no satisfaction and won him no affection or approval. As a toilet-trained child he saved his mother labor, just as household machines saved her labor. As a machine he was not loved for his performance, nor could he love himself.

So it had been with all other aspects of Joey's existence with his parents. Their reactions to his eating or noneating, sleeping or wakening, urinating or defecating, being dressed or undressed, washed or bathed did not flow from any unitary interest in him, deeply embedded in their personalities. By treating him mechanically his parents made him a machine. The various functions of life — even the parts of his body — bore no integrating relationship to one another or to any sense of self that was acknowledged and confirmed by others. Though he had acquired mastery over some functions, such as toilet-training and speech, he had acquired them separately and kept them isolated from each other. Toilet-training had thus not gained him a pleasant feeling of body mastery; speech had not led to communication of thought or feeling. On the contrary, each achievement only steered him away from self-mastery and integration. Toilet-training had enslaved him. Speech left him talking in neologisms that obstructed his and our ability to relate to each other. In Joey's development the normal process of growth had been made to run backward. Whatever he had learned put him not at the end of his infantile development toward integration but, on the contrary, farther behind than he was at its very beginning.

Had we understood this sooner, his first years with us would have been less baffling.

It is unlikely that Joey's calamity could befall a child in any time and culture but our own. He suffered no physical deprivation; he starved for human contact. Just to be taken care of is not enough for relating. It is a necessary but not a sufficient condition. At the extreme where utter scarcity reigns, the forming of relationships is certainly hampered. But our society of mechanized plenty often makes for equal difficulties in a child's learning to relate. Where parents can provide the simple creature-comforts for their children only at the cost of significant effort, it is likely that they will feel pleasure in being able to provide for them; it is this, the parents' pleasure, that gives children a sense of personal worth and sets the process of relating in motion. But if comfort is so readily available that the parents feel no particular pleasure in winning it for their children, then the children cannot develop the feeling of being worthwhile around the satisfaction of their basic needs. Of course parents and children can and do develop relationships around other situations. But matters are then no longer so simple and direct. The child must be on the receiving end of care and concern given with pleasure and without the exaction of return if he is to feel loved and worthy of respect and consideration. This feeling gives him the ability to trust; he can entrust his well-being to persons to whom he is so important. Out of such trust the child learns to form close and stable relationships.

For Joey relationship with his parents was empty of pleasure in comfort-giving as in all other situations. His was an extreme instance of a plight that sends many schizophrenic children to our clinics and hospitals. Many months passed before he could relate to us; his despair that anybody could like him made contact impossible.

When Joey could finally trust us enough to let himself become more infantile, he began to play at being a papoose. There was a corresponding change in his fantasies. He drew endless pictures of himself as an electrical papoose. Totally enclosed, suspended in empty space, he is run by unknown, unseen powers through wireless electricity.

As we eventually came to understand, the heart of Joey's delusional system was the artificial, mechanical womb he had created and into which he had locked himself. In his papoose fantasies lay the wish to be entirely reborn in a womb. His new experiences in the school suggested that life, after all, might be worth living. Now he was searching for a way to be reborn in a better way. Since machines were better than men, what was more natural than to try rebirth through them? This was the deeper meaning of his electrical papoose.

As Joey made progress, his pictures of himself became more dominant in his drawings. Though still machine-operated, he has grown in self-importance. Now he has acquired hands that do something, and he has had the courage to make a picture of the machine that runs him. Later still the papoose became a person, rather than a robot encased in glass.

Eventually Joey began to create an imaginary family at the school: the "Carr" family. Why the Carr family? In the car he was enclosed as he had been in his papoose, but at least the car was not stationary; it could move. More important, in a car one was not only driven but also could drive. The Carr family was Joey's way of exploring the possibility of leaving the school, of living with a good family in a safe, protecting car.

Joey at last broke through his prison. In this brief account it has not been possible to trace the painfully slow process of his first true relations with other human beings. Suffice it to say that he ceased to be a mechanical boy and became a human child. This newborn child was, however, nearly twelve years old. To recover the lost time is a tremendous task. That work has occupied Joey and us ever since. Sometimes he sets to it with a will; at other times the difficulty of real life makes him regret that he ever came out of his shell. But he has never wanted to return to his mechanical life.

One last detail and this fragment of Joey's story has been told. When Joey was twelve, he made a float for our Memorial Day parade. It carried the slogan: "Feelings are more important than anything under the sun." Feelings, Joey had learned, are what make for humanity; their absence, for a mechanical existence. With this knowledge Joey entered the human condition.

QUESTIONS

1. Write a paragraph outline (see page 78) of Bettelheim's essay, and compare it to another possible structure for the same material.

2. Bettelheim suggests that the parents' behavior was mainly responsible for Joey's condition, but he also suggests that our "time and culture," "our society of . . . plenty," is partly responsible. Explain how he tries to link these two. How adequate is the entire explanation when applied to Joey?

To Lie or Not to Lie? —
The Doctor's Dilemma

Sissela Bok

Should doctors ever lie to benefit their patients — to speed recovery or to conceal the approach of death? In medicine as in law, government, and other lines of work, the requirements of honesty often seem dwarfed by greater needs: the need to shelter from brutal news or to uphold a promise of secrecy; to expose corruption or to promote the public interest.

What should doctors say, for example, to a forty-six-year-old man coming in for a routine physical checkup just before going on vacation with his family who, though he feels in perfect health, is found to have a form of cancer that will cause him to die within six months? Is it best to tell him the truth? If he asks, should the doctors deny that he is ill, or minimize the gravity of the prognosis? Should they at least conceal the truth until after the family vacation?

Doctors confront such choices often and urgently. At times, they see important reasons to lie for the patient's own sake; in their eyes, such lies differ sharply from self-serving ones.

Studies show that most doctors sincerely believe that the seriously ill do not want to know the truth about their condition, and that informing them risks destroying their hope, so that they may recover more slowly, or deteriorate faster, perhaps even commit suicide. As one physician wrote: "Ours is a profession which traditionally has been guided by a precept that transcends the virtue of uttering the truth for truth's sake, and that is 'as far as possible do not harm.'"

Armed with such a precept, a number of doctors may slip into deceptive practices that they assume will "do no harm" and may well help their patients. They may prescribe innumerable placebos, sound more encouraging than the facts warrant, and distort grave news, especially to the incurably ill and the dying.

But the illusory nature of the benefits such deception is meant to bestow is now coming to be documented. Studies show that, contrary to the belief of many physicians, an overwhelming majority of patients do want to be told the truth, even about grave illness, and feel betrayed when they learn that they have been misled. We are also learning that truthful information, humanely conveyed, helps patients cope with illness: helps them tolerate pain better, need less medication, and even recover faster after surgery.

Not only do lies not provide the "help" hoped for by advocates of benevolent deception; they invade the autonomy of patients and render them unable to make informed choices concerning their own health, including the choice of whether to *be* a patient in the first place. We are becoming increasingly aware of all that can befall patients in the course of their illness when information is denied or distorted.

Dying patients especially — who are easiest to mislead and most often kept in the dark — can then not make decisions about the end of life: about whether or not to enter a hospital, or to have surgery; about where and with whom to spend their remaining time; about how to bring their affairs to a close and take leave.

Lies also do harm to those who tell them: harm to their integrity and, in the long run, to their credibility. Lies hurt their colleagues as well. The suspicion of deceit undercuts the work of the many doctors who are scrupulously honest with their patients; it contributes to the spiral of litigation and of "defensive medicine," and thus it injures, in turn, the entire medical profession.

Sharp conflicts are now arising. Patients are learning to press for answers. Patients' bills of rights require that they be informed about their condition and about alternatives for treatment. Many doctors go to great lengths to provide such information. Yet even in hospitals with the most eloquent bill of rights, believers in benevolent deception continue their age-old practices. Colleagues may disapprove but refrain from remonstrating. Nurses may bitterly resent having to take part, day after day, in deceiving patients, but feel powerless to take a stand.

There is urgent need to debate this issue openly. Not only in medicine, but in other professions as well, practitioners may find themselves repeatedly in straits where serious consequences seem avoidable only through deception. Yet the public has every reason to be wary of professional deception, for such practices are peculiarly likely to become ingrained, to spread, and to erode trust. Neither in medicine, nor in law, government, or the social sciences can there be comfort in the old saw, "What you don't know can't hurt you."

QUESTIONS

1. Is there anything in Bok's opening paragraph that prepares the reader for Bok's own position on whether or not lying is ever justifiable?

2. List the reasons Bok offers on behalf of telling the truth to patients. Are some of these reasons presented more convincingly than others? If any are unconvincing, rewrite them to make them more convincing.

3. Suppose Bok's last sentence was revised to read thus: "In medicine, law, government, and the social sciences, what you don't know *can* hurt you." Which version do you prefer, and why?

4. "What you don't know can't hurt you." Weigh the truth of this assertion in your own life. Were there instances of a truth being withheld from you that did hurt you? Were there occasions when you were told a truth that you now judge would have been better withheld? On the whole, do you come out in favor of the assertion, against it, or somewhere in between?

5. How much should adopted children be told about their biological parents? Consider reasons both for and against telling all. Use not only your own experiences and opinions but those of others, such as friends and classmates. If you read some relevant books or articles, see pages 333–56 on acknowledging sources.

The Gaucho and the City: Stories of Horsemen

Jorge Luis Borges

They are many and they may be countless. My first story is quite modest; those that follow will lend it greater depth.

A rancher from Uruguay had bought a country establishment (I am sure this is the word he used) in the province of Buenos Aires. From Paso de los Toros, in the middle of Uruguay, he brought a horse breaker, a man who had his complete trust but was extremely shy. The rancher put the man up in an inn near the Once markets. Three days later, on going to see him, the rancher found his horseman brewing maté in his room on the upper floor. When asked what he thought of Buenos Aires, the man admitted that he had not once stuck his head out in the street.

The second story is not much different. In 1903, Aparicio Saravia staged an uprising in the Uruguayan provinces; at a certain point of the campaign, it was feared that his men might break into Montevideo. My father, who happened to be there at the time, went to ask advice of a relative of his, the historian Luis Melián Lafinur, only to be told that there was no danger "because the gaucho stands in fear of cities." In fact, Saravia's troops did change their route, and somewhat to his amazement my father found out that the study of history could be useful as well as pleasurable.

My third story also belongs to the oral tradition of my family. Toward the end of 1870, forces of the Entre Ríos caudillo, López Jordán, commanded by a gaucho who was called (because he had a bullet embedded in him) "El Chumbiao," surrounded the city of Paraná. One night, catching the garrison off guard, the rebels broke through the defenses and rode right around the central square, whooping like Indians and hurling insults. Then, still shouting and whistling, they galloped off. To them war was not a systematic plan of action but a manly sport.

The fourth of these stories, and my last, comes from the pages of an excellent book, *L'Empire des Steppes* (1939), by the Orientalist René Grousset. Two passages from the second chapter are particularly relevant. Here is the first:

> Genghis Khan's war against the Chin, begun in 1211, was the last — with brief periods of truce — until his death (1227), only to be finished by his successor (1234). With their mobile cavalry, the Mongols could devastate the countryside and open settlements, but for a long time they knew nothing of the art of taking towns fortified by Chinese engineers. Besides, they fought in China as on the steppe, in a series of raids, after which they withdrew with their booty, leaving the Chinese behind them to reoccupy their towns, rebuild the ruins, repair the breaches in the walls, and reconstruct the fortifications, so that in the course of that war the Mongol generals found themselves obliged to reconquer the same places two or three times.

Here is the second passage:

> The Mongols took Peking, massacred the whole population, looted the houses, and then set fire to them. The devastation lasted a month. Clearly, the nomads had no idea what to do with a great city or how to use it for the consolidation and expansion of their power. We have here a highly interesting case for specialists in human geography: the predicament of the peoples of the steppe when, without a period of transition, chance hands them old countries with an urban civilization.

They burn and kill not out of sadism but because they find themselves out of their element and simply know no better.

I now give a story that all the authorities agree upon. During Genghis Khan's last campaign, one of his generals remarked that his new Chinese subjects were of no use to him, since they were inept in war, and that, consequently, the wisest course was to exterminate them all, raze the cities, and turn the almost boundless Middle Kingdom into one enormous pasture for the Mongol horses. In this way, at least, use could be made of the land, since nothing else was of any value. The Khan was about to follow this counsel when another adviser pointed out to him that it would be more advantageous to levy taxes on the land and on goods. Civilization was saved, the Mongols grew old in the cities that they had once longed to destroy, and doubtless they ended up, in symmetrical gardens, appreciating the despised and peaceable arts of prosody and pottery.

Distant in time and space, the stories I have assembled are really one. The protagonist is eternal, and the wary ranch hand who spends three days behind a door that looks out into a backyard — although he has come down in life — is the same one who, with two bows, a lasso made of horse hair, and a scimitar, was poised to raze and obliterate the world's most ancient kingdom under the hooves of his steppe pony. There is a pleasure in detecting beneath the masks of time the eternal species of horseman and city. This pleasure, in the case of these stories, may leave the Argentine with a melancholy aftertaste, since (through Hernández's gaucho, Martín Fierro, or through the weight of our past) we identify with the horseman, who in the end is the loser. The centaurs defeated by the Lapiths; the death of the shepherd Abel at the hand of Cain, who was a farmer; the defeat of Napoleon's cavalry by British infantry at Waterloo are all emblems and portents of such a destiny.

The horseman vanishing into the distance with a hint of defeat is, in our literature, the gaucho. And so we read in *Martín Fierro*:

Cruz y Fierro de una estancia
una tropilla se arriaron;
por delante se la echaron
como criollos entendidos,
y pronto, sin ser sentidos,
por la frontera cruzaron.

Y cuando la habían pasao,
una madrugada clara,

le dijo Cruz que mirara
las últimas poblaciones;
y a Fierro dos lagrimones
le rodaron por la cara.

Y siguiendo el fiel del rumbo
se entraron en el desierto . . .

From a ranch, Cruz and Fierro rounded up a herd of horses and, being practical gauchos, drove it before them. Undetected, they soon crossed over the border.

After this was done, early one morning Cruz told Fierro to look back on the last settlements. Two big tears rolled down Fierro's face.

Then, continuing on their course, the men set off into the wilderness
. . .

And in Lugones's *El Payador*:

In the fading twilight, turning brown as a dove's wing, we may have seen him vanish beyond the familiar hillocks, trotting on his horse, slowly, so that no one would think him afraid, under his gloomy hat and the poncho that hung from his shoulders in the limp folds of a flag at half mast.

And in *Don Segundo Sombra*:

Still smaller now, my godfather's silhouette appeared on the slope. My eyes concentrated on that tiny movement on the sleepy plain. He was about to reach the crest of the trail and vanish. He grew smaller and smaller, as if he were being whittled away from below. My gaze clung to the black speck of his hat, trying to preserve that last trace of him.

In the texts just quoted, space stands for time and history.

The figure of the man on the horse is, secretly, poignant. Under Attila, the "Scourge of God," under Genghis Khan, and under Tamerlane, the horseman tempestuously destroys and founds extensive empires, but all he destroys and founds is illusory. His work, like him, is ephemeral. From the farmer comes the word "culture" and from cities the word "civilization," but the horseman is a storm that fades away. In his book *Die Germanen der Völkerwanderung* (Stuttgart, 1939), Capelle remarks apropos of this that the Greeks, the Romans, and the Germans were agricultural peoples.

QUESTIONS

1. Are you a city person or a country (farm, mountain) person? Explain, in an essay of 250–500 words.

2. Briefly set forth a narrative of a kind of person (again, city, farm, mountain, or similar category) and then offer a paragraph of reflection on the kind. (If, like Borges, you can give more than one narrative, do so.)

On Keeping a Notebook

Joan Didion

" 'That woman Estelle,' " the note reads, " 'is partly the reason why George Sharp and I are separated today.' *Dirty crepe-de-Chine wrapper, hotel bar, Wilmington RR, 9:45 a.m. August Monday morning.*"

Since the note is in my notebook, it presumably has some meaning to me. I study it for a long while. At first I have only the most general notion of what I was doing on an August Monday morning in the bar of the hotel across from the Pennsylvania Railroad station in Wilmington, Delaware (waiting for a train? missing one? 1960? 1961? why Wilmington?), but I do remember being there. The woman in the dirty crepe-de-Chine wrapper had come down from her room for a beer, and the bartender had heard before the reason why George Sharp and she were separated today. "Sure," he said, and went on mopping the floor. "You told me." At the other end of the bar is a girl. She is talking, pointedly, not to the man beside her but to a cat lying in the triangle of sunlight cast through the open door. She is wearing a plaid silk dress from Peck & Peck, and the hem is coming down.

Here is what it is: the girl has been on the Eastern Shore, and now she is going back to the city, leaving the man beside her, and all she can see ahead are the viscous summer sidewalks and the 3 a.m. long-distance calls that will make her lie awake and then sleep drugged through all the steaming mornings left in August (1960? 1961?). Because she must go directly from the train to lunch in New York, she wishes that she had a safety pin for the hem of the plaid silk dress, and she also wishes that she could forget about the hem and the lunch and stay in the cool bar that smells of disinfectant and malt and make friends with the woman in the crepe-de-Chine wrapper. She is afflicted by a little self-pity, and she wants to compare Estelles. That is what that was all about.

Why did I write it down? In order to remember, of course, but exactly what was it I wanted to remember? How much of it actually happened? Did any of it? Why do I keep a notebook at all? It is easy to deceive oneself on all those scores. The impulse to write things down is a peculiarly compulsive one, inexplicable to those who do not share it, useful only accidentally, only secondarily, in the way that any compulsion tries to justify itself. I suppose that it begins or does not begin in the cradle. Although I have felt compelled to write things down since I was five years old, I doubt that my daughter ever will, for she is a singularly blessed and accepting child, delighted with life exactly as life presents itself to her, unafraid to go to sleep and unafraid to wake up. Keepers of private notebooks are a different breed altogether, lonely and resistant rearrangers of things, anxious malcontents, children afflicted apparently at birth with some presentiment of loss.

My first notebook was a Big Five tablet, given to me by my mother with the sensible suggestion that I stop whining and learn to amuse myself by writing down my thoughts. She returned the tablet to me a few years ago; the first entry is an account of a woman who believed herself to be freezing to death in the Arctic night, only to find, when day broke, that she had stumbled onto the Sahara Desert, where she would die of the heat before lunch. I have no idea what turn of a five-year-old's mind could have prompted so insistently "ironic" and exotic a story, but it does reveal a certain predilection for the extreme which has dogged me into adult life; perhaps if I were analytically inclined I would find it a truer story than any I might have told about Donald Johnson's birthday party or the day my cousin Brenda put Kitty Litter in the aquarium.

So the point of my keeping a notebook has never been, nor is it now, to have an accurate factual record of what I have been doing or thinking. That would be a different impulse entirely, an instinct for reality which I sometimes envy but do not possess. At no point have I ever been able successfully to keep a diary; my approach to daily life ranges from the grossly negligent to the merely absent, and on those few occasions when I have tried dutifully to record a day's events, boredom has so overcome me that the results are mysterious at best. What is this business about "shopping, typing piece, dinner with E, depressed"? Shopping for what? Typing what piece? Who is E? Was this "E" depressed, or was I depressed? Who cares?

In fact I have abandoned altogether that kind of pointless entry; instead I tell what some would call lies. "That's simply not true," the members of my family frequently tell me when they come up against my memory of a shared event. "The party was *not* for you, the spider was *not* a black widow, *it wasn't that way at all.*" Very likely they are right, for not only have I always had trouble distinguishing between what happened and what merely might have happened, but I remain unconvinced that the distinction, for my purposes, matters. The cracked crab that I recall having for lunch the day my father came home from Detroit in 1945 must certainly be embroidery, worked into the day's pattern to lend verisimilitude; I was ten years old and would not now remember the cracked crab. The day's events did not turn on cracked crab. And yet it is precisely that fictitious crab that makes me see the afternoon all over again, a home movie run all too often, the father bearing gifts, the child weeping, an exercise in family love and guilt. Or that is what it was to me. Similarly, perhaps it never did snow that August in Vermont; perhaps there never were flurries in the night wind, and maybe no one else felt the ground hardening and summer already dead even as we pretended to bask in it, but that was how it felt to me, and it might as well have snowed, could have snowed, did snow.

How it felt to me: that is getting closer to the truth about a notebook. I sometimes delude myself about why I keep a notebook, imagine that some thrifty virtue derives from preserving everything observed. See enough and write it down, I tell myself, and then some morning when the world seems drained of wonder, some day when I am only going through the motions of doing what I am supposed to do, which is write — on that bankrupt morning I will simply open my notebook and there it will all be, a forgotten account with accumulated interest, paid passage back to the world out there: dialogue overheard in hotels and elevators and at the hat-check counter in Pavillon (one middle-aged man shows his hat check to another and says, "That's my old football number"); impressions of Bettina Aptheker and Benjamin Sonnenberg and Teddy ("Mr. Acapulco") Stauffer; careful *aperçus* about tennis bums and failed fashion models and Greek shipping heiresses, one of whom taught me a significant lesson (a lesson I could have learned from F. Scott Fitzgerald, but perhaps we all must meet the very rich for ourselves) by asking, when I arrived to interview her in her orchid-filled sitting room on the second day of a paralyzing New York blizzard, whether it was snowing outside.

I imagine, in other words, that the notebook is about other people. But of course it is not. I have no real business with what one stranger said to another at the hat-check counter in Pavillon; in fact I suspect that the line "That's my old football number" touched not my own imagination at all, but merely some memory of something once read, probably "The Eighty-Yard Run." Nor is my concern with a woman in a dirty crepe-de-Chine wrapper in a Wilmington bar. My stake is always, of course, in the unmentioned girl in the plaid silk dress. *Remember what it was to be me:* that is always the point.

It is a difficult point to admit. We are brought up in the ethic that others, any others, all others, are by definition more interesting than ourselves; taught to be diffident, just this side of self-effacing. ("You're the least important person in the room and don't forget it," Jessica Mitford's governess would hiss in her ear on the advent of any social occasion; I copied that into my notebook because it is only recently that I have been able to enter a room without hearing some such phrase in my inner ear.) Only the very young and the very old may recount their dreams at breakfast, dwell upon self, interrupt with memories of beach picnics and favorite Liberty lawn dresses and the rainbow trout in a creek near Colorado Springs. The rest of us are expected, rightly, to affect absorption in other people's favorite dresses, other people's trout.

And so we do. But our notebooks give us away, for however dutifully we record what we see around us, the common denominator of all we see is always, transparently, shamelessly, the implacable "I." We are not talking here about the kind of notebook that is patently for public consumption, a structural conceit for binding together a series of graceful *pensées;* we are talking about something private, about bits of the mind's string too short to use, an indiscriminate and erratic assemblage with meaning only for its maker.

And sometimes even the maker has difficulty with the meaning. There does not seem to be, for example, any point in my knowing for the rest of my life that, during 1964, 720 tons of soot fell on every square mile of New York City, yet there it is in my notebook, labeled "FACT." Nor do I really need to remember that Ambrose Bierce liked to spell Leland Stanford's name "£eland $tanford" or that "smart women almost always wear black in Cuba," a fashion hint without much potential for practical application. And does not the relevance of these notes seem marginal at best?:

In the basement museum of the Inyo County Courthouse in Independence, California, sign pinned to a mandarin coat: "This MANDARIN COAT was often worn by Mrs. Minnie S. Brooks when giving lectures on her TEAPOT COLLECTION."

Redhead getting out of car in front of Beverly Wilshire Hotel, chinchilla stole, Vuitton bags with tags reading:

MRS. LOU FOX

HOTEL SAHARA

VEGAS

Well, perhaps not entirely marginal. As a matter of fact, Mrs. Minnie S. Brooks and her MANDARIN COAT pull me back into my own childhood, for although I never knew Mrs. Brooks and did not visit Inyo County until I was thirty, I grew up in just such a world, in houses cluttered with Indian relics and bits of gold ore and ambergris and the souvenirs my Aunt Mercy Farnsworth brought back from the Orient. It is a long way from that world to Mrs. Lou Fox's world, where we all live now, and is it not just as well to remember that? Might not Mrs. Minnie S. Brooks help me to remember what I am? Might not Mrs. Lou Fox help me to remember what I am not?

But sometimes the point is harder to discern. What exactly did I have in mind when I noted down that it cost the father of someone I know $650 a month to light the place on the Hudson in which he lived before the Crash? What use was I planning to make of this line by Jimmy Hoffa: "I may have my faults, but being wrong ain't one of them"? And although I think it interesting to know where the girls who travel with the Syndicate have their hair done when they find themselves on the West Coast, will I ever make suitable use of it? Might I not be better off just passing it on to John O'Hara? What is a recipe for sauerkraut doing in my notebook? What kind of magpie keeps this notebook? *"He was born the night the Titanic went down."* That seems a nice enough line, and I even recall who said it, but is it not really a better line in life than it could ever be in fiction?

But of course that is exactly it: not that I should ever use the line, but that I should remember the woman who said it and the afternoon I heard it. We were on her terrace by the sea, and we were finishing the wine left from lunch, trying to get what sun there was, a California winter sun. The woman whose husband was born the night the *Titanic* went down wanted to rent her house, wanted to go back to her children in Paris. I remember wishing that I could afford the house, which cost $1,000 a month. "Someday you will," she said lazily. "Someday it all comes." There in the sun on her terrace it seemed easy to believe in someday, but later I had a low-grade afternoon hangover and ran over a black snake on the way to the supermarket and was flooded with inexplicable fear when I heard the checkout clerk explaining to the man ahead of me why she was finally divorcing her husband. "He left me no choice," she said over and over as she punched the register. "He has a little seven-month-old baby by her, he left me no choice." I would like to believe that my dread then was for the human condition, but of course it was for me, because I wanted a baby and did not then have one and because I wanted to own a house that cost $1,000 a month to rent and because I had a hangover.

It all comes back. Perhaps it is difficult to see the value in having one's self back in that kind of mood, but I do see it; I think we are well advised to keep on nodding terms with the people we used to be, whether we find them attractive company or not. Otherwise they turn up unannounced and surprise us, come hammering on the mind's door at 4 a.m. of a bad night and demand to know who deserted them, who betrayed them, who is going to make amends. We forget all too soon the things we thought we could never forget. We forget the loves and the betrayals alike, forget what we whispered and what we screamed, forget who we were. I have already lost touch with a couple of people I used to be; one of them, a seventeen-year-old, presents little threat, although it would be of some interest to me to know again what it feels like to sit on a river levee drinking vodka-and-orange-juice and listening to Les Paul and Mary Ford and their echoes sing "How High the Moon" on the car radio. (You see I still have the scenes, but I no longer perceive myself among those present, no longer could even improvise the dialogue.) The other one, a twenty-three-year-old, bothers me more. She was always a good deal of trouble, and I suspect she will reappear when I least want to see her, skirts too long, shy to the point of aggravation, always the injured party, full of recriminations and little hurts and stories I do not want to hear again, at once saddening me and angering me with her vulnerability and ignorance, an apparition all the more insistent for being so long banished.

It is a good idea, then, to keep in touch, and I suppose that keeping in touch is what notebooks are all about. And we are all on our own when it comes to keeping those lines open to ourselves: your notebook will never help me, nor mine you. *"So what's new in the whiskey business?"* What could that possibly mean to you? To me it means a blonde in a Pucci bathing suit sitting with a couple of fat men by the pool at the Beverly Hills Hotel. Another man approaches, and they all regard one another in silence for a while. "So what's new in the whiskey business?" one of the fat men finally says by way of welcome, and the blonde stands up, arches one foot and dips it in the pool, looking all the while at the cabaña where Baby Pignatari is talking on the telephone. That is all there is to that, except that several years later I saw the blonde coming out of Saks Fifth Avenue in New York with her California complexion and a voluminous mink coat. In the harsh wind that day she looked old and irrevocably tired to me, and even the skins in the mink coat were not worked the way they were doing them that year, not the way she would have wanted them done, and there is the point of the story. For a while after that I did not like to look in the mirror, and my eyes would skim the newspapers and pick out only the deaths, the cancer victims, the premature coronaries, the suicides, and I stopped riding the Lexington Avenue IRT because I noticed for the first time that all the strangers I had seen for years — the man with the Seeing Eye dog, the spinster who read the classified pages every day, the fat girl who always got off with me at Grand Central — looked older than they once had.

It all comes back. Even that recipe for sauerkraut: even that brings it back. I was on Fire Island when I first made that sauerkraut, and it was raining, and we drank a lot of bourbon and ate the sauerkraut and went to bed at ten, and I listened to the rain and the Atlantic and felt safe. I made the sauerkraut again last night and it did not make me feel any safer, but that is, as they say, another story.

QUESTIONS

1. In the fourth paragraph, beginning "Why did I write it down?" (page 593), Didion says that "it is easy to deceive oneself" about the reasons for keeping a notebook. What self-deceptive reasons does she go on to give? What others can be added? And exactly why *does* she keep a notebook? (Didion in her last three paragraphs — and especially in the first two of these — makes explicit her reasons, but try to state her reasons in a paragraph of your own.)

2. In the paragraph beginning *"How it felt to me"* (page 594), Didion refers to a lesson she might have learned from F. Scott Fitzgerald and goes on to say, "but perhaps we all must meet the very rich for ourselves." If you have read a book by Fitzgerald, explain (in a paragraph) the point to someone who doesn't get it.

3. In the paragraph beginning "Well, perhaps not entirely marginal" (page 596), Didion says, "It is a long way from that world to Mrs. Lou Fox's world, where we all live now." What does she mean?

4. If you keep a notebook (or diary or journal), explain in one to three paragraphs why you keep it. Following Didion's example, use one entry or two to illustrate the notebook's usefulness to you. If you don't keep a notebook, explain in one to three paragraphs why you don't, and explain what effect, if any, Didion's essay had on you. Do you now think it would be a good idea to keep a notebook? Or did the essay reenforce your belief that there's nothing useful in it for you? Explain.

A Few Words about Breasts:
Shaping Up Absurd

Nora Ephron

I have to begin with a few words about androgyny. In grammar school, in the fifth and sixth grades, we were all tyrannized by a rigid set of rules that supposedly determined whether we were boys or girls. The episode in *Huckleberry Finn* where Huck is disguised as a girl and gives himself away by the way he threads a needle and catches a ball — that kind of thing. We learned that the way you sat, crossed your legs, held a cigarette and looked at your nails, your wristwatch, the way you did these things instinctively was absolute proof of your sex. Now obviously most children did not take this literally, but I did. I thought that just one slip, just one incorrect cross of my legs or flick of an imaginary cigarette ash would turn me from whatever I was into the other thing; that would be all it took, really. Even though I was outwardly a girl and had many of the trappings generally associated with the field of girldom

— a girl's name, for example, and dresses, my own telephone, an autograph book — I spent the early years of my adolescence absolutely certain that I might at any point gum it up. I did not feel at all like a girl. I was boyish. I was athletic, ambitious, outspoken, competitive, noisy, rambunctious. I had scabs on my knees and my socks slid into my loafers and I could throw a football. I wanted desperately not to be that way, not to be a mixture of both things but instead just one, a girl, a definite indisputable girl. As soft and as pink as a nursery. And nothing would do that for me, I felt, but breasts.

I was about six months younger than everyone in my class, and so for about six months after it began, for six months after my friends had begun to develop — that was the word we used, develop — I was not particularly worried. I would sit in the bathtub and look down at my breasts and know that any day now, any second now, they would start growing like everyone else's. They didn't. "I want to buy a bra," I said to my mother one night. "What for?" she said. My mother was really hateful about bras, and by the time my third sister had gotten to that point where she was ready to want one, my mother had worked the whole business into a comedy routine. "Why not use a Band-Aid instead?" she would say. It was a source of great pride to my mother that she had never even had to wear a brassiere until she had her fourth child, and then only because her gynecologist made her. It was incomprehensible to me that anyone would ever be proud of something like that. It was the 1950's, for God's sake. Jane Russell. Cashmere sweaters. Couldn't my mother see that? *"I am too old to wear an undershirt."* Screaming. Weeping. Shouting. "Then don't wear an undershirt," said my mother. "But I want to buy a bra." "What for?"

I suppose that for most girls, breasts, brassieres, that entire thing, has more trauma, more to do with the coming of adolescence, of becoming a woman, than anything else. Certainly more than getting your period, although that too was traumatic, symbolic. But you could *see* breasts; they were there; they were visible. Whereas a girl could claim to have her period for months before she actually got it and nobody would ever know the difference. Which is exactly what I did. All you had to do was make a great fuss over having enough nickels for the Kotex machine and walk around clutching your stomach and moaning for three to five days a month about The Curse and you could convince anybody. There is a school of thought somewhere in the women's lib/women's mag/ gynecology establishment that claims that menstrual cramps are purely psychological, and I lean toward it. Not that I didn't have them finally. Agonizing cramps, heating-pad cramps, go-down-to-the-school-nurse-and-lie-on-the-cot cramps. But unlike any pain I had ever suffered, I adored the pain of cramps, welcomed it, wallowed in it, bragged about it. "I can't go. I have cramps." "I can't do that. I have cramps." And most of all, gigglingly, blushingly: "I can't swim. I have cramps." Nobody ever used the hard-core word. Menstruation. God, what an awful word. Never that. "I have cramps."

The morning I first got my period, I went into my mother's bedroom to tell her. And my mother, my utterly-hateful-about-bras mother, burst into tears. It was really a lovely moment, and I remember it so clearly not just because it was one of the two times I ever saw my mother cry on my account (the other was when I was caught being a six-year-old kleptomaniac), but also because the incident did not mean to me what it meant to her. Her little girl, her firstborn, had finally become a woman. That was what she was crying about. My reaction to the event, however, was that I might well be a woman in some scientific, textbook sense (and could at least stop faking every month and stop wasting all those nickels). But in another sense — in a visible sense — I was as androgynous and as liable to tip over into boyhood as ever.

I started with a 28AA bra. I don't think they made them any smaller in those days, although I gather that now you can buy bras for five year olds that don't have any cups whatsoever in them; trainer bras they are called. My first brassiere came from Robinson's Department Store in Beverly Hills. I went there alone, shaking, positive they would look me over and smile and tell me to come back next year. An actual fitter took me into the dressing room and stood over me while I took off my blouse and tried the first one on. The little puffs stood out on my chest. "Lean over," said the fitter (to this day I am not sure what fitters in bra departments do except to tell you to lean over). I leaned over, with the fleeting hope that my breasts would miraculously fall out of my body and into the puffs. Nothing.

"Don't worry about it," said my friend Libby some months later, when things had not improved. "You'll get them after you're married."

"What are you talking about?" I said.

"When you get married," Libby explained, "your husband will touch your breasts and rub them and kiss them and they'll grow."

That was the killer. Necking I could deal with. Intercourse I could deal with. But it had never crossed my mind that a man was going to touch my breasts, that breasts had something to do with all that, petting, my God they never mentioned petting in my little sex manual about the fertilization of the ovum. I became dizzy. For I knew instantly — as naïve as I had been only a moment before — that only part of what she was saying was true: the touching, rubbing, kissing part, not the growing part. And I knew that no one would ever want to marry me. I had no breasts. I would never have breasts.

My best friend in school was Diana Raskob. She lived a block from me in a house full of wonders. English muffins, for instance. The Raskobs were the first people in Beverly Hills to have English muffins for breakfast. They also had an apricot tree in the back, and a badminton court, and a subscription to *Seventeen* magazine, and hundreds of games like Sorry and Parcheesi and Treasure Hunt and Anagrams. Diana and I spent three or four afternoons a week in their den reading and playing and eating. Diana's mother's kitchen was full of the most colossal assortment of junk food I have ever been exposed to. My house was full of apples and peaches and milk and homemade chocolate-chip cookies — which were nice, and good for you, but-not-right-before-dinner-or-you'll-spoil-your-appetite. Diana's house had nothing in it that was good for you, and what's more, you could stuff it in right up until dinner and nobody cared. Bar-B-Q potato chips (they were the first in them, too), giant bottles of ginger ale, fresh popcorn with melted butter, hot fudge sauce on Baskin-Robbins jamoca ice cream, powdered-sugar doughnuts from Van de Kamps. Diana and I had been best friends since we were seven; we were about equally popular in school (which is to say, not particularly), we had about the same success with boys (extremely intermittent) and we looked much the same. Dark. Tall. Gangly.

It is September, just before school begins. I am eleven years old, about to enter the seventh grade, and Diana and I have not seen each other all summer. I have been to camp and she has been somewhere like Banff with her parents. We are meeting, as we often do, on the street midway between our two houses and we will walk back to Diana's and eat junk and talk about what has happened to each of us that summer. I am walking down Walden Drive in my jeans and my father's shirt hanging out and my old red loafers with the socks falling into them and coming toward me is . . . I take a deep breath . . . a young woman. Diana. Her hair is curled and she has a waist and hips and a bust and she is wearing a straight skirt, an article of clothing I have been repeatedly told I will be unable to wear until I have the hips to hold it up. My jaw drops, and suddenly I am crying, crying hysterically, can't catch my breath sobbing. My best friend has betrayed me. She has gone ahead without me and done it. She has shaped up.

Here are some things I did to help:
Bought a Mark Eden Bust Developer.
Slept on my back for four years.
Splashed cold water on them every night because some French actress said in *Life* magazine that that was what *she* did for her perfect bustline.

Ultimately, I resigned myself to a bad toss and began to wear padded bras. I think about them now, think about all those years in high school I went around in them, my three padded bras, every single one of them with different sized breasts. Each time I changed bras I changed sizes: one week nice perky but not too obtrusive breasts, the next medium-sized slightly pointed ones, the next week knockers, true knockers; all the time, whatever size I was, carrying around this rubberized appendage on my chest that occasionally crashed into a wall and was poked inward and had to be poked outward — I think about all that and wonder how anyone kept a straight face through it. My parents, who normally had no restraints about needling me — why did they say nothing as they watched my chest go up and down? My friends, who would periodically inspect my breasts for signs of growth and reassure me — why didn't they at least counsel consistency?

And the bathing suits. I die when I think about the bathing suits. That was the era when you could lay an uninhabited bathing suit on the beach and someone would make a pass at it. I would put one on, an absurd swimsuit with its enormous bust built into it, the bones from the suit stabbing me in the rib cage and leaving little red welts on my body, and there I would be, my chest plunging straight downward absolutely vertically from my collarbone to the top of my suit and then suddenly, wham, out came all that padding and material and wiring absolutely horizontally.

Buster Klepper was the first boy who ever touched them. He was my boyfriend my senior year of high school. There is a picture of him in my high-school yearbook that makes him look quite attractive in a Jewish, horn-rimmed glasses sort of way, but the picture does not show the pimples, which were air-brushed out, or the dumbness. Well, that isn't really fair. He wasn't dumb. He just wasn't terribly bright. His mother refused to accept it, refused to accept the relentlessly average report cards, refused to deal with her son's inevitable destiny in some junior college or other. "He was tested," she would say to me, apropos of nothing, "and it came out 145. That's near-genius." Had the word underachiever been coined, she probably would have lobbed that one at me, too. Anyway, Buster was really very sweet — which is, I know, damning with faint praise, but there it is. I was the editor of the front page of the high-school newspaper and he was editor of the back page; we had to work together, side by side, in the print shop, and that was how it started. On our first date, we went to see *April Love* starring Pat Boone. Then we started going together. Buster had a green coupe, a 1950 Ford with an engine he had handchromed until it shone, dazzled, reflected the image of anyone who looked into it, anyone usually being Buster polishing it or the gas-station attendants he constantly asked to check the oil in order for them to be over-whelmed by the sparkle on the valves. The car also had a boot stretched over the back seat for reasons I never understood; hanging from the rearview mirror, as was the custom, was a pair of angora dice. A previous girl friend named Solange who was famous throughout Beverly Hills High School for having no pigment in her right eyebrow had knitted them for him. Buster and I would ride around town, the two of us seated to the left of the steering wheel. I would shift gears. It was nice.

There was necking. Terrific necking. First in the car, overlooking Los Angeles from what is now the Trousdale Estates. Then on the bed of his parents' cabana at Ocean House. Incredibly wonder-ful, frustrating necking, I loved it, really, but no further than neck-ing, please don't, please, because there I was absolutely terrified of the general implications of going-a-step-further with a near-dummy and also terrified of his finding out there was next to nothing there (which he knew, of course; he wasn't that dumb).

I broke up with him at one point. I think we were apart for about two weeks. At the end of that time I drove down to see a friend at a boarding school in Palos Verdes Estates and a disc jockey played *April Love* on the radio four times during the trip. I took it as a sign. I drove straight back to Griffith Park to a golf tournament Buster was playing in (he was the sixth-seeded teen-age golf player in Southern California) and presented myself back to him on the green of the 18th hole. It was all very dramatic. That night we went to a drive-in and I let him get his hand under my protuberances and onto my breasts. He really didn't seem to mind at all.

"Do you want to marry my son?" the woman asked me.

"Yes," I said.

I was nineteen years old, a virgin, going with this woman's son, this big strange woman who was married to a Lutheran minister in New Hampshire and pretended she was Gentile and had this son, by her first husband, this total fool of a son who ran the hero-sandwich concession at Harvard Business School and whom for one moment one December in New Hampshire I said — as much out of politeness as anything else — that I wanted to marry.

"Fine," she said. "Now, here's what you do. Always make sure you're on top of him so you won't seem so small. My bust is very large, you see, so I always lie on my back to make it look smaller, but you'll have to be on top most of the time."

I nodded. "Thank you," I said.

"I have a book for you to read," she went on. "Take it with you when you leave. Keep it." She went to the bookshelf, found it, and gave it to me. It was a book on frigidity.

"Thank you," I said.

That is a true story. Everything in this article is a true story, but I feel I have to point out that that story in particular is true. It happened on December 30, 1960. I think about it often. When it first happened, I naturally assumed that the woman's son, my boy-friend, was responsible. I invented a scenario where he had had a little heart-to-heart with his mother and had confessed that his only objection to me was that my breasts were small; his mother then took it upon herself to help out. Now I think I was wrong about the incident. The mother was acting on her own, I think: that was her way of being cruel and competitive under the guise of being helpful and maternal. You have small breasts, she was saying; there-fore you will never make him as happy as I have. Or you have small breasts; therefore you will doubtless have sexual problems. Or you have small breasts; therefore you are less woman than I am. She was, as it happens, only the first of what seems to me to be a never-ending string of women who have made competitive remarks to me about breast size. "I would love to wear a dress like that," my friend Emily says to me, "but my bust is too big." Like that. Why do women say these things to me? Do I attract these remarks the way other women attract married men or alcoholics or homosexuals? This summer, for example. I am at a party in East Hampton and I am introduced to a woman from Washington. She is a minor celebrity, very pretty and Southern and blonde and outspoken and I am flattered because she has read something I have written. We are talking animatedly, we have been talking no more than five minutes, when a man comes up to join us. "Look at the two of us," the woman says to the man, indicating me and her. "The two of us together couldn't fill an A cup." Why does she say that? It isn't even true, dammit, so why? Is she even more addled than I am on this subject? Does she honestly believe there is something wrong with her size breasts, which, it seems to me, now that I look hard at them, are just right. Do I unconsciously bring out competitiveness in women? In that form? What did I do to deserve it?

As for men.

There were men who minded and let me know they minded. There were men who did not mind. In any case, I always minded.

And even now, now that I have been countlessly reassured that my figure is a good one, now that I am grown up enough to understand that most of my feelings have very little to do with the reality of my shape, I am nonetheless obsessed by breasts. I cannot help it. I grew up in the terrible Fifties — with rigid stereotypical sex roles, the insistence that men be men and dress like men and women be women and dress like women, the intolerance of androgyny — and I cannot shake it, cannot shake my feelings of inadequacy. Well, that time is gone, right? All those exaggerated examples of breast worship are gone, right? Those women were freaks, right? I know all that. And yet, here I am, stuck with the psychological remains of it all, stuck with my own peculiar version of breast worship. You probably think I am crazy to go on like this: here I have set out to write a confession that is meant to hit you with the shock of recognition and instead you are sitting there thinking I am thoroughly warped. Well, what can I tell you? If I had had them, I would have been a completely different person. I honestly believe that.

After I went into therapy, a process that made it possible for me to tell total strangers at cocktail parties that breasts were the hang-up of my life, I was often told that I was insane to have been bothered by my condition. I was also frequently told, by close friends, that I was extremely boring on the subject. And my girl friends, the ones with nice big breasts, would go on endlessly about how their lives had been far more miserable than mine. Their bra straps were snapped in class. They couldn't sleep on their stomachs.

They were stared at whenever the word "mountain" cropped up in geography. And *Evangeline,* good God what they went through every time someone had to stand up and recite the Prologue to Longfellow's *Evangeline: ". . . stand like druids of eld . . . With beards that rest on their bosoms."* It was much worse for them, they tell me. They had a terrible time of it, they assure me. I don't know how lucky I was, they say.

I have thought about their remarks, tried to put myself in their place, considered their point of view. I think they are full of shit.

QUESTIONS

1. In her first paragraph Ephron says that Huck Finn gives himself away by his manner of threading a needle and catching a ball. In what ways does a boy supposedly differ from a girl in performing these activities? And how do they supposedly differ in the other activities that Ephron mentions in this paragraph?
2. Toward the end of the second paragraph Ephron writes several sentence fragments. How can you justify them?
3. Is the essay offensive? If so, why, and if not, why not?
4. On the basis of this essay characterize Nora Ephron, quoting a few words or phrases to support your characterization.

Very Like a Whale
Robert Finch

One day last week at sunset I went back to Corporation Beach in Dennis to see what traces, if any, might be left of the great, dead finback whale that had washed up there several weeks before. The beach was not as hospitable as it had been that sunny Saturday morning after Thanksgiving when thousands of us streamed over the sand to gaze and look. A few cars were parked in the lot, but these kept their inhabitants. Bundled up against a sharp wind, I set off along the twelve-foot swath of trampled beach grass, a raw highway made in a few hours by ten thousand feet that day.

I came to the spot where the whale had beached and marveled that such a magnitude of flesh could have been there one day and gone the next. But the carcass had been hauled off and the tide had smoothed and licked clean whatever vestiges had remained. The cold, salt wind had lifted from the sands the last trace of that pervasive stench of decay that clung to our clothes for days, and now blew clean and sharp into my nostrils.

The only sign that anything unusual had been there was that the beach was a little too clean, not quite so pebbly and littered as the surrounding areas, as the grass above a new grave is always fresher and greener. What had so manifestly occupied this space a short while ago was now utterly gone. And yet the whale still lay heavily on my mind; a question lingered, like a persistent odor in the air. And its dark shape, though now sunken somewhere beneath the waves, still loomed before me, beckoning, asking something.

What was it? What had we seen? Even the several thousand of us that managed to get down to the beach before it was closed off did not see much. Whales, dead or alive, are protected these days under the Federal Marine Mammals Act, and shortly after we arrived, local police kept anyone from actually touching the whale. I could hardly regret this, since in the past beached whales, still alive, have had cigarettes put out in their eyes and bits of flesh hacked off with pocket knives by souvenir seekers. And so, kept at a distance, we looked on while the specialists worked, white-coated, plastic-gloved autopsists from the New England Aquarium, hacking open the thick hide with carving knives and plumbing its depth for samples to be shipped to Canada for analysis and determination of causes of death. What was it they were pulling out? What fetid mystery would they pluck from that huge coffin of dead flesh? We would have to trust them for the answer.

But as the crowds continued to grow around the whale's body like flies around carrion, the question seemed to me, and still seems, not so much why did the whale die, as why had we come to see it? What made this dark bulk such a human magnet, spilling us over onto private lawns and fields? I watched electricians and oil truck drivers pulling their vehicles off the road and clambering down to the beach. Women in high heels and pearls, on their way to Filene's, stumbled through the loose sand to gaze at a corpse. The normal human pattern was broken and a carnival atmosphere was created, appropriate enough in the literal sense of "a farewell to the flesh." But there was also a sense of pilgrimage in those trekking across the beach, an obligation to view such a thing. But for what? Are we really such novices to death? Or so reverent toward it?

I could understand my own semiprofessional interest in the whale, but what had drawn these hordes? There are some obvious answers, of course: a break in the dull routine, "something different." An old human desire to associate ourselves with great and extraordinary events. We placed children and sweethearts in front of the corpse and clicked cameras. "Ruthie and the whale." "Having a whale of a time on Cape Cod."

Curiosity, the simplest answer, doesn't really answer anything. What, after all, did we learn by being there? We were more like children at a zoo, pointing and poking, or Indians on a pristine beach, gazing in innocent wonder at strange European ships come ashore. Yet, as the biologists looted it with vials and plastic bags and the press captured it on film, the spectators also tried to *make* something of the whale. Circling around it as though for some hold on its slippery bulk, we grappled it with metaphors, lashed similes around its immense girth. It lay upside down, overturned "like a trailer truck." Its black skin was cracked and peeling, red underneath, "like a used tire." The distended, corrugated lower jaw, "a giant accordion," was afloat with the gas of putrefaction and, when pushed, oscillated slowly "like an enormous waterbed." Like our primitive ancestors, we still tend to make images to try to comprehend the unknown.

But what were we looking at? Or more to the point, from what perspective were we looking at it? What did we see in it that might tell us why we had come? A male finback whale — *Balaenoptera physalus* — a baleen cetacean. The second largest creature ever to live on earth. An intelligent and complex mammal. A cause for conservationists. A remarkably adapted swimming and eating machine. Perfume, pet food, engineering oil. A magnificent scientific specimen. A tourist attraction. A media event, a "day to remember." A health menace, a "possible carrier of a communicable disease." A municipal headache and a navigational hazard. Material for an essay.

On the whale's own hide seemed to be written its life history, which we could remark but not read. The right fluke was almost entirely gone, lost in some distant accident or battle and now healed over with a white scar. The red eye, unexpectedly small and mammalian, gazed out at us with fiery blankness. Like the glacial scratches sometimes found on our boulders, there were strange marks or grooves in the skin around the anal area, perhaps caused by scraping the ocean bottom.

Yet we could not seem to scratch its surface. The whale — dead, immobile, in full view — nonetheless shifted kaleidoscopically before our eyes. The following morning it was gone, efficiently and sanitarily removed, like the week's garbage. What was it we saw?

I have a theory, though probably (as they say in New England) it hardly does.

There is a tendency these days to defend whales and other endangered animals by pointing out their similarities to human beings. Cetaceans, we are told, are very intelligent. They possess a highly complex language and have developed sophisticated communications systems that transmit over long distances. They form family groups, develop social structures and personal relationships, and express loyalty and affection toward one another. Much of their behavior seems to be recreational: they sing, they play. And so on.

These are not sentimental claims. Whales apparently do these things, at least as far as our sketchy information about their habits warrants such interpretations. And for my money, any argument that helps to preserve these magnificent creatures can't be all bad.

I take exception to this approach not because it is wrong, but because it is wrongheaded and misleading. It is exclusive, anthropocentric, and does not recognize nature in its own right. It implies that whales and other creatures have value only insofar as they reflect man himself and conform to his ideas of beauty and achievement. This attitude is not really far removed from that of the whalers themselves. To consume whales solely for their nourishment of human values is only a step from consuming them for meat and corset staves. It is not only presumptuous and patronizing, but it is misleading and does both whales and men a grave disservice. Whales have an inalienable right to exist, not because they resemble man *or* because they are useful to him, but simply because they do exist, because they have a proven fitness to the exactitudes of being on a global scale matched by few other species. If they deserve our admiration and respect, it is because, as Henry Beston put it, "They are other nations, caught with ourselves in the net of life and time, fellow prisoners of the splendour and travail of life."

But that still doesn't explain the throngs who came pell-mell to stare and conjecture at the dead whale that washed up at Corporation Beach and dominated it for a day like some extravagant *memento mori.*[1] Surely we were not flattering ourselves, consciously or unconsciously, with any human comparisons to that rotting hulk. Nor was there much, in its degenerate state, that it had to teach us. And yet we came — why?

---

[1] Editors' note: These Latin words mean "Remember that you must die"; hence a *memento mori* is a reminder of death.

The answer may be so obvious that we have ceased to recognize it. Man, I believe, has a crying need to confront otherness in the universe. Call it nature, wilderness, the "great outdoors," or what you will — we crave to look out and behold something other than our own human faces staring back at us, expectantly and increasingly frustrated. What the human spirit wants, as Robert Frost said, "Is not its own love back in copy-speech, / But counter-love, original response."

This sense of otherness is, I feel, as necessary a requirement to our personalities as food and warmth are to our bodies. Just as an individual, cut off from human contact and stimulation, may atrophy and die of loneliness and neglect, so mankind is today in a similar, though more subtle, danger of cutting himself off from the natural world he shares with all creatures. If our physical survival depends upon our devising a proper use of earth's materials and produce, our growth as a species depends equally upon our establishing a vital and generative relationship with what surrounds us.

We need plants, animals, weather, unfettered shores and unbroken woodland, not merely for a stable and healty environment, but as an antidote to introversion, a preventive against human inbreeding. Here in particular, in the splendor of natural life, we have an extraordinary reservoir of the Cape's untapped possibilities and modes of being, ways of experiencing life, of knowing wind and wave. After all, how many neighborhoods have whales wash up in their backyards? To confine this world in zoos or in exclusive human terms does injustice not only to nature, but to ourselves as well.

Ever since his beginnings, when primitive man adopted totems and animal spirits to himself and assumed their shapes in ritual dance, *Homo sapiens* has been a superbly imitative animal. He has looked out across the fields and seen and learned. Somewhere along the line, though, he decided that nature was his enemy, not his ally, and needed to be confined and controlled. He abstracted nature and lost sight of it. Only now are we slowly realizing that nature can be confined only by narrowing our own concepts of it, which in turn narrows us. That is why we came to see the whale.

We substitute human myth for natural reality and wonder why we starve for nourishment. "Your Cape" becomes "your Mall," as the local radio jingle has it. Thoreau's "huge and real Cape Cod . . . a wild, rank place with no flattery in it," becomes the Chamber of Commerce's "Rural Seaside Charm" — until forty tons of dead flesh wash ashore and give the lie to such thin, flattering conceptions, flesh whose stench is still the stench of life that stirs us to reaction and response. That is why we came to see the whale. Its mute, immobile bulk represented that ultimate, unknowable otherness that we both seek and recoil from, and shouted at us louder than the policeman's bullhorn that the universe is fraught, not merely with response or indifference, but incarnate assertion.

Later that day the Dennis Board of Health declared the whale carcass to be a "health menace" and warned us off the beach. A health menace? More likely an intoxicating, if strong, medicine that might literally bring us to our senses.

But if those of us in the crowd failed to grasp the whale that day, others did not have much better luck. Even in death the whale escaped us: the tissue samples taken in the autopsy proved insufficient for analysis and the biologists concluded, "We will never know why the whale died." The carcass, being towed tail-first by a Coast Guard cutter for a final dumping beyond Provincetown, snapped a six-inch hawser. Eluding further attempts to reattach it, it finally sank from sight. Even our powers of disposal, it seemed, were questioned that day.

And so, while we are left on shore with the memory of a deflated and stinking carcass and of bullhorns that blared and scattered us like flies, somewhere out beyond the rolled waters and the shining winter sun, the whale sings its own death in matchless, sirenian strains.

QUESTIONS

1. In a sentence or two or three state Finch's thesis. By the way, where in the essay does Finch come closest to stating his thesis explicitly? Should he have stated it earlier?

2. Finch (page 610) says that whales "have a proven fitness for the exactitudes of being on a global scale matched by few other species." Exactly what does this mean, and is it true? Offhand, can you name several other species that fit this description?

3. Finch often uses similes and metaphors. Some of these are so common that they are relatively inconspicuous (in the first paragraph people "streamed over the sand"), but many are fresh. For instance, in the second paragraph, "the tide had . . . licked clean whatever vestiges remained"; in the third paragraph, "a question lingered, like a persistent odor in the air"; in the fifth paragraph, "the crowds continued to grow around the whale's body like flies around carrion," the carcass is a "magnet," and there is both a "carnival atmosphere" and "a sense of

pilgrimage." In fact, two paragraphs later in the essay he says of the spectators looking at the whale, "We grappled it with metaphors." Take two or three figures, and in a paragraph evaluate them. Are they strained? Effective? Why? (You may want to take one figure that you consider effective and contrast it with another that you consider ineffective.)

4. Restate in your own words what Finch means (page 611) when he says that "nature can be confined only by narrowing our own concepts of it, which in turn narrows us."

5. How necessary are the last two paragraphs of the essay? Explain.

A Proposal to Abolish Grading
Paul Goodman

Monday

Let half a dozen of the prestigious Universities — Chicago, Stanford, the Ivy League — abolish grading, and use testing only and entirely for pedagogic purposes as teachers see fit.

Anyone who knows the frantic temper of the present schools will understand the transvaluation of values that would be effected by this modest innovation. For most of the students, the competitive grade has come to be the essence. The naïve teacher points to the beauty of the subject and the ingenuity of the research; the shrewd student asks if he is responsible for that on the final exam.

Let me at once dispose of an objection whose unanimity is quite fascinating. I think that the great majority of professors agree that grading hinders teaching and creates a bad spirit, going as far as cheating and plagiarizing. I have before me the collection of essays, *Examining in Harvard College,* and this is the consensus. It is uniformly asserted, however, that the grading is inevitable; for how else will the graduate schools, the foundations, the corporations *know* whom to accept, reward, hire? How will the talent scouts know whom to tap?

By testing the applicants, of course, according to the specific task-requirements of the inducting institution, just as applicants for the Civil Service or for licenses in medicine, law, and architecture are tested. Why should Harvard professors do the testing *for* corporations and graduate-schools?

The objection is ludicrous. Dean Whitla, of the Harvard Office of Tests, points out that the scholastic-aptitude and achievement tests used for *admission* to Harvard are a super-excellent index for all-around Harvard performance, better than high-school grades or particular Harvard course-grades. Presumably, these college-entrance tests are tailored for what Harvard and similar institutions want. By the same logic, would not an employer do far better to apply his own job-aptitude test rather than to rely on the vagaries of Harvard section-men? Indeed, I doubt that many employers bother to look at such grades; they are more likely to be interested merely in the fact of a Harvard diploma, whatever that connotes to them. The grades have most of their weight with the graduate schools — here, as elsewhere, the system runs mainly for its own sake.

It is really necessary to remind our academics of the ancient history of Examination. In the medieval university, the whole point of the grueling trial of the candidate was whether or not to accept him as a peer. His disputation and lecture for the Master's was just that, a master-piece to enter the guild. It was not to make comparative evaluations. It was not to weed out and select for an extramural licensor or employer. It was certainly not to pit one young fellow against another in an ugly competition. My philosophic impression is that the medievals thought they knew what a good job of work was and that we are competitive because we do not know. But the more status is achieved by largely irrelevant competitive evaluation, the less will we ever know.

(Of course, our American examinations never did have this purely guild orientation, just as our faculties have rarely had absolute autonomy; the examining was to satisfy Overseers, Elders, distant Regents — and they as paternal superiors have always doted on giving grades, rather than accepting peers. But I submit that this set-up itself makes it impossible for the student to *become* a master, to *have* grown up, and to commence on his own. He will always be making A or B for some overseer. And in the present atmosphere, he will always be climbing on his friend's neck.)

Perhaps the chief objectors to abolishing grading would be the students and their parents. The parents should be simply disregarded; their anxiety has done enough damage already. For the students, it seems to me that a primary duty of the university is to deprive them of their props, their dependence on extrinsic valuation and motivation, and to force them to confront the difficult enterprise itself and finally lose themselves in it.

A miserable effect of grading is to nullify the various uses of testing. Testing, for both student and teacher, is a means of structuring, and also of finding out what is blank or wrong and what has been assimilated and can be taken for granted. Review — including high-pressure review — is a means of bringing together the fragments, so that there are flashes of synoptic insight.

There are several good reasons for testing, and kinds of test. But if the aim is to discover weakness, what is the point of downgrading and punishing it, and thereby inviting the student to conceal his weakness, by faking and bulling, if not cheating? The natural conclusion of synthesis is the insight itself, not a grade for having had it. For the important purpose of placement, if one can establish in the student the belief that one is testing *not* to grade and make invidious comparisons but for his own advantage, the student should normally seek his own level, where he is challenged and yet capable, rather than trying to get by. If the student dares to accept himself as he is, a teacher's grade is a crude instrument compared with a student's self-awareness. But it is rare in our universities that students are encouraged to notice objectively their vast confusion. Unlike Socrates, our teachers rely on power-drives rather than shame and ingenuous idealism.

Many students are lazy, so teachers try to goad or threaten them by grading. In the long run this must do more harm than good. Laziness is a character-defense. It may be a way of avoiding learning, in order to protect the conceit that one is already perfect (deeper, the despair that one *never* can). It may be a way of avoiding just the risk of failing and being down-graded. Sometimes it is a way of politely saying, "I won't." But since it is the authoritarian grown-up demands that have created such attitudes in the first place, why repeat the trauma? There comes a time when we must treat people as adult, laziness and all. It is one thing courageously to fire a do-nothing out of your class; it is quite another thing to evaluate him with a lordly F.

Most important of all, it is often obvious that balking in doing the work, especially among bright young people who get to great universities, means exactly what it says: The work does not suit me, not this subject, or not at this time, or not in this school, or not in school altogether. The student might not be bookish; he might be school-tired; perhaps his development ought now to take another direction. Yet unfortunately, if such a student is intelligent and is not sure of himself, he *can* be bullied into passing, and this obscures everything. My hunch is that I am describing a common situation. What a grim waste of young life and teacherly effort! Such a student will retain nothing of what he has "passed" in. Sometimes he must get mononucleosis to tell his story and be believed.

And ironically, the converse is also probably commonly true. A student flunks and is mechanically weeded out, who is really ready and eager to learn in a scholastic setting, but he has not quite caught on. A good teacher can recognize the situation, but the computer wreaks its will.

QUESTIONS

1. In his opening paragraph Goodman limits his suggestion about grading and testing to "half a dozen of the prestigious Universities." Does he offer any reason for this limitation? Can you?

2. In the third paragraph Goodman says that "the great majority of professors agree that grading hinders teaching." What evidence does he offer to support this claim? What arguments might be offered that grading assists teaching? Should Goodman have offered them?

3. Have grades helped you to learn or hindered you? Explain.

Soaps, Cynicism, and Mind Control: Randomness in Everyday Life

Elizabeth Janeway

What does the powerful teaching tool of television have to say to its viewers about desirable attitudes toward life and its problems? And what does the Media Establishment assume that *we* assume about the way this world functions? With these questions, I approached soap operas and evening series — programs that claimed to present ordinary existence, though heightened for drama and catering to everyone's curiosity about how the other half lives.

In between commercial breaks, I noted a deeply disturbing factor in so many of the dramas: the lack of any sense of process, of the eternal truth that events have consequences, and that people can and do influence what happens to them and to others. What I saw instead was a consistent, insistent demonstration of *randomness,* a statement that life is unpredictable and out of control. With rare exceptions what happens on-screen suggests that no one can trust her or his own judgment and (other side of the same coin) that no one, friend, kin, or lover, is really trustworthy.

We may identify with the actors because we all face unpredictable events, but we get no clues to coping with them. No one seems talented at solving the puzzles of life: even J. R. Ewing was shot. Nobody shows us how to decide on the fidelity of kin or associates, no love is certain. Let a wedding date be set and you can be pretty sure the ceremony won't come off. Report a death and expect the corpse to show up in a future segment fleeing crime, amnesiac, or as survivor of a "fatal" plane crash. Says one of a pair of embracing lovers, "I don't know anything about you." Par for the course. Later in the same segment (of *Another World*) a young woman tells a young man she doesn't love him. But wait a minute! She has been hypnotized, it seems, in a program I missed, and here she is on tape declaring she *does* love him to the hypnotist. Not only don't we/ they know anything about the others in their lives, they/we don't understand ourselves either. The Guiding Lights we seek are shrouded in fog.

Now drama, and indeed fiction as a whole, has always aimed at surprising its audiences. But those surprises end by showing us something we hadn't known, some truth, about existence. It may be a tragic truth, but tragedy can strengthen us to face the future because it explains and illustrates the processes that lead to defeat instead of victory. And knowledge is power. Even when it tells us some things can't be changed, it differentiates inevitability for potentiality; and moreover, it gives us a chance to plan our own responses: we can't change the weather, but we can take an umbrella when we go out. Our intervention in ongoing existence is shown to be possible. Beginning with childhood fables and fairy tales, such stories bring us useful messages about the workings of the real world and what human beings can do to influence it.

That's not what the TV programs say. The people on the screen are adrift in a world of happenstance, and the messages warn that no action will do any good.

Certainly there's a lot of randomness in the world. Stable unchanging small-town life is fading from the American scene and close ties to extended families are rare. Most of us meet a lot of strangers from unfamiliar backgrounds. Women who have moved into formerly all-male preserves have had to learn or invent patterns of relationships as well as new processes of doing things. These women have begun to take risks and forget old lessons in helplessness. But daily there appears on the screen counsel that the world is unpredictable, that one can't hope to plan or gain control of events. Moreover when we see the rare realistic portrayal of work-life (where competence, daring, and imagination may be rewarded), attention is concentrated on the personal. Intimate relationships are chancy and dangerous, comes the word, but they're the only things that matter.

Randomness, like guilt, is a powerful tool for social control. Survivors of the Holocaust and refugees from Stalin's "Gulag Archipelago" record how personality was deliberately broken down by those in control disrupting their prisoners' normal expectations. Guards separated consequences from action and thus persuaded prisoners that it was hopeless for them to plan a particular behavior, hopeless for them to imagine a future. Survival became a matter of utter chance. Inmates of the camps were thus reduced to subhuman, mindless robots who moved as they were told to.

Today in El Salvador (and who can say how many other places?), terror activates the randomness of danger. No one knows where the death squads will strike next, and therefore people can't take any reasonable action and expect to ensure greater safety. If safety exists at all, it lies in passivity and hiding. *Time* magazine quotes an expert on Central America in a recent issue: "Anybody can be killed with virtual impunity. You do not want to investigate because you might find out, and finding out can itself be fatal."

But it's not only in extreme situations that randomness can be used to promote self-policing. If the powerful can divide the majority of ordinary folk into disconnected, self-protecting individuals, they need not fear organized resistance. And when television suggests to a woman that even her friends had better not be trusted, it is denying comradeship, sisterhood—and joint action.

I don't suggest that this is a conscious media conspiracy intended to keep women and other groups in their subordinate places. *It doesn't need to be.* Standard practice and the mythic ideology that enforces it have always played up individual effort as a way of establishing one's value and one's deserts. For instance, the Supreme

Court has underlined that message by limiting affirmative action remedies that can be awarded to a group or class. Legal recourse must now be sought by *individuals* rather than on a group basis. When the media repeats this message, it need only appeal to what we've often heard before: success means learning the rules and following them. Don't trust your colleagues. The big world of action is both dangerous and mysterious, you'll never really understand it. Stay out of it, sit still, don't try.

Will we follow that message more than two generations after women won the ballot? . . . Let us refuse the posture of the powerless. People who have begun to feel strong don't have to accept victimization.

QUESTIONS

1. In her second paragraph Janeway asserts that soap operas generally depict a world of randomness. Let's assume that you agree. Write a new third paragraph, in which you support this assertion by offering concrete examples drawn from a soap opera with which you are familiar. Or, if you disagree, write a paragraph in which you offer evidence to show that a particular program does not support Janeway's argument.

2. On page 617, in the paragraph beginning "Now drama, and indeed fiction as a whole," Janeway moves from soaps to "fiction as a whole." Why does she seem to desert her topic?

3. Formulate a thesis-sentence for Janeway's essay.

4. In the course of commenting on soaps, Janeway states or implies certain assumptions about real life. List these assumptions. Are they irrelevant to a discussion of soap operas? Explain.

5. This essay first appeared in *Ms* magazine. Where in the essay does Janeway appear to address the special interests of *Ms* readers? Does the essay as a whole seem to exclude a wider audience?

Who Killed King Kong?

X. J. Kennedy

The ordeal and spectacular death of King Kong, the giant ape, undoubtedly have been witnessed by more Americans than have ever seen a performance of *Hamlet, Iphigenia at Aulis,* or even *Tobacco Road.* Since RKO-Radio Pictures first released *King Kong,* a quarter-century has gone by; yet year after year, from prints that grow more rain-beaten, from sound tracks that grow more tinny, ticket-buyers by thousands still pursue Kong's luckless fight against the forces of technology, tabloid journalism, and the DAR. They see him chloroformed to sleep, see him whisked from his jungle isle to New York and placed on show, see him burst his chains to roam the city (lugging a frightened blonde), at last to plunge from the spire of the Empire State Building, machine-gunned by model airplanes.

Though Kong may die, one begins to think his legend unkillable. No clearer proof of his hold upon the popular imagination may be seen than what emerged one catastrophic week in March 1955, when New York WOR-TV programmed *Kong* for seven evenings in a row (a total of sixteen showings). Many a rival network vice-president must have scowled when surveys showed that *Kong* — the 1933 B-picture — had lured away fat segments of the viewing populace from such powerful competitors as Ed Sullivan, Groucho Marx and Bishop Sheen.

But even television has failed to run *King Kong* into oblivion. Coffee-in-the-lobby cinemas still show the old hunk of hokum, with the apology that in its use of composite shots and animated models the film remains technically interesting. And no other monster in movie history has won so devoted a popular audience. None of the plodding mummies, the stultified draculas, the white-coated Lugosis with their shiny pinball-machine laboratories, none of the invisible stranglers, berserk robots, or menaces from Mars has ever enjoyed so many resurrections.

Why does the American public refuse to let King Kong rest in peace? It is true, I'll admit, that *Kong* outdid every monster movie before or since in sheer carnage. Producers Cooper and Schoedsack crammed into it dinosaurs, headhunters, riots, aerial battles, bullets, bombs, bloodletting. Heroine Fay Wray, whose function is mainly to scream, shuts her mouth for hardly one uninterrupted minute from first reel to last. It is also true that *Kong* is larded with good healthy sadism, for those whose joy it is to see the frantic girl dangled from cliffs and harried by pterodactyls. But it seems to me that the abiding appeal of the giant ape rests on other foundations.

Kong has, first of all, the attraction of being manlike. His simian nature gives him one huge advantage over giant ants and walking vegetables in that an audience may conceivably identify with him. Kong's appeal has the quality that established the Tarzan series as American myth — for what man doesn't secretly image himself a huge hairy howler against whom no other monster has a chance? If Tarzan recalls the ape in us, then Kong may well appeal to that great-granddaddy primordial brute from whose tribe we have all deteriorated.

Intentionally or not, the producers of *King Kong* encourage this identification by etching the character of Kong with keen sympathy. For the ape is a figure in a tradition familiar to moviegoers: the tradition of the pitiable monster. We think of Lou Chaney in the role of Quasimodo, of Karloff in the original *Frankenstein*. As we watch the Frankenstein monster's fumbling and disastrous attempts to befriend a flower-picking child, our sympathies are enlisted with the monster in his impenetrable loneliness. And so with Kong. As he roars in his chains, while barkers sell tickets to boobs who gape at him, we perhaps feel something more deep than pathos. We begin to sense something of the problem that engaged Eugene O'Neill in *The Hairy Ape*: the dilemma of a displaced animal spirit forced to live in a jungle built by machines.

King Kong, it is true, had special relevance in 1933. Landscapes of the depression are glimpsed early in the film when an impresario, seeking some desperate pretty girl to play the lead in a jungle movie, visits souplines and a Woman's Home Mission. In Fay Wray — who's been caught snitching an apple from a fruitstand — his search is ended. When he gives her a big feed and a movie contract, the girl is magic-carpeted out of the world of the National Recovery Act. And when, in the film's climax, Kong smashes that very Third Avenue landscape in which Fay had wandered hungry, audiences of 1933 may well have felt a personal satisfaction.

What is curious is that audiences of 1960 remain hooked. For in the heart of urban man, one suspects, lurks the impulse to fling a bomb. Though machines speed him to the scene of his daily grind, though IBM comptometers ("freeing the human mind from drudgery") enable him to drudge more efficiently once he arrives, there comes a moment when he wishes to turn upon his machines and kick hell out of them. He wants to hurl his combination radioalarmclock out the bedroom window and listen to its smash. What sub-way commuter wouldn't love — just for once — to see the down-town express smack head-on into the uptown local? Such a wish is gratified in that memorable scene in *Kong* that opens with a wide-angle shot: interior of a railway car on the Third Avenue El. Strap-hangers are nodding, the literate refold their newspapers. Unknown to them, Kong has torn away a section of trestle toward which the train now speeds. The motorman spies Kong up ahead, jams on the brakes. Passengers hurtle together like so many peas in a pail. In a window of the car appear Kong's bloodshot eyes. Women shriek. Kong picks up the railway car as if it were a rat, flips it to the street and ties knots in it, or something. To any commuter the scene must appear one of the most satisfactory pieces of celluloid ever exposed.

Yet however violent his acts, Kong remains a gentleman. Re-markable is his sense of chivalry. Whenever a fresh boa constrictor threatens Fay, Kong first sees that the lady is safely parked, then manfully thrashes her attacker. (And she, the ingrate, runs away every time his back is turned.) Atop the Empire State Building, ignoring his pursuers, Kong places Fay on a ledge as tenderly as if she were a dozen eggs. He fondles her, then turns to face the Army Air Force. And Kong is perhaps the most disinterested lover since Cyrano: his attentions to the lady are utterly without hope of re-ward. After all, between a five-foot blonde and a fifty-foot ape, love can hardly be more than an intellectual flirtation. In his simian way King Kong is the hopelessly yearning lover of Petrarchan convention. His forced exit from his jungle, in chains, results di-rectly from his single-minded pursuit of Fay. He smashes a Broad-way theater when the notion enters his dull brain that the flashbulbs of photographers somehow endanger the lady. His perilous shin-nying up a skyscraper to pluck Fay from her boudoir is an act of the kindliest of hearts. He's impossible to discourage even though the love of his life can't lay eyes on him without shrieking murder.

The tragedy of King Kong then, is to be the beast who at the end of the fable fails to turn into the handsome prince. This is the conviction that the scriptwriters would leave with us in the film's closing line. As Kong's corpse lies blocking traffic in the street, the entrepreneur who brought Kong to New York turns to the assem-bled reporters and proclaims: "That's your story, boys — it was Beauty killed the Beast!" But greater forces than those of the scream-ing Lady have combined to lay Kong low, if you ask me. Kong lives for a time as one of those persecuted near-animal souls bewil-dered in the middle of an industrial order, whose simple desires are thwarted at every turn. He climbs the Empire State Building because in all New York it's the closest thing he can find to the clifftop of his jungle isle. He dies, a pitiful dolt, and the army brass and publicity-men cackle over him. His death is the only possible outcome to as neat a tragic dilemma as you can ask for. The machine-guns do him in, while the manicured human hero (a nice clean Dartmouth boy) carries away Kong's sweetheart to the altar. O, the misery of it all. There's far more truth about upper-middle-class American life in *King Kong* than in the last seven dozen novels of John P. Marquand.

A Negro friend from Atlanta tells me that in movie houses in colored neighborhoods throughout the South, *Kong* does a constant business. They show the thing in Atlanta at least every year, presumably to the same audiences. Perhaps this popularity may simply be due to the fact that Kong is one of the most watchable movies ever constructed, but I wonder whether Negro audiences may not find some archetypical appeal in this serio-comic tale of a huge black powerful free spirit whom all the hardworking white policemen are out to kill.

Every day in the week on a screen somewhere in the world, King Kong relives his agony. Again and again he expires on the Empire State Building, as audiences of the devout assist his sacrifice. We watch him die, and by extension kill the ape within our bones, but these little deaths of ours occur in prosaic surroundings. We do not die on a tower, New York before our feet, nor do we give our lives to smash a few flying machines. It is not for us to bring to a momentary standstill the civilization in which we move. King Kong does this for us. And so we kill him again and again, in much-spliced celluloid, while the ape in us expires from day to day, obscure, in desperation.

QUESTIONS

1. What is your response to Kennedy's colloquial expressions, such as "lugging a frightened blonde," "hunk of hokum," "snitching an apple"? Are they used for a purpose?
2. In the third paragraph Kennedy calls *King Kong* "the old hunk of hokum." Does he consistently maintain the attitude implied here?
3. How persuasive do you find Kennedy's analysis? Is any of it useful in explaining the appeal of other films you have seen?
4. Kennedy refers to *King Kong* as a "monster movie." Can you

think of other films you would place in that category? How would you define "horror movie" or "disaster film" or "science fiction film"? Are these, and "monster movie," distinct or overlapping categories?

"The Trouble with 'X' . . ."

C. S. Lewis

I suppose I may assume that seven out of ten of those who read these lines are in some kind of difficulty about some other human being. Either at work or at home, either the people who employ you or those whom you employ, either those who share your house or those whose house you share, either your in-laws or parents or children, your wife or your husband, are making life harder for you than it need be even in these days. It is to be hoped that we do not often mention these difficulties (especially the domestic ones) to outsiders. But sometimes we do. An outside friend asks us why we are looking so glum; and the truth comes out.

On such occasions the outside friend usually says, "But why don't you tell them? Why don't you go to your wife (or husband, or father, or daughter, or boss, or landlady, or lodger) and have it all out? People are usually reasonable. All you've got to do is to make them see things in the right light. Explain it to them in a reasonable, quiet, friendly way." And we, whatever we say outwardly, think sadly to ourselves, "He doesn't know 'X'." We do. We know how utterly hopeless it is to make "X" see reason. Either we've tried it over and over again — tried it till we are sick of trying it — or else we've never tried it because we saw from the beginning how useless it would be. We know that if we attempt to "have it all out with 'X'" there will either be a "scene," or else "X" will stare at us in blank amazement and say "I don't know what on earth you're talking about"; or else (which is perhaps worst of all) "X" will quite agree with us and promise to turn over a new leaf and put everything on a new footing — and then, twenty-four hours later, will be exactly the same as "X" has always been.

You know, in fact, that any attempt to talk things over with "X" will shipwreck on the old, fatal flaw in "X's" character. And you see, looking back, how all the plans you have ever made always have shipwrecked on that fatal flaw — on "X's" incurable jealousy, or laziness, or touchiness, or muddle-headedness, or bossiness, or ill temper, or changeableness. Up to a certain age you have perhaps had the illusion that some external stroke of good fortune — an improvement in health, a rise of salary, the end of the war — would solve your difficulty. But you know better now. The war is over, and you realize that even if the other things happened, "X" would still be "X," and you would still be up against the same old problem. Even if you became a millionaire, your husband would still be a bully, or your wife would still nag or your son would still drink, or you'd still have to have your mother-in-law to live with you.

It is a great step forward to realize that this is so; to face the fact that even if all external things went right, real happiness would still depend on the character of the people you have to live with — and that you can't alter their characters. And now comes the point. When you have seen this you have, for the first time, had a glimpse of what it must be like for God. For, of course, this is (in one way) just what God Himself is up against. He has provided a rich, beautiful world for people to live in. He has given them intelligence to show them how it can be used, and conscience to show them how it ought to be used. He has contrived that the things they need for their biological life (food, drink, rest, sleep, exercise) should be positively delightful to them. And, having done all this, He then sees all His plans spoiled — just as our little plans are spoiled — by the crookedness of the people themselves. All the things He has given them to be happy with they turn into occasions for quarreling and jealousy, and excess and hoarding, and tomfoolery.

You may say it is very different for God because He could, if He pleased, alter people's characters, and we can't. But this difference doesn't go quite as deep as we may at first think. God has made it a rule for Himself that He won't alter people's character by force. He can and will alter them — but only if the people will let Him. In that way He has really and truly limited His power. Sometimes we wonder why He has done so, or even wish that He hadn't. But apparently He thinks it worth doing. He would rather have a world of free beings, with all its risks, than a world of people who did right like machines because they couldn't do anything else. The more we succeed in imagining what a world of perfect automatic beings would be like, the more, I think, we shall see His wisdom.

I said that when we see how all our plans shipwreck on the characters of the people we have to deal with, we are "in *one* way" seeing what it must be like for God. But only in one way. There are two respects in which God's view must be very different from ours. In the first place, He sees (like you) how all the people in your home or your job are in various degrees awkward or difficult; but when He looks into that home or factory or office He sees one more person of the same kind — the one you never do see. I mean, of course, yourself. That is the next great step in wisdom — to realize that you also are just that sort of person. You also have a fatal flaw in your character. All the hopes and plans of others have again and again shipwrecked on your character just as your hopes and plans have shipwrecked on theirs.

It is no good passing this over with some vague, general admission such as "Of course, I know I have my faults." It is important to realize that there is some really fatal flaw in you: something which gives the others just that same feeling of *despair* which their flaws give you. And it is almost certainly something you don't know about — like what the advertisements call "halitosis," which everyone notices except the person who has it. But why, you ask, don't the others tell me? Believe me, they have tried to tell you over and over again, and you just couldn't "take it." Perhaps a good deal of what you call their "nagging" or "bad temper" or "queerness" are just their attempts to make you see the truth. And even the faults you do know you don't know fully. You say, "I admit I lost my temper last night"; but the others know that you're always doing it, that you are a bad-tempered person. You say, "I admit I drank too much last Saturday"; but everyone else knows that you are a habitual drunkard.

That is one way in which God's view must differ from mine. He sees all the characters: I see all except my own. But the second difference is this. He loves the people in spite of their faults. He goes on loving. He does not let go. Don't say, "It's all very well for Him; He hasn't got to live with them." He has. He is inside them as well as outside them. He is *with* them far more intimately and closely and incessantly than we can ever be. Every vile thought within their minds (and ours), every moment of spite, envy, arrogance, greed and self-conceit comes right up against His patient and longing love, and grieves His spirit more than it grieves ours.

The more we can imitate God in both these respects, the more progress we shall make. We must love "X" more; and we must learn to see ourselves as a person of exactly the same kind. Some people say it is morbid to be always thinking of one's own faults. That would be all very well if most of us could stop thinking of our own without soon beginning to think about those of other people. For unfortunately we *enjoy* thinking about other people's faults: and in the proper sense of the word "morbid," that is the most morbid pleasure in the world.

We don't like rationing which is imposed upon us, but I suggest one form of rationing which we ought to impose on ourselves. Abstain from all thinking about other people's faults, unless your duties as a teacher or parent make it necessary to think about them. Whenever the thoughts come unnecessarily into one's mind, why not simply shove them away? And think of one's own faults instead? For there, with God's help, one *can* do something. Of all the awkward people in your house or job there is only one whom you can improve very much. That is the practical end at which to begin. And really, we'd better. The job has to be tackled some day: and every day we put it off will make it harder to begin.

What, after all, is the alternative? You see clearly enough that nothing, not even God with all His power, can make "X" really happy as long as "X" remains envious, self-centered, and spiteful. Be sure there is something inside you which, unless it is altered, will put it out of God's power to prevent your being eternally miserable. While that something remains there can be no Heaven for you, just as there can be no sweet smells for a man with a cold in the nose, and no music for a man who is deaf. It's not a question of God "sending" us to Hell. In each of us there is something growing up which will of itself *be Hell* unless it is nipped in the bud. The matter is serious. Let us put ourselves in His hands at once — this very day, this hour.

QUESTIONS

1. Lewis assumes, rather than argues for, the existence of God, and he writes for an audience of believers. What value, if any, does his essay have for nonbelievers?
2. Lewis is preaching, and he therefore runs the risk of seeming smug or holier-than-thou. How successful is he in avoiding this image? If you think he is fairly (or completely) successful, list some of the devices he uses that contribute to his success.
3. On page 625, in the paragraph beginning "It is a great step forward," Lewis refers to "the crookedness of people." In this paragraph what does the word "crookedness" mean? What are its connotations?

4. On the basis of this essay, write one paragraph defining God as Lewis might.

Total Effect and the Eighth Grade

Flannery O'Connor

In two recent instances in Georgia, parents have objected to their eighth- and ninth-grade children's reading assignments in modern fiction. This seems to happen with some regularity in cases throughout the country. The unwitting parent picks up his child's book, glances through it, comes upon passages of erotic detail or profanity, and takes off at once to complain to the school board. Sometimes, as in one of the Georgia cases, the teacher is dismissed and hackles rise in liberal circles everywhere.

The two cases in Georgia, which involved Steinbeck's *East of Eden* and John Hersey's *A Bell for Adano*, provoked considerable newspaper comment. One columnist, in commending the enterprise of the teachers, announced that students do not like to read the fusty works of the nineteenth century, that their attention can best be held by novels dealing with the realities of our time, and that the Bible, too, is full of racy stories.

Mr. Hersey himself addressed a letter to the State School Superintendent in behalf of the teacher who had been dismissed. He pointed out that his book is not scandalous, that it attempts to convey an earnest message about the nature of democracy, and that it falls well within the limits of the principle of "total effect," that principle followed in legal cases by which a book is judged not for isolated parts but by the final effect of the whole book upon the general reader.

I do not want to comment on the merits of these particular cases. What concerns me is what novels ought to be assigned in the eighth and ninth grades as a matter of course, for if these cases indicate anything, they indicate the haphazard way in which fiction is approached in our high schools. Presumably there is a state reading list which contains "safe" books for teachers to assign; after that it is up to the teacher.

English teachers come in Good, Bad, and Indifferent, but too frequently in high schools anyone who can speak English is allowed to teach it. Since several novels can't easily be gathered into one textbook, the fiction that students are assigned depends upon their teacher's knowledge, ability, and taste: variable factors at best. More often than not, the teacher assigns what he thinks will hold the attention and interest of the students. Modern fiction will certainly hold it.

Ours is the first age in history which has asked the child what he would tolerate learning, but that is a part of the problem with which I am not equipped to deal. The devil of Educationism that possesses us is the kind that can be "cast out only by prayer and fasting." No one has yet come along strong enough to do it. In other ages the attention of children was held by Homer and Virgil, among others, but, by the reverse evolutionary process, that is no longer possible; our children are too stupid now to enter the past imaginatively. No one asks the student if algebra pleases him or if he finds it satisfactory that some French verbs are irregular, but if he prefers Hersey to Hawthorne, his taste must prevail.

I would like to put forward the proposition, repugnant to most English teachers, that fiction, if it is going to be taught in the high schools, should be taught as a subject and as a subject with a history. The total effect of a novel depends not only on its innate impact, but upon the experience, literary and otherwise, with which it is approached. No child needs to be assigned Hersey or Steinbeck until he is familiar with a certain amount of the best work of Cooper, Hawthorne, Melville, the early James, and Crane, and he does not need to be assigned these until he has been introduced to some of the better English novelists of the eighteenth and nineteenth centuries.

The fact that these works do not present him with the realities of his own time is all to the good. He is surrounded by the realities of his own time, and he has no perspective whatever from which to view them. Like the college student who wrote in her paper on Lincoln that he went to the movies and got shot, many students go to college unaware that the world was not made yesterday; their studies began with the present and dipped backward occasionally when it seemed necessary or unavoidable.

There is much to be enjoyed in the great British novels of the nineteenth century, much that a good teacher can open up in them for the young student. There is no reason why these novels should be either too simple or too difficult for the eighth grade. For the simple, they offer simple pleasures; for the more precocious, they can be made to yield subtler ones if the teacher is up to it. Let the student discover, after reading the nineteenth-century British novel, that the nineteenth-century American novel is quite different as to its literary characteristics, and he will thereby learn something not only about these individual works but about the sea-change which a new historical situation can effect in a literary form. Let him come to modern fiction with this experience behind him, and he will be better able to see and to deal with the more complicated demands of the best twentieth-century fiction.

Modern fiction often looks simpler than the fiction that preceded it, but in reality it is more complex. A natural evolution has taken place. The author has for the most part absented himself from direct participation in the work and has left the reader to make his own way amid experiences dramatically rendered and symbolically ordered. The modern novelist merges the reader in the experience; he tends to raise the passions he touches upon. If he is a good novelist, he raises them to effect by their order and clarity a new experience — the total effect — which is not in itself sensuous or simply of the moment. Unless the child has had some literary experience before, he is not going to be able to resolve the immediate passions the book arouses into any true, total picture.

It is here the moral problem will arise. It is one thing for a child to read about adultery in the Bible or in *Anna Karenina,* and quite another for him to read about it in most modern fiction. This is not only because in both the former instances adultery is considered a sin, and in the latter, at most, an inconvenience, but because modern writing involves the reader in the action with a new degree of intensity, and literary mores now permit him to be involved in any action a human being can perform.

In our fractured culture, we cannot agree on morals; we cannot even agree that moral matters should come before literary ones when there is a conflict between them. All this is another reason why the high schools would do well to return to their proper business of preparing foundations. Whether in the senior year students should be assigned modern novelists should depend both on their parents' consent and on what they have already read and understood.

The high-school English teacher will be fulfilling his responsibility if he furnishes the student a guided opportunity, through the best writing of the past, to come, in time, to an understanding of the best writing of the present. He will teach literature, not social studies or little lessons in democracy or the customs of many lands.

And if the student finds that this is not to his taste? Well, that is regrettable. Most regrettable. His taste should not be consulted; it is being formed.

QUESTIONS

1. What is the function of the first three paragraphs of "Total Effect and the Eighth Grade"? Can you justify O'Connor's abrupt dismissal ("I do not want to comment on the merits of these particular cases") of the opposing argument summarized in the second and third paragraphs? How?

2. "English teachers come in Good, Bad, and Indifferent, but too frequently in high schools anyone who can speak English is allowed to teach it." Can you, from your own experience, support this view?

3. Is the tone of the sixth paragraph, beginning "Ours is the first age," sarcastic? If not, how would you characterize it?

4. Which of O'Connor's arguments might be used to support the rating of movies X, R, PG, and G? Are you for or against these ratings? How would you support your position?

Politics and the English Language
George Orwell

Most people who bother with the matter at all would admit that the English language is in a bad way, but it is generally assumed that we cannot by conscious action do anything about it. Our civilization is decadent and our language — so the argument runs — must inevitably share in the general collapse. It follows that any struggle against the abuse of language is a sentimental archaism, like preferring candles to electric light or hansom cabs to aeroplanes. Underneath this lies the half-conscious belief that language is a natural growth and not an instrument which we shape for our own purposes.

Now, it is clear that the decline of a language must ultimately have political and economic causes: it is not due simply to the bad influence of this or that individual writer. But an effect can become a cause, reinforcing the original cause and producing the same effect in an intensified form, and so on indefinitely. A man may take to drink because he feels himself to be a failure, and then fail all the more completely because he drinks. It is rather the same thing that is happening to the English language. It becomes ugly and inaccurate because our thoughts are foolish, but the slovenliness of our language makes it easier for us to have foolish thoughts. The point is that the process is reversible. Modern English, especially written English, is full of bad habits which spread by imitation and which can be avoided if one is willing to take the necessary trouble. If one gets rid of these habits one can think more clearly, and to think clearly is a necessary first step towards political regeneration: so that the fight against bad English is not frivolous and is not the exclusive concern of professional writers. I will come back to this presently, and I hope that by that time the meaning of what I have said here will have become clearer. Meanwhile, here are five specimens of the English language as it is now habitually written.

These five passages have not been picked out because they are especially bad — I could have quoted far worse if I had chosen — but because they illustrate various of the mental vices from which we now suffer. They are a little below the average, but are fairly representative samples. I number them so that I can refer back to them when necessary:

(1) I am not, indeed, sure whether it is not true to say that the Milton who once seemed unlike a seventeenth-century Shelley had not become, out of an experience ever more bitter in each year, more alien [*sic*] to the founder of that Jesuit sect which nothing could induce him to tolerate.

— Professor Harold Laski (Essay in *Freedom of Expression*)

(2) Above all, we cannot play ducks and drakes with a native battery of idioms which prescribes such egregious collocations of vocables as the basic *put up with* for *tolerate* or *put at a loss* for *bewilder*.

— Professor Lancelot Hogben (*Interglossa*)

(3) On the one side we have the free personality: by definition it is not neurotic, for it has neither conflict nor dream. Its desires, such as they are, are transparent, for they are just what institutional approval keeps in the forefront of consciousness; another institutional pattern would alter their number and intensity; there is little in them that is natural, irreducible, or culturally dangerous. But *on the other side,* the social bond itself is nothing but the mutual reflection of these self-secure integrities. Recall the definition of love. Is not this the very picture of a small academic? Where is there a place in this hall of mirrors for either personality or fraternity?

— Essay on psychology in *Politics* (New York)

(4) All the "best people" from the gentlemen's clubs, and all the frantic fascist captains, united in common hatred of Socialism and bestial horror of the rising tide of the mass revolutionary movement, have turned to acts of provocation, to foul incendiarism, to medieval legends of poisoned wells, to legalize their own destruction of proletarian organizations, and rouse the agitated petty-bourgeoisie to chauvinistic fervor on behalf of the fight against the revolutionary way out of the crisis.

— Communist Pamphlet

(5) If a new spirit is to be infused into this old country, there is one thorny and contentious reform which must be tackled, and that is the humanization and galvanization of the B.B.C. Timidity here will bespeak canker and atrophy of the soul. The heart of Britain may be sound and of strong beat, for instance, but the British lion's roar at present is like that of Bottom in Shakespeare's *Midsummer Night's Dream* — as gentle as any sucking dove. A virile new Britain cannot continue indefinitely to be traduced in the eyes or rather ears, of the world by the effete languors of Langham Place, brazenly masquerading as "standard English." When the voice of Britain is heard at nine o'clock, better far and infinitely less ludicrous to hear aitches honestly dropped than the present priggish, inflated, school-ma'amish arch braying of blameless bashful mewing maidens!

— Letter in *Tribune*

Each of these passages has faults of its own, but, quite apart from avoidable ugliness, two qualities are common to all of them. The first is staleness of imagery; the other is lack of precision. The writer either has a meaning and cannot express it, or he inadvertently says something else, or he is almost indifferent as to whether his words mean anything or not. This mixture of vagueness and sheer incompetence is the most marked characteristic of modern English prose, and especially of any kind of political writing. As soon as certain topics are raised, the concrete melts into the abstract and no one seems able to think of turns of speech that are not hackneyed: prose consists less and less of *words* chosen for the sake of their meaning, and more and more of *phrases* tacked together like the sections of a prefabricated hen-house. I list below, with notes and examples, various of the tricks by means of which the work of prose-construction is habitually dodged:

Dying metaphors. A newly invented metaphor assists thought by evoking a visual image, while on the other hand a metaphor which is technically "dead" (e.g. *iron resolution*) has in effect reverted to being an ordinary word and can generally be used without loss of vividness. But in between these two classes there is a huge dump of worn-out metaphors which have lost all evocative power and are merely used because they save people the trouble of inventing phrases for themselves. Examples are: *Ring the changes on, take up the cudgels for, toe the line, ride roughshod over, stand shoulder to shoulder with, play into the hands of, no axe to grind, grist to the mill, fishing in troubled waters, on the order of the day, Achilles' heel, swan song, hotbed.* Many of these are used without knowledge of their meaning (what is "grist," for instance?), and incompatible metaphors are frequently mixed, a sure sign that the writer is not interested in what he is saying. Some metaphors now current have been twisted out of their original meaning without those who use them even being aware of the fact. For example, *toe the line* is sometimes written *tow the line.* Another example is the *hammer and the anvil,* now always used with the implication that the anvil 'gets the worst of it. In real life it is always the anvil that breaks the hammer, never the other way about: a writer who stopped to think what he was saying would be aware of this, and would avoid perverting the original phrase.

Operators or *verbal false limbs.* These save the trouble of picking out appropriate verbs and nouns, and at the same time pad each sentence with extra syllables which give it an appearance of symmetry. Characteristic phrases are *render inoperative, militate against, make contact with, be subjected to, give rise to, give grounds for, have the effect of, plays a leading part (role) in, make itself felt, take effect, exhibit a tendency to, serve the purpose of,* etc., etc. The keynote is the elimination of simple verbs. Instead of being a single word, such as *break, stop, spoil, mend, kill,* a verb becomes a *phrase,* made up of a noun or adjective tacked on to some general-purpose verb such as *prove, serve, form, play, render.* In addition, the passive voice is wherever possible used in preference to the active, and noun constructions are used instead of gerunds (*by examination of* instead of *by examining*). The range of verbs is further cut down by means of the *-ize* and *de-* formations, and the banal statements are given an appearance of profundity by means of the *not un-* formation. Simple conjunctions and prepositions are replaced by such phrases as *with respect to, having regard to, the fact that, by dint of, in view of, in the interests of, on the hypothesis that;* and the ends of sentences are saved from anticlimax by such resounding common-places as *greatly to be desired, cannot be left out of account, a development to be expected in the near future, deserving of serious consideration, brought to a satisfactory conclusion,* and so on and so forth.

Pretentious diction. Words like *phenomenon, element, individual* (as noun), *objective, categorical, effective, virtual, basic, primary, promote, constitute, exhibit, exploit, utilize, eliminate, liquidate,* are used to dress up simple statements and give an air of scientific impartiality to biased judgments. Adjectives like *epoch-making, epic, historic, unforgettable, triumphant, age-old, inevitable, inexorable, veritable,* are used to dignify the sordid processes of international politics, while writing that aims at glorifying war usually takes on an archaic color, its characteristic words being: *realm, throne, chariot, mailed fist, trident, sword, shield, buckler, banner, jackboot, clarion.* Foreign words and expressions such as *cul de sac, ancien régime, deus ex machina, mutatis mutandis, status quo, gleichschaaltung, weltanschauung,* are used to give an air of culture and elegance. Except for the useful abbreviations *i.e., e.g.,* and *etc.,* there is no real need for any of the hundreds of foreign phrases now current in English. Bad writers, and especially scientific, political and sociological writers, are nearly always haunted by the notion that Latin or Greek words are grander than Saxon ones, and unnecessary words like *expedite, ameliorate, predict, extraneous, deracinated, clandestine, subaqueous* and hundreds of others constantly gain ground from their Anglo–Saxon opposite numbers.[1] The jargon peculiar to Marxist writing (*hyena, hangman, cannibal, petty bourgeois, these gentry, lacquey, flunkey, mad dog, White Guard,* etc.) consists largely of words and phrases translated from Russian, German or French; but the normal way of coining a new word is to use a Latin or Greek root with the appropriate affix and, where necessary, the *-ize* formation. It is often easier to make up words of this kind (*deregionalize, impermissible, extramarital, non-fragmentary* and so forth) than to think up the English words that will cover one's meaning. The result, in general, is an increase in slovenliness and vagueness.

Meaningless words. In certain kinds of writing, particularly in art criticism and literary criticism, it is normal to come across long

[1] An interesting illustration of this is the way in which the English flower names which were in use till very recently are being ousted by Greek ones, *snapdragon* becoming *antirrhinum, forget-me-not* becoming *myosotis,* etc. It is hard to see any practical reason for this change of fashion: it is probably due to an instinctive turning-away from the more homely word and a vague feeling that the Greek word is scientific.

passages which are almost completely lacking in meaning.[2] Words like *romantic, plastic, values, human, dead, sentimental, natural, vitality,* as used in art criticism, are strictly meaningless, in the sense that they not only do not point to any discoverable object, but are hardly ever expected to do so by the reader. When one critic writes, "The outstanding feature of Mr. X's work is its living quality," while another writes, "The immediately striking thing about Mr. X's work is its peculiar deadness," the reader accepts this as a simple difference of opinion. If words like *black* and *white* were involved, instead of the jargon words *dead* and *living*, he would see at once that language was being used in an improper way. Many political words are similarly abused. The word *Fascism* has now no meaning except in so far as it signifies "something not desirable." The words *democracy, socialism, freedom, patriotic, realistic, justice,* have each of them several different meanings which cannot be reconciled with one another. In the case of a word like *democracy*, not only is there no agreed definition, but the attempt to make one is resisted from all sides. It is almost univerally felt that when we call a country democratic we are praising it: consequently the defenders of every kind of régime claim that it is a democracy, and fear that they might have to stop using the word if it were tied down to any one meaning. Words of this kind are often used in a consciously dishonest way. That is, the person who uses them has his own private definition, but allows his hearer to think he means something quite different. Statements like *Marshal Pétain was a true patriot, The Soviet Press is the freest in the world, The Catholic Church is opposed to persecution,* are almost always made with intent to deceive. Other words used in variable meanings, in most cases more or less dishonestly, are: *class, totalitarian, science, progressive, reactionary, bourgeois, equality.*

Now that I have made this catalogue of swindles and perversions, let me give another example of the kind of writing that they lead to. This time it must of its nature be an imaginary one. I am

---

[2] Example: "Comfort's catholicity of perception and image, strangely Whitmanesque in range, almost the exact opposite in aesthetic compulsion, continues to evoke that trembling atmospheric accumulative hinting at a cruel, an inexórably serene timelessness. . . . Wrey Gardiner scores by aiming at simple bull's-eyes with precision. Only they are not so simple, and through this contented sadness runs more than the surface bittersweet of resignation." (*Poetry Quarterly.*)

going to translate a passage of good English into modern English of the worst sort. Here is a well-known verse from *Ecclesiastes:*

> I returned and saw under the sun, that the race is not to the swift, nor the battle to the strong, neither yet bread to the wise, nor yet riches to men of understanding, nor yet favor to men of skill; but time and chance happeneth to them all.

Here it is in modern English:

> Objective consideration of contemporary phenomena compels the conclusion that success or failure in competitive activities exhibits no tendency to be commensurate with innate capacity, but that a considerable element of the unpredictable must invariably be taken into account.

This is a parody, but not a very gross one. Exhibit (3), above, for instance, contains several patches of the same kind of English. It will be seen that I have not made a full translation. The beginning and ending of the sentence follow the original meaning fairly closely, but in the middle the concrete illustrations — race, battle, bread — dissolve into the vague phrase "success or failure in competitive activities." This had to be so, because no modern writer of the kind I am discussing — no one capable of using phrases like "objective consideration of contemporary phenomena" — would ever tabulate his thoughts in that precise and detailed way. The whole tendency of modern prose is away from concreteness. Now analyse these two sentences a little more closely. The first contains forty-nine words but only sixty syllables, and all its words are those of everyday life. The second contains thirty-eight words of ninety syllables: eighteen of its words are from Latin roots, and one from Greek. The first sentence contains six vivid images, and only one phrase ("time and chance") that could be called vague. The second contains not a single fresh, arresting phrase, and in spite of its ninety syllables it gives only a shortened version of the meaning contained in the first. Yet without a doubt it is the second kind of sentence that is gaining ground in modern English. I do not want to exaggerate. This kind of writing is not yet universal, and outcrops of simplicity will occur here and there in the worst-written page. Still, if you or I were told to write a few lines on the uncertainty of human fortunes, we should probably come much nearer to my imaginary sentence than to the one from *Ecclesiastes.*

As I have tried to show, modern writing at its worst does not consist in picking out words for the sake of their meaning and inventing images in order to make the meaning clearer. It consists in gumming together long strips of words which have already been set in order by someone else, and making the results presentable by sheer humbug. The attraction of this way of writing is that it is easy. It is easier — even quicker, once you have the habit — to say *In my opinion it is not an unjustifiable assumption that* than to say *I think*. If you use ready-made phrases, you not only don't have to hunt about for words; you also don't have to bother with the rhythms of your sentences, since these phrases are generally so arranged as to be more or less euphonious. When you are composing in a hurry — when you are dictating to a stenographer, for instance, or making a public speech — it is natural to fall into a pretentious, Latinized style. Tags like *a consideration which we should do well to bear in mind* or *a conclusion to which all of us would readily assent* will save many a sentence from coming down with a bump. By using stale metaphors, similes and idioms, you save much mental effort, at the cost of leaving your meaning vague, not only for your reader but for yourself. This is the significance of mixed metaphors. The sole aim of a metaphor is to call up a visual image. When these images clash — as in *The Fascist octopus has sung its swan song, the jackboot is thrown into the melting pot* — it can be taken as certain that the writer is not seeing a mental image of the objects he is naming; in other words he is not really thinking. Look again at the examples I gave at the beginning of this essay. Professor Laski (1) uses five negatives in fifty-three words. One of these is superfluous, making nonsense of the whole passage, and in addition there is the slip *alien* for *akin,* making further nonsense, and several avoidable pieces of clumsiness which increase the general vagueness. Professor Hogben (2) plays ducks and drakes with a battery which is able to write prescriptions, and, while disapproving of the everyday phrase *put up with,* is unwilling to look *egregious* up in the dictionary and see what it means; (3), if one takes an uncharitable attitude towards it, is simply meaningless: probably one could work out its intended meaning by reading the whole of the article in which it occurs. In (4), the writer knows more or less what he wants to say, but an accumulation of stale phrases chokes him like tea leaves blocking a sink. In (5), words and meaning have almost parted company. People who write in this manner usually have a general emotional meaning — they dislike one thing and want to express solidarity with another — but they are not interested in the detail of what they are saying. A scrupulous writer, in every sentence that he writes, will ask himself at least four questions, thus: What am I trying to say? What words will express it? What image or idiom will make it clearer? Is this image fresh enough to have an effect? And he will probably ask himself two more: Could I put it more shortly? Have I said anything that is avoidably ugly? But you are not obliged to go to all this trouble. You can shirk it by simply throwing your mind open and letting the ready-made phrases come crowding in. They will construct your sentences for you — even think your thoughts for you, to a certain extent — and at need they will perform the important service of partially concealing your meaning even from yourself. It is at this point that the special connection between politics and the debasement of language becomes clear.

In our time it is broadly true that political writing is bad writing. Where it is not true it will generally be found that the writer is some kind of rebel, expressing his private opinions and not a "party line." Orthodoxy, of whatever color, seems to demand a lifeless, imitative style. The political dialects to be found in pamphlets, leading articles, manifestos, White Papers and the speeches of under-secretaries do, of course, vary from party to party, but they are all alike in that one almost never finds in them a fresh, vivid, home-made turn of speech. When one watches some tired hack on the platform mechanically repeating the familiar phrases — *bestial atrocities, iron heel, bloodstained tyranny, free peoples of the world, stand shoulder to shoulder* — one often has a curious feeling that one is not watching a live human being but some kind of dummy: a feeling which suddenly becomes stronger at moments when the light catches the speaker's spectacles and turns them into blank discs which seem to have no eyes behind them. And this is not altogether fanciful. A speaker who uses that kind of phraseology has gone some distance towards turning himself into a machine. The appropriate noises are coming out of his larynx but his brain is not involved as it would be if he were choosing his words for himself. If the speech he is making is one that he is accustomed to make over and over again, he may be almost unconscious of what he is saying, as one is when one utters the responses in church. And this reduced state of consciousness, if not indispensable, is at any rate favorable to political conformity.

In our time, political speech and writing are largely the defence of the indefensible. Things like the continuance of British rule in India, the Russian purges and deportations, the dropping of the atom bombs on Japan, can indeed be defended, but only by arguments which are too brutal for most people to face, and which do not square with the professed aims of political parties. Thus political language has to consist largely of euphemism, question-begging and sheer cloudy vagueness. Defenceless villages are bombarded from the air, the inhabitants driven out into the countryside, the cattle machine-gunned, the huts set on fire with incendiary bullets: this is called *pacification*. Millions of peasants are robbed of their farms and sent trudging along the roads with no more than they can carry: this is called *transfer of population* or *rectification of frontiers*. People are imprisoned for years without trial, or shot in the back of the neck or sent to die of scurvy in Arctic lumber camps: this is called *elimination of unreliable elements*. Such phraseology is needed if one wants to name things without calling up mental pictures of them. Consider for instance some comfortable English professor defending Russian totalitarianism. He cannot say outright, "I believe in killing off your opponents when you can get good results by doing so." Probably, therefore, he will say something like this:

> While freely conceding that the Soviet régime exhibits certain features which the humanitarian may be inclined to deplore, we must, I think, agree that a certain curtailment of the right to political opposition is an unavoidable concomitant of transitional periods, and that the rigors which the Russian people have been called upon to undergo have been amply justified in the sphere of concrete achievement.

The inflated style is itself a kind of euphemism. A mass of Latin words falls upon the facts like soft snow, blurring the outlines and covering up all the details. The great enemy of clear language is insincerity. When there is a gap between one's real and one's declared aims, one turns as it were instinctively to long words and exhausted idioms, like a cuttlefish squirting out ink. In our age there is no such thing as "keeping out of politics." All issues are political issues, and politics itself is a mass of lies, evasions, folly, hatred and schizophrenia. When the general atmosphere is bad, language must suffer. I should expect to find — this is a guess which I have not sufficient knowledge to verify — that the German, Russian and Italian languages have all deteriorated in the last ten to fifteen years, as a result of dictatorship.

But if thought corrupts language, language can also corrupt thought. A bad usage can spread by tradition and imitation, even among people who should and do know better. The debased language that I have been discussing is in some ways very convenient. Phrases like *a not unjustifiable assumption, leaves much to be desired, would serve no good purpose, a consideration which we should do well to bear in mind,* are a continuous temptation, a packet of aspirins always at one's elbow. Look back through this essay, and for certain you will find that I have again and again committed the very faults I am protesting against. By this morning's post I have received a pamphlet dealing with conditions in Germany. The author tells me that he "felt impelled" to write it. I open it at random, and here is almost the first sentence that I see: "[The Allies] have an opportunity not only of achieving a radical transformation of Germany's social and political structure in such a way as to avoid a nationalistic reaction in Germany itself, but at the same time of laying the foundations of a cooperative and unified Europe." You see, he "feels impelled" to write — feels, presumably, that he has something new to say — and yet his words, like cavalry horses answering the bugle, group themselves automatically into the familiar dreary pattern. This invasion of one's mind by ready-made phrases (*lay the foundations, achieve a radical transformation*) can only be prevented if one is constantly on guard against them, and every such phrase anaesthetizes a portion of one's brain.

I said earlier that the decadence of our language is probably curable. Those who deny this would argue, if they produced an argument at all, that language merely reflects existing social conditions, and that we cannot influence its development by any direct tinkering with words and constructions. So far as the general tone or spirit of a language goes, this may be true, but it is not true in detail. Silly words and expressions have often disappeared, not through any evolutionary process but owing to the conscious action of a minority. Two recent examples were *explore every avenue* and *leave no stone unturned,* which were killed by the jeers of a few journalists. There is a long list of flyblown metaphors which could similarly be got rid of if enough people would interest themselves in the job; and it should also be possible to laugh the *not un-*formation out of existence,[3] to reduce the amount of Latin and Greek in the average sentence, to drive out foreign phrases and strayed scientific words, and, in general, to make pretentiousness unfashionable. But all these are minor points. The defence of the English language implies more than this, and perhaps it is best to start by saying what it does *not* imply.

To begin with it has nothing to do with archaism, with the

---

[3] One can cure oneself of the *not un-* formation by memorizing this sentence: *A not unblack dog was chasing a not unsmall rabbit across a not ungreen field.*

salvaging of obsolete words and turns of speech, or with the setting up of a "standard English" which must never be departed from. On the contrary, it is especially concerned with the scrapping of every word or idiom which has outworn its usefulness. It has nothing to do with correct grammar and syntax, which are of no importance so long as one makes one's meaning clear, or with the avoidance of Americanisms, or with having what is called a "good prose style." On the other hand it is not concerned with fake simplicity and the attempt to make written English colloquial. Nor does it even imply in every case preferring the Saxon word to the Latin one, though it does imply using the fewest and shortest words that will cover one's meaning. What is above all needed is to let the meaning choose the word, and not the other way about. In prose, the worst thing one can do with words is to surrender to them. When you think of a concrete object, you think wordlessly, and then, if you want to describe the thing you have been visualizing you probably hunt about till you find the exact words that seem to fit it. When you think of something abstract you are more inclined to use words from the start, and unless you make a conscious effort to prevent it, the existing dialect will come rushing in and do the job for you, at the expense of blurring or even changing your meaning. Probably it is better to put off using words as long as possible and get one's meaning as clear as one can through pictures or sensations. Afterwards one can choose — not simply *accept* — the phrases that will best cover the meaning, and then switch round and decide what impression one's words are likely to make on another person. This last effort of the mind cuts out all stale or mixed images, all prefabricated phrases, needless repetitions, and humbug and vagueness generally. But one can often be in doubt about the effect of a word or a phrase, and one needs rules that one can rely on when instinct fails. I think the following rules will cover most cases:

(i)   Never use a metaphor, simile or other figure of speech which you are used to seeing in print.
(ii) Never use a long word where a short one will do.
(iii) If it is possible to cut a word out, always cut it out.
(iv) Never use the passive where you can use the active.
(v)   Never use a foreign phrase, a scientific word or a jargon word if you can think of an everyday English equivalent.
(vi) Break any of these rules sooner than say anything outright barbarous.

These rules sound elementary, and so they are, but they demand a deep change of attitude in anyone who has grown used to writing in the style now fashionable. One could keep all of them and still write bad English, but one could not write the kind of stuff that I quoted in those five specimens at the beginning of this article.

I have not here been considering the literary use of language, but merely language as an instrument for expressing and not for concealing or preventing thought. Stuart Chase and others have come near to claiming that all abstract words are meaningless, and have used this as a pretext for advocating a kind of political quietism. Since you don't know what Fascism is, how can you struggle against Fascism? One need not swallow such absurdities as this, but one ought to recognize that the present political chaos is connected with the decay of language, and that one can probably bring about some improvement by starting at the verbal end. If you simplify your English, you are freed from the worst follies of orthodoxy. You cannot speak any of the necessary dialects, and when you make a stupid remark its stupidity will be obvious, even to yourself. Political language — and with variations this is true of all political parties, from Conservatives to Anarchists — is designed to make lies sound truthful and murder respectable, and to give an appearance of solidity to pure wind. One cannot change this all in a moment, but one can at least change one's own habits, and from time to time one can even, if one jeers loudly enough, send some worn-out and useless phrase — some *jackboot, Achilles' heel, hotbed, melting pot, acid test, veritable inferno* or other lump of verbal refuse — into the dustbin where it belongs.

QUESTIONS

1. Revise one or two of Orwell's examples of bad writing.
2. Examine Orwell's metaphors. Do they fulfill his requirements for good writing?
3. Look again at Orwell's grotesque revision (page 637) of a passage from the Bible. Write a similar version of another passage from the Bible.
4. Examine an editorial on a political issue. Analyze the writing as Orwell might have.

Fathers and Sons

Studs Terkel

Glenn Stribling[1]

A casual encounter on a plane; a casual remark: he and his wife are returning from a summer cruise. It was their first vacation in twenty-five years. He is forty-eight.

He and his son are partners in the business: Glenn & Dave's Complete Auto Repair. They run a Texaco service station in a fairly affluent community some thirty miles outside Cleveland. "There's eight of us on the payroll, counting my son and I. Of course, the wife, she's the bookkeeper." There are three tow trucks.

"Glenn & Dave's is equipped to do all nature of repair work: everything from transmission, air conditioning, valves, all . . . everything. I refer to it as a garage because we do everything garages do.

"We have been here four years." He himself has been at it "steady" for twenty-nine years. "When I was a kid in high school I worked at the Studebaker garage part-time for seven dollars a week. And I paid seven dollars a week board and room." (Laughs.) "It more or less runs in our family. My great-grandfather used to make spokes for automobiles back in Pennsylvania when they used wooden wheels. I have a brother, he's a mechanic. I have another brother in California, he's in the same business as I'm in. My dad, he was a steam engine repairman.

"Another reason I went into this business: it's Depression-proof. A good repairman will always have a job. Even though they're making cars so they don't last so long and people trade 'em in more often, there's still gonna be people that have to know what they're doing."

I work eight days a week. (Laughs.) My average weeks usually run to eighty, ninety hours. We get every other Sunday off, my son and I. Alternate, you know. Oh, I love it. There's never a day long enough. We never get through. And that's a good way to have it, 'cause people rely on you and you rely on them, and it's one big

---

[1] Terkel's book *Working* consists of edited versions of more than a hundred interviews with workers of all sorts. Here we reprint an interview with Glenn Stribling and another with Stribling's son, Dave.

business. Sometimes, they're all three trucks goin'. All we sell is service, and if you can't give service, you might as well give up.

All our business has come to us from mouth to mouth. We've never run a big ad in the paper. That itself is a good sign that people are satisfied. Of course, there's some people that nobody could satisfy. I've learned: Why let one person spoil your whole day?

A new customer comes to town, he would say, "So-and-so, I met him on the train and he recommended you folks very highly." Oh, we've had a lot of compliments where people, they say they've never had anything like that done to a car. They are real happy that we did point out things and do things. Preventive maintenance I call it.

A man come in, we'd Xed his tires, sold him a set of shocks, repacked his wheel bearings, aligned his front, serviced his car — by service I mean lubricate, change oil, filter . . . But he had only one tail light working and didn't know it. So we fixed that and he'll be grateful for it. If it's something big, a matter of a set of tires or if he needs a valve job, we call the customer and discuss it with him.

Sometimes, but not very often, I've learned to relax. When I walk out of here I try to leave everything, 'cause we have a loud bell at home. If I'm out in the yard working, people call. They want to know about a car, maybe make a date for next week, or maybe there's a car here that we've had and there's a question on it. The night man will call me up at home. We have twenty-four-hour service, too, towing. My son and I, we take turns. So this phone is hooked up outside so you can hear it. And all the neighbors can hear it too. (Laughs.)

Turn down calls? No, never. Well, if it's some trucking outfit and they don't have an account with us — they're the worst risk there is. If they don't have a credit card or if the person they're delivering won't vouch for them, there's gotta be some sort of agreement on payment before we go out. Of course, if it's a stranger, if it's broke down, naturally we have the car.

Sometimes if we're busy, bad weather and this and that, why we won't get any lunch, unless the wife runs uptown and grabs a sandwich. I usually go home, it varies anywhere between six thirty, seven, eight. Whatever the public demands. In the wintertime, my God, we don't get out of here till nine. I have worked thirty-seven hours non-stop.

I don't do it for the money. People are in trouble and they call you and you feel obligated enough to go out there and straighten them out as much as you can. My wife tells me I take my business more serious than a doctor. Every now and then a competitor will come down and ask me to diagnose something. And I go ahead and do it. I'll tell anybody anything I know if it'll help him. That's a good way to be. You might want a favor from them sometime. Live and let live.

You get irritated a lot of times, but you keep it within yourself. You can't be too eccentric. You gotta be the same. Customers like people the same all the time. Another thing I noticed: the fact that I got gray hair, that helps in business. Even though my son's in with me and we have capable men working for us, they always want to talk to Glenn. They respect me and what I tell 'em.

If I'm tensed up and there'll be somebody pull in on the driveway, ring all the bells, park right in front of the door, then go in and use the washroom — those kind of people are the most inconsiderate kind of people there is. If you're out there in the back, say you're repacking wheel bearings. Your hands are full of grease. In order to go out in that drive, you have to clean your hands. And all the customer wanted to know was where the courtroom is. When I travel, if I want information, I'll park out on the apron. Sometimes we have as high as fifty, sixty people a day in here for information. They pull up, ring all the bells . . . You can imagine how much time it takes if you go out fifty, sixty times and you don't pump gas. I call 'em IWW: Information, wind, and water. It's worse the last four years we've been here. People don't care. They don't think of us. All they think of is themself.

Oh, I lose my temper sometimes. You wouldn't be a red-blooded American if you wouldn't, would you? At the same time you're dealing with the public. You have to control yourself. Like I say, people like an even-tempered person. When I do lose my temper, the wife, she can't get over it. She says, "Glenn, I don't know how you can blow your stack at one person and then five minutes later you're tellin' him a joke." I don't hold grudges. Why hold a grudge? Let people know what you think, express your opinion, and then forget it. Of course, you don't forget, you just don't keep harpin' on it.

In the summertime, when I get home I don't even go in the house. I grab a garden tool and go out and work till dark. I have a small garden — lettuce, onions, small vegetables. By the time you're on your feet all day you're ready to relax, watch television, sometimes have a fire in the fireplace. At social gatherings, if somebody's in the same business, we compare notes. If we run into something that's a time saver, we usually exchange. But not too much. Because who likes to talk shop?

There's a few good mechanics left. Most of 'em in this day and age, all they are is parts replacers. This is a new trend. You need an air conditioner, you don't repair 'em any more. You can get exchange units, factory guaranteed and much cheaper, much faster. People don't want to lay up their car long enough to get it fixed. If they can't look out and see their car in the driveway, they feel like they've lost something. They get nervous. It's very seldom people will overhaul a car. They'll trade it in instead.

This is something hard to find any more, a really good, conscientious worker. When the whistle blows, they're all washed up, ready to go before they're punched out. You don't get a guy who'll stay two or three hours later, just to get a job done.

Take my son, Dave. Say a person's car broke down. It's on a Sunday or a Saturday night. Maybe it would take an hour to fix. Why, I'll go ahead and fix it. Dave's the type that'll say, "Leave it sit till Monday." I put myself in the other guy's boots and I'll go ahead and fix his car, because time don't mean that much to me. Consequently we got a lot of good customers. Last winter we had a snowstorm. People wanted some snow tires. I put 'em on. He's a steady customer now. He just sold his house for $265,000.

When we took this last cruise, my customers told me Dave did a terrific job. "Before, we didn't think much of him. But he did a really good job this last time." I guess compared to the average young person Dave is above average as far as being conscientious. Although he does sleep in the morning. Today's Wednesday? Nine o'clock this morning. It was ten o'clock yesterday morning. He's supposed to be here at seven. Rather than argue and fight about it, I just forget it.

Another thing I trained myself: I know the address and phone number of all the places we do business with and a lot of our customers. I never even look in the phone book. (Dave had just made a phone call after leafing through the directory.) If he asked me, I coulda told him.

Dave Stribling

He is twenty-three, married, and has two baby children. He has been working with his father "more or less since I was twelve years old. It's one of those deals where the son does carry on the family tradition.

"I actually worked full-time when I was in junior high school. School was a bore. But when you stop and look back at it you wish to hell you'd

done a lot more. I wanted to go get that fast buck. Some people are fortunate to make it overnight. My dad and I had a few quarrels and I quit him. I used to work down at Chrysler while I was in high school. I worked at least eight hours a day. That was great. You don't work Saturdays and you don't work Sundays. Then I came back and worked for my dad."

How would I describe myself? Mixed up really. (Laughs.) I like my work. (Sighs.) But I wish I hadn't started that early. I wish I would have tried another trade, actually. At my age I could quit this. I could always come back. But I'm pretty deep now. If I were to walk out, it would be pretty bad. (Laughs.) I don't think I'll change my occupation, really.

I think I'da tried to be an architect or, hell, maybe even a real top-notch good salesman. Or maybe even a farmer. It's hard to say. The grass is always greener on the other side of the fence. You turn around and there's an attorney. It makes you feel different. You work during the day and you're dirty from this and that. The majority of the people overlook the fact as long as you're established and this and that. They don't really care what your occupation is as long as you're a pretty good citizen.

Where it really gets you down is, you're at some place and you'll meet a person and strike up a conversation with 'em. Naturally, sometime during that conversation he's going to ask about your occupation, what you do for a living. So this guy, he manages this, he manages that, see? When I tell him — and I've seen it happen lots of times — there's a kind of question mark in his head. Just what is this guy? You work. You just sweat. It's not mental. 'Cause a lot of these jobs that you do, you do so many of the same thing, it just becomes automatic. You know what you're doing blindfolded.

It's made me a pretty good livin' so far. But I don't have a lot of time that a lot of these guys do that are in my age and in the same status that I am. I put in every week at least sixty, sixty-five hours. And then at night, you never know. If somebody breaks down, you can't tell 'em no. You gotta go. My friends work forty hours a week and they're done. Five days a week. I work seven, actually. Every other Sunday. I have to come and open up.

I don't really like to talk about my work with my friends. They don't really seem to, either. A lot of times somebody will ask me something about their car. How much will this cost? How much will that cost? I don't really even want to quote my price to them. A couple of 'em work for the state, in an office. A couple of 'em are body men. One's a carpenter, one's a real estate salesman. A few of 'em, they just work.

I come home, I gotta go in the back door, 'cause I've got on greasy boots. (Laughs.) If it does happen to be about six thirty, then I won't get cleaned up before I eat. I'll sit down and eat with the wife and kids. If they've already eaten, I'll take a shower and I'll get cleaned up and I'll come down and eat. If it's a nice night, I might go out and putz around the yard. If it's not nice outside, I'll just sit and watch the TV. I don't really read that much. I probably read as much as the average American. But nothing any more. Sometimes you really put out a lot of work that day — in general, I'm tired. I'm asleep by ten o'clock at night. I come to work, it varies, I might come in between eight and nine, maybe even ten o'clock in the morning. I like my sleep. (Laughs.)

He's the one that opens it up. He believes the early bird gets the worm. But that's not always true either. I might come in late, but actually I do more work than he does here in a day. Most of it probably is as careful as his. I can't understand a lot of the stuff he does. But he can't understand a lot of the stuff I do either. (Laughs.) He's getting better. He's kinda come around. But he still does think old-fashioned.

Like tools. You can buy equipment, it might cost a lot more money but it'll do the job faster and easier. He'll go grab hand tools, that you gotta use your own muscle. He doesn't go in for power tools.

Like judging people. Anybody with long hair is no good to him — even me. If he caught me asleep, he'd probably give me a Yul Brynner. Hair doesn't have anything to do with it. I've met a lot of people with hair really long, just like a female. They're still the same. They still got their ideas and they're not hippies or anything. They go to work every day just like everybody else does. It gets him. Especially if someone will come in and ask him to do something, he'll let them know he doesn't like them. I don't give people that much static.

When somebody comes in and they're in a rage and it's all directed at you, I either go get the hell out of there or my rage is brought up towards them. I've definitely lost customers by tellin' 'em. I don't know how to just slough it off. In the majority of cases you're sorry for it.

I've seen my father flare up a lot of times. Somebody gives him a bad time during the day, he'll take it home. Whereas instead of tellin' 'em right there on the spot, he'll just keep it within himself. Then half-hour later he might be mumblin' somethin'. When I used to live at home, you could tell by thirty seconds after he got in the door that he either didn't feel good or somebody gave him a bad time. He just keeps it going through his mind. He won't forget it. Whereas when I go home to the wife and the two kids, I just like to forget it. I don't want to talk about it at all.

I yell a lot, cuss a lot. I might throw things around down here, take a hammer and hit the bench as hard as it'll go, I'm getting better though, really. I used to throw a lot of stuff. I'd just grab and throw a wrench or something. But I haven't done that in a long time now. When you get older and you start thinking about it, you really have changed a lot in the last few years. (Laughs.) It'll stay inside me. You learn to absorb more of it. More so than when you were a kid. You realize you're not doing any good. Lotta times you might damage something. It's just gonna come out of your pocket.

When I was younger, if there was something I didn't agree upon, I was ready to go right then against it. But now I don't. I kinda step back a half a step and think it out. I've gotten into pretty good arguments with my buddies. It never really comes down to fists, but if you're with somebody long enough, it's bound to happen, you're gonna fight. You had a hard day and somebody gave you a hard time and, say you went out to eat and the waitress, she screwed something up? Yeah, it'll flare up. But not as much as it used to be.

As far as customers goes, there's not too many of 'em I like. A lot of customers, you can joke with, you can kid with. There are a lot of 'em, they don't want to hear any of it. They don't want to discuss anything else but the business while they're here. Older people, yeah, they're pretty hard. Because they've gone through a change from a Model T to what you got nowadays. Nowadays a lot of 'em will put up the hood and they just shake their heads. They just can't figure it out.

Some of 'em, when they get old they get real grumpy. Anything you say, you're just a kid and you don't know what you're doin'. (Laughs.) They don't want to listen to you, they want to talk to somebody else. There's a lot of 'em that'll just talk to him. But there's a lot of 'em that want to talk to me and don't want to talk to him. My-age people. It's a mixed-up generation. (Laughs.)

I have pride in what I do. This day and age, you don't always repair something. You renew. Whereas in his era you could buy a kit to rebuild pretty near anything. Take a water pump. You can buy 'em. You can put on a new one. I wouldn't even bother to repair a water pump. You can buy rebuilts, factory rebuilts. Back in his time you rebuilt water pumps.

His ideas are old, really. You gotta do this a certain way and this a certain way. There's short cuts found that you could just eliminate half the stuff you do. But he won't. A lot of the new stuff that comes out, he won't believe anybody. He won't even believe me. He might call three or four people before he'll believe it. Why he won't believe me I don't know. I guess he must figure I bull him a lot. (Laughs.)

When he was working for a living as a mechanic, his ability was pretty good. Actually, he doesn't do that much work. I mean, he more or less is a front. (Laughs.) Many people come in here that think he does work on their car. But he doesn't. He's mostly the one that meets people. He brings the work in. In his own mind he believes he's putting out the work. But we're the ones that put out the work.

He's kind of funny to figure out. (Laughs.) He has no hobbies, really. When he's out he'll still talk his trade. He just can't forget it, leave it go.

I'd like to go bigger in this business, but father says no for right now. He's too skeptical. We're limited here. He doesn't want to go in debt. But you gotta spend money to make money. He's had to work harder than I have. There's nobody that ever really gave him anything. He's had to work for everything he's got. He's given me a lot. Sometimes he gives too much. His grand-kids, they've got clothes at home still in boxes, brand-new as they got 'em. He just goes overboard. If I need money, he'll loan it to me. He's lent me money that I haven't even paid back, really. (Laughs.)

(Sighs.) I used to play music. I used to play in a rock group. Bass. I didn't know very much on the bass. Everybody that was in the band really didn't know all that much. We more or less progressed together. We played together for a year and a half, then everything just broke up. Oh yeah, we enjoyed it. It was altogether different. I like to play music now but don't have the time . . . I like to play, but you can't do both. This is my living. You have to look at it that way.

QUESTIONS

1. How accurate do you think Glenn Stribling's view of his son is?

2. How accurate do you think Dave Stribling's view of his father is?

On Natural Death

Lewis Thomas

There are so many new books about dying that there are now special shelves set aside for them in bookshops, along with the health-diet and home-repair paperbacks and the sex manuals. Some of them are so packed with detailed information and step-by-step instructions for performing the function that you'd think this was a new sort of skill which all of us are now required to learn. The strongest impression the casual reader gets, leafing through, is that proper dying has become an extraordinary, even an exotic experience, something only the specially trained get to do.

Also, you could be led to believe that we are the only creatures capable of the awareness of death, that when all the rest of nature is being cycled through dying, one generation after another, it is a different kind of process, done automatically and trivially, more "natural," as we say.

An elm in our backyard caught the blight this summer and dropped stone dead, leafless, almost overnight. One weekend it was a normal-looking elm, maybe a little bare in spots but nothing alarming, and the next weekend it was gone, passed over, departed, taken. Taken is right, for the tree surgeon came by yesterday with his crew of young helpers and their cherry picker, and took it down branch by branch and carted it off in the back of a red truck, everyone singing.

The dying of a field mouse, at the jaws of an amiable household cat, is a spectacle I have beheld many times. It used to make me wince. Early in life I gave up throwing sticks at the cat to make him drop the mouse, because the dropped mouse regularly went ahead and died anyway, but I always shouted unaffections at the cat to let him know the sort of animal he had become. Nature, I thought, was an abomination.

Recently I've done some thinking about that mouse, and I wonder if his dying is necessarily all that different from the passing of our elm. The main difference, if there is one, would be in the matter of pain. I do not believe that an elm tree has pain receptors, and even so, the blight seems to me a relatively painless way to go even if there were nerve endings in a tree, which there are not. But the mouse dangling tail-down from the teeth of a gray cat is something else again, with pain beyond bearing, you'd think, all over his small body.

There are now some plausible reaons for thinking it is not like that at all, and you can make up an entirely different story about the mouse and his dying if you like. At the instant of being trapped and penetrated by teeth, peptide hormones are released by cells in the hypothalamus and the pituitary gland; instantly these substances, called endorphins, are attached to the surfaces of other cells responsible for pain perception; the hormones have the pharmacologic properties of opium; there is no pain. Thus it is that the mouse seems always to dangle so languidly from the jaws, lies there so quietly when dropped, dies of his injuries without a struggle. If a mouse could shrug, he'd shrug.

I do not know if this is true or not, nor do I know how to prove it if it is true. Maybe if you could get in there quickly enough and administer naloxone, a specific morphine antagonist, you could turn off the endorphins and observe the restoration of pain, but this is not something I would care to do or see. I think I will leave it there, as a good guess about the dying of a cat-chewed mouse, perhaps about dying in general.

Montaigne had a hunch about dying, based on his own close call in a riding accident. He was so badly injured as to be believed dead by his companions, and was carried home with lamentations, "all bloody, stained all over with the blood I had thrown up." He remembers the entire episode, despite having been "dead, for two full hours," with wonderment:

> It seemed to me that my life was hanging only by the tip of my lips. I closed my eyes in order, it seemed to me, to help push it out, and took pleasure in growing languid and letting myself go. It was an idea that was only floating on the surface of my soul, as delicate and feeble as all the rest, but in truth not only free from distress but mingled with that sweet feeling that people have who have let themselves slide into sleep. I believe that this is the same state in which people find themselves whom we see fainting in the agony of death, and I maintain that we pity them without cause. . . . In order to get used to the idea of death, I find there is nothing like coming close to it.

Later, in another essay, Montaigne returns to it:

> If you know not how to die, never trouble yourself; Nature will in a moment fully and sufficiently instruct you; she will exactly do that business for you; take you no care for it.

The worst accident I've ever seen was on Okinawa, in the early days of the invasion, when a jeep ran into a troop carrier and was crushed nearly flat. Inside were two young MPs, trapped in bent steel, both mortally hurt, with only their heads and shoulders visible. We had a conversation while people with the right tools were prying them free. Sorry about the accident, they said. No, they said, they felt fine. Is everyone else okay, one of them said. Well, the other one said, no hurry now. And then they died.

Pain is useful for avoidance, for getting away when there's time to get away, but when it is end game, and no way back, pain is likely to be turned off, and the mechanisms for this are wonderfully precise and quick. If I had to design an ecosystem in which creatures had to live off each other and in which dying was an indispensable part of living, I could not think of a better way to manage.

QUESTIONS

1. We find the first paragraph witty, in a quiet way. In a paragraph point out the wit to a friend who missed it.
2. Make a rough outline of Thomas's essay — perhaps a sentence for each paragraph or group of closely related paragraphs — and then, on the basis of this outline, explain the organization of the essay. In particular, account for the relation between the first paragraph and the last.
3. Thomas uses "I" fairly often. Does he talk too much about himself? Explain.

The Battle of the Ants
Henry David Thoreau

I was witness to events of a less peaceful character. One day when I went out to my wood-pile, or rather my pile of stumps, I observed two large ants, the one red, the other much larger, nearly half an inch long, and black, fiercely contending with one another.

Having once got hold they never let go, but struggled and wrestled and rolled on the chips incessantly. Looking farther, I was surprised to find that the chips were covered with such combatants, that it was not a *duellum,* but a *bellum,*[1] a war between two races of ants, the red always pitted against the black, and frequently two red ones to one black. The legions of these Myrmidons[2] covered all the hills and vales in my wood-yard, and the ground was already strewn with the dead and dying, both red and black. It was the only battle which I have ever witnessed, the only battle-field I ever trod while the battle was raging; internecine war; the red republicans on the one hand, and the black imperialists on the other. On every side they were engaged in deadly combat, yet without any noise that I could hear, and human soldiers never fought so resolutely. I watched a couple that were fast locked in each other's embraces, in a little sunny valley amid the chips, now at noonday prepared to fight till the sun went down, or life went out. The smaller red champion had fastened himself like a vice to his adversary's front, and through all the tumblings on that field never for an instant ceased to gnaw at one of his feelers near the root, having already caused the other to go by the board; while the stronger black one dashed him from side to side, and, as I saw on looking nearer, had already divested him of several of his members. They fought with more pertinacity than bulldogs. Neither manifested the least disposition to retreat. It was evident that their battle-cry was "Conquer or die." In the meanwhile there came along a single red ant on the hillside of this valley, evidently full of excitement, who either had despatched his foe, or had not yet taken part in the battle; probably the latter, for he had lost none of his limbs; whose mother had charged him to return with his shield or upon it. Or perchance he was some Achilles, who had nourished his wrath apart, and had now come to avenge or rescue his Patroclus.[3] He saw this unequal combat from afar, — for the blacks were nearly twice the size of the red, — he drew near with rapid pace till he stood on his guard within half an inch of the combatants; then, watching his opportunity, he sprang upon the black warrior, and commenced his operations near the root of his right fore leg, leaving the foe to select among his own members; and so there were three united for life, as if a new kind

---

[1] *Duellum* and *bellum* are Latin words for, respectively, a combat of two persons, and a war. (All notes to this selection are by the editors.)

[2] Myrmidons were legendary Greek warriers.

[3] In the *Iliad* Achilles avenges the death of his friend Patroclus.

of attraction had been invented which put all other locks and cements to shame. I should not have wondered by this time to find that they had their respective musical bands stationed on some eminent chip, and playing their national airs the while, to excite the slow and cheer the dying combatants. I was myself excited somewhat even as if they had been men. The more you think of it, the less the difference. And certainly there is not the fight recorded in Concord history, at least, if in the history of America, that will bear a moment's comparison with this, whether for the numbers engaged in it, or for the patriotism and heroism displayed. For numbers and for carnage it was an Austerlitz or Dresden.[4] Concord Fight! Two killed on the patriots' side, and Luther Blanchard wounded! Why here every ant was a Buttrick, — "Fire! for God's sake fire!" — and thousands shared the fate of Davis and Hosmer. There was not one hireling there. I have no doubt that it was a principle they fought for, as much as our ancestors, and not to avoid a three-penny tax on their tea; and the results of this battle will be as important and memorable to those whom it concerns as those of the battle of Bunker Hill, at least.

I took up the chip on which the three I have particularly described were struggling, carried it into my house, and placed it under a tumbler on my window-sill, in order to see the issue. Holding a microscope to the first-mentioned red ant, I saw that, though he was assiduously gnawing at the near fore leg of his enemy, having severed his remaining feeler, his own breast was all torn away, exposing what vitals he had there to the jaws of the black warrior, whose breastplate was apparently too thick for him to pierce; and the dark carbuncles of the sufferer's eyes shone with ferocity such as war only could excite. They struggled half an hour longer under the tumbler, and when I looked again the black soldier had severed the heads of his foes from their bodies, and the still living heads were hanging on either side of him like ghastly trophies at his saddle-bow, still apparently as firmly fastened as ever, and he was endeavoring with feeble struggles, being without feelers and with only the remnant of a leg, and I know not how many other wounds to divest himself of them; which at length, after half an hour more, he accomplished. I raised the glass, and he went off over the window-sill in that crippled state. Whether he finally survived that combat, and spent the remainder of his days in some Hôtel des Invalides, I do not know; but I thought that his industry

---

[4] Battles during the Napoleonic wars.

would not be worth much thereafter. I never learned which party was victorious, nor the cause of the war; but I felt for the rest of that day as if I had had my feelings excited and harrowed by witnessing the struggle, the ferocity and carnage, of a human battle before my door.

Kirby and Spence tell us that the battles of ants have long been celebrated and the date of them recorded, though they say that Huber[5] is the only modern author who appears to have witnessed them. "Æneas Sylvius," say they, "after giving a very circumstantial account of one contested with great obstinacy by a great and small species on the trunk of a pear tree," adds that "'this action was fought in the pontificate of Eugenius the Fourth, in the presence of Nicholas Pistoriensis, an eminent lawyer, who related the whole history of the battle with the greatest fidelity.' A similar engagement between great and small ants is recorded by Olaus Magnus, in which the small ones, being victorious, are said to have buried the bodies of their own soldiers, but left those of their giant enemies a prey to the birds. This event happened previous to the expulsion of the tyrant Christiern the Second from Sweden." The battle which I witnessed took place in the Presidency of Polk, five years before the passage of Webster's Fugitive-Slave Bill.

QUESTIONS

1. The final sentence refers to Daniel Webster's Fugitive-Slave Bill. What is the relevance of this sentence to Thoreau's essay?
2. Are the metaphors of war serious or playful, or both? Do they glorify ants? Trivialize human beings? Or what? What is Thoreau's attitude toward his material, that is toward ants, human beings, and war? To what degree does Thoreau directly express his feelings? In what ways does he indirectly express them?
3. Thoreau says, "I have no doubt that it was a principle they fought for." Does this statement make sense?
4. In a paragraph or two describe Thoreau's persona here, supporting your characterization with concrete references to the essay. (On persona, see page 506.)
5. In a paragraph set forth your interpretation of Thoreau's essay. (You may want to consider if the essay has a point — or is it mere description?)

[5] Kirby and Spence were nineteenth-century American entomologists; Huber was a Swiss entomologist.

6. Watching the battle, Thoreau says, "I was myself excited some- what even as if they had been men." If you have ever felt excited by some aspect of nature, narrate the experience and try to account for your feeling.

Why Women Are Paid Less Than Men
Lester C. Thurow

In the 40 years from 1939 to 1979 white women who work full time have with monotonous regularity made slightly less than 60 percent as much as white men. Why?

Over the same time period, minorities have made substantial progress in catching up with whites, with minority women making even more progress than minority men. Black men now earn 72 percent as much as white men (up 16 percentage points since the mid-1950's) but black women earn 92 percent as much as white women. Hispanic men make 71 percent of what their white coun- terparts do, but Hispanic women make 82 percent as much as white women. As a result of their faster progress, fully employed black women make 75 percent as much as fully employed black men while Hispanic women earn 68 percent as much as Hispanic men.

This faster progress may, however, end when minority women finally catch up with white women. In the bible of the New Right, George Gilder's *Wealth and Poverty,* the 60 percent is just one of Mother Nature's constants like the speed of light or the force of gravity. Men are programmed to provide for their families econom- ically while women are programmed to take care of their families emotionally and physically. As a result men put more effort into their jobs than women. The net result is a difference in work intensity that leads to that 40 percent gap in earnings. But there is no discrimination against women — only the biological facts of life.

The problem with this assertion is just that. It is an assertion with no evidence for it other than the fact that white women have made 60 percent as much as men for a long period of time.

"Discrimination against women" is an easy answer but it also has its problems as an adequate explanation. Why is discrimination against women not declining under the same social forces that are leading to a lessening of discrimination against minorities? In recent years women have made more use of the enforcement provisions of the Equal Employment Opportunities Commission and the courts than minorities. Why do the laws that prohibit discrimination against women and minorities work for minorities but not for women?

When men discriminate against women, they run into a problem. To discriminate against women is to discriminate against your own wife and to lower your own family income. To prevent women from working is to force men to work more.

When whites discriminate against blacks, they can at least think that they are raising their own incomes. When men discriminate against women they have to know that they are lowering their own family income and increasing their own work effort.

While discrimination undoubtedly explains part of the male-female earnings differential, one has to believe that men are monumentally stupid or irrational to explain all of the earnings gap in terms of discrimination. There must be something else going on.

Back in 1939 it was possible to attribute the earnings gap to large differences in educational attainments. But the educational gap between men and women has been eliminated since World War II. It is no longer possible to use education as an explanation for the lower earnings of women. Some observers have argued that women earn less money since they are less reliable workers who are more apt to leave the labor force. But it is difficult to maintain this position since women are less apt to quit one job to take another and as a result they tend to work as long, or longer, for any one employer. From any employer's perspective they are more reliable, not less reliable, than men.

Part of the answer is visible if you look at the lifetime earnings profile of men. Suppose that you were asked to predict which men in a group of 25-year-olds would become economically successful. At age 25 it is difficult to tell who will be economically successful and your predictions are apt to be highly inaccurate. But suppose that you were asked to predict which men in a group of 35-year-olds would become economically successful. If you are successful at age 35, you are very likely to remain successful for the rest of your life. If you have not become economically successful by age 35, you are very unlikely to do so later.

The decade between 25 and 35 is when men either succeed or fail. It is the decade when lawyers become partners in the good firms, when business managers make it onto the "fast track," when academics get tenure at good universities, and when blue collar workers find the job opportunities that will lead to training opportunities and the skills that will generate high earnings. If there is any one decade when it pays to work hard and to be consistently in the labor force, it is the decade between 25 and 35. For those who succeed, earnings will rise rapidly. For those who fail, earnings will remain flat for the rest of their lives.

But the decade between 25 and 35 is precisely the decade when women are most apt to leave the labor force or become part-time workers to have children. When they do, the current system of promotion and skill acquisition will extract an enormous lifetime price.

This leaves essentially two avenues for equalizing male and female earnings. Families where women who wish to have successful careers, compete with men, and achieve the same earnings should alter their family plans and have their children either before 25 or after 35. Or society can attempt to alter the existing promotion and skill acquisition system so that there is a longer time period in which both men and women can attempt to successfully enter the labor force. Without some combination of these two factors, a substantial fraction of the male-female earnings differentials are apt to persist for the next 40 years, even if discrimination against women is eliminated.

QUESTIONS

1. Thurow assumes that discrimination against women can't possibly be the whole explanation for their lower earnings. On what does he base this assumption? Do you agree with his assumption?
2. Evaluate Thurow's opening paragraph, explaining why you find it effective or ineffective.
3. Where in the essay does Thurow provide an answer to the question asked in his title? State his answer as a syllogism, with a major premise, a minor premise, and a conclusion. (On syllogism, see page 202.)
4. After giving his analysis, Thurow ends the essay be suggesting two ways in which the differential in earnings may be decreased. Does he convey enthusiasm? Optimism? Is the tone or the ending consistent with the tone of the rest of the essay?

The Door

E. B. White

Everything (he kept saying) is something it isn't. And everybody is always somewhere else. Maybe it was the city, being in the city, that made him feel how queer everything was and that it was something else. Maybe (he kept thinking) it was the names of the things. The names were tex and frequently koid. Or they were flex and oid or they were duroid (sani) or flexsan (duro), but everything was glass (but not quite glass) and the thing that you touched (the surface, washable, crease-resistant) was rubber, only it wasn't quite rubber and you didn't quite touch it but almost. The wall, which was glass but thrutex, turned out on being approached not to be a wall, it was something else, it was an opening or doorway — and the doorway (through which he saw himself approaching) turned out to be something else, it was a wall. And what he had eaten not having agreed with him.

He was in a washable house, but he wasn't sure. Now about those rats, he kept saying to himself. He meant the rats that the Professor had driven crazy by forcing them to deal with problems which were beyond the scope of rats, the insoluble problems. He meant the rats that had been trained to jump at the square card with the circle in the middle, and the card (because it was something it wasn't) would give way and let the rat into a place where the food was, but then one day it would be a trick played on the rat, and the card would be changed, and the rat would jump but the card wouldn't give way, and it was an impossible situation (for a rat) and the rat would go insane and into its eyes would come the unspeakably bright imploring look of the frustrated, and after the convulsions were over and the frantic racing around, then the passive stage would set in and the willingness to let anything be done to it, even if it was something else.

He didn't know which door (or wall) or opening in the house to jump at, to get through, because one was an opening that wasn't a door (it was a void, or koid) and the other was a wall that wasn't an opening, it was a sanitary cupboard of the same color. He caught a glimpse of his eyes staring into his eyes, in the thrutex, and in them was the expression he had seen in the picture of the rats — weary after convulsions and the frantic racing around, when they were willing and did not mind having anything done to them. More and more (he kept saying) I am confronted by a problem which is incapable of solution (for this time even if he chose the right door, there would be no food behind it) and that is what madness is, and things seeming different from what they are. He heard, in the house where he was, in the city to which he had gone (as toward a door which might, or might not, give way), a noise — not a loud noise but more of a low prefabricated humming. It came from a place in the base of the wall (or stat) where the flue carrying the filterable air was, and not far from the Minipiano, which was made of the same material nailbrushes are made of, and which was under the stairs. "This, too, has been tested," she said, pointing, but not at it, "and found viable." It wasn't a loud noise, he kept thinking, sorry that he had seen his eyes, even though it was through his own eyes that he had seen them.

First will come the convulsions (he said), then the exhaustion, then the willingness to let anything be done. "And you better believe it *will* be."

All his life he had been confronted by situations which were incapable of being solved, and there was a deliberateness behind all this, behind this changing of the card (or door), because they would always wait till you had learned to jump at the certain card (or door) — the one with the circle — and then they would change it on you. There have been so many doors changed on me, he said, in the last twenty years, but it is now becoming clear that it is an impossible situation, and the question is whether to jump again, even though they ruffle you in the rump with a blast of air — to make you jump. He wished he wasn't standing by the Minipiano. First they would teach you the prayers and the Psalms, and that would be the right door (the one with the circle) and the long sweet words with the holy sound, and that would be the one to jump at to get where the food was. Then one day you jumped and it didn't give way, so that all you got was the bump on the nose, and the first bewilderment, the first young bewilderment.

I don't know whether to tell her about the door they substituted or not, he said, the one with the equation on it and the picture of the amoeba reproducing itself by division. Or the one with the photostatic copy of the check for thirty-two dollars and fifty cents. But the jumping was so long ago, although the bump is . . . how those old wounds hurt! Being crazy this way wouldn't be so bad if only, if only. If only when you put your foot forward to take a step, the ground wouldn't come up to meet your foot the way it does. And the same way in the street (only I never get back to the street unless I jump at the right door), the curb coming up to meet your foot, anticipating ever so delicately the weight of the body, which is somewhere else. "We could take your name," she said, "and send it to you." And it wouldn't be so bad if only you could read a sentence all the way through without jumping (your eye) to something else on the same page; and then (he kept thinking) there was that man out in Jersey, the one who started to chop his trees down, one by one, the man who began talking about how he would take his house to pieces, brick by brick, because he faced a problem incapable of solution, probably, so he began to hack at the trees in the yard, began to pluck with trembling fingers at the bricks in the house. Even if a house is not washable, it is worth taking down. It is not till later that the exhaustion sets in.

But it is inevitable that they will keep changing the doors on you, he said, because that is what they are for; and the thing is to get used to it and not let it unsettle the mind. But that would mean not jumping, and you can't. Nobody can not jump. There will be no not-jumping. Among rats, perhaps, but among people never. Everybody has to keep jumping at a door (the one with the circle on it) because that is the way everybody is, especially some people. You wouldn't want me, standing here, to tell you, would you, about my friend the poet (deceased) who said, "My heart has followed all my days something I cannot name"? (It had the circle on it.) And like many poets, although few so beloved, he is gone. It killed him, the jumping. First, of course, there were the preliminary bouts, the convulsions, and the calm and the willingness.

I remember the door with the picture of the girl on it (only it was spring), her arms outstretched in loveliness, her dress (it was the one with the circle on it) uncaught, beginning the slow, clear, blinding cascade — and I guess we would all like to try that door again, for it seemed like the way and for a while it was the way, the door would open and you would go through winged and exalted (like any rat) and the food would be there, the way the Professor had it arranged, everything O.K., and you had chosen the right door for the world was young. The time they changed that door on me, my nose bled for a hundred hours — how do you like that, Madam? Or would you prefer to show me further through this so strange house, or you could take my name and send it to me, for although my heart has followed all my days something I cannot name, I am tired of the jumping and I do not know which way to go, Madam, and I am not even sure that I am not tried beyond the endurance of man (rat, if you will) and have taken leave of sanity. What are you following these days, old friend, after your recovery from the last bump? What is the name, or is it something you cannot name? The rats have a name for it by this time, perhaps, but I don't know what they call it. I call it plexikoid and it comes in sheets, something like insulating board, unattainable and ugli-proof.

And there was the man out in Jersey, because I keep thinking about his terrible necessity and the passion and trouble he had gone to all those years in the indescribable abundance of a householder's detail, building the estate and the planting of the trees and in spring the lawn-dressing and in fall the bulbs for the spring burgeoning, and the watering of the grass on the long light evenings in summer and the gravel for the driveway (all had to be thought out, planned) and the decorative borders, probably, the perennials and the bug spray, and the building of the house from plans of the architect, first the sills, then the studs, then the full corn in the ear, the floors laid on the floor timbers, smoothed, and then the carpets upon the smooth floors and the curtains and the rods therefor. And then, almost without warning, he would be jumping at the same old door and it wouldn't give: they had changed it on him, making life no longer supportable under the elms in the elm shade, under the maples in the maple shade.

"Here you have the maximum of openness in a small room."

It was impossible to say (maybe it was the city) what made him feel the way he did, and I am not the only one either, he kept thinking — ask any doctor if I am. The doctors, they know how many there are, they even know where the trouble is only they don't like to tell you about the prefrontal lobe because that means making a hole in your skull and removing the work of centuries. It took so long coming, this lobe, so many, many years. (Is it something you read in the paper, perhaps?) And now, the strain being so great, the door having been changed by the Professor once too often . . . but it only means a whiff of ether, a few deft strokes, and the higher animal becomes a little easier in his mind and more like the lower one. From now on, you see, that's the way it will be, the ones with the small prefrontal lobes will win because the other ones are hurt too much by this incessant bumping. They can stand just so much, eh, Doctor? (And what is that, pray, that you have in your hand?) Still, you never can tell, eh, Madam?

He crossed (carefully) the room, the thick carpet under him softly, and went toward the door carefully, which was glass and he could see himself in it, and which, at his approach, opened to allow him to pass through; and beyond he half expected to find one of the old doors that he had known, perhaps the one with the circle, the one with the girl her arms outstretched in loveliness and beauty before him. But he saw instead a moving stairway, and descended in light (he kept thinking) to the street below and to the other people. As he stepped off, the ground came up slightly, to meet his foot.

QUESTIONS

1. What information does the first paragraph give us about the story's setting and about the main character? What is the effect of all the parenthetical interruptions? How can White's use of a fragmentary sentence at the end of the paragraph be defended?

2. In the second paragraph, the man recalls an account of a psychologist's experiment. What was the experiment's purpose? Why does the man recall it?

3. Beginning with the fifth paragraph ("All his life"), the man reflects on the last twenty years of his life and on the "doors" that were constantly changed on him. What do the doors and their constant changing symbolize? He gives four examples. What are they, and what does each represent? Do the examples suggest that the man's problem is unique, or that it is shared by many of us?

4. What do the "man out in Jersey" and the "poet (deceased)" and the man have in common? How are they dissimilar?

5. In the next-to-last paragraph, the doctor offers the man a solution of a kind. What is it? What does White think of this solution?

6. Does the story have a happy ending? Explain.

PART FIVE

Editing

No iron can stab the heart
with such force as a period
put just at the right place.
— ISAAC BABEL

18

Manuscript Form

To edit a manuscript is to refine it for others to read. When your essay at last says what you want to say, you are ready to get it into good physical shape, into an edited manuscript.

BASIC MANUSCRIPT FORM

Much of what follows is nothing more than common sense. Unless your instructor specifies something different, you can adopt these principles as a guide.

1. Use 8½-by-11-inch paper of good weight. Keep as lightweight a carbon copy as you wish — or make a photocopy — but hand in a sturdy original. Do not use paper torn out of a spiral notebook; the ragged edges will distract the reader. If you have written your essay on a computer and have printed it on a continuous roll of paper, remove the perforated strips from each side of the paper and separate the sheets before you hand in the essay.

2. Write on one side of the page only. If you typewrite, double-space, typing with a reasonably fresh ribbon. If you write on a word processor, use a letter-quality printer or a dot-matrix printer that closely approaches letter quality.

3. In the upper right-hand corner, one inch from the top, put your name, your instructor's name, and the course number. Double-space between lines. It's a good idea to put your last name before the page number (in the upper right-hand corner) of each

subsequent page, so the instructor can easily reassemble your essay if somehow a page gets detached and mixed with other papers. (If you write your paper on a word processor, you can instruct it to print your name before each page number.)

4. Double-space after the number or title of the course, and then center the title of your essay. Capitalize the first letter of the first and last words of your title, the first word after a semicolon or colon if you use either one, and the first letter of all the other words except articles, conjunctions, and prepositions, thus:

`The Diabolic and Celestial Images in `<u>`The Scarlet Letter`</u>

Notice that your title is neither underlined nor enclosed in quotation marks (though of course if, as here, it includes material that would normally be italicized or in quotation marks, that material continues to be so written). If the title runs more than one line, double-space between the lines.

5. Begin the essay by double-spacing *twice* below the title. If your instructor prefers a title page, begin the essay on the next page and number it 1. The title page is not numbered.

6. Except for page numbers, leave a one-inch margin at top, bottom, and sides of the text.

7. Number the pages consecutively, using arabic numerals in the upper right-hand corner, half an inch from the top. Do not put a period or a hyphen after the numeral, and do not precede the numeral with "page" or "p." And, to repeat, do not number the title page. If you give the title on a separate sheet, the page that follows it is page 1.

8. Indent the first word of each paragraph five spaces from the left margin.

9. Fasten the pages of your paper with a paper clip in the upper left-hand corner. Stiff binders are unnecessary; indeed, they are a nuisance to the instructor, adding bulk and making it awkward to write annotations.

CORRECTIONS IN THE FINAL COPY

Your extensive revisions should have been made in your drafts, but minor last-minute revisions may be made on the finished copy. Proofreading may catch some typographical errors, and you may notice some small weaknesses. For example, you may notice in the final copy an error in agreement between subject and verb, as in "The insistent demands for drastic reform has disappeared from most of the nation's campuses." The subject is "demands" and so the verb should be plural, "have" rather than "has." You need not retype the page, or even erase. You can make corrections with the following proofreader's symbols.

Proofread the messages in the three triangles. If you find nothing wrong, read again.

Changes in wording may be made by crossing through words and rewriting just above them, either on the typewriter or by hand in pen:

```
                                       have
The insistent demands for drastic reform has disappeared from most of

the nation's campuses.
```

Additions should be made above the line, with a caret (∧) below the line at the appropriate place:

```
                                                   from
The insistent demands for drastic reform have disappeared∧most of the

nation's campuses.
```

Transpositions of letters may be made thus:

```
The insistent demands for drastic reform have disappeared from most of

the nation's campuses.
```

Deletions are indicated by a horizontal line through the word or words to be deleted. Delete a single letter by drawing a vertical or diagonal line through it.

```
The insistent demands for drastic reform ~~reform~~ have disappeared from

most of the nation's campuse/s.
```

Separation of words accidentally run together is indicated by a vertical line, *closure* by a curved line connecting the things to be closed up.

```
The insistent|demands for drastic reform have disappeared f⌒rom most of

the nation's campuses.
```

Paragraphing may be indicated by the symbol ¶ before the word that is to begin the new paragraph.

```
The insistent demands for drastic reform have disappeared from most of

the nation's campuses.¶Another sign that the country's mood has
```

QUOTATIONS AND QUOTATION MARKS

Quotations from the material you are writing about are indispensable. They not only let your readers know what you are talking about; they give your readers the material you are responding to, thus letting them share your responses. But quote sparingly and quote briefly. Use quotations as evidence, not as padding. If the exact wording of the original is crucial, or especially effective, quote it directly, but if it is not, don't bore the reader with material that can be effectively reduced either by summarizing or by cutting. And make sure, by a comment before or after a quotation, that your reader understands why you find the quotation relevant. Don't count on a quotation to make your point for you.

Here are some additional matters to keep in mind.

1. Identify the speaker or writer of the quotation, so that readers are not left with a sense of uncertainty. Usually this identification precedes the quoted material (e.g., "Smith says . . .") in accordance with the principle of letting readers know where they are going, but occasionally it may follow the quotation, especially if it will provide something of a pleasant surprise. For example, in

a discussion of T. S. Eliot's poetry, you might quote a hostile comment on one of the poems and then reveal that Eliot himself was the speaker.

Consider also using verbs other than "says" to introduce a quotation. Depending on the context — that is, on the substance of the quotation and its place in your essay — it might be more accurate to say "Smith argues," "adds," "contends," "points out," "admits," or "comments." Or, again with just the right verb, you might introduce the quotation with a transitional phrase: "In another context Smith had observed that . . ." or "To clarify this point Smith refers to . . ." or "In an apparent contradiction Smith suggests . . ." But avoid such inflated words as "opines," "avers," and "is of the opinion that." The point is not to add "elegant variation" (see page 481) to your introduction of someone else's words, but accuracy and grace. A verb often used inaccurately is "feels." Ralph Linton does not "feel" that "the term *primitive art* has come to be used with at least three distinct meanings." He "points out," "writes," "observes," or "says" so.

2. Distinguish between short and long quotations, and treat each appropriately. Short quotations (usually defined as not more than four lines of typing) are enclosed within quotation marks and run into the text (rather than set off, without quotation marks).

LeRoi Jones's "Preface to a Twenty Volume Suicide Note" ends with a glimpse of the speaker's daughter peeking into her "clasped hands," either playfully or madly.

Pope's Essay on Criticism begins informally with a contraction, but the couplets nevertheless have an authoritative ring: "'Tis hard to say, if greater want of skill / Appear in writing or in judging ill."

Notice that in the second example a slash (diagonal line, virgule) is used to indicate the end of a line of verse other than the last line quoted. The slash is, of course, not used if the poetry is set off, indented, and printed as verse, thus:

Pope's Essay on criticism begins informally with a contraction, but the couplets nevertheless have an authoritative ring:

```
'Tis hard to say, if greater want of skill

Appear in writing or in judging ill;

But of the two less dangerous is the offense

To tire our patience than mislead our sense.
```

Material that is set off (more than four lines of typing) is *not* enclosed within quotation marks. To set it off, begin a new line, indent ten spaces from the left margin, and type the quotation, double-spaced. If you are quoting two or more paragraphs of prose, indent the first line of each paragraph an additional three spaces, but indent the first line of your first paragraph these extra three spaces only if it was the beginning of a paragraph in your source. If you are setting off very short lines of poetry, you may center the passage so that the page does not look unbalanced. If you are setting off very long lines of poetry, you may indent them fewer than ten spaces.

Long quotations, whether poetry or prose, are usually introduced by a sentence ending with a colon, something like "Jones presents a forceful argument:" or "In his first soliloquy Hamlet condemns his uncle, but chiefly condemns his own mother: [the long quotation follows, on the next line]. Don't try to introduce a long quotation (say, more than a complete sentence) into the middle of one of your own sentences. It is almost impossible for the reader to come out of the quotation and to pick up the thread of your own sentence. It is better to lead into the long quotation with "Jones says . . ." and then, after the quotation, to begin a new sentence of your own.

3. An embedded quotation (that is, a quotation embedded into a sentence of your own) must fit grammatically into the sentence of which it is a part. For example, suppose you want to use Othello's line "I have done the state some service."

Incorrect

Near the end of the play Othello says that he "have done the state some service."

Correct

Near the end of the play Othello says that he has "done the state some service."

Correct

Near the end of the play, Othello says, "I have done the state some service."

4. The quotation must be exact. Any material that you add must be in square brackets (not parentheses), thus:

```
When Pope says that Belinda is "the rival of his [i.e., the sun's]
beams," he uses comic hyperbole.

Stephen Dedalus sees the ball as a "greasy leather orb [that] flew like
a heavy bird through the grey light."
```

If you wish to omit material from within a quotation, indicate the ellipsis by three periods, with a space before and after each period. If a sentence ends with the omission of the last part of the original sentence, put a period immediately after the last word quoted, and then put three spaced periods to indicate the omission. The following example is based on a quotation from the sentences immediately above this one:

```
The manual says, "If you . . . omit material from within a quotation,
[you must] indicate the ellipsis. . . . If a sentence ends with the
omission of the last part of the original sentence, put a period . . .
and then put three spaced periods. . . ."
```

Notice that if you begin the quotation with the beginning of a sentence (in the example we have just given, "If you" is the beginning of a quoted sentence) you do *not* indicate that material preceded the words you are quoting. Similarly, if you end your quotation with the end of the quoted sentence, you give only a single period, not four periods, although of course the material from which you are quoting may have gone on for many more sentences. But if you begin quoting from the middle of a sentence, or end quoting before you reach the end of a sentence in your source, it is customary to indicate the omissions. But even such omissions need not be indicated when the quoted material is obviously incomplete — when, for instance, it is a word or phrase.

When a line or more of verse is omitted from a passage that is set off, the three spaced periods are printed on a separate line.

5. Commas and periods go inside the quotation marks; semi-colons and colons go outside. Question marks, exclamation points, and dashes go inside if they are part of the quotation, outside if they are your own. Notice that in the following example, the first question mark is part of the quotation, and therefore it is enclosed within the quotation marks, but the second question mark is *not* part of the quotation and therefore it is outside the quotation marks.

```
Amanda ironically says to her daughter, "How old are you, Laura?" Is it
possible to fail to hear Laura's weariness in her reply, "Mother, you
know my age"?
```

The closing punctuation of a quotation thus depends on where the quotation fits into your sentence. Suppose you want to quote Laura's sentence, "Mother, you know my age." We have seen that if you use this quotation at the end of an interrogative sentence, you will need to put a question mark after the closing quotation mark. If you use it within a declarative sentence of your own, you will put a comma at the end of the quotation:

```
When Laura says, "Mother, you know my age," she reveals a touch of wear-
iness.
```

or:

```
"Mother, you know my age," Laura says wearily.
```

6. If you use parenthetic citations to document your sources (see pages 333–51), be sure to close the quotation *before* giving the citation. And be sure to put the terminal period, which ordinarily would be inside the quotation marks, *after* the parentheses. (See page 334.)

7. Use *single* quotation marks for material contained within a quotation that itself is within quotation marks, thus:

```
T. S. Eliot says, "Mr. Richards observes that 'poetry is capable of sav-
ing us.'"
```

8. Use quotation marks around titles of short works, that is, for titles of chapters in books and for stories, essays, short poems, songs, lectures, and speeches. Titles of unpublished works, even book-length dissertations, are also enclosed in quotation marks. But underline — to indicate *italics* — titles of pamphlets and of books, that is, novels, periodicals, collections of essays, and long poems, such as *The Rime of the Ancient Mariner* and *Paradise Lost*. Underline also titles of films, record albums, radio and television programs, ballets and operas, works of art, and the names of planes, ships, and trains.

Exception: titles of sacred works (for example, the Old Testament, the Bible, Genesis, Acts, the Gospels, the Koran) are neither underlined nor enclosed within quotation marks. To cite a book of the Bible with chapter and verse, give the name of the book, then a space, then an arabic numeral for the chapter, a period, and an arabic numeral (*not* preceded by a space) for the verse, thus: Exodus 20.14–15. Standard abbreviations for the books of the Bible (for example, Chron.) are permissible in footnotes and in parenthetic citations within the text.

19

Punctuation

Speakers can raise or lower the volume or pitch of their voices; they can speak a phrase slowly and distinctly and then (making a parenthetical remark, perhaps) quicken the pace. They can wave their arms, pound a table, or pause meaningfully. But writers, physically isolated from their audience, have only paper and ink to work with. Nevertheless, they can embody some of the tones and gestures of speech — in the patterns of their written sentences, and in the dots, hooks, and dashes of punctuation that clarify those patterns.

Punctuation clarifies, first of all, by removing or reducing ambiguity. Consider this headline from a story in a newspaper:

SQUAD HELPS DOG BITE VICTIM

Of course there is no real ambiguity here — only a laugh — because the stated meaning is so clearly absurd, and on second reading we supply the necessary hyphen in *dog-bite*. But other ill-punctuated sentences may be troublesome rather than entertaining. Take the following sentence:

He arrived late for the rehearsal didn't end until midnight.

Almost surely you stumbled in the middle of the sentence, thinking that it was about someone arriving tardily at a rehearsal, and then, since what followed made no sense, you probably went back and mentally added the comma (by pausing) at the necessary place:

He arrived late, for the rehearsal didn't end until midnight.

Punctuation helps to keep the reader on the right path. And the path is your train of thought. If your punctuation is faulty, you unintentionally point the reader off your path and toward dead end streets and quagmires. Let's look at an example.

Once more, with feeling.

Once more with feeling.

Is there a difference between these two sentences or do they have identical meanings? Well, if punctuation is not just ink on paper, the first sentence means something like "Let's do it again, but this time do it with feeling," while the second sentence means "The last performance had feeling, and so let's do it once more, keeping the feeling."

Even when punctuation is not the key to meaning, it usually helps you to get your meaning across neatly. Consider the following sentences:

> There are two kinds of feminism — one is the growing struggle of women to understand and change the shape of their lives and the other is a narrow ideology whose adherents are anxious to clear away whatever does not conform to their view.

This is clear enough, but by changing the punctuation it can be sharpened. Because a dash usually indicates an abrupt interruption — it usually precedes a sort of afterthought — a colon would be better. The colon, usually the signal of an amplification of what precedes it, here would suggest that the two classifications are not impromptu thoughts but carefully considered ones. Second, and more important, in the original version the two classifications are run together without any intervening punctuation, but since the point is that the two are utterly different, it is advisable to separate them by inserting a comma or a semicolon, indicating a pause. A comma before "and the other" would do, but probably a semicolon — without the "and" — is preferable because it is a heavier pause, thereby making the separation clearer. Here is the sentence, revised:

> There are two kinds of feminism: one is the growing struggle of women to understand and change the shape of their lives; the other is a narrow ideology whose adherents are anxious to clear away whatever does not conform to their view.

The right punctuation enables the reader to move easily through the sentence.

Now, although punctuation helps a reader to move through a sentence, it must be admitted that some of the rules of punctuation do not contribute to meaning or greatly facilitate reading. For example, in American usage a period never comes immediately after quotation marks; it precedes quotation marks, thus:

She said, "Put the period inside the quotation marks."

If you put the period after the closing quotation mark, the meaning remains the same, but you are also informing your reader that you don't know the relevant convention. Since a misspelled word or a misplaced period often gives the impression of laziness, ignorance, or incompetence, why not generate as little friction as possible by learning the chief conventions?

THREE COMMON ERRORS: FRAGMENTS, COMMA SPLICES, AND RUN-ON SENTENCES

Fragments and How to Correct Them

A fragment is a part of a sentence set off as if it were a complete sentence: *Because I didn't care. Being an accident. Later in the week. For several reasons. My oldest sister.* Fragments are common in speech, but they are used sparingly in writing, for particular effects (see pages 479–98). A fragment used carelessly in writing often looks like an afterthought — usually because it *was* an afterthought, that is, an explanation or other addition that really belongs to the previous sentence. With appropriate punctuation (and sometimes with no punctuation at all) a fragment can usually be connected to the previous sentence.

1. *Incorrect*

Many nineteenth-century horror stories have been made into films. Such as *Dracula* and *Frankenstein*.

Correct

Many nineteenth-century horror stories have been made into films, such as *Dracula* and *Frankenstein*.

2. *Incorrect*

Many schools are putting renewed emphasis on writing. Because SAT scores have declined for ten years.

Correct

Many schools are putting renewed emphasis on writing because SAT scores have declined for ten years.

3. *Incorrect*

He practiced doing card tricks. In order to fool his friends.

Correct

He practiced doing card tricks in order to fool his friends.

4. *Incorrect*

She wore only rope sandals. Being a strict vegetarian.

Correct

Being a strict vegetarian, she wore only rope sandals.
She wore only rope sandals because she was a strict vegetarian.

5. *Incorrect*

A fragment often looks like an afterthought. Perhaps because it *was* an afterthought.

Correct

A fragment often looks like an afterthought — perhaps because it *was* an afterthought.

6. *Incorrect*

He hoped to get credit for two summer school courses. Batik and Hang-Gliding.

Correct

He hoped to get credit for two summer school courses: Batik and Hang-Gliding.

Notice in the examples above that, depending upon the relationship between the two parts, the fragment and the preceding statement can be joined by a comma, a dash, a colon, or by no punctuation at all.

Notice also that unintentional fragments often follow subordinating conjunctions, such as *because* and *although*. Subordinating conjunctions introduce a subordinate (dependent) clause; such a clause cannot stand as a sentence. Here is a list of the commonest subordinating conjunctions.

after	though
although	unless
because	until
before	when
if	where
provided	whereas
since	while

Fragments also commonly occur when the writer, as in the fourth example, mistakenly uses *being* as a main verb.

Comma Splices and Run-on Sentences, and How to Correct Them

An error known as a *comma splice* or *comma fault* results when a comma is mistakenly placed between two independent clauses that are not joined by a coordinating conjunction: *and, or, nor, but, for, yet, so.* If the comma is omitted, the error is called a *run-on sentence.*

Examples of the two errors:

Comma splice (or *comma fault*): In the second picture the man leans on the woman's body, he is obviously in pain.

Run-on sentence: In the second picture the man leans on the woman's body he is obviously in pain.

Run-on sentences and comma splices may be corrected in five principal ways.

1. Use a period. Write two sentences.

In the second picture the man leans on the woman's body. He is obviously in pain.

2. Use a semicolon.

In the second picture the man leans on the woman's body; he is obviously in pain.

3. Use a comma and a coordinating conjunction (and, or, not, but, for, yet, so).

In the second picture the man leans on the woman's body, and he is obviously in pain.

4. Make one of the clauses dependent (subordinate). Use a subordinating conjunction such as *after, although, because, before, if, since, though, unless, until, when, where, while.*

In the second picture the man leans on the woman's body because he is in pain.

5. Reduce one of the independent clauses to a phrase, or even to a single word.

In the second picture the man, obviously in pain, leans on the woman's body.

Run-on sentences and comma splices are especially common in sentences containing transitional words or phrases such as the following:

also	however
besides	indeed
consequently	in fact
for example	nevertheless
furthermore	therefore
hence	whereas

When these words join independent clauses, the clauses cannot be linked by a comma.

Incorrect: She argued from faulty premises, however the conclusions happened to be correct.

Here are five correct revisions, following the five rules we have just given. (In the first two revisions we place "however" after, rather than before, "the conclusions" because we prefer the increase in emphasis, but the grammatical point is the same.)

1. She argued from faulty premises. The conclusions, however, happened to be correct. (Two sentences)
2. She argued from faulty premises; the conclusions, however, happened to be correct. (Semicolon)
3. She argued from faulty premises, but the conclusions happened to be correct. (Coordinating conjunction)
4. Although she argued from faulty premises, the conclusions happened to be correct. (Subordinating conjunction)

    5. She argued from faulty premises to correct conclusions. (Reduction of an independent clause to a phrase)

It should now be evident that the following sentence contains a comma splice:

    The husband is not pleased, in fact, he is embarrassed.

And the ways of repairing it are equally evident.

THE PERIOD

    1. Periods are used to mark the ends of sentences (or intentional sentence fragments) other than questions and exclamations.

    A sentence normally ends with a period.

    She said, "I'll pass."

    Yes.

    Once more, with feeling.

But a sentence within a sentence is punctuated according to the needs of the longer sentence. Notice, in the following example, that periods are *not* used after "pass" or directly after "said."

    "I'll pass," she said (but meant she hoped she would).

If a sentence ends with a quotation, the period goes *inside* the quotation marks unless parenthetic material follows the quotation.

    Brutus says, "Antony is but a limb of Caesar."

    Brutus says, "Antony is but a limb of Caesar" (*Julius Caesar*, II.i.165).

    2. Periods are used with abbreviations of titles and terms of reference.

    Dr., Mr., Mrs., Ms.

    p., pp. (for "page" and "pages"), i.e., e.g., etc.

But when the capitalized initial letters of the words naming an organization are used in place of the full name, the periods are commonly omitted:

    CBS, CORE, IBM, NBA, UCLA, UNICEF, USAF

3. Periods are also used to separate chapter from verse in the Bible.

Genesis 3.2, Mark 6.10

For further details on references to the Bible, see page 677.

THE COLON

The colon has three chief uses: to introduce a list or series of examples; to introduce an amplification or explanation of what precedes the colon; and to introduce a quotation (though a quotation can be introduced by other means). A fourth, less important, use is in the indication of time.

1. The colon may introduce a list or series.

> Students are required to take one of the following sciences: biology, chemistry, geology, physics.

Note, however, that a colon is *not* used if the series is introduced by *such as, for example,* or a similar transitional phrase.

2. As a formal introduction to an amplification or explanation, the colon is almost equivalent to *namely,* or *that is.* What is on one side of the colon more or less equals what is on the other side. The material on either side of the colon can stand as a separate sentence.

> She explained her fondness for wrestling: she did it to shock her parents.

> The forces which in China created a central government were absent in Japan: farming had to be on a small scale, there was no need for extensive canal works, and a standing army was not required to protect the country from foreign invaders.

> Many of the best of the Civil War photographs must be read as the fossils of earlier events: The caissons with their mud-encrusted wheels, the dead on the field, the empty landscapes, all speak of deeds already past.

> — John Szarkowski

Notice in this last example that the writer uses a capital letter after the colon; the usage is acceptable when a complete sentence follows the colon, as long as that style is followed consistently throughout a paper. But most students find it easier to use lowercase letters after colons, the prevalent style in writing today.

The use of a colon before an amplification or explanation should not be confused with the use of a *semicolon* before closely related independent clauses that are not joined by coordinating conjunctions. Note the difference between the previous example on Civil War photographs, which required a colon, and the following example, which requires a semicolon:

> Many of the best of the Civil War photographs must be read as the fossils of earlier events; paintings only rarely can be read so.

3. The colon, like the comma, may be used to introduce a quotation; it is more formal than the comma, setting off the quotation to a greater degree.

> The black sculptor Ed Wilson tells his students: "Malcolm X is my brother, Martin Luther King is my brother, Eldridge Cleaver is my brother! But Michelangelo is my grandfather!"
>
> — Albert E. Elsen

4. A colon is used to separate the hour from the minutes when the time is given in figures.

> 9:15, 12:00

Colons (like semicolons) go outside of closing quotation marks if they are not part of the quotation.

> "There is no such thing as a free lunch": the truth of these words is confirmed every day.

THE SEMICOLON

Typographically a semicolon is part comma, part period; and it does indeed function as a strong comma or as a weak period. It can never function as a colon.

1. As a strong comma, the semicolon can be used as follows:

> Only in countries touching on the Mediterranean has the nude been at home; and even there its meaning was often forgotten.

> In the greatest age of painting, the nude inspired the greatest works; and even when it ceased to be a compulsive subject it held its position as an academic exercise and a demonstration of mastery.

As a strong comma, it can be used to separate a series of phrases or clauses with internal commas.

> He had a car, which he hadn't paid for; a wife, whom he didn't love; and a father, who was unemployed.

But:

> He had a car, a wife, and a father.

2. As a weak period, the semicolon joins independent statements that the writer wishes to bring together more closely than a period allows. Lewis Thomas puts it thus: "The period tells you that that is that; if you didn't get all the meaning you wanted or expected, anyway you got all the writer intended to parcel out and now you have to move along. But with a semicolon there you get a pleasant little feeling of expectancy; there is more to come; read on; it will get clearer." Here are some examples of a semicolon joining independent but related statements.

> When a cat washes its face it does not move its paw; it moves its face.

> Others merely live; I vegetate.

> All the windows seemed to be in the wrong places; it was a house designed to hold the darkness.
>
> — Sharon R. Curtin

> The catacombs were not underground churches where Christians secretly worshiped; they were burial chambers connected by long passages, and they were well known to official Rome.

> He never complained; he knew it wouldn't do any good.

With short clauses, such as those in the last example, a comma could be used, but some purists would object, saying that joining even short clauses with a comma would produce a run-on sentence of the sort known as a comma splice or a comma fault (see pages 682–84).

Use a semicolon also before a conjunctive adverb (that is, a transitional word such as *also, consequently, furthermore, however, moreover, nevertheless, therefore*) connecting independent clauses, and put a comma after the conjunctive adverb.

Her hair was black and wavy; however, it was false.

Semicolons (like colons) go outside of closing quotation marks if they are not part of the quotation.

He said, "I do"; moreover, he repeated the words.

THE COMMA

A comma (from a Greek word meaning "to cut") indicates a relatively slight pause within a sentence. If after checking the rules you are still uncertain of whether or not to use a comma in a given sentence read the sentence aloud and see if it sounds better with or without a pause, and then add or omit the comma. A women's shoe store in New York has a sign on the door:

NO MEN PLEASE.

If the proprietors would read the sign aloud, they might want to change it to

NO MEN, PLEASE

In typing, always follow a comma with a space.

We outline below the correct uses of the comma. For your reference, here is a table of contents for the following pages:

A note on the position of the comma with other punctuation, pages 694–95

1. Independent clauses (unless short) joined by a coordinating conjunction (*and, or, nor, but, for, yet, so*) take a comma before the conjunction.

> Most students see at least a few football games, and many go to every game of the season.

> Most students seem to have an intuitive sense of when to use a comma, but in fact the "intuition" is the result of long training.

If the introductory independent clause is short, the comma is usually omitted:

> She dieted but she continued to gain weight.

2. An introductory subordinate clause or long phrase is usually followed by a comma.

> Having revised his manuscript for the third time, he went to bed.

> In order to demonstrate her point, the instructor stood on her head.

If the introductory subordinate clause or phrase is short, say four words or fewer, the comma may be omitted, provided no ambiguity results from the omission.

> Having left he soon forgot.

But compare this last example with the following:

> Having left, the instructor soon forgot.

If the comma is omitted, the sentence is misread. Where are commas needed in the following sentences?

> Instead of discussing the book she wrote a summary.

> When Shakespeare wrote comedies were already popular.

> While he ate his poodle would sit by the table.

> As we age small things become killers.

3. A subordinate clause or long modifying phrase tacked on as an afterthought is usually preceded by a comma.

> I have decided not to be nostalgic about the 1950's, despite the hoopla over Elvis.

> Buster Keaton fell down a flight of stairs without busting, thereby gaining his nickname from Harry Houdini.

> By the time he retired Hank Aaron had 755 home runs, breaking Babe Ruth's record by 41.

With afterthoughts, the comma may be omitted if there is a clear sequence of cause and effect, signaled by such words as *because, for,* and *so.* Compare the two following examples:

> In 1601 Shakespeare wrote *Hamlet,* probably his best-known play.

> In 1601 Shakespeare wrote *Hamlet* because revenge tragedy was in demand.

4. A pair of commas can serve as a pair of unobtrusive parentheses. Be sure not to omit the second comma.

> Doctors, I think, have an insufficient knowledge of acupuncture.

> The earliest known paintings of Christ, dating from the third century, are found in the catacombs outside of Rome.

> Medicare and Medicaid, the chief sources of federal support for patients in nursing homes, are frequently confused.

Under this heading we can include a conjunctive adverb (a transitional adverb such as *also, besides, consequently, however, likewise, nevertheless, therefore*) inserted within a sentence. These transitional words are set off between a pair of commas.

> Her hair, however, was stringy.

If one of these words begins a sentence, the comma after it is optional. Notice, however, that the presence of such a word as "however" is not always a safeguard against a run-on sentence or comma splice; if the word occurs between two independent clauses and it goes with the second clause, you need a semicolon before it and a comma after it.

> Her hair was black and wavy; however, it was false.

(See the discussion of comma splice on pages 682–84.)

5. Use a comma to set off a nonrestrictive modifier. A nonrestrictive modifier, as the following examples will make clear, is a sort of parenthetical addition; it gives supplementary information about the subject, but it can be omitted without changing the subject. A restrictive modifier, however, is not supplementary but essential; if a restrictive modifier is omitted, the subject becomes more general. In Dorothy Parker's celebrated poem,

> Men seldom make passes
> At girls who wear glasses,

"who wear glasses" is a restrictive modifier, narrowing or restricting the subject down from "girls" to a particular group of girls, "girls who wear glasses."
Here is a *non*restrictive modifier:

> For the majority of immigrants, who have no knowledge of English, language is the chief problem.

Now a restrictive modifier:

> For the majority of immigrants who have no knowledge of English, language is the chief problem.

The first version says — in addition to its obvious message that language is the chief problem — that the majority of immigrants have no knowledge of English. The second version makes no such assertion; it talks not about the majority of immigrants but only about a more restricted group — those immigrants who have no knowledge of English.
Other examples:

> Shakespeare's shortest tragedy, *Macbeth*, is one of his greatest plays.

In this sentence, "*Macbeth*" is nonrestrictive because the subject is already as restricted as possible; Shakespeare can have written only one "shortest tragedy." That is, "*Macbeth*" is merely an explanatory equivalent of "Shakespeare's shortest tragedy" and it is therefore enclosed in commas. (A noun or noun phrase serving as an explanatory equivalent to another, and in the same syntactical relation to other elements in the sentence, is said to be in apposition.) But compare

> Shakespeare's tragedy *Macbeth* is one of his greatest plays.

with the misleadingly punctuated sentence,

> Shakespeare's tragedy, *Macbeth*, is one of his greatest plays.

The first of these is restrictive, narrowing or restricting the subject "tragedy" down to one particular tragedy, and so it rightly does not separate the modifier from the subject by a comma. The second, punctuated so that it is nonrestrictive, falsely implies that *Macbeth* is Shakespeare's only tragedy. Here is an example of a nonrestrictive modifier correctly punctuated:

> Women, who constitute 51.3 percent of the population and 53 percent of the electorate, constitute only 2.5 percent of the House of Representatives and 1 percent of the Senate.

In the next two examples, the first illustrates the correct use of commas after a nonrestrictive appositive, and the second illustrates the correct omission of commas after a restrictive appositive.

> Houdini, the American magician, died in 1926.
> The American magician Houdini died in 1926.

6. Words, phrases, and clauses in series take a comma after each item except the last. The comma between the last two items may be omitted if there is no ambiguity.

> Photography is a matter of eyes, intuition, and intellect.
> — John Szarkowski

> She wrote plays, poems, and stories.

> He wrote plays, sang songs, and danced jigs.

> She wrote a wise, witty, humane book.

But adjectives in a series may cause difficulty. The next two examples correctly omit the commas.

> a funny silent film
> a famous French professor

In each of these last two examples, the adjective immediately before the noun forms with the noun a compound that is modified by the earlier adjective. That is, the adjectives are not a coordinate series (what is funny is not simply a film but a silent film, what is famous is not simply a professor but a French professor) and so commas are not used. Compare:

> a famous French professor
>
> a famous, arrogant French professor

In the second example, only "famous" and "arrogant" form a coordinate series. If in doubt, see if you can replace the commas with "and"; if you can, the commas are correct. In the example given, you could insert "and" between "famous" and "arrogant," but not between "famous" and "French."

Commas are not needed if all the members of the series are connected by conjunctions.

> He ate steak for breakfast and lunch and supper.

7. Use a comma to set off direct discourse.

> "It's a total failure," she said.
>
> She said, "It's a total failure."

But do not use a comma for indirect discourse.

> She said that it is a total failure.
>
> She said it is a total failure.

8. Use a comma to set off "yes" and "no."

> Yes, he could take Freshman English at ten o'clock.

9. Use a comma to set off words of address.

> Look, Bill, take Freshman English at ten o'clock.

10. Use a comma to separate a geographical location within another geographical location.

> She was born in Brooklyn, New York, in 1895.

Another way of putting it is to say that a comma is used after each unit of an address, except that a comma is *not* used between the name of the state and the zip code.

11. Use a comma to set off the year from the month or day.

> He was born on June 10, 1965. (No comma is needed if you use the form "10 June 1965.")

A note on the position of the comma when used with other punctuation: If a comma is required with parenthetic material, it follows the second parenthesis.

> Because Japan was secure from invasion (even the Mongols were beaten back), her history is unusually self-contained.

The only time a comma may precede a parenthesis is when parentheses surround a digit or letter used to enumerate a series.

> Questions usually fall into one of three categories: (1) true-false, (2) multiple choice, (3) essay.

A comma always goes inside closing quotation marks unless the quotation is followed by a parenthesis.

> "Sayonara," he said.
>
> "Sayonara" (Japanese for "goodbye"), he said.

THE DASH

A dash — made by typing two hyphens without hitting the space-bar before, between, or after — indicates an abrupt break or pause. Overuse of the dash gives writing an unpleasantly explosive quality.

1. The material within dashes may be, in a sense, parenthetic, though the dashes indicate that it is less dispensable than is parenthetic material.

> The bathroom — that private place — has rarely been the subject of scholarly study.
>
> The Great Wall of China forms a continuous line over 1400 miles long — the distance from New York to Kansas City — running from Peking to the edge of the mountains of Central Asia.
>
> The old try to survive by cutting corners — eating less, giving up small pleasures like tobacco and movies, doing without warm clothes — and pay the price of ill-health and a shortened life-span.
>
> — Sharon R. Curtin

Notice that when two dashes are used, if the material within them is deleted the remainder still forms a grammatical sentence.

2. A dash can serve, somewhat like a colon, as a pause before a series. It is more casual than a colon.

> The earliest Shinto holy places were natural objects — trees, boulders, mountains, islands.

> Each of the brothers had his distinct comic style — Groucho's double-talk, Chico's artfully stupid malapropisms, Harpo's horse-play.
>
> — Gerald Mast

Especially in this last example, where the series is elaborated, a colon could have been used, but it would have been more formal; here the dash is more appropriate to the subject.

A dash is never used next to a comma, and it is used before a period only to indicate that the sentence is interrupted. When used with closing quotation marks it goes inside if it is part of the quotation, outside if it is not.

PARENTHESES

First, a caution: avoid using parentheses to explain pronouns: "In his speech he (Hamlet) says . . ." If "he" needs to be explained by "Hamlet," omit the "he" and just say "Hamlet."

1. Parentheses subordinate material; what is in parentheses is almost a casual aside, less essential than similar material set off in commas, less vigorously spoken than similar material set off in dashes.

> While guest curator for the Whitney (he has since returned to the Denver Art Museum), Feder assembled a magnificent collection of masks, totems, paintings, clothing, and beadwork.

Two cautions: avoid an abundance of these interruptions, and avoid a long parenthesis within a sentence (you are now reading a simple example of this annoying but common habit of writers who have trouble sticking to the point) because the reader will lose track of the main sentence.

2. Use parentheses to enclose digits or letters in a list that is given in running text.

The exhibition included: (1) decorative screens, (2) ceramics, (3) ink paintings, (4) kimonos.

3. Do not confuse parentheses with square brackets, which are used around material you add to a quotation. See pages 674–75.

4. For the use of parentheses in documentation, see pages 333–54.

A note on the position of other punctuation with a parenthesis: The example under rule number 2, of commas preceding parentheses enclosing digits or letters in a list given in running text, is the rare exception to the rule that within a sentence, punctuation other than quotation marks never immediately precedes an opening parenthesis. Notice that in the example under rule number 1, the comma *follows* the closing parenthesis:

> While guest curator for the Whitney (he has since returned to the Denver Art Museum), Feder assembled a magnificent collection of masks, totems, paintings, clothing, and beadwork.

If an entire sentence is in parentheses, put the final punctuation (period, question mark, or exclamation mark) inside the closing parenthesis.

QUOTATION MARKS

1. Use quotation marks to attribute words to a speaker or writer. (Long quotations that are set off do not take quotation marks. See pages 673–74.) If your quotation includes a passage that was enclosed in quotation marks, alter these inner quotation marks to single quotation marks.

> According to Professor Hugo, "The male dragon in Chinese art has deep-set eyes, the female has bulging eyes, but as one Chinese scholar put it, 'This is a matter of interest only to dragons.'"

British quotation marks are just the reverse: single for ordinary quotations, double for inner quotations. If you are quoting from a passage that includes such quotation marks, change them to the American form.

2. Use quotation marks to indicate the title of unpublished works, like dissertations, and of short works — for example, a lecture, speech, newspaper article, essay, chapter, short story, or song, as well as a poem of less than, say, twenty pages. (But magazines and pamphlets, like books, are underlined.)

3. Use quotation marks to identify a word or term to which you wish to call special attention. (But italics, indicated by underlining, may be used instead of quotation marks.)

> By "comedy" I mean not only a funny play, but any play that ends happily.

Do *not* use quotation marks to enclose slang or a term that you fear is low; use the term or don't use it, but don't apologize by putting it in quotation marks, as in these examples.

Incorrect

"Streaking" was first popularized by Lady Godiva.

Incorrect

Because of "red tape" it took three years.

Incorrect

At last I was able to "put in my two cents."

In all three of these sentences the writers are signaling their uneasiness; in neither the first nor the second is there any cause for uneasiness, but probably the third should be rewritten to get rid of the cliché.

Be sparing, too, in using quotation marks to convey sarcasm, as in

> These "poets" are mere dispensers of fantasies.

Sarcasm is usually a poor form of argument, best avoided. But of course there are borderline cases when you may want to convey your dissatisfaction with a word used by others.

> African sculpture has a long continuous tradition, but this tradition has been jeopardized recently by the introduction of "civilization" to Africa.

Perhaps the quotation marks here are acceptable, because the writer's distaste has not yet become a sneer and because she is, in effect, quoting. But why not change "civilization" to "western culture," omitting the quotation marks?

Commas and periods go inside closing quotation marks except when the quotation marks are followed by parentheses, in which case they follow the closing parenthesis. Colons, semicolons, and footnote numbers go outside closing quotation marks. Question marks and exclamation points go inside if they are part of the quotation, outside if they are not.

> While Thelma Todd paddles the canoe, Groucho listens to her chatter, looks at a duck swimming near the canoe, and asks, "Did that come out of you or the duck?"

> What is funny about Groucho saying, "Whatever it is, I'm against it"?

ITALICS

In typewritten material underlining is the equivalent of italic type.

1. Underline the name of a plane, ship, train, movie, radio or television program, record album, musical work, statue, painting, play, pamphlet, and book (except sacred works such as the Bible, the Koran, Acts of the Apostles). Notice that when you write of *The New York Times,* you underline *New York* because it is part of the title, but when you write of the London *Times,* you do not underline "London" because "London" is not part of the title, only information added for clarity. Similarly, when you refer to *Time* magazine do not underline "magazine."

2. As suggested on page 490, use italics only sparingly for emphasis. Sometimes, however, this method of indicating your tone of voice is exactly right.

> In 1911 Jacques Henri Lartigue was not merely as unprejudiced as a child; he *was* a child.
>
> — John Szarkowski

3. Use italics for foreign words that have not become a part of the English language.

> Acupuncture aims to affect the *ch'i,* a sort of vital spirit which circulates through the bodily organs.

But:

> He ate a pizza.
>
> She behaved like a prima donna.
>
> Avoid clichés.

4. You may use italics in place of quotation marks to identify a word or term to which you wish to call special attention.

> Claude Lévi-Strauss tells us that one of the great purposes of art is that of *miniaturization.* He points out that most works of art are miniatures, being smaller (and therefore more easily understood) than the objects they represent.

CAPITAL LETTERS

Certain obvious conventions — the use of a capital for the first word in a sentence, for names (of days of the week, holidays, months, people, countries), and for words derived from names (such as pro-French) — need not be discussed here.

1. Titles of works in English are usually given according to the following formula. Use a capital for the first letter of the first word, for the first letter of the last word, and for the first letter of all other words that are not articles, conjunctions, or prepositions.

> *The Merchant of Venice*
>
> *A Midsummer Night's Dream*
>
> *Up and Out*
>
> "The Short Happy Life of Francis Macomber"
>
> *The New York Times*

2. Use a capital for a quoted sentence within a sentence, but not for a quoted phrase (unless it is at the beginning of your sentence) and not for indirect discourse.

> He said, "You can even fool some of the people all of the time."
>
> He said you can fool some people "all of the time."
>
> He said that you can even fool some of the people all of the time.

3. Use a capital for a rank or title preceding a proper name or for a title substituting for a proper name.

> She said she was Dr. Perez.
>
> He told President Reagan that the Vice President was away.

But:

> Why would anyone wish to be president?
>
> Washington was the first president.

4. Use a capital when the noun designating a family relationship is used as a substitute for a proper noun.

> If Mother is busy, ask Tim.

But:

> Because my mother was busy, I asked Tim.

5. Formal geographical locations (but not mere points on the compass) are capitalized.

> North America, Southeast Asia, the Far East
>
> In the Southwest, rain sometimes evaporates before touching the ground.
>
> Is Texas part of the South?
>
> The North has its share of racism.

But:

> The wind came from the south.
>
> Czechoslovakia is adjoined on the north by East Germany.

Do *not* capitalize the names of the seasons.

THE HYPHEN

The hyphen has five uses, all drawing on the etymology of the word *hyphen,* which comes from the Greek for "in one," "together."

1. Use a hyphen to attach certain prefixes from root words. *All-, pro-, ex-,* and *self-* are the most common of these ("all-

powerful," "ex-wife," "pro-labor," "self-made"), but note that even these prefixes are not always followed by a hyphen. If in doubt, check a dictionary. Prefixes before proper names are always followed by a hyphen:

> anti-Semite, pro-Kennedy, un-American

Prefixes ending in *i* are hyphenated before a word beginning with *i*:

> anti-intellectual, semi-intelligible

A hyphen is normally used to break up a triple consonant resulting from the addition of a prefix:

> ill-lit, all-loving

2. Use a hyphen to tie compound adjectives into a single visual unit:

> out-of-date theory, twenty-three books, long-term loan
> eighteenth- and nineteenth-century novels
> The sea-tossed raft was a common nineteenth-century symbol of man's tragic condition.

But if a compound modifier follows the modified term, it is usually not hyphenated, thus:

> The theory was out of date.

3. Use a hyphen to join some compound nouns:

> Scholar-teacher, philosopher-poet

4. Use a hyphen to divide a word at the end of a line. Because words may be divided only as indicated by a dictionary, it is easier to end the line with the last complete word you can type than to keep reaching for a dictionary. But here are some principles governing the division of words at the end of a line:

a. Never hyphenate words of one syllable, such as *called, doubt, right, through.*
b. Never hyphenate so that a single letter stands alone: *a-bout, hairy.*
c. If a word already has a hyphen, divide it at the hyphen: *anti-intellectual, semi-intelligible.*

d. Divide prefixes and suffixes from the root: *mis-spell, pro-vide, drunken-ness, walk-ing.*

e. Divide between syllables. If you aren't sure of the proper sylla-bification, check a dictionary.

5. Use a hyphen to indicate a span of dates or page numbers:

1957-59, pp. 162-68.

THE APOSTROPHE

Use an apostrophe to indicate the possessive, to indicate a contraction, and for certain unusual plurals.

1. The possessive. The most common way to indicate the possessive of a singular noun is to add an apostrophe and then an *s.*

> A dog's life, a week's work
>
> a mouse's tail, Keats's poems, Marx's doctrines

But some authorities suggest that for a proper noun of more than one syllable that ends in *s* or another sibilant (*-cks, -x, -z*), it is better to add only an apostrophe:

> Jesus' parables, Sophocles' plays, Chavez' ideas

When in doubt, say the name aloud and notice if you are adding an *s.* If you are adding an *s* when you say it, add an apostrophe and an *s* when you write it. Our own strong preference, however, is to add an apostrophe and an *s* to all proper nouns:

> Jones's book
>
> Kansas's highways

Pronouns do not take an apostrophe.

> his book, its fur ("it's fur" is short for "it is fur")
>
> The book is hers, not ours.
>
> The book is theirs.

(Exception: indefinite pronouns take an apostrophe, as in "one's hopes" and "others' opinions.")

For plurals ending in *s*, add only an apostrophe to indicate the possessive:

the boys' father, the Smiths' house, the Joneses' car

If the plural does not end in *s*, add an apostrophe and an *s*.

women's clothing, mice's eyes

Don't try to form the possessive of the title of a work (for example, of a play, a book, or a film): Write "the imagery in *The Merchant of Venice*" rather than "*The Merchant of Venice*'s imagery." Using an apostrophe gets you into the problem of whether or not to italicize the *s*; similarly, if you use an apostrophe for a work normally enclosed in quotation marks, you can't put the apostrophe and the *s* after the quotation marks, but you can't put them inside either. And the work really can't possess anything anyway — the imagery, or whatever else, is the author's.

2. Contractions. Use an apostrophe to indicate the omitted letters or numbers in contractions.

She won't.

It's time to go.

the class of '87

3. Unusual plurals. Use an apostrophe to make plurals of words that do not usually have a plural, and (this is optional) to make the plurals of digits and letters.

Her speech was full of if's and and's and but's.

Ph.D.'s don't know everything.

Mind your p's and q's.

I got two A's and two B's.

He makes his 4's in two ways.

the 1920's

But if the number is written out, it does not take an apostrophe:

In the envelope were two tens and two fives.

She is in her twenties.

ABBREVIATIONS

In general, avoid abbreviations except in footnotes and except for certain common ones listed below. And don't use an ampersand (&) unless it appears in material you are quoting, or in a title. Abundant use of abbreviations makes an essay sound like a series of newspaper headlines. Usually *United States* is better than *U.S.* and *the Soviet Union* better than *U.S.S.R.*

1. Abbreviations, with the first letter capitalized, are used before a name.

Dr. Bellini, Ms. Smith, St. Thomas

But:

The doctor took her temperature and ten dollars.

2. Degrees that follow a name are abbreviated:

B.A., D.D.S., M.D., Ph.D.

3. Other acceptable abbbreviations include:

A.D., B.C., A.M., P.M., e.g., i.e.

(By the way, *e.g.* means *for example;* *i.e.* means *that is.* The two ought not to be confused. See pages 725 and 728.)

4. The name of an agency or institution (for instance, the Committee on Racial Equality; International Business Machines; Southern Methodist University) may be abbreviated by using the initial letters, capitalized and usually without periods (e.g., CORE), but it is advisable to give the name in full when first mentioning it (not everyone knows that AARP means American Association of Retired Persons, for instance), and to use the abbreviation in subsequent references.

NUMBERS

1. Write them out if you can do so in fewer than three words; otherwise, use figures.

sixteen, seventy-two, ten thousand, one sixth

10,200; 10,200,000

There are 336 dimples on a golf ball

But write out round millions and billions, to avoid a string of zeroes.

>a hundred and ten million

For large round numbers you can also use a combination of figures and words, such as

>about 350 million

Note, however, that because a figure cannot be capitalized, if a number begins a sentence it should always be written out:

>Two hundred and fifty . . .

2. Use figures in dates, addresses, decimals, percentages, page numbers, and hours followed by A.M. or P.M.

>February 29, 1900; .06 percent; 6 percent; 8:16 A.M.

But hours unmodified by minutes are usually written out, and followed by *o'clock*.

>Executions in England regularly took place at eight o'clock.

3. To make the plural of figures (but not of numbers written out) use an apostrophe.

>three 6's

>two tens

Use an apostrophe to indicate omitted figures.

>class of '79

>the '80s (but: the eighties)

Use a hyphen to indicate a span.

>1975–79

In giving inclusive numbers, give the second number in full for the numbers up through ninety-nine (2–5, 8–11, 28–34). For larger numbers, give only the last two digits of the second number (101–06; 112–14) unless the full number is necessary (198–202).

4. Dates can be given with the month first, followed by numerals, a comma, and the year

> February 10, 1986

or they can be given with the day first, then the month and then the year (without a comma after the day or month)

> 10 February 1986

On decades, see item 3 above.

5. BC (no periods and no space between the letters) follows the year, but AD precedes it.

> 10 BC
>
> AD 200

6. <u>Roman numerals are less used than formerly.</u> Capital roman numerals were used to indicate a volume number, but volume numbers are now commonly given in arabic numerals. Capital roman numerals still are used, however, for the names of individuals in a series (Elizabeth II) and for the primary divisions of an outline; lowercase roman numerals are used for the pages of a preface. The old custom of citing acts and scenes of a play in roman numerals and lines in arabic numerals (II.iv.17–25) is still preferred by many instructors, but the use of arabic numerals throughout (2.4.17–25) is gaining acceptance.

EXERCISES

1. Correct the following sentence fragments. You may join fragments to independent clauses, or you may recast them as complete sentences.

   a. He left the sentence fragments in the final version of his essay. Instead of trying to fix them.
   b. Her associate left the country. Although their project was unfinished.

    c. Philip Roth argues that closing Newark's libraries will be a costly mistake. That the action will be an insult to Newark's citizens.

    d. He made corrections on the final copy of his essay by hand. Being unwilling to retype the whole paper.

    e. She spent three hours waiting in line in the rain to buy tickets to his concert. Since she was an irrepressibly enthusiastic Springsteen fan.

2. Determine which of the following sentences are run-ons and which contain comma splices. Label them accordingly and correct them appropriately — using any of the five methods shown on pages 682–84.

    a. *CATCH-22* is one of his favorite books, he's reading it now for the fifth time.

    b. Don't write run-on sentences they are not acceptable.

    c. The quarterback was intercepted on fourteen consecutive passes, he was traded the following season.

    d. Ambiguously punctuated sentences are usually confusing often they are humorous.

    e. There are those who warn that computers are dehumanizing students, however such people have produced no verifiable evidence.

3. Correct the following sentences, inserting the necessary colons and semicolons.

    a. I signed up for four courses this semester Spanish, geology, calculus, and composition.

    b. "Every dark cloud has a silver lining" I've found that the cliché doesn't always hold true.

    c. The semicolon is tricky it can be effective, but it is often misused.

    d. I finished my final papers three weeks early consequently, I had nothing to do while everyone else was working.

    e. The case for nuclear power has always rested on two claims that reactors were reasonably safe, and that they were indispensable as a source of energy.

    f. Dinner was a disaster he broiled fish, which he burned he steamed broccoli, which came out soggy and he baked a souffle, which fell.

4. In these sentences insert commas where necessary to set off phrases and clauses.

a. While she was cooking the cat jumped onto the refrigerator.
b. Geometry is a prerequisite for trigonometry and calculus is a prerequisite for physics.
c. He wanted to go to Europe in the summer so he had to take a part-time job.
d. Although she's aware of the dangers of smoking it seems impossible for her to quit.
e. Final exams they thought were a waste of time.
f. Turner's painting *The Slave Ship* probably his greatest work was donated to Boston's Museum of Fine Arts.

5. Insert commas to make the restrictive elements in the following sentences nonrestrictive. Be prepared to explain how changing the punctuation changes each sentence's meaning.

a. My uncle who owns a farm breeds racehorses.
b. The circus which returns to New York every winter is attended by thousands.
c. Teachers who are the ones chiefly entrusted with educating people formally should concentrate more heavily on developing their students' analytical skills.
d. Athletes who ought to know better sometimes play while injured.

6. Punctuate these sentences using the instructions given in items 6–11 on pages 692–93 as guidelines.

a. A lone masked silent gunman robbed the only bank in Albuquerque New Mexico on March 10 1885.
b. Yes it's a sentimental story but I like it.
c. "You have no taste" he said.
d. The plot of his detective novel was flimsy weak and unoriginal.
e. I would prefer not to receive a partridge in a pear tree two French hens three turtle doves and all that other stuff again this Christmas.

7. Place commas correctly in the following sentences.

a. "Don't write sentence fragments" the instructor said "they are unacceptable."
b. Arguing with him was useless (he was most stubborn when he was wrong) so she decided to drop the subject.
c. To revise Mrs. Beeton's famous recipe: you must (1) find your hare (2) catch it (3) cook it.
d. "A Good Man Is Hard to Find" "Petrified Man" and "A Rose for Emily" are three of his favorite short stories.

8. Correct the following sentences, adding apostrophes where needed. Label each word you correct to indicate whether it is a possessive, a contraction, or an unusual plural.

   a. Its easy to learn to use apostrophes.
   b. The boys books are on their shelves, under their beds, and in their closets.
   c. There are three copies of *Barnet and Stubbs Practical Guide to Writing* in the professors office.
   d. My copys falling apart
   e. In the 1940s ones dollars went farther.

9. In the following sentences, decide what punctuation is needed, and then add it. If the sentence is correctly punctuated, place a check mark to the left of it.

   a. Around his neck is a scarf knotted in front and covering his head is a wide brimmed hat.
   b. Buffalo Bill radiates confidence in his bold stance and looks self assured with his head held high.
   c. The demands that men and women make on marriage will never be fully met they cannot be.
   d. The Polish painter Oskar Kokoschka once said to a man who had posed for a portrait those who know you wont recognize you but those who dont will.
   e. Boys on the whole do not keep diaries.
   f. Children are unwelcome in most New York restaurants that are not Chinese.
   g. Shlomo a giraffe in the Tel Aviv zoo succumbed to the effects of falling down after efforts to raise him with ropes and pulleys were unsuccessful.
   h. Character like a photograph develops in darkness.
   i. In a grief reaction especially when the person has suffered a loss crying comes easily and produces a healthy release from pent up emotion.
   j. There is no God but Allah and Mohammed is His prophet.

10. We reprint below the fourth paragraph of Jeff Greenfield's essay, "Columbo Knows the Butler Didn't Do It," but without punctuation. Go through the paragraph, adding the punctuation you find necessary. Check your work against the original paragraph on page 65. If you find differences between your

punctuation and Greenfield's, try to explain why Greenfield made the choices he did.

columbos villains are not simply rich they are privileged.they live the lives that are for most of us hopeless daydreams.houses on top of mountains with pools servants and sliding doors.parties with women in slinky dresses and endless food and drink.plush enclosed box seats at professional sports events the envy and admiration of the crowd while we choose between johnny carson and *invasion of the body snatchers*.they are at screenings of movies the rest of us wait in line for on third avenue three months later.

11. Here are the first two paragraphs — but without punctuation — of Raymond A. Sokolov's review of a book by Sarah Stage, *Female Complaints: Lydia Pinkham and the Business of Women's Medicine*. Add the necessary punctuation.

home at the range victorian women in america suffered in shame from all manner of female complaints too intimate to name.many of them were the fault of men gonorrhea or men doctors.prolapsed uterus and women shrewdly kept shy of the ineffectual and often positively harmful doctors of their day.instead they doctored themselves with so called patent medicines.the most famous of these was lydia pinkhams vegetable compound.mrs pinkham actually existed in lynn mass a center of the progressive spirit hotbed of abolition and feminism.

sarah stage who has taught american history at williams college had the acuity to see that lydia pinkham was more than a quaint picture on a label.that she was a paradigm of the independent woman of her day.building a big business with a home remedy to save her family from bankruptcy caused by a neer do well husband.she saw furthermore that many of the important themes and forces of american society before world war I clustered around the medicine itself which was largely alcoholic but respectably bitter

20
Spelling

Life would be easier if a sound were always represented by the same letter. Some modern European languages come close to this principle, but English is not among them. "You" and "ewe" are pronounced identically, but they do not have even a single letter in common. George Bernard Shaw once called attention to some of the oddities of English spelling by saying that *fish* might be spelled *ghoti*. How? *Gh* is *f,* as in *enough; o* is *i,* as in *women; ti* is *sh,* as in *notion.* So, *ghoti* spells *fish.*

This is not the place to explain why English spelling is so erratic, but it may be consoling to know that the trouble goes back at least to the Norman French Conquest of England in 1066; after the Conquest, French scribes spelled English words more or less as though the words were French. Moreover, though pronunciation kept changing, spelling became relatively fixed, so that even in Shakespeare's time spelling often reflected a pronunciation that had long been abandoned. And today the spelling of many words still reflects the long-lost medieval pronunciation. The silent *e* in *life,* and the silent consonants in *knight* and *through,* for example, were pronounced in Chaucer's day.

But medieval pronunciation accounts for only some of our spellings. There are many other reasons for the oddities: the *s* in *island* is there, for example, because scholars mistakenly thought the word came into English through the Latin *insula.* (*Isle* indeed comes from *insula,* but *island* comes from Old English *iland.*) Most rules for spelling, then, must immediately be modified with lists of exceptions. Even the most famous,

> *I* before *e* except after *c*
> Or when sounded as *a*
> In *neighbor* and *sleigh,*

No, no it's ⟨⟩ before ⟨⟩ except after ⟨⟩ !

Reprinted with permission of Joseph Kohl.

has more exceptions than cheery handbooks admit. Always *ei* after *c*? What about *ancient, efficient,* and *sufficient*? Oh, but in these words the *c* is pronounced *sh,* an easy enough exception to keep in mind. But how can we explain *financier*? And of words where a *c* does not precede the letters in question, does the rule *ie* really govern all those not "sounded as *a* / In *neighbor* and *sleigh*"? How about *counterfeit, deity, either, foreign, forfeit, heifer, height, neither, leisure, protein, seize, their, weird*?

Instead of offering rules with menacing lists of exceptions, we offer a single list of words commonly misspelled in college writing. And here are four suggestions:

1. Read the list, mark any words whose spelling surprises you, and make a conscientious effort to memorize them.

2. Keep a dictionary at hand, and consult it while you are editing your final draft. If you have not formed a habit of consulting the dictionary, you may have to work at it. Begin by noticing what words or groups of words you have trouble with. Then cultivate the habit of doubting your own spellings of these words. When in doubt, don't guess; look the word up.

3. In a notebook, keep a list of words you misspell and try to classify your errors. Most spelling errors occur in characteristic and even predictable patterns. Some errors originate in mispronunciation, or the dropping or slurring of sounds in speech. (Notice, for example, gover*n*ment, Feb*r*uary, prejudic*e*d.) On the other hand, words with a vowel in an unaccented syllable are troublesome because those vowels all sound alike. You'll have to learn to visualize the correct vowel in such words as: dist*a*nt, it*e*m, ed*i*ble, gall*o*p, circ*u*s. Still other errors stem from confusing pairs of words such as: accept/except, conscience/conscious, past/passed, capital/capitol. But you don't have to be aware of all possible errors any more than you need to know all the rules. You need only to classify the errors you do make and work on reducing those. The task is really not hopeless.

4. For words that you persistently misspell, invent some device to assist your memory. For example, if you erroneously put an *a* in *cemetery* in place of an *e,* say to yourself "people r*e*st in a cemetery." When you next have to write the word *cemetery* you will remember the associative device (*rest*), and you will spell *cemetery* with an *e.* Another example: if you repeatedly leave out an *l* from *balloon,* say to yourself — really say it — "a balloon is a ball." The next time you have to write *balloon* you will remember *ball.* Similarly, tell yourself there's *a rat* in *separate.* A last example, for people who mistakenly put an *n* in *dilemma*: "Emma is in a dilemma." Generally speaking, the sillier the phrase, the more memorable it will be.

Words Commonly Misspelled

abridgment	accidentally	acknowledgment
absence	accommodate	acquire
accessible	achievement	across

actually
address
adjacent
adolescence
adolescent
advice (noun)
advise (verb)
aggravate
aggressive
aging
alcohol
allege
all right (*not* alright)
a lot (*not* alot)
already (*not* all ready)
alter (to change)
altogether
analysis
analyze
apparent
appearance
appreciate
arctic
argument
assassin
assistance
assistant
athlete
attendance
balloon
beggar
beginner
believe
benefit
bourgeois
bourgeoisie
Britain
bureau
bureaucracy
burglar

business
calendar
capital (noun: seat of government, money; adjective: chief)
capitol (building)
category
ceiling
cemetery
changeable
chief
choose (present tense)
chose (past tense)
chosen (participle)
commit
committee
comparative
competent
complement (noun: that which completes; verb: to complete)
compliment (praise)
conferred
congratulate
conscience
conscious
consistent
controlled
controversy
coolly
corollary
counterfeit
criticism
criticize
curiosity
deceive
decision
defendant

definite
deity
dependent
description
desirable
despair
desperate
develop, develops
development
dilemma
disappear
disappoint
disastrous
divide
divine
dormitory
eighth
embarrass
envelop (verb)
envelope (noun)
environment
equipped
equivalent
especially
essence
exaggerate
exceed
excellence
excellent
exhilarate
existence
experience
explanation
familiar
fascinate
fiend
fiery
foreign
foreword (preface)
forty
fourth
friend

gauge
genealogy
goddess
government
grammar
grievance
guarantee
height
heroes
hoping
humorous
hypocrisy
imagery
imagination
immediately
impel
incidentally
incredible
independence
independent
indispensable
insistence
insistent
intelligent
interest
interpretation
interrupt
irrelevant
irresistible
judgment
led (past tense of *to lead*)
leisure
license
loneliness
loose (adjective)
lose (verb)
losing
maneuver
marriage
mathematics
medicine

mischievous
misspell
naive
necessary
necessity
niece
ninety
noncommittal
noticeable
occasion
occasionally
occur
occurred
occurrence
omit
omitted
original
parallel
pastime
peaceable
performance
permanent
persistent
playwright
possession
practically
precede
predominant
preferred
prejudice
prevalent
principal (adjective: foremost; noun: chief)
principle (noun: rule)
privilege
probably
procedure
proceed
prominent
prophecy (noun)

prophesy (verb)
pursue
quantity
realize
really
receipt
receiving
recommend
reference
referring
relevance
relevant
relieve
remembrance
repentance
repetition
resistance
rhyme
rhythm
sacrifice
secretary
seize
sense
separate
shining
shriek
siege
significance
similar
solely
specimen
sponsor
stationary (still)
stationery (paper)
strength
subtlety
subtly
succeed
supersede
surprise
syllable
temperament

tendency

theories

therefore

thorough

tragedy

transferred

tried

truly

unforgettable

unnecessary

useful

usually

various

vengeance

villain

weird

wholly

who's (contraction: who is)

whose (possessive pronoun: belonging to whom)

withhold

writing

Finally, a few words about spelling programs designed for use with computers. Programs such as Word Plus or Easy Speller flag any word you use that is not in the program's dictionary. A misspelled word is of course not in the dictionary and thus flagged. But a word flagged is not necessarily misspelled; it may simply not be in the program's dictionary. Proper names, past participles, possessives, and contractions, for example, regularly get flagged. Keep in mind also that most programs cannot distinguish between homophones (*to, too, two; there, their; alter, altar*), nor can they tell you that you should have written *accept* instead of *except*. Since all of these words appear in the program's dictionary, they arouse no response — even when you may use them incorrectly.

Although the limitations in spelling programs will probably be overcome soon, we nevertheless think it reasonable to suggest that (if you are a poor speller) you learn to spell correctly. After all, even if you regularly use a word processor, you can't assume that you will have one available for every writing task. There are, for instance, quizzes and final examinations. Study our list of words, then, and make yourself independent (*not* independant) of spelling programs.

21
Usage

Some things are said or written and some are not. More precisely, anything can be said or written, but only some things are acceptable to the ears and minds of many readers. "I don't know nothing about it" has been said and will be said again, but many readers who encounter this expression might judge the speaker as a person with nothing of interest to say — and immediately tune out.

Although such a double negative today is not acceptable, it used to be: Chaucer's courteous Knight never spoke no baseness, and Shakespeare's courtly Mercutio, in *Romeo and Juliet*, "will not budge for no man." But things have changed; what was acceptable in the Middle Ages and the Renaissance (for example, emptying chamber pots into the gutter) is not always acceptable now. And some of what was once unacceptable has become acceptable. At the beginning of the twentieth century, grammarians suggested that one cannot use *drive* in speaking of a car; one drives (forces into motion) an ox, or even a person ("He drove her to distraction"), but not a machine. Some seventy years of usage, however, have erased all objections.

This chapter presents a list of expressions that, although commonly used, set many teeth on edge. Seventy years from now some of these expressions may be as acceptable as "drive a car"; but we are writing for today, and we might as well try to hold today's readers by following today's taste. If our essays are thoughtful, they will provide enough challenges to the reader; we should not use constructions that will arouse antagonism or that will allow the reader to brush us off as ignoramuses.

You may not be familiar with some of the abuses in the following list; if so, our citing them will not instruct you, but may entertain you.

A NOTE ON IDIOMS

An idiom (from a Greek word meaning "peculiar") is a fixed group of words, peculiar to a given language. Thus, in English we say "I caught a cold" but we do not say "I seized a cold." If someone who is not a native speaker of English tells us that she thought "catch" and "seize" are synonymous, we may sympathize with her problem but we can only insist that in English one cannot seize a cold. Anyone who says or writes "I seized a cold" is using *un*idiomatic English, just as anyone who says he knows a poem "at heart" instead of "by heart" is using unidiomatic English.

Probably most unidiomatic expressions use the wrong preposition. Examples:

Unidiomatic	Idiomatic
comply to	comply with
superior with	superior to

Sometimes while we write, or even while we speak, we are unsure of the idiom and we pause to try an alternative — "parallel with?" "parallel to?" — and we don't know which sounds more natural, more idiomatic. At such moments, more often than not, either is acceptable, but if you are in doubt, check a dictionary when you are editing your work. (The *American Heritage Dictionary* has notes on usage following the definitions of hundreds of its words.)

In any case, if you are a native speaker of English, when you read your draft you will probably detect unidiomatic expressions such as *superior with*; that is, you will hear something that sounds odd, and so you will change it to something that sounds familiar, idiomatic — here, *superior to*. If any unidiomatic expressions remain in your essay, the trouble may be that an effort to write impressively has led you to use unfamiliar language. A reader who sees such unidiomatic language will know that you are trying to gain stature by walking on stilts.

GLOSSARY

a, an Use *a* before words beginning with a consonant ("a book") or with a vowel sounded as a consonant ("a one-way ticket," "a university"). Use *an* before words beginning with a vowel or a vowel sound, including those beginning with a silent *h* ("an egg," "an hour"). If an initial *h* is pronounced but the accent is not on the first syllable, *an* is acceptable, as in "*an* historian" (but "*a* history course").

above Try to avoid writing *for the above reasons, in view of the above,* or *as above.* These expressions sound unpleasantly legalistic. Substitute *for these reasons,* or *therefore,* or some such expression or word.

academics Only two meanings of this noun are widely accepted: (1) "members of an institution of higher learning," and (2) "persons who are academic in background or outlook." Avoid using it to mean "academic subjects," as in "A student should pay attention not only to academics but also to recreation."

accept, except *Accept* means "to receive with consent." *Except* means "to exclude" or "excluding."

affect, effect *Affect* is usually a verb, meaning (1) "to influence, to produce an effect, to impress," or (2) "to pretend, to put on," as in "He affected an English accent." Psychologists use it as a noun for "feeling," e.g., "The patient experienced no affect." *Effect,* as a verb, means "to bring about" ("The workers effected the rescue in less than an hour"). As a noun, *effect* means "result" ("The effect was negligible").

aggravate "To worsen, to increase for the worse," as in "Smoking aggravated the irritation." Although it is widely used to mean "annoy" ("He aggravated me"), many readers are annoyed by such a use.

all ready, already *All ready* means "everything is ready." *Already* means "by this time."

all right, alright The first of these is the preferable spelling; for some readers it is the only acceptable spelling.

all together, altogether *All together* means that members of a group act or are gathered together ("They voted all together");

altogether is an adverb meaning "entirely," "wholly" ("This is altogether unnecessary").

allusion, reference, illusion An *allusion* is an implied or indirect reference. "As Lincoln says" is a *reference* to Lincoln, but "As a great man has said," along with a phrase quoted from the Gettysburg Address, constitutes an *allusion* to Lincoln. The student who, in a demonstration at Berkeley, carried a placard saying "I am a human being — please do not fold, spindle, or mutilate" *referred* to himself and *alluded* to a computer card. *Allusion* has nothing to do with *illusion* (a deception). Note the spelling (especially the second *i*) in "disillusioned" (left without illusions, disenchanted).

a lot Two words (not *alot*).

almost See *most*.

among, between See *between*.

amount, number *Amount* refers to bulk or quantity: "A small amount of gas was still in the tank." Use *number*, not *amount*, to refer to separate (countable) units: "A large number of people heard the lecture" (not "a large amount of people"). Similarly, "an amount of money," but "a number of dollars."

analyzation Unacceptable; use *analysis*.

and/or Acceptable, but a legalism and unpleasant-sounding. Often *or* by itself will do, as in "students who know Latin or Italian." When *or* is not enough ("The script was written by Groucho and/or Harpo") it is better to recast ("The script was written by Groucho or Harpo, or both").

and etc. Because *etc.* is an abbreviation for *et cetera* ("and others"), the *and* in *and etc.* is redundant. (See also the entry on *et cetera*.)

ante, anti *Ante* means "before" (*antebellum*, "before the Civil War"); *anti* means "against" (*antivivisectionist*). Hyphenate *anti* before capitals (*anti-Semitism*) and before *i* (*anti-intellectual*).

anthology, collection Because an *anthology* is a collection of writings by several authors, one cannot speak of "an anthology of poems by Robert Frost"; one can speak of a "collection of poems by Robert Frost."

anxious Best reserved for uses that suggest anxiety ("He was anxious before the examination"), though some authorities now accept it in the sense of "eager" ("He was anxious to serve the community").

anybody An indefinite pronoun, written as one word; if two words (*any body*), you mean any corpse ("Several people died in the fire, but the police cannot identify any body").

anyone One word, unless you mean "any one thing," as in "Here are three books; you may take any one."

area of Like *field of* and *topic of* ("the field of literature," "the topic of politics"), *area of* can usually be deleted. "The area of literature" equals "literature."

around Avoid using *around* in place of *about*: "He wrote it in about three hours." See also *centers on*.

as, like *As* is a conjunction; use it in forming comparisons, to introduce clauses. (A clause has a subject and a verb.)

> You can learn to write, as you can learn to swim.
>
> Huck speaks the truth as he sees it.
>
> He is as tall as I.

In "He is as tall as I," notice that the clause introduced by the second "as" consists of the subject "I" and the implied verb "am."

> He is as tall as I (am).

As can also introduce a clause in which both the subject and the verb are implied:

> Rose distrusts him as much as (she distrusts) me.

But notice that the last sentence means something different from the next:

> Rose distrusts him as much as I (do).

Like is a preposition; use it to introduce prepositional phrases:

> He looks like me.
>
> Like Hamlet, Laertes has lost a father.
>
> She thinks like a lawyer.

Writers who are fearful of incorrectly using *like* resort to cumbersome evasions: "He eats in the same manner that a pig eats." But there's nothing wrong with "He eats like a pig."

as of now Best deleted, or replaced by *now*. Not "As of now I don't smoke" but "Now I don't smoke" or "I don't smoke now" or "I don't smoke."

aspect Literally, "a view from a particular point," but it has come to mean *topic*, as in "There are several aspects to be considered." Try to get a sharper word; for example, "There are several problems to be considered," or "There are several consequences to be considered."

as such Often meaningless, as in "Tragedy as such evokes pity."

as to Usually *about* is preferable. Not "I know nothing as to the charges," but "I know nothing about the charges."

bad, badly *Bad* used to be only an adjective ("a bad movie"), and *badly* was an adverb ("she sings badly"). In "I felt bad," *bad* describes the subject, not the verb. (Compare "I felt happy." After verbs of appearing, such as "feel," "look," "seem," "taste," an adjective, not an adverb, is used.) But today "I feel badly" is acceptable and even preferred by many. Note, however, this distinction: "This meat smells bad" (an adjective describing the meat), and "Because I have a stuffed nose I smell badly" (an adverb describing my ability to smell something).

being Do not use *being* as a main verb, as in "The trouble being that his reflexes were too slow." The result is a sentence fragment. See pages 680–82.

being that, being as A sentence such as "Being that she was a stranger . . ." sounds like an awkward translation from the Latin. Use *because*.

beside, besides *Beside* means "at the side of." Because *besides* can mean either "in addition to" or "other than," it is ambiguous, as in "Something besides TB caused his death." It is best, then, to use *in addition to* or *other than*, depending on what you mean.

between Only English teachers who have had a course in Middle English are likely to know that it comes from *by twain*. And only English teachers and editors are likely to object to its use (and to call for *among*) when more than two are concerned, as in "among the three of us." Note, too, that even conservative usage accepts *between* in reference to more than two when the items are at the moment paired: "Negotiations *between* Israel and Egypt, Syria, and Lebanon seem stalled." *Between*, a preposition, takes an object ("between you and me"); only people who mistakenly think that "me" is vulgar say "between you and I".

biannually, bimonthly, biweekly Every two years, every two months, every two weeks (*not* twice a year, etc.). Twice a year is *semiannually*. Because *biannually, bimonthly,* and *biweekly* are commonly misunderstood, it is best to avoid them and to say "every two . . ."

Black, black Although one sometimes sees the word capitalized when it refers to race, most publishers use a lowercase letter, making it consistent with *white*, which is never capitalized.

can, may When schoolchildren asked "Can I leave the room," their teachers used to correct them thus: "You *can* leave the room if you have legs, but you *may not* leave the room until you receive permission." In short, *can* indicates physical possibility, *may* indicates permission. But because "you may not" and "why mayn't I?" sound not merely polite but stiff, *can* is usually preferred except in formal contexts.

centers on, centers around Use *centers on*, because *center* refers to a point, not to a movement around.

collection, anthology See *anthology*.

collective nouns A collective noun, singular in form, names a collection of individuals. Examples: *audience, band, committee, crowd, jury, majority, minority, team.* When you are thinking chiefly of the whole as a unit, use a singular verb (and a singular pronoun, if any): "The majority rules"; "The jury is announcing its verdict." But when you are thinking of the individuals, use a plural verb (and pronoun, if any): "The majority are lawyers"; "The jury are divided and they probably cannot agree." If the plural sounds odd, you can usually rewrite: "The jurors are divided and they probably cannot agree."

compare, contrast To *compare* is to note likenesses or differences: "Compare a motorcycle with a bicycle." To *contrast* is to emphasize differences.

complement, compliment *Complement* as a noun means "that which completes"; as a verb, "to fill out, to complete." *Compliment* as a noun is an expression of praise; as a verb it means "to offer praise."

comprise "To include, contain, consist of ": "The university comprises two colleges and a medical school" (not "is comprised of "). Conservative authorities hold that "to be comprised of " is always incorrect, and they reject the form one often hears: "Two colleges and a medical school comprise the university." Here the word should be *compose*, not *comprise*.

concept Should often be deleted. For "The concept of the sales tax is regressive" write "The sales tax is regressive."

contact Because it is vague, avoid using *contact* as a verb. *Not* "I contacted him" but "I spoke with him" or "I wrote to him," or whatever.

continual, continuous Conservative authorities hold that *continuous* means "uninterrupted," as in "It rained continuously for six hours"; *continually* means "repeated often, recurring at short intervals," as in "For a year he continually wrote letters to her."

contrast, compare See *compare.*

could have, could of See *of.*

criteria Plural of *criterion,* hence it is always incorrect to speak of "a criteria," or to say "The criteria is . . ."

data Plural of *datum.* Although some social scientists speak of "this data," "these data" is preferable: "These data are puzzling." Because the singular, *datum,* is rare and sounds odd, it is best to substitute *fact* or *figure* for *datum.*

different from Prefer it to *different than,* unless you are convinced that in a specific sentence *different from* sounds terribly wrong, as in "These two books are more different than I had expected." (In this example, "more," not "different," governs "than." But this sentence, though correct, is awkward and therefore it should be revised: "These two books differ more than I had expected.")

dilemma A situation requiring a choice between equally undesirable alternatives; not every difficulty or plight or predicament is a *dilemma.* Not "Her dilemma was that she had nowhere to go," but "Her dilemma was whether to go out or to stay home: one was frightening, the other was embarrassing." And note the spelling (two *m*'s, no *n*).

disinterested Though the word is often used to mean "indifferent," "unconcerned," "uninterested," reserve it to mean "impartial": "A judge should be disinterested."

due to Some people, holding that *due to* cannot modify a verb (as in "He failed due to illness"), tolerate it only when it modifies a noun or pronoun ("His failure was due to illness"). They also insist that it cannot begin a sentence ("Due to illness, he failed"). In fact, however, daily usage accepts both. But because it almost always sounds stiff, try to substitute *because of,* or *through*.

due to the fact that Wordy for *because*.

each Although many authorities hold that *each,* as a subject, is singular, even when followed by "them" ("Each of them is satisfactory"), some authorities accept and even favor the plural ("Each of them are satisfactory"). But it is usually better to avoid the awkwardness by substituting *all* for *each*: "All of them are satisfactory." When *each* is in apposition with a plural subject, the verb must be plural: "They each have a book"; "We each are trying." *Each* cannot be made into a possessive; you cannot say "Each's opinion is acceptable."

effect See *affect*.

e.g. Abbreviation for *exempli gratia,* meaning "for example." It is thus different from *i.e.* (an abbreviation for *id est,* meaning "that is"). E.g. (not italicized) introduces an example; i.e. (also not italicized) introduces a definition. Because these two abbreviations of Latin words are often confused, it may be preferable to avoid them and use their English equivalents.

either . . . or, neither . . . nor If the subjects are singular, use a singular verb: "Either the boy or the girl is lying." If one of the subjects joined by *or* or *nor* is plural, most grammarians say that the verb agrees with the nearer subject, thus: "A tree or two shrubs are enough," or "Two shrubs or a tree is enough." But because the singular verb in the second of these sentences may sound odd, follow the first construction; that is, put the plural subject nearer to the verb and use a plural verb. Another point about *either . . . or*. In this construction, "either" serves as advance notice that two equal possibilities are in the offing. Beware of putting "either" too soon, as in "Either he is a genius or a lunatic." Better: "He is either a genius or a lunatic."

enthuse Objectionable to many readers. For "He enthused," say "He was enthusiastic." Use *enthuse* only in the sense of "to be excessively enthusiastic," "to gush."

et cetera, etc. Latin for "and other things"; if you mean "and other people," you need *et al.,* short for *et alii*. Because *etc.* is vague, its use is usually inadvisable. Not "He studied mathematics, etc." but "He studied mathematics, history, economics, and French." Or, if the list is long, cut it by saying something a little more informative than *etc.* — for example, "He studied mathematics, history, and other liberal arts subjects." Even *and so forth* or *and so on* is preferable to *etc.* Confine *etc.* (and most other abbreviations, including *et al.*) to footnotes, and even in footnotes try to avoid it.

everybody, everyone These take a singular verb ("Everybody is here"), and a pronoun referring to them is usually singular ("Everybody thinks his problems are suitable topics of conversation"), but use a plural pronoun if the singular would seem unnatural ("Everybody was there, weren't they?"). To avoid the sexism of "Everybody thinks his problems . . ." revise to "All people think their problems . . ."

examples, instances See *instances.*

except See *accept.*

exists Often unnecessary and a sign of wordiness. Not "The problem that *exists* here is" but "The problem here is."

expound Usually pretentious for *explain* or *say.* To *expound* is to give a methodical explanation of theological matters.

facet Literally "little face," especially one of the surfaces of a gem. Don't use it (and don't use *aspect* or *factor* either) to mean "part" or "topic." It is most acceptable when, close to its literal meaning, it suggests a new appearance, as when a gem is turned: "Another *facet* appears when we see this law from the taxpayer's point of view."

the fact that Usually wordy. "Because of the fact that boys played female roles in Elizabethan drama" can be reduced to "Because boys played female roles in Elizabethan drama."

factor Strictly speaking, a *factor* helps to produce a result, but students commonly use it in the sense of "point": "Another factor to be studied is. . . ." Used with the sense of "point" it usually sounds pretentious: "The possibility of plagiarism is a factor that must be considered" simply adds up to "The possibility of plagiarism must be considered." *Factor* is almost never the precise word: "the factors behind Gatsby's actions" are, more precisely, "Gatsby's motives."

famous, notorious See *notorious.*

farther, further Some purists claim that *farther* always refers to distance and *further* to time ("The gymnasium is farther than the library"; "Let us think further about this").

fatalistic, pessimistic *Fatalistic* means "characterized by the belief that all events are predetermined and therefore inevitable"; *pessimistic,* "characterized by the belief that the world is evil," or, less gloomily, "expecting the worst."

fewer, less See *less.*

field of See *area of.*

firstly, secondly Acceptable, but it is better to use *first, second.*

former, latter These words are acceptable, but they are often annoying because they force the reader to reread earlier material in order to locate what *the former* and *the latter* refer to. The expressions are legitimately used in order to avoid repeating lengthy terms, but if you are talking about an easily repeated subject — say, Lincoln and Grant — don't hesitate to replace *the former* and *the latter* with their names. The repetition will clarify rather than bore.

good, well *Good* is an adjective ("a good book"), *well* is usually an adverb ("She writes well"). Standard English does not accept "She writes good." But Standard English requires *good* after verbs of appearing, such as "seems," "looks," "sounds," "tastes": "it looks good," "it sounds good." *Well* can also be an adjective meaning "healthy": "I am well."

graduate, graduate from Use *from* if you name the institution or if you use a substitute word as in "She graduated from high school"; if the institution (or substitute) is not named, *from* is omitted: "She graduated in 1983." The use of the passive ("She was graduated from high school") is acceptable but sounds fussy to many.

he or she, his or her These expressions are awkward, but the implicit male chauvinism in the generic use of the male pronoun ("A citizen should exercise his right to vote") may be more offensive than the awkwardness of *he or she* and *his or her.* Moreover, sometimes the male pronoun, when used for males and females, is ludicrous, as in "The more violence a youngster sees on television, regardless of his age or sex, the more aggressive he is likely to be." Do what you can to avoid the dilemma. Sometimes you can use the plural *their:* "Students are expected to hand in their papers on Monday" (instead of "The student is expected to hand in his or her paper on Monday"). Or eliminate the possessive: "The student must hand in a paper on Monday." See also *man, mankind.*

hopefully Commonly used to mean "I hope" or "It is hoped" ("*Hopefully,* the rain will stop soon"), but it is best to avoid what some consider a dangling modifier. After all, the rain itself is not hopeful. If you mean "I hope the rain will soon stop," say exactly that. Notice, too, that *hopefully* is often evasive; if the president of the college says, "Hopefully tuition will not rise next year," don't think that you have heard a promise to fight against an increase; you only have heard someone evade making a promise. In short, confine *hopefully* to its adverbial use, meaning "in a hopeful manner": "Hopefully he uttered a prayer."

however It is preferable not to begin a sentence with *however* unless it is an adverb meaning "to whatever extent or degree," as in "However hard he studied, he couldn't remember irregular verbs." When *however* is a conjunctive adverb, it usually gains emphasis if you put it later in the sentence, between commas: "He failed the examination, however, and didn't graduate." (Compare, "However, he failed the examination and didn't graduate.") Unless *however* is set off in commas it usually sounds insufficiently emphatic. If you want to begin a sentence with a sharp contrast, use *but* or *nevertheless.* Note too that you cannot link independent clauses with a *however* preceded by a comma; you need a semicolon ("He tried; however, he failed"). Even here, however, *but* is usually preferable, without a semicolon.

the idea that Usually dull and wordy. Not "The idea that we grow old is frightening," but "That we grow old is frightening," or (probably better) "Growing old is frightening."

identify When used in the psychological sense, "to associate oneself closely with a person or an institution," it is preferable to include a reflexive pronoun, thus: "He identified himself with Hamlet," *not* "He identified with Hamlet."

i.e. Latin for *id est,* "that is." The English words are preferable to the Latin abbreviation. On the distinction between *i.e.* and *e.g.,* see *e.g.*

immanent, imminent *Immanent,* "remaining within, intrinsic"; *imminent,* "likely to occur soon, impending."

imply, infer The writer or speaker *implies* (suggests); the perceiver *infers* (draws a conclusion): "Karl Marx implied that . . . but his modern disciples infer from his writings that . . ." Although *infer* is widely used for *imply,* preserve the distinction.

individual Avoid using the word to mean only "person": "He was a generous individual." But it is precise when it implicitly makes a contrast with a group: "In a money-mad society, he was a generous individual"; "Although the faculty did not take a stand on this issue, faculty members as individuals spoke out."

instances Instead of *in many instances* use *often.* Strictly speaking an *instance* is not an object or incident in itself but one offered as an example. Thus "another instance of his failure to do his duty" (not "In three instances he failed to do his duty").

irregardless Unacceptable; use *regardless.*

it is Usually this expression needlessly delays the subject: "It is unlikely that many students will attend the lecture" could just as well be "Few students are likely to attend the lecture."

its, it's The first is a possessive pronoun ("The flock lost its leader"); the second is a contraction of *it is* ("It's a wise father that knows his child.") You'll have no trouble if you remember that the possessive pronoun *its,* like other possessive pronouns such as *our, his, their,* does *not* use an apostrophe.

kind of Singular, as in "That kind of movie bothers me." (*Not:* "Those kind of movies bother me.") If, however, you are really talking about more than one kind, use *kinds* and be sure that the demonstrative pronoun and the verb are plural: "Those kinds of movies bother me." Notice also that the phrase is *kind of,* not *kind of a.* Not "What *kind of a* car does she drive?" but "What *kind of* car does she drive?"

latter See under *former.*

lay, lie To *lay* means "to put, to set, to cause to rest." It takes an object: "May I lay the coats on the table?" The past tense and the participle are *laid:* "I laid the coats on the table"; "I have laid the coats on the table." To *lie* means "to recline," and it does not take an object: "When I am tired I lie down." The past tense is *lay,* the participle is *lain:* "Yesterday I lay down"; "I have lain down hundreds of times without wishing to get up."

lend, loan The usual verb is *lend*: "Lend me a pen." The past tense and the participle are both *lent*. *Loan* is a noun: "This isn't a gift, it's a loan." But, curiously, *loan* as a verb is acceptable in past forms: "I loaned him my bicycle." In its present form ("I often loan money") it is used chiefly by bankers.

less, fewer *Less* (as an adjective) refers to bulk amounts (also called mass nouns): less milk, less money, less time. *Fewer* refers to separate (countable) items: fewer glasses of milk, fewer dollars, fewer hours.

lifestyle, life–style, life style All three forms are acceptable, but because many readers regard the expression as imprecise and faddish, try to find a substitute such as *values*.

like, as See under *as*.

literally It means "strictly in accord with the primary meaning; not metaphorically." It is not a mere intensive. "He was literally dead" means that he was a corpse; if he was merely exhausted, *literally* won't do. You cannot be "literally stewed" (except by cannibals), "literally tickled pink," or "literally head over heels in love."

loose, lose *Loose* is an adjective ("The nail is loose"); *lose* is a verb ("Don't lose the nail").

the majority of Usually a wordy way of saying *most*. Of course if you mean "a bare majority," say so; otherwise *most* will usually do. Certainly "The majority of the basement is used for a cafeteria" should be changed to "Most of the basement is used for a cafeteria."

man, mankind Because these words strike many readers as sexist, expressions such as "man's brain" and "the greatness of mankind" should be revised where possible. Consider using such words as *human being, person, humanity, people*.

may, can See under *can*.

me The right word in such expressions as "between you and me" and "They gave it to John and me." It is the object of verbs and of prepositions. In fact, *me* rather than *I* is the usual form after any verb, including the verb *to be*; "It is me" is nothing to be ashamed of.

medium, media *Medium* is singular, *media* is plural: "TV is the medium to which most children are most exposed. Other media include film, radio, and publishing." It follows, then, that *mass* *media* takes a plural verb: "The mass media exert an enormous influence."

more Avoid writing a false comparison such as: "His essay includes several anecdotes, making it more enjoyable." Delete "more" unless there really is a comparison with another essay.

most, almost Although it is acceptable in speech to say "most everyone" and "most anybody," it is preferable in writing to use "almost everyone," "almost anybody." But of course: "Most students passed."

nature You can usually delete *the nature of,* as in "The nature of my contribution is not political but psychological."

needless to say The reader may well wonder why you go on to say it. Of course this expression is used to let readers know that they are probably familiar with what comes next, but usually *of course* will better serve as this sign.

Negro Capitalized, whether a noun or an adjective, though *white* is not. In recent years *Negro* has been replaced by *black.*

neither . . . nor See *either . . . or.*

nobody, no one, none *Nobody* and *no one* are singular, requiring a singular verb ("Nobody believes this," "No one knows"); but they can be referred to by a plural pronoun: "Nobody believes this, do they?" "No one knows, do they?" *None,* though it comes from *no one,* almost always requires a plural verb when it refers to people ("Of the ten people present, none are freshmen") and a singular verb when it refers to things ("Of the five assigned books, none is worth reading").

not only . . . but also Keep in mind these two points: 1) many readers object to the omission of "also" in such a sentence as "She not only brought up two children but practiced law," and 2) all readers dislike a faulty parallel, as in "She not only is bringing up two children but practices law." ("Is bringing up" needs to be paralleled with "is also practicing.")

not . . . un- Such an expression as "not unfamiliar" is useful only if it conveys something different from the affirmative. Compare the frostiness of "I am not unfamiliar with your methods" with "I am familiar with your methods." If the negative has no evident advantage, use the affirmative. See pages 443–44.

notorious Widely and unfavorably known; not merely famous, but famous for some discreditable trait or deed.

a number of requires a plural verb: "A number of women are presidents of corporations." But when *number* is preceded by *the* it requires a singular verb: "The number of women who are presidents is small." (The plural noun after *number* of course may require a plural verb, as in "women are," but *the number* itself remains singular, hence its verb is singular, as in "is small.")

of Be careful not to use *of* when *have* is required. Not "He might of died in the woods," but "He might have died in the woods." Note that what we often hear as "would've" or "should've" or "must've" or "could've" is "would have" or "should have" or "must have" or "could have," *not* "would of," etc.

off of Use *off* or *from:* "Take it off the table"; "He jumped from the bridge."

often-times Use *often* instead.

old-fashioned, old-fashion Only the first is acceptable.

one British usage accepts the shift from *one* to *he* in "One begins to die the moment he is born," but American usage prefers "One begins to die the moment one is born." A shift from *one* to *you* ("One begins to die the moment you are born") is unacceptable. As a pronoun, *one* can be useful in impersonal statements such as the sentence about dying, at the beginning of this entry, where it means "a person," but don't use it as a disguise for yourself ("One objects to Smith's argument"). Try to avoid *one;* one *one* usually leads to another, resulting in a sentence that, in James Thurber's words, "sounds like a trombone solo" ("If one takes oneself too seriously, one begins to . . ."). See *you,* pages 740–41.

one of Takes a plural noun, and if this is followed by a clause, the preferred verb is plural: "one of those students who are," "one of those who feel." Thus, in such a sentence as "One of the coaches who have resigned is now seeking reinstatement," notice that "have" is correct; the antecedent of "who" (the subject of the verb) is "coaches," which is plural. Coaches have resigned, though "one . . . is seeking reinstatement." But in such an expression as "one out of a hundred," the following verb may be singular or plural ("One out of a hundred is," "One out of a hundred are").

only Be careful where you put it. The classic textbook example points out that in the sentence "I hit him in the eye," *only* can be inserted in seven places (beginning in front of "I" and ending after "eye") with at least six different meanings. Try to put it just before the expression it qualifies. Thus, not "Presidential aides are only responsible to one man," but "Presidential aides are responsible to only one man" (or "to one man only"). See page 476.

oral, verbal See *verbal*.

other Often necessary in comparisons. "No American president served as many terms as Franklin Roosevelt" falsely implies that Roosevelt was not an American president. The sentence should be revised to "No other American president served as many terms as Franklin Roosevelt."

per Usually it sounds needlessly technical ("twice per hour") or disturbingly impersonal ("as per your request"). Preferable: "twice an hour," "according to your request," or "as you requested."

per cent, percent, percentage The first two of these are interchangeable; both mean "per hundred," "out of a hundred," as in "Ninety per cent (or percent) of the students were white." *Per cent* and *percent* are always accompanied by a number (written out, or in figures). It is usually better to write out *per cent* or *percent* than to use a per cent sign (12%), except in technical or statistical papers. *Percentage* means "a proportion or share in relation to the whole," as in "A very large percentage of the student body is white." Many authorities insist that *percentage* is never preceded by a number. Do not use percentage to mean "a few," as in "Only a percentage of students attended the lecture"; a percentage can be as large as 99.99. It is usually said that with *per cent, percent,* and *percentage,* whether the verb is singular or plural depends on the number of the noun that follows the word, thus: "Ninety percent of his books are paperbacks"; "Fifty percent of his library is worthless"; "A large percentage of his books are worthless." But some readers (including the authors of this book) prefer a singular verb after *percentage* unless the resulting sentence is as grotesque as this one: "A large percentage of the students is unmarried." Still, rather than say a "percentage . . . are," we would recast the sentence: "A large percentage of the student body is unmarried," or "Many (or "Most," or whatever) of the students are unmarried."

per se Latin for "by itself." Usually sounds legalistic or pedantic, as in "Meter per se has an effect."

pessimistic See *fatalistic.*

phenomenon, phenomena The plural is *phenomena*; thus, "these phenomena" but "this phenomenon."

plus Unattractive and imprecise as a noun meaning "asset" or "advantage" ("When he applied for the job, his appearance was a plus"), and equally unattractive as a substitute for *moreover* ("The examination was easy, plus I had studied") or as a substitute for *and* ("I studied the introduction plus the first chapter").

politics Preferably singular ("Ethnic politics has been a strong force for a century") but a plural verb is acceptable.

prejudice, prejudiced *Prejudice* is a noun: "It is impossible to live entirely without prejudice." But use the past participle *prejudiced* as an adjective: "He was prejudiced against me from the start."

preventative, preventive Both are acceptable but the second form is the form now used by writers on medicine ("preventive medicine"); *preventative* therefore has come to seem amateurish.

prior to Pretentious for *before.*

protagonist Literally, the first actor, and, by extension, the chief actor. It is odd, therefore, to speak of "the protagonists" in a single literary work or occurrence. Note also that the prefix is *proto*, "first," not *pro*, "for"; it does *not* mean one who strives for something.

quite Usually a word to delete, along with *definitely, pretty, rather,* and *very.* See page 437. *Quite* used to mean "completely" ("I quite understand") but it has come also to mean "to a considerable degree," and so it is ambiguous as well as vague.

quotation, quote The first is a noun, the second a verb. "I will quote Churchill" is fine, but not "these quotes from Churchill." And remember, you may *quote* one of Hamlet's speeches, but Hamlet does not *quote* them; he says them.

rather Avoid use with strong adjectives. "Rather intelligent" makes sense, but "rather tremendous" does not. "Rather brilliant" probably means "bright"; "rather terrifying" probably means "frightening," "rather unique" probably means "unusual." Get the right adjective, not *rather* and the wrong adjective.

the reason . . . is because Usually *because* is enough (not "The reason they fail is because they don't study," but simply "They fail because they don't study"). Similarly, *the reason why* can usually be reduced to *why*. Notice, too, that because *reason* is a noun, it cannot neatly govern a *because* clause: not "The reason for his absence is because he was sick," but "The reason for his absence was illness."

rebut, refute To rebut is to argue against, but not necessarily successfully. If you mean "to disprove," use *disprove* or *refute*.

in regard to, with regard to Often wordy for *about, concerning,* or *on,* and sometimes even these words are unnecessary. Compare: "He knew a great deal in regard to jazz"; "He knew a great deal about jazz." Compare: "Hemingway's story is often misunderstood with regard to Robert Wilson's treatment of Margot Macomber"; "In Hemingway's story, Robert Wilson's treatment of Margot Macomber is often misunderstood."

relate to Usually a vague expression, best avoided, as in "I can relate to Hedda Gabler." Does it mean "respond favorably to," "identify myself with," "interact with" (and how can a reader "interact with" a character in a play?). Use *relate to* only in the sense of "have connection with" (as in "How does your answer relate to my question?"); even in such a sentence a more exact expression is preferable.

repel, repulse Both verbs mean "to drive back," but only *repel* can mean "to cause distaste," "to disgust," as in "His obscenities repelled the audience."

sarcasm Heavy, malicious sneering ("Oh, you're really a great friend, aren't you?" addressed to someone who won't lend the speaker ten dollars). If the apparent praise, which really communicates dispraise, is at all clever, conveying, say, a delicate mockery or wryness, it is irony, not sarcasm. The passages by Szarkowski on page 509 are ironic, not sarcastic.

seem Properly it suggests a suspicion that appearances may be deceptive: "He seems honest (but . . .)." Don't say "The book seems to lack focus" if you believe it does lack focus.

semiannually, semimonthly semiweekly See *biannually*.

shall, will, should, would The old principle held that in the first person *shall* is the future indicative of *to be* and *should* the conditional ("I shall go," "We should like to be asked"); and that *will* and *would* are the forms for the second and third persons. When the forms are reversed ("I will go," "Government of the people . . . shall not perish from the earth"), determination is expressed. But today almost nobody adheres to these principles. Indeed, *shall* (except in questions) sounds stilted to many ears.

simplistic Means "falsely simplified by ignoring complications." Do not confuse it with *simplified,* whose meanings include "reduced to essentials" and "clarified."

since, because Traditional objections to *since,* in the sense of "because," have all but vanished. Note, however, that when *since* is ambiguous and may also refer to time ("Since he joined the navy, she found another boyfriend") it is better to say *because* or *after,* depending on which you mean.

situation Overused, vague, and often unnecessary. "His situation was that he was unemployed" adds up to "He was unemployed." And "an emergency situation" is probably an emergency.

split infinitives The infinitive is the verb form that merely names the action, without indicating when or by whom performed ("walk," rather than "walked" or "I walk"). Grammarians, however, developed the idea that the infinitive was "to walk," and they held that one cannot separate or split the two words: "to quickly walk." But James Thurber says this idea is "of a piece with the sentimental and outworn notion that it is always wrong to strike a lady." Notice, however, that often the inserted word can be deleted ("to really understand" is "to understand"), and that if many words are inserted between *to* and the verb, the reader may get lost ("to quickly and in the remaining few pages before examining the next question conclude").

stanza See under *verse.*

subjunctive For the use of the subjunctive with conditions contrary to fact (for instance, "If I were you"), see the entry on *was/were.* The subjunctive is also used in *that* clauses followed by verbs demanding, requesting, or recommending: "He asked that the students be prepared to take a test." But because this last sort of sentence sounds stiff, it is better to use an alternate construction, such as "He asked the students to prepare for a test."

than, then *Than* is used chiefly in making comparisons ("German is harder than French"), but also after "rather," "other," "different," and "else" ("I'd rather take French than German"; "He thinks of nothing other than sex"). *Then* commonly indicates time ("She took German then, but now she takes French"; "Until then, I'll save you a seat"), but it may also mean "in that case" ("It's agreed, then, that we'll all go") or "on the other hand" ("Then again, she may find German easy"). The simplest guide: use *than* after comparisons and after "rather," "other," "different," "else"; otherwise use *then*.

that, which, who Many pages have been written on these words; opinions differ, but you will offend no one if you observe the following principles. (1) Use *that* in restrictive (that is, limiting) clauses: "The rocking chair that creaks is on the porch." (2) Use *which* in nonrestrictive (in effect, parenthetic) clauses: "The rocking chair, which creaks, is on the porch." (See pages 691–92.) The difference between these two sentences is this: in the first, one rocking chair is singled out from several — the one that creaks; in the second, the fact that the rocking chair creaks is simply tossed in, and is not added for the purpose of identifying the one chair out of several. (3) Use *who* for people, in restrictive and in nonrestrictive clauses: "The men who were playing poker ignored the women"; "The men, who were playing poker, ignored the women." But note that often *that, which,* and *who* can be omitted: "The creaky rocking chair is on the porch"; "The men, playing poker, ignored the women." In general, omit these words if the sentence remains clear. See pages 445–46.

their, there, they're The first is a possessive pronoun: "Chaplin and Keaton made their first films before sound tracks were developed." The second, *there,* sometimes refers to a place ("Go there," "Do you live there?"), and sometimes is what is known in grammar as an introductory expletive ("There are no solutions to this problem"). The third, *they're,* is a contraction of "they are" ("They're going to stay for dinner").

this Often refers vaguely to "what I have been saying." Does it refer to the previous sentence, the previous paragraph, the previous page? Try to modify it by being specific: "This last point"; "This clue gave the police all they needed."

thusly Unacceptable; *thus* is an adverb and needs no adverbial ending.

till, until Both are acceptable, but *until* is preferable because *till* — though common in speech — looks literary in print. The following are *not* acceptable: *til, 'til, 'till.*

to, too, two *To* is toward; *too* is either "also" ("She's a lawyer, too") or "excessively" ("It's too hot"); *two* is one more than one ("Two is company").

topic of See *area of.*

toward, towards Both are standard English; *toward* is more common in the United States, *towards* in Great Britain.

type Often colloquial (and unacceptable in most writing) for *type of,* as in "this type teacher." But *type of* is not especially pleasing either. Better to write "this kind of teacher." And avoid using *type* as a suffix: "essay-type examinations" are essay examinations; "natural-type ice cream" is natural ice cream. Sneaky manufacturers make "Italian-type cheese," implying that their domestic cheese is imported and at the same time protecting themselves against charges of misrepresentation.

unique The only one of its kind. Someone or something cannot be "rather unique" or "very unique" or "somewhat unique," any more than a woman can be somewhat pregnant. Instead of saying "rather unique," then, say *rare,* or *unusual,* or *extraordinary,* or whatever seems to be the best word.

U.S., United States Generally, *United States* is preferable to *U.S.;* similarly, *the Soviet Union* is preferable to *the U.S.S.R.*

usage Don't use *usage* where *use* will do, as in "Here Vonnegut completes his usage of dark images." *Usage* properly implies a customary practice that has created a standard: "Usage has eroded the difference between 'shall' and 'will.'"

use of The use of *use of* is usually unnecessary. "Through the use of setting he conveys a sense of foreboding" may be reduced to "The setting conveys . . ." or "His setting conveys . . ."

utilize, utilization Often inflated for *use* and *using,* as in "The infirmary has noted that it is freshmen who have most utilized the counseling service."

verbal Often used where *oral* would be more exact. *Verbal* simply means "expressed in words," and thus a *verbal agreement* may be either written or spoken. If you mean spoken, call it an *oral agreement.*

verse, stanza A *verse* is a single line of a poem; a *stanza* is a group of lines, commonly bound by a rhyme scheme. But in speaking or writing about songs, usage sanctions *verse* for *stanza,* as in "Second verse, same as the first."

viable A term from physiology, meaning "capable of living" (for example, referring to a fetus at a stage of its development). Now pretentiously used and overused, especially by politicians and journalists, to mean "workable," as in "a viable presidency." Avoid it.

was, were Use the subjunctive form — *were* (rather than *was*) — in expressing a wish ("I wish I were younger") and in "if-clauses" that are contrary to fact ("If I were rich," "If I were you . . .").

we If you mean *I,* say *I.* Not "The first fairy tale we heard" but "the first fairy tale I heard." (But of course *we* is appropriate in some statements: "We have all heard fairy tales"; "If we look closely at the evidence, we can agree that. . . .") The rule: don't use *we* as a disguise for *I.* See pages 471–72.

well See *good.*

well known, widely known Athletes, performers, politicians, and such folk are not really *well known* except perhaps by a few of their friends and their relatives; use *widely known* if you mean they are known (however slightly) to many people.

which Often can be deleted. "Students are required to fill out scholarship applications which are lengthy" can be written "Students are required to fill out lengthy scholarship applications." Another example: "*The Tempest,* which is Shakespeare's last play, was written in 1611"; "*The Tempest,* Shakespeare's last play, was written in 1611," or "Shakespeare wrote his last play, *The Tempest,* in 1611." For the distinction between *which* and *that,* see the entry on *that.*

while Best used in a temporal sense, meaning "during the time": "While I was speaking, I suddenly realized that I didn't know what I was talking about." While it is not wrong to use *while* in a nontemporal sense, meaning "although" (as at the beginning of this sentence), it is better to use *although* in order to avoid any ambiguity. Note the ambiguity in: "While he was fond of movies he chiefly saw westerns." Does it mean "Although he was fond of movies," or does it mean "During the time when he was fond of movies"? Another point: do not use *while* if you mean *and*: "Freshmen take English 1–2, while sophomores take English 10–11" (substitute *and* for *while*).

who, whom Strictly speaking, *who* must be used for subjects, even when they look like objects: "He guessed who would be chosen." (Here *who* is the subject of the clause "who would be chosen.") *Whom* must be used for the objects of a verb, verbal (gerund, participle), or preposition: "Whom did he choose?"; "Whom do you want me to choose?"; "To whom did he show it?" We may feel stuffy in writing "Whom did he choose?" or "Whom are you talking about?" but to use *who* is certain to annoy some reader. Often you can avoid the dilemma by re-writing: "Who was chosen?"; "Who is the topic of conversation?" See also the entry on *that*.

whoever, whomever The second of these is the objective form. It is often incorrectly used as the subject of a clause. "Open the class to whomever wants to take it" is incorrect. The object of "to" is not "whomever" but is the entire clause — "whoever wants to take it" — and of course "whoever" is the subject of "wants."

who's, whose The first is a contraction of *who is* ("I'm everybody who's nobody"). The second is a possessive pronoun: "Whose book is it?" "I know whose it is."

will, would See *shall* and also *would*.

would "I would think that" is a wordy version of "I think that." (On the mistaken use of *would of* for *would have*, see *of*, page 732.)

you In relatively informal writing, *you* is ordinarily preferable to the somewhat stiff *one*: "If you are addicted to cigarettes, you may find it helpful to join Smokenders." (Compare: "If one is addicted to cigarettes, one may . . .") But because the direct address of *you* may sometimes descend into nagging, it is usually better to write: "Cigarette addicts may find it helpful . . ." Certainly a writer (you?) should not assume that the reader is guilty of vices ("You should not molest children") unless the essay is clearly aimed at an audience that admits to these vices, say a pamphlet directed to child molesters who are seeking help. Thus, it is acceptable to say, "If you are a poor speller," but it is not acceptable to say, to the general reader, "You should improve your spelling"; the reader's spelling may not need improvement. And avoid *you* when the word cannot possibly apply to the reader: "A hundred years ago you were faced with many diseases that now have been eradicated." Something like "A hundred years ago people were faced . . ." is preferable.

your, you're The first is a possessive pronoun ("your book"); the second is a contraction of *you are* ("You're mistaken").

LAST WORDS

A rich patron once gave money to the painter Chu Ta, asking him to paint a picture of a fish. Three years later, when he still had not received the painting, the patron went to Chu Ta's house to ask why the picture was not done. Chu Ta did not answer, but dipped a brush in ink and with a few strokes drew a splendid fish. "If it is so easy," asked the patron, "why didn't you give me the picture three years ago?" Again Chu Ta did not answer. Instead, he opened the door of a large cabinet. Thousands of pictures of fish tumbled out.

AUTHOR
BIOGRAPHIES

Maya Angelou was born in St. Louis in 1928. Among her writings are two books of poetry and three autobiographical books. "Graduation" (editors' title) is from the first autobiographical volume, *I Know Why the Caged Bird Sings.*

Russell Baker, born in Virginia in 1925, has been a professional journalist since 1947, when he joined the *Baltimore Sun.* Later he covered Washington for *The New York Times,* and he now writes a widely syndicated column, "The Observer." "The Flag" was originally published in this column, and reprinted in a collection of his essays entitled *So This Is Depravity* (1980). "Coming to Grips with Death" is from *Growing Up,* an autobiography that won the 1982 Pulitzer Prize for biography. The title of the selection is ours.

James Baldwin was born in Harlem in 1924, and graduated from De Witt Clinton High School. At first he did odd jobs while he wrote, but in 1948 he received a fellowship that enabled him to go to Paris, where he wrote two novels (*Go Tell It on the Mountain* and *Giovanni's Room*), as well as essays published in *Notes of a Native Son.* He returned to the United States in 1955, where he has continued to publish fiction, plays, and essays.

Robert Benchley (1889–1945) was educated at Harvard, where, he said, he learned that one cannot attend two courses at the same hour, and that one can wear a sock with a hole in the toe if one turns the sock inside out. Benchley wrote humorous essays and performed on radio and in films.

Bruno Bettelheim was born in Vienna in 1903. He came to the United States in 1939, and became a naturalized citizen in 1944. From 1943 to 1973 he was head of the Sonia Shankman Orthogenic School in Chicago, where he also taught psychology at the University of Chicago. He is now retired, but continues to write on psychology.

Black Elk, a *wichasha wakon* (holy man) of the Oglala Sioux, as a small boy witnessed the Battle of Little Bighorn (1876). He lived to see his people all but annihilated and his hopes for them extinguished. In 1931, toward the end of his life, he told his life story to the poet and scholar John G. Neihardt in order to preserve a sacred vision given him. "High Horse's Courting" provides a comic interlude in a predominantly tragic memoir.

Sissela Bok teaches courses in medical ethics and in decision-making at the Harvard Medical School. She is the author of *Lying*, a book concerned with such problems as whether or not to lie to people for their own good.

Jorge Luis Borges was born in Argentina in 1899. Poet, essayist, story writer, and teacher, he is widely regarded as the greatest living man of letters writing in Spanish.

J. Bronowski (1908–1974) was born in Poland and was educated in England. Trained as a mathematician, Bronowski distinguished himself as a writer not only about science but also about literature and psychology.

Leonard Cammer (1914–1978), a specialist in the treatment of severe depression and schizophrenia, taught and practiced psychiatry in New York City.

Bruce Catton (1899–1978), after serving as a reporter for several newspapers, turned much of his attention to studying the Civil War, but he continued to work in journalism, for example by serving as Director of Information for the United States Department of Commerce. His historical writing won him a Pulitzer Prize and a National Book Award.

Joan Didion was born in California in 1934 and educated at the University of California, Berkeley. While she was still a senior she wrote a prize-winning essay for a contest sponsored by *Vogue*, and soon she became an associate feature editor for *Vogue*. She has written novels, essays, and screenplays.

Jim Doherty, a writer and editor, served as executive editor for *National Wildlife*.

Nora Ephron, born in 1941, is the daughter of two Hollywood writers. She has published several volumes of essays.

Bergen Evans (1904–1978) taught English at Northwestern University for many years, and achieved national prominence as the moderator of several television programs and as the author of *The Natural History of Nonsense* and other books.

Robert Finch is publications director of the Cape Cod Museum of Natural History and a member of the Breadloaf Writers' Conference at Middlebury College. This essay is from his first book, *Common Ground: A Naturalist's Cape Cod* (1981).

E[dward] M[organ] Forster (1879–1970) was born in London and was graduated from King's College, Cambridge. He traveled widely and lived for a while in India, but most of his life was spent back at King's College. His best-known novel is *A Passage to India* (1926).

Paul Goodman (1911–1972) received his bachelor's degree from City College in New York, and his Ph.D. from the University of Chicago. He taught in several colleges and universities, and wrote prolifically on literature, politics, and education.

Jeff Greenfield has written speeches for Robert F. Kennedy and John V. Lindsay, and has exchanged sharp words with William F. Buckley on television. He has published essays on sports and on other popular entertainments.

Jane Jacobs was born in Scranton, Pennsylvania, in 1916. From 1952 until 1962 she served as an associate editor of *Architectural Forum*. In addition to writing *The Death and Life of Great American Cities*, from which our selection comes, she has written *The Economy of Cities*.

Elizabeth Janeway was born in Brooklyn and educated at Swarthmore and Barnard. A novelist, critic, and lecturer, she is especially concerned with the social context that has produced the women's movement.

Susan Jacoby has worked as a reporter for the *Washington Post* and as a columnist for *The New York Times*.

X. J. Kennedy was born in 1929 in New Jersey. He has published several books of poetry (including a book for children) and several textbooks.

Martin Luther King (1929–1968), clergyman and civil rights leader, achieved national fame in 1955–56 when he led the boycott against segregated bus lines in Montgomery, Alabama. In 1964 he was awarded the Nobel Peace Prize, but he continued to encounter strong opposition. On 4 April 1968, while in Memphis to support striking sanitation workers, he was shot and killed.

Edward Koch, born in 1924 in New York City, was educated at City College and at New York University Law School. Long active in Democratic politics, Mr. Koch has served as mayor of New York since 1978.

Jonathan Kozol, born in 1936, has taught in elementary schools in Massachusetts. The author of several books, he is best known for *Death at an Early Age: The Destruction of the Hearts and Minds of Negro Children in the Boston Public Schools*.

Chuck Kraemer was born in 1945 in Marysville, Kansas. He received a bachelor's degree from the University of Kansas and did graduate work in film at Boston University. He has written essays, chiefly on film, for *The New York Times* and for other newspapers.

Barbara Lawrence was born in Hanover, New Hampshire, and was educated at Connecticut College and at New York University. She teaches at the State University of New York, at Old Westbury.

C[live] S[taples] Lewis (1898–1963) taught medieval and Renaissance literature at Oxford and later at Cambridge. In addition to writing about literature, he wrote fiction (including children's books), poetry, and numerous essays and books on moral and religious topics.

Alan Lightman was born in Memphis in 1948, and educated at Princeton and California Institute of Technology. A theoretical astrophysicist who teaches at Harvard, for this essay, published in *The New York Times Magazine,* he looked inward rather than upward.

Malcolm X, born Malcolm Little in Nebraska in 1925, was the son of a Baptist minister. He completed the eighth grade but then got into trouble and was sent to a reformatory. After his release he became a thief, dope peddler, and pimp; in 1944 he was sent to jail, where he spent six and a half years. During his years in jail he became a convert to the Black Muslim faith. Paroled in 1950, he served as a minister and founded Muslim temples throughout the United States. In 1964, however, he broke with Elijah Muhammad, leader of the Black Muslims, and formed a new group, the Organization of Afro-American Unity. The next year he was assassinated in New York.

Anne Hebald Mandelbaum was born in New York City in 1944, and was educated at Radcliffe College and Yale University. She is a free-lance writer.

Margaret Mead (1901–1978) was born in Philadelphia and educated at De Pauw University, Barnard College, and Columbia University. She lived in Samoa in 1925 and 1926; in 1928 she published the book that promptly established her reputation, *Coming of Age in Samoa.* Throughout the next fifty years she wrote prolifically and lectured widely on sociological and anthropological subjects.

Rhoda Metraux was born in Brooklyn in 1914. An anthropologist who has done field work in many parts of the world, she is a research associate of the American Museum of Natural History.

Jonathan Miller, an Englishman born in 1934, is widely known as a writer, actor, and director of plays, operas, and television programs. But he is also a physician and a student of the history of medicine. His medical background enabled him to write and direct a series of television programs entitled *The Body in Question*.

Flannery O'Connor (1925–1964) was born in Georgia and spent most of her short life there. *The Complete Stories of Flannery O'Connor* received the National Book Award for fiction in 1971; another posthumous volume, *Mystery and Manners*, includes essays on literature and an account of her experiences raising peacocks in Georgia.

George Orwell (1903–1950), an Englishman, adopted this name; he was born Eric Blair, in India. He was educated at Eton, in England, but in 1921 he returned to the East and served for five years as a police officer in Burma. He then returned to Europe, doing odd jobs while writing novels and stories. In 1936 he fought in the Spanish Civil War on the side of the Republicans, an experience reported in *Homage to Catalonia* (1938). His last years were spent writing in England.

Noel Perrin, born in New York in 1927, farms in Vermont and teaches American literature at Dartmouth College. Among his publications are three books of essays, chiefly on rural subjects.

Robert M. Pirsig, born in Minneapolis in 1928, has published one book, *Zen and the Art of Motorcycle Maintenance*, a narrative of a motorcycle trip taken by a father and his eleven-year-old, who travel from Minneapolis to the Pacific. As our extract on "Mechanic's Feel" suggests, the book is highly meditative, in large part an account of complex relationships with our environment.

Sylvia Plath (1932–1963), educated at Smith College, is known chiefly as a poet, but she also wrote fiction, letters, and a journal.

Philip Roth was born in Newark, New Jersey, in 1933. His first book, *Goodbye, Columbus*, won a National Book Award for fiction. Among his other notable books are *Letting Go, Portnoy's Complaint,* and *Reading Myself and Others*.

Nancy Masterson Sakamoto, professor of Buddhism at the University of Hawaii, lived for a while in Osaka, where she taught English to Japanese people. The essay we print is a chapter from a textbook written in English, used by Japanese students taking a course in conversational English.

Sei Shōnagon was born about 965 in Japan; for some ten years she served as lady-in-waiting to the Empress Sadako. The tradition that she died poor and alone may be true, or it may be the moralists' attempt to reply to her sensual life.

Max Shulman, born in St. Paul in 1919, is the author of many humorous books and of the television series *Dobie Gillis.*

Christopher D. Stone was born in 1937 in New York City. He holds a law degree from Yale, and teaches law at the University of Southern California.

I[sidore] F[einstein] Stone, born in Philadelphia in 1907, was educated at the University of Pennsylvania. For some twenty years he worked as a reporter and edited a leftist newsletter, *I. F. Stone's Bi-weekly,* noted for its incisive criticism of American politics. He now occasionally publishes in *The New York Review of Books.*

Studs Terkel was born Louis Terkel in New York City in 1912. He was brought up in Chicago and was graduated from the University of Chicago. Terkel has been an actor, playwright, columnist, and disc jockey, but he is best known as the man who makes books out of tape recordings of people he gets to talk. These oral histories are *Division Street: America* (1966), *Hard Times* (1970), *Working* (1974), and *American Dreams: Lost and Found* (1980). In 1978 Terkel published his memoirs, *Talking to Myself.*

Paul Theroux was born in 1941 in Medford, Massachusetts, and was educated at the University of Maine, the University of Massachusetts, and Syracuse University. He served as a Peace Corps volunteer in Africa, and has spent much of his adult life abroad, in Africa, Asia, Europe, and Central America. Though best known as a novelist and writer of travel books, he is also a poet and essayist. This essay originally appeared in *The New York Times Magazine.*

Lewis Thomas was born in 1913. A distinguished medical researcher and administrator, he is president of the Memorial Sloan-Kettering Cancer Center in New York. He is also a writer; he has published *Lives of a Cell,* a collection of twenty-nine short essays, which won a National Book Award in 1974, and *The Medusa and the Snail.*

Henry David Thoreau (1817–1862), naturalist, social and political activist, and (of course) writer, in 1845 went to live for a while at Walden Pond in Massachusetts, where he hoped to be free enough from distractions to study life closely, or, as he put it, "to drive life into a corner, . . . to know it by experience, and be able to give a true account of it."

Lester Thurow was born in Montana and educated at Williams College, Balliol College, and Harvard. A professor of economics at MIT, he is the author of books and articles not only for specialists but also for the general reader. This essay appeared in *The New York Times,* 8 March 1981.

John Updike was born in Shillington, Pennsylvania, in 1932. He has published stories, novels, and essays. In 1963, *The Centaur,* a novel, received a National Book Award.

E[lwyn] B[rooks] White wrote poetry and fiction, but he is most widely known as an essayist and as the coauthor (with William Strunk) of *Elements of Style.* After a long career at *The New Yorker* he retired to Maine, but he continued to write until the year before his death at the age of 86.

Virginia Woolf (1882–1941) was born in London into an upper-middle class literary family. In 1912 she married a writer, and with him she founded The Hogarth Press, whose important publications included not only books by T. S. Eliot but her own novels.

(Continued from page iv)

Russell Baker, "The Flag." Reprinted by permission of Don Congdon Associates, Inc. Copyright © 1975 by Russell Baker.

James Baldwin, "Stranger in the Village." From *Notes of a Native Son* by James Baldwin. Copyright © 1955 by James Baldwin. Reprinted by permission of Beacon Press.

Pat Bellanca, "Jimmy Buffett is Going Coconuts" from *The Wellesley News*, 13 March 1981. Reprinted by permission of the author.

Saul Bellow, excerpt reprinted from *The Victim* by Saul Bellow by permission of the publisher, Vanguard Press, Inc. Copyright 1947 by Saul Bellow. Copyright renewed 1974 by Saul Bellow.

Robert Benchley, "How to Get Things Done" by Robert Benchley from *The Benchley Roundup*, selected by Nathaniel Benchley. Copyright, 1930 by Chicago Tribune/New York News Syndicate, Inc. By permission of Harper & Row, Publishers, Inc.

Bruno Bettelheim, "Joey: A Mechanical Boy," *Scientific American*, March 1959. Reprinted with permission; copyright © 1959 by Scientific American, Inc. All rights reserved.

Robert Bly, "Love Poem" from *Silence in the Snowy Fields* (Middletown, Conn.: Wesleyan University Press, 1962). Copyright © 1962 by Robert Bly. Reprinted by permission of the author.

Sissela Bok, "To Lie or Not to Lie? — The Doctor's Dilemma," *The New York Times*, 18 April, 1978. Copyright © 1978 by The New York Times Company. Reprinted by permission.

Jose Luis Borges, "The Gaucho and the City: Stories of Horsemen," *The New Republic*, May 19, 1982. Reprinted by permission of *The New Republic*, © 1982 The New Republic, Inc.

Jacob Bronowski, "The Reach of Imagination." From *A Sense of the Future* (Cambridge, Mass.: MIT Press, 1977), pp. 21–31. Originally in *Proceedings of the American Academy of Arts and Letters and the National Institute of Arts and Letters* (1967), 2d series II, and reprinted with their permission.

Anthony Burgess, excerpt from *Language Made Plain*. Copyright © 1964 by Anthony Burgess. Reprinted by permission.

Leonard Cammer, "How to Deal with the Crying," from *Up from Depression*. Copyright © 1969 by Leonard Cammer, M.D. Reprinted by permission of Simon & Schuster, Inc.

Bruce Catton, "Grant and Lee: A Study in Contrasts" from *The American Story*, Earl Schenck Miers, editor. © 1956 by Broadcast Music, Inc. Copyright renewed 1984. Reprinted by permission.

Confidential Chat, a feature of *The Boston Globe*. Letters by Three Begonias and The First Waffle used by permission.

Sharon Curtin, excerpts from *Nobody Ever Died of Old Age* by Sharon Curtin. Copyright © 1972 by Sharon Curtin. By permission of Little, Brown and Company in association with the Atlantic Monthly Press.

Joan Didion, "Los Angeles Notebook." Reprinted by permission of Farrar, Straus and Giroux, Inc. from *Slouching Towards Bethlehem* by Joan Didion. Copyright © 1967, 1968 by Joan Didion.

Joan Didion, "On Keeping a Notebook." Reprinted by permission of Farrar, Straus & Giroux, Inc. from *Slouching Towards Bethlehem* by Joan Didion. Copyright © 19 , 1968 by Joan Didion.

Paul Diederich, from *Measuring Growth In English*, pp. 21–22. Copyright © 1974 National Council of Teachers of English. Reprinted by permission of the publisher.

Jim Doherty, "How Cemeteries Bring Us Back to Earth," *The New York Times*, 31 May 1982. Copyright © 1982 by The New York Times Company. Reprinted by permission.

Mamie Duff, "Dedication Doth Not a Good Teacher Make." Reprinted by permission of Mamie Duff, Staff, Lockwood Press.

Nora Ephron, "A Few Words about Breasts: Shaping Up Absurd." From *Crazy Salad: Some Things About Women*, by Nora Ephron. Copyright © 1972 by Nora Ephron. Reprinted by permission of Alfred A. Knopf, Inc.

Bergen Evans, "Sophistication," *The New York Times Book Review*, 7 September 1971. Copyright © 1971 by The New York Times Company. Reprinted by permission.

Robert Finch, "Very Like a Whale." From *Common Ground: A Naturalist's Cape Cod* by Robert Finch. Copyright © 1981 by Robert Finch. Reprinted by permission of David R. Godine, Publisher, Boston.

E. M. Forster, "My Wood" from *Abinger Harvest*, copyright 1936, 1964 by E. M. Forster. Reprinted by permission of Harcourt Brace Jovanovich, Inc. and Edward Arnold (Publishers) Ltd.

Patricia Freeman, "The Einstein of Happiness," *California Living*, 23 October 1983. Reprinted by permission.

Eileen Garred, "Ethnobotanists Race Against Time to Save Useful Plants," *Harvard University Gazette*, 24 May 1985. Reprinted by permission of the *Harvard University Gazette*.

Margaret Gooch, library exercises (following research paper in Chapter 10) reprinted by permission of Margaret Gooch, Wessell Library, Tufts University.

Paul Goodman, "A Proposal to Abolish Grading" (editors' title). Reprinted from *Compulsory Mis-Education* by Paul Goodman, copyright 1964, by permission of the publisher, Horizon Press, New York.

Jeff Greenfield, "Columbo Knows the Butler Didn't Do It," *The New York Times*, 22 April 1973. Copyright © 1973 by The New York Times Company. Reprinted by permission.

"In Search of the Elusive Pingo" (Ideas and Trends), *The New York Times*, 5 May 1974. Copyright © 1974 by The New York Times Company. Reprinted by permission.

Jane Jacobs, "The Use of Sidewalks" (original title, "The Uses of Sidewalk Safety") from *The Death and Life of Great American Cities*, by Jane Jacobs. Copyright © 1961 by Jane Jacobs. Reprinted by permission of Random House, Inc.

Susan Jacoby, "Too Many Women Are Misconstruing Feminism's Nature," *The New York Times*, 14 April 1983. Reprinted by permission of the author. Copyright © 1983 by Susan Jacoby.

Elizabeth Janeway, "Soaps, Cynicism, and Mind Control," *Ms.* Magazine, January 1985. Reprinted by permission of the author.

James Weldon Johnson, lines from "Lift Ev'ry Voice and Sing," © Copyright: Edward B. Marks Music Corporation. Reprinted by permission.

George Kane, "Traveler's Diarist," *The New Republic*, 14 March 1981. © 1981 The New Republic, Inc. Reprinted by permission.

X. J. Kennedy, "Who Killed King Kong?" *Dissent* Magazine, Spring 1960. Reprinted by permission of the publisher and author.

Martin Luther King, Jr., "Nonviolent Resistance," (editors' title). From pp. 211–216 in *Stride Toward Freedom* by Martin Luther King, Jr. Copyright © 1958 by Martin Luther King, Jr. By permission of Harper and Row, Publishers, Inc.

Carole Klein, "The Tough Got Going," *The New York Times Book Review*, 17 February 1985. Copyright © 1985 by The New York Times Company. Reprinted by permission.

Edward I. Koch, "Death and Justice: How Capital Punishment Affirms Life," *The New Republic*, April 15, 1985. Reprinted by permission of *The New Republic*. © 1985 The New Republic, Inc.

Jonathan Kozol, "Operation Illiteracy," *The New York Times*, 5 March 1979. Copyright © 1979 by The New York Times Company. Reprinted by permission.

Chuck Kraemer, "Indecent Exposure," *The Real Paper*, 4 June 1975. Reprinted by permission of *The Real Paper*.

Barbara Lawrence, "Four Letter Words Can Hurt You," (original title, "___ Isn't a Dirty Word"), *The New York Times*, 27 October 1973. Copyright © 1973 by The New York Times Company. Reprinted by permission.

"Letter to the Editor" by Leonard S. Charlap, *The New York Times*, 19 December 1977. Copyright © 1977 by The New York Times Company. Reprinted by permission.

"Letter to the Editor" by Ruth H. Cohn, *The New York Times*, 20 July 1978. Copyright © 1978 by The New York Times Company. Reprinted by permission.

C. S. Lewis, "The Trouble with X" from *God in the Dock*, edited by Walter Hooper (British title, *Undeceptions*). Copyright © 1970, 1971 by the Trustees of the Estate of C. S. Lewis. Reprinted by permission of Curtis Brown Ltd. and William Collins Sons & Co. Ltd.

C. S. Lewis, "Vivisection" from *God in the Dock*, edited by Walter Hooper (British title, *Undeceptions*). Copyright © 1970, 1971 by the Trustees of the Estate of C. S. Lewis. Reprinted by permission of Curtis Brown Ltd. and William Collins Sons & Co. Ltd.

Alan P. Lightman, "Elapsed Expectations," *The New York Times Magazine*, 25 March 1984. Copyright © 1984 by The New York Times Company. Reprinted by permission.

Walter Lippmann, excerpt from column in *The New York Times*, 20 February 1942. Copyright © 1942 by The New York Times Company. Reprinted by permission.

K. N. Llewellyn, excerpt reprinted with permission from Llewellyn, K. N., *The Bramble Bush: On Law and Its Study* (Oceana Publications, Inc., 1981).

Malcolm X, "Rejected" (editors' title) from *The Autobiography of Malcolm X*, by Malcolm X., with the assistance of Alex Haley. Copyright © 1964 by Alex Haley and Malcolm X. Copyright © 1965 by Alex Haley and Betty Shabazz. Reprinted by permission of Random House, Inc.

Anne Hebald Mandelbaum, "It's the Portly Penguin That Gets the Girl, French Biologist Claims," *Harvard University Gazette*, 30 January 1976. Reprinted by permission of the *Harvard University Gazette*.

Jack Margolis, "And All Those Others" from *The Poetry of Richard Milhous Nixon* (Los Angeles: Cliff House Books, 1974). Reprinted by permission of the author and publisher.

Sister Lydia Martin-Boyle, H.O.O.M., "Adman's Atlanta." Reprinted by permission of the author.

Gerald Mast, excerpts from *The Comic Mind*, pp. 281–283. Copyright © 1973 by Gerald Mast. Reprinted by permission of the Bobbs-Merrill Co., Inc.

Margaret Mead and Rhoda Metraux, "On Friendship — August 1966" from *A Way of Seeing* (1970) by Margaret Mead and Rhoda Metraux. Copyright © 1966 by Margaret Mead and Rhoda Metraux. By permission of William Morrow & Company.

Jonathan Miller, from *The Body In Question*, by Jonathan Miller. Copyright © 1978 by Jonathan Miller. Reprinted by permission of Random House, Inc. and Jonathan Cape Ltd.

Anne Moody, excerpt from *Coming of Age in Mississippi* by Anne Moody. Copyright © 1968 by Anne Moody. Reprinted by permission of Doubleday & Company, Inc.

Joseph Morgenstern, excerpt from "On the Road," *Newsweek*, 21 July 1969. Copyright 1969, by Newsweek, Inc. All Rights Reserved. Reprinted by permission.

John G. Neihardt, "High Horse's Courting" from *Black Elk Speaks* by John G. Neihardt, copyright 1959, 1961; courtesy John G. Neihardt Trust.

"Notes and Comment," *The New Yorker*, 10 January 1970. Reprinted by permission; © 1970 The New Yorker Magazine, Inc.

"Notes and Comment," *The New Yorker*, 22 September 1975. Reprinted by permission; © 1975 The New Yorker Magazine, Inc.

Flannery O'Connor, "Total Effect and the Eighth Grade," from *Mystery and Manners* by Flannery O'Connor, ed. by Sally and Robert Fitzgerald, pp. 135–140. Copyright © 1957, 1961, 1963, 1964, 1966, 1967, 1969 by the Estate of Mary Flannery O'Connor. Copyright © 1962 by Flannery O'Connor. Reprinted by permission of Farrar, Straus and Giroux, Inc.

George Orwell, excerpt from "England Your England" from *The Collected Essays, Journalism, and Letters of George Orwell*, Vol. II, Angus Ian and Sonia Orwell, eds., 1968. Reprinted by permission of Harcourt Brace Jovanovich, Inc., the estate of the late Sonia Brownell Orwell, and Martin Secker & Warburg Ltd.

George Orwell, "Politics and the English Language" from *Shooting an Elephant and Other Essays*. Copyright 1950 by Sonia Brownell Orwell; renewed 1978 by Sonia Pitt-Rivers. Reprinted by permission of Harcourt Brace Jovanovich, Inc., the estate of the late Sonia Brownell Orwell, and Martin Secker & Warburg Ltd.

George Orwell, "Shooting an Elephant" from *Shooting an Elephant and Other Essays*. Copyright 1945, 1946, 1949, 1950, by Sonia Brownell Orwell; renewed 1978 by Sonia Pitt-Rivers. Reprinted by permission of Harcourt Brace Jovanovich, Inc., the estate of the late Sonia Brownell Orwell, and Martin Secker & Warburg Ltd.

Dorothy Parker, "News Item" from *The Portable Dorothy Parker*. Revised and enlarged edition. Copyright 1936, copyright © renewed 1964 by Dorothy Parker. Reprinted by permission of Viking Penguin Inc.

Noel Perrin, "The Androgynous Man," *The New York Times Magazine*, 5 February 1984. Copyright © 1984 by The New York Times Company. Reprinted by permission.

Marge Piercy, lines from "Rough Times" from *Living in the Open* by Marge Piercy. Copyright © 1972, 1976 by Marge Piercy. Reprinted by permission of Alfred A. Knopf, Inc.

Robert M. Pirsig, excerpts from p. 14 and pp. 323–4 in *Zen and the Art of Motorcycle Maintenance* by Robert M. Pirsig. Copyright © 1974 by Robert M. Pirsig. By permission of William Morrow and Company.

Sylvia Plath, from *The Journals of Sylvia Plath*, edited by Frances McCullough. Copyright © 1982 by Ted Hughes as Executor of the estate of Sylvia Plath. Additional text copyright © 1982 by Frances McCullough. Reprinted by permission of The Dial Press.

Susan Pope, "Tennis Tips to a Beginner." Reprinted by permission of the author.

Charles T. Powers, "Say One Word and I'll Cut Your Throat," *Los Angeles Times*, 13 January 1974. Copyright, 1974, Los Angeles Times. Reprinted by permission.

Random House Dictionary of the English Language definition of *feminism*. Copyright © 1966 by Random House, Inc. Reprinted by permission.

Reuters, "Fish Eat Brazilian Fisherman," *The Boston Globe*, 17 January 1971. Reprinted by permission of Reuters.

Philip Roth, "The Newark Public Library" (original title, "Topics: Reflections on the Death of a Library"), *The New York Times*, 1 March 1969. Copyright © 1969 by The New York Times Company. Reprinted by permission.

David Royce, excerpt from "Moby Balloon," *The New York Times Magazine*, 26 May 1974. Copyright © 1974 by The New York Times Company. Reprinted by permission.

Nancy Sakamoto, "Conversational Ballgames" from *Polite Fictions* (Tokyo: Kinseido Ltd., 1982). Reprinted by permission of Kinseido Ltd.

Sei Shōnagon, "The Pillow Book of Sei Shonagon" from *The Pillow Book of Sei Shōnagon*, translated and edited by Ivan Morris (1967). Reprinted by permission of Columbia University Press and Oxford University Press.

Max Shulman, "Love is a Fallacy." Copyright 1951, © renewed 1979 by Max Shulman. Reprinted by permission of Harold Matson Company.

Gary Snyder, "Hitch Haiku" from *The Back Country* by Gary Snyder. Copyright © 1968 by Gary Snyder. Reprinted by permission of New Directions Publishing Corporation.

Christopher D. Stone, "Putting the Outside Inside the Fence of the Law," *The New York Times*, 29 August 1974. Copyright © 1974 by The New York Times Company. Reprinted by permission.

I. F. Stone, "A New Solution for the CIA," *The New York Review of Books*, 20 February 1975. Reprinted with permission from *The New York Review of Books*. Copyright © 1975 Nyrev, Inc.

Rebecca W. Strehlow, "The New Science Center at Wellesley College — An Eyesore?" from *Wellesley*, the alumnae magazine of Wellesley College, Winter 1985. Reprinted by permission.

Lisa Temple, "Beyond the Institution: The Effects of Labeling on Ex-Mental Patients," © 1986 by Lisa Temple. Used by permission of the author.

Studs Terkel, "Glenn Stribling" and "Dave Stribling" from *Working: What People Do All Day and How They Feel About What They Do*, by Studs Terkel. Copyright © 1972, 1974 by Studs Terkel. Reprinted by permission of Pantheon Books, a Division of Random House, Inc.

Paul Theroux, "The Male Myth," *The New York Times Magazine*, 27 November 1983. Copyright © 1983 by The New York Times Company. Reprinted by permission.

Lewis Thomas, "The Iks" from *The Lives of a Cell* by Lewis Thomas. Copyright © 1973 by the Massachusetts Medical Society. Originally published in the *New England Journal of Medicine*. Reprinted by permission of Viking Penguin Inc.

Lewis Thomas, "On Natural Death" from *The Medusa and the Snail: More Notes of a Biology Watcher* by Lewis Thomas. Copyright © 1979 by Lewis Thomas. Reprinted by permission of Viking Penguin Inc.

Lester C. Thurow, "Why Women Are Paid Less than Men," *The New York Times*, 8 March 1981. Copyright © 1981 by The New York Times Company. Reprinted by permission.

Time, excerpt from "Lord, They've Done It All," 6 May 1974. Copyright 1974 Time Inc. All rights reserved. Reprinted by permission from *Time*.

Sheila Tobias, excerpt from "Who's Afraid of Math and Why?" is reprinted from *Overcoming Math Anxiety* by Sheila Tobias, by permission of W. W. Norton and Company, Inc. Copyright © 1978 by Sheila Tobias.

John Updike, "Beer Can." Copyright © 1964 by John Updike. Originally appeared in *The New Yorker*. Reprinted from *Assorted Prose*, by John Updike, by permission of Alfred A. Knopf, Inc.

Alex Ward, excerpt from an article in *The New York Times Magazine*, 24 February 1985. Copyright © 1985 by The New York Times Company. Reprinted by permission.

E. B. White, "The Door" from *The Second Tree From the Corner* by E. B. White. Copyright 1939, 1967 by E. E. White. Reprinted by permission of Harper & Row, Publishers, Inc. Originally appeared in *The New Yorker*.

E. B. White, "Education — March 1939" (first section from *One Man's Meat* by E. B. White. Copyright 1939, 1967 by E. B. White. Reprinted by permission of Harper & Row, Publishers, Inc.

Virginia Woolf, "Professions for Women" from *The Death of the Moth and Other Essays* by Virginia Woolf. Copyright 1942 by Harcourt Brace Jovanovich;

Virginia Woolf, "Professions for Women" from *The Death of the Moth and Other Essays* by Virginia Woolf. Copyright 1942 by Harcourt Brace Jovanovich; copyright 1970 by Marjorie T. Powers, executrix. Reprinted by permission of Harcourt Brace Jovanovich, Inc. and The Hogarth Press Ltd.

William Butler Yeats, lines from "The Balloon of the Mind" reprinted with permission of Macmillan Publishing Company. Michael B. Yeats, and Macmillan London from *Collected Poems* by W. B. Yeats. Copyright 1919 by Macmillan Publishing Company, renewed 1947 by Bertha Georgie Yeats.

William Butler Yeats, lines from "The friends that have it I do wrong" reprinted with permission of Macmillan Publishing Company, Michael B. Yeats, and Macmillan London from *The Variorum Edition of the Poems of W. B. Yeats*, edited by Peter Allt and Russell K. Alspach (New York: Macmillan, 1957).

Art

Pieter Brueghel, *The Painter and the Connoisseur*. Graphische Sammlung Albertina, Wien.

Shaka nyorai. Japanese, Heian Period. Late 10th century. Single wood-block construction, painted and gilded. H 82.5 cm. Denman Waldo Ross Collection. 09.72. Courtesy, Museum of Fine Arts, Boston.

Bodhisattva Kuan Yin Seated in Royal Ease Position. Chinese, Sung dynasty. Carved wood, decorated in gold, lacquer, and polychrome. Reportedly from Chishan, Shansi province. H 1.41 m × W .88 m × D .88 m. Harvey Edward Wetzel Fund. 20.590. Courtesy, Museum of Fine Arts, Boston.

William Notman, Sitting Bull, and Buffalo Bill. Courtesy, Notman Photographic Archives, McCord Museum, McGill University.

Woman Holding Up Her Dying Lover. Francisco de Goya y Lucientes. Spanish, 1746–1828. Brush and gray wash, touched with brown wash. 9¼ × 5¹¹⁄₁₆ in. (234 × 145 mm). Gift of Frederick J. Kennedy Memorial Foundation. 1973. 700b. Courtesy, Museum of Fine Arts, Boston.

Francisco de Goya y Lucientes, *El amor y la muerte*. Courtesy, Museo del Prado, Madrid.

Covered Car — Long Beach, California. Copyright, Robert Frank, from *The Americans*, 1958.

Westchester, New York, Farm House. Courtesy, John T. Hill, Executor, Estate of Walker Evans.

Leonardo da Vinci, Mona Lisa. Alinari/Art Resource, New York.

"Spaghetti," from MAZES II by Vladimir Koziakin. Copyright 1972 by Vladimir Koziakin. Reprinted by permission of the Berkley Publishing Group.

"Atlanta" advertisement reprinted by permission of Atlanta Chamber of Commerce.

Index

SYMBOLS COMMONLY USED
IN MARKING PAPERS

All instructors have their own techniques for annotating essays, but many instructors make substantial use of the following symbols.

ab   faulty or undesirable abbreviation (see page 704)

agr   faulty agreement between subject and verb (page 480) or between pronoun and antecedent (page 479)

apos   apostrophe (pages 702–03)

awk (k)   awkward

cap   use a capital letter (pages 699–700)

cf   comma fault (pages 682–84)

choppy   too many short sentences—subordinate (pages 492–95)

cl   cliché (pages 464–65)

coh   paragraph lacks coherence (pages 94–97); sentence lacks coherence (pages 472–82)

cs   comma splice (pages 682–84)

dev   paragraph poorly developed (pages 82–88)

dm   dangling modifier (pages 476–77)

emph   emphasis obscured (pages 490–501)

good   a good point; or, well expressed

frag   fragmentary sentence (pages 497–98, 680–82)

id   unidiomatic expression (page 718)

ital   underline to indicate italics (page 698)

k (awk)   awkward

Lewis Thomas, "On Natural Death" ___ ___ ___
Henry David Thoreau, "The Battle of the Ants" ___ ___ ___
Lester C. Thurow, "Why Women Are Paid Less
    Than Men" ___ ___ ___
E. B. White, "The Door" ___ ___ ___

7. Do you think the professor should continue to assign this book next

   year? _____

   Did you tell her or him? _____

8. What would you have us change next time? _____

   _____

   _____

9. May we quote you in our promotion efforts for this book?

   _____Yes _____No

_____
Date   Signature
_____
Mailing address

3. Were the exercises useful? _____

4. Did you like the examples? _____

5. Please give us your reactions to the following readings:

	Keep	Drop	Didn't read
Martin Luther King, Jr., "Nonviolent Resistance"	—	—	—
Bruce Catton, "Grant and Lee: A Study in Contrasts"	—	—	—
E. B. White, "Education"	—	—	—
Margaret Mead and Rhoda Metraux, "On Friendship"	—	—	—
Jonathan Miller, "The Body in Question"	—	—	—
Anonymous, "Eclipse"	—	—	—
Sylvia Plath, "The Journals of Sylvia Plath"	—	—	—

6. Please give us your reactions to the additional readings in Part Four

	Keep	Drop	Didn't read
Russell Baker, "The Flag"	—	—	—
James Baldwin, "Stranger in the Village"	—	—	—
Robert Benchley, "How to Get Things Done"	—	—	—
Bruno Bettelheim, "Joey: A 'Mechanical Boy'"	—	—	—
Sissela Bok, "To Lie or Not to Lie? — The Doctor's Dilemma"	—	—	—
Jorge Luis Borges, "The Gaucho and the City: Stories of Horsemen"	—	—	—
Joan Didion, "On Keeping a Notebook"	—	—	—
Nora Ephron, "A Few Words about Breasts: Shaping Up Absurd"	—	—	—
Robert Finch, "Very Like a Whale"	—	—	—
Paul Goodman, "A Proposal to Abolish Grading"	—	—	—
Elizabeth Janeway, "Soaps, Cynicism, and Mind Control"	—	—	—
X. J. Kennedy, "Who Killed King Kong?"	—	—	—
C. S. Lewis, "The Trouble with 'X' . . ."	—	—	—
Flannery O'Connor, "Total Effect and the Eighth Grade"	—	—	—
George Orwell, "Politics and the English Language"	—	—	—
Studs Terkel, "Fathers and Sons"	—	—	—

To the Student

Please help us make *Barnet & Stubbs's Practical Guide to Writing, With Additional Readings,* an even better book. To improve our textbooks, we revise them every few years, taking into account the experiences of both instructors and students with the previous editions. At some time, your instructor will most likely be asked to comment extensively on *Barnet & Stubbs's Practical Guide to Writing, With Additional Readings*. Now we would like to hear from you.

Complete this questionnaire and return it to:

College English Developmental Group
Little, Brown and Company
34 Beacon St.
Boston, MA 02106

School _____

City, State, Zip Code _____

Course title _____

Instructor's full name _____

Other books required _____

_____

1. Did you like the book? _____

2. Was it too easy? _____ Too difficult? _____

   Did you read it all? _____

   Which chapters were most useful? Why? _____

   _____

   _____

   Which chapters were least useful? Why? _____

   _____

   _____